Contents

Note: There are a further 24 discount coupons available upon application. Please call 0800 316 8900

Birds, Butterflies & Bees

Bedford Butterfly Park
Renhold Road Wilden Bedford Bedfordshire MK44 2PX
[J13 off M1, follow A421 for Bedford, take bypass towards Cambridge follow signs for Wilden. Plenty of on site parking]
Tel: 01234 772770 Fax: 01234 772773
A global conservation park centered on a tropical glasshouse with waterfalls, ponds, exotic plants and spectacular butterflies. Additional attractions include a bugs room, leaf-cutting ant display, adventure playground, nature trails and pygmy goats. Tea-room serving light lunches and afternoon teas.
visitor comments: Variety of things to do. Lovely picnic areas outside. Staff helpful and welcoming.
Mar-Nov daily 10.00-17.00. Dec-Mar seasonal opening call for details. Guided tours by prior arrangement
Last Admission: 16.00
A£4.00 C(under 3)£Free C£2.50 Family Ticket (A2+C2)£10.00
discount offer: 25% Discount on Admission Prices. Valid for up to Four Persons. Mar-Nov 2000

Country Parks & Estates

Dunstable Downs
Dunstable Downs Countryside Centre Whipsnade Road Kensworth Dunstable Bedfordshire LU6 2TA
[J11 M1 Luton, take A505 to Dunstable Town Centre follow signs for Whipsnade Zoo. Turn L into Whipsnade Road, turn R into Downs car park, plenty of spaces.]
Tel: 01582 608489 Fax: 01582 671826
Located on NW tip of Chiltern Hills. Highest point in Bedfordshire with stunning views over the Vale of Aylesbury. Come and watch the gliders or fly a kite. There are also picturesque walks, an outside picnic area and a countryside centre with an exhibition, souvenirs and kites for sale. A kite festival is planned with demonstrations of trick kite flying, kite making, teddy bear parachute drop. Kites for sale.
Park: All year daily. Countryside Centre: Apr-Oct Tue-Sat 10.00-17.00, Sun & Bank Hol 10.00-18.00. Nov-Mar Sat & Sun only 10.00-16.00
Admission Free. School Groups £1.50 per head

Festivals & Shows

Bedford River Festival 2000
Bedford Bedfordshire
[major trunk roads to Bedford. BR: Bedford. There are 3 festival car parks with disabled parking available, please phone for details]
Tel: 01234 343992 Fax: 01234 343992
Main entertainment stage, motor village, arts village, sports village, road procession, river activities and living history heritage village. Held every 2 years since 1978, a major community event.
May 27-28 2000 Sat 13.00-23.00, Sun 13.00-18.00
Admission Free

↓*special events*

▶ **Bedford River Festival 2000**
27/5/00-28/5/00

£

Military & Defence Museums

Shuttleworth Collection
Old Warden Aerodrome Biggleswade Bedfordshire SG18 9EP
[2m W on A1 Biggleswade]
Tel: 09068 323310 Fax: 01767 626229
www.shuttleworth.org
A traditional grass aerodrome, with a world famous collection of aircraft from a 1909 Bleriot to a 1942 Spitfire, plus veteran and vintage motor vehicles and a coachroom of 19th century horse-drawn vehicles all displayed indoors. The aircraft and the vehicles are kept in working order.
visitor comments: Easy access to well exhibited aircraft. Plenty of information, with photographs. The flying days are unique and spectacular. Good toilet facilities.
All year daily 1 Apr-31 Oct 10.00-16.00, 1 Nov-

31 Mar daily 10.00-15.00. Closed Christmas week
Last Admission: 1hr before closing
A£6.00 C(accompanied)£Free OAPs Reduction (Mon ONLY)£3.00. Group rates 20+ A£5.00 School Parties £2.00. Prices on flying days: One Person in Car £10.00, Two Persons in Car £15.00, Three Persons in Car £20.00, Four Persons in Car £25.00, thereafter £5.00 per person. Coach passenger, pedestrian & cyclist £5.00

↓*special events*

▶ **Kite Society Spring Festival**
9/4/00-9/4/00
Come fly your kites in the skies over Shuttleworth, trade stands and catering

▶ **Model Aircraft Weekends**
23/4/00-8/10/00
Something of interest for all ages, on the following dates: 23 & 24 Apr, 13 & 14 May, 10 & 11 June; 22 & 23 July; 12 & 13 Aug, 7 & 8 Oct

▶ **Classic Car Show**
30/4/00-1/5/00
A real mecca for all car lovers, is a must... 10.00-17.00. A£5.00 C(5-16)£1.00 OAPs£4.00

▶ **Spring Air Display**
7/5/00-7/5/00
Featuring aerobatics and stunt flying plus a chance to step back in time to the pre-war air display era

▶ **Sunset Display 1 & Rally**
20/5/00-20/5/00
The first of several Sunset Displays. The YFC County Rally held in Old Warden Park also today

▶ **Great British Picnic Air Show**
4/6/00-4/6/00
Open to anyone who arrives in or on any form of road transport manufactured before 1 January 1960. Features a demonstration race round a short course near Old Warden Airfield

▶ **Schools Day**
7/6/00-7/6/00
A short air display put on especially for the children

▶ **Sunset Display 2**
17/6/00-17/6/00
Featuring the oldest of the aeroplanes from the Collection

▶ **Moth Club Charity Flying Weekend**
24/6/00-25/6/00
Buy a flight in a Tiger Moth, Puss Moth, Hornet Moth or Leopard Moth

▶ **Summer Air Show**
2/7/00-2/7/00
A large gathering of specialist car clubs at this event add interest to the varied flying display

▶ **SAM35 Model Weekend**
8/7/00-9/7/00
Antique models and small scale flying

▶ **Sunset Display 3**
15/7/00-15/7/00
Aircraft ranging from World War II to the pioneers of flight and include one or two sole survivors from World War I

Railways

Leighton Buzzard Railway

Page's Park Station Billington Road Leighton Buzzard Bedfordshire LU7 8TN
[on A4146 Hemel Hempstead road, near J with A505 Dunstable / Aylesbury road]
Tel: 01525 373888 (24hours) Fax: 01525 377814
www.btinternet.com/~buzzrail

The Leighton Buzzard Railway lets you experience public transport as it was in the early part of the late 20th century. The 65-minute return journey takes you through the edge of the town and out into the countryside, and features level crossings, sharp curves and steep gradients. Most trains are hauled by one of the historic steam engines from Britain's largest collection of narrow-gauge locomotives. The railway, originally built for sand traffic, dates from 1919. Anextra attraction this year is Beaudesert, our new diesel locomotive.

Sundays, Mar 19-Oct 29. Mondays Apr 24, May 1 & 29, Aug 28. Tuesdays Aug 1-29. Wednesdays Apr 26, May 31-Aug 30, Oct 25. Thursdays Aug 3-31. Fridays Apr 21, Sept 1 (eve). Saturdays Apr 22 & 29, May 27, June 10 &17, Aug 5-Sept 2. Christmas trains Dec 2, 3, 9, 10, 16, 17, 23, 24, 27, 28.
Last Admission: 15.45
A£5.00 C(0-2)£Free C£(2-15)£1.50 OAPs£4.00 Day Rover £8.50
discount offer: One Child Travels Free With Fare Paying Adult

↓*special events*

▶ **Mothering Sunday**
2/4/00-2/4/00
Treat Mum to a train ride and free chocolate cake!

▶ **Easter Fun**
21/4/00-24/4/00
Free Easter Gifts to all fare paying children. Easter clown on Sunday, prize competition on Monday. Also heritage demonstrations Saturday to Monday

▶ **European Steam Weekend**
10/6/00-11/6/00
Help us celebrate steam preservation right across Europe. Intensive train service with lots of engines in steam

▶ **Family Fun Days**
6/8/00-20/8/00
Helping you survive the long summer holidays! family entertainment and fun rides (extra charges apply). Free gifts for all fare-paying children

▶ **September Steam-Up**
1/9/00-3/9/00

Everything that can move will move, including a visiting loco. BBQ Friday evening, Quarry Digger demonstration Saturday and Industry trains display on Sunday

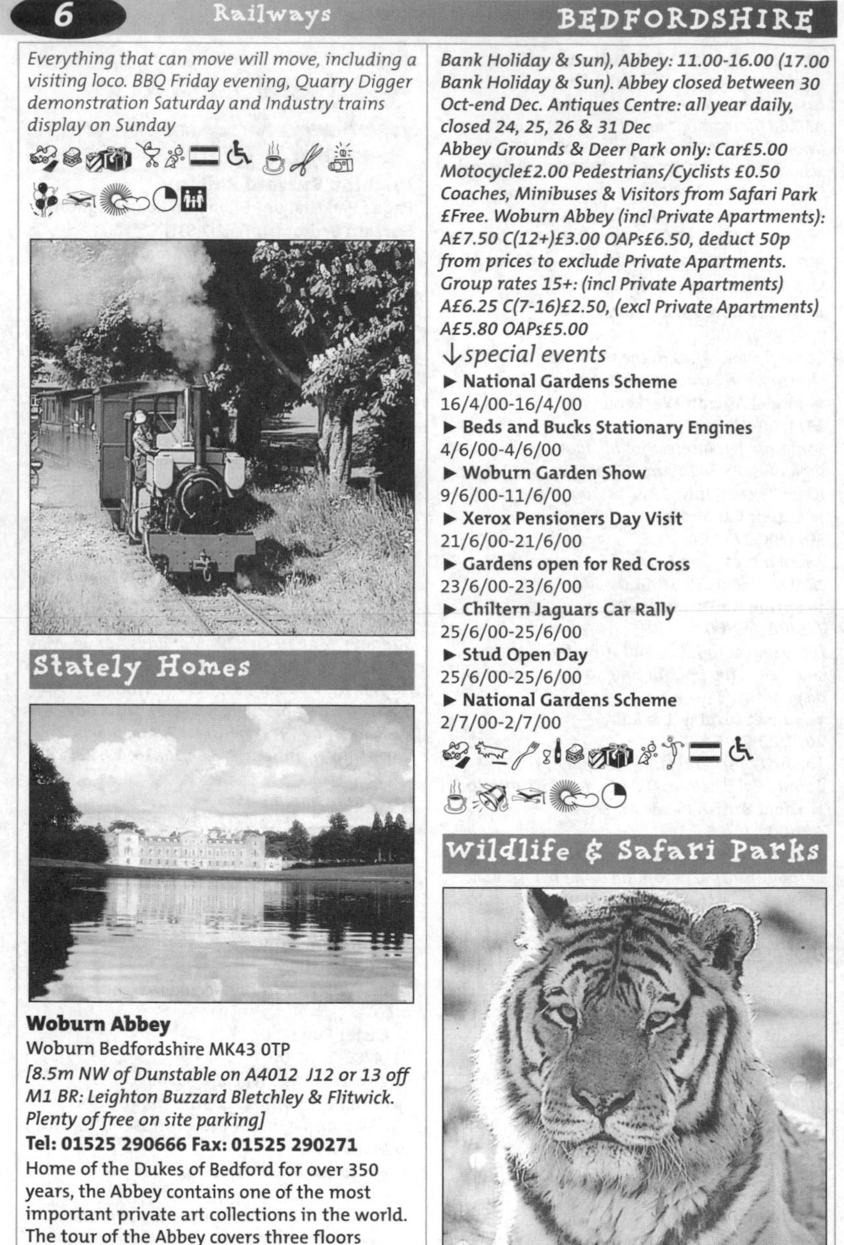

Stately Homes

Woburn Abbey

Woburn Bedfordshire MK43 0TP

[8.5m NW of Dunstable on A4012 J12 or 13 off M1 BR: Leighton Buzzard Bletchley & Flitwick. Plenty of free on site parking]

Tel: 01525 290666 Fax: 01525 290271

Home of the Dukes of Bedford for over 350 years, the Abbey contains one of the most important private art collections in the world. The tour of the Abbey covers three floors including the Crypt. The 3,000 acre Deer Park has lots of wildlife, including nine species of deer, roaming freely.

visitor comments: Our trip was a little expensive, but still a lovely day - worth it.

26 Mar-1 Oct daily Park: Mon-Sat 10.00-16.30 (16.45 Bank Holday & Sun), Abbey: Mon-Sat 11.00-16.00 (17.00 Bank Holiday & Sun). 2 Oct-29 Oct Weekends only Park: 10.30-15.45 (16.45 Bank Holiday & Sun), Abbey: 11.00-16.00 (17.00 Bank Holiday & Sun). Abbey closed between 30 Oct-end Dec. Antiques Centre: all year daily, closed 24, 25, 26 & 31 Dec

Abbey Grounds & Deer Park only: Car£5.00 Motocycle£2.00 Pedestrians/Cyclists £0.50 Coaches, Minibuses & Visitors from Safari Park £Free. Woburn Abbey (incl Private Apartments): A£7.50 C(12+)£3.00 OAPs£6.50, deduct 50p from prices to exclude Private Apartments. Group rates 15+: (incl Private Apartments) A£6.25 C(7-16)£2.50, (excl Private Apartments) A£5.80 OAPs£5.00

↓special events

▶ **National Gardens Scheme**
16/4/00-16/4/00

▶ **Beds and Bucks Stationary Engines**
4/6/00-4/6/00

▶ **Woburn Garden Show**
9/6/00-11/6/00

▶ **Xerox Pensioners Day Visit**
21/6/00-21/6/00

▶ **Gardens open for Red Cross**
23/6/00-23/6/00

▶ **Chiltern Jaguars Car Rally**
25/6/00-25/6/00

▶ **Stud Open Day**
25/6/00-25/6/00

▶ **National Gardens Scheme**
2/7/00-2/7/00

Wildlife & Safari Parks

Whipsnade Wild Animal Park

Whipsnade Dunstable Bedfordshire LU6 2LF

[just off J9 / 12 M1 and only 20mins from J21 M25]

Tel: 01582 872171 Fax: 01582 872649

www.whipsnade.co.uk

Set in 600 acres of beautiful parkland,

Whipsnade is home to over 2500 of the world's most incredible creatures. One of the largest wildlife conservation centres in Europe, the collection has many rare and endangered animals, including the family favourites - tigers, elephants, penguins, giraffe, bears, chimpanzees, hippopotamus and more! Get a taste of animal action at our free daily demonstrations; Elephant Walk, free-flying Birds of the World, Sealion Demonstration and penguin feeding. Take the Free Safari Tour Bus, and steam through herds of Asian animals on an unforgettable journey aboard the Great Whipsnade Railway. There is plenty for the children with the Run Wild Adventure Playground and children's farm... and who knows what wonderful creatures may be lurking around the corner in the Discovery Centre! Sorry, NO dogs allowed.

visitor comments: Educational, entertaining, and tiring! Don't miss the sea-lions or the elephants. Park is clean and animals seem content. Plenty to see.

Easter-end Sept Mon-Sat 10.00-18.00, Sun & Bank Hol Mon 10.00-19.00, for winter opening times please call. Closed Christmas Day

Last Admission: 60mins before closing

A£9.90 C(3-15)£7.50 OAPs/Students£7.50 Car(optional entrance) £8.00

discount offer: One Child Free When Accompanied By Two Full Paying Adults - Not Valid On Bank Holiday Weekends

Woburn Safari Park

Woburn Park Woburn Bedfordshire MK17 9QN

[J13 M1, or leave the A5 at Hockliffe for the A4012. Woburn Safari Park is well signed from these locations. Plenty of parking on site.]

Tel: 01525 290407 Fax: 01525 290489

www.woburnsafari.co.uk

Set in 300 of the 3000 acres of parkland surrounding Woburn Abbey, this award-winning safari park is well known, due to its collection of species of animals. A new leisure complex offers a boating lake, adventure playgrounds, Animal Encounters and Friends in the Forest, a woodland walk with tame deer. Many special events throughout the year in cluding the giant Tiger Crop Maze - 4 acres of maize maze for the summer holidays only.

Mar-Oct daily 10.00-17.00. Nov-Mar weekends only 11.00-15.00

Last Admission: 17.00 & 15.00

11 Mar-29 Oct: A£12.00 C£8.50 OAPs£9.00. Beds Schools Summer Holidays: A£12.50 C£9.00 OAPs£9.00. Family Tickets: £2.00 discount for every second or further child when 2A pay full price OR £2.00 discount for every third child when 1A pays full price. Group rates 15+ on application

↓special events

▶ **Bedfordshire Spring Craft Fair**

4/3/00-5/3/00

A variety of craft stalls, entry is included in Park admission price.

▶ **Bedfordshire Christmas Craft Fair**

4/11/00-5/11/00

A beautiful Christmas craft fair to buy those unusual gifts. Entry is included in Park Ticket

Animal Attractions

Bucklebury Farm Park

Bucklebury Reading Berkshire RG7 6RR

[BR: Thatcham or Midgham]

Tel: 0118 971 4002 Fax: 01734 714151

Magnificent red deer in sixty acres of beautiful parkland, lambs, calves, piglets, ducks, hens, rabbits, adventure playground, free tractor trailer rides, Nature Trail through ancient woodlands, picnic areas, refreshments. Water play through the summer. Free children's entertainment every Sunday through the summer holidays.

visitor comments: Nice and friendly. Picnic essential as no savoury snacks available. Tractor trailor ride to feed deer is great and best taken in June which is calving season.

Easter-Oct Sat & Sun School and Bank Hol 10.00-18.00

A£2.50 C£1.50 C(0-3)£Free

Courage Shire Horse Centre
Cherry Garden Lane Maidenhead Berkshire SL6 3QD
[off A4, 0.5m W of A4 / A423 / A423M. Plenty of on site parking available]
Tel: 01628 824848/823917 Fax: 01628 828472
Visitors are free to wander around and meet the horses, or take a free tour with a guide who will introduce you to the horses and explain the care and history of these 'gentle giants' of the equestrian world. You can see the harness maker at work and on selected days the farrier. Dray rides available.
Mar-Oct 10.30-17.00
Last Admission: 16.00
A£3.50 C&OAPs£2.50. Group rates 10+ call for details.

Lambourn Trainers Association
Windsor House Crowle Road Lambourn Hungerford Berkshire RG17 8NR
[Rail: Newbury. M4 J14]
Tel: 01488 71347 Fax: 01488 72664
Lambourn Trainers Association will escort visitors around their stables, giving a fascinating insight into the racing world not seen by the public before. Lambourn - Valley of the Racehorse, is highly respected for its enviable record for success, including the winners of the 1995 Champion Hurdle, Gold Cup and Grand national.
All year Mon-Sat 10.00-12.00 by appointment. Closed Bank Hol
Tours £5.00 + VAT

↓*special events*
▶ **Lambourn Racehorse Trainers Open Day**
21/4/00-21/4/00

Country Parks & Estates

Wellington Country Park
Odiham Road Riseley Reading Berkshire RG7 1SP
[signposted off A33]
Tel: 0118 932 6444 Fax: 0118 932 6445
Set in 350 acres of woodland & meadows, set around a lake, part of the Duke og Wellington's Estate. Other attractions include the collection of farm animals, a deer park, miniature railway, a fitness course & adventure playground. Fishing, pedaloes and row boats, private and company BBQ's, camping and caravanning site.
visitor comments: Beautiful setting - idyllic. Perfect for children. Peaceful and tranquil for those private family picnics.
Mar-Oct daily 10.00-17.30
Last Admission: 16.30
Queuing Times: 5mins
A£4.00 C£2.00
discount offer: Two For The Price Of One

↓*special events*
▶ **Husky Day**
26/3/00-26/3/00
100 teams of two-four dogs will compete in wheeled sled races
▶ **Easter Fun Days**
23/4/00-24/4/00
Grand Easter Egg Hunt and much more to keep the kids occupied
▶ **Animal Day**
1/5/00-1/5/00
An animalistic day for all the family including a fun dog show
▶ **Teddy Bear's Picnic**
11/6/00-11/6/00
A Bear-tastic day for all teddies and their owners. Meet Paddington Bear
▶ **Heavy Horse Spectacular**

9/7/00-9/7/00
Gentle giants, magnificent beasts, heavy horses; come and meet over 60 of them here today! An affiliated show with Cuntry Crafts

► **Firework Fiesta**
4/11/00-4/11/00
A stunning, professional display. Sideshows, entertainment, BBQs and refreshments. Entrance fees donated to charity

Festivals & Shows

Royal Windsor Horse Show 2000
RWHS Office The Royal Mews Windsor Castle Windsor Berkshire SL4 1NG
[The Home Park, Windsor. J5 M4, B470 to Windsor RAC signposted. Rail: Thames Line (via Slough) to Windsor Station, 10mins walk, or South Western Line to Windsor Riverside Station 5mins walk. Trains leave Windsor Riverside Station 30mins after the end of the evening performance. Car Parking £6.00 per day]
Tel: 01753 860633 venue Fax: 01753 831074
www.royal-windsor-horse-show.co.uk/
World's largest outdoor equestrian event - a great show of equestrian and country life for all the family. Brings together top International Show Jumping, Carriage Driving, Dressage and Showing. The country life displays and demonstrations combined with the shopping village and The Mad Hatters Tea Party (a home farm and maze with characters from Alice in Wonderland) are just some of the attractions which make it a perfect family day out. This year, in addition to the Kings Troop RHA, the Royal Mounted Canadian Police will be performing a spectacular ridden display to music. Set against the backdrop of Windsor Castle this is the ultimate sporting and country experience for all the family
May 10-14 2000. 9.00-22.30
Last Admission: Wed-Thur 17.30, Fri-Sun 20.30
Queuing Times: None
On site bookings: Wed-Thur A£7.00, C/Con£4.00. Fri A£8.00, C/Con£5.00. Sat A£10.00, C/Con£6.00. Sun A£11.00, C/Con £7.00. Seats Fri (eve only), Sat-Sun (aft and eve) £5.00. Advance booking discounts available, please call for details.

Historical

Basildon Park
Lower Basildon Reading Berkshire RG8 9NR
[J12 M4 between Pangbourne & Streatley, 7m NW of Reading on W side of A329]
Tel: 0118 984 3040 Fax: 0118 984 1267
A classical Georgian house standing in 400 acres of parkland overlooking the Thames Valley. After providing a billet for soldiers in both World Wars, the house was restored by Lord and Lady Iliffe. The Property contains a fine collection of furniture and pictures, an octagonal drawing room and a shell room. New for this season the Graham Sutherland Gallery where visitors can view his studies for the tapestry "Christ in Glory." There are also gardens, woodland walks, a tea room and National Trust Shop.
House: 1 Apr-31 Oct Wed-Sun & Bank Hol Mon 13.00-17.30. Closed Good Fri. Park, Gardens & Woodland Walks: as House 12.00-17.30. Tea Room & Shop: as House 12.00-17.30; Christmas Opening: 5 Nov-19 Dec Fri-Sun 12.00-16.00. NB: Property Closes at 17.00 on 11 & 12 Aug for concerts. Guided Tours: Wed-Fri 11.00 or evening (pre-booked). Terms discretionary for closed days, weekends or evenings. Group visits: Wed-Sun afternoons only and must be pre-booked
Last Admission: 17.00
House: £4.20 C£2.10 Family Ticket (A2+C3)£10.50, Park & Garden only: £1.80 C£0.90 Family Ticket £4.50. Group rates 15+ A£3.00 pre-booked

↓*special events*

► **Childrens' Theatre Production**
3/6/00-3/6/00
'The Pied Piper' presented by Openwide

► **Candlelight Concert**
6/6/00-6/6/00
'Fiori Musicali', a performance by the London Chamber Group

► **Candlelight Concert**
27/6/00-27/6/00
A performance by Concert Royale

► **Childrens' Theatre Production**
8/7/00-8/7/00
'The Emperor's New Clothes' presented by Illyria

► **Candlelight Concert**
11/7/00-11/7/00
A performance by the Delme String Quartet

► **Live Crafts Fair**
28/7/00-30/7/00
Contemporary and traditional crafts with live demonstrations

► **60's Concert with Fireworks**
11/8/00-11/8/00
With Marc Robinson and The Counterfeit Crickets (Buddy Holly tribute band), The Strolling Bones (Rolling Stones Tribute Band) and The Swinging Blue Jeans (with original members)

► **Jazz Concert with Fireworks**
12/8/00-12/8/00
Trevor Anthony's Dixieland All-Stars and the Pete Allen Jazz Band

Cliveden

Taplow Maidenhead Slough Berkshire SL6 0JA
[2m N of Taplow leave J7 M4 onto A4 or J4 M40 onto A404 to Marlow and follow signs BR: Taplow. Car parking 400m from house]
Tel: 01628 605069
New in 1999: Audio guide for the visually impaired and restored Spring Cottage Garden. The present house, built in 1851 by Sir Charles Barry, and once the home of Nancy, Lady Astor, is now let as a hotel. The 152ha garden and woodland include a magnificent parterre, a water garden and miles of woodland walks.
Estate & Garden: 13 Mar-31 Dec daily 11.00-18.00 (closes at 16.00 from 1 Nov-Mar 2000). Mansion (3 rooms) & Octagon Temple (Chapel): Apr-Oct Thur & Sun 15.00-18.00, entry by timed ticket from information kiosk. Spring Cottage Garden: June-Oct Thur 15.00-18.00 to holders of Mansion tickets only. Woodlands car park: All year daily 11.00-18.00 (closes at 16.00 from 1 Nov-Mar 2000)
Last Admission: 17.30
Queuing Times: Timed Tickets
Grounds: £5.00 C£2.50 Family Ticket £12.50. Mansion: A£1.00 C£0.50 extra. Pre-booked Group rates A£4.50 C£2.25. Woodland Car Park: £3.00 C£1.50 Family Ticket £7.50. Mooring Charge on Cliveden Reach: 24hrs £6.00, upto 4hrs £2.00, Season Ticket £30.00 inc. NT Members (does not include entry fee to Cliveden)

↓*special events*

- **Woodlands in Spring**
30/4/00-30/4/00
- **Open Air Theatre Festival**
28/6/00-9/7/00
Two of Shakespeare's best-loved works in the gardens: Twelfth Night and Romeo and Juliet
- **South Bucks Millennium Play**
13/7/00-16/7/00

Donnington Castle

Newbury Berkshire *[1m N of Newbury off B4494, BR: Newbury, Bus: 110 / 118 from Newbury]*
Built in the late 14th century, the twin towered gatehouse of this castle survives amidst some impressive earthworks.
All year any reasonable time
Admission Free

Highclere Castle

Highclere Newbury Berkshire RG20 9RN
[4.5m S of Newbury, off A34]
Tel: 01635 253210 Fax: 01635 255066
www.highclerecastle.co.uk
This splendid early Victorian mansion stands in beautiful parkland. It has sumptuous interiors and numerous Old Master pictures. Also shown are early finds by the 5th Earl of Carnarvon, one of the discoverer's of Tutankhamun's tomb. There is also a Racing Exhibition. Member of the Historic Houses Association.
visitor comments: Lovely gardens - especially the secret garden.
1 July-3 Sept Tue-Sun 11.00-17.00
Last Admission: Mon-Fri & Sun 16.00, Sat 14.30
A£6.50 C£3.00 OAPs&Students£5.00. Grounds & Gardens: A£3.00 C£1.50. Disabled Visitors: A£5.00 C£3.00 Wheelchair pushers £Free. Annual VIP Season Ticket (A2+C3)£25.00 includes many discounted admission prices. Groups rates 20+ A£5.00 C£3.00. Educational Groups C£3.00 1A£Free with every 10 Children

↓*special events*

- **Country Homes and Gardens Show**
6/5/00-7/5/00
- **Southern Counties Game and Country Fair**
28/5/00-29/5/00
- **"Romeo and Juliet" presented by Castle Theatre Company**
11/7/00-11/7/00
- **Porshe Rally**
22/7/00-23/7/00
Rally open to the public on Jul 23. Castle closed both days

Windsor Castle

Windsor Berkshire SL4 1NJ
[signposted from J6 M4 / J3 M3. BR: Waterloo-Windsor Riverside every 30mins Mon-Sat and hourly on Sun, Paddington - Windsor Central every 30mins all week]
Tel: 01753 831118 Fax: 01753 832290
www.royal.gov.uk
Over 900 years ago William the Conqueror, with the help of his victorious army, commenced the construction of Windsor Castle. The site was chosen with great care, high above the River Thames, on the edge of a Saxon hunting ground. The Castle was a day's march from the Tower of London and was designed to guard the Western approaches to the capital. Today, nine centuries after its foundation, the Castle continues to perform its prime role as one of the Official Residences of The Queen, who spends Easter, part of June and the majority of her private weekends at the Castle. The restoration of a major section of the Castle, severely damaged by fire in 1992, is now complete. This project, which cost over £35m and took the finest craftsmen from this country and abroad five years to complete, is

the largest restoration project completed this century. During the winter months additional rooms in the restored area of the Castle are included in the visitor route. These rooms, known collectively as the Semi State Rooms are as follows: The Green Drawing Room (view only), the Crimson Drawing Room, the State Dining Room, the Octagon Dining Room and the China Corridor. These rooms are scheduled to be open between October and the end of March. New visitor admissions building and audio's tours (in 6 languages) will be open/added in the summer.
Nov-Feb daily 09.45-16.15. Mar-Oct daily 09.45-17.15. Closed 1 Jan, 16 Feb, 23 May, 19 June, 25-26 Dec all day, other dates may be added. St George's Chapel is closed to visitors on Sun, worshippers are welcome. Changing of the Guard: Apr-end June Mon-Sat at 11.00
Last Admission: Summer 16.00, Winter 15.00
All areas: Mon-Sat A£10.50 C(0-17)£5.00 OAPs£8.00

↓*special events*

► **Changing of the Guard**
1/4/00-30/6/00

On the Water

French Brothers Thames Passenger Boat Operators
Clewer Boat House Clewer Court Road Windsor Berkshire SL4 5JH
[on A308. BR: Windsor / Eton Central or Windsor / Eton Riverside]
Tel: 01753 851900 Fax: 01753 832303
www.boat-trips.co.uk
Large fleet of modern, all-weather vessels offering a range of public scheduled cruises and short return trips from Windsor Promenade or Runnymede. Other group trips available at points between Maidenhead and Hampton Court. Well stocked bars on longer cruises and large range of on-board catering available if pre-booked. Guide Dogs allowed.
Easter-Nov for public sailings. All Year for group bookings and private hire
Public sailings from: £3.80 C(0-14)£half price. Private Hire and Group rates on application

Kris Cruisers
The Waterfront Southlea Road Datchet Berkshire SL3 9BU
[on the Waterfront in Datchet, 1.25m SE of Windsor]
Tel: 01753 543930 Fax: 01753 584866
Self drive boat hire. Perfect for that warm balmy day on the water. NEW for 1998 the 12 seater pontoon day boat with superior comfort. Choose from 6-12 seat day boats, 4-5 seat rowing boats, or how about the Cabin Cruisers: available from 2 berth to 11 berth for a weekend or weekly holiday on the river.
28 Mar-31 Oct 09.00-17.30
Rowing Boats: 4 seater from £5.00 per hour, 5 seater from £6.00 per hour. Day Boats: 6 seater from £13.00 per hour or from £60.00 per day, 8 seater from £14.50 per hour or from £80.00 per day, 10 seater from £16.00 per hour or from £100.00 per day, 12 seater from £17.50 per hour of from £110.00 per day. Call for Cabin Cruiser rates

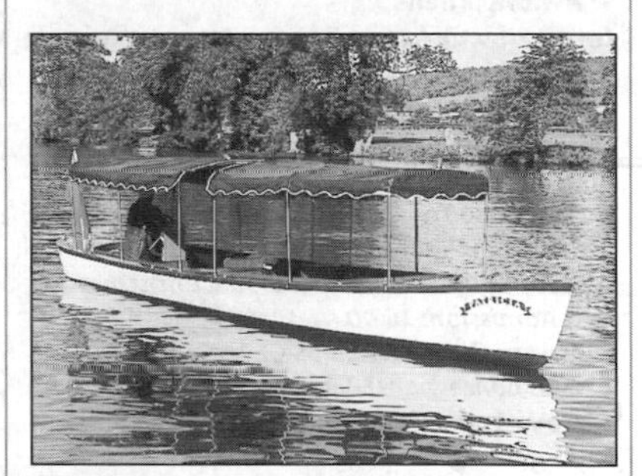

Rivertime
Whytegates House Berries Road Cookham Maidenhead Berkshire SL6 9SD
[BR: Maidenhead]
Tel: 01628 530600 Fax: 01628 810550
www.rivertime.com
Rivertime operates self-drive electric launches

which can carry up to 8 people each. Alternatively there are two classic launches, 'Rivertime' and 'Windsor Lady' both of which are perfect for up to 12 persons and are skippered for you.
All year, call for details
Prices vary please call for details
discount offer: 10% Discount Per Boat

Science - Earth & Planetary

Look Out Discovery Park
Nine Mile Ride Bracknell Berkshire RG12 7QW
[J10 M4, J3 M3 off the A322 on B3430. BR: Bracknell. Limited parking on site]
Tel: 01344 354400 Fax: 01344 354422
www.bracknell-forest.gov.uk/council/departments/leisure/recreation/lookout.htm
Education and fun Hands-On Science exhibition - Discovery Outpost. Over 70 exhibits suitable for all the family. Other attractions include 2,600 acres of Crown Estate Woodland, Mountain Bike Hire, Walks, Play Area.
All year daily 10.00-17.00. Closed Christmas
Last Admission: 16.00
Discovery Outpost: A£3.85 C£2.55 Family Ticket £10.20 Concessions£2.30
discount offer: One Child Free With A Full Paying Adult
↓*special events*
▶ **Workshops for 6-8 year olds**
21/2/00-27/10/00
Workshops run on Feb 21-25 - Evolution Week, Apr 17-20 and 25-28 - Light & Sound Weeks, May 30-June 2 - Mini Beasts and Aug 14-17 - Weather, Machines & Conservation Days, Oct 23-27 - Forces Week. C£6.00, start at 10.00-12.30. Please bring packed lunch. Booking essential
▶ **Friday Fun Days for 9-13 year olds**
18/8/00-1/9/00
Fri 18 - Who Dunnit? Fri 25 - Who's Stolen Eric? - track the kidnapper through the woods. Fri 1 Sept - Team building in the woods. From 10.00-15.00 each Friday. C£8.50 per session. Bring a packed lunch, booking is essential

Theme & Adventure Parks

LEGOLAND® Windsor
Winkfield Road Windsor Berkshire SL4 4AY
[on B3022 Windsor / Ascot road, well signposted from M4 & M3]
Tel: 08705 040404 Fax: 01753 626300
www.legoland.co.uk
With over 50 rides, shows and attractions, LEGOLAND® Windsor offers a full and exciting day out for children and their families. Plus five new attractions during 2000! You can watch the model makers at work in the brand new Creation Centre, surf the waves on the Adventure Wave Rider and race your own customised LEGO® car with the LEGO® Racer attraction. In Miniland you can see the brand new LEGO® Millennium Dome and Airport.
visitor comments: Editor's Choice. Excellent value, only two things my 2 year old could not go on! Food is plentiful, and staff obliging. Go out of season to beat the queues - ride in the morning and look at the models in the afternoon. Don't bother taking pushchairs, hire them there! Save your pennies for main shop, where you can see it all.
11 Mar-3 Jan 2001 daily: 10.00-18.00. English school holidays 10.00-20.00. Please call to confirm opening details after 31 Oct 2000 (0875 040404)
A£17.50 C£14.50 OAPs£11.50

Wildlife & Safari Parks

Beale Park
Lower Basildon Reading Berkshire RG8 9NH
[signposted from J12 M4, follow brown tourist signs]
Tel: 0118 984 5172 Fax: 0118 984 5171
This glorious Thameside Wildlife and Leisure Park has something for everyone. Unique collection of rare and endangered birds, Pets Corner, Deer Park, paddling pools, huge adventure playground, gardens, trails, education department, narrow gauge railway, picnic areas, Model boat collection, shops, cafeteria, fishing and much more.
Mar-Sept daily 10.00-18.00, Oct-Dec daily 10.00-17.00
Last Admission: 60mins before closing
A£4.50 C£3.00
discount offer: One Child Free With One Adult Paying Full Admission Price
↓*special events*
▶ **Beale Park Model Boat Festival**
29/4/00-1/5/00

Arts, Crafts & Textiles

Birmingham Museum And Art Gallery
Chamberlain Square Birmingham B3 3DH
[Birmingham city centre]
Tel: 0121 303 2834 Fax: 0121 303 1394
www.birmingham.gov.uk/bmag
Home to the world's finest collection of Pre-Raphaelite paintings, and many other prestigious works from the renowned Old Masters. Historic interest comes in the prehistoric form of Tyrannosaurus Rex. Egyptian mummies and the elegant Edwardian Tea room complete your journey through time and art.
All year Mon-Thur 10.00-17.00, Fri 10.30-17.00, Sat 10.00-17.00, Sun 12.30-17.00
Admission Free. Exhibitions in Gas Hall charged

↓*special events*
▶ **Gallery in the Trees**
5/10/99-30/3/00
An exciting and innovative project providing training and advice to graduate artists on public art commissions, and culminating in new art for the Lickey Hills
▶ **Visions of Birmingham**
25/11/99-28/2/00
▶ **20th Century Art**
2/12/99-1/5/00
Turbulent history and rapidly changing ideas and technologies are reflected in this major exhibition of over 200 British works in a range of media

Dudley Museum and Art Gallery
St James's Road Dudley DY1 1HU
[signposted within town centre]
Tel: 01384 815571/815575 Fax: 01384 815576
One of the Midland's most exciting exhibition venues, famous for its popular temporary shows. Permanent displays include the acclaimed 'Time Trail' geology gallery featuring spectacular fossils from the local rocks. Also the Brooke Robinson collection of 17th-19th century paintings, furniture, ceramics and enamels.
All year Mon-Sat 10.00-16.00
Admission Free
↓*special events*
▶ **The Black Country at War**
16/10/99-28/10/00
A fascinating look at life on the Home Front in the Black Country during the Second World War
▶ **Reflections: A Retrospective View**
12/2/00-29/4/00
A colourful exhibition displaying work from the

▶ **Live Craft Show**
2/9/00-3/9/00
*Tickets A£3.00, C£1.00, OAP£2.50**

▶ **Julian Bream in Concert**
23/9/00-23/9/00
*Britain's top classical guitarist. All tickets £16.00**

Waddesdon Manor
Aylesbury Buckinghamshire HP18 0JH
[at W end of Waddesdon village, 6m NW of Aylesbury on Bicester Road A41. Aylesbury Buses: Red Rover 1, 15, 16 from Aylesbury]
Tel: 01296 653211 Fax: 01296 653208
www.waddesdon.org.uk
Waddesdon Manor was built (1874-89) for Baron Ferdinand de Rothschild to display his vast collection of 18th century art treasures, which include French Royal furniture, Savonnerie carpets and Sevres porcelain as well as important portraits by Gainsborough and Reynolds. It has one of the finest Victorian Gardens in Britain, a fully stocked Rococo-style aviary, wine cellars, shops and a licensed restaurant. Many events are organised throughout the year. For more information call 01296 653226. During 2000 essential repairs are being made to a section of the roof, unfortunately this means part of the house will be covered with scaffolding.
visitor comments: A spectacular collection of French furniture, and the grounds are immaculate. The audio guide is well worth using.
Garden, Aviary, Shops & Restaurant: 1 Mar-24 Dec Wed-Sun & Bank Hol Mon 10.00-17.00. House & Wine Cellars: 30 Mar-29 Oct Thur-Sun, also Bank Hol Mon & Wed in July & Aug 11.00-16.00. Bachelors' Wing: Thur & Fri, & Wed in July & Aug 11.00-16.00 (access cannot be guaranteed)
Last Admission: recommended 14.30
House & Grounds: A£10.00 C£7.50. Grounds only: A£3.00 C£1.50 Bachelors' Wing £1.00. NT Members £Free. Timed tickets to the House can be purchased on site or reserved in advance by phoning 01296 653226 Mon-Fri 10.00-16.00. Advance booking fee: £3.00 per transaction

West Wycombe Park
West Wycombe Buckinghamshire HP14 3AJ
[at W end of West Wycombe, S of Oxford Road A40, 2.5m W High Wycombe Bus: Greenline from Victoria 290 to West Wycombe Village]
Tel: 01494 524411 Fax: 01494 471617
A Palladian house with frescos and painted ceilings owned by the National Trust. 18th century landscape garden with lake and various classical temples. Dogs are allowed in car park only, the house is unsuitable for wheelchairs and entry to the house by timed tickets on weekdays.
Grounds: 1 April-May Sun & Wed 14.00-18.00, Easter, May & Spring Bank Hol Sun & Mon 14.00-18.00, House & Gardens: June-Aug Sun-Thur 14.00-18.00
Last Admission: 17.15
Queuing Times: Timed tickets on weekdays
House & Grounds: A£4.40 Grounds only: A£2.60 C£1.75 Family Ticket £11.00. No reduction for parties

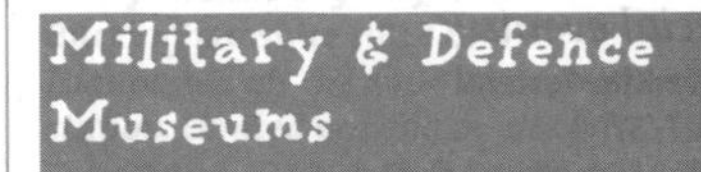

Military & Defence Museums

Bletchley Park Museum
The Mansion Wilton Avenue, Bletchley Park Bletchley Milton Keynes Buckinghamshire MK3 6EB
[300yds from Bletchley Station. Plenty of parking on site]
Tel: 01908 640404 Fax: 01908 274381
www.bletchleypark.org.uk
Privately run museum at the second world war codebreaking centre, where German, Italian and Japanese signals were broken, interpreted, and their substance distributed to Allied commanders - as featured in Enigma, Robert Harris's bestseller. Don't miss the reconstruction of Colossus, the world's first large electronic valve computer, that helped crack Hitler's messages. Photography in the grounds only.
All year every other weekend from 8 Jan 2000, 10.30-17.00
Last Admission: 15.30
A£4.50 C(under 8)£Free C&OAPs£3.50

Model Towns & Villages

Bekonscot Model Village
Warwick Road Beaconsfield Buckinghamshire

HP9 2PL
[2.7m from J2 M40, signposted, 4m from J16 M25]
Tel: 01494 672919 Fax: 01494 675284
www.bekonscot.org.uk
Bekonscot is a miniature world where time has stood still for 70 years. Showing rural England in the 1930's this wonderland of make-believe has a working model railway, airfield, castles, mine and an elevated walk-way. Two picnic areas - one undercover and a well equipped childrens' playground.
visitor comments: Beautiful. Great for young 'Thomas' fans. Very good value - we keep going again and again. Leave your pushchair behind if possible (some narrow paths). Covered picnic area if weather inclement.
19 Feb-29 Oct daily 10.00-17.00
Last Admission: 17.00
Queuing Times: not normally
A£4.50 C£2.50 OAPs&Students£3.00. Groups of 13+ A£3.75 C£2.25. Special rates for school groups
discount offer: One Child Free With One Full Paying Adult. Offer Valid Until 29 Oct 2000

Sport & Recreation

Wycombe Summit Ski and Snowboard Centre
Abbey Barn Lane High Wycombe Buckinghamshire HP10 9QQ
[between J3/4 of M40 just 30mins from London. Plenty of parking on site]
Tel: 01494 474711 Fax: 01494 443757
www.ski.co.uk/wycombesummit
England's longest slope and world class ski and snowboard school, Wycombe Summit is suitable for experts and beginners alike. 300m main slope, 100m trainer slope and several nursery areas with three lifts, all floodlit and fully lubricated. A wide range of lessons are available to meet all your requirements, from Big Foot Club for the children. Competent skiers and boarders may use the slopes for their own open practice. The Summit bar and restaurant is open all day for delicious food and refreshments. Wycombe has excellent facilities for entertainment and celebrations and regularly hosts national race competitions and training sessions.
All year 10.00-22.00 Closed Christmas Day
Last Admission: 21.00
1 Hour from: A£8.50-£10.00 C(under 16)£6.50-£7.50. 2 Hours: £15.00 C£12.50. All day from: A£10.00-£20.00 C£7.00-£15.00. Lessons are extra, please call for details
discount offer: Two For The Price Of One

XScape
Avebury Boulevard 602 Marlborough Gate Central Milton Keynes Buckinghamshire MK9
[M1 J14, central Milton Keynes, Avebury Boulevard]
Tel: 01908 200020 Fax: 01908 607199
www.xscape.co.uk/
Opening May 2000 Xscape™ is set to become the ultimate entertainment destination. A real snow indoor ski centre, 16 screen Cineworld multiplex, City Limits Family Entertainment Centre, Healthland fitness Centre, restaurants, cafés, bars and shops all under one enormous roof. A great day out. There just aren't enough hours in the day!
Due to open in May 2000. Please consult internet site
Due to opening, prices yet to be confirmed. Please consult internet site

Stately Homes

Hughenden Manor Estate
Hughenden Manor High Wycombe Buckinghamshire HP14 4LA
[1.5m N of High Wycombe on W side Gt Missenden Road A4128. BR: High Wycombe]
Tel: 01494 755573/755565 Fax: 01494 463310
New for 2000: Upgrading of Stable Tea Room to The Stableyard Restaurant, serving more extensive lunch menu. Further refurbishment of upper show rooms in the Manor. Home of Benjamin Disraeli, the red brick gothicised Manor is set in colourful Victorian style gardens and surrounded by parkland and woodland. The House is filled with fascinating mementoes of Disraeli's life as statesmen and writer, with much of the original furniture, pictures and books.
House: 1-30 Mar Sat & Sun only, 1 Apr-31 Oct

Maritime

Fort Grey Shipwreck Museum
Rocquaine Bay St Pierre Du Bois Guernsey Channel Islands GY7 9BY
[located on the Rocquaine coastal road twoards Pleimont]
Tel: 01481 65036 Fax: 01481 63279
www.museum.guernsey.net
Built in 1804 to defend the Island from French invasion, this delightful fort is known locally as 'The Cup & Saucer'. Set in one of the most picturesque areas of the Island, with the last manned lighthouse 'The Hanois' in the distance, Fort Grey's Martello tower now houses an excellent Shipwreck Museum. On special days the staff are dressed as Victorian characters from the nineteenth century.
Easter-Oct 10.00-17.00
A£2.00 C£Free OAPs£1.00. Joint Ticket with Castle Cornet & Guernsey Museum: A£6.00 C£Free OAPs£3.00. Students in full time education £Free. Season Tickets: A(1)£15.00 OAPs£10.00 A(2)£25.00. Groups rates pre-booked 10% discount. Educational Groups pre-booked £Free
discount offer: 10% Discount On Full Admission Prices

↓*special events*

▶ **Art for the Millennium 'Future Memories'**
1/6/00-1/12/00
An exhibition of artists with local connections from the Bailiwick and beyond

▶ **The Reluctant Recruits**
13/6/00-19/6/00
(not 15 June) It is 1807. An English Sergeant, seconded to the West regiment of the Guernsey Militia, to instruct new recruits two of which are not quite as he expects! A dramatisation by Echoes From The Past

▶ **The Sinking of the Boreas 1807**
16/6/00-17/6/00
A dramatised recounting of the loss of the Frigate HMS Boreas on the Hanois reef on the 28 Nov 1807

Zoos

Jersey Zoological Park
La Profonde Rue Trinity Jersey Channel Islands JE3 5BP
[signposted 4m N of St Helier]
Tel: 01534 860000 Fax: 01534 860001
aea@itl.net
Jersey Zoo offers visitors an extraordinary experience. Green open spaces, free-living animals and an exciting programme of visitor activities encourage the discovery of how this world leader in wildlife conservation is helping to save animals from extinction. 'First Impressions' an exciting new multi-species habitat opening 26 March 1999 to provide visitors with a dramatic first impression of wildlife conservation at work.
All year daily 9.30-18.00, dusk in winter. Closed 25 Dec
from 1 Mar 99: A£6.00 C£3.50 OAPs£5.00

Communication Museums

On the Air: The Broadcasting Museum
42 Bridge Street Row Chester Cheshire CH1 1NN
[in centre of Chester not far from The Cross]
Tel: 01244 348468 Fax: 01244 348468
"On the Air" tells the story of British radio & tv broadcasting from the 'Cat's Whisker' to digital tv. The exhibition is built around a fascinating collection, with period settings from the 1920's to the 1950's. Also includes the Vintage Sound Shop, selling original wireless sets and gramophones, books, records and tapes.
All year Easter-Dec daily 10.00-17.00. Dec-Easter Tue-Sat 10.00-17.00. Closed Sun except Bank Holidays weekends, 25-26 Dec
Last Admission: 16.45
A£1.95 C(0-5)£Free C£1.00 Family Ticket £5.50 OAPs£1.50
discount offer: Two For The Price Of One

Country Parks & Estates

Dunham Massey Hall, Garden and Park
Altrincham Cheshire WA14 4SJ
[3m SW of Altrincham off A56 J19 off M6 J7 off M56. BR: Altrincham & Hale. Plenty of parking on site]
Tel: 0161 941 1025 Fax: 0161 929 7508
A friendly treasure-filled mansion and one of the North-West's great gardens are set in an ancient park where deer graze under 300 year old trees. Guided tours or children's trails provide something for everyone and there's a fun packed events programme, from picnics with Rupert Bear to workshops with the Head Gardener. The informal Stables Restaurant caters for every appetite from a children's lunch-box to a gourmet meal. Find a souvenir of your day in the well-stocked gift shop.
Park, Restaurant and shop: Daily all year. House and Garden: 1 Apr-1 Nov. House: Sat-Wed 12.00-17.00 (11.00-17.00 Bank Hol Sun & Mon,

12.00-16.00 in Oct) Garden: Open Daily, 11.00-17.30 (11.00-16.30 in Oct)
Last Admission: 30mins before closing
House & Garden: A£5.00 C£2.50 Family Ticket £12.50. House or Garden: A£3.00 C£1.50 NT members Free. Groups 15+ £4.00 each, not available Sun & Bank Hol. Car: £3.00. Coach/Minibus: £5.00 (£Free to pre-booked groups). Motorcycle: £1.00. Discounted admission to House & Garden available to visitors who have used public transport
discount offer: Up To Three Children Free When Accompanied By Two Full Paying Adults to House & Garden. Car Entry Free. Valid Until 1 Nov 2000

Tatton Park
Knutsford Cheshire WA16 6QN
[5m from J19 M6 & J7 M56]
Tel: 01625 534400 Fax: 01625 534403
One of the most complete historic estates open to visitors. Neo-Classical Mansion, Tudor Old Hall, 1930's Working Farm and 60 acres of gardens surrounded by 1000 acre deerpark with meres and a children's playground Garden, Gift and Speciality Food Shops offer a variety of estate and local produce and gift wear. Special events include the Hallé firework concert and the RHS Flower Show. Managed and financed by Cheshire County Council. Event information will be available no more than 14 days prior to an event on 01625 534435. Most daytime events have a Park entry fee. For those events marked with an * booking is essential on either 0161 247 2220 or 01625 534400.
High Season: Apr-Oct, Park & Restaurant daily, Attractions Tue-Sun. Low Season: Nov-Mar, Park & Gardens Tue-Sun only
Last Admission: 17.00
Mansion & Garden: A£3.00 C(4-15)£2.00 Family Ticket (A2+C3)£8.00 Group 12+ A£2.40 C£1.50. Farm (inc. Stables) & Old Hall: A£2.50 C£1.50 Family Ticket £8.00 Group 12+ A£2.00 C£1.20. Discovery "Saver" Ticket (valid for one visit to any two attractions excl. car charge): A£4.50 C£2.50 Family Ticket £12.50 Group 12+ A£3.60 C£2.00

↓*special events*

▶ **Historic Costumed Tours**
21/5/00-21/5/00
Tatton's hidden gem, the Old Hall, built over 200 years before the Mansion. Noon-16.00. Usual charges apply - call to book

▶ **Classic Car Spectacular & Cheshire Autojumble**
3/6/00-4/6/00
Over 70 classic car clubs exhibiting some of the finest cars in the country. 350 autojumble / classic car specialists stands, collector's car auction (Sunday). Family attractions and refreshments. A£5.00 C£Free

▶ **Close Encounters of the Classical Kind with Fireworks**
10/6/00-10/6/00
Spooky space themes. An evening with an extra-terrestrial firework finale! A£17.50 (advance), £20.00 on the night. C(5-16)£10.00. Gates open from 17.00, Concert: 20.00-22.30

▶ **The Woman's Touch**
10/6/00-11/6/00
Patchwork and quilting groups from Cheshire and North Wales exhibit their work in the historic setting of the Old Hall. 11.00-16.30. A£2.50 C£Free Concessions£2.00

▶ **Catch the Dream**
18/6/00-18/6/00
A Christian Celebration. Gates open from 11.00, Procession: Noon. A Service at 17.00, local bands 18.00, Worldwide Message Tribe at 19.00. A£5.00 C(5-17)&Concessions £2.00 Family Ticket £12.00

▶ **RHS Flower Show**
19/7/00-23/7/00
Magnificent floral marquees, show gardens, specialist plant displays, RHS Advise Desk and 1,000s of plants and gardening products to buy. Wed-Sat 10.00-19.00, Sun 10.00-17.00. Wed tickets in advance only £16.00. Other days: from A£13.00-£16.00 C(5-15)£5.00 - ticket hotline 0870 906 3811 - tickets NOT available from Tatton

▶ **Historic Costumed Tours**
20/8/00-20/8/00
See entry for 21st May

▶ **Last Night of the Proms**
3/9/00-3/9/00
Sing heartily to Rule Britannia, Jerusalem and Land of Hope and Glory, wave Union Jacks and watch over 1,000 fireworks burst into a fizzing and bubbling mass of colourful explosions high up in the dark night sky. Gates open: 17.00, Concert commences: 19.30-22.00. A£17.00 (advance) A£20.00 on the night, C£(5-16)£10.00

▶ **Wood Weekend - A Wood Exhibition**
16/9/00-17/9/00
See and learn about the many uses of wood. Working demonstrations and displays. 10.30-17.00. A£2.70 C(4-17(£0.50p Family Ticket (A2+C3)£6.40

▶ **Historic Costumed Tours**
17/9/00-17/9/00
See entry for 21st May

▶ **The Really Good Deal Fashion Sale**
4/10/00-7/10/00
Many top brand names at reduced prices. Open: 10.00-18.00 both days. Call for ticket details on 01634 226203

▶ **Cheshire Crafts and Design Fair**
14/10/00-15/10/00
Featuring an abundance of creativity in tradi-

▶ **Medieval Entertainers**
8/7/00-9/7/00
From Noon. Play authentic medieval games, learn about cures and folklore, plus a children's play about the formative years of Parliament
▶ **Hoodwinked**
15/7/00-16/7/00
From Noon. Robin and Marian return to Sherwood to sort out truth from legend, with hilarious results!

Capesthorne Hall

Capesthorne Siddington Macclesfield Cheshire SK11 9JY
[J18 / J19 M6 J6 M56 approx 10m from either motorway, A34 between Congleton / Wilmslow]
Tel: 0161 9762729 Fax: 0161 9762758

Dating back to the Domesday times, Capesthorne contains a great variety of sculptures, paintings, & other contents including a collection of American Colonial furnishings. There are gardens, a nature trail & woodland walks. Member of the Historic Houses Association.

Garden: Apr-Oct Wed Sun & Bank 12.00-18.00. Hall: Apr-Oct Wed Sun & Bank Hol 13.30-15.30 Last Admission: Gardens 16.30 Hall 15.30 Gardens & Chapel: A£3.50 C£1.50 OAPs£3.00. Hall & Gardens: A£6.00 C(5-18)£2.50 OAPs£5.50 Family Ticket £12.00. Groups 25+ call for details

↓*special events*

▶ **Cheshire Kit Car Show**
21/5/00-21/5/00
▶ **6th Cheshire Classic Car and Motorcycle Show**
28/5/00-29/5/00
▶ **Costume talk in Theatre (Victorian)**
3/6/00-3/6/00
A talk on Victorian costume by Lesley Edwards, an expert in costume through the ages
▶ **National Gardens Scheme Open Day**
2/8/00-2/8/00
Normal admission times and charges with proceeds going to various charities
▶ **Fireworks and Laser Spectacular**
6/8/00-6/8/00
Tickets A£19.50 in advance and £22.00 on the night. C£10.00 (aged 5-16) Delicious pre-concert picnics, wonderful music and unsurpassable spectacular!
▶ **Classic Sports Car Show**
27/8/00-28/8/00

Dorfold Hall

Chester Road Acton Nantwich Cheshire CW5 8LD
[1m W of Nantwich on A534 BR: Nantwich 1.5m. Plenty of parking on site]
Tel: 01270 625245 Fax: 01270 628723

Jacobean country house built 1616. Beautiful plaster ceilings and panelling. Interesting furniture and pictures. Attractive gardens including spectacular spring garden and herbaceous borders. All visits by guided tour with a visit to the Gardens included. Member of the Historic Houses Association.

Apr-Oct Tue & Bank Hol Mon 14.00-17.00. Other times by appointment only, please call for details. Guided Tours 14.15, 15.15 & 16.15 or on other weekdays by appointment A£4.50 C£3.00. No parking facilities for coaches due to narrow driveway

discount offer: Two For The Price Of One

Gawsworth Hall

Church Lane Gawsworth Macclesfield Cheshire SK11 9RN
[2.5m S of Macclesfield on A536. BR: Macclesfield]
Tel: 01260 223456 Fax: 01260 223469
www.gawsworthhall.com

This fine Tudor black & white manor house was the birthplace of Mary Fitton (allegedly the 'Dark Lady' of Shakespeare's sonnets). Pictures & armour can be seen in the house, which also has a tilting ground, thought to be a rare example of an Elizabethan pleasure garden. Open air theatre performances held during the summer. For all special events marked with an *, please contact the venue for times and ticket details.

20 Apr-1 Oct 14.00-17.00. Not open Sat in Apr, May & Sept. Evening parties call for details A£4.20 C£2.10 Group rates 20+ £3.00

↓*special events*

▶ **Antique and Collectors Fayre**
23/4/00-24/4/00
Held on Apr 23-24 and Sept 2-3 2000
▶ **Pride and Prejudice**
12/7/00-15/7/00
*The world premiere of a new adaptation of Pride and Prejudice. A spectacular production for the family. **
▶ **Barber of Seville**
16/7/00-16/7/00
*Presented by European Chamber Opera. A fully costumed & staged production with orchestra. **
▶ **Piccadilly Dance Band**
19/7/00-19/7/00
*A Marvellous Party to celebrate Noel Coward's Centenary. **
▶ **The Grimethorpe Colliery Brass Band**
20/7/00-22/7/00
*Great evenings of superb brass band music. Don't forget your flag for our evenings of Heroism and Valour.**
▶ **Country Jamboree**
23/7/00-23/7/00
An evening featuring some of the top British

*Country stars. **

► **The Monarchs of All They Savoy**
26/7/00-26/7/00
*Tells the story of Gilbert & Sullivan and D'Oyly Carte at a cracking pace, cramming the action with music from all their collaborations! **

► **Miller Magic**
27/7/00-27/7/00
*We welcome the return of John Miller, Fiona Paige and the Miller Magic - a splendid night out! **

Tabley House
Knutsford Cheshire WA16 0HB
[J19 M6 A556, 2m W of Knutsford, entrance on A5033]
Tel: 01565 750151 Fax: 01565 653230
Home of the Leicester family since 1272, this magnificent 18th century Grade I mansion was designed by John Carr of York. Tabley has the first great collection of English pictures in the State Rooms, together with furniture and other fascinating family memorabilia. Friendly stewards are available to talk about the Leicester's 700 years at Tabley. Civil Wedding Licence.
Apr-Oct Thur, Fri-Sun & Bank Hol 14.00-17.00
Last Admission: 16.30
A£4.00 C&Students£1.50
discount offer: One Child Free With One Full Paying Adult. Offer ends 31 Oct 2000

Tabley House
Knutsford Cheshire WA16 0HB
[J19 M6 A556, 2m W of Knutsford, entrance on A5033]
Tel: 01565 750151 Fax: 01565 653230
Home of the Leicester family since 1272, this magnificent 18th century Grade I mansion was designed by John Carr of York. Tabley has the first great collection of English pictures in the State Rooms, together with furniture and other fascinating family memorabilia. Friendly stewards are available to talk about the Leicester's 700 years at Tabley. Civil Wedding Licence.
Apr-Oct Thur, Fri-Sun & Bank Hol 14.00-17.00
Last Admission: 16.30
A£4.00 C&Students£1.50
discount offer: One Child Free With One Full Paying Adult. Offer ends 31 Oct 2000

Water Tower
City Walls Chester Cheshire *[directional signs for City Walls]*
Tel: 01244 402008
www.chestercc.gov.uk
Built in 1324 to protect ships on the River Dee, these two linked Towers retain their medieval appearance. Audio Guide tells scenes from local history together with small display on City Walls. Many steep steps within Tower.
High season only 11.00-16.00, telephone for dates
Last Admission: 15.00
A£1.00 C£0.40 Family Ticket £2.25

Military & Defence Museums

Cheshire Military Museum
The Castle Chester Cheshire CH1 2DN
[edge of Chester City centre]
Tel: 01244 327617 Fax: 01244 401700
The 22nd (Cheshire) Regiment, Cheshire Yeomanry and representative collections of 3rd Carabiniers and 5th Royal Inniskilling Dragoon Guards. Displays of uniforms, old arms, awards, campaign medals, regimental colours, pictures, trophies and souvenirs. There are tableaux of the two wars and much else of interest. We are currently trying to raise the £0.5million needed to modernise and refurbish the Museum, donations will be much appreciated.
All year daily 10.00-17.00. Closed 22 Dec-2 Jan
A£1.00 Concessions£0.50
discount offer: Two For The Price Of One

↓*special events*

► **South Africa Exhibition**
1/10/99-31/12/00
An exhibition to commemorate the Boer War 1899-1902. Through objects and archival material, the display looks at the stories of individuals from Cheshire who served in South Africa. Complimented by a quiz for children.

► **Out from Behind the Glass**
1/5/00-4/6/00
Come and have a closer look at objects and uniforms of Cheshire soldiers which are usually behind glass and take home a photograph.

Zoos

Chester Zoo
Upton-by-Chester Chester Cheshire CH2 1LH
[2m N of city centre off A41]
Tel: 01244 380280 Fax: 01244 371273
www.demon.co.uk/chesterzoo
This is one of Europe's finest zoological gardens, with 5000 animals in 110 acres of enclosures & landscaped gardens. Over 40% of the species are considered endangered. Added attractions are the tropical realm, aquarium, waterbus rides & a zoofari overhead railway. Discover our NEW Bat Cave and Penguin Pool, and opening in Spring 'Islands in Danger', for endangered species that live on islands, including Komodo Dragons and Birds of Paradise. Ask about our corporate and celebration facilities.
visitor comments: Plenty of picnic spots indoor & outdoor. Animals well cared for.
All year daily from 10.00
Last Admission: Summer 17.30 Winter 15.30
Queuing Times: minimal
A£9.50 C(3-15)£7.00 Family Ticket (A2+C3)£34.00 OAPs£7.50

Animal Attractions

Newham Grange Leisure Farm
Wykeham Way Coulby Newham Middlesbrough Cleveland TS8 0TG
[A19, A174 Parkway, B1365 to Coulby Newham then signposted]
Tel: 01642 300261 Fax: 01642 300276
Newham Grange Leisure Farm is a working farm which is open to the public. It is a recognised Rare Breeds Survival Trust centre with pigs, cattle, sheep, poultry and ponies, café, picnic area, play area and museums. Guided Tours by arrangement, limited access for wheelchairs. A unique and enjoyable day out for all the family.
All year Apr-Septdaily 09.30-17.30. Oct-Feb Sat & Sun only 10.00-16.00
Last Admission: 60mins before closing
A£1.65 C&OAPs£0.85 Family Ticket £4.40
discount offer: One Child Free When Accompanied By A Full Paying Adult (Not OAP)

Birds, Butterflies & Bees

Butterfly World
Preston Park Yarm Road Stockton-On-Tees Cleveland TS18 3RH
[off A66]
Tel: 01642 791414 Fax: 01642 791212
An indoor tropical rainforest populated by exotic free-flying butterflies and birds complemented by a display of fascinating insects. Humming birds, Koi Carp and unusual flowering plants.
All year daily 10.00-17.00. Winter close 16.30 Closed Jan-Feb
Last Admission: Summer 16.30 Winter 16.00
A£2.90 C&OAPs£2.20 Family Ticket A2+C3) £8.50 Group rates, call for details

Owl Centre
Kirkleatham Redcar Cleveland TS10 5NW
[in village of Kirkleatham 2m from Redcar, easy access from A1, A19 & A66. Plenty of coach and car parking on site]
Tel: 01642 480512 Fax: 01642 492790
www.jillsowls.co.uk
Displaying owls, hawks, falcons, vultures and kites, the Owl Centre houses one of the largest collection of birds of prey in the UK. Photograph these magnificent creatures of darkness at close quarters, see the baby owls playing in the spring and summer sunshine and thrill to the free flying displays. Sorry, no dogs allowed.
All year daily 10.30-16.30
Last Admission: Summer 16.30
A£3.00 C(0-3)£Free C(4-15)£1.75 Family Ticket £7.95 OAPs£2.00
discount offer: One Child Free With A Full Paying Adult

Historical

Captain Cook Birthplace Museum
Stewart Park Marton Middlesborough Cleveland TS7 6AS
[3M S on A172 at Stewart Park, Marton. Plenty of on site parking available]
Tel: 01642 311211 Fax: 01642 317419
The museum has recently undergone a £1.2 million refurbishment. It was opened to mark the 250th anniversary of the birth of the voyager in 1728, and illustrates the early life of James Cook and his discoveries. On three great voyages Cook and his crew encountered many new peoples and lands. Artists and scientists

recorded strange plants and animals of the South Seas and Americas. A special resource centre is equipped with computers and other interactive educational aids, which help to give an account of life 200 years ago and what it was like to sail around the world!
All year Summer: Tue-Sun 10.00-17.30. Winter: 09.00-16.00. Closed 25-26 Dec & 1 Jan
Last Admission: 45mins before closing
A£2.40 C&OAPs£1.20 Family Ticket £6.00
discount offer: Two For The Price Of One. NOT Valid Bank Hol. One Coupon Per Party

Ormesby Hall
Church Lane Ormesby Middlesborough
Cleveland TS7 9AS
[3m SE of Middlesborough W of A171 from A19 take the A174 to the A172 follow signs for Ormesby Hall car entrance on Ladgate Lane B1380. Plenty of on site parking]
Tel: 01642 324188 Fax: 01642 300937
A mid 18th century house, home of the Pennyman family, with fine plasterwork and card woodwork; Victorian laundry and kitchen with scullery and game larders. A large model railway exhibition housed in the 17th century wing, where the family crest survives over the door from the earlier house. An attractive 2ha garden will holly walk. The stable block, attributed to Carr of York, is a particularly fine mid 18th century building which is leased to Cleveland Constabulary Mounted Police. Children's play area. School groups on Wed-Fri mornings during season, Laundry and Kitchen visits, Tuesdays.
28 Mar-31 Oct Tue, Wed Thur & Sun, Bank Hol Mon & Good Fri 14.00-17.00
Last Admission: 17.00
Combined entry: A£3.50 C£1.70 Family Ticket (A2+C3)£9.00. Garden & Exhibitions only: A£2.20 C£1.10. Party rates for 15+

↓special events

▶ **Wedding Fayre**
26/3/00-26/3/00
12.00-16.00 offering one stop wedding shopping from cakes to cars, bouquets to bridal wear. £1.00

▶ **Mother's Day**
2/4/00-2/4/00
A perfect chance for Mothers to be pampered, colour consultants, hairdressers and children's activities

▶ **Garden Tours**
27/4/00-26/10/00
Last Thursday in each month, call for details

▶ **Proms in the Park**
26/8/00-26/8/00
Northern Sinfonia performing Last Night of the Proms with a Millennium theme. Call for details and booking

▶ **Promos in the Park**
9/9/00-9/9/00
See entry for 26 August

▶ **North East Counties Ho,e Garden and Leisure Autumn Show**
16/9/00-19/9/00
See entry for 27 May

▶ **Halloween Haunts**
29/10/00-29/10/00
Scary fun with storytelling, crafts, traditional games etc. Wear your best Halloween outfit and bring your lanterns for the competitions. 14.00-16.30, booking essential

Maritime

HMS Trincomalee Trust
Jackson Dock Hartlepool Cleveland TS24 OSQ
[follow brown heritage signs A689 & A19 A1M]
Tel: 01429 223193 Fax: 01429 864385
Situated at Hartlepool Historic Quay, HMS Trincomalee was built in 1817 and is the oldest British Warship afloat today. The Ship is now under restoration. Guided tours.
All year from 10.30. Closed Christmas, Boxing Day and New Years' Day
A£2.50 C&Concessions £1.50 Family Ticket (A2+C3)£6.50

Nature & Conservation Parks

Nature's World
Ladgate Lane Acklam Middlesbrough
Cleveland TS5 7YN
[follow Brown tourist signs from A19 onto A174]
Tel: 01642 594895
Unique environmental attraction featuring a 400 metre working model of the River Tees. Also over 20 acres of organic demonstration gardens, ponds and wildlife areas. Opening

ment and professional performances around Bodmin culminating in Riding and Heritage Day, a traditional Cornish Feast Day.
June 24-July 1 2000 Please phone before for programme details
Prices vary, concessions available and some free events.

↓*special events*

▶ **Cornwall Theatre and Heritage Festival**
24/6/00-1/7/00

Daphne du Maurier Festival 2000

Fowey Cornwall *[Fowey and surrounding areas. M5 at Exeter, A38 or A30. BR: St Austell (9m). Bus: National Express runs between St Austell / Fowey]*
Tel: 01726 77477 Box Office Fax: 01726 68339
Celtic and folk music, art exhibitions, guided walks, street fayres, drama, comedy, day schools, camera clubs, orchestras and more. Most venues are not suitable for wheelchairs. Full list available on request from Festival Information Line: 01726 223535.
May 12-21 2000
Various. Some venues £Free.

↓*special events*

▶ **Daphne du Maurier Festival**
12/5/00-21/5/00

Falmouth Big Green Fair

Falmouth School Trescobees Road Falmouth Cornwall *[BR: Penmere 1m]*
Tel: 01326 375158
Music (drumming, hurdy-gurdy, belly dancing and other exotica), vegan food stalls, local cider and ale, environmental stalls. Bouncy castles, workshops, complimentary healing tasters such as reflexology, massage etc. Due to some steep slopes and steps, access for disabled is slightly curtailed. However, help is available upon request.
July 1 2000
Admission Free if travel by bus, cycle or foot. Full cars free but charges if contain 1-2 people.

↓*special events*

▶ **Falmouth Big Green Fair**
1/7/00-1/7/00

Fowey Royal Regatta and Carnival

Fowey Cornwall *[Fowey. B3269 / A3082 to Fowey. BR: Par (3m) / St Austell (9m). Bus: National Express St Austell. Hoppa Bus 24 from St Austell]*
Tel: 01726 832133
Gig racing, male voice choir, children's entertainment, torchlight procession on river, great fun for all.
Aug 13-19 2000
Voluntary donation appreciated. C£Free

↓*special events*

▶ **Fowey Royal Regatta and Carnival**
13/9/00-19/9/00

Helston Flora Day 2000

Helston Cornwall *[Helston town centre. Town centre closed to all traffice from 06.30-early eve]*
Tel: 01326 572082
Continuous programme of dancing. Children's dance featuring over 1000 children dressed in white, the Hal-An-Tow pageant about the history of Helston. Early dance and evening dance. Thousands dance their way through the town in colourful costumes and top hats.
May 6 2000. First dance starts 07.00
Admission Free

↓*special events*

▶ **Helston Flora Day**
6/5/00-6/5/00

Folk & Local History Museums

North Cornwall Museum and Gallery

The Clease Camelford Cornwall PL32 9PL
[follow signs to TIC which is in the same building]
Tel: 01840 212954 Fax: 01840 212954
The museum is set in a building that was used for making coaches and wagons. There are sections on agriculture, slate and granite quarrying, and wheelwright's tools, and other displays include cobbling, dairy work and the domestic scene from lace bonnets to early vacuum cleaners.
Apr-Sept Mon-Sat 10.00-17.00
Last Admission: 16.30
A£1.50 C£1.00 OAPs&Students£1.25
discount offer: Two For The Price of One

Royal Cornwall Museum

River Street Truro Cornwall TR1 2SJ
[in the centre of Truro]
Tel: 01872 272205 Fax: 01872 240514
www.royalcornwallmuseum.org.uk
Museum houses exhibits of the area including archaeology, paintings, pottery and an Egyptian Mummy, as well as a natural history gallery.
All year Mon-Sat 10.00-17.00. Closed Bank Hol
Last Admission: 16.30
A2.50 AccompaniedC£Free
UnaccompaniedC£0.50 Concessions£1.50,

School parties £Free
discount offer: Two Adults For The Price Of One

↓*special events*

▶ **The History of Christianity in Cornwall**
11/12/99-16/9/00
Treffry and De Pass Galleries. Christianity in Cornwall from 500 to 2000 AD featuring archaeology, architecture, fine and decorative arts, photography and archival material.

▶ **Kurt Jackson: Western Ireland**
26/2/00-25/3/00
Recent work from Kerry in the Philbrick Gallery

▶ **Niel Ballingal**
1/4/00-13/5/00
A selling exhibition of paintings held in the Cafè Gallery, admission free

Smugglers at Jamaica Inn
Bolventor Launceston Cornwall PL15 7TS
[on the A30 Launceston / Bodmin road. Plenty of free on site parking.]
Tel: 01566 86025 Fax: 01566 86177
www.jamaicainn.co.uk
An attraction in three parts, designed to appeal to the whole family. Employing the latest digital technology with traditional methods of interpretation. Visitors are first welcomed with an introduction to the life and works of Daphne Du Maurier, before entering a theatrical presentation of the Jamaica Inn story told in Tableaux, light and sound, then on to see probably the finest collection of smugglers relics, dating from today - back into the mists of time.
visitor comments: Great food, great prices, great day!
Mid season daily 10.00-17.00. Summer daily 10.00-19.00
One Museum Passport: A£2.50 C&OAPs£2.00 Family Ticket £6.95 Group rates 10+ £1.50. Two Attraction Passport: A£4.00 C&OAPs£3.00 Family Ticket £8.95 Group rates 10+ £3.00

↓*special events*

▶ **Karoake evening**
3/3/00-3/3/00
An excellent night with fun to be had by all. Starts 20.00. Admission Free

▶ **Codachrome Discotheque**
10/3/00-10/3/00
Dance the night away. Starts 20.00. Admission Free

▶ **Quiz Night**
17/3/00-17/3/00
Great prizes on offer. Starts 20.30. Admission £1.00

Zennor Wayside Folk Museum
Zennor St. Ives Cornwall TR26 3DA
[4m W of St Ives on B3306]
Tel: 01736 796945
Cornwall's oldest private museum. A unique collection of over 5,000 items in 14 display rooms covering all aspects of life in the area. A museum that is different!
Apr & Oct Sun-Fri 11.00-17.00. May-Sept Sun-Fri 10.00-18.00. Sat in school and public hol. weekends
Last Admission: 45mins before closing
A£2.20 C£1.50 (includes free Quiz Trail and Certificate) Over 60s£2.00 Party rates on request
discount offer: Free Guidebook/Brochure (value £1.25) Per Voucher

Gardens & Horticulture

Bosvigo
Bosvigo Lane Truro Cornwall TR1 3NH
[off the A390 at Highertown, turn down Dobbs Lane near Sainsbury roundabout, 500 yards down Dobbs Lane on the left hand side. Limited on site parking available]
Tel: 01872 275774 Fax: 01872 275774
A series of enclosed and walled gardens planted with mainly herbaceous material for colour and foliage effect. Unlike most Cornish gardens, at its best in Summer. Small specialist herbaceous nursery attached.
Mar-end Sept Thur-Sat 11.00-18.00
A£3.00 C(under 5)£Free C(5-15)£1.00 Season Ticket £12.00 admits two throughout the year during normal opening times
discount offer: Two For The Price Of One

Lost Gardens of Heligan
Pentewan St. Austell Cornwall PL26 6EN
[signposted from A390 / B3273]
Tel: 01726 845100 Fax: 01726 845101
www.heligan.com
Covering an area of 80 acres, this is the largest garden reclamation project in Britain. Four walled gardens have been restored to their former glory including the re-planting of Victorian varieties of fruit and vegetables. The 'Jungle' is a feature - with palms, tree ferns and bamboo. Please call venue for details on the following events.
All year daily 10.00-18.00. Closed 24 & 25 Dec
Last Admission: 16.30
A£5.50 C£2.50 FamilyTicket £15.00 OAPs£5.00

↓*special events*

▶ **Miracle Theatre**
12/7/00-12/7/00
An evening performance, please call for details.

▶ **Kneehigh Theatre**
18/7/00-22/7/00
Evening performances, please call for details.

▶ **Theatre Set-Up**
17/8/00-17/8/00
An evening performance, please call for details.

Trebah Garden
Mawnan Smith Falmouth Cornwall TR11 5JZ
[signposted at Treliever Cross roundabout on A39. Plenty of on site parking available]
Tel: 01326 250448 Fax: 01326 250781
www.trebah-garden.co.uk
A 25-acre wooded ravine garden descending 200ft. from the 18th century house down to a private cove on the Helford River. The cascading Water Garden has pools of giant Koi carp and exotic water plants. The beach is open to visitors and Tarzan's Camp provides an exciting play area for children. New routes and powered vehicles for disabled, with major new plantings.
visitor comments: Large enough to find some quiet spots. An opportunity to paddle in the sea! Definitely worth a visit.
All year daily 10.30-17.00. Guided tours by arrangement
Last Admission: 17.00
A£3.50 C&Disabled£1.75 OAPs£3.20. Groups A£3.00 C&Disabled£1.50 OAPs£3.00. Nov-Feb A£2.00 C/Disabled&OAPs£1.25. Group rates: A£2.00 C&Disabled & OAPs£1.00
discount offer: Two For The Price Of One Adult

↓*special events*

▶ **Millennium Bug Trail**
19/2/00-27/2/00

▶ **Daffy Down Dilly Day**
12/3/00-12/3/00
Welcome the spring with music, dancing and a display of 30,000 daffodils

▶ **Easter Egg Hunt**
15/4/00-30/4/00
Free entry for children under 16. Trails cost £1.95 and are available 10.30-16.00

▶ **Barn Dance**
4/6/00-4/6/00

▶ **Caribbean Evening**
6/6/00-6/6/00

▶ **Salsa Evening**
8/6/00-8/6/00

▶ **Santa Trail**
10/12/00-24/12/00
Held on Dec 10, 17, 20, 24 only. Find Santa beside a log fire in his grotto and receive a present

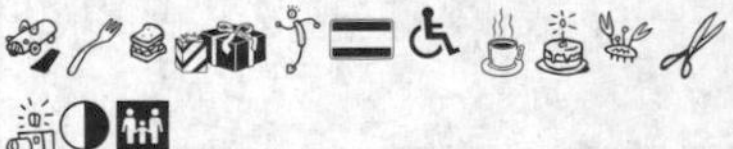

Heritage & Industrial

Charlestown Shipwreck and Heritage Centre
Quay Road Charlestown St. Austell Cornwall PL25 3NJ
[1.25m SE A3061 2m from St Austell]
Tel: 01726 69897 Fax: 01726 68025
Charlestown is a small and unspoilt village with a unique sea-lock china-clay port. It was purpose built in the 18th century by Charles Rashleigh. The Shipwreck and Heritage Centre houses the largest display of shipwreck artefacts in the UK, along with a series of lifesize tableaux and photographs depicting village life.
1 Mar-31 Oct daily 10.00-17.00 later in high season
Last Admission: 60mins before closing
A£3.95 C£Free when accompanied by paying Adult OAPs Student & Disabled £2.95
discount offer: 10% Off Admission Price. Valid Until 31 Oct 99

Land's End Visitor Centre
Sennen Penzance Cornwall TR19 7AA
[at the end of the A30]
Tel: 01736 871220 infoline Fax: 01736 871812
www.landsend-landmark.co.uk
Famous rugged coastline at the end of the road - Britain's most westerly point. New exhibitions include Air Sea Rescue - a motion theatre experience filmed in the wild Atlantic ocean, The Hall of Fame, The Lost City of Lyonesse and the Longships Family Restaurant and Bar. Popular attractions include the Lost Labyrinth, an award winning audio visual show. Shopping village now open throughout the year and a brand new children's adventure playground. Coaches, school parties and overseas visitors especially welcome.
All year daily. Closed 24 & 25 Dec. Attractions and Exhibitions open from 10.00. The Land's End Hotel open all year daily, reservations 01736 871844
Site Admission Free. Small car parking charge. Attractions & Exhibitions: Individual tickets available, Family Ticket (A2+C2) available
discount offer: One Child Free When One Ticket Is Paid For At The Normal Rate For Top Five Attractions Only

Lanhydrock
Lanhydrock House Bodmin Cornwall PL30 5AD
[2.5m SE of Bodmin. Follow signposts from either A30, A38 Bodmin / Liskeard or B3268 Bodmin / Lostwithiel]
Tel: 01208 73320 Fax: 01208 74084
www.nationaltrust.org.uk
Lanhydrock is set in 450 acres of woods, parkland and gardens of rare shrubs and trees. Built in 1651 and largely rebuilt after a fire in 1881, this Victorian house has 48 rooms open to view including vast kitchens, a nursery wing, servants quarters and an original long gallery with plaster barrel ceiling.
visitor comments: Well worth the entrance fee. Good insight into Victorian domestic service. Excellent catering.
House: Apr-Oct Tue-Sun & Bank Hol Mon 11.00-17.30, Oct 11.00-17.00, Gardens: Mar-Oct
Last Admission: House & Gardens 30mins before closing
House & Grounds: A£6.60 C£3.30 OAPs£6.60 Family Ticket £16.50, Garden only: A£3.60 C£1.80 OAPs£3.60, Groups: (15+) A£5.50 C£2.75

Pendennis Castle
Pendennis Headland Falmouth Cornwall TR11 4LP
[1m SE of Falmouth on Pendennis Head]
Tel: 01326 316594 Fax: 01326 319911
www.english-heritage.org.uk
This castle is a testament to the quality of the coastal defences erected by Henry VIII. The well preserved granite gun fort and outer ramparts with great angled bastions defended against invasion from the sea, but was captured from the land after a long siege during the Civil War.
1 Apr Mar-31 Oct daily, 09.00 in July & Aug, 10.00-18.00, 17.00 in Oct. 1 Nov-31 Mar daily 10.00-16.00. Closed 24-26 Dec & 1 Jan.
Restaurant: seasonal opening
£3.80 C(5-16)£1.90 Concessions£2.90

↓*special events*

► **Easter Egg Hunt**
23/4/00-24/4/00
Easter family fun

► **Boffins and Bangs!**
3/6/00-4/6/00
1913: Spy into a fictional and none too serious world of top secret military invention. Extremely silly!

St Mawes Castle

St Mawes Truro Cornwall TR2 3AA
[in St Mawes on A3078, Ferry from Falmouth]
Tel: 01326 270 526
www.english-heritage.org.uk
The castle was built by Henry VIII in the 1540's, roughly the same time as Pendennis Castle in Falmouth. Together they were to guard the mouth of the Falmouth estuary, their present state of excellent preservation is largely due to their comparatively trouble-free history. Renowned as an example of military architecture.
All year Apr-Oct daily 10.00-18.00, 17.00 in Oct. Nov-Mar Fri-Tue 10.00-16.00. Closed 24-26 Dec & 1 Jan
A£2.50 C£1.30 Concessions£1.90

↓*special events*

▶ **A Tudor Garrison**
23/4/00-24/4/00
Find out about life as a 16th century soldier

Tintagel Castle
Tintagel Cornwall PL34 0HE
[on Tintagel Head; access by foot only 0.5m along uneven track from Tintagel; no vehicles]
Tel: 01840 770328 Fax: 01840 770328
www.english-heritage.org.uk
Legendary birthplace of King Arthur. Clinging precariously to the edge of the cliff face are the extensive ruins of a medieval Royal Castle built by Richard, Earl of Cornwall, younger brother of Henry III. Despite extensive excavation since the 1930's and a mass of picturesque legend, Tintagel is still an enigma, its history full of gaps and the nature of its earlier occupation quite uncertain.
visitor comments: Access via very steep long flight of steps. Landrover shuttle from village (£1.00 each way).
1 Apr-8 July & 27 Aug-31 Oct daily 10.00-18.00, 17.00 in Oct, 9 July-26 Aug daily10.00-19.00,1 Nov-31 Mar daily 10.00-16.00. Closed 24-26 Dec, call for details for 1 Jan
A£2.80 C(5-16)£1.40 Concessions£2.10. Price increase from 1 Apr A£2.90 C(5-16)£1.50 Concessions£2.20

↓*special events*

▶ **Masquerade**
26/7/00-26/7/00
Music and dance on a summers evening, bring a rug and a picnic

▶ **Music on a Summers Evening**
26/7/00-26/7/00
Music and dance on a summers evening amid the romantic ruins. Bring a rug and a picnic, 18.15-19.45

▶ **Tintagel Battle Re-enactment**
4/8/00-6/8/00
Call for further information

Historical

Barbara Hepworth Museum and Sculpture Garden
Barnoon Hill St. Ives Cornwall TR26 1AD
[Barnoon Hill, St Ives town centre close to Trewyn Gardens]
Tel: 01736 796226 Fax: 01736 794480
www.tate.org.uk
Sculptures in wood, stone and bronze can be seen in the late Dame Barbara Hepworth's house, studio and sub-tropical garden, where she lived and worked from 1949-75. Photographs, documents and other memorabilia are also exhibited, as are workshops housing a selection of tools and some unfinished carvings.The Museum is managed by Tate St Ives.
All year Tue-Sun 10.30-17.30 & Mon in July & Aug. Also open Bank Hol 10.30-17.30
A£3.50 Concessions£1.80

Restormel Castle
Restormel Road Lostwithiel Cornwall PL22 0DB
[1.5m N of Lostwithiel off A390]
Tel: 01208 872687 Fax: 01208
With a commanding view over the Fowey Valley, the castle perched on a high mound is surrounded by a deep moat. The huge circular keep of this splendid Norman castle survives in remarkably good condition.
1 Apr-31 Oct daily 10.00-18.00 dusk in Oct £1.60 C£0.80 Concessions£1.20

↓*special events*

▶ **Medieval Entertainers**
29/7/00-30/7/00
Authentic medieval games, cures, folklore and early machinery, plus a children's play about the formative years of Parliament

▶ **Storytelling**
5/8/00-6/8/00
See enty for 15 July

▶ **Medieval Music**
12/8/00-13/8/00
Enjoy melodies and dance tunes dating back to the 12th century

▶ **Storytelling**
19/8/00-20/8/00
See entry for 15 July

▶ **Medieval Music**
27/8/00-28/8/00
Lively music and song from the 11th to 16th centuries

Trerice
Kestle Mill Newquay Cornwall TR8 4PG
[3m SE of Newquay via A392 / A3058 turn right at Kestle Mill. BR: Quintrell Downs. Plenty of free on site parking]
Tel: 01637 875404 Fax: 01637 879300
A delightful small, secluded Elizabethan manor house built in 1571 with an early gabled façade, containing fireplaces, plaster ceilings, oak and walnut furnishings. A small museum in the barn traces the development of the lawn mower. The summer garden has some unusual plants and an orchard of old varieties of fruit trees. Toddlers corner in Tea Room. Photography allowed in the garden only.
2 April-30 Oct Mon Wed Thur Fri & Sun, daily from 24 July-10 Sept 11.00-17.30. Oct 11.00-17.00
Last Admission: 30mins before closing
House: A£4.20 C£2.00 Family Ticket (A2+C3)£10.50. Pre-booked Groups £3.50. Garden: £Free

Nature & Conservation Parks

Cornwall Wildlife Trust
Five Acres Allet Truro Cornwall TR4 9DJ
[see individual sites under Wildlife Reserves]
Tel: 01872 273939 Fax: 01872 225476
www.wildlifetrust.org.uk/cornwall/
The Trust has 47 nature reserves across the county. We seek to raise awareness amongst the adult public of today and, through schools and youth groups, the decision makers of tomorrow. As well as providing a range of educational services, we run two junior clubs - Fox Club and Cornwall Wildlife Watch. All you have to do to join us is call!
Office: all year Mon-Fri 08.30-16.30. Sites: All year daily any reasonable time
Sites: Admission Free. Membership: Ordinary £15.00, Concessions£10.00, Additional family members at the same address £1.00

Eden Project
Bodelva Parr St Austell Cornwall PL26 6BE
[off the A390 between St Austell and Liskeard, turn off at St Blazey Gate]
Tel: 01726 222900 Fax: 01726 222901
www.edenproject.com
In the spring of 2000 Eden will open its doors to visitors to enable them to share in the excitement of the "re-creation" of Eden. In this first phase the Visitor Centre, situated on the lip of the crater, will house an exhibition designed by the Eden Team, working with artists and makers, to bring the challenges they have faced in creating this masterpiece, to life. We shall also outline the future plans and philosophy for Eden. From its stunning vantage point visitors will be able, for the first time, to glimpse work in progress on the two giant conservatories that frame the breathtaking panorama of Eden, unfolding on the pit floor, far below. Eden Project in mid Cornwall welcomes visitors to a once in a lifetime

opportunity to experience the building of 'The living theatre of plants and people'.
Experience the building of the largest conservatories in the country in a vast crater the size of 35 football pitches.
A unique opportunity to find out the how's, what's and why's behind the building of Eden.
opens 15th May 2000 10.00-17.00
A£4.00 OAPs£3.00 C(5-15)£1.00 Group 12+ 20% discount

Hidden Valley
Tredidon St Thomas Launceston Cornwall PL15 8SJ
[signposted off the A395,4m W of Launceston, 1m from the A30]
Tel: 01566 86463 Fax: 01566 86288
www.hiddenvalley.co.uk
Hidden Valley, Adventure & Conservation Park. One of it's kind Adventure park, exciting treasure hunts themed around an old shipwreck and gold mine. Lots of levels for all the family. Adventure 18 hole pitch & putt golf, Pets Paddock, farm animals to hold, woodland play area, Nature Reserve, walks, model railway, coffee shop, gift shop, fishing and accommodation.
Easter-end Sept daily Bank Hol Weekends & School Holidays 10.30-18.00
Last Admission: 17.00
A£3.00 C(0-3)£Free C(4-15)£2.50 OAPs£2.50. Discounts for families and pre-booked groups
discount offer: Two For The Price Of One

Railways

Launceston Steam Railway
St. Thomas Road Launceston Cornwall PL15 8DA
[signposted from the A30]
Tel: 01566 775665
The Launceston Steam Railway links the historic town of Launceston with the hamlet of New Mills. Travelling through the countryside of the Kensey Valley, the trains are hauled by locomotives built in Victoria's reign. At New Mills there are a range of waymarked footpaths, a riverside picnic area and a water mill. Launceston Station houses railway workshops, a transport museum, café, gift shop and book shop. Dogs on leads welcome.
Easter Good Fri-Tue, Tue-Sun until Spring Bank Hol, June-Sept Sun-Fri 10.30-16.30, Tue & Sun in Oct
Last Admission: 16.30
A£5.20 C(3-16)£3.50 Family Ticket (A2+C4)£17.00
discount offer: One Child Free When Accompanied By Two Full Paying Adults

World of Model Railways
Meadow Street Mevagissey Cornwall PL26 6UL
[behind the Kings Arms]
Tel: 01726 842457
www.model-railway.co.uk
Over 2000 British Continental and American models are on display in this museum, which also features an impressively realistic layout for the models to run through, with urban and rural areas, a 'working' fairground, an Alpine ski resort with cable cars, and a cornish china clay pit. Also an impressive docks complex and new additions to a special children's layout and expanded shop.
23 Mar-31 Oct daily from 10.00, Nov-22 Mar Sun only
£2.95 C&OAPs£2.45 C(2-5)£1.00: Includes 2 free tokens to operate Junior Junction
discount offer: One Child Free With Two Full Paying Adults

Science - Earth & Planetary

Goonhilly Earth Station
The Visitor Centre Goonhilly Downs Helston Cornwall TR12 6LQ
[Goonhilly Downs. 7m from Helston on B3293 St. Keverne Rd]
Tel: 0800 679593/01872 325400 Fax: 01326 221/438/639
www.goonhilly.bt.com
Goonhilly Earth Station is the largest operational satellite earth station in the world with over 40 experimental and operational dishes within the site. Viewed from afar, Arthur, Merlin and the other satellite dishes at Goonhilly Downs appear to be deceptively small. Seen close up, they tower above you, silent monoliths in almost reverent contemplative of the heavens. Over the last 37 years the satellite dishes at Goonhilly have probably transmitted and received more notable events than any other around the world - from pictures of the Apollo 11 moon landing in 1969 to pictures from the Olympic Games in Atlanta, simultaneously handles hundreds of thoushands of international phone, fax, data and video calls. The Earth Station Centre includes: guided tour, Internet Zone, video phones, gift shop and the Big Dish Café. Average visit time approx 2.5-3.5 hours, but your visit time is not restricted.
visitor comments: Excellent value for money. Good gift shop.

Mar 22-Nov 3 daily
Last Admission: alters, call for details
A£4.00 C(6-16)£2.50 C(0-5)£Free Concessions £3.00 Family Ticket £11.00 Group Rates A£3.00 C£1.50 OAPs£2.00. School Groups £1.50. School Groups in Cornwall & Devon are FREE

Sealife Centres & Aquariums

Newquay Sea Life Centre
Towan Promenade Newquay Cornwall TR7 1DU
[follow brown tourist sings in town centre]
Tel: 01637 872822/878134 Fax: 01637 872578
Newquay Sea Life overlooks one of England's most popular surfing beaches... and houses the amazing creatures that live beneath those crashing waves! From sharks to seahorses, octopus to eels... and many more. Journey through the wonderful underwater worlds from rock pools and sandy shores to the mysterious ocean deep without getting wet!
All year Summer daily from 10.00, last admission 17.00. Winter weekends only from 10.00 to avoid disappointment please call to check times as they alter
A£5.25 C(4-14)£3.95 OAPs£4.25. Discounts for groups, students, disabled - call for details

Sport & Recreation

Ben's Play World
Stadium Retail Park Par St Austell Cornwall PL25 3RP
[take the A390 to Britannia Inn roundabout and follow the signs]
Tel: 01726 815553 Fax: 01726 812346
www.bensplayworld.co.uk
Ben's Play World is the largest children's indoor play area in the South West. Several large slides, ball pools, soft play climbing system, ghost house, maze, punchball alley and so much more. Plus outdoor attractions: train ride; mini-cars and bikes; crazy golf. For children aged 2-12 years old.
visitor comments: Plenty for kids to do, safe, and best of all, free newspapers and Sky TV to enjoy whilst kids entertain themselves. Refreshements a little pricey!
All year daily 10.00-19.00. Closed 25 & 26 Dec, 1 Jan
Last Admission: 18.00
A£Free C£2.50-£3.50 Group rates 10+ 50p discount each. Schools 15+ £1.50

Theme & Adventure Parks

Dobwalls Family Adventure Park
Dobwalls Liskeard Cornwall PL14 6HD
[venue is 0.5m from A38 follow brown tourist signs]
Tel: 01579 320325/321129 Fax: 01579 321345
A 25 acre parking incorporating Forest Railway - one of Europe's most extensive miniature railroad, Adventureland - 8 amazing outdoor play areas, Krazee Kavern and Mr. Blobbymania - children's indoor adventure play experience and The Steven Townsend Centre - where there is a superb selection of Limited Edition prints for sale. We have Supakart Go-karts and Supakart driving school, great fun for kids. Daily appearances by Mr Blobby!
All year daily 10.00-18.00. Oct Weekends only & school half term
Last Admission: 16.30
Admission times and prices vary, please call 01579 320325 (24hr) for details
discount offer: One Child Free With One Full Paying Adult

Flambards Village Theme Park
Helston Cornwall TR13 0QA
[0.5m S on A3083 from Helston near Redruth or Penzance]
Tel: 01326 564093 info line Fax: 01326 573344

Cornwall

www.flambards.co.uk
1999Cornwall Family Attraction of the Year. Victorian Village - recreation of streets, shops and house interiors from the turn of the century. Britain in the Blitz, Cornwall Aero Park covers the history of aviation. There are many rides including the Hornet Rollercoaster, Flambards Family Log Flume, the fabulous Cyclopter Monorail, Balloon Race, Space Mission, Superbob and many other attractions. New for 2000: Bats in the Belfry children's high ride, Pirate Sip Radio Controlled Boats, Audio tour of the renowned Flambards Victorian Village, Furriers Shop in Victorian Village opening in summer 2000
visitor comments: Good value for money! Expect queues in peak season.
Spring: 15 Apr-23 July daily 10.30-17.00. Closed 8, 12, 15, 19 & 22 May. Summer: 24 July-31 Aug daily 10.00-18.00. Autumn: 1 Sept-29 Oct daily 10.30-17.00. Closed 22, 25 & 29 Sept & 2, 6, 9, 11, 13, 16 & 20 Oct
Last Admission: 15.30
Queuing Times: 10mins
Family Ticket (4 persons) £27.00 A£7.95 (Standard Ticket) C(4-11)£6.95 (Junior Ticket) OAPs£5.00 (Senior Ticket) Under 4 and over 80 £Free. Loyalty Packcard seasonal Return scheme £2.50 per person. Group booking rates available

Shires Family Adventure Park
Trelow Farm St. Issey Wadebridge Cornwall PL27 7RA
[off A39, fully signposted. Plenty of free on site parking]
Tel: 01841 541215 Fax: 01841 540276
This year we are bigger than ever! For the most fantastic day out in Cornwall, come to Shires Family Adventure Park. We have five major attractions in one, magnificent shire horses, the thrilling World of Adventure, the Play house for the younger children, Old MacDonald's Farm full of baby animals, plus a Jungle Fantasy, a day out on its own. We also have a wonderful Dragon Kingdom. The whole family will be entertained for hours on end, regardless of the weather and for one all inclusive entry price.
visitor comments: Hard to get the kids out of the play areas! A fun and educational show. Need 5-6 hours for visit. Clean, with equipment in good condition.
Good Fri-Oct daily 10.00-17.00. Closed Sat in Oct
Last Admission: 16.00
A£5.95 C(3-14)£3.95 C(0-3)£Free OAPs£4.95

Trethorne Leisure Farm
Kennards House Launceston Cornwall PL15 8QE
[3m W of Launceston just off the A30 on the A395. Plenty of on site parking]
Tel: 01566 86324 Fax: 01566 86981
www.cornwall-online.co.uk/trethorne
Situated in beautiful North Cornwall Trethorne Leisure Farm is the perfect solution for a fantastic fun filled day for the whole family - whatever the weather! With timed activities, massive indoor play area and fascinating collection of rare breeds. Try our state-of-the-art Ten Pin Bowling and our bar and restaurant. Picnic facilities undercover.
visitor comments: Good range of activities, lots of handwashing facilities. Good value for money - it's a whole day out.
All year Mon-Sat 10.00-18.00. Ten Pin Bowling Mon-Sat until 23.00. Closed Sun
Last Admission: 17.00
A£4.50 C&OAPs£4.00 Family Ticket (A2&C2)£16.00 Group rates 15+ A£4.00 C£3.50, school parties from £3.00
discount offer: One Adult Free With Two Full Paying Children. Valid until Mar 2001

Zoos

Newquay Zoo
Trenance Gardens Newquay Cornwall TR7 2LZ
[A30 Indian Queens, A392 to Newquay, turn right into Trevemper Road, follow brown and white signs]
Tel: 01637 873342 Fax: 01637 851318
www.thisiscornwall.co.uk/
'Zoo' is an abbreviation for Zoological Gardens - peaceful and delightful areas of exotic plants, shrubs and trees, of colour and scent. The homes of the world's wonderful and mystical animals. Newquay Zoo is all of that and more, a place for you to relax, be entertained

and educated and most of all enjoy yourself. A typical day starting at 10.45: Capybara feeding time, 11.30: Feeding the Monkeys, 12.00: Meet the animals, 12.30: Penguins feeding time, 12.45: Feeding the otters, 14.00: Meet the animals again and visit the hospital, 14.30: Big cat feeding time, 15.00: Capybaras again, 15.30: and now to the monkeys, 16.15: Let's talk to the penguins. Sorry NO DOGS whatsoever, due to the freerange animals roaming the park.
visitor comments: Feed and meet the animals, sessions have good commentaries and information.
Easter-Oct daily 09.30-18.00. Nov-Easter daily 10.00-17.00. Closed 25 Dec
Last Admission: 1 hour before closing
A£5.00 C£3.30 Family Ticket £15.50 OAPs£3.80

Paradise Park
Hayle Nr. St. Ives Cornwall TR27 4HB
[A30 to Hayle/St. Ives roundabout, follow brown signs]
Tel: 01736 757407info
Come and see Britain's No. 1 conservation zoo! See the world's rarest and most beautiful birds, fascinating otters, squirrels and little monkeys. Young visitors love to meet our breeding group of endangered penguins and enjoy free flying fun with the eagles and owls. The sheltered walled gardens and sub-tropical plants are paradise for gardeners. Exciting daily events, superb gardens and plenty of fun for children.
visitor comments: There is a good variety of birds and animals to be seen. Well laid-out, with good paths for pushchairs.
May-Sept 10.00-17.00. Mar, Apr, Oct 10.00-16.00. Winter 10.00-15.00

Animal Attractions

Hall Hill Farm
Lanchester County Durham DH7 0TA
[A691/A68 Farm is located half way between Tow Law and Lanchester]
Tel: 01388 730300
www.hallhillfarm.co.uk
Family farm set in attractive countryside with opportunity to see and touch animals at close quarters. Farm trailer rides, woodland and riverside walks. Farm tea-shop and chilren's play area. Special lambing days during April.
visitor comments: Dress sensibly, with comfy shoes. Suitable for young children. Good value for money.
28 Mar-end Aug 10.30-17.00. Sept & Oct Sun only 10.30-17.00. At other times by arrangement for Schools, groups etc
A£3.30 C£(3-15)£2.20
discount offer: Two For The Price Of One

Hall Hill Farm
Lanchester County Durham DH7 0TA
[A691/A68 Farm is located half way between Tow Law and Lanchester]
Tel: 01388 730300
www.hallhillfarm.co.uk
Family farm set in attractive countryside with opportunity to see and touch animals at close quarters. Farm trailer rides, woodland and riverside walks. Farm tea-shop and chilren's play area. Special lambing days during April.
visitor comments: Dress sensibly, with comfy shoes. Suitable for young children. Good value for money.
28 Mar-end Aug 10.30-17.00. Sept & Oct Sun only 10.30-17.00. At other times by arrangement for Schools, groups etc
A£3.30 C£(3-15)£2.20
discount offer: Two For The Price Of One

Archaeology

Durham University Museum of Archaeology
The Old Fulling Mill The Banks Durham County Durham DH1 3EB
[on river bank between Framwelgate and Prebends Bridges, no vehicular access]
Tel: 0191 374 3623
Archaeological museum illustrating the history of Durham City. Displays include material of international importance from excavations in and around the city and elsewhere. The museum also holds a variety of temporary exhibitions.
visitor comments: The hands-on activities are really good and well thought out, where parallels are made between Roman life and modern life. Excellent value for money.
Nov-Mar Mon, Thur, Fri 12.30-15.00, Sat & Sun 11.30-15.30, Apr-Oct daily 11.00-16.00.
Christmas / New Year: Closed 21-29 Dec 1999. Open 30 Dec 1999-3 Jan 2000
A£1.00 C&Concessions£0.50 Family Ticket £2.50
discount offer: Two For The Price Of One

Arts, Crafts & Textiles

Josephine and John Bowes Museum
Newgate Barnard Castle County Durham DL12 8NP
[just over .25m E of Market Place in Barnard

Castle]
Tel: 01833 690606 Fax: 01833 637163
www.durham.gov.uk/LT/bowes/bowesho me.htm
A French-style chateau housing one of Britain's finest museums, opened in 1892. Collections include paintings (the largest collection of French paintings in the country and one of the largest collections of Spanish paintings), furniture, ceramics and textiles in period settings as well as local antiquities. Attractive gardens with parterre. Café open all year.
Museum: All year Mon-Sun 11.00-17.00
A£3.90 C&OAPs£2.90. Prices subject to change
discount offer: Two For The Price Of One, With Every Adult Ticket Purchased (applicable only to the lowest priced member of the party)

Heritage & Industrial

Killhope Lead Mining Centre
Cowshill Weardale County Durham DL13 1AR
[3m W of Wearhead on A689]
Tel: 01388 537505 Fax: 01388 537617
A great day out full of hands-on activities for the whole family. Work as a washerboy and find lead ore, experience the living conditions of Victorian lead miners, and walk the woodland trail. Park Level Mine, the only lead mine open to the public in the region, is an exciting trip deep underground splashing through water by the light of your caplamp. We provide hard hats, lights and overshoes!
Apr-Oct daily 10.30-17.00, Nov Sun 10.30-16.00
Last Admission: 16.30
A£3.40 C&Disabled&UB40s£1.70 Seniors£2.40
Additional charge of mine tour.
discount offer: Two For The Price Of One (excludes Mine Tour)

Historical

Auckland Castle
Bishop Auckland County Durham DL14 7NR
[at the eastern end of the Market Place in Bishop Auckland]
Tel: 01388 601627 Fax: 01388 609323
www.auckland-castle.co.uk
Home of the Bishops of Durham for over 800 years, this magnificent building has architecture from the 12th, 14th, 16th and 18th century. Also houses the largest private chapel in Europe and a fine collection of paintings. Group bookings welcome, guided tours available.
1 May-16 July Fri & Sun 14.00-17.00, 17 July-31 Aug Sun-Fri 14.00-17.00
Last Admission: 30mins before closing
A£3.00 C(12-16)&OAPs£2.00 C(0-12)£Free

↓*special events*

▶ **Auckland Castle 10K Road Race**
30/4/00-30/4/00

▶ **Slava Grigoryan**
19/5/00-19/5/00

▶ **Summer Craft Exhibition**
3/6/00-4/6/00

▶ **Millennium Flower Show**
22/8/00-28/8/00

▶ **Antiques and Collectors Fair**
8/10/00-8/10/00

▶ **Christmas Craft Exhibition**
11/11/00-12/11/00
Quality Northumbrian Craft Exhibition, presented by Eurocraft, tel: 0191 386 3050 for further details

Barnard Castle
Newgate Barnard Castle County Durham DL12 8NP
[in Barnard Castle town centre]
Tel: 01833 638212
The town's name comes from Bernard Baliol, who built the castle in 1125. The castle clings to the steep banks of the Tees and is now a ruin, but it still has a 12th century keep, and the remains of a 14th century hall. Inclusive audio tour.
27 Mar-31 Oct daily 10.00-18.00 or dusk if sooner. 1 Nov-26 Mar Wed-Sun 10.00-16.00
Last Admission: 1 hour before closing
A£2.20 C£1.10 Concessions£1.70

↓*special events*

▶ **Medieval Music**
30/4/00-30/4/00
Lively medieval music and song, from Noon

▶ **Medieval Entertainers**
3/6/00-4/6/00
Play authentic medieval games, learn about cures, folklore and early machinery, plus a children's play about the formative years of Parliament

▶ **Traditional Song**
1/7/00-2/7/00
A performance of delightful unaccompanied song

▶ **A Medieval Siege**
22/7/00-23/7/00
How a 15th century siege could have looked, with siege equipment, exciting skirmishes and assaults.

▶ **Wind in the Willows**
29/7/00-30/7/00
Meet Toad, Ratty, Mole and Badger in this enchanting children's fantasy

▶ **The History Man**
19/8/00-20/8/00

Enjoy unusual guided tours with the presenter of the BBC's popular History Man programmes

Durham Castle
Palace Green Durham County Durham DH1 3RW
[Central Durham adjacent to Cathedral. BR: Durham 0.5m]
Tel: 0191 374 3863 Fax: 0191 374 7470
www.dur.ac.uk/-dunOwww/
Durham Castle, the former home of the Prince Bishops of Durham, was founded in the 1072. Since 1832 it has been the foundation College of the University of Durham. With the Cathedral it is a World Heritage Site. During holidays the Castle is a conference and holiday centre and is superb venue for wedding receptions.
Guided Tours only Apr-Sept 10.00-12.00 & 14.00-16.30. Oct-March 14.00-16.00
A£3.00 C£2.00 Family Ticket £6.50. Guide Book £2.50. Group rate up to 40 on application

Raby Castle
PO Box 50 Staindrop Darlington County Durham DL2 3AY
[1m N off A688]
Tel: 01833 660202 Fax: 01833 660169
www.rabycastle.com
The stronghold of the powerful Nevill family until 1569, and the home of the Vane family since 1626. the fortress is built around a courtyard and surrounded by a dry moat. There are about 5 acres of gardens and a 200 acre park which is home to red and fallow deer. No photography in castle. Member of the Historic Houses Association.
Bank Hol Sat-Wed May-Jun Wed & Sun, July-Sept Sun-Fri. Castle: 13.00-17.00 Park & Gardens: 11.00-17.30
Castle: A£4.00 C£1.50 OAPs£3.00. Park & Gardens: A£1.50 C£1.00 OAPs£2.75. Parties 25+ ring for prices

↓*special events*

► **Voyage 2000: A Classical Journey with Fireworks**
3/6/00-3/6/00
Tickets A£17.50 (£20.00 on night) C£10.00 (aged 5-16). Wide-ranging popular orchestral music followed by breathtaking fireworks set to Ravel's Bolero!

Places of Worship

Durham Cathedral
The College Durham County Durham DH1 3EH
[any bus or train to Durham and a short uphill walk, or City Courier minibus (not Sun) to Palace Green in front of cathedral]
Tel: 0191 386 4266 Fax: 0191 386 4267
www.durhamcathedral.co.uk
The cathedral was founded in 1093 as a shrine to St Cuthbert. His bones still rest in his shrine. The cathedral is a remarkable example of Norman architecture set within an imposing site high above the River Wear. Visit the Monks' Dormitory from 10.00-15.30. Guided tours please call in advance for booking. Cathedral Tower closes at 15.00 in winter and is a very strenuous climb.
visitor comments: Almost as imposing inside, as the site is outside.
27 May-30 Sept daily 09.30-20.00, 1 Oct-7 Apr daily 09.30-18.00. Cathedral Tours: 27 May-30 Sept Mon-Sat at 10.30 & 14.00. Access may be restricted owing to services and events
Cathedral: donation £2.50 Tower: A£2.00 C(under 16)£1.00 Family Ticket £5.00. Treasury A£2.00 C£0.50. Monks Dormitory A£0.80 C£0.20. Audio-Visual Exhibition A£0.80 C£0.20. Cathedral Tours: A£3.00 C£Free

↓*special events*

► **Chester Cycle of Mystery Plays**
24/6/00-24/6/00
Performed at various times during the day

Social History Museums

Beamish, The North of England Open Air Museum
Beamish County Durham DH9 0RG
[from the N or S - follow the A1(M) to J63, Chester-le-Street exit, 10m N of Durham City, 6m S of Newcastle upon Tyne.
Take the Chester-le-Street exit and follow the Beamish Museum signs, for 4m, along the A693 towards Stanley. From the NW - take the A68 S to Castleside, near Consett in County Durham, and follow the Beamish Museum signs along the A692, then A693, via. Stanley. Plenty of on site parking]
Tel: 01207 231811 Fax: 01207 290933

There's loads for the whole family to see and do at Beamish - Britain's favourite open air museum. Reduced operation in the Winter months - allow 1-2 hours for visit.

visitor comments: Wonderfully interesting portrayal of history, in a beautiful setting.

All year daily from 10.00 in the Summer. Closed Mon & Fri in Winter
Last Admission: Summer: 16.00 Winter: 15.00
Summer: A£10.00 C(under 5)£Free C(5-16)£6.00 A(60+)£7.00. Winter: A/C(5-16)/A(60+)£3.00

↓*special events*

▶ **The Story of Light**
8/4/00-14/4/00
A week of activities and demonstrations focussing on the history of lighting

▶ **Sunday School Anniversary**
11/6/00-11/6/00
Recitations, readings and hymn singing by children in period costume

▶ **Morgan Car Meet**
11/6/00-11/6/00
Fine examples of these cars, old and new, on show and in action

▶ **School Sports Day**
18/6/00-18/6/00
Children in period costume compete in customary events including potato, skipping and three-legged races

▶ **Clippy Mat Exhibition**
8/7/00-30/7/00
See how they are made and discover the difference between proggies and hookies

▶ **1913 Military Camp**
29/7/00-30/7/00
Fill out Attestation Forms and learn to drill. Members of The Great War Society re-enact this pre First World War encampment with gunfire, skirmishes and authentic military uniforms

Transport Museums

Darlington Railway Centre and Museum

North Road Station Station Road Darlington County Durham DL3 6ST
[J59 A1(M) 0.75m N of Town Centre off A167 signposted]
Tel: 01325 460532

Restored Victorian station, dating from 1842, on the original route of the Stockton and Darlington Railway, now a museum devoted to railway heritage of North-East England. Exhibits include Stephenson's "Locomotion" (1825), other steam engines and many smaller exhibits.

Feb-Dec daily 10.00-17.00
A£2.10 C£1.05

Timothy Hackworth Victorian Railway Museum

Soho Cottages Hackworth Close Shildon County Durham DL4 1PQ
[.25m SE of Shildon town centre, S of Bishop Auckland, trains to Shildon station. Plenty of parking on site]
Tel: 01388 777999 Fax: 01388 777999
www.sedgefield.gov.uk

Home and workplace of the Superintendant Engineer to the Stockton and Darlington Railway. Restored house with period rooms and display on Hackworth's life and achievements. Early railway structures include stables, coal drops and locomotive sheds. Occasional passenger rides along 400 yards of original 1825 Stockton & Darlington Railway track bed. New display of Hackworth built 1834 Beam Engine. Passenger rides on event days, at other times by prior arrangement

Easter-end Oct Wed-Sun & Bank Hol 10.00-17.00.
Last Admission: 16.15
A£1.50 C£1.00 Family Ticket £4.00. Ticket may entitle the holder to a concession for Darlington Railway Centre and Museum. Train rides £0.50

discount offer: Two For The Price Of One

↓*special events*

▶ **Mothering Sunday**
2/4/00-2/4/00

▶ **Church Festival Day**
29/5/00-29/5/00

▶ **Grand Railway Cavalcade**
26/8/00-28/8/00

▶ **Museum Festival and Steam Day**
1/10/00-1/10/00

▶ **Santa's Special Days**
10/12/00-17/12/00
Held on Dec 10, 16-17 only

Animal Attractions

Lakeland Sheep and Wool Centre

Egremont Road Cockermouth Cumbria CA13 0QX
[J40 M6, head W, A66 to Cockermouth on A66 & A5086 junction]
Tel: 01900 822673 Fax: 01900 822673

The Lakeland Sheep and Wool Centre is a purpose built centre, which houses and demonstrates to visitors LIVE sheep. You can learn about 19 different breeds, have fun watching each individual character, view the skills of shearing and see a 'one man and his dog' demonstration, indoors, before your very eyes. Children, and the young at heart adults also

love to feed our pet lambs and then feel the qualitiy of the fleece of the sheep. An educational and exciting show. The Cumwest slide show depicts the beauty, inhabitants and attractions to be found in the West.
All year daily 09.00-18.00. Closed Christmas Day
Last Admission: 15.30 last show 17.45 exhibition & shop
Sheep Show: A£3.00 C£2.00

Trotters and Friends Animal Farm

Coalbeck Farm Bassenthwaite Keswick Cumbria CA12 4RD
[5m NE of Cockermouth near north end of Bassenthwaite lake]
Tel: 017687 76239 Fax: 017687 76220
In the heart of the Lake District is this collection of old-fashioned breeds including Tamworth pigs, Herdwick sheep and White Park cattle. Donkeys and peacock's roam the grounds and small visitors can bottle-feed baby goats or hug a bunny, and may even catch sight of a chick emerging from an egg in the hatchery. Displays of milking and birds of prey flying, plus daily audiences with reptiles like Monty, the Burmese python. Tearoom serving hot and cold food and picnics and a British Wildlife Section.
visitor comments: Take plenty of animal feed (available at the entrance) you will run out very quickly. Lovely place for young children.
All year 1 Mar-31 Oct daily 10.00-17.30. Nov-Feb Sat & Sun 11.00-16.00 Open daily Christmas week except Christmas day
A£3.60 C£2.50
discount offer: One Child Free With A Full Paying Adult

Arts, Crafts & Textiles

Abbot Hall Art Gallery

Kendal Cumbria LA9 5AL
[J36 M6, signposted on A6 brown museum signs. Plenty of on site parking available]
Tel: 01539 722464 Fax: 01539 722494
www.abbothall.org.uk
One of Britain's finest small art galleries showing changing displays of contemporary art and touring exhibitions. The gallery is housed in a Grade I listed Georgian Villa and the ground floor rooms have been restored to provide a perfect setting for showing the permanent collection of portraits and paintings by George Romney and 18th century furniture. The adjacent museum looks back at 200 years of Lakeland life.
12 Feb-22 Dec daily 10.30-17.00, Feb, Mar, Nov & Dec closing 16.00
A£3.00 C&Student£1.50 Family Ticket £7.50 OAPs£2.80 Season Tickets start from £3.80

Exhibition & Visitor Centres

Rheged

Redhills Penrith Cumbria CA11 0DQ
[2m from M6 J40 at Penrith on the A66 in the direction of Keswick]
Tel: 01768 868000 Fax: 01768 868002
www.rheged.com
Opening Easter 2000 - Rheged will be Cumbria - the Lake District's newest, largest and most dramatic visitor attraction. Named after the ancient Celtic Kingdom, Rheged is Britain's largest grass covered building with seven levels including a showcase of rather special shops and restaurants combining local delicacies with mountain views. Rheged's centrepiece is the first British made large format film, shown on a six storey high cinema screen, revealing a dramatic journey through 2000 years of Cumbria's history, mystery and magic. Rheged will also feature a 180° cinerama experience and a magical exhibition revealing the hidden treasures of Cumbria. Disabled access to all levels. Children warmly welcomed.

Opens Easter 2000: All year daily, 10.00-18.00, call for further details around May 1999
Last Admission: 17.00
A£5.00 C£3.50 OAPs£4.25 Family Ticket (2A+2C) £14.50. Please call for special discounts for advanced group bookings (10+ people)

Folk & Local History Museums

Tullie House Museum and Art Gallery
Castle Street Carlisle Cumbria CA3 8TP
[J's 42, 43, 44 M6 follow brown signs to city centre Tullie House opposite Carisle Castle]
Tel: 01228 534781 Fax: 01228 810249
Award-winning museum and art gallery. Stunning and imaginative displays covering Border History from Roman times to the Reivers and beyond. A rich collection of regional importance includes archaeology, natural history and Carlisle's social history. Many interactives to fascinate and delight all ages plus Art Gallery, shop, restaurant and Herb Garden - all go to make Tulie House a treasure house of discovery for the whole family. (Please note that the House will be closed to the public for essential refurbishment between Jan 15-23)
All year daily Mon-Sat 10.00-17.00, Sun 12.00-17.00, Sun in July & Aug 11.00-17.00
Last Admission: 16.30
A£3.75 Family Ticket £12.00
Concessions£2.75/£2.25. Half price admission before 11.00 Mon-Sat. Group discounts available

↓*special events*

► **Revelation exhibition**
5/2/00-19/3/00
Open 10.00-17.00

► **Making Mosaics**
4/3/00-5/3/00
Weekend workshop, 10.00 start on Sat and 10.30 on Sun

► **Explorations in Cumbrian Cyberspace**
17/3/00-19/3/00
A weekend workshop, starts 19.00 on Fri, 10.00 on Sat and 10.30 on Sun

Historical

Brantwood
Coniston Cumbria LA21 8AD
[2.5m SE off B5285 unclassified road. Plent of on site parking available]
Tel: 015394 41396
www.brantwood.org.uk
Brantwood formerly home of John Ruskin is one of the most beautifully situated houses in the Lake District with fine views across Coniston Water. Inside there is a large collection of Ruskin paintings and other memorabilia.
Mid Mar-mid Nov daily 11.00-17.30. Mid Nov-mid Mar Wed-Sun 11.00-16.30
A£4.00 C£1.00 Family Ticket £9.50
Student£2.80. Group rates on request
discount offer: Two Children Free With One Full Paying Adult

Brough Castle
Brough Cumbria CA10
[S of A66 on A685]
Tel: 0191 261 1585 Fax: 0191 269 1209
Standing on the site of the Roman Verterae, the castle was built in the 12th & 13th centuries to replace a stronghold ruined by the Scots. English Heritage.
All year at any reasonable time
Admission Free

Brougham Castle
Brougham Penrith Cumbria CA10 2AA
[1.5m SE of Penrith on minor road off A66]
Tel: 01768 862488
The ruins of one of the strongest castles in the region lie on the quiet banks of the River Eden. Founded in the 13th century & restored in the 17th by strong minded Lady Anne Clifford. There is an exhibition of Roman tombstones from the nearby fort.
27 Mar-31 Oct daily 10.00-18.00 or dusk if sooner
A£1.90 C£1.00 Concessions£1.40

↓*special events*

► **Medieval Living History**
17/6/00-18/6/00
Encampment, drill, archery, mumming plays and dancing

► **Medieval Combat**
22/7/00-23/7/00
13th century knights, combat, archery contest and games

► **Have-a-go-Archery**
19/8/00-20/8/00
Arrowflight. 14th century archers introduce visitors to the art of archery

Dove Cottage and The Wordsworth Museum
Dove Cottage Grasmere Ambleside Cumbria LA22 9SH
[S of Grasmere village, on the main A591 Kendal / Keswick road. Hourly bus service (555. In summer open top bus (W1) Winderemere / Grasmere every 20mins call 01946 63222. Limited parking on site]
Tel: 015394 35544/35547 Fax: 015394 35748
www.wordsworth.org.uk
The award-winning museum displays the Wordsworth Trust's unique collections of manuscripts, books and paintings interpreting the life and work of Wordsworth, his family and circle. There is a major exhibition every year. Dove Cottage was William Wordsworth's home from 1799-1808. Visitors are offered guided tours of the cottage. The garden, "a little nook of mountain-ground," is open when weather permits. How Foot Lodge is a beautiful mid-Victorian Country Guest Hotel with views of Grasmere lake and has six spacious, ensuite bedrooms (015394 35366). Dove Cottage Tea Rooms provide a welcoming atmosphere. Meals and snacks made with high-quality local produce are served throughout the day. Evening meals during high season (015394 35268). An excellent shop sells books, gifts and local crafts relating to English literature and the Lake District. Coach and car parking next to tea rooms; additional parking in Grasmere village car park 250yds.
All year daily 09.30-17.30
Last Admission: 17.00
A£5.00 C£2.50 OAPs£4.70 Students/YHA£4.20 Group rates 15+ £4.40
↓*special events*
► **English Poetry**
22/4/00-31/12/00
The First Thousand Years

Holker Hall and Gardens
Cark in Cartmel Grange-Over-Sands Cumbria LA11 7PL
[on A590, follow brown and white signs. Plenty of on site parking]
Tel: 015395 58328 Fax: 015395 58776
Cumbria's premier stately home, still lived in by Lord and Lady Cavendish. No ropes or barriers bar your way at this, the friendliest of stately homes. Plus 25 acres of magnificent award-winning gardens, superb Lakeland Motor Museum, exhibitions, deer park, adventure playground, cafe, gift shop and picnic area. Home to The Holker Garden Festival, 2nd - 4th June 2000 see details below.
2 Apr-31 Oct Sun-Fri 10.00-18.00
Last Admission: 16.30
Gardens, Grounds & Exhibitions: A£3.50 C(over 6)£2.00 Family Ticket(2A+4C) £10.35
↓*special events*
► **Holker Garden Festival**
2/6/00-4/6/00
A magical mix of all that is good in the garden and countryside. A£7.50 C£(12+)£3.50 C(under 12)£Free OAPs£6.00. Discounted tickets available in advance, call the Show Office on 015395 58838 for further information

Hutton in the Forest
Penrith Cumbria CA11 9TH
[J41 M6 3m on B5305]
Tel: 017684 84449 Fax: 017684 84571
Set in magnificent woods, this beautiful historic house consists of a 14th century pele tower with 17th, 18th and 19th century additions. Inside is a fine collection of furniture, portraits, tapestries and china, a 17th century gallery and cupid staircase. The lovely 1730's walled garden is a wonderful setting for the large collection of herbaceous plants. Woodland walk with named specimen trees. Member of the Historic Houses Association.
Grounds: All year Sun-Fri 11.00-17.00. House & Tea Room: 20 Apr-1 Oct Thu Fri Sun & Bank Hol Mon House:12.30-16.00,Tea Room: 11.00-16.30
Last Admission: 16.00
House & Gardens: A£4.50 C(0-6)£Free C(7-16)£2.50 Family Ticket £12.00 Students£3.50
Grounds: A£2.50 C£Free Students£1.50
discount offer: £0.50 Off Per Adult
↓*special events*
► **Sculpture Exhibition**
26/5/00-26/10/00

Mirehouse Historic House and Gardens
Keswick Cumbria CA12 4QE

[J40 M6 signs from A66 3m N of Keswick on A591. Limited on site parking available]
Tel: 017687 72287 tel/fax
1999 NPI Heritage Award Winner. Our visitors return for many reasons: the spectacular setting between mountains and lake, the varied gardens, changing displays in the Poetry walk, peaceful sheltered seating, lakeside walks, free children's nature notes, four woodland adventure playgrounds, indoor and outdoor picnic areas, connections with many famous writers and painters, live classical piano music in the house, excellent cooking in the tearoom and, above all, for the relaxed welcome.
Grounds: Apr-Oct 10.00-17.30, House: Apr-Oct Sun, Wed (Fri in Aug) 14.00-16.30 Groups at any time by appointment
Last Admission: House: 16.30
House & Gardens: A£4.00 C£2.00 Family Ticket £11.50. Gardens: A£1.70 C£1.00
discount offer: Two Full Price Adults For The Price Of One. One Coupon Per Party. Valid Sun, Wed (also Fri in Aug) Only

Muncaster Castle, Gardens and Owl Centre
Muncaster Castle Ravenglass Cumbria CA18 1RQ
[1m S of Ravenglass on A595]
Tel: 01229 717614 Fax: 01229 717010
www.muncastercastle.co.uk
Diverse attractions are offered at this castle, the seat of the Pennington family since the 13th century. Inside is a fine collection of 16th and 17th century furnishings, embroideries and portraits whilst the grounds have a nature trail, a children's play area, and a profusion of flowers. Talk and Bird Display from the World Owl Trust daily at 14.30 throughout the season. Development of the grounds includes a Himalayan Walk, walks and trails through meadows and opportunities to wach wildlife. Member of the Historic Houses Assocation.
Castle End Mar-End Oct Sun-Fri 12.00-17.00. Gardens & Owl Centre: all year daily 10.00-18.00
Castle, Gardens & Owl Centre: A£6.00 C£4.00 C(0-5)£Free Family Ticket £17.00
discount offer: One Child Free With A Full Paying Adult

↓*special events*

► **Medieval Re-enactment**
29/4/00-1/5/00
A fun day of medieval entertainment for all the family. Please call to confirm dates

► **"Cushions 2000"**
8/7/00-28/8/00
The Embroiderers Guild of Britain are presenting an exhibition of cushions for the Millennium

► **Family Fundays**
6/8/00-27/8/00
Held every Sunday in Aug, 6, 13, 20, and 27. A wide variety of family entertainment to vary each week

Rydal Mount and Gardens
Rydal Ambleside Cumbria LA22 9LU
[1.5m on A591 to Grasmere. Limited on site parking]
Tel: 015394 33002 Fax: 015394 31738
The family home of William Wordsworth from 1813 until his death in 1850, Rydal Mount incorporates a pre-1574 farmer's cottage. Now owned by descendents of Wordsworth, the house contains important family portraits, furniture and many of the poet's personal possessions. With a beautiful garden landscaped by the poet. Member of the Historic Houses Association. Photography permissable in the Gardens only, and disabled access limited.
Mar-Oct daily 09.30-17.00, Nov-Feb daily 10.00-16.00. Closed Tue in winter
A£3.75 C£1.25 OAPs£3.25 Students£3.00. Garden only A£1.75. Groups 10+ A£3.25. Pre-booked Groups A£2.75
discount offer: Two For The Price Of One

Maritime

Windermere Steamboat Museum
Rayrigg Road Windermere Cumbria LA23 1BN
[0.5m N of Bowness Bay. Plenty of on site parking available]
Tel: 015394 45565 Fax: 015394 48769
www.steamboat.co.uk
A unique and historical collection of Victorian and Edwardian steamboats and vintage motorboats reflecting the enormous part boating has played over many years in the his-

tory of Lake Windermere. Steamboat trips, weather permitting. Shop, refreshments, model boat pond. Special events held.
18 Mar-29 Oct daily 10.00-17.00
A£3.25 C£2.00 Family Ticket(A2+C3)£8.00
discount offer: Two For The Price Of One

Natural History Museums

Kendal Museum

Station Road Kendal Cumbria LA9 6BT
[Limited parking on site]
Tel: 01539 721374 Fax: 01539 722494
www.kendalmuseum.org.uk
One of the oldest surviving museums in the country, it houses outstanding displays of archaeology and natural history, both local and global. With many examples of Lakeland flora and fauna, the museum charts developments from prehistoric times and into the 20th century. Explore the new interactive Kendal Castle display or discover more about Alfred Wainwright, who was the Honorary Curator. Pre-booked guided tours available.
10 Feb-22 Dec Mon-Sat 10.30-17.00. Feb, Mar, Nov & Dec closing at 16.00
A£3.00 Family Ticket £7.50 Concessions£1.50 Senior Citizen£2.80

Nature & Conservation Parks

Lake District Visitor Centre at Brockhole

Windermere Cumbria LA23 1LJ
[on A591 between Windermere / Ambleside. Plenty of on site parking available]
Tel: 01539 446601 Fax: 01539 445555
www.lake-district.gov.uk
Outstanding setting on the shores of Lake Windermere. 30 acres of award winning gardens and grounds. Cruises on Lake Windermere, adventure playground, walks, trails, events and activities, two floors of exciting interactive exhibitions, film auditorium and programme, plus an information centre gift shop and café. For further details of over 1000 events held throughout the year, please call the Cente.
Visitor Centre: Apr-Oct daily 10.00-17.00.
Grounds & Gardens: all year daily
Admission Free. Parking Full Day £4.00, Half Day £3.00
discount offer: Full Day's Parking For £3.00, Leave Your Coupon In The Windscreen

↓*special events*

▶ **Special Events Days**
1/1/00-31/12/00
Join us on all major bank holidays and enjoy seasonal activities for all the family including: guided walks, tours, gardening events, painting days and exhibitions

▶ **Furness Artists at Brockhole**
12/2/00-27/4/00
Artists identify with the landscape producing works which are sensitive and varied, reflecting the atmosphere of Cumbria

▶ **Elements and Medium**
29/4/00-26/5/00
The beautiful effects of sunlight and rain, and the atmospheric feeling of the elements on our surroundings explored by Sarah Appleby.

▶ **Intimate Views**
28/5/00-29/6/00
Artists and scientists use underwater photography to reveal brilliant and exotic marine animals that live near our beaches

Sealife Centres & Aquariums

Aquarium of the Lakes
Lakeside Newby Bridge Cumbria LA12 8AS
[15mins from J36 M6. S end of Lake Windermere follow signs for Barrow and Southern Lakes on the A590 to Newby Bridge. Turn R over the bridge and follow the Hawkshead road to the Aquarium, or follow the brown and white signs for Lakeside Steamers from the M6]
Tel: 015395 30153 Fax: 015395 30152
Britain's only freshwater Aquarium. Follow the journey of a Lakeland river and meet the UK's largest collection of freshwater fish, including the predatory pike and giant carp. Encounter mischievous otters, and enjoy close-up views in Aquaquest, the ever-changing seasonal lab. Walk in the Lake District's only underwater tunnel on Windermere's recreated lakebed to marvel at diving ducks. Undercover displays - a great visit whatever the weather.
visitor comments: Interesting for all ages, with easily recognisable exhibits. Combine your trip with a steam train ride (purchase inclusive tickets at aquarium).
All year daily 09.00. Closed Christmas Day
Last Admission: Summer 17.00, Winter 16.00
A£5.25 C(3-15)£3.95 Family Ticket (A2+C3)£16.95. Group rates available, please call for details

Theme & Adventure Parks

Lowther Leisure and Wildlife Park
Hackthorpe Penrith Cumbria CA10 2HG
[on the A6 4m S of Penrith, J39 N or J40 S of M6]
Tel: 01931 712523 Fax: 01931 712747
Lowther Leisure & Wildlife Park is three great days out in one: Theme Park with over 40 family attractions including rides, slides, swings, adventure play areas, miniature railway and boating lake; Live Entertainment in the Big Top with International Circus and a Puppet Theatre; Wildlife Area with a collection of exotic and familiar animals and birds.
visitor comments: Reasonably priced and plenty to do for a whole day.
31 May-12 Sept daily 10.00-18.00. Guided tours available for groups by prior appointment
Last Admission: approx 5hrs needed, suggested 14.00
A&C(3yrs +)£7.45 C(0-3)£Free OAPs£5.25. Groups 12+ £5.25, 20+ 1 person £FREE with every 10 paying, school parties and other children's groups on application
discount offer: Three For The Price Of Two Full Paying Adults/Child

World of Beatrix Potter
The Old Laundry Crag Brow Bowness-On-Windermere Windermere Cumbria LA23 3BX
[J36 M6 then follow A591 to Windermere, AA signposted]
Tel: 015394 88444 Fax: 015394 88444
www.hop-skip-jump.com
Visit this award winning attraction and discover Peter Rabbit™, Jemima Puddle-Duck™ and all their freinds in a magical indoor recreation of Beatrix Potter's little books, complete with the sights, sounds and even smells of the countryside. On their journey through the attraction in the year 2000 visitors will experience our new Peter Rabbit™ interactive tasks and puzzles. These, together with new information 'storybooks', will make their visit even more exciting.
Easter-Sept daily 10.00-17.30, Oct-Easter daily 10.00-16.30. Closed 25 Dec & 1 Jan 2000 (also 11-31 Jan 2000 to install new display)
Last Admission: 16.30
A£3.25 C£2.00 OAPs£3.25 Group rates A£2.99 C£1.80, School Parties £1.80 per child

Toy & Childhood Museums

Cumberland Toy and Model Museum
Bank's Court Market Place Cockermouth Cumbria CA13 9NG
[just off Market Place, follow brown signs from car parks]
Tel: 01900 827606
100 years of mainly British toys. Working tinplate Hornby trains, Scalextric cars, Lego and many more toys and models. Winner of the 1995 National Heritage Shoestring Award for achieving best results with limited resources. Free quiz and 'Find The Teddies' worksheets based on the National Curriculum.
1 Feb-30 Nov daily 10.00-17.00. Dec & Jan times vary please phone
A£2.60 C£1.30 Family Ticket £6.80 OAPs£2.20.

Cumbria

Groups rates A£2.20 C&Schools£1.10

discount offer: Two For The Price Of One. Valid until 30 Nov 2000

Transport Museums

Cars of the Stars Museum

Standish Street Keswick Cumbria CA12 5LS

[from the Town Centre walk through Pack Horse Court]

Tel: 017687 73757 Fax: 01687 72090

http://members.aol.com/cotsmm

Film set displays and vehicles from Mad Max, Magmun, The Saint, The Prisoner, Bergerac, The Avengers, Noddy, Postman Pat, The A Team amd James Dean's Porsche recreation. Plus many other famous vehicles and motorcycles.

5-20 Feb, 15 Apr-30 Nov daily 10.00-17.00. Weekends only during December

Last Admission: 16.00

A£3.00 C£2.00

discount offer: One Child Free With Every Two Full Paying Adults

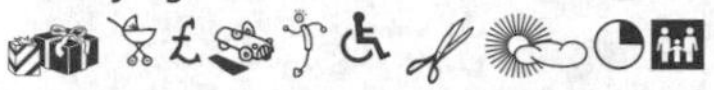

Zoos

Lakeland Wildlife Oasis

Hale Milnthorpe Cumbria LA7 7BW

[nr M6 J's35/36 on the A6 2.5m S of Milnthorpe]

Tel: 015395 63027

Half zoo, half museum and totally fascinating, the Lakeland Wildlife Oasis takes you on an amazing journey through the world of wildlife using a unique combination of live animals and interactive 'hands-on' displays. Educational, yet great fun, our exhibits range from chameleons to computers; from microscopes to meerkats and include creatures rarely seen in captivity, such as flying foxes and poison arrow frogs. Our friendly staff are always on hand to answer your questions and let you meet some of the residents face to face. So if you want to stroke a snake, weigh a whale or just relax in this unspoiled corner of Cumbria, the Lakeland Wildlife Oasis is the place to be.

visitor comments: Reasonable price for a compact, easy afternoon out. Baby changing/feeding facilities would be welcome.

All year daily from 10.00 closing times vary according to season. Closed 25 & 26 Dec

Last Admission: 16.00

A£4.50 C£2.50 Family Ticket £12.50 OAPs£3.00. Group rates A£4.00 C£2.40 OAPs£2.50

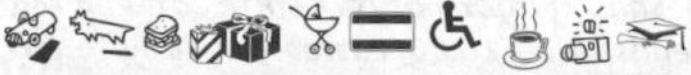

South Lakes Wild Animal Park

Crossgates Dalton-in-Furness Cumbria LA15 8JR

[M6 J36, A590 to Dalton-in-Furness signposted. Trains from Dalton and Askam - bus connections to the Zoo]

Tel: 01229 466086 Fax: 01229 466086

www.wildanimalpark.co.uk

The Lake District's only zoological park, recognised as one of Europe's leading conservation zoos. The rolling 17 acres are home to the rarest animals on earth, they are participants in programmes to save them from almost certain extinction in the wild. We are the only zoo in Britain to hold both Amur and Sumatran Tigers, the biggest and smallest tigers left in the world. We have been called the most animal friendly zoo in Britain because of our unique way of looking after animals. Daily events include meeting a snake, mee the rhinos, lemur feeding, tiger feeding, as well as seeing the new Giraffes. We also have a safari railway, a primate centre and an exciting Australian Bush Experience.

visitor comments: A well laid out trail around enclosures. Some animals are in the open to feed. Best time to visit is midday - feeding time, when they're awake.

All year daily 10.00-18.00. Winter 10.00-Dusk. Closed 25 Dec

Last Admission: 17.00

A£6.50 C(3-16)&OAPs£3.25 Family Ticket (A2+C2)£17.00. Half price admission 1 Nov-1 Mar. Group rates available. Wheelchair Users £Free.

discount offer: Free Colour Guide Book With Two Full Paying Adults

Arts, Crafts & Textiles

Rookes Pottery

Mill Lane Hartington Buxton Derbyshire SK17 0AN

[10m from Ashbourne, Buxton and Leek, easily found near to the centre of Hartington on the B5054 road to Warslow. Plenty of local parking]

Tel: 01298 84650 Fax: 01298 84806

www.rookespottery.co.uk

An original range of terracotta garden pots and planters. Everything from plain flower pots to decorative wall-pots of animals, birds and hmans. Well made and high fired these pots will surely make a splendid addition to any garden or patio. Seconds always available. All the pots are deisgned and made on the premises.

All year Mon-Fri 09.00-17.00, Sat 10.00-16.00 Sun 11.00-16.00. Closed some weekends in Winter
Last Admission: 16.00
Admission £Free
discount offer: 10% On Shop Purchases Over £10.00

Caverns & Caves

Heights of Abraham - Cable Cars, Country Park and Caverns

Matlock Bath Matlock Derbyshire DE4 3PD
[on A6 N of Derby]
Tel: 01629 582365 Fax: 01629 580279
www.heights-of-abraham.co.uk
High above the village of Matlock Bath are the Grounds of The Heights of Abraham. Cable cars provide a spectacular way of reaching the top. Two famous show caverns provide fascinating tours underground. There is also a nature trail, Owl Maze, the Explorers Challenge and landscaped water gardens. Allow 3 hrs minimum.
visitor comments: Lovely views. Elderley people may find it difficult. The caves are worth visiting and the tours are really enjoyable, although quite expensive.
Easter-Oct 10.00-17.00, later in high season
Last Admission: Last cable car advertised at office
A£6.20 C£4.10 OAPs£5.20. Groups rates 10+ A£5.20 C£3.60 OAPs£4.10 (1999 prices)
discount offer: One Child Free For The Cable Car & Caverns With One Full Paying Adult.

Speedwell Cavern

Castleton Hope Valley Derbyshire S33 8WA
[off A625 0.5m W of Castleton Village]
Tel: 01433 620512 Fax: 01433 621888
www.speedwellcavern.co.uk
Visitors descend 105 steps to a boat which takes them on a one-mile underground exploration of the floodlit cavern with its 'bottomless pit.'
All year daily, Summer: 09.30-17.00, Winter: 10.00-16.00
A5.25 C£3.25 Concessions£4.25. Group rates on application

Country Parks & Estates

Ilam Park

Home Farm South Peak Estate Ilam Ashbourne Derbyshire DE6 2AZ
[4.5m NW of Ashbourne]
Tel: 01335 350245/350503 Fax: 01335 350511
Attractive park and woodland on both banks of the River Manifold in the South Peak Estate, with magnificent views towards Thorpe Cloud and the entrance to Dovedale. Limited access for wheelchairs. Dogs on leads only. Hall let to YHA, not open to the public. For events requiring bookings call 01335 350503
Grounds & Park: all year daily during daylight hours. Shop & Information Centre: Jan-end Mar Weekends 11.00-16.00, Easter- Oct daily 11.00-

17.00, Nov-20 Dec Weekends 11.00-16.00 Admission Free. Car Park charge for non National Trust members. No coaches on Sun or Bank Hol. Guided Tours for pre-booked groups

↓*special events*

▶ **Easter Egg Trail**
21/4/00-21/4/00
Follow the trail and find a prize. C£1.50, 11.00-16.00

▶ **Simple Crafts with a Countryside Theme**
27/4/00-10/8/00
Apr 27 & Aug 10 only. Crafts on paper and other materials. £2.50, 10.30-12.30 and 13.30-15.30

▶ **Land Rover Safaris**
13/7/00-24/8/00
Thur 13 & 27 July, 10 & 24 Aug only. See Dovedale with a National Trust Warden on patrol. £2.00, 09.30, book early

▶ **Children's Nature Day**
4/8/00-4/8/00
Fun environmental activities, for ages 5-10. From 11.00, C£1.50

▶ **Pirate's Treasure Trail**
13/8/00-13/8/00
Follow a seafarers chart to find the hidden treasure! Open 11.00-16.00 C£1.00

▶ **Paint the Landscape**
20/8/00-20/8/00
Open anytime between 11.00-16.00. Small donation for materials

Sudbury Hall and the Museum
Sudbury Ashbourne Derbyshire DE6 5HT
[6m E of Uttoxeter at the crossing point of A50 Derby / Stoke and A515 Lichfield / Ashbourne roads]
Tel: 01283 585305 Fax: 01283 585139
One of the most individual and richly decorated late 17th century country houses with superb wood carvings and plasterwork. The great staircase is one of the finest in England. The Museum of Childhood contains fascinating displays about growing up in Victorian and Edwardian times. 'Sweep sized' visitors can try the chimney climb before admiring the fine collections of toys and dolls.
visitor comments: The gardens and grounds are meticulously kept.
Hall & Museum: 1 Apr-31 Oct Wed-Sun & Bank Hol Mon 13.00-17.30. Closed Good Fri. Coach House Tea Room 12.00-17.30 (last orders 17.00). Shop 12.30-17.30
Last Admission: 30mins before closing
Hall: A£3.70 C(under 5)£Free C(5-16)£1.80 Family Ticket £9.20. Museum: A£3.70 C(under 5)£Free C(5-16)£1.80 Family Ticket £9.20. Hall & Museum: A£5.90 C(under 5)£Free C(5-16)£2.80 Family Ticket £14.60

↓*special events*

▶ **Recital and Supper**
1/4/00-1/4/00
Equinox Strings in the Long Gallery. £18.50. Booking essential

▶ **Family Fun**
19/4/00-28/4/00
Held on Apr 19, 20, 21, 26, 27 and 28 only. Family activities from 13.00-16.00

▶ **Golden Egg Hunt**
22/4/00-24/4/00
£1.50 per child. Children must be accompanied by an adult. Open 13.00-17.00

▶ **May Day Plant Fair**
1/5/00-1/5/00
From 12.00, entry £1.00

▶ **Creative Writing Workshop**
25/5/00-25/5/00
Limited tickets available from Ashbourne Library or Jenny Edgar, tel: 01629 580000.

▶ **Never Grow Up!**
27/5/00-23/7/00
Peter Pan Quest held on May 27 and July 23 only, C£0.50, 13.00-16.00

Folk & Local History Museums

The Old House Museum
Cunningham Place Bakewell Derbyshire DE45 1AX
[situated on A6, 12m S of Buxton and 8m N of Matlock]
Tel: 01629 813165
Bakewell Old House Museum is a Tudor house with a collection of social life exhibits. It contains a Victorian kitchen, costume displays on models, old toys, artesan's craft workshops and tools, lace and early cameras, etc
1 Apr-31 Oct daily 13.30-16.00, July & Aug 11.00-16.00. Group bookings at other times
Last Admission: 15.30
A£2.50 C£1.00
discount offer: Two For The Price Of One. Valid Until 31 Oct 2000

Wind In The Willows
Peak Village Rowsley Derbyshire DE4 2NP
[off A6 between Bakewell and Matlock, easily accessible from the M1, follow the signs to Chatsworth House. Plenty of on site parking available]
Tel: 01539 488444 Fax: 01539
A brand new family attraction based on the story of the Wind in the Willows. Watch a short film telling you of the story, then walk around the magical trail where E H Shepard's original illustrations are brought to life using

models, lighting and sound effects. In the 'Wide World' learn about real Moles, Badgers, Toads and Water Rats and take home a souvenir from 'Heroes', the children's character shop.

visitor comments: Simply wonderful! The displays are magical. Visit Peak Village for fabulous Arts and Crafts goodies.

All year daily: Mon-Sat 10.00-17.30 Sun 10.00-17.00. Closed 25 Dec

Last Admission: 30mins before closing

A£3.25 C(under 4)£Free C(4-14)£2.00 Group Rates 15+ A£2.60 C£1.60

Forests & Woods

Heart of the National Forest Visitor Centre

Bath Lane Moira Derbyshire DE12 6BD

[Follow brown signs on B5003]

Tel: 01283 216633 Fax: 01283 210321

Here in the heart of England, the National Forest is not just a dream it is a happening. There's plenty to see both indoors and out, learning about the Forest and experience for yourself the growth of new woodlands as they emerge alongside the traditional wooded areas. The main visitor centre for the National Forest, set in 16 acres of woodland landscape, include exhibitions, lakeside restaurant, trails, canopy walk, an adventure playground, "Once a Tree" Shop, outdoor amphitheatre and craft workshops. There is also a plant centre, cycle hire (seasonal) and a forest products outlet.

visitor comments: Wonderful inexpensive gifts, and the adventure park is not to be missed! Lovely walks and good restaurant.

All year daily summer: 10.00-18.00, winter: 10.00-16.30 (please call to confirm)

Last Admission: 17.30

A£2.95 C£1.95 OAPs£2.00 Family Ticket £8.00 Group rates available

discount offer: One Child Free With A Full Paying Adult

Historical

Bolsover Castle

Castle Bungalows Castle Street Bolsover Chesterfield Derbyshire S44 6PR

[J29 M1 6m E of Chesterfield on A632]

Tel: 01246 823349 Fax: 01246 241569

www.english-heritage.org.uk

Built on the site of a Norman Castle this is largely 17th century mansion, explore the romanticism of the 'Little Castle' a unique celebration of Jacobean romanticism and the impressive internal seventeenth century riding school.

1 Apr-31 Oct daily 10.00-18.00 (17.00 in Oct) or dusk, 1 Nov-31 Mar Wed-Sun 10.00-16.00. Closed 24-26 Dec

A£4.20 C£2.10 OAPs&Students&UB40£3.20

↓*special events*

▶ **Castle Music of the Cavaliers and Roundheads**
1/4/00-2/4/00

▶ **Meet the Custodian**
8/4/00-9/4/00
At 11.00, 14.00 & 15.30. Tours of sites by the people who know them best

▶ **Wellington's Army British Redcoats of the Napoleonic Wars**
23/4/00-24/4/00

▶ **Military Vehicle and Living History Display**
29/4/00-1/5/00
From 10.00.Battle re-enactments, Home Guard and firepower demonstrations, plus military vehicles

▶ **Bolsover's Best Bits**
16/9/00-17/9/00
From 19.00.A visual extravaganza performed by local people

▶ **Conflict at the Castle**
23/9/00-24/9/00
From 10.00.Miniature war games and demonstrations.

▶ **A Victorian Christmas & Lantern Parade**
25/11/00-25/11/00

Calke Abbey

The National Trust Ticknall Derbyshire DE73 1LE

[10m S of Derby on A514 at Ticknall between Swadlincote & Melbourne. BR: Derby & Burton on Trent. Plenty of on site parking available]

Tel: 01332 863822 Fax: 01332 865272

A great house with a big difference! Calke Abbey is a baroque house built in 1703-4 for Sir John Harpur and contains rooms almost unchanged since the 1880s. Extensive natural history collections. Chinese silk state bed. Other features include: walled garden, pleasure ground, Orangery, stables with collection of carriages, church, restaurant and shop, and landscape park.

visitor comments: The Spring Plant Sale is lovely - take along a basket!

House, Garden & Church: Apr-Oct Sat-Wed & Bank Hol Mon. Closed Good Fri and 12 Aug.

House & Church: 13.00-17.30 Garden: 11.00-17.30. Ticket Office 11.00-17.00

Last Admission: House and garden: 17.00

Queuing Times: possible at peak times

All sites: A£5.10 C£2.50 Family Ticket £12.70. Garden only: £2.40. NT Members £Free. Discount for Groups. Refundable vehicle charge on entry to house when open

↓*special events*

▶ **From Winter to Spring**
17/3/00-17/3/00
The Kilwardby Singers with a programme of catches, arias and part-songs welcome spring. Includes meal. 7.30pm. £12.50. Booking essential.

▶ **Lambing**
17/3/00-31/3/00
Sheep and lambs to view during daylight hours. Vehicle charge, £2.50.

▶ **Writer in Residence**
8/4/00-14/4/00
Creative writing 'drop-in' sessions in the house. Details from property.

▶ **Kite Flying**
9/4/00-9/4/00
Fly your kite, make a kite. From 11.00. Vehicle entry charge, £2.50

▶ **Plant Sale**
16/4/00-16/4/00
Huge selection of plants, 11.00-16.00. Entry to sale £1.00

▶ **Easter Egg Trail**
24/4/00-24/4/00
£1.50 per entrant. Children must be accompanied by an adult. Usual admission. 12.00-15.30

▶ **Craft Fair**
29/4/00-1/5/00
Exquisite craftsmanship on show. Children's activities. A£2.50 C£Free OAPs£2.00

▶ **Tour and Tipple in the Garden**
4/5/00-4/5/00
Tour the gardens with Head Gardener, enjoy a glass of wine and a bite to eat. 18.30-20.00. £6.00. Booking essential

Chatsworth

Bakewell Derbyshire DE45 1PP
[8m N of Matlock off B6012. 16m from J29 M1 signposted via Chesterfield. 30m from J19 M6. BR: Chesterfield]
Tel: 01246 582204/565300 Fax: 01246 583536
www.chatsworth-house.co.uk

Chatsworth is the palatial home of the Duke and Duchess of Devonshire and has one of the richest collections of fine and decorative arts in private hands. Garden with fountain and maze. The park is one of the finest in Britain, laid out by Capability Brown. Thrilling playground has been built to conform to the highest international safety standards. Young children enjoy the sand and water play areas, while older children test their skills and daring on the towers, ropewalks, spiral slide and commando wire.

visitor comments: A whole day to visit, you will be left gasping! Gardens are wonderful - you can walk up the waterfall steps, the maze was a real challenge. A walker's paradise, we never tire of visiting.

15 Mar-29 Oct, House: 11.00-17.30. Garden: 11.00-18.00 June-Aug Garden opens at 10.30. Farmyard & Adventure Playground: 10.30-17.30. Last entry to Scots Rooms, when open is 16.00. House & Garden open Sept for Country Fair Visitors at a reduced rate
Last Admission: House: 16.30 Garden: 17.00
House & Garden: A£6.75 C£3.00 Family Ticket £16.75 OAPs&Students£5.50, including Scots Bedrooms: A£7.75 C£3.50 Family Ticket £19.00 OAPs&Students£6.50. Scots Bedrooms only: A£1.00 C£0.50. Garden only: A£3.85 C£1.75 Family Ticket £9.50 OAPs&Students£3.00. Farmyard & Adventure Playground: A&C£3.50 C(under 3)£Free, groups 5+ £3.00 each, School Parties £2.60. Family Pass for all attractions £26.00. Car Park £1.00. Pre-booked groups: A£6.00 OAPs&Students£4.75, including Scots Bedrooms: A£7.00 OAPs&Students£5.75. Private guided tours of the House are available at an extra charge, and by prior arrangement only, please contact Sue Gregory

↓*special events*

▶ **Lecture: History of the Garden**
29/3/00-29/3/00
A portrait of the Garden in its 450 year history

▶ **Housekeeping Demonstration**
29/3/00-25/10/00
The variety of skills and the work involved in maintaining the public side of the House, on 29 Mar, 27 Sept & 25 Oct

▶ **Behind The Scenes Days**
29/3/00-2/11/00
Spend a day backstage at Chatsworth and meet the people who look after the House and its collections, the Garden and Park. On the following dates: 29 Mar, 24 May, 3 & 28 June, 16 & 27 Sept, 7, 25, 28 & 31 Oct & 2 Nov. Book on 01246 582204 contact Mrs Sue Gregory

▶ **Textiles**
24/5/00-28/10/00
Examples of work undertaken on the textiles in the House and elsewhere, on 24 May, 7 & 28 Oct

▶ **Tour: Waterworks and Turbine**
3/6/00-7/10/00
Tour of the waterworks in the Garden ending with a visit to the Turbine House (not normally open), 3 June & 7 Oct

▶ **Chatsworth at the Turn of the Century**
28/6/00-28/6/00
An Introduction. The day will begin with a brief talk with slides, describing Chatsworth as it was at the end of the 19th century

▶ **Tour: The Garden**

28/6/00-28/6/00
A walk which emcompasses some of the working parts of the Garden as it was around the turn of the last century, call for details
▶ **Country Fair**
2/9/00-3/9/00
Including massed pipe and military bans, hot-air balloons, free-fall parachuting and trade stands, House and Garden open to Country Fair visitors only. Sat & Sun 09.00-18.00, A£8.00
▶ **Housekeeping, Textiles and a Lecture on Chatsworth 1950-2000**
31/10/00-2/11/00
Extended talks and demonstrations including rooms on and off the public route. The Lecture: see entry for 16 Sept. On 31 Oct & 2 Nov

Eyam Hall

Eyam Hope Valley Derbyshire S32 5QW
[approximately 10m from Sheffield / Chesterfield / Buxton. Eyam Hall is off the A623 which runs between Stockport / Chesterfield in the centre of the village past the church]
Tel: 01433 631976 Fax: 01433 631603
www.eyamhall.co.uk
Robert and Nicola Wright welcome you to their family home, Eyam Hall and hope you will enjoy your visit to this fascinating 17th century house, with its collections of portraits, tapestries, costumes and family memorabilia. Tours of the house give a very personal interpretation of the domestic and social history of previous Wright ancestors inhabiting the Hall. Extend your stay with a visit to the Craft Centre within the restored buildings of the Hall Farm and housing seven working craft shops, including stained glass design, stencilling, leatherwork and musical instrument making. Don't leave without indulging yourself at The Buttery which offers an exceptional menu of home-made cakes (Mary's Russian Cake is a must!) and unusual delicious light lunch dishes such as Spinakopita. Member of the Historic Houses Association.
House: Easter-Oct incl Wed, Thur, Sun & Bank Hol 11.00-17.00. Craft Centre & Buttery: All year Tue-Sun 10.30-17.00
Last Admission: 16.00
Craft Centre: Admission Free. House: A£4.00 Family Ticket £12.50 C£3.00 Concessions£3.50
discount offer: Two For The Price Of One

↓*special events*

▶ **Danielle Perrett - Harp Recital**
8/4/00-8/4/00
▶ **A Programme of French Music**
20/5/00-20/5/00
Featuring Douglas Hollick - Harpsichord and Iva Fleischansova -Baroque violin
▶ **Piano and Soprano**
3/6/00-3/6/00
Featuring Paul Webster on piano and Moira Harris, soprano
▶ **Baslow Choir**
1/7/00-1/7/00
An outdoor concert of sumer music

Hardwick Hall

The National Trust Doe Lea Chesterfield Derbyshire S44 5QJ
[J29 M1 follow brown signs 6.5m W of Mansfield 9.5m SE of Chesterfield via A6175 to Clay Cross Access only via Stainsby Mill Exit only via Hardwick Inn one-way traffic system operates in the Park. Plenty of on site parking available]
Tel: 01246 850430 Fax: 01246 854200
A late 16th century house designed by Robert Smythson for Bess of Hardwick. Outstanding furniture, tapestries and needlework with a permanent exhibition. Walled courtyards, fine gardens, orchards and herb garden. Country park has Herdwick sheep & Longhorn cattle. Dogs on leads in Country Park. Limited house access for wheelchairs.
Hall: 1 Apr-31 Oct Wed, Thur, Sat, Sun & Bank Hol Mon 12.30-15.00. Closed Good Fri. Garden: dates as above but daily 12.00-17.30. Country Park: All year daily dawn-dusk. Car Park gates close at 18.00. Stainsby Mill: 1 Apr-31 Oct open as per Hall 11.00-16.30 also July-Sept Fri 11.00-16.30
Last Admission: Hall 16.30 Stainsby Mill 16.00
Queuing Times: Timed tickets possible at peak times
Hall & Gardens: A£6.00 C(under 5)£Free C(5-16)£3.00 Family Ticket £15.00. Garden only: A£3.20 C(under 5)£Free C(5-16)£1.60 Family Ticket £8.00. Group rates available, pre-booking essential (sae please)

↓*special events*

▶ **Stonemason's Yard Tours**
29/3/00-26/10/00
Wed and Thur afternoons throughout season call for details
▶ **Elizabethan Music**
16/4/00-16/4/00
Musician Peter Bull performs in the High Great Chamber, call for further details
▶ **Birds Before Breakfast**
14/5/00-14/5/00
Meet: 04.00 at Information Centre. £12.00 Booking essential
▶ **Airborne Forces Memorial Parade**
14/5/00-14/5/00
Commences 10.00, call for further details
▶ **Birds Before Breakfast**
21/5/00-21/5/00

See entry for 14 May

▶ **Kite Flying**
4/6/00-4/6/00
Bring a picnic. 11.00-17.00

▶ **Evening Entertainment**
16/6/00-16/6/00
Elizabethan Meal after a garden walk at 18.30, £26.00. Booking essential

▶ **Paint the Plant**
25/8/00-25/8/00
See entry for 18 August

▶ **Open Air Theatre**
27/8/00-27/8/00
Romeo and Juliet with Illyria at 19.00. Bring rugs and picnics. A£12.00 C£6.00. Booking is advisable

▶ **Paint the Plant**
1/9/00-1/9/00
See entry for 18 August

Melbourne Hall and Gardens

Church Square Melbourne Derbyshire DE73 1EN
[9m S of Derby on A514]
Tel: 01332 862502 Fax: 01332 862263
1133 saw Henry I give the manor of Melbourne to the first Bishop of Carlisle, sold to Sir John Coke (Charles I Secretary of State in 1628) and still owned by his descendants. Converted over time to a grander residence, the home of two Prime Ministers Palmerston and Melbourne, now houses collections of art and antiques with formal gardens laid out in the french style. Member of the Historic Houses Association.
Gardens: Apr-Sept Wed, Sat, Sun & Bank Hol Mon 14.00-18.00. House: Aug only Tue-Sat 14.00-17.00. Sun & Bank Hol Mon (No Guided Tours)
Last Admission: Gardens 17.30 House 16.30
House Guided Tour: A£2.50 C£1.00 OAPs£2.00. House: A£2.00 OAPs£1.50 C£0.75. House & Garden: Aug only A£4.50 OAPs£3.50 C£2.50. Garden only: A£3.00 OAPs£2.00 Family Ticket £8.00
discount offer: Two For The Price Of One, For House Only. Valid For Aug 2000

Wingfield Manor

Garner Lane South Wingfield Derbyshire *[17m N of Derby 11m S of Chesterfield on B5035, 0.5m S of South Wingfield. From J28 M1 W on A38 / A615 at Alfreton and turn onto B5035 after 1.5m. BR: Alfreton and Mansfield Parkway 4m]*
Tel: 01773 832060
Huge, ruined medieval country mansion built in mid-15th century. Mary Queen of Scots was imprisoned at Wingfield in 1569. Most of the manor has been unoccupied since the 1770's but the late-Gothic Great Hall and the 'High Tower' are fine testaments to Wingfield in its heyday. Used as a film location for 'Peak Practice' and Zeffirelli's 'Jane Austen'
1 Apr-31 Oct Wed-Sun 10.00-18.00, 17.00 in Oct. 1 Nov-31 Mar Sat & Sun only 10.00-16.00. Closed 13.00-14.00. Closed 24-26 Dec
A£3.00 C£1.50 Concessions£2.30

↓*special events*

▶ **Meet the Custodian**
1/4/00-2/4/00
Tours of sites by the people who know them best

▶ **Meet the Custodian**
1/4/00-2/4/00
Tours of sites by the people who know them best

▶ **Children's Easter Lollipop Trail**
23/4/00-24/4/00
Find Easter Bunny and Easter Chick hidden in the grounds and solve their clues to win a lollipop

▶ **A Victorian Weekend**
30/4/00-1/5/00
Enjoy a country fair of 1900, complete with a Boer War recruiting party. Why not come in Victorian costume?

▶ **Guided Tours of the Gardens**
7/5/00-7/5/00
A look at the remains of the Victorian parterres, plus the Woodland Gardens, extensively replanted with rhododendrons. Advance booking recommended

▶ **Music 2000**
28/5/00-29/5/00

▶ **A Mid-Summer Night's Dream**
15/6/00-15/6/00
Shakespeare's classic with additional music by Terence Hawes and sunrise-coloured costumes to greet the dawning of a new millennium. Bring a picnic, rug or folding chair

▶ **Guided Tours of the Gardens**
18/6/00-18/6/00
See entry for 7 May

▶ **Meet the Head Gardener & Housekeeper**
24/6/00-25/6/00
Learn about servants' lives at the end of the 19th century and the part the house played in the community

Mills - Water & Wind

Arkwright's Cromford Mill

Mill Road Cromford Matlock Derbyshire DE4 3RQ
[turn off A6 at Cromford follow brown tourist signs. BR: on Derby-Matlock branch line]
Tel: 01629 824297 Fax: 01629 823256
The world's first successful water powered cotton spinning mill. Guided tours, shops, restau-

rant. 1996 has seen massive a excavation uncovering exciting archaeological remains of the 1776 mill. There is an on going restoration programme and a guide will explain the history and plans for the future.

All year daily 09.00-17.00. Guided tours 09.00-17.00. Closed 25 Dec

Last Admission: 16.00

Guided tours & exhibitions: A£2.00 C&OAPs£1.50. Mill: Admission Free

Caudwell's Mill and Craft Centre

Bakewell Road Rowsley Matlock Derbyshire DE4 2EB

[off J28 or J29 M1, on A6 in village of Rowsley between Matlock and Bakewell]

Tel: 01629 734374 Fax: 01629 734374

Victorian, grade II* listed, water turbine-powered roller flour mill. Four floors of fascinating original machinery, exhibitions and hands-on models to explore. Guided tours for pre-booked parties. Range of high quality flours and free recipes from our Mill Shop. Working craftspeople in Stable Courtyard, café.

visitor comments: See craftspeople at work - very interesting.

1 Mar-end Oct daily 10.00-18.00 Weekends only in winter 10.00-16.30. Open for flour sale daily. Closed 24-26 Dec

Last Admission: 30mins before closing

A£3.00 C(under 5)£Free C(5-16)£1.00 OAPs£2.00

discount offer: Two For The Price Of One

↓*special events*

▶ **Wheat and Bread**

1/4/00-30/4/00

Exhibition illustrating the story of wheat growing, milling and bread making.

▶ **The Saving of Caudwell's Mill**

1/5/00-31/5/00

History of the Trust to celebrate 20 years of our work

Sporting History Museums

Donington Grand Prix Collection

Donington Park Castle Donington Derby Derbyshire DE74 2RP

[approximately 2m from J23a / 24 M1 & M42 / A42, close to Nottingham, Derby and Leicester]

Tel: 01332 811027 Fax: 01332 812829

The largest collection of Grand Prix racing cars in the World, now features a recently expanded McLaren Hall, which includes Mika Hakkinen's 1997 West McLaren-Mercedes, and the car in which Ayrton Senna won the European Grand Prix at Donington Park in 1993. In total, over one hundred cars driven by Mansell, Moss, Clark, Fangio, Ascari and Nuvolari. The cars exhibited include the largest complete collection of Vanwalls in the World, and also features an ever expanding World Champions Helmet collection. Non-Grand Prix cars include a Rolls Royce Silver Ghost and Bugatti Royale. Also featured is the Senna-Fangio memorial, dedicated to these two great drivers. Conference facilities are available.

All year daily 10.00-17.00. Closed Christmas & New Year

Last Admission: 16.00

A£7.00 C(0-5)£Free C(6-16)£2.50 Family Ticket (A2+C3)£14.00 OAPs&Students£5.00. Coach parties welcome

Theme & Adventure Parks

American Adventure

Ilkeston Derbyshire DE7 5SX

[follow tourist signposts from J26 M1 and major trunk roads]

Tel: 01773 531521 Fax: 01773 716140

www.adventureworld.co.uk

The American Adventure Theme Park is tops for fun, action and excitement with rides for thrill junkies, rides for tots and rides that get you soaking wet! Home to Europe's tallest Skycoaster, the 200 foot high face first freefall is more terrifying than any rollercoaster in the world! The amazing Flying Island, which soars majestically skyward over Lake Reflection takes your breath away...without taking your breath away! Don't miss our superb motion master action adventure experience, The Secrets of the Lost Temple, and with old favourites like Nightmare Niagra, the world's highest triple drop log flume and the Missile,

our gravity defying six looper rollercoaster, there's enough thrills and excitement to blow your socks clean off. If loops (we've got the most), freefalls (we've got the biggest), log flumes, (we've got the highest) and runaway trains (we've got the naughtiest) aren't your thing, then sit back to watch dazzling shows of great courage and skill on stage, on horseback and on bar tops. With over 100 rides and attractions set within magnificent Derbyshire countryside and free from unacceptably long queues, you're sure to have a great day out at The American Adventure.
visitor comments: Good value, no queues on out-of-season days. Water rides were great.
27 Mar-31 Oct daily 10.00 onwards
A£12.99 C(0.9meters-aged 11)£9.99 C(under 0.9metres)£Free Family Ticket(4 people max 2 adults)£39.00 Family Ticket(5 people max 2 adults)£47.00 OAPs£2.50

Transport Museums

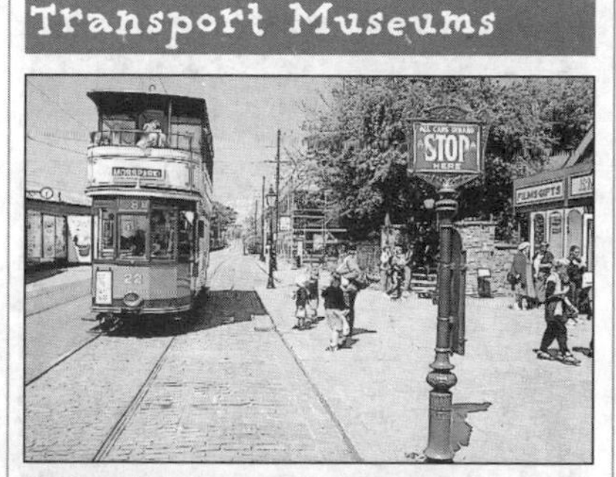

National Tramway Museum
Crich Matlock Derbyshire DE4 5DP
[J28 M1, signs from A6 and A38, off B5035. Plenty parking on site]
Tel: 01773 852565 Fax: 01773 852326
www.tramway.co.uk
Ride on vintage trams from all over the world as many times as you like through period townscape to open countryside. Explore indoor attractions and exhibitions plus tea rooms, refreshment pavilion, shops, picnic areas, indoor and outdoor playgrounds. Dogs (on leads) are welcome to enjoy your visit with you! Braille Guide books plus text version for sighted companions, ramps to all facilities, specially converted tram to lift and carry wheelchairs, free car and coach parking.
April-Oct 10.00-17.30 (18.30 Sat & Sun in June, July & Aug & Bank Hol Weekends) Nov-March Sun & Mon 10.30-16.00
Last Admission: 16.00
A£6.70 C£3.30 Family Ticket £18.20 OAPs£5.80 Group rates available
discount offer: One Child Free With Every Full Paying Adult
↓*special events*
▶ **The Millennium Mini Meet**
4/6/00-4/6/00
Still chic and crammed with character, the mini's timeless appeal is displayed in a monumental meeting of these great little cars.
▶ **In Living Memory**
16/7/00-16/7/00
Dare you! We'll reward you if you do! Come in full Edwardian or Victorian period costume and you can get in free!

Animal Attractions

Hedgehog Hospital at Prickly Ball Farm
Denbury Road East Ogwell Newton Abbot Devon TQ12 6BZ
[A381 follow brown tourist signs, turn off A38 to Newton Abbot at the Trago Mills turn off. Plenty of on site parking available]
Tel: 01626 362319 Fax: 01626 362319
www.hedgehog.org.uk
Possibly the only Hedgehog hospital open to the public. A busy 'hands on' and educational farm experience as well. See, touch and learn about this delightful wild animal. In mid season see baby hogs bottle feeding. Conservation, preservation and care of the environment. How to encourage hedgehogs into the garden and how we put them back onto the wild. Video information with subtitles. Come rain, come shine, lots under cover including picnic facilities. Bottle feed lambs, groom a pony, collect eggs, ride a donkey, cuddle a rabbit, see chicks hatching. Babies, tots and toddlers. Excellent child and baby care facilities.
visitor comments: Free nappies & wipes available. Informative for all age groups. Steep hill from main car park to entrance. Friendly and helpful staff.
26 Mar-end Sept daily 10.00-17.00. Hospital open daily
Last Admission: Mar-Sept 16.00
A£5.25 C(4-14)£3.95 Family Ticket (A2+C2)£12.00 OAPs & Students £4.20

National Shire Horse Adventure Park
Yealmpton Plymouth Devon PL8 2EL
[on A379 Plymouth-Kingsbridge road]
Tel: 01752 880268 Fax: 01752 881014
Fine old farm buildings are at the hub of this 100 acre farm with over 40 Shire horses. A but-

terfly house permits a range of exotic butterflies to be seen in the real habitat. A craft centre, showing the skills of the saddler and the potter, among others, pets corner, falconry centre and new indoor children's adventure playground.
1 May-Sept daily 10.00-17.00. Call for winter opening. Closed 24-26 Dec
Last Admission: 15.30
A£3.95 C£2.75 OAPs£3.40

World of Country Life
Sandy Bay Exmouth Devon EX8 5BU
[J30 M5 (25mins). B3178]
Tel: 01395 274533 Fax: 01392 873533
Marvel at a bird of prey in flight. Mingle amongst the lambs and baby goats; climb in with the rabbits and the guinea pigs or take the Safari Train for a closer look at the red deer and llamas. There's always so much to see and do at The World of Country Life.
visitor comments: Great day out for the children.
6 Apr-31 Oct daily 10.00-17.00. Open until 18.00 June, July & Aug
A£5.25 C(2+)£4.00 Family Ticket (A2+C4)£17.50 OAPs£4.75 Disabled & Helper £3.50. Group rates 10+ A£4.50 C£3.25 OAPs£3.75. Schools: 1 adult free to 10 children. Playgroups: 1 adult free to 5 children. Half price Sat (except July & Aug) & from 24-31 Oct.

Caverns & Caves

Kents Cavern Showcaves
The Caves Wellswood Torquay Devon TQ1 2JF
[1.5m N from Torquay Harbour follow tourist signs]
Tel: 01803 215136 Fax: 01803 211034
www.kents-cavern.co.uk
Tour through the mysterious chambers and passages of this 2 million year old cavern. Experience the caves by candlelight and see the very places where cave people and prehistoric animals sheltered. Wander through an exhibition with sounds and displays recreating scenes of the cave dwellers and the first archaeological excavations and experience our NEW Sound & Light Show.
All year daily July &Aug 09.45-17.00, Apr-June & Sept 10.00-16.30, Oct-Mar 10.00-16.00. Evening Encounters: A Theatrical & Special Effects Tour 15 June-2 Sept 18.00-22.00
A£4.40 C(4-15)£2.80 Family Ticket £13.00 OAPs£3.80. Evening Encounters need to be pre-booked call for prices and booking

Costume & Jewellery Museums

Croyde Gem, Rock and Shell Museum
10 Hobbs Hill Croyde Devon EX33 1LZ
[in centre of Croyde village, follow B3237 from Braunton]
Tel: 01271 890407
A unique museum of gem rocks and shells showing the world's gem stones in their natural and cut and polished state and a comprehensive display of the world's shells. Jewellery made on the premises, cut and polished stones and lapidary machinery may be obtained from the museum shop.
visitor comments: Interesting collection, with a selection of gifts from shop.
31 Mar-31 Oct daily 10.00-17.30, July-Aug daily 10.00-21.30. Winter Opening by telephone appointment 0127 1890407
A£0.30 C£0.10. Schools A£0.15 C£0.05

Country Parks & Estates

Canonteign Falls and Lakeland
Lower Ashton Exeter Devon EX6 7NT
[3m off A38 Chudleigh Teign Valley turning on B3193. Plenty of on site parking available]
Tel: 01647 252434 Fax: 01647 252617
Lakes, wildfowl, a children's play area and miniature horses can be found in this beautiful country park. Covering 80 acres of ancient woodland. Canonteign is also the setting of the highest waterfall in England. A superb day out for the whole family. Indoor and outdoor

picnic areas.
visitor comments: Kids had a great time on the 2 large trampolines. Great view from the top.
Mar-mid Nov daily 10.00-17.30. Nov-Mar Sun, 1 Jan, Feb half term 11.00-16.00
Last Admission: 60mins before closing
A£4.25 C£2.75 Family Ticket (A2+C2)£12.50 OAPs£3.50. Group discounts available. Free souvenir guide
discount offer: One Child Free When Accompanied By A Full Paying Adult

Escot Country Park and Gardens
Escot Ottery St. Mary Devon EX11 1LU
[0.5m off the A30 Exeter to Honiton road at Fairmile signposted. Plenty of on site parking available]
Tel: 01404 822188 Fax: 01404 822903
Escot is a traditionally run family estate and a visit is a day to remember. The extensive park and gardens mix entertainment, animals and natural beauty. Our hand reared pair of otters and a pair of snowy owls are firm favourites. They are fed at 11.00 and 15.00. During the summer months our birds of prey are flown daily (except Saturday) whilst our resident falconer gives an informative introduction to these magnificent raptors. Escot is also a nationally acclaimed, award winning Pet and Aquatic centre. Adjacent is a 2 acre walled Victorian rose garden which includes a pets corner, barn owls, and a trampoline for the children. Worth a visit just to see our collection of wild boar in their woodland enclosures. 25 acres of tranquility and serene splendour. Amongst this is a playground for the children. Next the wetlands and waterfowl park awaits - an enchanting area of natural beauty. The beautifully restored Coach House restaurant beckons with coffees & home cooked lunches. In summary, Escot is absorbing, yet refreshingly uncommercialised.
1 Mar-31 Oct 10.00-18.00, 1 Nov-28 Feb Gardens closed
A£3.50 C(4-15)&OAPs£3.00 C(0-4)£Free Family of 4 £12.00 Dogs£0.45
discount offer: Two For The price Of One

Saltram
Plympton Plymouth Devon PL7 1UH
[3.5m E of Plymouth city centre between Plymouth/Exeter road A38 and Plymouth/Kingsbridge road A379. Take Plympton turn at Marsh Mills roundabout BR: Plymouth North Road. Plenty of on site parking available]
Tel: 01752 336500 Fax: 01752 336474
With Palladian facades wrapped around its Tudor core, this perfectly proportioned mansion boasts some exceptional plasterwork by Robert Adam and a virtually intact Georgian painting collection, including ten by Sir Joshua Reynolds. Also of interest are the Great Kitchen, a gallery of local art in the chapel and an orangery in the garden. The house starred as Norland Park, the Dashwood's family home in the film Sense and Sensibility.
House & Chapel Art Gallery: 27 Mar-31 Oct daily except Fri & Sat 12.00-17.00. Timed tickets issued at busy times. Garden: 6-21 Mar Sat & Sun only 11.00-16.00, 27 Mar-31 Oct daily except Fri & Sat 10.30-17.00. Great Kitchen : 27 Mar-31 Oct daily except Fri & Sat 10.30-17.00. All areas Open Good Fri
Last Admission: House: 16.30
Queuing Times: Timed ticket system used in busy periods
House & Garden: A£5.80 Family Ticket £14.50. Pre-booked Group rates £5.10. Garden only: A£2.90, Parking £1.50

Factory Outlets & Tours

Dartington Crystal
Torrington Devon EX38 7AN
[follow brown tourist signs]
Tel: 01805 626242 Fax: 01805 626263
www.dartington.co.uk
Be amazed at the craftsmen's blowing skills. Enjoy activity in the hands-on glass art area. Be enticed by the factory shop bargains and then enjoy homemade fayre in the licensed restaurant.
visitor comments: Interesting, worth a visit. Some real bargains available in shop.
All year daily 09.30-15.30. Visitor Centre, Shop and Restaurant 09.30-17.00
A£3.50 C£1.00
discount offer: One Child Free With Each Full Paying Adult

Gardens & Horticulture

Bicton Park
Bicton Park Bicton East Budleigh Budleigh Salterton Devon EX9 7BJ
[J30 M5 brown tourist signs 2m N of Budleigh Salterton on B3178]
Tel: 01395 568465 Fax: 01395 568889
Gotha land has now closed! we need new edit!
Mar-Oct 10.00-18.00 Oct-1 Mar 10.00-16.00
A£4.00 C&Concessions £3.50 Family Ticket £13.00

Coleton Fishacre Garden
Brownstone Road Kingswear Dartmouth Devon TQ6 0EQ
[3m from Kingswear, turn off at Tollhouse]
Tel: 01803 752466 Fax: 01803 752466
The house, set in a stream fed valley on a beautiful stretch of the South Devon coastline, was designed in the 1920s for Rupert and Lady Dorothy D'Oyly Carte who created the luxuriant garden around it. It reflects the Arts & Crafts tradition, but has refreshingly modern interiors; the garden has year round interest from early spring flowers to glorious autumn colours. Also a gazebo, water features and a fine collection of rare and exotic plants. Limited access for wheelchairs to house and garden.
House: 5 May-31 Oct daily except Mon & Tue (open Bank Hol Mon) 11.00-16.00. Garden: 7, 14 & 21 Mar 14.00-17.00, 27 Mar-31 Oct daily except Mon & Tue (open Bank Hol Mon) 10.30-17.30 or duck if sooner
Last Admission: 17.00. Timed tickets maybe in operation
House & Garden: A£4.60 Family Ticket £11.50. Pre-booked Group rates A£3.80. Garden only: £3.60 Pre-booked Group rates A£2.90.

Docton Mill
Near Elmscott Hartland Bideford Devon EX39 6EA
[A39 to Hartland follow flower signs to Hartland Stoke, before Elmscott Gardens]
Tel: 01237 441369 Fax: 01237 441369
Less than a mile from the sea, nestling in one of Devon's outstanding natural beauty spots, lies Docton Mill. A restored Mill of Saxon origins, surrounded by 8 acres of internationally renowned gardens, created around the original Mill streams, encompassing an exceptional bog garden, orchard and natural woodland. Televised on several occasions by both the BBC and ITV.
1 Mar-31 Oct daily including Bank Hol 10.00-17.00
A£2.50 C(0-14)£0.50 no coaches

Marwood Hill Gardens
Marwood Barnstaple Devon EX31 4EB
[signposted off A361 Barnstaple-Ilfracombe road]
Tel: 01271 42528
The gardens with their three small lakes cover 18 acres and have many rare trees and shrubs. There is a large bog garden and a walled garden, collections of Clematis, Camelias and Eucalyptus, as well as alpine plants.
All year daily dawn to dusk
A£3.00 Accompanied C(0-12)£Free

RHS Garden Rosemoor
Great Torrington Devon EX38 8PH
[1m SE of town on B3220]
Tel: 01805 624067 Fax: 01805 624717
www.rhs.org.uk
40 acres of superb garden in the stunning setting of the Torridge Valley. Inspirational for gardeners. Walk from Lady Anne's old garden through the Arboretum and stream in a rocky gorge planted with Ferns to a magnificent lake and large formal area of individual gardens, including 2000 roses of 200 different varieties. Fruit & vegetable garden, and also a new winter garden. Award winning Visitor Centre in a beautiful Devon valley setting, surrounded by a 40 acre RHS Garden of great variety and interest. The attractive Restaurant specialises in good home make cooking with Devon cream teas. It has a magnificent view over the Garden and Valley and is adjacent to the Alpine Terrace, with external seating.
Gardens & Visitor Centre all year Apr-Sept 10.00-18.00, Oct-Mar 10.00-17.00
A£4.00 C(6-16)£1.00

Heritage & Industrial

Coldharbour Mill Working Wool Museum
Uffculme Cullompton Devon EX15 3EE
[situated in the Culm Valley just 2m from J27 M5, off the B3181 and follow brown signs]
Tel: 01884 840960 Fax: 01884 840858
Situated in the beautiful Culm valley, the 200 year old mill houses an impressive array of working spinning and weaving machinery, some of which date back to Victorian times. The giant mill engines are "in steam" every bank holiday on Sundays and Mondays. The new World Tapestry is also on permanent dis-

play. Other facilities include a licensed restaurant, Mill Shop and riverside picnic area.
Easter-Oct daily 10.30-17.00, Nov-Mar Mon-Fri Last Admission: Last entry 16.00, Last tour 15.30
Mill & Tapestry: A£5.50 C(5-16)£2.50 Family Ticket £15.00. Tapestry only: A£4.00. Group rates 20+ please call
discount offer: Two For The Price Of One

Historical

Berry Pomeroy Castle
Berry Pomeroy Totnes Devon TQ9 6NJ
[2.5m E of Totnes off A385]
Tel: 01803 866618
A romantic late-medieval castle, unusual in combining the remains of a large castle with a flamboyant courtier's mansion. It is reputed to be haunted. It has a picnic area of exceptional beauty.
1 Apr-31 Oct daily 10.00-18.00, dusk in Oct
A£2.20 C£1.10 Concessions£1.70

↓*special events*

▶ **Late 15th Century Music**
6/5/00-6/5/00
From Noon. From Gothic to Renaissance, lively 16th century music and song also

▶ **Medieval Living History**
17/6/00-18/6/00
From noon, 15th century living history, medieval music, artillery and combat displays with skirmish

▶ **Twelfth Night**
2/7/00-2/7/00
From 15.00,Shakespeare's classic comedy

Dartmouth Castle
Castle Road Dartmouth Devon TQ6 0JN
[1m SE off B3205, narrow approach road. Limited parking on site]
Tel: 01803 833588 Fax: 01803 834445
www.english-heritage.org.uk
This brilliantly positioned defensive castle juts out into the narrow entrance of the Dart estuary with the sea lapping at its feet. It was one of the first castles constructed with artillery in mind and has seen 450 years of fortification and preparation for war.
1 Apr-31 Oct daily 10.00-18.00, 17.00 in Oct. 1 Nov-31 Mar Wed-Sun 10.00-16.00. Closed 24-26 Dec & 1 Jan
A£2.90 C£1.50 Concessions£2.20

↓*special events*

▶ **Elizabethan Gems**
23/4/00-24/4/00
From Noon. Popular song and dance in the reign of Good Queen Bess

▶ **Medieval Music**
6/5/00-7/5/00
From Noon. Lively music and song from the 11-16 centuries

▶ **Thunder of the Guns**
28/5/00-29/5/00
From Noon. Hear the crash of cannons echo around the castle

▶ **Music from Henry VIII's era**
3/6/00-4/6/00
From Noon. Lively 16th century music and song

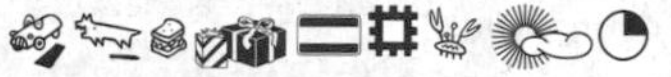

High Cross House
Dartington Hall Totnes Devon TQ9 6ED
[between Exeter & Plymouth 2m from Totnes on A385]
Tel: 01803 864114 Fax: 01803 867057
High Cross contains a unique private collection of early 20th century paintings and ceramics belonging to the Dartington Hall Trust. The first International Modernist House in Britain to be open to the public. Built in 1932, set in a most beautiful 800 acre medieval estate.
1 June-27 Oct Tue-Fri 14.00-16.30. Closed Bank Hol out of season by arrangement
A£2.50 Concessions£1.50 Parties pre-booked special rates

Hound Tor Deserted Medieval Village
Dartmoor Devon
[1.50m S of Manaton off Ashburton road. Park in Hound Tor car park 0.50m walk. Bus: Western National 170/1 Newton Abbo / Tavistock Summer Suns only Tel: 01392 382800]
Tel: 0117 975 0700 Fax: 0117 975 0701
Remains of three or four medieval farmsteads, first occupied in the Bronze Age.
Any reasonable time
Admission Free

Killerton House and Garden
Broadclyst Exeter Devon EX5 3LE
[M5 J28 southbound, J29 northbound, 6m NE of Exeter off B3181, entrance off B3185]
Tel: 01392 881345 Fax: 01392 881954
The house, home of the Acland family, was rebuilt in 1778 to the design of John Johnson. It is furnished as a comfortable family home and includes a display of the National Trust's finest costume collection dating from the 18th century to present day. The 8 hectare hillside garden is beautiful throughout the year, with rhododendrons, magnolias, herbaceous borders and rare trees from all over the world. A network of footpaths through the parkland,

woods and meadows, as well as the garden can be enjoyed all year round. Special exhibitions are planned for 1999.
visitor comments: Good value for money. Lovely in May with bluebells and rhododendrons. Facilities of high standard.
House: 13 Mar-31 Oct daily except Tue 11.00-17.30. Christmas 11-22 Dec. Gardens & Park: All year daily from 10.30
Last Admission: 17.00
House & Gardens: A£5.00 C£2.50 Family Ticket £12.50. Grounds only: A£3.50 C£1.75. Pre-booked Group rates £4.00. Garden and Park reduce during Winter

Powderham Castle
Estate Office Powderham Castle Exeter Devon EX6 8JQ
[signposted off A379 Exeter-Dawlish]
Tel: 01626 890243 Fax: 01626 890729
www.powderham.co.uk
Built between 1390-1420. Ancestral home of the Earls of Devon, damaged in Civil War. The house was restored and altered later. Fine furnishings and portraits are displayed. Rose gardens with views of Deer park and Exe Estuary. Member of the Historic Houses Association.
2 Apr-29 Oct Mon-Fri & Sun 10.00-17.30
Last Admission: 17.00
A£5.85 C£2.95 OAPs£5.35 Family Ticket £14.65
discount offer: Two For The Price Of One
↓*special events*
▶ **Last Night of the Powderham Proms**
4/8/00-4/8/00
Bournemouth Symphony Orchestra conducted by Pablo Gonzales. Call 01202 669925 for details. Tickets: from £14.00-£19.00 C&Students half price

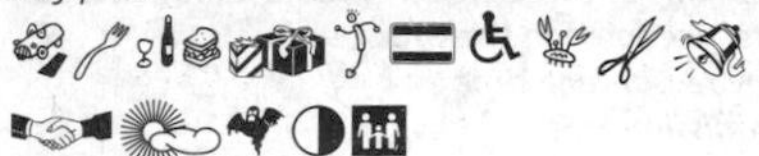

Prysten House
Catherine Street Plymouth Devon PL1 2AD
[city centre]
Tel: 01752 661414 Fax: 01752 661414
Erected as a Town House by merchant Thomas Yogge who bought land in two lots 1487 and 1498. Believed to be a 'priest's house' for Augustinian Order at Plymouth Priory in 1530's. Then into secular hands as wine store and bacon factory. Since 1923 owned by St Andrew's Church and looked after by local people for national heritage. Heritage weekend in September. Guided Tours by arrangement.
All year Mon-Sat 10.00-15.30. Closed Christmas & New Year.
Last Admission: 15.00
A£0.70 C&OAPs£0.35. Groups 15+ £0.35
discount offer: Two Adults For The Price Of One

Sand
Sidbury Sidmouth Devon EX10 0QN
[0.75m NE of Sidbury, 400yds from A375. Plenty of on site parking available]
Tel: 01395 597230
www.eastdevon.net/sand
Lived in Manor house owned by Huyshe family since 1560, rebuilt 1592-4, situated in unspoilt valley. Screens passage, panelling, family documents, heraldry. Also Sand Lodge roof structure of late 15th century Hall House.
House: 23, 24 & 30 Apr, 1, 28 &29 May, 2, 3, 16, 17, 30 & 31 July, 13, 14, 27 & 28 Aug from 14.00. Garden: 1 Apr-31 Aug, Sun-Tues from 14.00
Last Admission: 17.00
A£4.00 C&Students£1.00 Garden only A2.50 C(under16)£Free

Tiverton Castle
Park Hill Tiverton Devon EX16 6RP
[in Tiverton 7m from J27 M5 A361 to Tiverton - signposted]
Tel: 01884 253200/255200 Fax: 01884 254200
Few buildings evoke such immediate feeling of history. Originally built in 1106, rebuilt 14th Century. Many architectural styles. Castle witnessed extremes of peace and turbulence, but is now a peaceful, private house. Fine Civil War Armoury, come and try some on. Old Walls, New Gardens. Superb holiday apartments. Licensed for Civil Weddings. Member of the Historic Houses Association.
Easter-June & Sept Sun, Thur & Bank Hol Mon 14.30-17.30 July & Aug Sun-Thur 14.30-17.30
Last Admission: 17.00
A£3.00 C(under 7)£Free C(7-16)£2.00
discount offer: Two For The Price Of One. Valid until end Sept 2000

Torre Abbey Historic House and Gallery
The Kings Drive The Kings Drive Torquay TQ2 5JE
[on Torquay sea front next to the Riviera Centre]
Tel: 01803 293593 Fax: 01803 215948
www.torbay.gov.uk
From monastery to Mayor's parlour, Torre Abbey is Torquay's most historic building. Situated by the sea, and surrounded by colourful gardens, the Abbey offers you a delightful

visit. Over 20 historic rooms, Monastic ruins, stunning paintings, memorials of crime-writer Agatha Christie, special children's quest.
Apr-1 Nov daily 09.30-18.00
Last Admission: 17.00
A£3.00 C(8-15)£1.50 Family Ticket £7.25 OAP/Students£2.50. Group rates £2.25
discount offer: One Child Free With Every Full Paying Adult

Totnes Castle
Castle Street Totnes Devon TQ9 5NU
[on the hill overlooking the town of Totnes]
Tel: 01803 864406
A classic example of the Norman motte-and-bailey castle. Totnes dates from the 11th century. The circular shell-keep is protected by a curtain wall erected in the 13th century and reconstructed in the 14th. Marvellous views from the walls of the keep across the town to the Dart Valley.
1 Apr-Sept daily 10.00-18.00. Oct daily 10.00-16.00. Nov-Mar Wed-Sun 10.00-16.00. Closed 24-26 Dec & 1 Jan
A£1.60 C£0.80 Concessions£1.20

↓*special events*

▶ **Carry on Piping!**
23/4/00-24/4/00
Lively, humorous, have-a-go family show with 16th century rock 'n' roll!

▶ **The Soldier's Tale**
30/4/00-1/5/00
Four centuries of warfare as seen through the eyes of a soldier

▶ **Storytelling**
9/5/00-9/7/00
Ancient tales to enjoy, on 9 May, 1/2 & 8/9 July

▶ **Medieval Entertainment and Combat**
24/5/00-24/5/00
Fighting knights, fire eating, juggling, children's games, and more - part of the Totnes Millennium Festival

▶ **The King's Shilling**
28/5/00-29/5/00
Listen to tales of valour and find out about taking the King's shilling to enlist as a marine

▶ **The Totnes Taborer - Strolling Medieval Musician**
4/7/00-29/8/00
Costumed entertainer performing on pipes and drums throughout the day, on 4, 11, 18 & 25 July & 29 Aug

▶ **Medieval Living History**
15/7/00-16/7/00
15th century living hisotry, medieval music, artillery and combat displays with skirmish

▶ **Medieval Music**
22/7/00-23/7/00
Enjoy melodies and dance tunes dating back to the 12th century

▶ **Medieval Cookery**
29/7/00-30/7/00

▶ **Stories & Mask-making**
5/8/00-6/8/00
Traditional folk tales, myths, legends and mask-making

Ugbrooke House
Ugbrooke Chudleigh Newton Abbot Devon TQ13 0AD
[just off the A380 Exeter / Torbay road. Follow the historic house signs]
Tel: 01626 852179 Fax: 01626 853322
The original house and church were built about 1200, and redesigned by Robert Adam. Ugbrooke contains fine furniture, paintings, embroideries, porcelain and an extremely rare family military collection. Capability Brown landscaped park with lakes, majestic trees and scenic views to Dartmoor. Guided tours relate stories of Clifford Castles and Lady Anne Clifford who defied Cromwell. Member of the Historic Houses Association.
Grounds: 2nd Sun in July-1st Thur in Sept Sun Tue-Thur 13.00-17.30. Guided Tours of House: 14.00 & 15.45. Orangery Tearooms 14.00-17.00
Last Admission: 17.00
A£4.80 C(5-16)£2.00. Parties 20+ £4.20 per head. Private parties by arrangement
discount offer: Two Adults For The Price Of One. Valid until 7 Sept 2000

Maritime

Plymouth Dome
The Hoe Plymouth Devon PL1 2NZ
[follow signs to Plymouth City centre from A38 then signs to the Hoe and Seafront]
Tel: 01752 603300/600608 Fax: 01752 256361
www.plymouth.gov.uk
Award-winning Visitor Centre in Plymouth Hoe, overlooking Plymouth Sound and telling the story of the great voyages that sailed from Plymouth to change the world. From Sir Francis Drake and his voyages on the Golden Hinde to the voyage of the Pilgrims on the Mayflower, from Captain Cook on the Endeavour to Darwin and the Beagle. They all sailed from Plymouth. Allow two hours for your visit. Printed translations available in French, German, Spanish and Japanese. Group Information Packs also available in French and Spanish. Excellent gift shop and cafe.
All year daily Spring & Autumn: 09.00-18.00. Summer: 09.00-18.00. Winter: 09.30-17.00. Closed 24 Dec-4 Jan

Last Admission: 60mins before closing
A£3.95
discount offer: Two For The Price Of One

Mills - Water & Wind

Otterton Mill Centre
Otterton Budleigh Salterton Devon EX9 7HG
[off A376]
Tel: 01395 568521 Fax: 01395 568521
Mentioned in Doomsday Book this waterpowered Mill grinds wholemeal flour, used in bread and cake making sold on premises. Gallery house holds exhibitions, studio workshops for stained glass, pottery, woodturning and printing. Craft shop, riverside walks and annual furniture design exhibition in October for West Country workshops.
All year daily Summer: 10.30-17.30, Winter: 10.30-16.00
Last Admission: 30mins before closing
A£1.75 C£0.90
discount offer: Two For The Price Of One

Nature & Conservation Parks

Lydford Gorge
The Stables Lydford Okehampton Devon EX20 4BH
[at W end of Lydford village halfway between Okehampton / Tavistock, 1m W off A386 opposite Dartmoor Inn. Main entrance at W end of Lydford near the Mucky Duck. BR: Exeter - St David's]
Tel: 01822 820441 Fax: 01822 820320
This famous gorge is 1.5 miles long, giving walks along the top of a steep-sided, oak wooded ravine leading to the spectacular 90ft White Lady Waterfall and sown to enchanting riverside walks along the River Lyd as it plunges into a series of whirlpools including the thrilling Devil's Cauldron. Home to a wide variety of animals, birds and plants. Wear stout footwear and take care at all times. Expect delays at the Devil's Cauldron during busy periods.
1 Apr-Sept daily 10.00-17.30, 1-31 Oct daily 10.00-16.00, Nov-Mar (waterfall entrance only) daily 10.30-15.00
Last Admission: 17.00
Queuing Times: At Devil's Cauldron peak season
A£3.40 C(5-16)£1.70. Pre-arranged Group rates A£2.80 C£1.40. NT members Free
discount offer: One Child Free With Two Full Paying Adults

Railways

Exmoor Steam Railway
Bratton Fleming Barnstaple Devon EX32 7JN
[on A399 midway between Blackmoor Gate and Brayford]
Tel: 01598 710711 Fax: 01598 710711
Beautifully situated on the edge of Exmoor National Park this unique half-size narrow gauge steam railway runs on over a mile of track through delightful gardens with stunning views of Exmoor beyond. Our admission charges include access to our garden walks, exhibits and not forgetting our awe inspiring South African giants. A perfect day out!
visitor comments: Excellent day out.
19 Mar-Apr & Oct: Sun & Wed; May: Sun, Tues & Wed, June, July & Sept: Sun, Tues, Wed & Thurs; Aug: Sun-Fri
Last Admission: 16.00
A£3.75 C(2-14)£2.75 OAPs£3.25, prices include unlimited train rides
discount offer: 10% Off Admission Charges

Pecorama
Underleys Beer Seaton Devon EX12 3NA
[A3052 E from Exeter W from Lyme Regis. Leave Beer at turning B3174 follow Brown signs to Pecorama]
Tel: 01297 21542 Fax: 01297 20229
www.peco-uk.com
Wonderful views of Lyme Bay from flower-filled gardens offering a variety of children's activity areas. Children's entertainers on many summer dates. Special dates to remember are 10th and 11th June (Steam and Model festival) and 23rd July (Opening of PECO Millennium Garden). Mile-long miniature steam and diesel passenger carrying railway plus PECO Model Railway Exhibition and Model Shop.

Devon

visitor comments: The gardens are beautiful - well maintained and peaceful, and the staff are very helpful. The activity areas are great for children of all ages.
Easter-end Sept & Oct Half-Term Mon-Fri 10.00-17.30, Sat 10.00-13.00, Sun 10.00-17.30 23 Apr then 28 May-3 Sept
A£3.75 C£2.25 C(0-4)£Free OAPs£3.25 over 80's & Disabled Person's Helper £Free. Small increase expected in 2000

↓special events

► **Pecorama Steam and Model Festival**
10/6/00-11/6/00
A two day festival of live steam with exhibits ranging from miniature locomotives to full size vintage traction engines.

► **Official Opening: Peco Millennium Garden**
23/7/00-23/7/00
The opening of a new attraction at Pecorama - The Peco Millennium Garden.

South Devon Railway

The Railway Station Buckfast Leigh Devon TQ11 ODZ
[between Exeter / Plymouth on A38 from Dart Bridge junction, follow signs]
Tel: 01364 642338 Fax: 01364 642338
The Steam Trains of the South Devon Railway link the historic town of Totnes with the popular tourist centres of Buckfastleigh and Buckfast Abbey on the edge of the Dartmoor National Park. Running for 7 miles along the east bank of the River Dart, the line traverses some of Devon's most glorious scenery. Wildlife abounds in and around both river and railway with herons, swans, badgers, foxes and kingfishers amongst the birds and animals sometimes seen. Combine a nostalgic trip behind a steam locomotive along a branch of the legendary Great Western Railway with a chance to view at leisure an almost inaccessible part of the countryside.
visitor comments: Excellent value. Interesting engines but viewing sheds not very organised. Small play and picnic areas adequate.
Apr-Oct Wed, Sat & Sun, Easter Hol,15 May, 4 Oct, Oct half-term daily, May Tues, Wed, Sat & Sun
Return tickets A£5.90 C(under 5)£Free C£3.90 Family Saver Return (A2+C2) £17.60

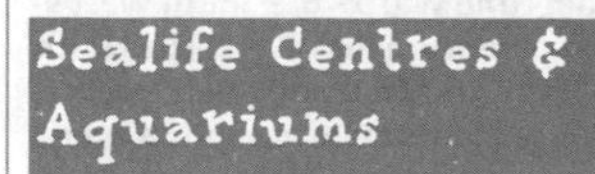

Sealife Centres & Aquariums

National Marine Aquarium

Rope Walk Coxside Plymouth Devon PL4 0LF
[follow signs to City Centre, Barbican and Aquarium]
Tel: 01752 600301 Fax: 01752 600593
www.national-aquarium.co.uk
Take a journey through an amazing underwater world at the new National Marine Aquarium in Plymouth. Experience some of Europs's largest underwater displays and come face to face with over 3000 animals - from seahorses to tropical sharks. New for 2000! - see Britain's largest Sahrk Exhibition (Easter - 30 Sept only). Voted Devon Family Attraction of the Year 2000!
visitor comments: Very popular, try and go off peak!
All year daily 1 Apr-31 Oct 10.00-18.00, 1 Nov-Mar 11.00-17.00
Last Admission: 1hr before closing
A£6.50 C(4-16)£4.00 Family Ticket (A2+C2)£18.00 Concessions£5.00. Group rates 12+ £5.50 School parties from £3.00
discount offer: One Child Free With Two Full Paying Adults

Sport & Recreation

Woodlands Leisure Park

Blackawton Totnes Devon TQ9 7DQ
[on the A3122 6m from Dartmouth. Plenty of parking on site]
Tel: 01803 712598 Fax: 01803 712680
www.woodlands-leisure-park.co.uk
A beautiful 60 acre park with indoor and outdoor attractions for all the family. There are 12 outstanding Playzones including three Dry-ride Watercoasters, 500m TornadoToboggan run, excellent Commando Course, Action Tracks, Amazin Matrix. Paradise for preschoolers with 4 zones. 46,000 sq.ft. of undercover play. Falconry centre and animals galore. New

for this year: The Sea Dragon's Empire - a vast ocean of indoor ad venture, the ultimate play experience!
Mar-Nov daily 09.30-18.00
A£5.95 C£5.40 Family Ticket (A2+C2)£20.95 OAPs£3.50

↓*special events*

▶ **Easter Extravaganza**
15/4/00-2/5/00
Live entertainment, workshops and competitions including, Easter egg hunt on Apr 23-24 and Easter Bonnet competition on Apr 24

▶ **Spring Holiday Fun**
27/5/00-4/6/00
Live entertainers everyday!

▶ **The Best Live Entertainment Programme Anywhere!**
1/7/00-3/9/00

▶ **Halloween Spooktacular**
28/10/00-28/10/00
With the Wicked Witch of the Woods, free pumpkins, lantern procession, workshops and best costume!

▶ **Woodlands Firework Festival**
4/11/00-4/11/00
18.00-20.30. Watch the Spooky Galleon burn! Jazz band, spangles and magnificent firework display

Theme & Adventure Parks

Crealy Park
Sidmouth Road Clyst St Mary Exeter Devon EX5 1DR
[J30 M5 onto A3052 Exeter / Sidmouth road]
Tel: 01395 233200 Fax: 01395 233211
www.crealy.co.uk
Six unique realms combine magic and adventure to create an unforgettable day out for families at the award-winning Crealy Adventure Park near Exeter, the West Country's No.1 Attraction, where Maximum FUN is Guaranteed.
Apr-Oct daily10.00-18.00, Nov-Mar daily 10.00-17.00. Closed 24-26 Dec
Last Admission: 1 hour before closing
Queuing Times: Not excessive
Admission: £5.50 C(Under2)£Free OAPs£4.25 Four-or-more ticket £5.25 Group Rates (20+) £4.25/£4.50

↓*special events*

▶ **Woodcraft Folk Day Out**
19/3/00-19/3/00

▶ **Card Making**
26/3/00-26/3/00

▶ **Mothering Sunday**
2/4/00-2/4/00
A free gift and a piece of Simnel cake for every Mother visiting Crealy

▶ **Teachers Open Day**
8/4/00-14/10/00

▶ **Good Friday - Gigantic Easter Egg Hunt**
21/4/00-21/4/00
Hunt the counters throughout the park and find some of the thousands of chocolate eggs!

▶ **Easter Bunny Day**
22/4/00-22/4/00
Meet the rabbits and babies in the World of Pets

▶ **St George's Day Easter Egg Hunt**
23/4/00-23/4/00
Hunt the Chocolate Dragon Eggs!

▶ **Easter Egg Hunts**
24/4/00-24/4/00
For the bank holiday with over ten thousand chocolate eggs hidden all around the Park.

▶ **May-Day Lost Toys' Treasure Hunt**
30/4/00-1/5/00
A free toy for every child when you find the counters hidden throughout the Park

▶ **Fun Yacht Sail**
7/5/00-7/5/00

▶ **Yacht Racing**
21/5/00-21/5/00

Milky Way Adventure Park
Clovelly Bideford Devon EX39 5RY
[A39, 2m from Clovelly]
Tel: 01237 431255 Fax: 01237 431735
The Day in the Country that's out of this world! Attractions include The Clone Zone - An Alien Encounter, Europe's 1st interactive adventure ride, Time Warp - the South West's largest indoor adventure Play Zone, The North Devon Bird of Prey and Sheepdog Centres, Pets Corner. Amusing and fascinating shows every hour, archery centre, laser target shooting, Toddler Town soft play area, puppet shows, railway and more.

visitor comments: Good entertainment whatever the weather for all ages. Very safe for small children.

Easter-Oct daily 10.30-18.00. Please call for winter variations

A£5.50 C&Concessions£4.50 Family Ticket (A2+C2)£19.00

Once Upon A Time Theme Park

The Old Station Station Road Woolacombe Devon EX34 9SL

[J27 M5, A39 & A361, B3343]

Tel: 01271 867474 Fax: 01271 865864

Once Upon A Time really is the place where children's dreams come true. As well as four carriages brimming with fairy tail scenes, there are two kiddies driving schools, a young scientists room, fantasy train rides, bumper boats, autokid wash - one for the hot days! Old penny slot machines, carousels animated animal band, crazy golf, crazy bikes, disco scooters and so much more.

visitor comments: Excellent entertainment for school age children. Allow half a day.

May 18-July 18 Sun-Fri 11.00-16.00, July 20-Aug 29 Sun-Fri 10.00-16.00, Aug 31 -Sept 19 Sun-Fri 11.00-16.00, Sept 21-Oct 2 Sun-Thur 14.00-16.00, closed winter

A£2.50 C(3-13)£4.75 C(2-3)£3.75 C(0-2)£Free. Price increase likely in the near future

Transport Museums

Combe Martin Motorcycle Collection

Cross Street Combe Martin Ilfracombe Devon EX34 0DH

[off A399 adjacent to the main car park behind the beach]

Tel: 01271 882346 Fax: 01271 882346

The collection was formed in 1979 and contains over 50 British motorcycles, displayed against a background of old petrol pumps, signs and garage equipment, exhibiting motoring nostalgia in an old world atmosphere. Also houses an exhibition of Motorised Invacars. All visitors are given a entry free competition on arrival based on observation around the museum, high scorers receive a prize. Why not enter the yearly Prize Draw to win a 'motorcycle' only 50p a ticket.

visitor comments: Great collection. Original machines.

22 May-29 Oct daily 10.00-17.00

A£2.50 AccompaniedC(0-10)£Free C(10-16)&OAPs£1.50. Pre-booked groups 10+ 10% discount

Wildlife & Safari Parks

Combe Martin Wildlife and Dinosaur Park

Combe Martin Ilfracombe Devon EX34 0NG

[J27 M5. Go W on A361 towards Barnstaple. Turn right onto A399 following signs for Ilfracombe and Combe Martin]

Tel: 01271 882486 Fax: 01271 882486

30 acres of Woodland, complete with streams, cascading waterfalls, ornamental gardens, tropical plants and rare trees make this the most natural wildlife park in Britain. Over 250 species of animals and plants including Snow Leopards, Meerkats, Sealions and free flying Parrots. As well as life-size animated Dinosaurs, there are Falconry Displays, animal handling sessions and a spectacular Earthquake Train Ride. New for 1999 is the Indoor Dinosaur Museum. Visitors can stay in the Park's own Hotel.

1 Apr-Nov daily from 10.00

Last Admission: 16.00

A£6.95 C£3.95 OAPs£4.95 Family Ticket (2A+2C)£21.00

discount offer: One Child Free With Every Two Paying Adults. Valid until 30 November 2000

Zoos

Paignton Zoo, Environmental Park

Totnes Road Paignton Devon TQ4 7EU

[1m from Paignton centre, on the A385]

Tel: 01803 527936 Fax: 01803 523457

www.paigntonzoo.demon.co.uk

Tour the world at one of England's biggest Zoos with hundreds of animals in the natural setting of 75 acres of the world's threatened habitats - Savannah, Forest, Wetland and Desert. Many exciting new features opened in '97 including a new centre for endangered orang utans and gorillas. Daily keeper talks, children's activities, feeding times and displays. The Clennon Gorge Nature Trail, officially opened on 10th September 1998, a circular route through the woodland covering the side of this limestone valley. The woodland here has developed a huge variety of plants and animals, having been in existence for many hundreds of years. You may possibly recognise some of Paignton Zoo's Keepers from the BBC fly-on-the-wall documentary 'Zoo Keepers'

visitor comments: Nice sized enclosures in lovely layout and surroundings. Very educational. Restaurant has a good choice.

All year daily 10.00-18.30 (16.30 in winter)

Last Admission: Summer 17.00, Winter 16.00

Jan 99-26 Mar 99: A£5.40 C£3.75 Family Ticket £16.50 OAPs&Students£4.20. Group rates

A£4.40 C£3.00 OAPs&Students£3.40. From 27 Mar-31 Sept: A£7.00 C£4.90 Family Ticket £21.80 OAPs&Students£5.40. Group rates A£6.00 C£3.90 OAPs&Students£4.40.

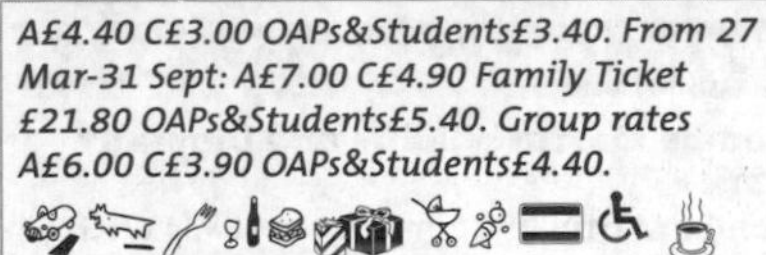

Animal Attractions

Dorset Heavy Horse and Pony Centre

Grains Hill Edmondsham Nr Verwood
Wimborne Dorset BH21 5RJ
[1.25m NW signposted from Verwood on B3081]
Tel: 01202 824040 Fax: 01202 821407

Set in the beautiful Dorset countryside on the edge of the New Forest. Our aim is to preserve and breed the different heavy horses, and to give you the opportunity to enjoy these magnificent animals. Home of the ever popular Shire, the Clydesdale, Percheron, Suffolk and Ardenne. Visit them in their stables and see them paraded daily. We have a lovely display of harness and a small collection of horse drawn implements.

visitor comments: A mixture of animals. Limited hand basins (more on the way), take wet wipes.

Easter-31 Oct daily 10.00-17.00. Live commentaries 11.30, 14.00 & 16.00
A£3.95 C(3-14)£2.25 C(0-3)£Free OAPs£3.50 Family Ticket(A2+C2)£11.00

Monkey World Ape Rescue Centre

Longthorns Wareham Dorset BH20 6HH
[between Bere Regis and Wool off the A35, signposted from Bere Regis]
Tel: 01929 462537 Fax: 01929 405414

Monkey World was set up in 1987 to provide a permanent home for abused Spanish Beach Chimpanzees. We work with foreign governments from all over the world to stop the illegal smuggling and use of primates. The chimpanzees at the centre have been rescued from all across the world where they were being used as beach photographer's props, exotic pets, in laboratories, and in circuses. The animal's exact histories may vary but the majority of them share part of the same story. Here they are rehabilitated into social groups and live in large natural areas. You can see them living as they would in the wild, but you are not allowed to touch. Whilst we participate in breeding programmes for certain species we do not breed chimpanzees, as there are still many chimps who need rescuing. For those who are as lively as our primates we have a fifteen stage obstacle course and three outdoor plays areas (and indoor for wet weather) including Mini Bikes; Mini Boats, swings and slides.

visitor comments: Not so good on wet days. Excellent toilet/baby changing facilities. Great, so much to do. An affordable family day out.

All year daily 10.00-17.00, July & Aug 10.00-18.00. Closed 25 Dec
Last Admission: 60mins before closing
A£5.25 C£3.00 Family Ticket (A1+C2)£10.50 & (A2+C2)£15.00 OAPs£3.50. Groups rates available on request. School Parties C£2.50 Teacher £Free on (1:10 ratio)

Putlake Adventure Farm

Langton Matravers Swanage Dorset BH19 3EU
[on the B3069 Langton Matravers at the bottom end of the village between the Kings Arms and the Ship Inn]
Tel: 01929 422917 Fax: 01929 422917

Visitors are encouraged to explores and make contact with a variety of friendly animals in a relaxed atmoshpere. You can bottle feed the lambs and goats throughout the day and at 4pm you can have a go at the hand milking! It is well worth a trailer ride around the farm and see the stunning views over the Isle of Purbeck, or you can wander along the interesting Farm Trail. We especially cater for the disabled and school parties (it is wise to prebook). If it rains - no worry we have 8600sq ft under cover. The Dairy Tea Shop offers beverages and locally made pastries and gateaux and light meals.

Mar-Oct daily 11.00-18.00 School groups 09.30-18.00
A£3.70 C£2.70 Family Ticket £11.80 OAPs£3.00

Birds, Butterflies & Bees

Abbotsbury Swannery

New Barn Road Abbotsbury Weymouth Dorset DT3 4JG
[9m NW of Weymouth on B3157 coastal road to Bridport. During July & Aug a regular bus service runs daily from Weymouth]
Tel: 01305 871858/871130 Fax: 01305 871092

For over 600 years this colony of friendly mute swans has made its home at the Abbotsbury Sanctuary. Sheltered by the famous Chesil Beach, this ancient and special site provides protection for hundreds of nesting swans and their broods. Incredibly, from the end of May, you can wander safely around the nests, observing at close quarters the antics of the

fluffy cygnets. Mass feeding of the herd takes place everyday at 12.00 and 16.00 and an audio visual show about the Swannery runs hourly during the day. Families will particularly enjoy the wealth of educational information and the ugly duckling trail.
visitor comments: Amazing to see all the swans at feeding time. You can get really close to the swans.
21 Mar-30 Oct daily 10.00-18.00. 1000 Times: Easter-29 Oct daily 10.00-18.00
Last Admission: 17.00
A£4.80 C£2.50 Family Ticket (A2+C2)£13.00 OAPs&Students£4.40
discount offer: Up To £3.00 Off. 50p Off Per Adult/OAP, Maximum Of Six Persons. Valid Until 29th October 1999

↓*special events*

▶ **Baby Swans Hatching**
18/5/00-30/6/00
Watch baby swans hatching in their natural habitat

Country Parks & Estates

Kingston Lacy

Wimborne Minster Dorset BH21 4EA
[on B3082 Blandford-Wimborne road, 1.5m W of Wimborne. Bus: Wilts & Dorset occasional service from Bournemouth tel 01202 673555. BR: Poole]
Tel: 01202 883402
17th century house designed for Sir Ralph Bankes by Sir Roger Pratt. Set in formal gardens and woodland walks surrounded by a park of 103 hectares.
House: Apr 1-Oct 29 Sat-Wed 12.00-17.30. Garden & Park: Apr 1-Oct 29 daily (except 18 Aug) 11.00-18.00, Nov & Dec Fri-Sun 11.00-16.00. Open weekends for snowdrops call infoline in Jan for details.
Last Admission: 16.30 House
House, Park & Garden: A6.00 C£3.00 Family Ticket £15.00. Group rates A£5.00. Park & Garden: A£2.50 C£1.25

↓*special events*

▶ **Easter Egg Hunt**
22/4/00-22/4/00
11.00-16.00, no extra charge

▶ **In Celebration of Wildflowers**
10/5/00-10/5/00
£12.00 to include roast dinner

▶ **Back in Time-Activities**
29/5/00-2/6/00
Go back to the 19th Century, usual admission charge, NT members free. 11.00-16.00.

▶ **A Ride Through the Park**
7/6/00-7/6/00
£10.00 to include supper. 18.30

▶ **A Summer Evening in the Countryside**
29/6/00-29/6/00
£10.00 to include supper. 18.45

Moors Valley Country Park Visitor Centre

Ashley Heath Horton Dorset *[off A31, then take the Horton Road at Ashley Heath roundabout, 10m N of Bournemouth]*
Tel: 01425 470721
Relax beside the lake, have a picnic or hire a BBQ. The Castle and Sandworks are a toddlers paradise, plenty of Adventure for children on the Forest Play Trail, the Spiders Web is just one of ten play strctures ideal for children. Enjoy views of the forest and beyond from the Lookout or get a bird's eye view of the forest on the Trail through the Tree Tops. Play 11 or 18 holes, improve your swing in the practice area or maybe treat yourself in the Gold Shop. Steam through the park in a traditional way, explore over 12 miles of tracks on foot or hire a bike. For the less mobile Easiriders and Tandems are available. Why not complete your day trip by popping into the Visitor Centre, the Tea Room or the Country Shop with its exhibitions. A fun filled, action packed day!
visitor comments: Excellent visit for children. Caters well for children. Plenty of other facilities.
All year daily dawn-dusk. Visitor Centre & tea Room: 09.30-16.30 (later in Summer). Country Shop: 10.30-16.30 (later in Summer). Railway School Holidays and late May-September: 10.45-17.00. Golf COurse: 08.00-1 hour before dusk. Walks, play areas and trails 07.00-1 hour before dusk. Closed Christmas Day
Admission Free. Car Parking Charges vary during the year from a peak charge of £3.50 per car a day to free parking on weekdays Nov-Mar. Railway: single, return and shuttle tickets available. Golf: Green fees payable on the day

↓*special events*

▶ **Chris Walker's Quintet with Dave Shepherd**
10/3/00-10/3/00

▶ **Mad as a March Hare Barn Dance**
31/3/00-31/3/00

Folk & Local History Museums

Priest's House Museum and Garden

23-27 High Street Wimborne Dorset BH21 1HR
[A31 centre of Winborne Minster. BR: Poole / Bournemouth]

Tel: 01202 882533 Fax: 01202 882533
A fascinating historic town house of medieval origin with many Tudor and Georgian features. Set in an exquisite walled garden, the displays include an 18th century parlour, Victorian stationer's shop and working kitchen plus regular special exhibitions. An award winning museum with a hands-on childhood gallery and free children's quizzes. There is plenty to see and do. The ground floor of the house has disabled access and there is a guide filled with photos and information on other floors available on request.
1 Apr-31 Oct Mon-Sat 10.30-17.00. June-Sept Sun & Bank Hol Weekends 14.00-17.00
A£2.20 C£1.00 OAPs£1.75

↓special events

▶ **East Dorset Villages Gallery**
1/4/00-1/4/00
The opening of this brand new interactive attraction which features a Victorian village school room and street scene.

▶ **"From Dinosaurs to Star Wars"**
1/4/00-31/10/00
A Multi-Millennium Celebration of the Museum's Collections

▶ **"Out of this World - A Space Odyssey"**
30/5/00-30/5/00
An event for the whole family

▶ **National Gardens Scheme Open Day**
25/6/00-25/6/00

▶ **The President's Georgian Fair**
12/8/00-12/8/00

▶ **"Beatrix Potter and Friends"**
24/8/00-24/8/00
An event for families in the Garden, so bring a picnic!

▶ **Civic Trust Weekend**
16/9/00-17/9/00
A weekend of special events and free admission

▶ **Witches and Wizards**
25/10/00-25/10/00
A spooktacular family event

Gardens & Horticulture

Abbotsbury Sub Tropical Gardens
Abbotsbury Weymouth Dorset DT3 4LA
[9m NW of Weymouth on B3157 coastal road to Bridport. During July & Aug a regular bus service runs daily from Weymouth]
Tel: 01305 871130
Established in 1765 by the first Countess of Ilchester as a kitchen garden to her nearby castle. It has since developed into a magnificent 20 acre garden filled with rare and exotic plants from all over the world. Most of these were new introductions to this country, found by the plant hunting descendents of the Countess. It now has a mixture for formal and informal gardens, with charming walled garden walks and spectacular woodland valley views. World famous for its Camellia Groves and Magnolias, noted for its Rhododendrons and Hydrangea collections. New for 1998 a colonial style wooden, self service restaurant with verandah and views. The Educational Explorers Trail is popular with families and schools. 70% of the gardens are wheelchair accessible. Dogs are allowed on leads.
visitor comments: Large, clean baby changing facilities. Plenty of seating around. Not 100% pushchair accessible.
All year daily Mar-Nov 10.00-18.00. Dec-Feb 10.00-16.00 or dusk if sooner. Closed 25-26 Dec & 1 Jan
Last Admission: 60mins before closing
A£4.20 C(5-15)£2.00 C(0-4)Free Family Ticket (A2+C2)£10.50 OAPs&Students£3.80 disabled with free helper £3.80. Group rates 10+: A£3.80 OAPs£3.50

↓special events

▶ **The Giant Easter Egg Hunt**
21/4/00-24/4/00

▶ **Baby Swans Hatching**
15/5/00-30/6/00
Dates to be confirmed

▶ **The 2000 Garden Festival**
17/6/00-18/6/00

▶ **'Fiesta in the Gardens'**
8/7/00-8/7/00

▶ **Outdoor Barn Dance**
15/7/00-15/7/00

▶ **Show of Hands**
22/7/00-22/7/00
Summer Festival Concert

Knoll Gardens and Nursery
Stapehill Road Hampreston Ferndown Dorset BH21 7ND
[exit A31 Canford Bottom roundabout onto B3073 Hampreston signposted, 3m E between Wimborne / Ferndown]
Tel: 01202 873931 Fax: 01202 870842
www.knollgardens.co.uk
Winners: Southern England in Bloom top landscaping award. Over 6000 plant species from around the world. Beautiful Water Gardnes, Mediterranean stlye Gravel Garden. Formal 'Dragon' garden. National collections: Ceanothus (deciduous) and Phygelius (Cape Fuchsia). In partnership with Dorset Wildlife Trust, see their wildlife project in action throughout the Garden. Specialist Nursery.
Apr-Sep daily 10.00-17.00, Mar & Oct Wed-Sun 10.00-16.30
Last Admission: 16.00
A£3.75 C£1.80 Students£2.50 OAPs£3.25. Free guide to gardens included with admission. Groups of 15+ on request with optional lunch

or cream tea included

discount offer: One Adult or OAP Admission at Half Price With One Full Paying Adult. Valid to 29 Oct 2000. Excluding Bank Holidays. Maximum Two Persons Per Card

Mapperton Gardens

Mapperton Beaminster Dorset DT8 3NR

[2m SE off A356 & B3163]

Tel: 01308 862645 Fax: 01308 863348

www.mapperton.com

Terraced valley gardens surrounding a delightful Tudor/Jacobean manor house, stable blocks, and dovecote. There is a 17th century Summer House, with specimen shrubs and rare trees, leading to woodland and spring gardens. Magnificent walks and views. Main location for the BBC's Tom Jones. Member of the Historic Houses Association. Partial disabled access, please telephone first.

Mar-Oct daily 14.00-18.00

A£3.50 C£1.50

discount offer: Two Adults For The Price Of One. Valid Until 31 Oct 2000

↓*special events*

▶ **Jazz Evening**

8/7/00-8/7/00

Jazz evening in the gardens. Bring your own picnic and rug. Times to be confirmed

▶ **Mapperton Courtyard Fair**

19/8/00-19/8/00

An annual and popular event with stalls, crafts, children's competitions and teas, 14.00-17.00

Heritage & Industrial

Brewers Quay and the Timewalk Journey

Brewers Quay Hope Square Weymouth Dorset DT4 8TR

[by the harbour]

Tel: 01305 777622 Fax: 01305 761680

Converted Victorian Brewery at the heart of Weymouth's picturesque old Harbour now housing a superb range of attractions for visitors of all ages. Step back in time at the award-winning Timewalk Journey attraction and experience the sights, sounds and smells of 600 years of Weymouth's fascinating history. Other attractions include a speciality Shopping Village with craft centre and Courtyard Restaurant, Weymouth Museum, Discovery hands-on science centre and Bowlingo tenpin bowling. Full programme of free events. Disables access is limited to the Shopping Village only.

All year daily 10.00-17.30. Open until 21.30 during 24 July-1 Sept. Closed 25-27 Dec & last 2 weeks in Jan

Last Admission: Timewalk: 60mins before closing

Queuing Times: Timed tickets during peak times

Admission to Events, Exhibitions and Complex: £Free. Admission to Timewalk: A£4.25 C£3.00 Family Ticket £12.50 Students&OAPs£3.75

discount offer: £1.50 Off A Family Ticket To Timewalk Journey Attraction

↓*special events*

▶ **Two Faces: Weymouth Museum Exhibition Gallery**

7/2/00-26/3/00

A photographic exhibition by Jim Tampin featuring pictures taken when a photojournalist in Africa and recently a wildlife photographer

▶ **Easter Eggstravaganza**

21/4/00-24/4/00

Four fabulous Easter Fun Days featuring top class entertainers, workshops and competitions

▶ **Weymouth Old Harbour 10th Annual Oyster Festival**

28/5/00-28/5/00

A unique fun-filled festival with live musical entertainment, competitions and side shows plus oysters galore!

▶ **Jazz in June**

8/6/00-11/6/00

Four fabulous days of FREE JAZZ in character venues around Weymouth's picturesque Old Harbour, including open air performances in Hope Square

▶ **Half Term Festival of Fun**

21/10/00-29/10/00

A week long programme of special events and entertainment for ghosties, ghoulies and long-legged beasties of all ages

▶ **Christmas Festival**

13/11/00-24/12/00

Six week festival celebrating the traditional sights, sounds and tastes of Christmas including Santa in his grotto and carol singing

Portland Castle
Castle Town Portland Dorset DT5 1AX
[overlooking Portland harbour adjacent to the Helicopter Base]
Tel: 01305 820539
www.english-heritage.org.uk
One of the best preserved of Henry VIII's coastal forts, built of white Portland stone. It was originally intended to thwart attack by the Spanish and French, and changed hands several times during the Civil War.
1 Apr-31 Oct daily 10.00-18.00, 17.00 in Oct A£2.80 C£1.40 Concessions£2.10. Personal stereo tour included in admission

↓*special events*

▶ **Tudor Living History**
30/4/00-1/5/00
Tudor family life

▶ **Wessex Millennium Festival**
28/5/00-28/5/00

▶ **Production**
17/6/00-18/6/00

▶ **Medieval Music**
1/7/00-2/7/00
Enjoy melodies and dance tunes dating back to the 12th century

▶ **Victorian Surgeons**
8/7/00-9/7/00

▶ **Civil War Living History**
9/9/00-10/9/00

▶ **Jazz Festival**
30/9/00-1/10/00

▶ **Traditional Song**
7/10/00-8/10/00
A performance of delightful unaccompanied song

Historical

Athelhampton House and Gardens
Athelhampton Dorchester Dorset DT2 7LG
[off the A35 1m E of Puddletown, 5m E of Dorchester. Plenty of free on site parking.]
Tel: 01305 848363 Fax: 01305 848135
www.athelhampton.co.uk
Athelhampton is one of the finest 15th century houses in England, containing many magnificently furnished rooms including The Great Hall of 1485 and the newly opened Library. The glorious Grade I gardens, dating from 1891, contain the world-famous Topiary pyramids, fountains, the River Piddle and collections of Tulips, Magnolias, Roses, Clematis and Lilies in season. Member of the Historic Houses Association and Christies Garden of the Year Winner.
Mar-Oct daily (exc Sat) 10.30-17.00. Nov-Feb Sun only 10.30-Dusk
Last Admission: 16.30
House & Gardens: A£5.40 OAPs£4.95 C£1.50 Family Ticket (A/OAPs2+C4) £12.00. Garden only: £3.80
discount offer: £1.00 Off Adult & OAPs Admission To House & Garden OR £2.00 Off Family Ticket

↓*special events*

▶ **Easter Celebrations**
21/4/00-21/4/00
Birds of Prey Flying Displays and Medieval Reinactment. Standard admission applies

▶ **Flower Festival - 'As You Like It'**
28/5/00-1/6/00
Fresh and Dried flower arrangements in the House with special Garden displays.

▶ **MG Car Rally**
2/7/00-2/7/00
Display of MG cars of all ages with cars from all MG clubs in the South of England.

Corfe Castle
The Square Corfe Castle Wareham Dorset BH20 5EZ

[on A351 Wareham-Swanage road. Bus: Wilts & Dorset Nos.142/3/4 tel 01202 673555. BR: Wareham Corfe Castle (Swanage Railway) & Norden]

Tel: 01929 481294

Corfe Castle is one of the most impressive ruins in England. An important medieval royal fortification commanding a cleft in the Purbeck Hills.

5-25 Mar 10.00-16.30, 26 Mar-29 Oct daily 10.00-17.30, 30 Oct-3 Mar 2001 daily 11.00-15.30. Closed 25 & 26 Dec (and two days at end of Jan for staff training)

A£4.00 C£2.00 Family Ticket (A2+C2)£10.00 & (A1+C3)£6.00. Group rates A£3.50 C£1.80

↓*special events*

▶ **Spring on the Common**
2/4/00-2/4/00
Meet at 11.00 at the Castle ticket office, no charge

▶ **Medieval Weekend**
30/4/00-1/5/00
Historical societies led by the Gylda Cinque Portman, no extra charge

▶ **Corfe Castle Common: 300 years occupation**
7/5/00-7/5/00
Meet at the Castle ticket office at 11.00, no extra charge

▶ **Digging up the Dirt**
4/6/00-4/6/00
An archaeological tour, meet at Castle ticket office at 11.00, no extra charge

▶ **Midsummer Festival of Traditional Crafts**
17/6/00-18/6/00
A working Castle Dorset craftsmen demonstrating their skills. No extra charge

Lulworth Castle

East Lulworth Wareham Dorset BH20 5QS

[off B3070]

Tel: 01929 400352

Beautiful 17th century Castle and Chapel in delightful parkland. Spectacular views from the tower, interesting artefacts and displays. Lots for children, including a special room full of puzzles and games and a children's farm open May to September. Free parking and access to Stable Cafe and Courtyard Gift and Food Shop.

All year Sun-Fri. Mar Oct: 10.00-18.00. Nov-Mar: 10.00-16.00. Closed 24-25 Dec

A£4.50 C£3.00 Family Ticket £12.00 Concessions£3.50

discount offer: Two For The Price Of One (adult or child free with a full paying adult)

↓*special events*

▶ **Lulworth Easter Bunny Hunt**
23/4/00-23/4/00

▶ **Country Gardening Festival**
13/5/00-14/5/00
Gardening and food fair

▶ **Lulworth 'Classic' Car Event**
25/6/00-25/6/00

▶ **Lulworth Horse Trials and Country Fair**
29/7/00-30/7/00

▶ **International Floral Design Show and Competition**
22/9/00-24/9/00

Maritime

Deep Sea Adventure and Sharky's Play Area

9 Custom House Quay Old Harbour Weymouth Dorset DT4 8BG

[take the A35 into Weymouth. Follow the brown signs for the Deep Sea Adventure - park in the Pavilion car park. Deep Sea Adventure is located on the Old Harbour between the Pavilion and the Town Bridge - on the corner of Custom House Quay and East Street]

Tel: 01305 760690 Fax: 01305 760690

Deep Sea Adventure: family attraction telling the story of underwater exploration and marine history since the 17th century. A wealth of animated and interactive displays. Sharky's Play Zone: Swing, jump, slide and climb. Fun for children of all ages including a separate toddler area for the under 5s. Sharky's Galley offers meals for both parents and children.

visitor comments: Hunt the oyster game kept the children occupied during the visit, excellent idea that worked. Titanic floor was interesting.

All year daily 09.30-19.00. Closed 25 & 26 Dec & 1 Jan

Last Admission: 17.00

A£3.50 C£2.50 OAPs£3.00 Family Tickets £10.95 & £14.95

Military & Defence Museums

Blandford Forum Royal Signals Museum

Blandford Camp Blandford Forum Dorset DT11 8RH

[signposted off the B3082 Blandford to Wimborne road]

Tel: 01258 482258 Fax: 01258 482084

www.royalsignals.army.org.uk/museum/

The Royal Signals Museum depicts the history of Military technology and communications from the Crimea to the Gulf. With displays on the Great War, Second World War, the SOE, the ATS, the Long Range Desert Group and SAS Signals. Featuring military vehicles and motorbikes, uniforms and equipment, medals and memorabilia.

Jan-Dec Mon-Fri 10.00-17.00, 29 Feb-30 Oct Sat, Sun & Bank Hol 10.00-16.00. Closed 10 days over Christmas

Last Admission: Weekdays 16.30, Weekends 15.30

A£4.00 C£2.00 Family Ticket £9.00 OAPs£3.00. Group rate 10+ 10% discount

discount offer: Two For The Price Of One

Tank Museum

Bovington Camp Wareham Dorset BH20 6JG

[A35, then off A352 Dorchester / Wareham road]

Tel: 01929 405096 Fax: 01929 405360

www.tankmuseum.co.uk

With thousands of fascinating artefacts and over 300 vehicles from 28 countries, The Tank Museum is the finest of its kind in the world. Myriad displays, interactive exhibits, video theatres. Spectacular FREE Firepower and Mobility displays every Thursday at noon throughout July, August and September. You will need at least 3 hours for each visit. Braille and Audio Tours, Guide Dogs only in the Museum, Guided Tours by appointment only. NEW Schools Education Programme.

visitor comments: An excellent and well laid out museum, but only if you like tanks. Pleasant staff and interesting gift shop.

All year daily 10.00-17.00. Closed from 17.00 Tue 21 Dec-27 Dec 10.00 & again from 30 Dec at 17.00-2 Jan 2000 10.00

Last Admission: 16.30

A£6.50 C(5-16)£4.50 C(0-5)£Free Family Ticket (A2+C2)£17.50 OAPs£5.50 Group/Coach rates of 10+ call for details

Model Towns & Villages

Wimborne Minster Model Town and Gardens

King Street Wimborne Dorset BH21 1DY

[situated in King St, only a few minutes walk from the town centre, 200yds W of the Minster and opposite public car park]

Tel: 01202 881924

Much care has been taken to provide a charming and colourful setting for your visit. You will be delighted by the beautiful landscaped prize winning gardens surrounding the Model Town. The gardens are also open for the National Gardens Scheme on selected Sundays. There is so much to admire on your trip down memory lane - from buildings built over 40 years ago and accurately recording the period down to the smallest detail, including goods displayed in the shop windows. Relax and enjoy the peaceful setting from the many seats provided. The view is delightful: rivers in miniature, a waterfall and ponds and beyond the grounds the tranquil vista over the Stour Valley and meadows. Children and adults enjoy comparing the town of today with the one-tenth scale models of the 1950's as they wander through the model town's narrow streets.

visitor comments: Enjoyable, peaceful, small and not commercialised.

Easter-last Sun in Sept, daily 10.00-17.00

A£2.50 C(3-15)£1.00 C(0-3)£Free OAPs£2.00. Season Tickets: A£6.00 C(3-15)£2.50. Educational visits and other groups by prior arrangement. Special rates for coach parties

↓*special events*

▶ **Easter Bonnet Parade**

24/4/00-24/4/00

▶ **National Gardens Scheme**

4/6/00-3/9/00

To be held on June 4, July 7 and Sept 3 only

▶ **Annual Teddy Bears' Picnic**

10/9/00-10/9/00

Performing Arts

Pavilion Complex

The Esplanade Weymouth Dorset DT4 8ED

[on the beachfront]

Tel: 01305 785747 Fax: 01305 761654

www.weymouth.gov.uk

Tourist information, conference centre and home of the Weymouth & Portland entertainments and tourism department.

All year except christmas day

↓*special events*

▶ **The Vintage Motorcycle Display**

21/5/00-21/5/00

Held on the Forecourt

▶ **Summer Spectaculars**

10/7/00-30/8/00

Call Box Office on 01305 783225

▶ **International Maritime Modelling Festival**

15/7/00-16/7/00

Held at Pavilion, Radipole Lake, Pleasure Pier

Sealife Centres & Aquariums

Oceanarium

Pier Approach West Beach Bournemouth
Dorset BH2 8AA
[From A338 Wessex Way, follow Oceanarium signs]
Tel: 01202 311993 Fax: 01202 311990

Oceanarium will take you on a fascinating tour of the world from the Antarctic to the Caribbean. From the darkest depths of the Atlantic to the vividly coloured corals of the Great Barrier Reef - teeming with exotic fish. Dive down beneath the reef in our tropical lagoon tunnel and relish the experience of being amongst sharks and colourful creatures.

visitor comments: Excellent - the kids were fascinated, and wanted to return later! Good cafe with views over the sea.

All year daily from 10.00, except Christmas
A£5.25 C£3.95 OAPs£4.50 Family Ticket(2A+3C) £17.50 Group rates available

Sea Life Park - Dorset

Lodmoor Country Park Greenhill Weymouth
Dorset DT4 7SX
[on A353]
Tel: 01305 788255 Fax: 01305 760165

The Sea Life Park is situated at the beautiful Lodmoor Country Park and you can marvel at the mysteries of the deep and discover amazing sea creatures from around our own shores. Sea Life brings you closer than ever before to the mysterious and amazing creatures found in and around our shores. On entry every visitor enrols as a shark cadet before graduating in thrilling style from Europe's first 3D interactive Shark Academy. Black tipped, Leopard and Nurse sharks cruise perilously close by in the Tropical Shark Lagoon. All this and much more including exciting new features for 1999.

visitor comments: Efficient, knowledgeable and friendly staff. Displays were entertaining and educational. Good value for money.

All year daily from 10.00. Please call for winter opening hours
Queuing Times: 30mins
A£5.95 C£3.95 OAPs£3.95. Groups 10+ call for details

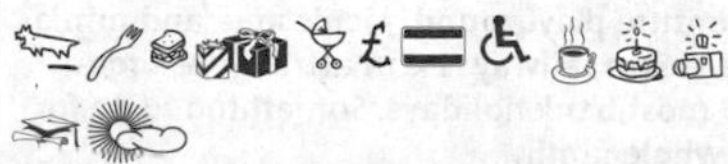

Social History Museums

Dorset County Museum

High West Street Dorchester Dorset DT1 1XA
[on the main road through the town of Dorchester]
Tel: 01305 262735 Fax: 01305 257180

Best Museum of Social History Award 1998. A visit to the museum is a must for anyone interested in the Dorset area and its fascinating archaeology. Displays cover prehistoric and Roman times, including sites such as Maiden Castle. There is also a major new child friendly gallery on Dorset's renowned writers including Thomas Hardy, the Wessex author and poet.

All year Mon-Sat 10.00-17.00 and daily in July & Aug including Bank Hol
A£3.00 C£1.50 Family Ticket £7.50 Concessions£2.00. Group 15+ call for details

discount offer: Second Adult/Child Free With One Full Admission Paid

Stately Homes

Forde Abbey

Chard Dorset TA20 4LU
[A358, B3167 follow the brown signs from Chard to Forde Abbey]
Tel: 01460 221290 Fax: 01460 220296

This 12th-century Cistercian monastery was converted into a private dwelling in the mid-17th century by Cromwell's attorney general. In the house there are good pictures and furniture and an outstanding set of Mortlake tapestries. The large gardens are some of the finest in Dorset and include an historic kitchen garden, rock garden and bog garden.

Gardens: All year daily 10.00-16.30. House: 1 Apr-31 Oct Tue, Wed, Thur, Sun & Bank Holiday afternoons 13.00-16.30
Last Admission: 16.30

House & Gardens: A£5.20 C(0-15)£Free OAPs£5.00. Gardens: A£4.00 C(0-15)£Free OAPs£3.80. Discounts for pre-book groups 20+ can be arranged for any day of the week during the season. Please tel: 01460 220 231 for details

discount offer: 50p Off Full Admission Prices

↓special events

▶ **Wonderful Flowers**
29/4/00-1/5/00

▶ **Jazz in the Garden**
28/5/00-28/5/00

Animal Attractions

Ada Cole Rescue Stables
Epping Road Nazeing Waltham Abbey Essex EN9 2DH
[on B181 on outskirts of Harlow]
Tel: 01992 892133 Fax: 01992 893841
Home for rescued horses, ponies and donkeys. Visitors can walk through the stables and view the fields, browse in the gift shop and watch the animals at pets corner.
visitor comments: Friendly staff, pleasant tour, animals well looked after.
All year daily 14.00-17.00. Closed 25 Dec
A£1.50 C£Free Green Card Holders Free

Dedham Vale Family Farm
Mill Street Dedham Essex CO7 6DH
[off A12 at Dedham Village turning, entrance located adjacent to the Dedham Village car park]
Tel: 01206 323111
19 acres site set in beautiful Dedham Vale. Rare British farm animals are kept in large paddocks divided by wire walkways. Area where children can pet and feed the animals. Playground and picnic areas. Partially suitable for wheelchairs, dogs on leads only.
8 Mar-30 Sept daily 10.30-17.30
A£3.35 C(0-3)£Free C(3-16)£2.10 OAPs£2.85

Hobbs Cross Open Farm
Theydon Garnon Epping Essex CM16 7NY
Tel: 01992 814862/814764
Real working livestock farm with pigs, calves, ewes, lambs, hens and chicks. Other attractions include an adventure playground and straw jump.
All year daily 09.30-18.00
A£2.50 C&OAPs£2.00

Jakapeni Rare Breeds Farm
Burlington Gardens Hullbridge Essex SS5 6BE
[A127 or A130]
Tel: 01702 232394
Smallholding displaying various rare breeds of farm animals and poultry, and organic farming practices. Fishing lake, country walks and pets corner. Camping facilities available.
Easter Sun-Oct Sun & Bank Hol 10.30-17.30, mid week by prior arrangement for groups
A£1.50 C£0.75. 20% discount for pre-booked groups

Marsh Farm Country Park
Marsh Farm Road South Woodham Ferrers Chelmsford Essex CM3 5WP
[A130 Chelmsford / Southend road, venue is off this road, follow brown tourist signs saying Open Farm and Country Park]
Tel: 01245 321552 Fax: 01245 324191
Part working farm, part animal centre. Extensive farm walks take you through up-to-date Piggery units with educational area. Cattle and sheep. Feed the free-range chickens. Play in the soft play area or in the outside adventure playground.
visitor comments: Good family day out. Inexpensive catering. Very friendly welcoming staff. Excellent for picnics.
14 Feb-1 Nov Mon-Fri 10.00-16.30, Weekends and Bank Hol 10.00-17.30. 7 Nov-20 Dec Weekends only 10.00-17.30
Last Admission: 30mins before closing
A£2.40 C(0-2)£Free C&OAPs£1.60 Family Season Ticket (A2+C3)£27.00 provides unlimited visits to the farm

Folk & Local History Museums

Barleylands Farm Museum and Visitors Centre
Barleylands Farm Barleylands Road Billericay Essex CM11 2UD
[J29 M25 onto A127, then take A176 exit onto South Wash Road, 2nd left into Barleylands Road follow signposts]
Tel: 01268 282090/532253 Fax: 01268 532032
A Unique visitors centre comprising of farm museum with over 2,000 exhibits depicting rural life of days gone by, farm animal centre, gift shop, craft studios, tea rooms/restaurant, adventure playground, picnic area and miniature steam railway. Extra attractions organised most bank holidays. Something to do for the whole family.

1 Mar-31 Oct 10.00-17.00. Groups by arrangement
Last Admission: 16.30
A£3.25 C(5-16)&OAPs&Students£1.75, wheelchairs users half price
discount offer: Two For The Price Of One. Valid Until 31 Oct 99

Colchester Castle Museum
Castle Park Colchester Essex CO1 1TJ
[off the A12 in Colchester town centre. Pay & Display parking in town centre. On site parking for disabled visitors.]
Tel: 01206 282931/282932 Fax: 01206 282925
This is the largest Norman Castle Keep in Europe. It was built over the remains of the magnificent Roman Temple of Claudius which was detroyed by Boadicea in AD60. The archeological collections are among the finest in the country. Displays including 'hands-on' learning, and an exhibition on medieval Colchester. Phone for details of holiday events. Disabled acccess limied to ground floor and first floor, not to castle vaults and roof.
visitor comments: Superb museum on the history of this ancient town.
All year Mon-Sat 10.00-17.00, Mar-Nov also Sun 13.00-17.00
Last Admission: 16.30
A£3.80 C(0-5)£Free C(5-15)&Concessions£2.50 Saver Ticket (A2+C2 or A1+C3)£10.20. Guided tours by arrangement on arrival: A£1.20 C&Concessions£0.70
discount offer: Two For The Price Of One

Gardens & Horticulture

Open Garden
Wickham Place Farm Station Road Wickham Bishops Witham Essex CM8 3JB
[Take B1018 from Witham towards Maldon. After going under the A12 take 3rd L (Station Rd), 1st property on the L. Plenty of on site parking available]
Tel: 01621 891282 (after 18.00) Fax: 01621 891721
A two acre walled garden with a further 12 acres of woodland. Huge climbers, roses and wisterias cascade down into wide borders filled with shurbs, perennials and blubs. Planted for year round colour. Knot garden and natural pond. Mixed woodland with plants and bulbs. Profits to Farleigh Hospice and National Gardens Scheme.
May-Sept (closed Aug) Fri only 11.00-16.00
Last Admission: 16.00
A£1.50 C(over 5)£0.50p
discount offer: 25% Off Plant Sales

RHS Garden Hyde Hall
Buckhatch Lane Rettendon Chelmsford Essex CM3 8ET
[A130 follow tourist signs. Plenty of parking on site]
Tel: 01245 400256 Fax: 01245 402100
www.rhs.org.uk
This Royal Horticultural Society garden occupies a delightful hilltop site with fine views across the surrounding area. The Garden has been developed over the last 36 years and hosts a wide variety of plants including a large selection of roses. The plantsman's garden extends to 8 acres and includes a national collection of Viburnum. New for this year is a rose garden with modern roses and a visitor centre.
22 Mar-29 Oct daily 11.00-18.00, Sept-Oct

11.00-17.00
Last Admission: 60mins before closing
A£3.00 C(6-16)£0.70 C(0-6)£Free. Parties 10+ £2.50 per head. Carer for disabled visitor and blind visitors free
discount offer: Free Child Entry. Valid Until 29 Oct 2000

Historical

Audley End House

Audley End Saffron Walden Essex CB11 4JF
[1m W of Saffron Walden on B1383, J8 J9 & J10 M11 Northbound only]
Tel: 01799 522399 Fax: 01799 521276
www.english-heritage.org.uk

Built by Thomas Howard, Earl of Suffolk to entertain King James I, Audley End House was gradually demolished and by the 1750's it was about the size seen today. There are still over 30 rooms to see, each with period furnishings and a stunning collection of art.

1 Apr-30 Sept Wed-Sun & Bank Hol 11.00-18.00. Guided tour of house in Oct
Last Admission: 17.00
House & Grounds: A£6.00 C£3.00 Family Ticket £15.00 Concessions£4.50. Grounds only: A£4.00 C£2.00 Family Ticket £10.00 Concessions£3.00

↓*special events*

▶ **Garden Workshop**
12/3/00-8/10/00
On 12 March, 11 June, 10 Sept, 8 Oct

▶ **Spring Craft Festival**
1/4/00-2/4/00
From 10.00. Craft exhibitors and demonstrators, farm animals, music and childrens entertainment

▶ **Easter Weekend**
23/4/00-24/4/00
From Noon. Easter in the Farmyard

▶ **A Country Weekend**
23/4/00-24/4/00
A variety of country pursuits and sports for Easter

▶ **Spring Gardeners' Weekend**
29/4/00-1/5/00
From 10.00. Includes garden plants, accessories and furniture, free gardening advise and entertainment.

▶ **Medieval Living History Encampment**
13/5/00-14/5/00
From Noon. Drill, archery, mumming plays and dancing.

▶ **Dog Displays**
14/5/00-14/5/00
From Noon. Exciting dog agility races and displays by the country's premier dog team

▶ **Food and Drink Fair**
28/5/00-29/5/00
From 10.00. Up to 100 exhibitors, plus music, competitions, cookery demonstrations and much more

▶ **Medieval Entertainers**
1/7/00-2/7/00
From Noon. Authentic medieval games, learn about cures, folklore and early machinery, plus a children's play about the formative years of Parliament

▶ **A Children's Day**
16/7/00-16/7/00
A wonderful day out for children, including puppet and magic shows, circus skills and more!

▶ **Wind in the Willows**
22/7/00-23/7/00
At 12.30 & 15.00. Meet Toad, Ratty, Mole and Badger in this enchanting children's fantasy

▶ **Autumn Gardeners' Weekend**
26/8/00-28/8/00
Get the garden into shape for autumn flowering and winter colour! Includes entertainment

Hedingham Castle

Castle Hedingham Halstead Essex CO9 3DJ
[on B1058 1m off A1017. Plenty of parking on site.]
Tel: 01787 460261 Fax: 01787 461473

This majestic Norman castle was built in 1140 and is a member of Historic Houses Association. The Keep is one of the finest and best preserved in England and stands 100ft high. Children will love to explore the castle with its splendid banqueting hall and minstrels gallery. There is also a peaceful woodland for walks and picnics. Dogs on leads only. Unfortunately, disabled access is limited to grounds.

visitor comments: Lovely gardens and picnic areas, with lots of open space.

Easter-Oct daily 10.00-17.00

A£3.50 C£2.50 Family Ticket £10.50. Special events may be charged extra

discount offer: Two For The Price Of One

↓*special events*

▶ **Life in Tudor England**
23/4/00-24/4/00
Tudor History Matters, falconry and Archery displays.

▶ **Jousting Tournament**
30/4/00-1/5/00
Two lively days of entertainment and full regalia.

▶ **Medieval Festival**
28/5/00-29/5/00
Dancing, minstrels, jugglers, archery, drama and knights in combat.

▶ **Jousting Tournament**
30/7/00-30/7/00
Presented by The Knights of Royal England. Two lively days of entertainment and full regalia.

▶ **Jousting Tournament**
27/8/00-28/8/00
Presented by The Knights of Royal England. Two lively days of entertainment and full regalia.

▶ **Craft Fair**
14/10/00-15/10/00
Rainbow Fair craft fair.

Museum- Farms

Barleylands Farm Museum and Visitors Centre
Barleylands Farm Barleylands Road Billericay Essex CM11 2UD
[J29 M25 onto A127, then take A176 exit onto South Wash Road, 2nd left into Barleylands Road follow signposts]
Tel: 01268 282090/532253 Fax: 01268 532032

A Unique visitors centre comprising of farm museum with over 2,000 exhibits depicting rural life of days gone by, farm animal centre, gift shop, craft studios, tea rooms/restaurant, adventure playground, picnic area and miniature steam railway. Extra attractions organised most bank holidays. Something to do for the whole family.

1 Mar-31 Oct 10.00-17.00. Groups by arrangement
Last Admission: 16.30
A£3.25 C(5-16)&OAPs&Students£1.75, wheelchairs users half price

discount offer: Two For The Price Of One. Valid Until 31 Oct 99

Sealife Centres & Aquariums

Southend Sea Life Centre
Eastern Esplanade Southend-On-Sea Essex SS1 2ER
[on seafront 0.5m E of the pier]
Tel: 01702 601834 Fax: 01702 462444

Occupying a key position on the bustling Eastern Esplanade and overlooking the busy Thames Estuary, Southend Sea Life Centre focuses on the rich marine life to be found where the Thames meets the North Sea. Seahorses have amazed and enchanted human beings throughout the centuries. In Kingdom of the Seahorse take a privileged peek into their magical kingdom. Full range of talks and activities and feeding demonstrations daily.

visitor comments: A lot to see and keep children entertained. Ideal wet weather attraction.

Summer: daily 10.00-18.00. Telephone for Winter opening hours
Last Admission: 60mins before closing
A£4.95 C(4-14)£3.50 OAPs£3.50

Zoos

Colchester Zoo
Maldon Road Stanway Colchester Essex CO3 5SL
[follow signs along A1124 exit from A12 S of town]
Tel: 01206 331292 Fax: 01206 331392
www.colchester-zoo.co.uk

Colchester Zoo has over 175 species of animals, with informative daily displays. New enclosures include Elephant Kingdom - Spirit of Africa, Penguin Shores, the Wilds of Asia and Chimp World. There is an undercover soft play complex, road train, two adventure play areas set in forty acres of beautiful gardens.

visitor comments: Great day out. Viewing enclosures excellent. Partly on very steep hills. Good picnic facilities and special places to buy food.

All year daily from 09.30. Closed 25 Dec
Last Admission: 17.30, 60mins before dusk out of season
A£7.95 C(3-13)£5.25 OAPs£5.25 Disabled£3.50. Family Super Saver for 3-8 people (must include at least one paying child) 5% off admission. Prices may vary from 10/7/99

Abbeys

Prinknash Abbey

Cranham Gloucester Gloucestershire GL4 8EX
[take A46 or J11a M5. Plenty of on site parking]
Tel: 01452 812066 Fax: 01452 812066
The abbey has become famous for its pottery in the 20th century, but its origins lie in the Middle Ages. The old abbey building is a 12th to 16th century house still used by Bendictine monks and guests. Set in one of the most breathtaking beauty spots in Gloucestershire, many come for the views, some for the solitude and tranquility, some for the friendly shops & tearoom. Prinknash Pottery allows visitors to view the factory via a guided tour. A low cost and memorable day out for all ages.
visitor comments: In addition to the Abbey and Pottery, there is a lovely bird and deer park and a beautiful wendy house. Some deer are tame enough to touch - a wonderful experience. A great day out!
Abbey: daily 05.00-20.00. Shop & Tearoom: daily 09.30-17.00
Last Admission: Shop 17.00, Abbey 20.00
Pottery Viewing gallery fee: A£1.00 C£0.50. Sept-Feb £Free, (No guide)
discount offer: 10% Off Pottery Firsts

Animal Attractions

Cotswold Farm Park

Guiting Power Stow on the Wold Cheltenham Gloucestershire GL54 5UG
[J9 M5 off B4077 Tewkesbury / Stow road. Plenty of free parking available]
Tel: 01451 850307 Fax: 01451 850423
The home of Rare Breed Conservation. Over 50 breeding flocks and herds of our rarest British Farm animals on top of the Cotswold hills. Pets Corner, Touch barn, Adventure Playground, Lambing, Shearing and other seasonal demonstrations. Daily milking July-Sept 12.00-16.00. New for 2000: Technofarm; Farm Safari and an audio tour entitled 'Animals Through The Ages.'
visitor comments: Excellent value for money. Good playground. Plenty of car parking. Restaurant good value for money.
1 Apr-1 Oct Mon-Sat 10.30-17.00, Sun & Hols 10.30-18.00.
Last Admission: 16.30
A£4.50 C£2.30 Family Ticket £12.00 OAPs£4.00. Group rates 10% discount
discount offer: One Child Free With A Full Paying Adult. Valid Until 1 Oct 2000

↓*special events*

▶ **Lambing Time**
1/4/00-7/5/00
Oohhhhh, aaahh, how sweet. See the lambs coming into the world for yourself

▶ **Shearing Time**
27/5/00-7/7/00
Watch the experts relieve our 950 sheep of their winter woollies

▶ **Milk!**
1/7/00-31/10/00
Discover the origin of the milk you pour on your cereal and find out how WE get it for you.

Arts, Crafts & Textiles

Nature in Art

Wallsworth Hall Twigworth Gloucester Gloucestershire GL2 9PA
[on A38, 2m N of Gloucester. Plenty free parking on site]
Tel: 01452 731422 Fax: 01452 730937
www.nature-in-art.org.uk
The world's first museum dedicated to art inspired by nature, from Picasso to David Shepherd, ethnic art to Flemish Masters, plus sculpture, tapestries and ceramics. Artists from around the world demonstrate from February to October. Collection includes work

by over 600 artists from nearly 60 countries, spanning 1500 years. All housed in fine Georgian Mansion. Twice specially commended in the National Heritage Museum of the Year Awards.

visitor comments: Interesting and fun galleries and grounds. Nice café, with reasonable prices.

All year Tue-Sun & Bank Hol 10.00-17.00, Mon by arrangement. Closed 24-26 Dec

A£3.10 C&OAPs&Students£2.40 C(0-8)£Free Family Ticket £9.50

discount offer: One Child Free With Every Full Paying Adult

↓special events

▶ **John James Audubon Prints**

22/2/00-2/4/00

An exhibition of prints, including over 20 plates from his most famous book 'Birds of America'

▶ **San Art from the Kalahari**

19/4/00-14/5/00

Exhibition of original contemporary work

▶ **Nature in Art Anniversary Exhibition**

9/5/00-4/6/00

This exhibition highlights some of the most exciting additions to our own collection over the past 10 years

▶ **Wildlife Sculptures in Bronze**

13/7/00-30/7/00

Some of the very best in contemporary sculpture

▶ **Heather Angel Wildlife Photography - Provisional dates**

8/8/00-10/9/00

Never previously seen exhibition to mark the publication of her latest book

▶ **Picasso Exhibition**

12/9/00-8/10/00

Buffon Suit by Picasso - a fascinating show of over 50 items

▶ **Anthony Gibbs Exhibition**

31/10/00-12/11/00

Especially famous for his paintings of big cats

▶ **British Contemporary Crafts**

14/11/00-17/12/00

Annual selling exhibition

Caverns & Caves

Clearwell Caves Ancient Iron Mines
Royal Forest of Dean Coleford Gloucestershire GL16 8JR
[1.5m S of Coleford town centre on B4228 signposted from Coleford Town Centre. Plenty of on site parking available.]
Tel: 01594 832535 Fax: 01594 833362
www.clearwellcaves.com
The mines have worked from Iron Age times, 2500 years ago. Today nine large caverns can be explored. Visitors descend 100 feet underground. Deeper trips can be arranged for the more adventurous. Geological and mining displays, blacksmith's shop, Ochre Room, shop and tearoom. Working continues today.
Mar-Oct daily 10.00-17.00, all other times by arrangement only
Last Admission: 17.00
A£3.50 C£2.20 Concessions£3.00
discount offer: Two For The Price Of One

Communication Museums

Robert Opie Collection Museum of Advertising and Packaging
Albert Warehouse The Docks Gloucester Gloucestershire GL1 2EH
[J10,11 or 12 M5 head for the Docks]
Tel: 01452 302309 Fax: 01452 308507
This museum is not only a feast of nostalgia, it is an exploration of the changes in advertising and packaging from 1870 to the present day. Based on the Robert Opie Collection, the museum is the first of its kind in the world. Project Sheets on History & Design & Technology for Schools. Old T.V. ads shown continuously in Tea

Room.
Mar-Sept 100.00-18.00, Oct-Feb Tues-Sun 10.00-17.00. Open Bank Holidays. Closed 25-26 Dec A£3.50 C£1.25 OAPs&Students£2.30 Family Ticket £8.50
discount offer: 30% Off Admission Price

Gardens & Horticulture

Barnsley House Garden

Barnsley Village Cirencester Gloucestershire GL7 5EE
[3m NE of Cirencester on B4425]
Tel: 01285 740561 Fax: 01285 740628
This lovely garden is the creation of Rosemary Verey, who since 1960 has transformed the older garden that was here. There are herbs, a knot garden and a vegetable garden to include mixed borders. The garden is not purely for show all produce is picked and used by the family. Member of the Historic Houses Association.
1 Feb-16 Dec Mon, Wed, Thur & Sat 10.00-17.30. Closed Tue, Fri & Sun
A£3.75 C£Free OAPs£3.00. Guided tours available for groups

Hidcote Manor Garden

Hidcote Bartrim Chipping Campden Gloucestershire GL55 6LR
[4m NW of Chipping Camden, 1m E of B4632 originally A46 off B4081. BR: Honeybourne]
Tel: 01386 438333 Fax: 01386 433817
www.ntrustsevern.org.uk
One of the most delightful gardens in England, created by the great horticulturist Major Lawrence Johnston. A series of small gardens separated by walls and hedges. Hidcote is famous for rare shrubs, trees, herbaceous borders, 'old' roses and interesting plant species. Limited access for disabled visitors, contact to arrange assistance.
Apr-21 May daily except Tue & Fri 11.00-18.00, 22 May-end July daily except Fri 11.00-18.00, Aug-5 Nov daily except Tue & Fri 11.00-18.00 (17.00 from Oct onwards). Shop & Restaurant open additionally 6 Nov-12 Dec Fri-Sun 12.00.16.00
Last Admission: 1 hour before closing or dusk if earlier
Queuing Times: Possible on Bank Hol Mon & Sundays
A£5.60 C£2.80 Family Ticket £14.00. NT Members Free. No group concessions

Painswick Rococo Garden

Gloucester Road Painswick Stroud Gloucestershire GL6 6TH
[on B4073. Plenty parking on site]
Tel: 01452 813204 Fax: 01452 813204
www.beta.co.uk/painswick
This beautiful Rococo garden is the only one of its period to survive completely and is nearing the end of an ambitious restoration programme. It consists of contemporary buildings, woodland walks, and magnificent vistas. NEWLY planted anniversary maze. Charitable Trust No. 299792. Member of the Historic Houses Association.
2nd Wed in Jan-30 Nov Wed-Sun & daily during May-Sept 11.00-17.00
A£3.30 C£1.75 OAPs£3.00
discount offer: Two For The Price Of One. Valid Until 30 Nov 2000

↓*special events*

► **The Tempest**
14/6/00-15/6/00
Outdoor Shakespeare with covered seating, picnic first in the gardens. Please telephone for fur-

ther information.

▶ **Twelfth Night**
18/7/00-22/7/00

Heritage & Industrial

Cotswold Heritage Centre
Fosseway Northleach Cheltenham
Gloucestershire GL54 3JH
[12m E of Cheltenham on A429]
Tel: 01451 860715 Fax: 01451 860091
www.cotswold.gov.uk/museum.htm
The story of everyday rural life in the Cotswolds is told in this museum, housed in the remaining buildings of the Northleach House of correction.
1 Apr-1 Nov Mon-Sat 10.00-17.00, Sun 14.00-17.00, Bank Hol 10.00-17.00, Nov-Christmas Sat only 10.00-16.00
Last Admission: 16.30
A£2.50 C£0.80 Students£1.00 Family Ticket£5.00
discount offer: Two For The Price Of One

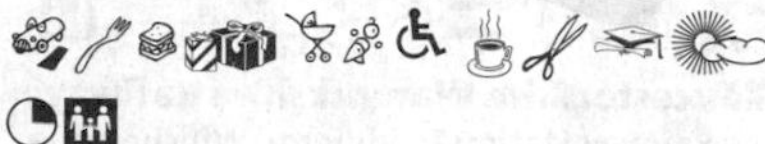

Dean Heritage Centre
Camp Mill Soudley Cinderford Gloucestershire GL14 2UB
[on B4227 between Blakeney / Cinderford]
Tel: 01594 822170
In the heart of the Forest of Dean, the centre is set around a restored mill and pond. The Museum explores the area from prehistoric times until the present day with hands-on models and activities. Grounds include a Victorian cottage, with pigs, ducks and hens, woodland sculptures and an adventure playground, as well as a traditional charcoal burn taking place twice a year. The centre has craft shops and a café, in addition to picnic and barbeque facilities. Nature trails start from the museum. The centre has an active programme of temporary exhibitions and special events.
visitor comments: A fun, educational place to visit for all ages.
Oct-Mar daily 10.00-16.00, Apr-Sept 10.00-18.00
Last Admission: 45mins before closing
A£3.50 C£2.00 Concessions£3.00 Family Ticket (A2+C2)£10.00 . Group Rates: A£3.00 C£1.50 OAPs£2.50. Season Ticket: A£10.00 C£6.00 Family Ticket £24.00 Concessions£8.00
discount offer: One Child Free With Every Full Paying Adult

Historical

Berkeley Castle
Berkeley Gloucestershire GL13 9BQ
[on B4509 1.5m W of A38.]
Tel: 01453 810332
Home of the Berkeley's for almost 850 years, the castle is all one might expect - a great rambling place surrounded by 14ft thick walls, with a Norman keep, a great hall, medieval kitchens and some splendid apartments. It is famous for the dungeon where Edward II was gruesomely murdered in 1327. Member of the Historic Houses Association.
Apr & May daily Tue-Sun 14.00-17.00, June-Sept Tue-Sat 14.00-17.00, Sun 14.00-17.00, July-Aug Mon-Sat 11.00-17.00, Sun 14.00-17.00. Oct Sun only 14.00-16.30. Bank Hol Mon 11.00-17.00. Closed Christmas
Last Admission: 16.30
Castle & Gardens: A£5.40 C£2.90 OAPs£4.40. Gardens only: A£2.00 C£1.00. Butterfly Farm only: A£2.00 Family Ticket (A2+C2) £5.00 C&OAPs£1.00 School Groups £0.80

Kelmscott Manor
Kelmscott Lechlade Gloucestershire GL7 3HJ

[2m SE of Lechlade off the Lechlade / Faringdon road]
Tel: 01367 252486 Fax: 01367 253754
Kelmscott Manor was the country home of William Morris, poet, craftsman and socialist from 1871 until his death in 1896. The house contains a collection of the possessions and works of Morris and his associates including furniture, textiles carpets and ceramics. Member of the Historic Houses Association.
Apr-Sept Wed 11.00-13.00 & 14.00-17.00. Third Sat in Apr, May, June & Sept 14.00-17.00. First & Third Sat in July & Aug 14.00-17.00
Last Admission: 16.30
A£6.00 C&Students£3.00

Owlpen Manor
Owlpen Uley Dursley Gloucestershire GL11 5BZ
[3m E of Dursley off B4066 signposted]
Tel: 01453 860261 Fax: 01453 860819
www.1travel/owlpen
A romantic Tudor manor house dating from 1450 to 1616. Housing unique 17th century painted cloth wallhangings, furniture, textiles and pictures. Set in formal terraced gardens and part of a picturesque Cotswold manorial group including a watermill, a Victorian church and medieval tithe barn. Member of the Historic Houses Association.
1 Apr-31 Oct Tue-Sun & Bank Hol Mon 14.00-17.00
A£4.50 C£2.00 Family Ticket(2A+4C) £12.00
discount offer: Two For The Price Of One. Excludes Sundays and Bank Holiday Mondays

Dean Forest Railway
Norchard Centre Forest Road Lydney Gloucestershire GL15 4ET
[1m N of Lydney at New Mills on B4234. Plenty of free parking on site.]
Tel: 01594 843423 info line Fax: 01594 845840
Steam standard gauge line from Norchard to Lydney Junction (2 miles). Museum, gift shop, riverside walk, forest trail, large car park. Pre-booked guided tours available.
Trains Run: Apr-Oct Sun. June-Aug Wed. Aug Tue Thur & Sat. All Bank Hol & Special Events. Call above info line for running times
Last Admission:
Standard Fares: A£4.00 C£2.00 OAPs£3.00
discount offer: Two For The Price Of One

↓*special events*

► **Day Out With Thomas**
30/5/00-4/6/00
Come along and meet Thomas and Wilbert the Forest Engine

► **Day Out With Thomas**
1/9/00-3/9/00
Come along and meet Thomas and Wilbert the Forest Engine

► **Santa Specials**
3/12/00-24/12/00
Every Sat and Sun during Dec. Five trains each day all tickets £6.50 includes refreshment and gift. Credit Card bookings on 01594 845840

Gloucestershire Warwickshire Railway
The Railway Station Toddington Winchcombe Gloucestershire GL54 5DT
[J between B4632 / B4077 on Stow Road (8m from J9 M5)]
Tel: 01242 621405 Fax: 01242 233845
www.gwsr.plc.uk/
A thirteen mile preserved steam railway operating through the scenic Cotswolds from the beautifully restored stations at Toddington and Winchcombe. There is a large collection of locomotives and rolling stock to view at Toddington. Various events throughout the year, talking timetable: 01242 621405
visitor comments: The "Thomas the Tank" weekend was magical for my 3 year old. Staff are friendly and helpful. Take along a picnic - picnic place available.
Mar-mid Oct Sat Sun & Bank Hol Mon Dec weekends Easter week Spring Hol weeks and school summer hol Tue-Thur
Last Admission: 16.00
A£6.00 C(0-5)£Free C(5-15)£3.60 OAPs£4.00. Group rates 20+

Roman Era

Corinium Museum
Park Street Cirencester Gloucestershire GL7 2BX
[signposted from Market Sq]
Tel: 01285 655611ext206 Fax: 01285 643286

www.cotswold.gov.uk/museum.htm
Cirencester was the second largest town in Roman Britain and the Corinium Museum displays use full-scale reconstructions to bring alive the way of life during this period in history. New Roman Military Gallery and Medieval Gallery. Changing exhibitions and events throughout the year.
Apr-Oct Mon-Sat 10.00-17.00, Sun 14.00-17.00, Nov-Mar Mon-Sat 10.00-17.00, Sun 14.00-17.00, Bank Hol 10.00-17.00
Last Admission: 1hr before closing
A£2.50 C(5-16)£0.80 Family Ticket (A2+C2)£5.00 Students£1.00 OAPs£2.00. Free admission Fridays from 15.30
discount offer: Two For The Price Of One

Sport & Recreation

Cotswold Water Park and Keynes Country Park
Spratsgate Lane Cirencester Gloucestershire GL7 6DF
[on the Spine Road junction of the A419 the Cirencester to Swindon Road]
Tel: 01285 861459 Fax: 01285 860186
www.waterpark.org
Britain's largest Water Park. 50% larger than the Norfolk Broads. Plenty of outdoor activities including simple country walks to jet skiing, camping and caravanning, nature and bird-watching, cycling, sailing and fishing. The area's historic towns and villages such as Crickdale, South Cerney, Fairford and Lechlade are well worth a visit. You could even try the Thames Path national Trail. All the information on the park activities can be found at Keynes Country Park along with the visitor eco-centre, the famous bathing beach, children's play area, lakeside café, wood sculpture trails, boating and cycle hire. A great day out for the whole family.
All year daily 09.00-21.00
Parking charges for Keynes Country Park
discount offer: Car Parking Discount 50% for Keynes Country Park

Transport Museums

National Waterways Museum
Llanthony Warehouse Gloucester Docks Gloucester Gloucestershire GL1 2EH
[Js 11, 12a & 12 M5, A38 & A40 then follow brown signs for Historic Docks]
Tel: 01452 318054 Fax: 01452 318066
www.nwm.org.uk
Award winning National Museum based within historic Gloucester Docks, on three floors of a listed seven storey Victorian Warehouse. Entry is via a lock Chamber with running water, where a sense of adventure takes you into the secret world of canals. Relive the 200 year story of Britain's first transport system, its tale of pioneering men, fortunes gained/lost. View the national collection of British Waterways. Working models/engines, archive film, hands-on exhibits, new galleries and interactives brings all of this to life. Two sides of quay, where cargoes were once transferred, now sports boats of differing shapes and sizes including No 4 Steam Dredger and 100 year old 'Northwich.' Explore the Blacksmith's Workshop with its noises and smells. Activities in school holidays, giving all ages an opportunity to put their creative and constructive skills into practice. A flexible Museum ticket allows you freedom of entry on its day of purchase. Visit the new tea room opening in spring and our specialist book/gift shop, adding to the wide variety of things to do. Observe the water traffic negotiating Llanthony Bridge or take a boat trip along the Gloucester and Sharpness Canal. Tea Room re-opens in March 2000.
All year daily 10.00-17.00. Closed 25 & 31 Dec, 1 & 2 Jan 2000
Last Admission: 1 hour before closing
A£4.75 C&OAPs£3.75 Family Tickets:

(A2+C1)£11.00, (A2+C2)£12.00, (A2+C3)£13.00. Group rates call for details

discount offer: 20% Discount On Single Entry Ticket To The Museum

↓*special events*

▶ **Education Maths Week**
6/3/00-10/3/00

▶ **Victorians**
13/3/00-17/3/00
An education special for schools only

▶ **Education Science Week**
20/3/00-24/3/00
Dates to be confirmed

Animal Attractions

Animal World
Moss Bank Park Moss Bank Way Bolton Greater Manchester BL1 6NQ
Tel: 01204 846157
Moss Bank Park was the site of the Ainsworth's bleaching business. The family's tower and aviary now form part of Animal World with its landscaped gardens, tropical brids, small animals and adventure playground.
visitor comments: Excellent place to visit with children. Attractive, clean layout.
All year daily. Closed Christmas Hol
Admission Free

Arts, Crafts & Textiles

The Lowry
Pier 8 Salford Manchester M5 2AZ
[from the A5063, at the lights turn onto Broadway and follow the route to the Lowry]
Tel: 0161 876 2000 Fax: 0161 876 2001
www.thelowry.org.uk/
The Lowry, National Landmark Millennium Project for the Arts, will open all day, everyday, from 28 April 2000. A waterfront home for entertainment and innovation. The Lowry will house two theatres, art galleries (one showing the works of L S Lowry, the other for visiting exhibitions), Artworks - a creative interactive experience for everyone, plus bars and restaurants with stunning waterside views. No matter how many times you visit, twice a day or twice a year, there will always be something difference. The Lowry is there to be discovered, explored and enjoyed. It is there for everyone and much of it is free.
Opens 28 Apr 2000. All year daily. Closed Christmas Day
Admission Free. Individual performances and Artworks are charged separately. Please call for details
discount offer: 25% Discounts On Artwork Tickets

Science - Earth & Planetary

Museum of Science and Industry in Manchester
Liverpool Road Castlefield Manchester Greater Manchester M3 4FP
[BR: Deansgate (5min walk), Metrolink tramstop: G-Mex (5min walk). Brown tourist signs from approximately 2m radius of town centre]
Tel: 0161 832 2244 Fax: 0161 833 2184
www.msim.org.uk
The Museum offers endless fascination for adults and children. Located in the buildings of the world's oldest passenger railway station, the fun-filled galleries amaze and entertain. Take off to the Air and Space Gallery or visit the textile exhibition - Fibres, Fabrics and Fashion. The new Futures Gallery looks at how we have imagined the future.
All year daily 10.00-17.00. Closed 24-26 Dec
Last Admission: 16.30
A£6.50 C£Free Concessions£3.50

Animal Attractions

Finkley Down Farm Park
Finkley Down Andover Hampshire SP11 6NF
[signposted from A303 and A343]
Tel: 01264 352195
A wide range of farm animals and poultry can be seen here, including some rare breeds. The pets corner has tame, hand-reared baby ani-

mals that can be stroked and petted. There are also a Countryside Museum, housed in a barn, Romany caravans and rural bygones to see, an adventure playground and a large picnic area.
visitor comments: Very enjoyable, well presented.
16 Mar-2 Nov daily 10.00-18.00
Last Admission: 17.00
A£4.00 C(0-2)£Free C(2-14)£3.00 Family Ticket (A2+C2)£13.00 OAPs£3.50

Longdown Dairy Farm
Longdown Ashurst Southampton Hampshire SO40 4UH
[off A35 between Lyndhurst & Southampton]
Tel: 023 80293326 Fax: 023 80293376
A wonderful opportunity to get close to lots of friendly farm animals, from piglets to ducklings, from goats to cows, and many more. Visitors can touch and feed many of the residents, watch the afternoon milking from the viewing gallery and learn about modern farming methods.
visitor comments: A real hands-on experience. The staff are are very friendly and helpful.
22 Mar-2 Nov daily 10.00-17.00
Last Admission: 16.00
A£4.00 C(3-14)£2.80 Family Saver Ticket (A2+C2)£12.50, (A2+C2)£9.00 OAPs£3.50

Birds, Butterflies & Bees

Hawk Conservancy
Sarson Lane Weyhill Andover Hampshire SP11 8DY
[3m W of Andover signposted from A303]
Tel: 01264 773850 Fax: 01264 773772
This is the largest centre in the south for birds of prey from all over the world including eagles, hawks, falcons, owls, vultures and kites. Exciting birds of prey demonstrations are held daily at noon, 14.00 & 15.30 & at 16.15. Heron, Vulture and Raptor feeds. Children have the opportunity to hold a bird and adults can fly a Harris Hawk. Take a trip on the Raptor Safari Trailer rides.
visitor comments: A good day out - stimulating. A little costly, however spend a day. Remember to take your camera!
Mar-Oct daily from 10.30
Last Admission: Spring & Winter 16.00, Summer 17.00
A£5.75 C£3.250 Family Ticket (A2+C2)£16.50 OAPs£5.25

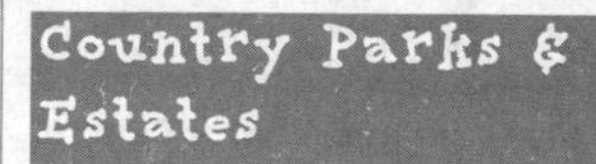

Staunton Country Park
Middle Park Way Havant Hampshire PO9 5HB
[off B2149 between A27(T) and A3(M) N of Havant. BR: 2m. Bus: No.21]
Tel: 023 92453405 Fax: 023 92498156
www.hants.gov.uk/leisure/coparks/staunton
Superb historic Ornamental Farm with exotic and domestic animals, from Chipmunks to Shire horses, and wildfowl. Tropical glasshouses including the giant Amazonian water lily, 1,000 acres of parkland, lake and follies. Delightful Regency tearooms, with famous home-baked cakes.
visitor comments: Good value for money. Designed with children in mind. Cosy tearoom.
Apr-Oct daily 10.00-17.00, Nov-Mar daily 10.00-16.00
Last Admission: 17.00 & 16.00
A£3.60 C(3-16)£2.60 Family Ticket £10.50 OAPs£3.20. Group rates A£2.90 C£2.20
discount offer: Two For The Price Of One

Ordnance Survey Balloon and Flower Festival 2000
Southampton Common Southampton Hampshire *[The Avenue (A33) Southampton, follow AA signs]*
Tel: 023 80832755 Fax: 023 80832929
www.Southampton.gov.uk
Over 150,000 people are expected to watch the 80 hot air balloons lift majestically from the ground in the early mornings and evenings (weather permitting). The Nightglow on the Friday evening promises an exciting mix of colour light and sound featuring special balloons and fireworks. During the day plenty of family entertainment will be available in the form of arena events and live music. If you are a lover of horticulture the spectacular flower displays (organised by the Southamoton Horticultural Society) will delight both the eye and nose!
June 30-July 2 2000, Fri 18.30-23.00, Sat & Sun 06.00-23.00
Free admission, site parking £5.00

↓*special events*

▶ **Ordnance Survey Balloon and Flower Festival 2000**
30/7/00-2/8/00

Hampshire

Forests & Woods

New Forest Museum and Visitor Centre
Main Car Park High Street Lyndhurst
Hampshire SO43 7NY
[A337 or A35]
Tel: 023 80283914 Fax: 023 80284236
www.hants.gov.uk/leisure/museum
For any visitors to the New Forest, a visit to the New Forest Museum and Visitor Centre is a must. The Living Forest audio-visual show and exhibition displays, that include life-size models of Forest characters and the famous New Forest embroidery, bring to life the Forest's history, traditions, characters and wildlife. Pre-booked guided tours only.
Apr-Oct 10.00-18.00. End Oct-end Mar 10.00-17.00
Last Admission: 1hr before closing
A£2.75 C£1.75 Family Ticket (A2+C4)£7.50 OAPs£2.25. Group rates: A£2.25 C£1.25 OAPs£1.75. One person free for each 10
discount offer: £1.00 Off 2 Adults Admission Or £1.00 Off Family Ticket

Gardens & Horticulture

Exbury Gardens
The Estate Office Exbury Southampton
Hampshire SO45 1AZ
[3m from Beaulieu off B3054, 20mins from J2 M27]
Tel: 023 80891203 Fax: 023 80899940
www.exbury.co.uk
A 200 acre landscaped woodland garden on the East bank of the Beaulieu River containing a fine collection of rhododendrons, azaleas, camellias and magnolias along with many rare and beautiful shrubs and trees. A labyrinth of tracks and paths enable the visitor to explore and enjoy the countless intricate plantings, cascades and ponds.
26 Feb-5 Nov daily 10.00-17.30 or dusk if sooner
26 Feb-mid Mar & mid June-5 Nov: A£3.50 C(0-10)£Free C£(10-15)£2.50 OAPs&Groups£3.00. +Mid Mar-mid June A£5.00 C(0-10)£Free C(10-15)£4.00 OAPs&Groups£4.50. +Subject to alteration depending on flowering conditions. *OAPs £4.00 on Tue, Wed & Thur*

↓*special events*

▶ **Summer Classics**
30/6/00-30/6/00
Bournemouth Symphony Orchestra with Pablo Gonzales as conductor. Call for further details on 01202 669925. Tickets from £13.00-19.00 C&Students half price

Hinton Ampner Garden
Hinton Ampner Bramdean Alresford
Hampshire SO24 0LA
[on A272 1m W of Bramdean village 8m E on Winchester, leave M3 J9 and follow signs to Petersfield. BR: Alresford & Winchester]
Tel: 01962 771305 Fax: 01962 771305
The garden, set in superb Hampshire countryside, combines formal design with informal planting, producing delightful walks with many unexpected vistas. After 5 years of restoration the garden is now flourishing and highlights include the dell and a sunken garden.
visitor comments: Lots of hidden areas for children to explore. Expensive for the 90min visit. Not over suitable for young families.
Garden: 15 & 22 Mar then 28 Mar-30 Sept Sat, Sun, Tue, Wed & Bank Hol Mon 13.30-17.30. House: 31 Mar-30 Sept Tues & Wed only, Plus Sat & Sun in Aug 13.30-17.30
Last Admission: 17.00
House & Garden: A£4.00 C(5-16)£2.00. Garden only: £3.20 C(5-16)£1.60 C(under 5) & NT Members £Free

↓*special events*

▶ **Meet the Gardner Walk**
9/4/00-3/9/00
Monthly walk with the Gardener. A formal garden with a few steps but wheelchair users welcome. Meet at the entry kiosk. Sorry, no dogs, £1 plus normal property admission. 14.15-16.15

▶ **Spring Plant Fair**
14/5/00-14/5/00
Come and buy some plants and enjoy a walk around Hinton Ampner. Usual admission, 10.00-15.00

Heritage & Industrial

Holycombe Steam Collection
Midhurst Road Liphook Hampshire GU30 7LP
[off A3 2m SE on unclass road]
Tel: 01428 724900
All-encompassing collection of steam-driven equipment including a Bioscope showing old films, fairground organs, steam-driven roundabouts, big wheel, steam yacht, razzle dazzle, steam farm and paddle steamer engine. Demonstrations of threshing and steam rolling, and traction engine rides. Steam hauled trains run through woodland with spectacular views of the South Downs.
Good Friday, Bank Hols & Sun until 2nd week Oct daily last 2 weeks in Aug
A£5.50 C&OAPs£4.50 Family Ticket £17.00. Group rates 15+ call for details

Historical

Broadlands
Romsey Hampshire SO51 9ZD
[main entrance on A3090 Romsey bypass. Plenty of parking available]
Tel: 01794 505010 Fax: 01794 505040
www.broadlands.net
The home of the late Lord Mountbatten, Broadlands is now lived in by his grandson Lord Romsey. An elegant Palladian mansion in a beautiful landscaped setting on the banks of the River Test. A house with fine furnishings and mementoes of the famous, superb views and Mountbatten audio-visual presentation. Wheelchair and pushchair access limited to ground floor of house and gardens.
12 June-1 Sept daily 12.00-17.30. Access to House by Guided tour only
Last Admission: 16.00
A£5.50 C(12-16)£3.85 C(0-12)£Free OAPs£4.70. Disabled & Students £4.70. Group rates for 15+ A4.70 OAPs£4.40 C(12-16)£3.60. Disabled & Students £4.40

↓*special events*

▶ **Romsey Show**
9/9/00-9/9/00
One of the largest agricultural events in the south

▶ **Christmas Craft Show**
11/11/00-12/11/00
Enjoy hundreds of unique ideas in floored and heated marquees with plenty of Christmas flavour

Medieval Merchant's House
58 French Street Southampton Hampshire SO1 0AT
[0.25m S of city centre. Bus: Southampton Citybus 17A/B. BR: Southampton]
Tel: 023 80221503
The life of a prosperous merchant in the Middle Ages is vividly evoked by the brightly painted cabinets, chests and colourful wall hanging authentically re-created for this faithfully restored 13th century town house, originally built as a shop and home for wine merchant John Fortin.
27 Mar-31 Oct 10.00-18.00 or dusk in Oct
A£2.00 C£1.00 OAP£1.50

↓*special events*

▶ **Medieval Living History**
5/8/00-6/8/00
A medieval house brought to life, with displays of everyday 15th century living history, including crafts

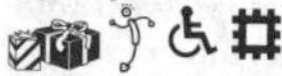

Portchester Castle
Castle Street Portchester Fareham Hampshire PO16 9QW
[J11 M27, on S side of Portchester off A27]
Tel: 023 9237 8291
A magnificent fortress with a history stretching back nearly 2,000 years. The Roman walls are the most complete in Europe and the site was the starting point of Henry V's victorious expedition to the Battle of Agincourt in 1415. Today the vast Keep offers breathtaking views over Portsmouth and the Solent but it once held 4,000 prisoners of war.
visitor comments: Lots of open spaces for running around and picnics, and lovely walks around the outside of the Castle.
All year 1 Apr-30 Sept daily 10.00-18.00, 1 Oct-31 Oct daily 10.00-17.00, 1 Nov-31 Mar daily 10.00-16.00. Closed 24-26 Dec & Jan 2001
A£2.70 C£1.40 Concessions£2.00

↓*special events*

▶ **Men and Women in Times of Conflict**
27/8/00-28/8/00
Famous characters from the Romans to World War II who faced war or strife, together with the experiences of ordinary people in extraordinary situations

▶ **English Civil War and Peace**
7/10/00-8/10/00
17th century military displays and musket-firing. Plus living history

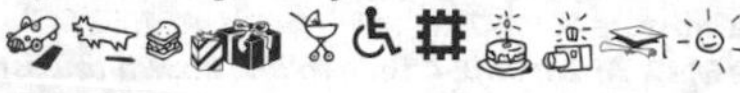

Uppark
South Harting Petersfield Hampshire GU31 5QR
[1.5m S of South Harting, West Sussex, on B2146]
Tel: 01730 825415
The National Trust's most ambitious restoration project: Georgian interior, paintings, ceramics, textiles, furniture, dolls house res-

cued from the 1989 fire. Multi-media exhibition. Interesting servants' rooms. H. G. Wells connections. Garden restored to Repton's design. The stables have now been opened for the first time since the 1989 fire.
visitor comments: Very nice countryside. Interesting house particularly exhibition showing the rebuilding and craftsmanship as a result of the fire.
28 Mar-28 Oct Sun-Thur Grounds, Garden etc 11.30-17.30. House: 13.00-17.00, 16.00 in October
Last Admission: 16.15
Queuing Times: Admission to house by timed ticket
A£5.50 Family Ticket £13.75, Groups (weekdays only) no reduction, must book in advance
discount offer: One Free When Accompanied By One Paying Or One NT Member

↓*special events*

▶ **Restoration / Creation of an Historic Garden**
21/3/00-21/3/00
Lecture followed by lunch from a specially themed historic menu. Send SAE and cheque to National Trust (Enterprises) Ltd. Telephone 01730 825256 for information. £14.95 including refreshments, 10.00-14.30

▶ **Romeo and Juliet**
10/6/00-10/6/00
Presented by Illyria. Tickets from Southern Region Box Office on 01372 451596 A£9.00 C£5.00 18.00 for 20.00

▶ **The Emperor's New Clothes**
1/7/00-1/7/00
Illyria's colourful new family show. Tickets from Southern Region Box Office on 01372 451596, A£6.50, C£4.50, 15.30 for 17.00

▶ **Designer Clothes Sale**
20/10/00-20/10/00
See entry for 12 May

Maritime

Buckler's Hard Village and Maritime Museum

Bucklers Hard Near Beaulieu Brockenhurst Hampshire SO42 7XB
[J2 M27, A326, B3054 then follow brown tourist signs]
Tel: 01590 616203 Fax: 01590 612283
www.bucklershard.co.uk
This historic and picturesque village is situated on the banks of the Beaulieu River, where ships of Nelson's fleet were built. The Maritime Museum shows the shipbuilding history of the village and displays of 18th century life. Cottage displays allow visitors to compare the lifestyle of 18th century village life with that of families today. In the summer months river cruises are available at an additional charge.
All year Easter-Sept daily 10.00-21.00, Winter months 10.00-16.00. Closed 25 Dec
1998 Prices: A£3.20 C£2.10 Family Ticket (A2+C3)£9.00 Senior Citizen & Students £2.50. (Price Review Apr 1999)

Flagship Portsmouth - at the Historic Dockyard

Porter's Lodge Building 1/7 College Road H M Naval Base Portsmouth Hampshire PO1 3LJ
[M27 / A27 follow brown 'Historic Ship' signs]
Tel: 01705 9286 1533 Fax: 023 9229 5252
www.flagship.org.uk
Flagship Portsmouth is home to the world's greatest historic ships: Henry VIII's favourite warship - Mary Rose; Nelson's flagship at the Battle of trafalgar - HMS Victory; and the pride of Queen Victoria's fleet - HMS Warrior 1860. The ships are set amongst the glorious Georgian storehouses, which are home to the royal Naval Museum and its three breathtaking new galleries: Horatio Nelson - The hero and the man; The Sailing Navy; and the new Victory Gallery featuring 'Trafalgar!' New for 2000: Action Stations - a £13.2 million multimedia attraction opening in the Autumn.
visitor comments: Too much to see in one day - passport ticket is definitely worth it, so that you can revisit.
Mar-Oct daily 10.00-17.30, Nov-Feb daily 10.00-17.00. Closed 25 Dec
Last Admission: 1hr before closing
Passport Ticket: £14.90 C£10.90 OAPs£12.90; All ships Ticket: A£11.90 C£8.90 OAPs £10.40; Individual Ship Tickets: A£5.95 C£4.45 OAPs £5.20
discount offer: Two For The Price Of One On Adult Passport Tickets Only

Royal Marines Museum
Eastney Esplanade Southsea Hampshire PO4 9PX
[M27, M3, A3M to Portsmouth Southsea front, at Eastney follow brown tourist signs. Plenty of on site parking and dog 'park' available]
Tel: 023 92819385 Fax: 023 92838420
www.royalmarinesmuseum.co.uk
The museum offers a series of exhibitions depicting the eventful history of the corps from the 17th century to the present day in all parts of the world, including its service with the United Nations. Audio visual shows and a multi-media cinema bring to life campaigns such as the Falklands War.
Spring Bank Hol-Aug daily 10.00-17.00, Sept-May daily 10.00-16.30. Closed 24-26 Dec
Last Admission: 60mins before closing
A£4.00 C&Students£2.15 Family Ticket (A2+C4)£12.00 OAPs£3.00. Army/RAF £2.25. Group rates 10+ 10% discount (organiser and coach driver Free) Schools rates £0.75 per head 1 Teacher Free for each 8 children, Cadets £0.60 per head
discount offer: Two For The Price Of One

Royal Navy Submarine Museum and HMS Alliance
Haslar Jetty Road Gosport Hampshire PO12 2AS
[M27 J11 follow signs for Fort Blockhouse / RNH Haslar]
Tel: 02392 529217 Fax: 02392 511349
www.submarine-museum.demon.co.uk/index.html
To See What's Really Going on...You Have to Look Under the Surface! Experience life on a real submarine at The Royal Navy Submarine Museum. Step on board the UK's only walk on submarine HMS Alliance. When the klaxon sounds prepare yourself for a depth-charge attack! Discover the stories of courage and see the heroic story of the Royal Navy's Submarine Service vividly brought to life. New for 1999 The Submarine Weapon Gallery featuring the development of submarine weapons from the tiny 19th century torpedo to a huge Polaris nuclear missile. Visit the Jolly Roger Café or relax in the waterfront picnic areas. Sorry - No wheelchair access to submarine but café and the lowers floors of the musuem building are accessible with a lift being installed during 1999. Research and photographic service available.
Apr-Oct daily 10.00-17.30, Nov-Mar 10.00-16.30. Last tour 1 hour before closing. Closed 24 Dec & 1 Jan.
Last Admission: Allow 3 hours for visit
Queuing Times: possible during Summer but plenty to do!
A£3.75 C&OAPs£2.50 Family Ticket (A2+C4)£10.00. Group rates 12+ call for details
discount offer: One Child Free With Every Full Paying Adult

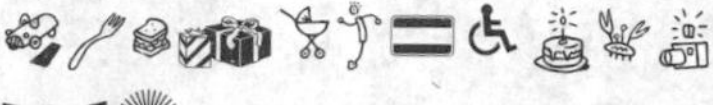

Military & Defence Museums

Airborne Forces Museum
Browning Barracks Aldershot Hampshire GU11 2BU
[J4 M3 follow A325 to Aldershot take next left. The Museum is easily identified by the Dakota aircraft outside]
Tel: 01252 349619 Fax: 01252 349203
The Museum traces the history of British Airborne Forces since their beginning in 1940 to the present day. With the help of weapons, equipment, dioramas and briefing models we tell the story of the many actions in which members of the Parachute Regiment and other Airborne soldiers took part: the early raids, D-Day, Arnhem, Rhine Crossing and the post war campaigns such as The Falklands.
All year daily 10.00-16.30
Last Admission: 15.45
A£2.50 C&Concessions£1.00
discount offer: One Child Free Per Family When Accompanied By Full Paying Adults. Excludes Bank Holiday Weekends

D-Day Museum and Overlord Embroidery
Clarence Esplanade Southsea Hampshire PO5 3NT
[adjacent to Southsea Castle. Plenty of parking on site]
Tel: 023 9282 7261 Fax: 023 9287 5276
Experience the world's largest ever seaborne invasion through the 1270ft long Overlord Embroidery with Soundalive commentary. The story of D-Day is told by an audio-visual show - step back in time to the sights and sounds of wartime Britain. Watch the airborne drop and board a genuine landing craft.
visitor comments: Exquisite embroidery. Lots to see (a good 2 hours).
All year, Apr-Oct daily 10.00-17.30, Nov-Mar Tue-Sun 10.00-17.00 Mon pm only 13.00-15.00. Closed 24-27 Dec
Last Admission: 30mins before closing

A£4.75 C£2.85 OAP£3.60 Family Ticket £12.35

Museum of Army Flying
Middle Wallop Stockbridge Hampshire SO20 8DY
[on A343 between Andover and Salisbury. Plenty of parking on site.]
Tel: 01980 674421 Fax: 01264 781694
www.flying-museum.org.uk
Celebrating over one hundred years of aviation, this award-winning museum is home to one of the country's finest historical collections of military kites, gliders, aircraft and helicopters. There are over 35 fixed wing and rotary aircraft to see at the museum including the largest collection of military gliders in Europe. The Museum's imaginative diroamas and static displays trace the developments of Army flying from pre World War I years through to today's modern Army Air Corps. Explorers World - the Interactive Science and Education Centre - features an imaginative range of hands-on activities and experiments for children of all ages. Experience the Hall of Mirrors, Sensory Trail, Light Waves Exhibition and the IT suite. Explorers' World also houses one of the finest camera obscuras in the country giving panoramic views of the surrounding Hampshire countryside.
All year daily 10.00-16.30. Closed week prior to Christmas
Last Admission: 16.00
A£4.50 C£3.00 OAPs&Student£3.50 Family Ticket (A2+C2)£12.50. Group Rates: A£4.00 C£2.50 OAPs&Student£3.00. Group Concessions: complimentary meal and admission for coach drivers
discount offer: Two For The Price Of One. NOT valid for Special Events & The International Air Show

Nature & Conservation Parks

Bramshaw Commons
c/o Motisfont Abbey Motisfont Romsey Hampshire SO51 0LP
Tel: 01794 340757 Fax: 01794 341492
↓*special events*
► **A Look at Bramshaw Commons**
25/6/00-25/6/00
Take a look at the work being undertaken through the LIFE project. Meet the Warden at the Furztey Crossroads (SU286164) for this 3-mile walk. Telephone 01794 340757 for information. £Free, 14.00-16.00

New Forest Nature Quest
Longdown Marchwood Southampton Hampshire SO40 4UH
[signposted off A35]
Tel: 023 80292408 Fax: 023 80293367
Discover Britain's magnificent animal kingdom at the New Forest Nature Quest and help preserve its future as you explore the first such wildlife project in the UK. Surrounded by the sights and sounds of this ancient woodland, more than 20 carefully re-created natural settings bring you face to face with a variety of forest characters.
All year. Closed 25 Dec call to confirm
A£5.50 C4-14£3.75 OAPs£3.75 Parties 10+ by arrangement

Places of Worship

Sandham Memorial Chapel
Burghclere Hampshire RG20 9JT
[4m S Newbury, 0.5m E of A34]
Tel: 01635 278394 Fax: 01635 278394
Considered by many to be Stanley Spencer's greatest achievement. The interior walls of the First World War chapel, built in the 1920's, are entirely covered with murals by Stanley Spencer. This extraordinary project illustrates the artist's experiences as a medical orderly during the Great War. He celebrates the everyday routine of a soldier's life with an intensely personal religious faith, reaching its triumphant climax with the huge Resurrection of the Soldiers which completely fills the east wall and dominates the entire chapel. The chapel sits amidst beautiful and tranquil scenery, with views across to Watership Down. Note: there is no lighting in the chapel, it is best to view the paintings on a bright day.

Wheelchair access via a portable ramp supplied. Dogs on leads only in grounds. Refreshments available in the Carpenter's Arms 100m away 11.00-15.00, parties must book in advance call 01635 278251.
Apr-Oct Wed-Sun 11.30-17.00, Nov & Mar Sat & Sun 11.30-16.00. Also open Bank Hol Mon. Group visits must be arranged in advance
Last Admission: 30min before closing
A£2.50 C£1.25
discount offer: Two For The Price Of One. Valid Until 26 Nov 2000

Winchester Cathedral
The Education Centre 10a The Close Winchester Hampshire SO23 9LS
[in city centre follow city heritage signs]
Tel: 01962 857200 Fax: 01962 857201
www.win.diocese.org.uk
This magnificent cathedral, the longest medieval church in Europe, was founded in 1079 on the site where Christian worship had already been offered for over 400 years. Among its treasures are the 12th-century illuminated Winchester Bible, the font, medieval wall paintings and pavement, six chantry chapels and Triforium Gallery Museum.
visitor comments: Guided tour is definitely worth it. Pleasant, warm and interesting.
All year daily 08.30-17.30. Access may be restricted during services and major events
Recommended donations requested: A£3.00 C£0.50 Family Ticket £6.00 OAPs&Students£2.50

↓*special events*

▶ **Sharing Good Practice in Spiritual Direction**
11/3/00-11/3/00

▶ **Staging Posts in the Work 'Journey'**
12/6/00-14/6/00
at Douai Abbey, Bernard Kilroy and Pam Ritchie lead this course which is both a retreat and a workshop. Tel: 01252 843133

Sealife Centres & Aquariums

Portsmouth Sea Life Centre
Clarence Esplanade Southsea Portsmouth Hampshire PO5 3PB
[signposted]
Tel: 023 92875222 Fax: 023 92294443
Overlooking the bustling Solent, Portsmouth Sea Life Centre is an exciting introduction to the mysterious world beneath the oceans. From the safety of our tropical reef observatory, enjoy the closest of encounters with this magical underwater wonderland. FinZone is a thrilling undersea adventure trail, track down the clues and solve the puzzles as you journey through the deep; explore Think Tank, our interactive Sea Life resource centre; then let off steam in the soft play area. There's endless enjoyment and entertainment for all ages.
All year daily from 10.00. Please call for Winter opening hours
A£5.50 C(0-3)£Free C(4-14)£4.00 OAPs£4.25

Stately Homes

Stansted House
Stansted Park Rowlands Castle Hampshire PO9 6DX
[2m East of Rowlands Castle. Follow brown signs from A3 or A27. Plenty of parking on site]
Tel: 023 9241 2265 Fax: 023 9241 3773
www.stanstedpark.co.uk
One of the South's most beautiful stately homes, set in 1750 acres of glorious park and woodland. Stansted House is a prime example of The Caroline revival, with elegant state rooms displaying fine period furniture and an important collection of paintings. Plus the recently restored "below stairs," a rare survival of servants quarters. Limited Disabled access.
1 March-31 Oct, Sun-Wed 13.00-17.00. Closed Nov-Feb
Last Admission: 16.15

A£3.80 C£1.90 OAPs£2.70 Family Ticket £11.00
discount offer: Two For The Price Of One. Valid Tuesdays and Wednesdays (excludes special events)

↓*special events*

▶ **Galloway Antiques Fair**
28/1/00-9/4/00
Held on Jan 28-31 and Apr 7-9 only. Three days of quality antiques and fine art.

▶ **Snowdrop Theatre Company**
29/3/00-1/4/00
Performing 'Table Manners' by Alan Ayckbourn

▶ **The Garden Show**
9/6/00-11/6/00
Specialist nurseries, garden product stalls and lectures, art and design tent. Open 10.00-17.00

▶ **"Twelfth Night"**
6/7/00-6/7/00
Groundlings Theatre Company present outdoor Shakespeare.

▶ **Last Night of the Proms**
22/7/00-22/7/00
A mid-summer evening of superb music and magnificent fireworks.

▶ **"Othello"**
30/7/00-30/7/00
Groundlings Theatre Company perform outdoor Shakespeare

▶ **Stansted Players**
6/9/00-9/9/00

Theme & Adventure Parks

Paultons Park
Paultons Park Ower Romsey Hampshire SO51 6AL
[J2 M27, near junction of A31 & A36. Plenty of on site parking available]
Tel: 023 80814455 24 hour Fax: 023 80813025

A great day out for all the family with over 40 attractions included in the price. Fast rides and slow rides, wet rides and dry rides, animated shows, play areas, museums, tranquil corners, exotic birds and animals - all in beautiful parkland. Great favourites are the raging River Log Flume, Teacup Ride, Tiny Tots Town, Kids Kingdom, Dinosaurs, Bumper Boats, Rabbit Ride and lots more. New for 2000 - The Stinger family roller coaster.

visitor comments: Season ticket well worth it, includes all rides, one can then call in for an afternoon. Good mix of activities and excellent park layout.

11 Mar-29 Oct daily 10.00-18.30. Earlier closing at certain times in the year. Weekends only Nov-Dec until Christmas
Last Admission: 16.30 at certain times of year
A£9.50 C(under 14)&OAPs£8.50 Family Supersavers for 3 £25.50, Family of 4 £33.00, Family of 5 £40.00. Children under 1 metre £Free

Transport Museums

Beaulieu
John Montagu Building Beaulieu Brockenhurst Hampshire SO42 7ZN
[J2 M27, A326, B3054 then follow brown tourist signs. Plenty of free on site parking.]
Tel: 01590 612345 Fax: 01590 612624
www.beaulieu.co.uk

Set in 75 acres of grounds at Beaulieu you can see the world famous National Motor Museum featuring 250 historic vehicles plus motoring memorabilia. Palace House and gardens, set on the banks of the Beaulieu River, Lord Montagu's ancestral home, Abbey Ruins and exhibition of monastic life. All this plus rides and drives for everyone. Guided tours for pre-booked groups.

All year May-Sept 10.00-18.00, Oct-Apr 10.00-17.00. Closed 25 Dec
Last Admission: 40mins before closing
A£9.25 C£6.50 Family Ticket (A2+C3 or A1+C4)£29.50 Student&OAPs£8.00

↓*special events*

▶ **Beaulieu Boat Jumble**
16/4/00-16/4/00
The place to be for everyone who's looking for a boating bargain, from 10.00. Please contact us for further details

▶ **Spring Autojumble and Car Mart**
8/5/00-9/5/00
One of the great motoring events of the year, from 10.00. Please contact us for further details

▶ **Motorcycle World**
22/7/00-23/7/00
Covers every aspect of the world of motorcycling, from 10.00. Please contact us for further details

▶ **Palace House Proms**
29/7/00-29/7/00
Gates open 18.30. Concert commences at 20.00. Beautiful Music in a Classic Setting 'Idyllic, Exciting, Magical'. Please call us for further information

▶ **International Autojumble and Automart**
9/9/00-10/9/00
Undoubtedly the biggest Autojumble in Europe. One day: A£9.00 C£6.50, Two day A£16.25 C£11.75.

▶ **Spooks and Sparks**
28/10/00-28/10/00
The fun starts at 15.00! Ghosts and Phantoms come out to play... See Sparks Flying... and then the grand finale of a Fireworks Spectacular

▶ **Christmas Festive Season**
16/12/00-31/12/00
Christmas at Beaulieu is a time of magic, with fun, activities, and entertainment for all the family.

Sammy Miller Museum
Bashley Cross Road New Milton Hampshire BH25 5SZ
[M27 J1, A35 towards Bournemouth, well sign-posted]
Tel: 01425 620777 Fax: 01425 619696
This museum has machines dating back to 1900 with many machines that are the only surviving ones in the world. The racing collection covers World Record Breaking Bikes and their history, including the first bike to lap a Grand Prix Course at over 100 miles per hour, the 4 cylinder supercharged 500cc AJS.
All year daily 10.00-16.30
A£3.50 C£1.50
discount offer: 50p Discount On Adult Admission

Zoos

Marwell Zoological Park
Colden Common Winchester Hampshire SO21 1JH
[J5 M27, J11 M3, BR: Eastleigh/ Winchester]
Tel: 01962 777407 Fax: 01962 777511
www.marwell.org.uk
Marwell has a worldwide reputation for conservation and the breeding of rare and endangered species, which can be seen grazing in paddocks or in large enclosures. The collection covers 100 acres of beautiful Hampshire parkland and is home to over 1000 animals and birds. Attractions include a children's Encounter Village, Owl Aviaries, Penguin World, Tropical World, Road and Rail Train's and an Adventure Playground. Regret no dogs allowed.
visitor comments: Excellent value for money for a whole day. A wide selection of endangered animals. Constantly improved site - large and spacious. Brilliant child facilities. A free land train around zoo (saves walking!)
All year daily, Summer 10.00-18.00, Winter 10.00-16.00. Closed 25 Dec
Last Admission: 90 mins before closing
A£8.80 C(3-14)£6.30 Family Ticket (A2+C2)£28.00 OAPs£7.80. Cars entering zoo circuit £7.50 (at Parks discretion). Free to orange badge holders. Group rates 20+ call for details

↓*special events*

▶ **Mad about Monkeys**
28/5/00-4/6/00
Raise money for monkeys in the wild with our fun activities

▶ **5th Annual Community Weekend**
1/4/00-2/4/00
Half price admission for residents of historic Twyford and Shawford

▶ **Caught on Camera**
21/4/00-20/8/00
Get snap happy and enter our photographic competition

▶ **Earthday at Marwell**
22/4/00-22/4/00
Come and learn how we can ALL help save endangered species

▶ **Swing into Spring**
23/4/00-23/4/00
Follow our traditional Easter Bunny Trail

▶ **Prowl in the Park**
21/5/00-21/5/00
A sponsored walk to raise funds for our own Carnivore projects

▶ **Sunset Safaris**
1/6/00-31/8/00
Book in for our special after hours look at the Park. Call for specific dates

▶ **Medieval to Modern**
1/6/00-31/8/00
Discover the fascinating history of Marwell. Call for specific dates

▶ **Tots and Toddlers Week**
12/6/00-18/6/00

Fun activities, entertainment and reduced admission for 3-5s (under 3s free)

▶ **8th Krazy Character Fun Day**
17/6/00-17/6/00
Fun and games with a host of costume characters

▶ **Sun-Day**
18/6/00-18/6/00
Join us on this special 'SUN-day' and find out about some energy alternatives

▶ **Face to Face**
26/7/00-30/8/00
Sundays and Wednesdays in July and Aug and Bank Holiday Monday. Call to check dates. Enter our quiz for your chance to meet an animal and its keeper

Gardens & Horticulture

Amazing Hedge Puzzle
Simonds Yat West Ross-On-Wye Herefordshire HR9 6DA
[200 meters from A40 at Whitchurch Junction]
Tel: 01600 890360 Fax: 01600 890360
www.btinternet.com/~mazes
The Jubilee Park houses the Jubilee Maze, built to celebrate the Queen's Jubilee in 1977, and the celebrated Museum of Mazes showing paths of mazes and labyrinth through the ages. The World of Butterflies, has hundreds of colourful butterflies from all over the world flying free in their large tropical indoor garden.
Good Fri-Sept daily 11.00-17.00. School Summer Hol daily 11.00-18.00. Winter Half-Term Hol daily 12.00-16.00. Mar & Oct Weekends only 11.00-16.00. Closed Christmas Last Admission: 30mins before closing A£2.80 C(0-4)£Free C(5yrs+)£1.80 Family Ticket(A2+C3) or (A1+C4)£8.50 Concessions&OAPs£2.25.

Hergest Croft Gardens
Kington Herefordshire HR5 3EG
[0.25m W of Kington, off A44. Plenty of on site parking available]
Tel: 01544 230160 Fax: 01544 230160
www.hergest.co.uk
From spring bulbs to autumn colour, this is garden for all seasons. One of the finest collections of trees and shrubs surround the Edwardian house, an old fashioned kitchen garden has spring and summer borders and Park Wood, a hidden valley, has rhododendrons up to 30ft tall. Member of the Historic Houses Association.
1 Apr-31 Oct daily 13.30-18.00 A3.50 C£Free Group rates 20+ A£3.00. Pre-booked Guided Tours 20+ A£4.50. Season tickets A£12.00
discount offer: Two For The Price Of One. Valid Apr-Oct (except 1 May - Flower Fair)

↓*special events*

▶ **May Flower Fair**
1/5/00-1/5/00
With specialist plant and craft stalls, charity auction for Matha Trust, garden walks and other attractions, A£5.00 C£Free. 10.30-17.30

▶ **Theatre Production**
20/8/00-20/8/00
The Rain or Shine Theatre Company perform Sheridan's The Rivals. Call for details

▶ **Autumn Plant Sale**
15/10/00-15/10/00
All garden enthusiasts come along to our plant fair.

Historical

Berrington Hall
Berrington Leominster Herefordshire HR6 0DW
[3m N of Leominster 7m S of Ludlow on W side of A49. BR: Leominster]
Tel: 01568 615721 Fax: 01568 613263
www.ntrustsevern.org.uk
An elegant neo-classical house of late 18th century set in a park landscaped by Capability Brown. Formal exterior belies the delicate interior with beautifully decorated ceilings and fine furniture. Nursery, Victorian laundry and Georgian dairy. Attractive garden and historic apple orchard. Children's quizzes indoor and outdoor. Servants Hall Licensed Restaurant

and Edwardian Tea Room.
visitor comments: One of the most pleasing houses we have visited, with lovely Georgian architecture and furnishings.
House: 1 Apr-30 Sept Sat-Wed & Bank Hol Mon & Good Fri 13.30-17.30. Oct-1 Nov Sat-Wed 13.30-16.30. Garden: as House 12.30-18.00, Oct 17.30. Park Walk: July-Oct same days and times as House. Shop: as House 12.30-17.30, also Nov & Dec Sat-Sun 12.30-16.30. Servants Hall Licensed Restaurant: as House, Lunch: 12.30-17.30. Oct 12.30-16.30, also Nov & Dec Sat-Sun 12.30-16.30. Edwardian Tea Room: Bank Hol weekends and pre-booked groups
Last Admission: 30mins before closing
A£4.20 C£2.10 Family Ticket £10.00. Grounds: £2.00
discount offer: Two For The Price Of One

↓*special events*

▶ **Snowdrop Tea**
12/3/00-12/3/00
Guided tour of the woodland walk with the gardener. £6.25 per person (includes afternoon tea) commencing at 14.00

▶ **Easter Egg Trail**
23/4/00-23/4/00
Come and hunt for hidden eggs. C£2.00 A£2.00, commencing at 14.00

▶ **British Horse Trials Association**
5/8/00-6/8/00
Horse Trials Dressage, 14.00. Horse Trials 09.00-17.30. £5.00 per car & normal admission rates

Eastnor Castle
Eastnor Ledbury Herefordshire HR8 1RL
[2m E of Ledbury on A438 Tewkesbury Rd. Alternatively, J2 M50 then A449/A438 to Eastnor]
Tel: 01531 633160 Fax: 01531 631776
A magnificent Georgian castle in a fairytale setting with a deer park, arboretum and lake. Inside tapestries, fine art and armour. The Italianate and Gothic interiors have been restored to a superb standard. There is a children's adventure playground and delightful nature trails and lakeside walks. Homemade teas are available. Member of the Historic Houses Association.
Easter-8 Oct Sun & Bank Hol Mon 11.00-17.00, July-Aug Sun-Fri 11.00-17.00
Last Admission: 16.30
Castle & Grounds: A£4.75 C£2.50. Family Ticket £12.00. Grounds: A£2.75 C£1.50. Groups 20+ £4.25, Guided Tours £5.75

Kinnersley Castle
Kinnersley Herefordshire HR3 6QF
[4m W of Weobley on A4112, Black and White Village Trail. BR: Hereford / Leominster]
Tel: 01544 327507 Fax: 01544 327663
www.kinnersley.com/castle
Medieval Welsh border Castle, reconstructed about 1588. Little changed since then, retaining fine plasterwork and panelling, leaded glass and stone tiled roof. Yew hedges, walled garden and fine trees including probably the largest example of a Ginkgo tree in the United Kingdom. Outdoor performances presented by Oddsocks, towards the end of July. Book by phone or online with our web site.
For Guided Tours: July 17-Aug 20 14.30 & 15.30 closed Mondays. Coach parties by arrangement A£2.50 C£1.50 OAPs&Students&UB40£2.00. Groups £2.00 by arrangement through the year
discount offer: Two For The Price Of One

Places of Worship

Hereford Cathedral
Cathedral Close Hereford Herefordshire HR1 2NG
[J7 M5, A4103 Worcester, venue signposted around the City]
Tel: 01432 359880 Fax: 01432 355929
Hereford's beautiful Romanesque Cathedral dates from 676, and contains the famous Mappa Mundi & Chained Library in the New Library Building, winner of the Royal Fine Art Commission's 'Building of the Year 1997'. The interpretative exhibition uses models, orginal artefacts and the latest interactive computer technology. Between July - October visit the most comprehensive exhibition of medieval world maps ever as part of the 1999 Mappa Mundi. Conference.
visitor comments: An extraordinary view of the medieval world.

Cathedral daily 08.00-18.00. Mappa Mundi & Chained Library Exhibition Easter-Oct Mon-Sat 10.00-16.15, Sun 11.00-15.15. Oct-Easter: Mon-Sat 11.00-15.15. The Mappa Mundi & Chained Library will be closed 11-24 Jan for cleaning, and 21-28 July to install the Internation Mappa Mundi Exhibition
Last Admission: 16.15
Mappa Mundi & Chained Library Exhibition: A£4.00 Family Ticket £10.00 Single Family Ticket £6.00 Concessions£3.00 Party 10+ A£3.50 Concessions£2.50 School Groups 10+ Primary £1.00 p/h Secondary £2.00 p/h

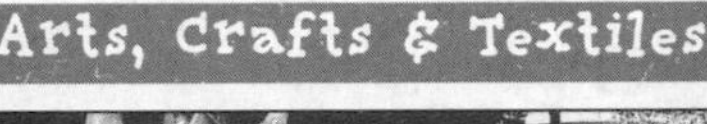

Arts, Crafts & Textiles

Henry Moore Foundation
Dane Tree House Perry Green Much Hadham Hertfordshire SG10 6EE
[M11 J8 no signposts. Limited parking on site]
Tel: 01279 843333 Fax: 01279 843647
www.henry-moore-fdn.co.uk
Major works are displayed in the grounds and in the studios where Moore worked. Visitors are guided around the grounds and into the studios. The guided tour lasts approxmiately 90 minutes.
By appointment, Apr-mid Oct weekday afternoons only. Guided Tour at 14.30. Morning educational visits can be arranged
A£3.00 C(0-18)&Students£Free OAPs£1.50

Letchworth Museum and Art Gallery
Broadway Letchworth Hertfordshire SG6 3PF
[approx 1m from A1, fingerposted in town centre, 200 yards from town centre parking, by Public Library]
Tel: 01462 685647 Fax: 01462 481879
Letchworth Museum opened in 1914 to house the collections of the Letchworth Naturalists' Society. Since then the collections have expanded greatly in both size and scope. The downstairs Natural History Gallery includes examples of local wildlife in realistic settings, as well as displays on the geology of the area. The Art Gallery upstairs houses monthly changing exhibitions of paintings, photography and craft, much of which is for sale. Along the corridor, the extensive Archaeology Gallery shows how people have lived in this area for many thousands of years. There is a museum shop with a range of souvenirs, an identification service, a regular programme of workshops and a school service with extensive school loan collection. Guided Tours by arrangement, an area where pushchairs can be left.
All year Mon-Sat 10.00-17.00. Closed Sun & Bank Hol
Admission Free

↓*special events*

▶ **Diane Kliszynska**
12/2/00-11/3/00
An exhibition of colourful oil paintings, drawings and some sculpture in the Mezzanine Gallery.

▶ **Letchworth Camera Club**
11/3/00-1/4/00
Variety of subjects captured on camera with a balance of full colour with black and white held in the Art Gallery

▶ **Recent paintings by Len Hobbs**
18/3/00-15/4/00
Colourful landscapes and seascapes in line and wash in the Mezzanine Gallery

▶ **ART 2000**
8/4/00-29/4/00
A dynamic exhibition in the Art Gallery by local school children on the theme 'Our World'

▶ **Fragments of Life**
22/4/00-20/5/00
Work by Carol Ayton in the Mezzanine Gallery. An attarctive display of mixed media still life paintings.

▶ **The Collecting Bug**
6/5/00-3/6/00
A community exhibition for Museums and Galleries Month in the Art Gallery. Collections lent by members of the public young and old

▶ **Krysia Michna-Novak**
27/5/00-24/6/00
Mono-prints based on cats, birds and flowers by an artist from Belgrave. In the Mezzanine Gallery

▶ **Yesterplays - A History of the Electric Guitar**
10/6/00-8/7/00
Major exhibition of classic electric guitars to coincide with the Letchworth Festival, June 10-17.

Country Parks & Estates

Ashridge Estate

Ringshall Berkhamsted Hertfordshire HP4 1LT
[between Northchurch & Ringshall just off B4506 3m N of A41 BR: Tring]
Tel: 01442 851227 Fax: 01442 842062
This magnificent and varied estate runs across the borders of Herts and Bucks, along the main ridge of the Chiltern Hills. There are woodlands, commons and chalk downland, supporting a rich variety of wildlife and offering splendid walks through outstanding scenery. The focal point of the area is the Monument, erected in 1832 to the Duke of Bridgwater. There are also breathtaking views from Ivinghoe Beacon, accessible from Steps Hill.
Estate: all year. Monument & Visitor Centre: 2 Apr-31 Oct Mon-Thur & Good Fri 14.00-17.00, Sat, Sun & Bank Hol Mon 14.00-17.30. Note WC's closed on Fri. Shop: as Visitor Centre and 6 Nov-12 Dec Sat & Sun 12.00-16.00 or dusk if earlier
Last Admission: 30mins before closing time
Monument: A£1.00 C£0.50

↓*special events*

▶ **Easter Egg Trail**
24/4/00-24/4/00
Family Fun on a woodland trail, 12.00-16.00 C£1.50

▶ **Woodland Birds**
13/5/00-13/5/00
Identification, song, behaviour and ecology of birds. 08.30-15.00. Cost: £15

▶ **Bat Walk**
19/7/00-19/7/00
Time: 19.00-22.00. Cost: £10.00

▶ **Children's Theatre**
5/8/00-5/8/00
The Big Catch: 11.00. A Wheelie Bin Ate My Sister: 13.30. The Town Mouse & The Country Mouse: 16.00.

Knebworth House, Gardens and Country Park

Knebworth Park Old Knebworth Knebworth Hertfordshire SG3 6PY
[direct access from J7 A1(M) at Stevenage]
Tel: 01438 812661 Fax: 01438 811908
www.knebworthhouse.com
Home of the Lytton family since 1490, the original Tudor manor was transformed in 1843 by the spectacular high Gothic decoration of Victorian novelist Sir Edward Bulwer Lytton. The interior includes a superb Jacobean Great Hall with a splendid plaster ceiling and magnificent panelling. There is a fascinating exhibition on the British Raj and some fine furniture and portraits. Guided tours most days. Member of the Historic Houses Association.
15 Apr-1 May, 27 May-4 June & 8 July-3 Sept Daily. 6 May-21 May Weekends and Bank Hol. 10 June-2 July, 9 Sept-1 Oct Weekend (closed 18 June) House: 12.00-17.00 Park, Gardens & Playground: 11.00-17.30
Last Admission: House: 16.15
House (incl exhibition): A£6.00 C(5-16)&OAPs£5.50. Park & Playground only: £5.00 Family Ticket (4 persons)£17.50. Groups 20+. Season Tickets available
discount offer: Two For The Price Of One

↓*special events*

▶ **Jousting**
23/4/00-24/4/00
Dates to be confirmed

▶ **Knebworth Country Show**
30/4/00-1/5/00

▶ **Garden Show**
13/5/00-14/5/00

▶ **Heavy Horse Show**
11/6/00-11/6/00
Dates to be confirmed

▶ **Pre-50 American Auto Club Rally**
15/7/00-16/7/00

▶ **Classic Corvettes Rally**
22/7/00-23/7/00

▶ **Fireworks and Laser Symphony Concert**
30/7/00-30/7/00

Gardens & Horticulture

Gardens of The Rose (Royal National Rose Society)

Chiswell Green Lane St. Albans Hertfordshire AL2 3NR
[2m S of St Albans on B4630. Bus: 321. BR: St Albans City]
Tel: 01727 850461 Fax: 01727 850360

www.roses.co.uk
Over 30 000 roses on display including old garden roses and modern roses, complimented by a rich variety of companion plants, such as clemantis, lavender, foxglove and iris. These landscaped gardens are Heaven Scent!
27 May-24 Sept Mon-Sat 09.00-17.00, Sun & Bank Hol 10.00-18.00
Last Admission: 30mins before closing
A£4.00 C(6-16)£1.50 OAPs£3.50 Groups 20+ £3.50
discount offer: Two For The Price Of One

↓*special events*

▶ **Spring Craft and Garden Show**
19/5/00-21/5/00
Over 80 craft and garden stalls. Admission A£2.00 C£1.00 from 10.00-17.00

▶ **National Show For Miniature Roses**
29/7/00-30/7/00
Garden admission allows entry.

▶ **Last Night Of The Proms**
19/8/00-19/8/00
Open-air concert with lasers and firework displays.

Historical

Hatfield House, Park and Gardens

Hatfield Hertfordshire AL9 5NQ
[7m from J23 M25 & 2m from J4 A1(M), opposite Hatfield railway station. Plenty of free on site parking.]
Tel: 01707 262823 Fax: 01707 275719
Celebrated Jacobean House with magnificent paintings, furniture and tapestries. Within the delightful and extensive formal gardens, which are all managed organically, stands a surviving wing of the Old Tudor Palace, the childhood home of Elizabeth I. 4000 acres of parkland with nature trails and a children's play area. The national collection of model soldiers is in the Stable Yard near the gift shops and licensed restaurant. Functions, weddings and banquets, call (01707) 262055.
25 Mar-24 Sept. House: Tue-Thur 12.00-16.00, Sat & Sun 13.00-16.30, Bank Hol 11.00-16.30. Park: Sat-Thur 10.30-18.00, (West Gardens: 11.00-18.00, closed Mon). Friday (Connoisseurs' Day): Park & all Gardens, 11.00-18.00 and special house tours for booked parties (20+)
Last Admission: Park: 17.00
House, Park & Gardens: A£6.20 C£3.10. Park only: A£1.80 C£0.90. Connoisseurs' Day (Fri) £5.20 (£4.00 for booked house tour) Pre-booked group rates 20+ House & Gardens: £5.20
discount offer: Two For The Price Of One (Excludes Mon & Fri and major special events)

↓*special events*

▶ **Bailey Antiques Fair**
10/3/00-12/3/00
Time: 11.00-17.00. Cost A£3.00 C£1.50 (Free entry to the Park) Tel: 01277 214677

▶ **Living Crafts**
4/5/00-7/5/00
Hundreds of crafts. Time: 10.00-18.00. Cost: A£6.80 C£3.40. Tel: 023 9242 6523

▶ **Model Soldiers Day**
14/5/00-14/5/00
Time: 11.00-16.30. A£1.80 C£0.90 Tel: 020 8979 7137

▶ **'Much Ado About Nothing'**
11/6/00-11/6/00
Shakespeare in the park. Time:16.00-19.00. Cost: A£8.50 C£5.00. Tel: 01707 332880

▶ **Festival of Gardening**
24/6/00-25/6/00
Annual garden spectacular. Time: 10.00-18.00. Cost: A£6.80 C£3.40. Tel: 01707 262823

▶ **National Rose Society Day**
30/6/00-30/6/00
Time: 11.00-18.00. Cost: £5.20 (no concessions). Tel: 01707 262823

▶ **Bailey Antiques Fair**
17/11/00-19/11/00
Time: 11.00-17.00. Cost A£3.00 C£1.50 (Free entry to the Park) Tel: 01277 214677

▶ **Book Fair**
26/11/00-26/11/00
Time: 10.00-16.30. Cost: A£0.70 C£Free (Free entry to the Park) Tel: 01707 260838

▶ **St. Etheldreda's Church Fair**
2/12/00-2/12/00
Time: 11.00-16.30. A£1.00 C£Free. Tel: 01707 267531

▶ **Christmas Tree Sales**
2/12/00-23/12/00
Time: 10.00-16.00. Free entry. Tel: 01707 273315

Living History Museums

Forge Museum and Victorian Cottage Garden

High Street Much Hadham Hertfordshire SG10 6BS
[from M25, take M11, then A414 towards Harlow then Hertford, take Hadhams turn off and follow signs, the Museum is on the B1004]
Tel: 01279 843301 Fax: 01279 843301
The Forge Museum is set in attractive Grade II Listed buildings situated in the picturesque village of Much Hadham. The living museum was the village smithy run by the Page family from 1811-1983. Our resident blacksmith can

be seen working here 6 days a week. The displays follow the crafts of blacksmithing and farriery over the years, as well as smaller exhibits about local village life. The Victorian Cottage Garden houses a rare early 19th century Bee Shelter and a recently reconstructed Granary building.
All year Fri-Sun & Bank Hol 11.00-17.00
Last Admission: 16.30
A£0.80 C&Concessions£0.40
discount offer: Two For The Price Of One

Mills - Water & Wind

Cromer Windmill
Cromer Stevenage Hertfordshire SG2 7QA
[adjoins the B1037 between Walkern and Cottered, 4m NE of Stevenage which is on A1(M)]
Tel: 01279 843301
Hertfordshire's unique 17th century Postmill restored to working order. Video, guided visits.
Mid-May-mid Sept Sun, Bank Hol, 2nd & 4th Sat 14.30-17.00
A£1.25 C£0.25. Groups by appointment
discount offer: Two Adults For The Price Of One

Mill Green Museum and Mill
Mill Green Hatfield Hertfordshire AL9 5PD
[between Hatfield and W.G.C. at the junction of the A1000 and the A414]
Tel: 01707 271362 Fax: 01707 272511
Enjoy the working watermill, which produces flour every week, as well as a local history museum with a temporary exhibition gallery. There are also various craft demonstrations and special events on Summer weekends.
Tue-Fri 10.00-17.00, Sat Sun & Bank Hol 14.00-17.00
Admission Free
discount offer: 20p Off A Bag Of Mill Green Flour Any Size

Natural History Museums

Walter Rothschild Zoological Museum
Akeman Street Tring Hertfordshire HP23 6AP
[Tring is on the A41, 7m SE of Aylesbury and 33m from London]
Tel: 020 7942 6160/6175 Fax: 020 7942 6150
www.nhm.ac.uk
This museum was once the private collection of Lionel Walter, 2nd Baron Rothschild, and is now part of the Natural History Museum. It houses more than 4000 specimens in a unique Victorian setting. The displays comprise of mounted specimans of animals from all parts of the world - from whales to fleas, hummingbirds to tigers, even a large collection of domestic dogs.
All year Mon-Sat 10.00-17.00 Sun 14.00-17.00. Closed 24-26 Dec
C(0-16) & OAPs£Free. Small charge for adults and concessions.
discount offer: Two For The Price Of One

↓*special events*

► **National Science Week Activities**
17/3/00-26/3/00
Skeletons and movement through trails and workshops

► **A Celebration of Fish through Contemporary Arts and Crafts**
17/3/00-7/5/00
From the quirky to the elegant, tableware to toys

► **Butterflies, Moths and Beetles - the work of Nuni Ryder**
12/5/00-18/6/00
An exquisite magnified vision of the beautiful colours and textures found in the wings of these creatures

► **Tring Art Show**
23/6/00-7/7/00
A selection of professional and amateur work as part of the Tring Festival. Call to confirm dates

► **Eating Creepy Crawlies**
15/7/00-10/9/00
The exotic creatures that are eaten across the world, complete with recipes. Call for confirmation of dates

► **Looking in Wonderland**
15/9/00-5/11/00
Prints taken from the original Tenniel wood blocks for the famous Alice books

► **National Poetry Week**
9/10/00-13/10/00
A week of poetic fun around the Galleries

► **BG Wildlife Photographer of the Year Exhibition**
15/12/00-31/1/01
A fantastic exhibition of award winning work

from across the world. Dates to be confirmed

▶ **An Anecdotal Eye - the work of Thomas Bewick**

9/2/01-1/4/01

Prints of an eighteenth century artist preoccupied with wildlife and its habitats

Places of Worship

St. Albans Cathedral

Sumpter Yard Holywell Hill St. Albans Hertfordshire AL1 1BY

[centre of St. Albans, J3 A1(M), M1 from N J7, from S J6, M25 from E J22, from W J21a]

Tel: 01727 860780 Fax: 01727 850944

www.stalbanscathedral.org.uk

An imposing Norman Abbey Church built on the site of the execution of St. Alban, Britain's first martyr circa 250AD, built from recycled Roman brick from nearby Verulanium. Features include a shrine to St. Alban, many 13th century wall paintings and a wide-screen audio-visual. Guided tours by arrangement.

All year daily 09.00-17.45

Suggested Donations: £2.50. Audio-visual presentation: A£1.50 C£1.00

↓*special events*

▶ **Easter Monday**

24/4/00-24/4/00

Diocesan Pilgrimage

▶ **Pilgrimage**

17/6/00-17/6/00

A Pilgrimage to the Shrine of St Alban

▶ **The Rose Service**

25/6/00-25/6/00

For the children of the Diocese

▶ **Alban 2000**

3/10/00-12/10/00

A Millennium experience in Light and Sound, call Box Office for details

Roman Era

Roman Theatre of Verulamium

Gorhambury Drive St. Michaels St. Albans Hertfordshire AL3 6AH

[off A4147 signposted]

Tel: 01727 835035

The theatre was first discovered on the Gorhambury Estate in 1847 and was fully excavated by Dr. Kathleen Kenyon in 1935. It is unique in England. First constructed AD 160, it is semi-circular in shape. 180ft across and could hold 2,000 spectators. Following modification over two centuries, the theatre was used for religious processions, ceremonies and plays.

All year daily 10.00-17.00. Winter 10.00-16.00. Closed 25-26 Dec

A£1.50 C(0-5)£Free C£0.50 Concessions £1.00

Roman Wall

St. Albans Hertfordshire *[on S side of St Albans 0.5m from centre off A4147. BR: St Albans Abbey 0.5m St Albans 1.25m]*

Tel: 01604 730320

Several hundred yards of the wall, built circa AD 200, which enclosed the Roman city of Verulamium. The remains of towers and foundations of a gateway can still be seen.

Any reasonable time

Admission Free

Verulamium Museum and Park

St. Michaels Street St. Albans Hertfordshire AL3 4SW

[A4147, J21A M25, J9 M1. Signed to Roman Verulamium]

Tel: 01727 819339 Fax: 01727 859919

Verulamium was one of the largest and most important Roman towns in Britain. By the 1st century it was declared a 'municipium', which gave its inhabitants the rights of Roman citizenship. The town was attacked by Boudicca in AD61, but rebuilt after her defeat. The site is set within a 100 acre park. Special events see Guide.

All year Mon-Fri 10.00-17.30, Sun 14.00-17.30

Last Admission: 17.00

A£3.00 Family Ticket £7.50 Concessions£1.70 Residents £Free

discount offer: Two For The Price Of One

Welwyn Roman Baths
Welwyn Village Welwyn Hertfordshire AL6 9HT
[under the A1M at its junction with the A1000, access off central roundabout of the Welwyn by-pass]
Tel: 01707 271362 Fax: 01707 272511
Third century AD bathing suite, the only visible remains of a Romano-British villa, ingeniously preserved within the embankment of the A1(M).
Jan-Nov Sat, Sun & Bank Hol 14.00-17.00 or dusk if earlier. Open daily during school half terms and holidays except Dec 14.00-17.00 or dusk if earlier
A£1.00 C£Free
discount offer: A Free Colour Postcard. Offer Valid Until 30 Nov 2000

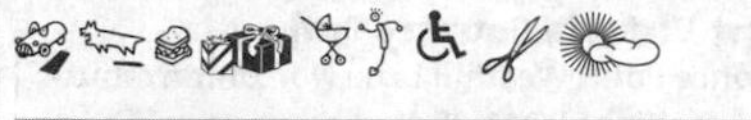

Wildlife & Safari Parks

Paradise Wildlife Park
White Stubbs Lane Broxbourne Hertfordshire EN10 7QA
[6m from J25 off M25 Motorway, follow brown signs]
Tel: 01992 470490
www.pwpark.com
At Paradise Park you can touch and feed our paddock animals, including zebras and camels, and meet the lion and tiger cubs too. Visit our adventure playground to burn off some enrgy, and then catch your breath in the jungle theatre.
visitor comments: A great day out! Wonderful for all ages.

Willersmill Wildlife Park
Station Road Shepreth Nr Royston Hertfordshire SG8 6PZ
[Off A10 between Royston and Cambridge]
Tel: 0891 715522 Fax: 01763 260582
Set in natural grounds with large lakes, Willersmill originally began as a refuge for injured and orphaned British birds and mammals. A famous collection of wild and domesticated animals including monkeys, wolves, reptiles, birds and much more. You can enjoy feeding the animals and giant fish.
visitor comments: My 3 year old loved feeding the fish.
Summer daily 10.00-18.00 Winter-28 Feb 10.00-dusk
A£4.50 C£3.20 OAPs£3.80
discount offer: One Child Free With A Full Paying Adult (One Per Family)

Historical

Castle Rushen, Kings and Lords of Mann
Castletown Isle of Man *[bus or steam train to Castletown from Douglas at regular intervals]*
Tel: 01624 648000 Fax: 01624 648001
Castle Rushen is situated in the Island's ancient capital Castletown. This castle is regarded as one of the most complete castles in the British Isles. The interior of the castle has exciting displays re-creating life in the medieval period.
Easter-Sept daily 10.00-17.00
A£4.00 C(5-15)£2.00 Family Ticket (A2+C2) £10.00. Pre-booked groups £2.70. Manx schools Free. Off-island schools and youth groups pre-booked £1.60

Peel Castle Trail
St Patrick's Isle Peel Isle of Man *[Bus: Douglas / Peel travel time 35mins]*
Tel: 01624 648000 Fax: 01624 648001
Situated on the scenic St. Patrick's Isle, this castle includes ruins from the 11th-century. The castle is significant in Manx history as the former ruling seat of the Norse Kingdom of Mann and the Isles. Free audio-guide available.
Easter-Sept daily 10.00-17.00
A£2.75 C£1.50 Family Ticket £7.00. Joint ticket with House of Manannan A£7.00 C£3.50 Family Ticket (A2+C2)£18.00
↓*special events*
► Shakespeare in Peel Castle
26/7/00-30/7/00

Tomb of Sir William Hillary
St George's Churchyard Douglas Isle of Man NE
[close to main entrance of churchyard on right hand side]
Tomb of Sir William Hillary (founder of RNLI) in St George's churchyard. Commemorative plaque on lifeboat house and bronze model (inside office building on Hillary's former home on Prospect Hill called Hillary House).
Any reasonable time
Admission Free

Mining

Great Laxey Wheel and Mines Trail
Laxey Isle of Man *[bus or electric railway from Douglas / Laxey 30 mins]*
Tel: 01624 648000 Fax: 01624 648001
The Great Laxey Wheel was built in 1854 and christened "Lady Isabella" after the wife of the then Lieutenant Governor of the Isle of Man. Designed to pump water from the mines of the Great Laxey Mining Company, this masterpiece of 19th century engineering has a diameter of 22 meters, and remains the largest working water wheel in the world.
Easter-end Sept daily 10.00-17.00
A£2.75 C(5-15)£1.50 Family Ticket (A2+C2) £7.00 Groups pre-booked A£1.90. Manx Schools £Free, Off Island Schools and all Youth Groups £1.20

Wildlife & Safari Parks

Curraghs Wildlife Park
Ballaugh Isle of Man IM7 5EA
Tel: 01624 897323 Fax: 01624 897327
Developed adjacent to the reserve area of the Ballaugh Curraghs is the wildlife park, which exhibits a large variety of animals and birds in natural settings. Large walk through enclosures let visitors explore the world of wildlife, including local habitats along the Curraghs nature trail. The miniature railway runs on Sundays.
Easter-Oct daily 10.00-18.00. Oct-Easter Sat & Sun 10.00-16.00
Last Admission: 45mins before closing
A£3.60 C£1.80. Group rates A£2.40 C£1.20
discount offer: One Third Off Admission Prices: A£2.40 C£1.20

Animal Attractions

Brickfields Horse Country
Newnham Lane Brinstead Rye Isle of Wight PO33 3TH
[situated on the outskirts of Ryde, .5m from the main A3054 and 2m from the Fishbourne Ferry. There is a free courtesy bus from Ryde sea front in high season]
Tel: 01983 566801 Fax: 01983 562649
www.brickfields.co.uk
So much to see and do...with parades, pony rides, guided tours and working demonstrations there will be little time for any visitors to be bored. Meet Bud and Weiser the world famous twin shire horses; visit the museum packed with things from bygone days; see Porkers Paradise, smile as you watch The Lester Piglet Derby; see all things small in Mini World ideal for the children; riding stables on site. A first class family day out!
visitor comments: Mid-day parade was especially good
All year daily 10.00-17.00. Closed 25 Dec
A£4.50 C£3.25 Family Ticket £14.00 OAPs£4.00

Country Parks & Estates

Fort Victoria Country Park
Sconce Point Westhill Lane Norton Yarmouth Isle of Wight PO41 0RW
[1m W off A3054]
Tel: 01983 760860/760283
Based around the remains of a fort built in 1855 to protect the western approach to Portsmouth, the wide grassy areas, coastal slopes, beach and sea wall have been made into a country park. Affording superb views of the Solent, there are picnic areas, a Marine Aquarium, Maritime Heritage Centre and a Model Railway.
Park daily, Aquarium: Easter-Oct daily 10.00-18.00, Planetarium: daily in season. Call 761555 for out of season opening times
Park Admission Free, Marine Aquarium, Maritime Heritage Centre and Model Railway all charged

Nunwell House and Gardens
West Lane Nunwell Sandown Isle of Wight PO36 0JQ
[signposted off Ryde-Sandown road A3055]
Tel: 01983 407240
Set in 5 acres of beautiful gardens, an impressive lived-in and much loved house where King Charles I spent his last night of freedom. Partake in a guided tour of the house containing fine furniture, Old Kitchen exhibition and interesting collections of family militaria.

Guided Tours at 13.30, 14.30 & 15.30. Member of the Historic Houses Association.
House & Gardens 92 June-17 Sept Mon-Wed 13.00-17.00 Closed 31 July-17 Aug
Last Admission: 16.30
A£4.00 (incl Guide Book) Couple£7.50 Accompanied C(under12) £1.00 OAPs£3.00

Robin Hill Country Park
Down End Newport Isle of Wight PO30 2NU
[2m E of Newport off A3056 nr Arreton]
Tel: 01983 527352 Fax: 01983 527347
80 acres of countryside with activities for all ages. Attractions include Squirrel Tower, Rabbit Run, Gypsy Camp, Woodland Temple, Forest Scultpures, Fir Tree Farm, Treetop Trail, Countryside Centre, Troll Island, Toboggan Run and Pine Cone Construction Company.
visitor comments: Lots of adventurous things for kids to do. Good educational areas, and excellent value for money.
22 Mar-31 Oct daily 10.00-17.30
Last Admission: 16.00
A£3.95 C(3-13)£2.95 OAPs£3.50 Disabled Concession£2.00. Toboggan Run £1.00 extra per person. Season Tickets for both Robin Hill and Blackgang Chine gives unlimited admission to both during 1999 A£19.50 C(3-13)£15.95 Disabled Concession£9.50

Gardens & Horticulture

Mottistone Manor Garden
Mottistone Newport Isle of Wight PO30 4ED
[at Mottistone 2m W of Brighstone on B3399. Ferry: Yarmouth (Wightlink) Tel 0870 5827744. E Cowes (Red Funnel) Tel 01703 334010]
Tel: 01983 741302
The colourful herbaceous borders, flowering fruit trees and delightful sea views combine to make a perfect setting for the 16th & 17th century manor house. Parties by written application only. Dogs on leads. Toilet facilities and teas available.
Garden: 26 Mar-29 Oct Sun, Tue & Bank Hol Mon 14.00-17.30. House: Aug Bank Hol Mon only
Last Admission: 17.00
Garden: A£2.10. No reduction for parties

↓*special events*

▶ **Garden Tour**
11/4/00-11/4/00
An easy stroll. Meet at the entrance kiosk (SZ406838), £1.00 (non-member), NT members free plus usual admission, 14.30 & 15.30

▶ **Archaeology and Restoration**
28/6/00-28/6/00
Meet in Mottistone car park (SZ403838) for this 2-mile walk, £1.00 (non-member), NT members free, 14.00-16.00

▶ **Summer Butterflies**
26/7/00-26/7/00
Meet at Mottistone Down car park (SZ420845) for this 1.5-mile walk. Sorry, no dogs, £1.00 (non-member), NT members free, 14.00-16.00

▶ **Mottistone Jazz**
28/7/00-29/7/00
Gates 18.30 for 19.30. Open-air concert, dress 1920s style, enjoy picnics and dancing. Call 01372 451596, Fri £10.00 Sat £12.00 C(under 5)£Free

▶ **Garden Tour**
5/9/00-5/9/00
Meet at the entrance kiosk (SZ406838). Sorry, no dogs, £1.00 (non-member), NT members free plus usual admission, 14.30-15.30

Historical

Appuldurcombe House
Appuldurcombe Road Wroxall Ventnor Isle of Wight PO38 3EW
[off B3327]
Tel: 01983 852484
www.english-heritage.org.uk
The manor house at Wroxall began as a priory in 1100. It later came into the hands of the Worsley family, who pulled down the original building and built Appuldurcombe in the Palladian style. Appuldurcombe has been a ruin since World War II. Its 11 acre grounds are perfect for picnics. NEW for 1999 is the Isle of Wight Owl and Falconry Centre, opening on 1st April 99. Call for combined ticket details
1 Apr-31 Oct daily 10.00-18.00
Last Admission: Oct 16.00
A£2.00 C£1.00 Concessions£1.50
discount offer: One Child Free When Accompanied by A Full Paying Adult (for Appuldurcombe House only). Valid Until 31 Oct 99

↓*special events*

▶ **Easter Egg Hunt**
23/4/00-23/4/00

From 10.00. Fun for all the family!

▶ **Giant Cluedo Game**

27/5/00-30/6/00

From 10.00. Family game, based loosely on the history of the house. Normal admission applies plus charge per Detective, with prizes

▶ **Sweeney Todd - The Demon Barber**

7/7/00-9/7/00

From 19.00 (Sat) 14.00 (Sun) Call for further details

▶ **Festival of Flowers**

15/7/00-16/7/00

From 10.00. Fantastic floral displays, plus vintage cars

▶ **Antique Fair**

3/9/00-3/9/00

From 10.00.Call for further details

Carisbrooke Castle

Newport Isle of Wight PO30 1XY

[1.25m SW of Newport off the B3323]

Tel: 01983 522107

Here are seven acres of castle and earthworks to explore. The oldest parts of the castle are 12th century, but the great mound - 71 steps hight - bore a wooden castle before that, and there are fragments of Roman wall at its base.

27 Mar-31 Oct daily 10.00-18.00, 1 Nov-26 Mar daily 10.00-16.00

A£4.00 C£2.00 Family Ticket (A2+C2)£15.00 Concessions£3.00

↓*special events*

▶ **Medieval Entertainments**

25/7/00-27/7/00

Meet the famous medieval Lord in all his armoured splendour!

▶ **Civil War Living History**

1/8/00-3/8/00

Visit a military encampment and meet soldiers, womenfolk and horses of the Civil War

▶ **A Medieval Knight and his Lady**

8/8/00-10/8/00

Find out about medieval life, from armour and archery to ladies and linen

▶ **The Bard and the Blade**

13/8/00-16/8/00

Shakespearean dialogue and dramatic duels with sword and dagger

▶ **Leeches and Bone Saws!**

20/8/00-23/8/00

Scientific but gruesome - learn about life as a 17th century surgeon. Not for the faint-hearted!

▶ **Nosher The Pig and The Black-hearted Baron**

27/8/00-28/8/00

A fantastic tale of a besieged town and crazy puppet characters, at 13.20 & 15.00

Haseley Manor

Heasley Lane Arreton Newport Isle of Wight PO30 3AN

Tel: 01983 865420 Fax: 01983 867547

This is the oldest and largest manor open to the public on the island. Parts of the south wing have some of the original building, c1350, but the rest of the house is a mixture of styles including Georgian and Victorian. There are lovely gardens, a children's farm, and pottery displays.

Easter-Oct daily 10.00-17.30

Last Admission: 16.30

A£4.75 C£3.45 OAPs£4.00

discount offer: One Child Free When Accompanied By A Full Paying Adult. Valid Until 31 Oct 2000

Morton Manor

Morton Manor Road Brading Sandown Isle of Wight PO36 0EP

[off A3055 in Brading]

Tel: 01983 406168

The manor dates back to 1249, but was rebuilt in 1680 with further changes during the Georgian period. The house contains furniture of both the 18th and 19th centuries.The Gardens are the main attraction with a vineyard. Winners of Southern England in bloom 1996.

Apr-Oct Sun-Fri 10.00-17.30

A£4.00 C£(6-16)£1.50 OAPs£3.50

discount offer: Two For The Price Of One

Osborne House

East Cowes Isle of Wight PO32 6JY

[1m SE of East Cowes off the A3021]

Tel: 01983 200022

www.english-heritage.org.uk

See the Royal Apartments and Victoria's Private Rooms. Take a free carriage ride to the Swiss Cottage where the royal children played. Superb gardens including, new for 2000, the Walled Garden. The Victorian Drama, Mrs Brown, was partly filmed at Osborne House.

visitor comments: Beautiful building - inside

and out. Get there early in high season, as it gets really busy.
1 Apr-30 Sept daily. House: 10.00-17.00, Garden: 10.00-18.00. 1-31 Oct 10.00-16.00. Winter: pre-booked guided tours only; tel 01983 200022
Last Admission: 60mins before closing
A£6.90 C£3.50 Concessions£5.20 Family Ticket £17.30

↓*special events*

▶ **Garden Tour**
23/4/00-22/10/00
At 13.00 on: 9, 23 Apr, 7, 14, 28 May, 11, 25 June, 9, 23 July, 13, 27 Aug, 10, 24 Sept, 8 & 22 Oct

▶ **Garden Show**
13/5/00-14/5/00
Beautiful blooms to enjoy, plus market stalls

▶ **Last Night of the Osborne Proms**
22/7/00-22/7/00
Bournemouth Symphony Orchestra with Christopher Bell as conductor. Call for details on 01202 669925. Tickets: from £14.00-£19.00 C&Students half price

Yarmouth Castle
Quay Street Yarmouth Isle of Wight PO41 0PB
[adjacent to car ferry terminal]
Tel: 01983 760678/852484

Now tucked away among newer buildings, this rather homely castle is in excellent repair. Visitors can see the Master Gunner's parlour and kitchen, plus an unusually small great hall. Built during the reign of Henry VIII as a coastal defence.
22 Mar-31 Oct daily 10.00-18.00 or dusk if sooner
A£2.00 C£1.00 Concessions£1.50

↓*special events*

▶ **Tudor Sailors**
3/6/00-4/6/00
Meet the officers, mariners and their families of Queen Elizabeth's navy

Maritime

Cowes Library and Maritime Museum
Beckford Road Cowes Isle of Wight PO31 7SG
[in town centre on the corner of West Hill road / Beckford road]
Tel: 01983 293394 / 293341

Models, paintings and archives concerning the maritime history of the Isle of Wight. Photographic and plans collections of the vessels built by J Samuel White & Co Ltd, collection of photographic material on yachting by Kirk of Cowes. Small craft designed and built by VFFA Fox. Approximately 7,000 maritime books and periodicals.
All year Mon-Wed & Fri 09.30-18.00 Sat 09.30-16.30. Closed Bank Hol & Sat before Bank Hol.
Appointment needed to see photographs
Admission Free

Isle of Wight Shipwreck Centre and Maritime Museum
Providence House Sherborne Street Bembridge Isle of Wight PO35 5SB
Tel: 01983 872223 / 873125 Fax: 01983 873125

This fine museum brings alive the maritime history of the Isle of Wight. There are six galleries displaying a unique collection of salvage and shipwreck items, early diving equipment, ship models HMS Swordfish and a model of the harbour.
Late Mar-Oct daily 10.00-17.00
A£2.35 C£1.35 OAPs&Students£1.70

Museum of Smuggling History
Botanic Gardens The Undercliffe Drive Ventnor Isle of Wight PO38 1UL
[on A3055 1m W of Ventnor]
Tel: 01983 853677

Situated in the Botanic gardens the museum is underground in extensive vaults, this unique museum shows methods of smuggling used over a 700-year period right up to the present day.
Easter-Sept daily 10.00-17.00
A£2.20 Concessions£1.10. Parties by arrangement

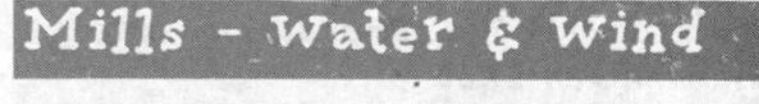

Mills - Water & Wind

Bembridge Windmill
High Street Bembridge Isle of Wight PO35 5SQ
[0.5m S of Bembridge on B3395. Ferry: Ryde (Wightlink Ltd) tel 0870 582 7744 & East Cowes

(Red Funnel) 01703 334010]
Tel: 01983 873945
Dating from around 1700 the only Windmill to survive on the Island and with much of its wooden machinery intact. Conducted school parties and special visits by written appointment Mar-Oct (but not July & Aug).
27 Mar-27 Oct Sun-Fri & Easter Sat, July & Aug daily 10.00-17.00
Last Admission: 16.30
A£1.50 C£0.75. No reductions for groups

Yafford Water Mill Farm Park
Yafford Shorwell Newport Isle of Wight PO30 3LH
[between Shorwell and Brightstone on B3399]
Tel: 01983 740610/741125 Fax: 01983 740610
The mill is situated in attractive surroundings with a large mill pond. The great overshot wheel still turns and all the milling machinery is in working order. An unusual attraction is the millpond, which is home to Sophie the seal. Sophie lives happily in the pool below the mill race. She is extremely friendly and enjoys showing off in front of visitors, especially if you call her name. Sophie is fed at 11.30, 14.30 and 16.30 daily. Around the park and in the display sheds are many examples of old farming machinery and equipment, undergoing restoration. Highlights include a working Traction Engine and Narrow Gauge Railway. There are many interesting and rare breeds to be seen at Yafford Mill, such as White Park and Highland Cattle, Portland, Hebridean and Jacob Sheep. Also goats, Shetland ponies, donkeys, pigs, rabbits and a Trout pond. Along with many breeds of ducks, and geese you will find turkeys, peacocks, pheasants and domestic fowl.
All year daily 10.00-18.00 or dusk in winter
Last Admission: 17.00
A£3.70 C£2.30 Concessions£2.70 Family Ticket £10.00
discount offer: Two For The Price Of One

Nature & Conservation Parks

Needles Old Battery
West High Down Totland Bay Isle of Wight PO39 0JH
[at Needles Headland W of Freshwater Bay and Alum Bay. Ferry: Yarmouth (Wightlink Ltd) Tel: 0990 827744 E Cowes (Red Funnel) Tel: 01703 334010]
Tel: 01983 754772
A Victorian coastal fort built in 1862 over 80 metres above sea level. A 65 metre tunnel leads to spectacular views of Needles Rocks, lighthouse and Hampshire and Dorset coastline. Two original Rifled Muzzle-Loader gunbarrels are mounted on carriages in the parade ground. Exhibitions, tea room and shop. Accompanied wheelchair users may park nearer by prior arrangement with the property only.
visitor comments: Walked down and got the chair lift up - my 2 year old loved it! Lots to do at the top. There's a boat trip around the needles if you fancy it.
21 Mar-28 Oct Sun-Thur Easter weekend daily in July & Aug 10.30-17.00. Please note property will close in adverse weather conditions, telephone property on day of visit to check
Last Admission: 16.30
A£2.50 Family Ticket £6.00. No reduction for parties. Paid for parking at Alum Bay is not NT

Shanklin Chine
12 Pomona Road Shanklin Isle of Wight PO37 6PF
[venue signposted on A3055]
Tel: 01983 866432 Fax: 01983 874215
Shanklin Chine is a natural gorge of great scenic beauty with a spectacular 45ft waterfall. A path winds down through the boulders, overhanging trees, ferns and other flora that cover its steep sides. The Heritage Centre features the Millennium Exhibition: "Century of Solent Sea and Sail."
visitor comments: Breathtakingly wonderful. Disabled are welcome and get reduced prices as they can't go too far in. A magical world of beauty - waterfalls, greenery.
3 Apr-18 May & 18 Sept-29 Oct 10.00-17.00. 19 May-17 Sept 10.00-22.00 subject to weather conditions
Last Admission: 30mins before closing
A£2.50 C(0-16)£1.00 OAPs&Students£1.50,

Children(schools)£1.00, Teachers&Carers£Free Mobility Impaired £1.00 due to restricted access. Groups excluding schools 10+ 10% discount
discount offer: Two For The Price Of One

Performing Arts

Waltzing Waters
Aqua Theatre Westridge Centre Brading Road Ryde Isle of Wight PO33 1QS
Tel: 01983 811333 Fax: 01983 811333
The world's most elaborate water, light and music production. 'It's like nothing you've ever seen before'... a triumph of artistry and engineering. Visitors are overwhelmed by thousands of dazzling patterns of moving water synchronised with music in spectacular fashion. This indoor production is an entertainment that one never forgets. The very first of its kind in England, this venue will provide a completely different set of musical selections on each day of the week, therefore appealing to all tastes and to all ages. So if you're looking for something entirely new in entertainment... don't miss this unique show.
visitor comments: Wonderfully entertaining. Staff are kind and friendly.
1 Feb-5 Dec daily from 10.00 on the hour every hour & 19.15 & 20.15 from 22 Mar-31 Oct
A£4.00 C£1.50 Concessions£3.50
discount offer: A Free Child With Each Adult

Railways

Isle of Wight Steam Railway
Station Road Havenstreet Village Ryde Isle of Wight PO33 4DS
[electric train to Smallbrook junction from Ryde]
Tel: 01983 882204 Fax: 01983 884515
When the Newport to Ryde railway was closed, Haven Street Station was taken over by a private company, the Isle of Wight Steam Railway. Steam trains now run the five miles from Wootton, via Haven Street to Smallbrook Junction, where there is a direct interchange with Island Line's Ryde-Shanklin Line.
visitor comments: Spent hours travelling up and down the line - you can get on and off wherever you like. A Rover Ticket will let you travel all day on the mainline trains and steam railway - great vlaue.
Operates 22 May-26 Sept daily, plus selected days during Mar, Apr & Oct, also over Christmas. Please telephone for departure times.
Return Fares: A£6.00 C(4-15)£4.00 Family Ticket £19.00

Theme & Adventure Parks

Blackgang Chine Fantasy Park
Blackgang Ventnor Isle of Wight PO38 2HN
[off A3055]
Tel: 01983 730330 Fax: 01983 731267
Opened as scenic gardens in 1843 covering some 40 acres, the park has imaginative play areas, water gardens, maze and coastal gardens and a water force high speed boat ride. Set on the steep wooded slopes of the Chine are the themed areas where you will find a magical mix of fantasy, legend and heritage.
visitor comments: A tiring day out with loads to do for all ages. On the whole good value, with reasonably priced restaurant.
22 Mar-31 Oct daily 10.00-17.30. Floodlit evenings during the Summer Holidays until 22.00
Last Admission: 60mins before closing
A£5.50 C£4.50 OAPs£5.00 Disabled Concesion£2.75 Family Ticket (A2+C2 or A1+C3)£18.00. Free return visit within 3 days (Special events excluded). Season Tickets offer unlimited admission to both Blackgang Chine and Robin Hill A£19.50 C(3-13)£15.95 Disabled Concession£9.50

Needles Pleasure Park
Alum Bay Totland Bay Isle of Wight PO39 0JD
[signposted on B3322]
Tel: 01983 752401 Fax: 01983 755260
Set in heritage coastline the park is a haven of fun and activity. The chairlift to the beach enables visitors to view the unique coloured sandcliffs, and the Island's most famous landmark, The Needles rocks and lighthouse. From daredevil rides to coloured sands, handmade crafts to crazy golf - there's something for everyone.
Easter-early Nov daily 10.00-17.00, hours extended during High Season
Admission Free to Pleasure Park. Charge for parking and chargeable attractions of your choice. Group rates available

Zoos

Isle of Wight Zoo
Yaverland's Seafront Sandown Isle of Wight PO36 8QB

[Bus: 1 & 22]
Tel: 01983 403883/405562 Fax: 01983 407049
On a conducted zoo tour you may well see TV & radio's Jack Corney with his big cats and lethal venomous snakes - you'll be safe, he won't! Be photographed with a small or large harmless snake. Take home your photo and snake handling certificate to prove it. Including many other endangered species - monkeys, birds, snakes and giant spiders. Parrot, snake and big cat shows and zoo chats. Kiddies play area and pets' corner.
visitor comments: They work very closely on the survival of big cats.
Feb-Easter 10.00-17.00, Easter-Nov 10.00-18.00. Closed Dec & Jan. Pre-booked groups welcome anytime of the year except 25 Dec.
A£4.95 C(0-5)£Free Concessions £3.95

Airfields / Flight Centres

Biggin Hill International Air Fair 2000
Air Displays Int Ltd Biggin Hill Airport Biggin Hill Westerham Kent TN16 3BN
[J4 M25. Shuttle bus service available from BR: Bromley South]
Tel: 01959 540959 Fax: 01959 575969
www.airdisplaysint.co.uk
One of the great British summertime events of the year and one of the biggest outside events held inside the M25. World famous 7 hour international flying display with top teams and pilots. Unique mixture of modern, military, vintage and civilian aircraft. The many family attractions combined with excellent value for family tickets make this event very popular with families as well as enthusiasts. Disabled facilities and privileged viewing area.
June 3-4 2000. Gates open 08.00, flying commences 11.00-18.00 each day
Queuing Times: possible
Advance tickets - Provisional: A£10.00 C(5-15)£4.00 Family Ticket (Car+5 people)£20.00. Car Park £Free. Gate Prices: A£12.50 C(5-15)£4.50 Family Ticket (Car+5 people)£25.00. Car Park £Free

↓*special events*

► **Biggin Hill International Air Fair 2000**
3/6/00-4/6/00

► **Battle of Britain Open Day**
17/9/00-17/9/00

Animal Attractions

South of England Rare Breeds Centre
Woodchurch Ashford Kent TN26 3RJ
[J10 M20 9m, on B2067 between Hamstreet / Tenterden follow brown tourist signs. Plenty of on site parking available]
Tel: 01233 861493 Fax: 01233 861457
www.rarebreeds.org.uk
A fun family day out with rare farm animals, many to touch. Children's Barn where children can play with young animals, also regular 'Meet the Animals' sessions. You can see the reconstruction of an historic Georgian farmstead, enjoy farm rides, woodland walks, toddler's sandpit and paddling pool, adventure playground. Low price children's menus in 'The Granary'.
All year Summer: daily 10.30-17.30, Winter: Tue-Sun 10.30-16.30. Closed 24 & 25 Dec
A£3.50 C(3-15)£1.90 OAPs£3.00. Group rates: A£2.75 C£1.50
discount offer: Up to Two Adults At Group Rate (£2.75)

↓*special events*

► **Pudding Day**
6/2/00-3/12/00
1st Sunday of every month: 6 Feb, 5 Mar, 2 Apr, 7 May, 4 June, 2 July, 6 Aug, 3 Sept, 1 Oct, 5 Nov & 3 Dec. British puds, served with steaming custard, cream or ice cream

► **Half Term - Half Price**
19/2/00-27/2/00

► **Easter Fun**
23/4/00-24/4/00
Lots of activities on an 'Easter' theme, including Bunny Hunt, craft fair and children's entertain-

ment

► **Real Ale Festival**
27/5/00-27/5/00
Annual CAMRA Beer festival with over 30 real ales, ciders and perry. Morris Dancing, music, games and fun

► **Piggy Picnics**
28/5/00-29/5/00
Piglet racing, piggy obstacle course, piggy bath-time, craft fair and a children's competition

► **Classic Car Rally**
25/6/00-25/6/00
6th Annual Car Rally - cars, bikes, coaches, lorries and bicycles from yesteryear. Bouncy castle, children's roundabout, arena concourse, competitions, beer tent and BBQ

► **A World of Difference**
24/7/00-6/8/00
Magical multi-sensory festival - explore the indoor exhibition and (from 31/7 to 6/8) the inflatable maze - full of light and colour

► **Rare Breeds Show and Country Fair**
20/8/00-20/8/00
Show of Rare and Minority Breeds, country craft displays, children's entertainment, local produce, trailer rides, beer tent, BBQ. See horses, dogs, birds of prey, rats, reptiles and ferrets!

Archaeology

Lullingstone Roman Villa

Lullingstone Lane Eynsford Kent DA4 0JA
[J3 M25 0.5m SW of Eynsford off A225, follow A20 towards Brands Hatch]
Tel: 01732 778000

The excavation of this roman villa in 1949 uncovered one of the most exciting archaeological finds of the century. Here you can see some of the most remarkable villa remains in Britain, including wonderful mosaic tiled floors, wall painting and the ruins of one of the earliest Christian chapels in Britain. Audio tape tour included in price.

27 Mar-31 Oct daily 10.00-18.00 or dusk if sooner. 1 Nov-26 Mar daily 10.00-16.00. Closed 24-26 Dec
Last Admission: 30mins before closing
A£2.50 C£1.90 OAPs&UB40 £1.30

↓*special events*

► **Bones, Skulls, Teeth & Diseases**
15/4/00-16/4/00
Renowed expert Trevor Anderson explains the fascinating facts discovered from medieval skeletons

► **Easter Activities**
22/4/00-22/4/00
Fun for children includng egg painting, colouring competition and Easter Bonnet making

► **Meet the Romans**
27/5/00-1/6/00
Meet a Roman couple living at the Villa and enjoy period activities including face painting and music

► **The Last Romans**
1/7/00-2/7/00
Meet soldiers and a horseman of the type that defended Britain after the departure of Rome's Legions

► **Roman Storytelling**
8/7/00-9/7/00
Enthralling Roman stories to enjoy

► **Roman Mosaics**
15/7/00-16/7/00
An insight into Roman domestic design, with the opportunity to create a mosaic

Arts, Crafts & Textiles

Maidstone Museum and Bentlif Art Gallery

St. Faiths Street Maidstone Kent ME14 1LH
[close to County Hall behind the Army & Navy]
Tel: 01622 754497 Fax: 01622 602193
www.museum.maidstone.gov.uk

Set in an Elizabethan manor house which has been much extended over the years, this museum houses a surprising and outstanding collection of fine and applied arts, including oil paintings and watercolours, furniture, Roman, Anglo-Saxon and Medieval archeology, ceramics, costumes and a collection of Japanese art and artefacts. Please apply for details of temporary exhibitions, workshops etc. Photography allowed by prior consent. Disabled access limited.

All year Mon-Sat 10.00-17.15, Sun 11.00-16.00. Closed 25-26 Dec
Last Admission: 17.00
Admission Free

↓*special events*

► **Magic People**
11/3/00-11/3/00
Where do tales of fairies and elves come from?

► **Embroiderers Guild**
23/9/00-29/10/00
One of the largest exhibitions of embroidery and textiles

► **Helen Sears/Photo Works**
6/11/00-3/12/00
Contemporary photography with a concurrent exhibition at Maidstone Library Gallery

► **Kent Field Club Annual Exhibition**
9/12/00-9/12/00
Kent wildlife and natural habitats with stalls and outdoor activities

► **Portrait Exhibition featuring Joan La Dell**
15/12/00-31/12/00
The concept of portrait painting including the

relationship between the artist and sitter

Tunbridge Wells Museum and Art Gallery
Civic Centre Mount Pleasant Royal Tunbridge Wells Kent TN1 1JN
[off A264, brown pedestrian signs, next to the Town Hall]
Tel: 01892 526121/554171 Fax: 01892 534227
www.tunbridgewells.gov.uk
The museum displays local and natural history, archaeology, toys and dolls, and domestic and agricultural bygones. There is a fine display of Tunbridge ware. The art gallery has regularly changing exhibitions which include showings of the Ashton Bequest of Victorian oil paintings.
All year Mon-Sat 09.30-17.00. Closed Bank Hol & Easter Sat
Admission Free

↓*special events*

▶ **Arts and Crafts 2000**
4/3/00-18/3/00
Annual arts and craft show by local residents

▶ **The Age of Steam**
16/3/00-16/3/00
George Holland describes his experiences as a local engine driver in the age of steam, starts 20.00

▶ **The Embroiderers' Guild**
27/3/00-8/4/00
Embroidery and textiles by the Tunbridge Wells and District Branch

▶ **Art Out East**
13/4/00-29/4/00
Multicultural, functional and decorative art and craft from East London

▶ **Women in Focus**
5/5/00-3/6/00
Portrait photographer Derek Tamea pays tribute to the leading women of today. Talk on May 5 at 19.15

▶ **Beyond Blue**
30/6/00-12/7/00
Contemporary, colourful and exciting pictures and 3D works by Elizabeth Major and Bill Hudson

▶ **Annual General Meeting**
3/10/00-3/10/00
19.15 in the art gallery

Birds, Butterflies & Bees

Wingham Wildlife Park
Rusham Road Shatterling Canterbury Kent CT3 1JL
[A257 between Canterbury and Sandwich]
Tel: 01227 720836 Fax: 01227 722452
A fascinating day out for the whole family. Wander around the landscaped gardens and walk through aviary to see our collection of birds and animals including: llamas, meerkats, otters, prarie dogs, wallabies, parrots, ducks, peafowl, emus and rheas. Then enjoy a snack in the tea-room and a browse through the gift shop.
All year daily 10.00-18.00, dusk in Winter months
Last Admission: 14.30
discount offer: One Free Child With Two Full Paying Adults

Country Parks & Estates

Knole
Knole Sevenoaks Kent TN15 0RP
[off M25 London Orbital at S end of Sevenoaks town just E of A225. BR: Sevenoaks]
Tel: 01732 450608 infoline Fax: 01732 465528
Tour 13 magnificent state rooms in one of the great treasure houses of England. Find exquisite silver furniture, fragile tapestries, rare carpets and other unique furniture including the first 'Knole' settee, state beds and even an early royal loo! Newly restored garden gates and railings; conserved curtains and counterpane on Lady Betty Germain's bed. Study a remarkable collection of historical portraits by masters such as Sir Joshua Reynolds, Van Dyck and Gainsborough. Uncover Knole's intriguing history of connections with the famous: Archbishops of Canterbury, Henry VIII, Elizabeth I, the Sackville family, Dukes of Dorset, Vita Sackville-West and Virginia Woolf whose novel Orlando is set at the house. Enjoy throughout the year the extensive deer park owned by Lord Sackville and visit the displays in the Bewhouse Tea Room. Dogs in park only on lead, do not feed the deer.

House: 27 Mar-31 Oct Wed-Sat 12.00-16.00, Sun, Bank Hol Mon & Good Fri 11.00-17.00. Garden: May-Sept first Wed in each month only. Last Admission: House: 15.30, 16.00
£5.00 C£2.50 Family Ticket £12.50. Pre-booked Groups £4.00. Parking (NT members free) £2.50. Garden: A£1.00 C£0.50. Special Offer: Concessions for NT members on BR London Charing Cross to Knole combined train/bus admission ticket call 0345 484950

↓*special events*

▶ **Recital by Amabile**
10/6/00-10/6/00
With readings by Gregory Warren Wilson. Tickets £11.00, starts at 19.30

▶ **Classical guitar with Julian Bream**
9/9/00-9/9/00
At 19.30, tickets £15.00

Festivals & Shows

Hever 2000

The Lakeside Theatre Hever Castle Hever Edenbridge Kent TN8 7NG
[situated 3m S/E of Edenbridge off B2026 between Seveoaks and East Grinstead. J5 or 6 of M25. Plenty of on site parking.]
Tel: 01732 866114 Box Office Fax: 01732 866796

Since it opened in the early eighties, the Lakeside Theatre has become one of the most popular outdoor venues in the south-east, attracting many thousands every summer, many of whom return year after year. Situated in the beautiful Italian Garden of Hever Castle in Kent, overlooking the lake, it offers the perfect setting for a pre-show picnic with family and friends. The tiered and covered seating make for an unusually initmate audiotrium to enjoy the programme of music, opera and drama which comprises the Summer Festival.

June 22-Aug 27 2000, Wed-Sun, all performances commences 20.00. Gates open for Picnic at 18.30
A£11.50-£18.00. Group rates 10+ 10%

↓*special events*

▶ **La Boheme**
22/6/00-24/6/00
Performed by Beaufort Opera.

▶ **The Tempest**
30/6/00-15/7/00
William Shakespeare's play performed by the Kent Repertory Company

▶ **Classic Jazz**
16/7/00-16/7/00
Humphrey Lyttelton with Stacey Kent.

▶ **Great Composers**
21/7/00-21/7/00
The Primavera Chamber Orchestra, musical and artistic director Paul Manley.

▶ **The Best of Gilbert & Sullivan**
22/7/00-22/7/00
Including 'Trial by Jury', performed by Opera Options.

▶ **Opera Classics**
23/7/00-23/7/00
Popular excerpts and arias from the greatest classical operas performed by the London Opera Players.

Kent Beer Festival 2000

Merton Farm Merton Lane Canterbury Kent CT2
[leave A2 at J for Canterbury. Take Hythe turning off ring road. Follow RAC signs to festival]
Tel: 01227 463478 Fax: 01227 463478

This is the 26th Kent Beer Festival held in a huge barn in a Kentish farmyard will feature the usual range of over 100 real ales and ciders from home and abroad. Food stalls, souvenir glasses and entertainment. The festival is run by volunteer members of the Campaign for Real Ale (CAMRA). Free festival programme available.

July 20-22 2000. Thur: 18.30-23.00, Fri: 12.00-16.00 & 18.30-23.00, Sat: 11.30-16.30 & 18.30-23.00
Thur: A£2.00, CAMRA members Free, Fri: Lunchtime free, evening A£4.00 in advance, Sat: A£2.00 each session (free after 21.00). C£Free

↓*special events*

▶ **Kent Beer Festival 2000**
20/7/00-22/7/00

Kent County Showground

Detling Hill Detling Maidstone Kent ME14 3JF
[off A249 Link Rd between M20 and M2]
Tel: 01622 630975 Fax: 01622 630978

County showground holding many special events. See Special Events

↓*special events*

▶ **Kent County Show 2000**
13/7/00-15/7/00
Kent's premier agricultural show featuring over 500 trade stands, livestock, equestrian events, demonstrations and other related attractions. Cheaper if pre paid 01622 630975

▶ **Detling Transport and Country Festival 2000**
12/8/00-13/8/00

Millennium Clocks Dover 2000

Dover College Grounds Effingham Crescent Dover Kent CT17 9RH
[Dover town centre - all town centre car parks FREE from 16.00 (31.12.99-1.1.00)]
Tel: 01304 872077

Free celebrations for all - New Year's Eve: Peace Light Lantern Processions and The Clock of the 2nd Millennium. New Year's Day: Carnival of the Planets and The Clock of the 3rd Millennium & Millennium Firework Spectacular at 20.00 from Dover Castle (best viewed from Dover Seafront).
Dec 31 1999 18.00-20.00 & Jan 1 2000 18.00-20.00
Admission and Workshops Free. Call 01303 244533 for information on the workshops

Folk & Local History Museums

Dover Museum

Market Square Dover Kent CT16 1PB
[adjacent to White Cliffs Experience in Market Square]
Tel: 01304 201066 Fax: 01304 241186
www.doveruk.com/museum/
New three-floor museum in the centre of Dover. History and archaeology of Dover on two floors with models and original objects including Roman, Saxon and medieval archaeology, Cinque Ports objects, portrait of Elizabeth I, Victorian and war items. Special exhibition gallery of temporary displays. The Dover Bronze Age Boat, believed to be the world's oldest seagoing boat is now on display in its superb gallery setting.
All year daily 10.00-17.30. Closed 25-26 Dec
A£1.70 C&OAPs£0.90. Local Resident Concession 50% discount
discount offer: Two For The Price Of One
↓*special events*
▶ **Rocks and Rex**
19/2/00-2/5/00
The Dover Geology and Fossil Show
▶ **The Fossil Roadshow**
18/3/00-19/3/00
An expert panel identify your rocks and fossils and answer any geology queries. Plus a chance to see and handle fossils and dinosaurs. Open 10.00-17.00
▶ **Belt Bosses**
22/4/00-22/4/00
Bronze Age Boat Gallery from 10.00-16.30
▶ **Bronze Age Boat Event**
22/4/00-24/4/00
Learn about the Bronze Age by participating in a range of hands-on activities at the Bronze Age Boat Gallery
▶ **'Highlights of the Millennia'**
13/5/00-29/10/00
A look at the definitive eras of the last 2000 years inluding the Roman, Saxon, Tudor and the Second World War periods.
▶ **Roman Mosaics**
30/5/00-30/5/00
Homes of the Millennium exhibition
▶ **Saxon Copper Jewellery**
17/6/00-17/6/00
Homes of the Millennium exhibition from 10.00-16.30
▶ **Tudor Woodblock Printing**
22/7/00-24/10/00
Held on July 22 and Oct 24 only. Homes of the Millennium exhibition, 10.00-16.30
▶ **Victorian Christmas Decorations**
9/12/00-9/12/00
Mezzanine at the Museum, 10.00-16.30

Old Town Hall Museum

Market Place Margate Kent CT9 1ER
[signposted from town and seafront]
Tel: 01843 231213 Fax: 01843 582359
Margate's development as a seaside resort; also old Court Room and Victorian Police cells. Reg Charity No: 288702.
All year Apr-Sept daily 10.00-17.00. Oct-Mar Mon-Fri 09.30-16.30
Last Admission: 30mins before closing
A£1.00 C&OAPs£0.50
discount offer: One Child Free When Accompanied By A Full Paying Adult

Food & Drink

Biddenden Vineyards

Little Whatmans Gribble Bridge Lane
Biddenden Kent TN27 8DH
[off A262, between Biddenden and Tenterden. Plenty of on site parking]
Tel: 01580 291726 Fax: 01580 291933
The present vineyard was established in 1969 and now covers 22 acres. Visitors are welcome to stroll around the vineyard and to taste

wines, ciders and apple juice available at the shop. Tea and coffee available. Guided tours for pre-booked groups.
All year Mar-Dec Mon-Sat 10.00-17.00, Sun & Bank Hol 11.00-17.00. Jan-Feb Mon-Sat 10.00-17.00. Closed Sun, also closed Dec 24 from 12.00 -1 Jan incl. Guided tours for pre-booked groups - call for details
Admission and Tastings £Free
discount offer: 10% Discount On All Shop Purchases

↓*special events*

▶ **Easter Bunny Hunt**
23/4/00-23/4/00
From 11.00 you can hunt for the Easter Bunny and meet the owls from Hawkhurst Owl Sanctuary

▶ **Special Christmas Promotion**
25/11/00-17/12/00
Free mince pies, mulled cider special offers and a Free Prize Draw every weekend - on following dates: Sat & Sun 25 & 26 Nov, Sat & Sun 2 & 3, 9 & 10, 16 & 17 Dec

Gardens & Horticulture

Doddington Place Gardens

Church Lane Doddington Sittingbourne Kent ME9 0BB
[off A2 at Teynham and Ospringe, also signposted on A20 at Lenham]
Tel: 01795 886101
Landscaped gardens in the grounds of a Victorian country house (not open) with good views over surrounding parkland and countryside. Edwardian rock garden and formal garden, rhododendrons and azaleas in a woodland setting, fine trees, yew hedges and a recently built folly.
May-Sept Sun 14.00-18.00, Wed and Bank Hol Mon 11.00-18.00. Groups at other times, by prior arrangement
A£2.50 C£0.25. Group rate £2.00. Coaches by prior arrangement only

Emmetts Garden

Ide Hill Sevenoaks Kent TN14 6AY
[4m from M25 J5. 1.5m S of A25 on Sundridge / Ide Hill road. 1.5m N of Ide Hill off B2042. BR: Sevenoaks / Penshurst]
Tel: 01732 868381/750367
Enjoy wonderful views across the Weald of Kent from this peaceful garden, one of the highest spots in the county. Follow the meandering paths among rare trees and shrubs planted by Victorian gardener William Robinson. Wander around the pretty rock garden and Italianate rose garden or follow the hillside woodland walk. Come and enjoy the plants in all seasons - daffodils and bluebells in Spring, roses in Summer, and glowing colours in Autumn. And don't forget to look out for the highest tree-top in Kent! Wheelchair availab le for access to parts of the garden. Dogs on leads only.
27 Mar-30 May Wed-Sun & Bank Hol Mon 11.00-17.30. 2 June-31 Oct Wed, Sat-Sun & Bank Hol Mon 11.00-17.30. Stable Tearoom and Shop: As Garden 11.30-16.30
Last Admission: 16.30
A£3.00 C£1.50 Family Ticket £7.50. Pre-booked Groups £2.20

↓*special events*

▶ **Bluebell Tour**
2/5/00-2/5/00
Tickets £6.00, starts at 18.30

▶ **Rhododendrons etc**
23/5/00-23/5/00
19.00, tickets £6.00

▶ **The Blues Band**
29/7/00-29/7/00
Open air concert at 19.30, tickets £13.00

▶ **Autumn Colours**
17/10/00-17/10/00
Starts at 14.00, a tour of the garden in its "autumn glory". Tickets £6.00

Goodnestone Park Gardens

Nr Wingham Canterbury Kent CT3 1PL
[8m SE of Canterbury 4m E of A2 0.25m SE of B2046 S of A257. BR: Adisham 2m. Plenty of parking on site]
Tel: 01304 840107 Fax: 01304 840107
The garden is approximately 14 acres with many fine trees, a woodland garden and the walled garden with a large collection of old roses and herbaceous plants. Jane Austen was a frequent visitor, her brother Edward having married a daughter of the house. The garden is continually being extended, with new plantings all the time. Member of the Historic Houses Association.
Gardens only: Mon Wed Thur Fri & Sun Mar-Oct 11.00-17.00, Sun Mar-Oct House open by

appointment for parties of not over 20. 1999 Times: Mar-Oct Mon, Wed-Sat 11.00-17.00 Sun 12.00-18.00
A£3.00 C(0-12)£0.30 OAPs£2.50 Family Ticket (A2+C2)£4.50 Wheelchair users £1.00. Groups rates 20+ £2.50. Guided Tours £3.50

↓*special events*

▶ **Ceramics Exhibition**
7/4/00-9/4/00

▶ **Garden Lectures**
9/5/00-18/7/00
Held on May 9, June 18 and July 18 only

▶ **Garden Opera**
11/8/00-11/8/00

▶ **Hardy Plant Society Sale**
19/8/00-20/8/00

Groombridge Place Gardens and The Enchanted Forest

Groombridge Place Groombridge Tunbridge Wells Kent TN3 9QG
[off A264 on B2100]
Tel: 01892 863999 Fax: 01892 863996
www.groombridgeplace.com

"Groombridge Place is wonderful because it's so different" is what our visitors say! Experience the history, mystery and excitement for yourself. Relax in the stunning formal gardens and enjoy the sheer magic of the Enchanted Forest. Take a canal boat cruise to the Forest, children love the "Dark Walk" and the Groms' Village and everyone is thrilled by the Romany Camp, the Giant Rabbits, the pig racing and the Birds of Prey. let your imagination run wild and you'll discover the best day out in the South East. Please call the venue to confirm dates for the following special events.
12 April-29 Oct daily 09.00-18.00
Last Admission: 17.00
A£7.50 C&OAPs£6.50 (prices subject to change in July)

↓*special events*

▶ **Millennium Easter Extravaganza**
23/4/00-24/4/00

▶ **The Robin Hood Legend Live on...**
30/4/00-1/5/00

▶ **Bank Holiday Family Fun**
28/5/00-29/5/00

▶ **11th London to Brighton Classic Car Run**
4/6/00-4/6/00
Route Two: Starts Crystal Place, London. Check point 1. Groombridge Gardens, Kent, Check Point 2. Michelham Priory, Sussex. Finishing at Maderia Drive, Brighton. No charge to visitors at the Start and Finish points

▶ **Take to the Skies**
18/6/00-18/6/00
Hot air balloons and kites

▶ **Living Heritage Craft Fair**
8/7/00-9/7/00

▶ **Wings, Wheels and Steam 2000**
6/8/00-6/8/00

▶ **Scarecrows, Shires and Sheepdogs**
27/8/00-28/8/00

▶ **King Henry V and The Battle of Agincourt**
3/9/00-3/9/00

▶ **Millennium Kent Hot Air Balloon Classic**
10/9/00-10/9/00

▶ **MG Car Club**
17/9/00-17/9/00
South East centre autumn gathering

▶ **Living Heritage Craft Fair**
7/10/00-8/10/00

▶ **Nearly Hallowe'en Adventure**
28/10/00-28/10/00

▶ **Firework Spectacular**
4/11/00-4/11/00

Mount Ephraim Gardens

Staple Street Hernhill Faversham Kent ME13 9TX
[1m off M2 A2 or A299]
Tel: 01227 751496 Fax: 01227 750940

8 acres of superb gardens set in the heart of family run orchards. The gardens offer an attractive balance of formal and informal with herbaceous border, a Topiary, a Japanese rock garden, water garden, rose terraces and a lake. Vineyard and orchard trails to follow. Tea is served in the Tea Rooms and the new Tea Terrace. Lunches served on Bank Holiday Sundays and Mondays. Craft centre and gift shop. Member of the Historic Houses Association. Dogs on leads allowed.
Gardens: Apr-Sept Mon, Wed, Thur, Sat & Sun 13.00-18.00. Craft Centre: Sun 14.00-18.00 only
A£3.00 C£1.00. Group rates £2.50
discount offer: £1.00 Off Entrance For Adults. Valid Until 30 Sept 2000

↓*special events*

▶ **NCCPG Spring Plant Fair**
9/4/00-9/4/00
National Council for the Conservation of Plants and Gardens. For further details call 01227 751496

▶ **Pat a Lamb**

30/4/00-1/5/00
Display of young lambs amid wonderful orchard blossom. For details call 01227 751496

▶ **Millennium Garden Festival**
28/5/00-29/5/00
Wine, craft, plants, farm strawberries, live music, homemade food, gardening demonstrations, children's entertainment and folk dancing. For details call 01227 751496

Heritage & Industrial

Fleur de Lis Heritage Centre
13 Preston Street Faversham Kent ME13 8NS
[off M2 at Faversham exit to A2. Near Central car-park]
Tel: 01795 534542
Http://www.faversham.org
A thousand years of history and architecture in Faversham are shown in award-winning displays, an audio-visual programme, and a working vintage telephone exchange in this 16th-century building (a former coaching inn). There is a Tourist Information Centre and a bookshop. The Centre, run by 100% voluntary effort, hopes to expand, and all profits go towards its expansion scheme.
All year daily 10.00-16.00, Sun 10.00-13.00. Guided town tours: Apr-Oct Sat 10.30
Last Admission: 15.30 (Sun 12.30)
A£1.50 OAPs£1.00 Concessions£0.50. Guided town tour £1.00
discount offer: Two For The Price Of One (Excludes Tour)

Historical

Chartwell
Mapleton Road Westerham Kent TN16 1PS
[2m S of Westerham, fork left off B2026 after 1.5m. BR: Edenbridge / Edenbridge Town / Sevenoaks]
Tel: 01732 866368 infoline Fax: 01732 868193
Home of Sir Winston Churchill from 1924 until the end of his life. The rooms, left as they were in his lifetime, evoke his career and interests, with pictures, maps, documents and personal mementoes. Two rooms are given over to a museum of his many gifts and uniforms. Terraced gardens descend towards the lake. New for this year the Chartwell Explorer Bus offering all-inclusive tickets from London, and a new leaflet on the countryside walks between Chartwell and Emmetts Garden.
visitor comments: A beautiful house and garden to see - all year long.
27 Mar-31 Oct Wed-Sun, Bank Hol Mon & Good Fri 11.00-17.00. Additionally Tue in July & Aug 11.00-17.00.
Last Admission: 16.30
Queuing Times: Timed ticket possible delays
House, garden & studio: A£5.50 C£2.75 Family Ticket £13.75. Garden & studio only: A£2.75. Coaches and groups by appointment.

↓*special events*

▶ **Music, Memories and Moonlight**
17/6/00-17/6/00
An evening with the Herb Miller Orchestra, starts 19.30, tickets £17.50

▶ **Churchill's Garden - A Guided Tour**
5/7/00-19/7/00
Held on July 5 and 19 only. Tour begins at 18.00, tickets £6.00

▶ **"Tails" of Chartwell**
11/8/00-22/8/00
Held on Aug 11 and 22 only. A storytelling event at 14.00, tickets £3.50

Cobham Hall
Cobham Gravesend Kent DA12 3BL
[adjacent to A2 / M2 between Gravesend / Rochester. 8m from J2 M25. 27m from London]
Tel: 01474 823371 Fax: 01474 822995/824171
Cobham Hall is an outstandingly beautiful, red brick mansion in Elizabethan, Jacobean, Carolian and 18th century styles. This former home of the Earls of Darnley is set in 150 acres of parkland. The Gothic Dairy and some of the

classical garden buildings are being renovated. Independent international boarding and day school. The grounds yield many delights for the lover of nature, especially in Spring, when the gardens and woods are resplendent with daffodils, narcissi and a myriad of rare bulbs. The House is open for Guided Tours each day from 13.00-16.00 with delicious cream teas available in the dining room.
Mar & Apr Wed, Sun & Easter Weekend 14.00-17.00, July-Aug Wed & Sun 14.00-17.00
Last Admission: 16.00
A3.50 C&OAPs£2.50
discount offer: £1.00 Off Admission to House/Garden. Valid until 29 Aug

Deal Castle
Victoria Road Deal Kent CT14 7BA
[SW of Deal town centre]
Tel: 01304 372762
www.english-heritage.org.uk
Crouching low and menacing, the huge, rounded bastions of this austere fort, built by Henry VIII, once carried 119 guns. Designed to resemble a Tudor Rose, Deal Castle is one of three artillery forts on the Kent coast built to counter the threat of invasion during the mid-16th century. Today the castle still appears exactly as it was originally intended to look: powerful and virtually impregnable. Its remarkable coastal position affords breathtaking views out to sea. It is a fascinating castle to explore, with long, dark passages, battlements and a massive basement with an exciting exhibition.
27 Mar-31 Oct daily 10.00-18.00 (dusk in Oct). 1 Nov-26 Mar Wed-Sun 10.00-16.00. Closed 24-26 Dec.
A£3.00 C£1.50 Concessions£2.30

↓*special events*

▶ **1940**
23/4/00-24/4/00
Meet members of the "Dad's Army" who defended Deal in 1940

▶ **King Henry's Mercenaries**
6/5/00-7/5/00
From Noon. Meet colourful German mercenaries of 1546 in garrison at the castle

▶ **Civil War Music and Dance**
28/5/00-29/5/00
From Noon. Courtly music and stately dance from the mid 17th century

▶ **Captaine Staffage's Cornucopia of ye Curious**
10/6/00-11/6/00
From Noon. Laugh and groan in equal measures as 17th century travelling players put on an hilarious show!

▶ **Schoole of Defence**
1/7/00-2/7/00
Soldiers and gentlemen duel for honour and glory

▶ **Puppet Making Workshops**
8/7/00-9/7/00
From Noon. The opportunity for younger visitors to make a puppet and take part in a puppet show

▶ **Passage to the New World, 1650**
15/7/00-16/7/00
From Noon. Find out why you should take ship to help found a new colony on Long Island, New England

▶ **Tudor Music**
22/7/00-23/7/00
From Noon. Lively music played on many instruments, with the opportunity to join in!

▶ **Recruiting for Wellington**
29/7/00-30/7/00
From Noon. Redcoat soldiers in camp, with living history displays, drill and musket-firing

▶ **The History Man**
5/8/00-6/8/00
From Noon. Enjoy unusual guided tours with the presenter of the BBC's History Man programmes

▶ **Tudor Printing**
12/8/00-13/8/00
From Noon. Tudor Printing Children can use wood blocks to print their own 1588 Armada newsheet

▶ **Traditional Song**
19/8/00-20/8/00
From Noon. A performance of delightful unaccompanied song

▶ **Tudor Living History**
27/8/00-28/8/00
From Noon. 16th century living history, sciences and entertainments

▶ **Soldiers from the Sea**
21/10/00-22/10/00
From Noon. Naval warfare from the Romans to the 20th century, with talks and demonstrations

▶ **Meet Father Christmas**
2/12/00-17/12/00
Meet Santa on 2, 3, 9, 10, 16 & 17 Dec

Dover Castle and Secret Wartime Tunnels
Dover Castle Dover Kent CT16 1HU
[on E side of Dover]
Tel: 01304 211067
www.english-heritage.org.uk
Discover 2000 years of history from the Iron Age to World War II. take the atmospheric tour deep underground in the secret wartime tunnels. See the reconstruction of preparations for Henry VIII's visit in the medieval Keep. Experience life under siege in 1216 in the fabulous sound and light presentation.

visitor comments: Really good value for money. Interesting and educational, very life-like. Great views.
All year 1 Apr-30 Sept daily 10.00-18.00. 1 Oct-31 Oct daily 10.00-17.00. 1 Nov-31 Mar daily 10.00-16.00. Closed 24-26 Dec
Last Admission: 1 hour before closure
A£6.90 C£3.50 Family Ticket £17.30 Concessions£5.20

↓special events

▶ **Castle Characters**
19/2/00-31/8/00
From 11.00. Meet colourful costumed characters and uniformed soldiers from Dover Castle's past. On 19-27 Feb, 21-24 Apr, 30 Apr-1 May & 1-31 Aug

▶ **The Imperial Roman Army**
30/4/00-1/5/00
At 12.30 & 15.00. Superbly armoured legionaries and auxiliaries 100AD on parade

▶ **Castle Characters**
27/5/00-4/6/00
From 11.00 Meet the 1940's inhabitants of the secret wartime tunnels

▶ **Their Finest House - Dover, 1940**
28/5/00-29/5/00
From Noon. The castle as it might have looked in 1940 the time of the "Miracle of Dunkirk", with military vehicles, checkpoints, "Dads Army" volunteers and much more

▶ **Archery Tournament**
22/7/00-23/7/00
From 11.00. The annual medieval "Archer of the Kingdom" festival. With combat, weapons displays and market traders

Dover Old Town Gaol
Dover Town Hall Biggin Street Dover Kent CT16 1DL
[M20 A2 signposted in Dover town]
Tel: 01304 201200 Fax: 01304 201200
High-tech animation, audio-visual techniques and 'talking heads' take visitors back to Victorian England to experience the horrors of life behind bars, listening, as they walk through the reconstructed courtroom, exercise yard, and cells, to the stories of the felons and their jailers. You can even try the prisoner's beds.
All year Tue-Sat 10.00-16.30, Sun 14.00-16.3. Closed Mon & Tue Oct-May call 01304 202723 for further information
Last Admission: 16.30
A£3.50 C&OAPs£2.10 (1999 prices)
discount offer: Two For The Price Of One

Dymchurch Martello Tower
Dymchurch Kent TN
[access from High Street, not from seafront]
Tel: 01732 778000
One of the many artillery towers which formed part of a chain of strongholds intended to resist an invasion by Napoleon. It is fully restored, with an original 24-pounder gun on the roof.
10-13 Apr & 2-4 May 14.00-17.30. 9 May-11 July Weekends & Bank Hol Mon 14.00-17.30. 18 July-31 Aug daily 14.00-17.30. 1-30 Sept Sat-Sun 14.00-17.30
A£1.00 C£0.50 Concessions£0.80

Hever Castle and Gardens
Hever Castle Hever Edenbridge Kent TN8 7NG
[off J5/6 M25, off B2026. 3m from BR: Victoria London to Edenbridge Town]
Tel: 01732 865224 Fax: 01732 866796
www.HeverCastle.co.uk
South East England Tourist Board Visitor Attraction of the Year Award - 1998. This romantic 13th century moated Castle was the childhood home of Anne Boleyn. In 1903 William Waldorf Astor acquired the Castle and created beautiful gardens. He filled the Castle with wonderful furniture, paintings and tapestries which visitors can see today. Children will enjoy the costumed figure exhibition of Henry VIII and his six wives, and the Anne Boleyn Books of Hours. The spectacular award winning gardens include topiary, Italian and Tudor Gardens, a 110 metre herbaceous border and a lake. Families will enjoy the yew maze (open May-Oct), the splashing water maze (open April-Oct), the Miniature Model Houses Exhibition and the Adventure Playground.
visitor comments: Excellent children's playground (bring a change of clothes for the water maze!) Somewhere to spend the whole day.
1 Mar-30 Nov daily, Castle: 12.00-18.00. Gardens: 11.00-18.00. Winter months 11.00-

Kent

16.00
Last Admission: 60mins before closing
Castle & Gardens: A£7.80 C(5-16)£4.20 Under 5's £Free Family Ticket (A2+C2)£19.80 OAPs£6.60. Gardens only: A£6.10 C(5-16)£4.00 Under 5's £Free Family Ticket (A2+C2)£16.20 OAPs£5.20. Group rates 15+ available on request

↓*special events*

▶ **Easter Weekend**
21/4/00-24/4/00
Easter egg trail and local bands in the garden

▶ **May Day Music and Dance**
29/4/00-1/5/00
A weekend of traditional music and dance featuring local Morris dancers

▶ **Merrie England Weekend**
27/5/00-29/5/00
A wekend of archery, medieval music and dance

▶ **Rose Festival**
24/6/00-25/6/00
Featuring specialist nurseries and tours of the garden

▶ **Longbow Warfare**
16/7/00-3/9/00
Demonstrations of the Longbow as a military weapon on the following dates: 16, 23 & 30 July, 27 & 28 Aug, 2 & 3 Sept

▶ **Jousting Tournaments**
22/7/00-26/8/00
Presented by the Knights of Royal England on the following dates in July 22 & 29, & Aug 5, 6, 12, 13, 19, 20 & 26

▶ **Patchwork and Quilting Exhibition**
8/9/00-10/9/00
A magnificent display of patchwork quilts

Ightham Mote

Mote Road Ivy Hatch Sevenoaks Kent TN15 0NT
[6m E of Sevenoaks off A25 and 2.5m S of Ightham off A227. BR: Borough Green / Wrotham / Hildenborough / Sevenoaks]
Tel: 01732 811145 Fax: 01732 811029

Explore 650 years of history in one house! Cross the walled moat and enter a medieval and Tudor manor house with rooms dating from as early as the 1340's. See the courtyard, the Great Hall and the Robinson Library laid out as seen in a 1960 edition of Homes and Gardens magazine. Enjoy the newly restored Tudor chapel, drawing room and Billiards room and visit the housekeeper's room and butler's pantry. Learn in a major exhibition about the methods and materials used in the restoration project - the largest of its kind ever undertaken by the National Trust. Enjoy extensive grounds - gardens, lakes, and woodland and estate walks.

28 Mar-31 Oct Mon, Wed-Fri, Sun, Bank Hol Mon & Good Fri 11.00-17.30. Car Park: All year dawn-dusk for estate walks
Last Admission: 16.30
A£5.00 C£2.50 Family Ticket £12.50. Group rates 15+ £4.00 - no reduction Sun & Bank Hol

↓*special events*

▶ **Flora and Fauna**
6/5/00-6/5/00
A guided walk of the garden. Tickets £6.00, begins at 14.30

▶ **Romeo and Juliet**
17/6/00-17/6/00
Open air theatre at 18.30. Tickets £9.00

▶ **Music at the Mote**
1/7/00-1/7/00
Commences at 19.30. Music and songs from the West End Shows. Tickets £16.00

▶ **The Emperor's New Clothes**
6/8/00-6/8/00
Open air theatre for families. Starts at 18.30, A£8.00 C£4.00

▶ **Family Fun Day with Treasure Hunt**
24/8/00-24/8/00
Normal opening times and prices

Ladham House

Ladham Road Goudhurst Cranbrook Kent TN17 1DB
[from Goudhurst, up hill past church on right. Keep on rd for 0.25m until you reach Chequers Inn on left, turn left - signpost B2079 to Horsmonden and Marden. Over small crossroads then first right signposted Blantyre House and Curtisden Green. Ladham House is on left with tall black wrought Iron gates]
Tel: 01580 211203/212674 Fax: 01580 212596

10 acres of rolling lawns, fine specimen trees, rhododendrons, azaleas, camellias, shrubs and magnolias. Newly planted arboretum. Spectacular twin mixed borders. Fountain garden and bog garden. Fine view. Reserected Old Rock garden with waterfall. Dogs on leads allowed.

House: by appointment only for private functions. Garden: All year daily (please ring owner first before making journey). Also open 2 & 16 May & 4 Oct for National Gardens Scheme 13.30-17.30 with tea & refreshments supplied on these days only
Gardens: A£2.50 C(under 12)£Free. Guided Tours: A£3.00

Leeds Castle
Maidstone Kent ME17 1PL
[4m at J8 of M20 A20]
Tel: 01622 765400 Fax: 01622 735616
www.leeds-castle.co.uk
The site of a manor of the Saxon royal family in the 9th century, Leeds Castle was described by Lord Conway as 'the loveliest Castle in the world.' Built on two islands in the middle of a lake and set in 500 acres of landscaped parkland, it was converted into a royal palace by Henry VIII and left to the nation by its last private owner, Olive, Lady Baillie, in 1975. The Lady Baillie Garden, opened in Spring 1999, is in memory of someone who spent so much of her life restoring the Castle and filling it with treasures. Other attractions include the Woodland Walk and Duckery, a unique Dog Collar Museum, exotic bird Aviary, Maze and Underground Grotto, Victorian Greenhouses, shops and restaurants. Full programme of special events.
visitor comments: A lovely castle - fantastic maze and beautiful gardens with small lakes and rivers.
All year, Mar-Oct daily Park & Gardens: 10.00-17.00, Castle: 11.00-17.30. Nov-Feb daily, Park: 10.00-15.00, Castle: 10.15-15.30 Closed 25 Dec, 24 June and 1 July
Last Admission: Stated closing times
Castle & Park: A£9.50 C(5-15)£6.00 Family Ticket £26.00 OAPs&Students£7.50. Park & Gardens: A£7.50 C(5-15)£4.50 Family Ticket £21.00 OAPs&Students£6.00
↓*special events*
▶ **Greenhouse Weekend**
8/4/00-9/4/00
Top advice from the Castle's professional plantsmen
▶ **Celebration of Easter**
22/4/00-24/4/00
Fun for the young and not-so-young, face painting, Punch and Judy, Circus Workshops and plenty of refreshments
▶ **Woodland Walk's Festival of English Food and Wine**
13/5/00-14/5/00
Samplings, talks, celebrity cooks, Morris Dancing and a jazz band add to the colourful atmosphere
▶ **Half Term Amazing Mazes**
27/5/00-4/6/00
Mazes of all shapes and sizes will be appearing throughout the Castle's beautiful grounds
▶ **Leeds Castle Open Air Concerts**
24/6/00-1/7/00
Carl Davis will conduct the Royal Liverpool Philharmonic Orchestra. Gates open at 16.00 - entertainment from 17.30. Concert begins at 20.00. Advance tickets sales only from the box office from 1 Feb Tel: 01622 880008. Book early to avoid disappointment
▶ **Kent Children's Promenade Concert**
28/6/00-28/6/00
A wonderful event by children for children. Children must be accompanied by an adult, and adults must be accompanied by a child! Gates open at 16.30. Concert commences at 18.00-19.30
▶ **Festival of Summer Floral Art**
20/7/00-23/7/00
A riot of colour and scent will enhance the splendid Castle rooms
▶ **Great Leeds Castle Balloon and Vintage Car Weekend**
9/9/00-10/9/00
With up to 30 hot air balloons, Tiger Moth displays, a cavalcade of vintage cars, veteran bicycles, Champagne and much more, there is plenty for all
▶ **Autumn Gold - A Festival of Flowers and Produce**
18/10/00-22/10/00
The Castle's magnificent interior is filled with exotic flower displays and presentations of produce from the Garden of England.
▶ **Half Term Fun - Halloween Week**
23/10/00-27/10/00
Children can learn all about the traditions of Halloween.
▶ **Grand Firework Spectacular**
4/11/00-4/11/00
Gates open at 17.00, extra entertainment from 17.30, with the display scheduled for 19.30. Call for further details after 1 Oct
▶ **Christmas at the Castle**
10/12/00-24/12/00
During December the Castle is traditionally decorated with trees, garlands and swags, lunchtime carols. Dates to be confirmed

Penshurst Place and Gardens
Penshurst Tonbridge Kent TN11 8DG
[BR: Tonbridge]
Tel: 01892 870307 Fax: 01892 870866
www.penshurstplace.com
The original manor house was built by Sir John de Pulteney between 1340 and 1345 and is

perfectly preserved. Successive owners enlarged it during the 15th, 16th and 17th centuries, and the great variety of architectural styles creates an elaborate and dramatic backdrop for the extensive collections of English, French and Italian furniture, tapestries and paintings.
Weekends only from 4 March. Daily from 1 April-31 Oct. Grounds: 10.30-18.00 House: 12.00-17.00 Shop and Plant Centre: 10.30-18.00 Last Admission: 17.00
House & Grounds: A£6.00 C(5-16)£4.00 Family Ticket £16.00 OAPs&Students&UB40£5.50 Adult Party (20+)£5.30. Grounds only: A£4.50 C(5-16)£3.50 Family Ticket £13.00 OAPs&Students&UB40£4.00. Garden Season Ticket £22.00. Pre-booked Guided House Tours: A£6.00 C(5-16)£3.20, Garden Tours: A£6.50 C(5-16)£4.00

↓*special events*

▶ **ARMADA!**
1/4/00-2/4/00
Penshurst Place in 1588

▶ **Easter at Penshurst**
23/4/00-24/4/00
An activity trail and tractor trailer rides

▶ **Craft Fair**
29/4/00-1/5/00
Leading showcase for crafts in the South East

▶ **Treasure Island**
14/5/00-13/8/00
Mrs Humphreys Productions in the Stage Garden held on May 14 and Aug 13 only

▶ **Classic Car Show**
28/5/00-29/5/00
Hundreds of classic cars on display. Open 10.00-17.00. A£5.00 C(5-16)£1.00 OAPs£4.00

▶ **Wind in the Willows**
18/6/00-18/6/00
Mrs Humphreys Productions in the Stage Garden

▶ **Sunday Falconry Displays**
2/7/00-27/8/00
July 2, 9, 16, 23, 20, Aug 6, 13, 20, 27 only. Static and flying displays of magnificent birds of prey

▶ **Jazz in the Barons Hall**
11/8/00-11/8/00
Black Cat jazz with Tina May

▶ **A Midsummer Night's Dream**
20/8/00-20/8/00
Theatre Set-up presents this Shakespearean classic in the Barons Hall

▶ **Weald of Kent Craft Show**
8/9/00-10/9/00
The leading craft showcase in the South East

▶ **Half-term Fun**
23/10/00-27/10/00
Activity trail and house quiz to amuse younger visitors

Quebec House
Quebec Square Westerham Kent TN16 1TD
[off A25]
Tel: 01892 890651 Fax: 01892 890110
Westerham was the birthplace of General Wolfe who spent his childhood in the multi-gabled, square brick house now renamed Quebec House. The house probably dates from the 16th Century but was extended and altered in th 17th Century. It contains a Wolfe museum and an exhibition on Wolfe and the Quebec campaign. The fax number given is for the National Trust Regional Office.
28 Mar-31 Oct Sun & Tue only 14.00-18.00 Last Admission: 17.30
A£2.50 C£1.25. Group rates £1.80

↓*special events*

▶ **The Regency Duo - Mozart and Haydn**
25/5/00-25/5/00
Held at 15.00 (£10.00) and 19.30 (£12.00)

▶ **The English Bach**
12/10/00-12/10/00
Presented by Oliver Davies at 15.00 (£10.00) and 19.30 (£12.00)

Quex House and Gardens, Powell-Cotton Museum
Quex Park Birchington Kent CT7 0BH
[in Birchington 0.5m S of Birchington Square, SW of Margate, 13m E of Canterbury. Signposted. BR: Birchington. Plenty of on site parking.]
Tel: 01843 842168 Fax: 01843 846661
Quex House was built as a Regency gentleman's Country residence and grew to become the Victorian mansion we see today. Still home to Powell-Cotton family, it has a mellow atmosphere, many of the rooms appearing much as they did during Major Powell-Cotton's lifetime and complimented by flowers from the walled gardens at Quex. There are some splendid pieces of oriental and period furniture, fine rugs and porcelain, as well as family portraits and an extensive collection of silver, clocks and memorabilia. The polished mahogany cases displaying Major Powell-

Cotton's treasures give Quex Museum its authentic quality, so often lacking in modern visitor attractions. There are eight galleries in all - three of them built by the Major himself - containing an amazing variety of items from the animal dioramas to striking tribal art, weapons, carvings and costumes, as well as valuable collections of European and Chinese porcelain and local archaeology. What began as one man's museum has been painstakingly cared for and added to by members of the Powell-Cotton family and now offers visitors an exciting insight into discoveries of a great Victorian Explorer. Member of the Historic Houses Association.

Gardens, Museum & Restaurant: Mar, Nov-Dec Sun only 11.00-17.00, Apr-Oct Tue-Thur, Sun & Bank Hol 11.00-18.00, Quex House 14.30-18.00

Last Admission: 17.00

Summer: A£3.50 C&OAPs £2.80. Winter: A£2.50 C&OAPs£1.80

Squerryes Court

Squerryes Westerham Kent TN16 1SJ

[J5 or J6 M52 0.5m W of Westerham, signposted from A25. Plenty of on site parking.]

Tel: 01959 562345/563118 Fax: 01959 565949

This beautiful 1681 manor house, has been the family home of the Wardes since 1731. It contains many fine Italian, 17th and 18th century Dutch and English pictures, as well as furniture, porcelain and tapestries. Also featured are items related to General James Wolfe of Quebec, a lovely 18th Century landscaped garden, a lake, a dovecot and a restored formal garden. Please note ONLY the three downstairs rooms pf the house are suitable for wheelchairs, and pushchairs access is for the garden only. Dogs are allowed on a lead in the garden only. Member of the Historic Houses Association.

1 Apr-30 Sept Wed, Sat, Sun & Bank Hol Mon, Garden: 12.00-17.30. House: 13.30-17.30. Pre-booked groups of 20+ welcome any day

Last Admission: 17.00

House & Grounds: A£4.20 C£2.50 OAPs£3.80

Grounds: A£2.50 C£1.50 OAPs£2.20

discount offer: Two For The Price Of One. Valid Until 1 Apr-30 Sept 2000

↓*special events*

▶ **National Garden Scheme**

8/7/00-9/7/00

Times: Grounds 12.00 House13.30-17.30. Last entry 17.00

▶ **Festival Of Flowers 2000**

14/7/00-16/7/00

Presented by Sevenoaks Flower Club. Donations to Cancer Research Campaign. Time: 11.00-17.30

Upnor Castle

High Street Upper Upnor Rochester Kent ME2 4XG

[on unclassified road off A228. Car parking is central in the Village and visitors should then walk the 200 yards following the sign to the Castle entrance overlooking the river]

Tel: 01634 827980

Upnor Castle, is set in the village of Upper Upnor on the banks of the river Medway. This attractive turreted Castle is backed by rolling wooded hills and fronted by a water battery jutting out into the river Medway. It survives as an impressive reminder of stirring and troubled times. Built in the year 1559 as a gun fort on the orders of Queen Elizabeth I to defend warships at anchor in the reaches of the Medway and Chatham Dockyard, Upnor saw action when in 1667 the Dutch, under the command of Admiral de Ruyter, sailed into the river to wreak havoc among the British fleet. Soon after this the Castle was converted into a gunpowder store (Magazine) and at one time it stored more powder than the Tower of London. If you like to sketch, draw or paint, Upnor Castle is for you, whether it be the buildings or the shore line, river birds, boats or trees.

Apr 1-Sept 30 daily 10.00-18.00. For other times call the Seasonal Custodian 01634 718742 or central office out of season 01634 827980

Last Admission: 17.30

A£3.50 C£2.50 Concessions£2.50 Family Ticket (A2+C2)£9.50

Walmer Castle

Kingsdown Road Walmer Deal Kent CT14 7LJ

[on coast S of Walmer on A258, J13 M20 or from M2 to Deal. Limited parking on site]

Tel: 01304 364288 Fax: 01304 364826

www.english-heritage.org.uk

Walmer Castle was built by Henry VIII, designed to withstand the mightiest bombardment. It is the official residence of the Lord Warden of the Cinque Ports, a post once held by the Duke of Wellington who died here. Wellington's famous boots can be seen. The castle is still used today by HM the Queen Mother in her official capacity as Warden of the Cinque Ports. A garden has been created to mark her 95th birthday.

1 Apr-30 Sept daily 10.00-18.00, 1 Oct-31 Oct daily 10.00-17.00, 1 Nov-31 Dec Wed-Sun 10.00-16.00. Closed 24-26 Dec. Closed Jan & Feb 2001. 1 Mar-31 Mar Wed-Sun 10.00-16.00. Closed when Lord Warden is in residence

A£4.50 C£2.30 Concessions£3.40 Personal

stereo tour included in admission price, also available for the partially sighted, those with learning difficulties, and in French & German. RHS members free

↓*special events*

▶ **Life Below Stairs**
15/4/00-28/8/00
Servant's gossip and tales, 15-24 Apr, 17/18 June, 29/30 July & 27/28 Aug

▶ **Garden Tours**
16/4/00-26/8/00
A look at the history and development of the Lord Warden's Gardens on 16 Apr, 7 May, 18 June, 13 & 26 Aug

▶ **Garden Tour**
21/4/00-21/4/00
Spring flowers at Walmer

▶ **Easter Egg Hunt**
22/4/00-22/4/00
Egg Hunt for C(under 5) from 13.00-14.00, with an Easter Trail competition from 13.00-16.00 for C(5+)

▶ **Garden Tour**
24/4/00-24/4/00
See entry for 21 April

▶ **Regency Murder Mystery**
30/4/00-1/5/00
A murder to solve, plots, sword fights and tight breeches!

▶ **Fantastical Fairy Tales!**
20/5/00-21/5/00
21st century versions of your favourite fairy tales, as told by the villainous Grimey Brothers!

▶ **Flower Festival**
23/6/00-25/6/00
Enjoy beautiful blooms and wonderful arrays of period flower arrangements. Not to be missed!

▶ **Garden Tour**
25/6/00-25/6/00
The Herbacous border in summer

▶ **More Fairy Tales...**
2/7/00-2/7/00
...from the Enchanted Garden Back by popular demand! Prepare yourself for a new magical adventure in the enchanted gardens...from the Enchanted Garden Back by popular demand! Prepare yourself for a new magical adventure in the enchanted gardens, on 28/ 29 May, 4, 11, June, 2, 9 July, 3, & 10 Sept

▶ **The Roaring Twenties!**
22/7/00-23/7/00
Enjoy a Brideshead Revisited-style garden party. Play croquet, listen to the gramophone, even learn to Fox-trot!

▶ **Garden Tour**
30/7/00-30/7/00
See entry for 25 June

▶ **The Wednesday Tour**
2/8/00-2/8/00
Looking at the history and development of the gardens

Living History Museums

Canterbury Roman Museum
Butchery Lane Longmarket Canterbury Kent CT1 2RA
[off A2 London / Dover road in Canterbury centre signposted]
Tel: 01227 785575 Fax: 01227 455047
Underground, at the level of the Roman town, you will find this famous Roman house with its mosaic floors. Following the discoveries of archaeologists, you walk through a fascinating reconstruction of Roman buildings, including a market place with stallholders wares of the period. Displays reveal a wealth of objects rescued by excavations. In the 'touch the past' area you can handle artefacts and take part in archaeological discovery.
All year Mon-Sat 10.00-17.00, Sun June-Oct 13.30-17.00. Closed Good Fri & Christmas period
Last Admission: 16.00
A£2.30 C(5-18)£1.15 Family Ticket £5.15 OAPs& Students£1.50. Group rates10+ 10% discount. Educational Ticket £0.35. Residents Ticket £0.50

Canterbury Tales
St. Margaret's Street Canterbury Kent CT1 2TG
[main routes into Canterbury are M2/A2. Located just off the pedestrianised High Street]
Tel: 01227 454888 Fax: 01227 765584
www.heritageattractions.co.uk/
Join us in 2000 as we celebrate 600 years of Chaucer's Canterbury Tales. Step back in time to join Chaucer's famous band of pilgrims on their journey to the shrine of St Thomas Becket in Canterbury Cathedral. Hear their tales of love, greed, chivalry and intrigue and experience life in the 14th century, complete with authentic sights, sounds and smells. Foreign language commentaries are available.
visitor comments: Good layout. Interesting and fun for all ages. Headphones available in 5 languages.
All year Mar, June, Sept & Oct daily 09.30-17.30, July-Aug daily 09.00-17.30, Nov-Feb Sun-Fri 10.00-16.30, Sat 09.30-17.30.
A£5.50 C(5-16)£4.60 Family Ticket £17.50 OAPs&Students£4.60
discount offer: One Child Free With Each Full Paying Adult

Maritime

World Naval Base, Chatham
Chatham Kent ME4 4TZ
[J3 M2 or from J6 M20 follow signs for Chatham and then Brown Anchor. BR: Chatham]
Tel: 01634 823800 Fax: 01634 823801
www.worldnavalbase.org.uk
This 80 acre site contains 48 ancient monuments and a range of other exhibits including "Wooden Walls" where visitors can walk through the dockyard of 1758 with William Crokwell, a new apprentice as he discovers the trades and skills required to construct Valiant, a 74 gun ship-o-the-line. "Lifeboat!" tells the story of the RNLI, fifteen lifeboats are on display with two open to the public. New for this year: "Battle Ships": HMS Cavalier - the last surviving British WWII destroyer. Once hailed as 'the fastest ship in the Fleet' now saved for the nation. HMS Ocelot - the last 'O' Class submarine built at Chatham for the Royal Navy and HMS Gannett - the last Victorian Sloop. A fine example of naval tradition from when The British Empire was at its peak.
29 Mar-31 Oct daily 10.00-18.00, Feb, Mar & Nov only Wed, Sat & Sun 10.00-16.00
Last Admission: 60mins before closing
A£8.50 C(5-16)£5.50 Family Ticket (A2+C2)£22.50

Military & Defence Museums

Royal Engineers Museum
Prince Arthur Road Gillingham Kent ME4 4UG
[off B2004]
Tel: 01634 406397 Fax: 01634 822371
The prize-winning museum tells the story of Britain's soldier engineers - the Sappers - and their work around the world in peace and war from 1066 to the present day. It is a treasure trove of the unexpected ranging from Wellington's battlemap of Waterloo to a Harrier Jump jet. The magnificent medal displays include 24 Victoria crosses and the regalia of Field Marshal Lord Kitchener. Something for everyone.
All year Mon-Thur 10.00-17.00, Sat-Sun 11.30-17.00, Bank Hol Mon 11.30-17.00. Closed Good Fri, 25-26 Dec & 1 Jan
A£3.50 C&OAPs&UB40s£2.00 Family Ticket £9.00. Guided Tour £5.00. Group rate 15+ 30% discount
discount offer: One Child Free With One Full Paying Adult

↓*special events*
▸ **The Anglo-Boer War**
2/10/99-2/5/02

Mills - Water & Wind

Crabble Corn Mill
Lower Road River Dover Kent CT17 0UY
[off A256 between Dover / Whitfield on A2]
Tel: 01304 823292 Fax: 01304 826040
www.invmed.demon.co.uk
Visit this beautifully restored Georgian watermill, built 1812. Now fully working, producing traditionally stoneground wholemeal flour from Kentish organic wheat (organic flour on sale). Tour the whole mill, see regular demonstrations of it working. Cafe serves 'Kentish Fare' local produce, including home-baking with mill's flour. Gallery with exhibitions of local artists. Riverside gardens being developed.
1 April-30 Sept daily 11.00-17.00. Winter opening Sundays only 11.00-17.00. Closed 25 Dec-31 Jan. Pre-booked tours any day or evening
A£2.00 C£1.00 Family Ticket £5.00 OAPs£1.50
discount offer: 50p Off Adult Ticket or £1.00 Off Family Ticket

Places of Worship

Canterbury Cathedral
Cathedral House The Precincts Canterbury Kent CT1 2EH
[in Canterbury town centre. Parking is not permitted within The Precincts except for a certain very limited provision for disabled drivers, by prior arrangement]
Tel: 01227 762862 Fax: 01227 865222
Permits for individual, personal photography in the Cathedral can be obtained at the Welcome Centre of the Cathedral Gift Stall. Audio-visual presentation lasts 14mins and runs regularly throughout the day in the Theodore (at the North-West corner of the Great Cloister) from mid February to 31 October. Ancient ghosts tread the flagstones: Archbishop Simon Sudbury, killed in 1381 by Wat Tyler is supposed to haunt the tower named after him for the doubtful reason that his head is buried in Suffolk and his torso within the walls of Canterbury. Another ghost is that of an unknown monk seen by several visitors in the last few years. When a member of the choir school attached to the cathedral

was walking round the cloisters one evening and saw the figure of the man approaching her, silently with his head bowed in contemplation or prayer. She merely glanced at him, thinking he was a member of the religious orders who carry out pilgrimage to the holy spot, and passed by. As the figure drew level, she suddenly felt extremely cold and turning to see the monk suddenly vanish.

General Visiting: Mon-Sat Easter-30 Sept 08.45-19.00, 1 Oct-Easter 08.45-17.00. The Crypt all year daily 10.00-16.30. Sun all year 12.30-14.30, Crypt 16.30-17.30. Guided Tours: Mon-Sat call for full details. For information on Church Services call above number

Last Admission: 30mins before closing

A£3.00 C&Concessions £2.00 C(0-4)£Free. Guided Tours: A£3.00 OAPs&Students£2.00 Accompanied C£1.20 Groups upto 9 £30.00 School Groups each £0.50. Audio Visual: A£1.00 OAPs&Students£0.70 Accompanied C£0.50 School Groups each £0.50. Audio Tours: A&OAPs£Students£2.70 Accompanied C&Students Groups 10+ £1.70 School Groups each £1.00. Toilets £0.20

Railways

Kent and East Sussex Steam Railway

Tenterden Town Station Tenterden Kent TN30 6HE

[on the A28 main road between Ashford and Hastings]

Tel: 01580 765155

There are engines and carriages dating from Victorian times waiting to take you for a ride through 7 miles of beautiful countryside on this charming rural railway. Refreshment Rooms, Video Theatre, Letterpress Printworks, Gift Shop, Museum, Play Area, Luxury Dining Cars, Dinners, Lunches and Teas, booking essential.

visitor comments: Enjoyable day for 2-100 year olds! A rather different way to enjoy a family roast Sunday Lunch

14-22 Feb, Mar Sun only, Apr-Oct weekends & school hol, June & Sept daily except Mon & Fri, July & Aug daily, Dec Santa Specials at weekends, 10.30-16.20

Last Admission: 16.20

A£6.50 C£3.25 Family Ticket £17.50 Concessions £5.60 School Parties £4.00 Group Rates £5.60

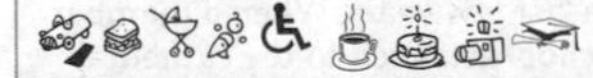

Romney Hythe and Dymchurch Railway

New Romney Station Littlestone Road New Romney Kent TN28 8PL

[J11 M20 signposted, Hythe station, other stations on A259. Plenty parking places]

Tel: 01797 362353/363256 Fax: 01797 363591

www.rhdr.demon.co.uk

The world's smallest public railway has its headquarters here. The concept of two enthusiasts coincided with Southern Railway's plans for expansion, and so the thirteen-and-a-half mile stretch of 15 inch gauge railway came into being, running from Hythe through New Romney and Dymchurch to Dungeness Lighthouse. Picnic areas available (indoor and outdoor). Visit can be anything from 1 hour to a full day.

visitor comments: Not to be missed. Stations are well kept, clean and tidy. A excellent train journey, with stops for tea.

Regular services Easter-Sept daily also weekends in Mar & Oct and October half-term daily

Fares depend on length of journey, C£half-price, discount for pre-booked parties of 15+. OAP concessions available

discount offer: One Adult or Child Travels Free with One Adult Paying Full Rate All Stations Return Ticket. Valid For One Person Per Coupon, Per Day. Not Valid Special Events or Bank Holidays

Theme & Adventure Parks

Dreamland Fun Park

Marine Terrace Margate Kent CT9 1XG

[off the M2, A28 to Margate]

Tel: 01843 227011 Fax: 01843 298667

The South East's largest seaside amusement park. A mix of traditional and new family attractions opposite Margate's sandy beach.

1998: Easter-late Oct daily 10.00-18.00, 10.00-22.00 during peak season. Opening Times under review

1998: A£12.00 C£8.00. Prices under review
discount offer: One Child Wristband Free With Every Full Paying Adult Wristband

White Cliffs Experience
Market Square Dover Kent CT16 1PB
[signposted on entry to Dover town centre for vehicles and from BR]
Tel: 01304 214566/210101 Fax: 01304 212057
www.dover.gov.uk/tourism/wce/wce-home.htm
Roman Encounters is an exciting hands-on experience where you can visit a Roman street, have a go at making a mosaic or building a Roman road. Enjoy a visit to our Magical Mechanical Theatre, our acclaimed 1940's Dover Street and Gromet's Challenge - our indoor playground for children. All this, plus a FREE visit to Dover Museum - where The Dover Bronze Age Boat, believed to be the world's oldest seagoing boat is now on display in its superb gallery setting.
visitor comments: Interesting presentation of historic facts for all ages.
All year 1 Apr-31 Oct daily 10.00-17.00, Nov-Mar 10.00-15.00
Last Admission: Apr-Oct: 17.00 Nov-Mar: 15.00
Full Visit: A£5.95 C(4-14)&UB40s£4.15 Family Ticket (A2+C2)£18.95 (up to 3 additional children)£3.50 OAPs&Students£4.80. Group discount: A£5.20 C(4-14)&UB40s£3.50 OAPs&Students£4.00. Travel Trade: A£4.20 C(4-14)&UB40s£3.15 OAPs&Students£3.70. School parties: UK children aged (5-18)£3.25 , Overseas (5-18)£3.60, One adult FREE per 10 children, additional adults same rate as children. Language Schools Students £3.60, One adult FREE per 10 students
discount offer: One Child Free With One Full Paying Adult

↓*special events*

► **Fascinating Food Quiz**
19/2/00-27/2/00

► **Be a Deteggtive**
12/4/00-25/4/00
Solve our puzzle going back 2000 years in our family quiz. On Apr 23 and 24, children will be rewarded with Easter eggs

► **Easter Card Workshop**
13/4/00-14/4/00
Children can make their own Easter card, we supply the materials

► **Pavement Picasso**
27/5/00-27/5/00
11.00-13.00, the theme is 2000 Years of History. Free to enter, all materials provided and prizes for all entrants

► **Commemorative Events**
27/5/00-1/6/00
For the 60th Anniversary of the Dunkirk Evacuation

► **Highlights of the Millennia Quiz**
27/5/00-4/6/00
A quiz to accompany the exhibition in Dover Museum

► **Roman Festival for Schools**
20/6/00-23/6/00
Children participate in a range of Roman related activities - mainly outdoors if dry. A visual spectacle!

Transport Museums

C M Booth Collection of Historic Vehicles
63-67 High Street Rolvenden Cranbrook Kent TN17 4LP
[based in Falstaff Antiques. On A28 6m from Cranbrook, 3m from Tenterden]
Tel: 01580 241234
The collection is made up of historic vehicles and other items of interest connected with transport. The main feature is the unique collection of three-wheel Morgan cars, dating from 1913. Also here is the only known Humber Tri-car of 1904; and items include a 1929 Morris van, a 1936 Bampton caravan, motorcycles and bicycles.
All year Mon-Sat 10.00-18.00
A£1.50 C£0.75

Tyrwhitt Drake Museum of Carriages
Mill Street Maidstone Kent ME15 6YE
[close to River Medway & Archbishops Palace well signposted.]
Tel: 01622 663006 Fax: 01622 682451
A wide array of horse-drawn carriages and

vehicles is displayed in these late-medieval stables, which are interesting in themselves. The exhibits include state, official and private carriages, and some are on loan from royal collections. Viewed as one of the finest collections in Europe

visitor comments: Amazing collection. Strong royal connection.

Mar-Oct daily 10.30-17.15, Nov-Feb 12.30-16.30. Closed 25-26 Dec

Last Admission: 45 mins before closing

A£1.50 C(0-5)£Free C&OAPs£1.00 Family Ticket £4.00 Disabled free - carer half-price.

Concession rates available telephone for details.

Wildlife & Safari Parks

Druidstone Wildlife Park

Honey Hill Blean Canterbury Kent CT2 9JR

[on the A290. Plenty of parking available on site]

Tel: 01227 765168 Fax: 01227 768860

A garden park with woodland walk, adventure playground and under 5's play area. Wallabies, deer, owls and parrots are among the animals and birds that make this park their home. New for 2000, squirrel monkeys.

April-end Oct daily 10.00-17.30. Nov 10.00-16.30

Last Admission: 16.45

A£3.50 C£2.50 OAPs£3.00

discount offer: Two For The price Of One. Valid Until 30 Nov 2000

Howletts Wild Animal Park

Bekesbourne Lane Bekesbourne Canterbury Kent CT4 5EL

[signposted off A2 3m S of Canterbury]

Tel: 0891 800 605 Info Line Fax: 01227 721853

www.howletts.co.uk

Howletts is one of John Aspinall's wild animal parks and has the world's largest breeding gorilla colony in captivity. It also has tigers, small cats, free-running deer and antelope, snow leopards, bison, ratel, the UK's most successful herd of breeding African elephants, and many endangered species of monkeys all housed in natural enclosures. Many new animals and enclosures for 1999.

visitor comments: Wonderful, friendly park with healthy, clean and content looking animals.

All year daily 10.00-17.00 or dusk in Winter. Closed 25 Dec

Last Admission: Summer 17.00 Winter 15.30

A£8.90 C(under 4's)£Free C(4-14)&OAPs£6.90 Family Ticket £26.00

discount offer: £2.00 Off Adult or Child Admission When Accompanied By A Full Paying Adult

Port Lympne Wild Animal Park

Aldington Road Lympne Hythe Kent CT21 4PD

[J11 M20. Park is 5mins away signposted from this juction]

Tel: 01303 264647 Fax: 01303 264944

John Aspinall's 300-acre wild animal park houses hundreds of rare animals: Black rhinos, Indian elephants, wolves, bison, black and snow leopards, Siberian and Indian tigers, gorillas and monkeys. The mansion designed by Sir Herbert Baker is surrounded by 15 acres of spectacular gardens. The Spencer Roberts mural room depicts over 300 animals and birds from South East Asia. Many new animals and enclosures for 1999.

visitor comments: Very clean. Take a picnic and enjoy the wonderful scenic views.

All year daily 10.00-17.00. Winter closing 15.30. Closed 25 Dec

Last Admission: Summer 17.00 Winter 15.30

A£8.90 C(under 4)£Free C(4-14)&OAPs£6.90 Family Ticket £26.00

Arts, Crafts & Textiles

Manchester City Art Galleries

Mosley Street Manchester Lancashire M2 3JL

[corner of Mosley St and Princess St near Manchester Town Hall]

Tel: 0161 234 1456 Fax: 0161 236 2880

www.u-net.com/set/mcag/cag.html

Manchester City Art Galleries, Mosley Street is a beautiful listed building, housing one of the most prestigious collections of fine and decorative arts in the country. City Art Galleries, Princess Street (just around the corner) is

renowned for its exciting and innovative programme of temporary exhibitions. The Princes Street Gallery will close in March 1998 and the Manchester City Art Gallery's multi-million pound expansion project gets underway this autumn. The extended and refurbished gallery will be of international importance, with world-class facilities, exhibitions and displays. The Gallery is closed until 2001, so that this transformation can take place. A full programme of events and activities continues at other venues in the service.
Manchester City Art Gallery is closed until 2001.
Last Admission: 17.15
Admission Free

Salford Museum and Art Gallery
Peel Park The Crescent Salford Lancashire M5 4WU
[A6 in front of Salford University to end of M602 signposted]
Tel: 0161 736 2649 Fax: 0161 745 9490
The Art Gallery houses the world's largest public collection of paintings and drawings by L.S. Lowry. There is also a gallery of Victorian art and a 20th century collection. In addition, the Art Gallery stages temporary exhibitions throughout the year. The Museum is home to Lark Hill Place, a reproduction Victorian Street with many shops and rooms.
All year Mon-Fri 10.00-16.45, Sat & Sun 13.00-17.00. Closed 25-26 Dec, 1 Jan, Good Fri & Easter Sat
Admission Free

Birds, Butterflies & Bees

WWT Martin Mere
Fish Lane Burscough Ormskirk Lancashire L40 0TA
[signposted from M61 / M58 / M6 off A59]
Tel: 01704 895181 Fax: 01704 892343
One of Britain's largest wetland sites where visitors can get really close to a variety of ducks, geese and swans including pink-footed geese, Bewick's, and Whooper swans from all over the world as well as two flocks of flamingos. Many birds will feed from your hand. Also featuring an adventure playground, exhibition gallery, craft area and educational centre. Free wheelchair loan, disabled toilets and braille notices.
All year daily Summer: 09.30-17.30. Winter: 09.30-16.00. Closed 25 Dec
A£4.75 C£2.75 Family Ticket £12.00 OAPs£3.75
discount offer: 20% Off Admission Prices (Excludes Family Tickets)

Forests & Woods

Sunnyhurst Wood and Visitor Centre
Sunnyhurst Wood Darwen Blackburn Lancashire *[off Earnsdale Road, Visitor Centre in Sunnyhurst Wood. Limited access for wheelchairs to both wood and Visitor Centre; access on Falcon Avenue]*
Tel: 01254 701545/55423
Sunnyhurst Wood is 85 acres of beautiful woodland set in a valley with a network of footpaths which lead onto the Moors and Darwen Tower. Information on walks, wildlife and local history at the Visitor Centre. Upstairs gallery is an exhibition venue for local artists.
Wood: All year 24 hours. Visitor Centre: Tue, Thur, Weekends 13.00-16.30. Closed 25-26 Dec & 1 Jan
Admission Free to Wood and Visitor Centre

Gardens & Horticulture

Williamson Park
Quernmore Road Lancaster Lancashire LA1 1UX
[follow Lancaster signs from J33 or J34 M6. Follow brown tourist signs from City]
Tel: 01524 33318 Fax: 01524 848338
The Tropical Butterfly House has exotic species of Butterflies flying free amidst it's beautiful plants and trees. Visit the Conservation Garden and explore the 'Mini Beasts' Cave, a shady world of insects and reptiles. Walk through the Bird enclosure, a garden aviary, home to many British bred foreign birds. Explore the Ashton Memorial, an Edwardian Folly and the Williamson Art Gallery on the second floor of the building. All these super attractions plus fifty six acres of beautiful parkland with lake and play area.
All year daily; Summer 10.00-17.00. Winter 10.00-16.00
Last Admission: 30mins before closing
A£2.95 C£1.50 Family Ticket £9.00 OAPs&Concessions£2.50. Group rates 10% discount. School parties £1.50 per head - A£Free

Heritage & Industrial

British Lawnmower Museum
106-114 Shakespeare Street Southport Lancashire PR8 5AJ

[off A565 or A570 or M6]
Tel: 01704 501336 Fax: 01704 500564
www.lawnmowerworld.co.uk/lmuseum
The award winning museum houses a private collection of over 200 exhibits of garden machinery. Built up over a period of 30 years, many of the machines were rescued from scrap yards and restored to pristine condition. A tribute to the garden machine industry over the last 150 years. Latest exhibis are Lawnmowers of the Rich & Famous; Princess Diana, Alan Tichmarsh, Venessa Feltz, garden machinery includes Atco Lawnmower from Prince Charles to Hilda Ogden Qualcast Panther also a pair of Nicholas Parson's secateurs. Designing fastest lawnmower in the World (100mph). The museum holds the complete set of Garden Machinery Patents dating from 1799 to 1900. This includes the original lawnmower made by Edwin Budding.
All year Mon-Sat 09.00-17.30
Last Admission: 17.30
A£1.00 C£0.50
discount offer: Two For The Price Of One

Historical

Rufford Old Hall
Liverpool Road Rufford Ormskirk Lancashire L40 1SG
[off A59]
Tel: 01704 821254 Fax: 01704 821254
There is a story that William Shakespeare performed here for the owner Sir Thomas Hesketh in the Great Hall of this, one of the finest 16th century buildings in Lancashire. The bard would have delighted in the magnificent hall, built in 1530, with its intricately carved movable wooden screen. The Carolean Wing, altered in 1821 features fine collections of 16th and 17th century oak furniture, arms, armour and tapestries.
Hall: Apr-Oct Sat-Wed 13.00-17.00. Garden & Shop: 12.00-17.30. Also open on Thur during School Hol call for details.
Last Admission: 16.30
A£3.80 C£1.90 Family Ticket £9.50, Garden only £2.00

Astley Hall
Astley Park Off Hall Gate Chorley Lancashire PR7 1NP
[J8 M61 off A565 Chorley - Southport road signposted]
Tel: 01257 515555 Fax: 01257 515556
www.astleyhall.fsnet.co.uk
A charming Tudor/Stuart building set in a beautiful parkland this lovely Hall retains a comfortable 'lived-in' atmosphere. There are pictures and pottery to see, as well as fine furniture and rare plasterwork ceilings.
Apr-Oct Tue-Sun 12.00-17.00. Nov-Mar Fri-Sun 12.00-16.00
Last Admission: 30mins before closing
A£2.90 Concessions£1.90 Family Ticket £6.50
discount offer: Two For The Price One

Leighton Hall
Leighton Hall Carnforth Lancashire LA5 9ST
[signposted from J35 M6 with A6 N of Carnforth]
Tel: 01524 734474 Fax: 01524 720357
A large collection of birds of prey can be seen, and flying displays are given at 15.30 each afternoon. Early Gillow furniture is displayed among other treasures in the fine interior of this neo-Gothic mansion. Member of the Historic Houses Association.
May-Sept Sun, Tue-Fri & Bank Hol Mon 14.00-17.00 Aug 11.30-17.00
Last Admission: 16.30
A£3.70 C£2.50 Family Ticket(A2+C3) £11.50
discount offer: Two For The Price Of One (Buy One £3.70 Admission, Get One Free). Not valid on Bank Holidays or Special Events

Turton Tower
Tower Drive Turton Bolton Lancashire BL7 0HG
[1.5m N off B6391]
Tel: 01204 852203 Fax: 01204 853759
Historic house incorporating a 15th century tower house and Elizabethan half-timbered buildings. Restored in the 19th century it features a major collection of mostly English carved and wood furniture and period rooms depicting Tudor, Stuart and Victorian eras. A product of the Renaissance, the house became associated with the Gothic Revival. The gardens have been restored in late Victorian style.
May-Sept Mon-Thur 10.00-12.00 & 13.00-17.00,

Sat-Sun 13.00-17.00. Apr Sat-Wed 14.00-17.00. Nov & Feb Sun 14.00-17.00. Mar & Oct Sat-Wed 13.00-16.00
A£1.00 C&OAPs£0.50 Family Ticket £2.75. Guided tour with supper / lunch
discount offer: Half Price Tea, Coffee and Cream Teas

On the Water

Wigan Pier
Wigan Pier Wallgate Wigan Lancashire WN3 4EU
Tel: 01942 323666 Fax: 01942 322031
Since Wigan Pier was opened by Her Majesty the Queen in 1986, over 4 million people have taken a step back in time to Victorian Lancashire and experienced one of the country's premier heritage attractions. Wigan Pier offers a lively mix of museum and theatre, with the past brought to life by the professional actors of the Wigan Pier Theatre Company. Exploring the past, visitors can visit the seaside of old, a strict Victorian School-lesson, go down the coal-mine, visit the music hall and the pub. A trip aboard a canal waterbus takes you to Trencherfield Mill, home of the world's biggest original mill steam engine - still in perfect working order! Along with a children's play area, Wigan Pier is a fantastic family day out.
All year Mon-Thur 10.00-17.00, Sat & Sun 11.00-17.00. Closed 25-26 Dec & Fri excluding Good Friday
Easter-Sept A£5.10 Family Ticket £14.50 Concessions£4.10. Oct-Apr A£4.60 Family Ticket £12.80 Concessions£3.40

Sealife Centres & Aquariums

Blackpool Sea Life Centre
Golden Mile Centre Promenade Blackpool Lancashire FY1 5AA
[Fleetwood Junction off M55, signposted to venue]
Tel: 01253 622445 Fax: 01253 751647
www.sealife.co.uk
Here at the Sea Life Centre you can take a journey underwater without actually getting wet. Marine life can be viewed at close quarters, and visitors can walk through the largest shark display in Europe. Talks and feeding demonstrations throughout the day. New for this year is the 'Lost City of Atlantis' the mythical city is back with our fantastic new feature exhibition.
All year daily. Winter: 10.00-16.30. Summer: 09.30-22.00. Closed 25 Dec
A£5.95 C(4-14)£4.95

Sporting History Museums

Manchester United Museum and Tour Centre
Sir Matt Busby Way Manchester Lancashire M16 0RA
[2m from city centre off A56]
Tel: 0161 877 4002 Fax: 0161 930 2902
Our NEW Museum was opened in April 1998, by the Legendary Pele. At a cost of £4million and spread over three floors, the Museum charts the History of the Club from 1878 to the present day through a mixture of traditional showcase displays, film footage as well as many 'Hands-on' activities.
All year daily 09.30-17.00. Match Day closing 2.5 hours before kickoff. Closed 25 Dec
Tour & Museum: A£7.50 C&OAPs£5.00 Family Ticket £20.00, Museum only: A£4.50 C&OAPs£3.00 Family Ticket £12.00

Theme & Adventure Parks

Blackpool Pleasure Beach
525 Promenade Ocean Boulevard Blackpool Lancashire FY4 1EZ
[M6 J32 then take M55, follow the brown tourist signs. Parking nearby and not so nearby... parking charged]
Tel: 0870 444 5566 Fax: 01253 407609
www.blackpoolpleasurebeach.co.uk
Rollercoaster capital of the world! More rollercoasters than any other amusement park, including the Pepsi Max Big One, the tallest, fastest rollercoaster in the world. Opening Spring 2000 is Valhalla, the biggest, most spectacular dark ride ever to be constructed - dare you ride the adventure? Over 145 rides and attractions for all the family. Beaver Creek Theme Park for the children. Spectacular shows including the Hot Ice Show, Mystique and award winning Eclipse.
15 Apr-5 Nov daily. Mar, Nov & Dec weekends only
Pay individually on rides or purchase discounted sheets of ride tickets or wristbands, also available for Beaver Creek Children's Park

Camelot Theme Park and Rare Breeds Farm

Park Hall Road Charnock Richard Chorley Lancashire PR7 5LP

[J27 N on M6, J28 S on M6, J8 M61]

Tel: 01257 453044/452100 Fax: 01257 452320

Camelot Theme Park combines the thrills of a modern theme park with the magic of the knights of Arthurian legend. Daily Jousting Tournaments in the arena can be enjoyed from the undercover seating for 2,000 people and NEW additions include 'Castle Camelot', a family indoor entertainment centre which will be open all year round and will include the world's first interactive attraction and a soft play area. There will also be a 200 seat theatre for a new Sooty Show and a new Food Court offering High Street brands.

visitor comments: The jousting displays are excellent. Helpful, friendly staff. Recommended for younger children.

9 Apr-29 Oct 10.00-17.00, may vary in the with some late night events, please call the 24hr info line on 01257 452100

A&C£8.99 OAPs£6.99 Family Ticket (2A+2C) £32.00. Children under 1 metre in height £Free. Group rates for 12+ available

discount offer: One Child Free When Accompanied By Two Full Paying Adults At £8.99. Valid 9/4-29/10/2000. Not Valid Bank Hol Weekends

Frontierland - Western Theme Park

The Promenade Marine Road West Morecambe Lancashire LA4 4DG

[J34 M6 Northbound of J35 M6 Southbound, 5 mins Morecambe station.]

Tel: 01524 410024 Fax: 01524 831399

One of the most popular tourist attractions in the North West, with over 1.3 million visitors a year. Situated directly on the Promenade, Frontierland is a western style theme park which offers over 40 rides and attractions ranging from the Morecambe Bay Polo Tower, a unique ride which ascends to 160ft with stunning views of the Lakeland Hills, to the Texas Tornado, a wooden rollercoaster. There are rides and attractions especially for young children. There is also live entertainment during the summer season. A day pass gives you unlimited use of the rides and attractions.

Apr: 4-19, 25 & 26 daily. May: 2-4 & 23-31 daily, 9-17 Fri & Sat only. June: 3-28 Wed-Sun. 1 July-31 Aug daily. Sept: 1-6 daily, 12-27 Fri & Sat only. Oct: 3-18 Fri & Sat only, 24-31 daily. Hours: 10.00-17.00

High Season Day: A£6.95 C(under 1.25m)£4.95 Family Ticket(4 people)£20.00

discount offer: Two For The Price Of One

Granada Studios

Water Street Manchester Lancashire M60 9EA

[0.5 m from the end of the M602, brown tourist signs on all major routes into the City]

Tel: 0161 832 4999 Fax: 0161 834 3684

Enter the world of television at Granada Studios in the heart of the City Centre. Only here can you walk down Coronation Street, Downing Street and Baker Street in just one day. See the spectacular Sooty Show called Sooty Heights, based on the new TV programme, then take part in a comedy debate in the House of Commons.

****This attraction closes on 30 Dec 99 for redevelopment and will re-open between Spring and Summer 2000. Check the info line for the latest information. Until closure opening times are: All year daily Summer: 09.45-19.00. Winter: 09.45-17.30, 09.45-18.30. Weekends & Bank Hol. Closed Mon & Tue first half of Feb, Mar & Dec except 2 & 29 Dec. Closed Mon May-Sept except Bank Hol. Closed 19-25 Dec. Open 1 & 2 Jan and weekends only*

Last Admission: Summer 16.00 Winter 13.00 Bank Hol 16.00

Prices until closure on 30 Dec 99: A£14.99 C(5-11)&OAPs£9.99 C(0-5)£Free. Group rates 12+ on application. Upon re-opening there will be a new price structure.

discount offer: Two For The Price Of One. Adult Ticket Must Be Purchased. ref: MISC/BOGOF. Please check the info line for year 2000 opening dates & times.

Haigh Hall and Country Park

Haigh Wigan Greater Manchester Lancashire WN2 1PE

[J27 M6 or J6 M61, follow brown and white tourist signs. Plenty of car parking on site]

Tel: 01942 832895 Fax: 01942 831081

A great day out doesn't cost a fortune at Haigh. It's FREE admission and pay as you go; bouncy castle, ladybird ride, model village, crazy golf, miniature railway, craft gallery and lots more. Special events include craft fairs, galas, motor show and lots of free entertainment.

visitor comments: Great place for kids. Good, but small craft gallery. Lots of extra activities for children.

All year daily dawn-dusk. Closed Christmas Hol

Admission Free. Car Park: £0.80

Wax Works

Louis Tussauds Waxworks
87/89 Central Promenade Blackpool
Lancashire FY1 5AA
[at the end of M55 on the Central Promenade]
Tel: 01253 625953 Fax: 01253 621611
Displays of wax models and tableaux; Grand Hall with models of Royal Family, Politicians, Film Stars, famous Artists and Authors; Chamber of Horrors; Anatomy Exhibition (adults only/optional charge). New for this year in the extended Chamber of Horrors you can see the effigies of infamous murderers and serial killers.
All year daily Summer: 10.00-19.00, during Blackpool Illuminations: 10.00-10.00, Winter: 10.00-17.00
A£3.50 C(0-5)£Free C(5-12)£1.80 Family Ticket (A2+C2)£10.00 OAPs£2.80
discount offer: One Child Free With Two Full Paying Adults (excludes the Anatomy Exhibition)

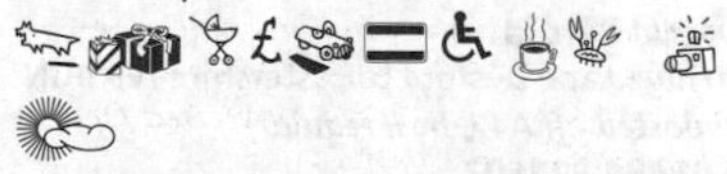

Animal Attractions

Farmworld
Stoughton Farm Park Gartree Road Oadby
Leicestershire LE2 2FB
[signposted off A6 / A47]
Tel: 0116 271 0355 Fax: 0116 271 3211
www.farmworld-stoughton.co.uk
Farmworld is a feast of fun and surprises for all the family. Children will enjoy the Children's Farmyard and the playground, while parents might appreciate the Edwardian Ale-House and working demonstrations. Also Shire horse and cart rides, lakeside and woodland walks, nature trails, collection of rare farm animals, and a toy tractor park with 'real' play-on tractors.
visitor comments: Hard work pushing a buggy. Bottle feeding lambs was great. Play area suited for range of ages.
Easter-Sept daily 10.00-17.00
Last Admission: 17.00
A£2.50 C&OAPs£2.00. Groups rates please call for details. Schools welcome
discount offer: One Child Free With Two Full Paying Adults

Halstead House Farm and Nature Trail
Oakham Road Tilton-on-the-Hill Leicestershire LE7 9DJ*[]*
Tel: 0116 259 7239
Bring the family to our farm in high East Leicestershire. Farm animals, nature trail, play and picnic areas (indoors and outdoors), tea room, garden, trailer rides, windmill museum, shop. Groups welcome.
visitor comments: A very friendly, welcoming place. Small friendly farm trail and nature trail. Excellent tea room with a relaxing garden.
Easter-end Sept Tue-Sun 10.00-17.30. Open Bank Hol Mon
A£3.00 C£2.00
discount offer: One Child Free With A Full Paying Adult

Manor Farm Animal Centre and Donkey Sanctuary
Castle Hill East Leake Loughborough
Leicestershire LE12 6LU
[take Costock J on A60 go through Costock village, as you enter East Leake take 2nd L (signposted Loughborough) - Castle Hill after 250yds Manor Farm is on the L over brow of hill. Limited on site parking.]
Tel: 01509 852525 Fax: 01509 852797
Great day out for all the family. Set in 100 acres with over 200 tame animals, nature

trails, pond dipping, straw maze, living willow sculpture, children's play area and fort adventure, donkey and quad rides. Indoor art and craft activity centre for wet days and lovely home made cakes and snacks in the café. In and outdoor picnic areas. Facilities for disabled and babies. Free car park - coach parties, school and OAP groups by special arrangement. Children's birthday parties a specialty.
Open weekends & Bank Hols Summer 10.00-17.00, Winter 10.00-16.00. Closed 24 Dec-2 Jan
Last Admission: Summer 16.00, Winter 15.00
A£3.50 C(0-2)£Free C(2+)£2.50 OAPs£3.50.
Group rates on application

Stonehurst Family Farm and Museum
Bond Lane Mountsorrel Village Nr Loughborough Leicestershire *[BR: Sileby 2m]*
Tel: 01509 413216
Enjoyment for the whole family will be found at Stonehurst Family Farm and Museum. It is the farm in the imagination of every child, where they can wander amongst and cuddle small sheep, pigs, rabbits, hens, horses, ponies and more, see traditional farm animals, a hatchery and pond dip, play in a strawbarn and activity playground, ride small tractors and on the farmer's tractor and trailer, and take a field walk. Farmer's Den Teashop and Restaurant. Accommodation on farm. Assistance given to disabled visitors, please telephone.
visitor comments: Excellent family-run working farm. Delicious restaurant.
All year daily 09.30-17.00
A£2.95 C£1.95

Tumbledown Farm
Melton Spinney Road Thorpe Arnold Melton Mowbray Leicestershire LE14 4SB
[1m N of Melton Mowbray signposted from A607 between Melton Mowbray / Grantham]
Tel: 01664 481811
A traditional family run working farm, set in unspoilt countryside. We breed animals, milk cows, sheep and goats and grow cereal crops. All year round you can watch us work with the animals and the land. Adventure field, indoor play barn, vintage machinery and much more.
visitor comments: Friendly staff and a lovely tea room. A nice enclosed playfarm for children.
All year daily Summer: 10.00-17.00, Winter: 10.00-16.00. Closed 24-26 Dec
All £2.95 C(0-2)£Free Family Ticket(A2+C2)£11.00

Birds, Butterflies & Bees

Butterfly Farm and Aquatic Centre
Sykes Lane Car Park North Shore Leicester Leicestershire **Tel: 01780 460515**
5,000 sq. ft. of walk-through jungle with free-flying butterflies and tropical birds. Ponds with Koi carp and terrapins. New extension featuring tropical creepy-crawlies, iguanas, tarantulas. New Monitor Lizard enclosure.
Apr-Oct daily 10.30-17.00, 16.30 Sept
A£2.95 C(5-16)£1.75 C(0-5)£Free Family Ticket £9.00 OAPs£2.25. Group rates on request

Falconry and Fishing Centre
The Mill on the Soar Centre Coventry Road Sutton in the Elms Leicestershire *[B4114]*
Tel: 01455 285924
Flying demonstrations by owls, hawks, falcons and buzzards. Fishing lake.
All year daily, Falconry Centre display times 12.00, 14.00, 16.00. Closed 25 Dec
Falconry Centre A£2.00 C£1.00, Fishing Lake day ticket £4.00

Tropical Birdland
Lindridge Lane Desford Leicestershire LE9 9GN
[signposted off A47, bus: regular]
Tel: 01455 824603
Experience birds of the rainforest on your doorstep. Over 85 species, walk through aviaries, chick room, woodland walk, koi ponds, bird shop.
visitor comments: Excellent day out. Memorable Moment: Sit just past the chick hatching room with a bag of monkey nuts and the small parrots will come out of the trees for their lunch. Watch your ears! Café basic and inexpensive.
Easter-end Oct daily 10.00-17.00
A£3.00 C&OAPs£2.00. Group discounts available

Country Parks & Estates

Bradgate Country Park Visitor Centre
Bradgate Park Newtown Linford Leicestershire
[6m NW of Leicester]
Tel: 0116 236 2713
Comprehensive Visitor Centre with displays on Lady Jane Grey (Nine Days Queen of England), ruins of Bradgate House, Old John Tower, History of Bradgate Park and Swithland Wood, the parks' geology, flora and fauna - with dioramas and models. Disabled visitors on

ground floor only.
Apr-Oct Tue-Fri 13.00-17.00; Sat, Sun, Bank Hol Mon & Tue 13.00-18.00. Nov-Mar Sat & Sun 13.00-17.00 (or dusk if earlier). Closed Dec-Feb inclusive. Pre-booked groups taken all year A£1.20 C/OAPs/Registered unemployed/Disabled£0.60. Groups rates 20+ A£1.00 Concessions£0.50. Parking Charge

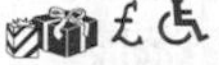

Foxton Locks Country Park
Gumley Road Foxton Market Harborough Leicestershire LE16 7RA
[on the A6 signposted]
Tel: 0116 267 1944 Fax: 0116 265 6962
Landscaped car park and picnic site with woodland footpath to Grand Union Canal tow-path, long flight of locks and remains of barge lift on inclined plane.
All year daily during daylight hours
Admission Free

£

Market Bosworth Country Park
The Park Nuneaton Leicestershire *[off B585 on outskirts of Market Bosworth. Plenty of on site parking available]*
Tel: 01455 290429 Fax: 01455 292841
87 acres of rural park, including 11 acre arboretum. Children's Adventure Playground, lake, Day tickets for fishing available (June-March).
All year daily during daylight hours
Admission Free

£

Melton Country Park
Visitor Centre Wymondham Way Melton Mowbray Leicestershire *[BR: Melton Mowbray 1.25m]*
Tel: 01664 480164
140 acres of informal parkland and a lake situated close to the town centre. Picnic sites, nature trails, children's play areas. See wildlife in grassland, hedgerows, wetland and open water. Visitor centre contains archaeological finds from the site.
Please telephone for opening times

Watermead Country Park
off Wanlip Road Syston Leicester Leicestershire *[off A6 via bypass and Syston then B673. Plenty of on site parking available]*
Tel: 0116 267 1944 Fax: 0116 267 1944
230 acres of Country Park, with lakes, nature reserve, woodland walks, footpaths. Access to River Soar and canal.
All year daily during daylight hours
Admission Free

Forests & Woods

Burbage Common and Woods
c/o Hinckley and Bosworth Boro Council Argents Mead Hinckley Leicestershire LE10 1BZ *[B4668 E of Hinckley. Another entrance is on Smithy Lane just off Sapcote Road A5070. BR: Hinckley 1.5m]*
Tel: 01455 633712

Burbage Woods - nationally important because of spectacular ground flora. Burbage Common - one of largest areas of natural grassland locally. Network of footpaths, wheelchair access, visitor centre, bird observation hide, picnic tables. Full colour brochure from Hinckley and Bosworth Borough Council, Argents Mead, Hinckley LE10 1BZ or from the visitor centre.
Woods: All year daily. Visitor Centre: All year Sat 14.00-16.00 Sun 11.00-13.00 & 14.00-16.00. Mar-Nov Tue-Thur 14.00-16.00. June-Aug Mon-Fri 14.00-16.00
Admission Free

Gardens & Horticulture

Kayes Garden Nursery
1700 Melton Road Rearsby Leicester Leicestershire LE7 4YR
[just inside Rearsby village NE of Leicester on A607 on left hand side approaching from Leicester]
Tel: 01664 424578
Hardy herbaceous perennials and good selection of climbers and shrubs. The garden and nursery are in Rearsby, in the Wreake Valley countryside North East of Leicestershire. Once an orchard, the one acre garden houses an extensive selection of herbaceous plants and climbers. Extensive stream and water garden.
Mar-Oct Tue-Sat 10.00-17.00, Sun-10.00-12.00. Nov-Feb Fri-Sat 10.00-16.00. Closed 25 Dec-31Jan
A£2.00 accompanied C£0.10
discount offer: Half Price Admission

Heritage & Industrial

Snibston Discovery Park
Ashby Road Coalville Leicestershire LE67 3LN
[10 mins from J22 of the M1 or J13 of the M42 / A42]
Tel: 01530 510851 Fax: 01530 813301
All weather 'hands-on' science and industrial heritage museum where visitors of all ages can discover the wonders of science or explore our rich industrial heritage. Other attractions include lively surface tours of Snibstons colliery buildings conducted by ex-miners and an outdoor science exhibit and playground.
visitor comments: Truly brilliant for all ages. Restaurant light and airy, with a well priced menu. Good for a wet day.
Apr-Aug daily 10.00-18.00, Sept-Mar daily 10.00-17.00. Closed 25-26 Dec. 6 Nov 1999 The Park will be closed to the public until 16.30 on this day
A£4.75 C£2.95 Concessions£3.25 Family Ticket £13.50. Group rates for parties of 10+ A£3.75 C£2.00 Concessions£2.50. School parties: A£2.30 C£1.80. Discount tickets for large groups. Colliery Tours: A£1.00 C£0.50
discount offer: One Child Free With One Full Paying Adult

Historical

Ashby-de-la-Zouch Castle
South Street Ashby-de-la-Zouch Leicestershire LE65 1BR
[in Ashby de la Zouch 12m S of Derby on A50, Bus: Stevensons 9 / 27 Burton-on-Trent - Ashby-de-la-Zouch. BR: Burton-on-Trent 9m]
Tel: 01530 413343
The impressive ruins of this late medieval castle are dominated by a magnificent tower, over 24 metres (80 feet) high, which was split in two during the Civil War. There are panoramic views of the surrounding countryside.
visitor comments: Excellent audio tape really brought the Castle's history to life. Kids will love the hidden passage, but bring your own torch!
1 Apr-31 Oct daily 10.00-18.00, 17.00 in Oct. 1 Nov-31 Mar Wed-Sun 10.00-16.00. Closed 13.00-14.00 in winter. Closed 24-26 Dec
A£2.60 C£1.30 Concessions£2.00

↓*special events*

▶ **Meet the Custodian**
15/4/00-16/4/00
Tours of sites by the people who know them best

▶ **A Medieval Knight and his Lady**
23/4/00-24/4/00
Find out about medieval life, from armour and archery to ladies and linen, from noon

▶ **Medieval Entertainments**
30/4/00-1/5/00
Medieval weaponry and combat from noon

▶ **Torchlit Tunnel Tours**
7/5/00-3/9/00
At 11.30 & 14.30. Hear about the famous siege and don a hard hat to tour the tunnel by torchlight, on 7 May, 4 June, 2 July, 6 Aug, 3 Sept

▶ **The Tragic Life of Mary Queen of Scots**
10/6/00-11/6/00
From Noon. Murder, intrigue, treachery and rebellion in the dramatic story of Mary Queen of Scots, with music, military displays and swashbuckling action
▶ **Wind in the Willows**
8/7/00-9/7/00
At 12.30 & 15.00. Meet Toad, Ratty, Mole and Badger in this enchanting children's fantasy
▶ **As You Like It**
26/7/00-26/7/00
At 19.30. Fun, intrigue, music and lust abound in, bring a picnic, rug or folding chair
▶ **Ivanhoe!**
27/8/00-28/8/00
Armoured knights demonstrate the ruthless efficiency of the Norman Army, from noon
▶ **17th Century Cuisine & Surgery**
16/9/00-17/9/00
From Noon

Bosworth Battlefield Visitor Centre and Country Park

Ambion Hill Sutton Cheney Market Bosworth Leicestershire CV13 0AD
[2.5m S of Market Bosworth]
Tel: 01455 290429 Fax: 01455 292841
www.leics.gov.uk
The Battle of Bosworth Field was fought in 1485 between the armies of Richard III and the future Henry VII. The visitor centre gives the viewer a comprehensive interpretation of the battle by means of exhibitions, models and a film theatre. Also illustrated trails around battlefield and medieval special events.
Country Park & Battle trails all year during daylight hours. Visitor Centre: Apr-Oct Mon-Fri 13.00-17.00. July-Aug from 11.00, weekends Bank Hol Mon & Good Fri 11.00-18.00
Visitor Centre A£2.80 C&OAPs&UB40£1.80 Family Ticket £7.40 Car Parking £1.00. Special charges on Event days

↓*special events*

▶ **Re-enactment of Battle of Bosworth Field (1485)**
19/8/00-20/8/00

Rockingham Castle

Rockingham Castle Estate Rockingham Market Harborough Leicestershire LE16 8TH

[2m N of Corby, 9m from Market Harborough, 14m from Stamford on A427, visitors entrance on A6003 S of J with A6116]

Tel: 01536 770240 Fax: 01536 771692
Set on a hill overlooking three counties, Rockingham Castle was built by William the Conqueror. The castle was a royal residence for 450 years. Then in the 16th century Henry VIII granted it to Edward Watson. New for 1999 are the Supper Tours by Candlelight which provides a pleasant and relaxed evening in beautiful surroundings of Rockingham Castle. Including light refreshments served by the staff, an unhurried and informal tour of the Castle followed by a walk around the grounds and then Supper by candlelight in Walker's House, provides a civilised occasion where you may feel justified in spoiling yourself. Parties can arrive from 18.30 onwards, please call for further details. Member of the Historic Houses Association. Photography allowed - outside the building ONLY.

Easter Sun 4 Apr-15 Oct Thur, Sun, Bank Hol Mon & following Tue also Tue in Aug 13.00-17.00, daily for pre-booked parties and schools. Grounds: Sun & Bank Hol Mon 11.30, 12.45 on other open days. Light refreshments from 12.45 on open days. Winter months daily by appointment for pre-booked parties and schools only

Last Admission: 16.30

House & Garden: A£4.40 C£2.90 Family Ticket (A2+C2)£12.00 Concessions£3.90. Group rates: £3.90 per head (minimum of £74.00), C£2.90. Schools: £1.50 per head (minimum charge £37.50) 1 adult free for every 15 children. Grounds: All £2.90 (may vary when special events are held in the grounds). Groups and school parties can be accommodated on any day by arrangement. Supper Tours by Candlelight: £17.60 per head.

discount offer: Two For The Price Of One House & Garden Admissions

Stanford Hall
Lutterworth Leicestershire LE17 6DH
[M1 J18 and 19 (from North only) M6 exit at A14/M1(N). Signposted off A426, A4304, A5199, A5, A14. 1.5m from Swinford. NB: No exit at J19 M1 northbound to A14 OR Swinford]
Tel: 01788 860250 Fax: 01788 860870
Beautiful William and Mary (1690's) house set in an attractive Park besides Shakespeare's River Avon. The house contains antique furniture, fine pictures (including the Stuart Collection) and family costumes. In the Grounds there is a Motorcycle Museum (extra charge), Craft Centre and Pottery (most Sundays), Walled Rose Garden, Nature Trail and a full-size replica of Percy Pilcher's 1898 Flying Machine, 'The Hawk.' The Tea Room is the perfect place to relax and enjoy a home-made cream tea. On Event Days breakfasts and light lunches are also served here. The Hall and Grounds are both available for Conferences, Company Incentive Days, Wedding Receptions, Dinners and Lunches. Coarse fishing is available on a half-mile stretch of the River Avon; Day or Season tickets may be purchased. All enquiries should be addressed to the Administrator. Member of the Historic Houses Association. Dogs on leads in grounds only. For the following special events, gates are normally open by 10.00, please call for further details. Also, for those events marked with an *, there are special admission prices.
Easter Sat-end Sept Sat, Sun, Bank Hol Mon & Tue following 14.30-17.30. Bank Hol and Event days Grounds: 12.00. House: 14.30
Last Admission: 17.00
House & Grounds: A£4.00 C£2.00. Grounds only: A£2.30 C£1.00. Motorcycle Museum: A£1.00 C£0.35
↓*special events*
▶ **Crafts at Stanford Hall ***
8/4/00-9/4/00
▶ **Volkswagen Owners Club Rally**
30/4/00-30/4/00
(Warks. and Leics. Branch)
▶ **Leicestershire Ford RS Owners Club Rally ***
21/5/00-21/5/00
▶ **Capri Club International National Rally ***
28/5/00-28/5/00
Also being held is the Honda S800 Sports Car Club Rally
▶ **Leicester Mercury Flower and Garden Festival ***
3/6/00-4/6/00
▶ **Lea-Francis Owners Club Rally**
4/6/00-4/6/00
▶ **Alfa-Romeo Owners Club National Rally ***
11/6/00-11/6/00
▶ **Ford AVO Owners Club Rally**
18/6/00-18/6/00
▶ **Honda Motorcycle Classic Gathering**
2/7/00-2/7/00
Also showing, Velocette Motorcycle Classic Gathering and Norton Rotary Enthusiasts' Club Rally
▶ **Sporting Escort Owners Club Rally ***
9/7/00-9/7/00
▶ **Afghan Hound Association Dog Show**
15/7/00-15/7/00
▶ **Ford RS Mk II Owners Club Rally ***
16/7/00-16/7/00
▶ **Triumph Sports 6 Owners Club Rally**
13/8/00-13/8/00
** Please call to confirm dates*
▶ **Zundapp Bella Enthusiasts Club Rally**
20/8/00-20/8/00
▶ **Scott Motorcycle Owners Club Rally**
3/9/00-3/9/00
Also showing, Midlands Austin 7 Car Club Rally
▶ **Mini Owners Club National Rally ***
10/9/00-10/9/00
▶ **L.E. Velo Motorcycle Owners Club Rally**
17/9/00-17/9/00
Minx and Hunters Galore Rally to be held also, please call for confirmation
▶ **Crafts at Stanford Hall ***
7/10/00-8/10/00

On the Water

Albion Narrowboats
The Albion Inn Canal Bank Bridge Street Loughborough Leicestershire *[BR: Loughborough 0.75m]*
Tel: 01509 213952
Traditional 70ft narrowboat offering 3 hour Sunday afternoon trips south to Barrow upon Soar or north to Zouch. Bar and Cream Teas available. Booking essential. Also available for charters. Santa cruises in December.
Mar-Dec departure 15.00
A£5.00

Ashby Boat Company
Canal Wharf Station Road Stoke Golding

Hinckley Leicestershire CV13 6EY
Tel: 01455 212671
Steer yourself along the picturesque lock free Ashby Canal. Three fully equipped traditional narrowboats provide comfort for 2-12 people. Weekly narrowboat hire. Canalside Tea Room, Souvenir Shop and Chandlery.
All year daily Mar-Oct 09.00-17.00
From £50.00 per day inclusive. Day Boats for 7.5 hours 09.30-17.00/10.00-17.30 please telephone in advance to reserve

Sport & Recreation

Rutland Water
Sykes Lane Empingham Oakham Leicestershire LE15 8PX
[A606 Oakham / Stamford]
Tel: 01780 460321/276427
Largest man made lake in Western Europe, 3100 acres. Information Centre Sykes Lane. Water and land based recreational facilities. Pleasure Cruiser and Church Museum, Butterfly and Aquatic Centre. You can hire bikes from Rutland Water Cycling (01780 460705) and from May 99 you'll be able to have a go at both outdoor and indoor climbing at the Rock Blok (01780 460060)
Water park all year daily during daylight hours
Attractions Easter-Oct
Varies according to activity

Animal Attractions

Bransby Home of Rest for Horses
Bransby Saxilby Lincoln Lincolnshire LN1 2PH
[off A57 on B1241, near Saxilby 8m from Lincoln]
Tel: 01427 788464 Fax: 01427 787657
Bransby Home of Rest for Horses cares for over 200 rescued horses, ponies and donkeys. Visitors can see the animals in the fields and in two large stable yards.
All year daily 08.00-16.00
Admission Free

Northcote Heavy Horse Centre
Great Steeping Spilsby Lincolnshire PE23 5PS
[3 m E of Spilsby (A16) on the B1195]
Tel: 01754 830286 Fax: 01754 830286
http://freespace.virgin.net/northcote.horses
This centre offers a most unique experience for those who like horses. A total hands on day out with some of the biggest horses in the world. As a charity we are always looking for anyone who can help us look after our retired and handicapped residents. Price includes a wagon ride.
Easter-Sept 11.00-15.00 Apr, May, June & Sept Sun-Wed, July & Aug Sun-Fri
A£4.00 C£2.80 Concessions£3.50 Family Ticket £12.00 Group rates 25+ less 10%

Rand Farm Park
Rand Lincoln Lincolnshire LN8 5NJ
[A158 Lincoln / Skegness road, 8m E of Lincoln visible from the road]
Tel: 01673 858904 Fax: 01673 858904
A genuine working farm with a touch of magic. The animals enjoy meeting people and respond when you touch and talk to them. Most live under cover - so you can enjoy your day at Rand Farm Park in any season, in any weather. Adventure playground and pets corner, indoor and outdoor picnic areas. Tractor rides.
All year Mar-Oct daily 10.00-18.00, Nov-Feb 10.00-16.00. Closed 25-26 Dec
£3.25 C(0-3)£Free

Skegness Natureland Seal Sanctuary
North Parade Skegness Lincolnshire PE25 1DB
[A52 & A158 signposted]
Tel: 01754 764345 Fax: 01754 764345
Natureland houses a specialised collection of animals including seals, penguins, tropical birds, aquarium, reptiles, pets' corner etc. Also free-flight tropical butterflies. Well known for its rescue of abandoned seal pups, and has successfully reared and returned to the wild a large number of these beautiful creatures. Also Sea Life Exhibition.
visitor comments: Excellent value for money. Staff are knowledgeable and friendly. Quiet and calm after the hustle and bustle of the sea

front.
All year daily Summer: 10.00-17.00. Winter: 10.00-16.00. Closed 25-26 Dec & 1 Jan
A£3.90 C£2.60 Family Ticket (A2+C2)£11.70 OAPs£3.20
discount offer: One Child Free When Accompanied By A Full Paying Adult

Gardens & Horticulture

Spalding Tropical Forest and Rose Cottage Water Garden Centre
Glenside North Pinchbeck Spalding Lincolnshire PE11 3SD
[A16 follow brown tourist signs. Plenty of on site parking available]
Tel: 01775 710882 Fax: 01775 710882
Spalding Tropical Forest is the largest of its kind in the British Isles. There are four zones: oriental, temperate, tropical and dry tropics. Cascading waterfalls and lush, colourful tropical plants, create a wonderful atmosphere heavy with scents. Water Garden Centre and Plant House where some unusual specimens are for sale.
Summer daily 10.00-17.30. Winter daily 10.00-16.00. Closed 25 Dec-2 Jan. Call for opening times of restaurant
A£2.45 C(5+)£1.40 OAPs£1.99

Springfields Gardens
Camelgate Spalding Lincolnshire PE12 6ET
[1m E of Spalding signposted]
Tel: 01775 724843 Fax: 01775 711209
www3.mistral.co.uk/springfields
The 25-acre gardens provide an amazing spectacle in the spring when thousands of bulbs are blooming among lawns and lakes. Semi-tropical greenhouse, maze, garden shop, self service restaurant, DO NOT miss the famous Spalding Flower Festival, 29 Apr-1 May. Special events marked with an * are free to Springfields members.
10 Mar-7 May (All year for events)
Last Admission: 17.00
A£3.50 C(accompanied)£Free OAPs£3.00. Groups 15+ 10% discount
discount offer: Two For The Price Of One

↓*special events*

▶ **Antiques Fair**
27/2/00-27/2/00

▶ **Spring Gift and Craft Fair** *
11/3/00-12/3/00

▶ **Cage Bird Show**
26/3/00-12/11/00
Held on Mar 26 and Nov 12 only

▶ **Toy Tractor Fair**
9/4/00-9/4/00

▶ **Antiques Fair**
16/4/00-8/10/00
Held on Apr 16 and Oct 8 only

▶ **Spalding Flower Parade and Country Fair** *
29/4/00-1/5/00
The 42nd Parade starts at 14.00 with floats decorated on themes representing "Hopes, Dreams and Innovations".

▶ **Toy, Train and Collectors Fair**
7/5/00-26/11/00
Held on May 7, July 23, Sept 10 and Nov 26 only

▶ **Amateur Radio Show**
4/6/00-4/6/00

▶ **Music in the Gardens**
15/7/00-15/7/00

▶ **Vintage Vehicle and Classic Car Show** *
16/7/00-16/7/00

▶ **National Cactus Show**
19/8/00-19/8/00

▶ **Model Railway Exhibition**
4/11/00-5/11/00

▶ **Christmas Gift and Craft Fair** *
18/11/00-19/11/00

Grimsthorpe Castle
Grimsthorpe Bourne Lincolnshire PE10 0NB
[8m E of A1 at Colsterworth on A151. Plenty of parking on site]
Tel: 01778 591205 Fax: 01778 591259
The historic seat of the Willoughby de Eresby family since 1516. A medieval tower and a Tudor quadrangular house with a Baroque north front by Vanbrugh. Formal gardens, parkland and lake. Member of the Historic Houses Association.
Castle: Easter Sun-24 Sept Sun, Thur & Bank Hol. Aug daily except Fri & Sat 13.00-18.00.
Park: 11.00-18.00
Last Admission: Castle: 16.30
Park & Gardens: A£3.00 C£1.50
Concessions£2.00. Castle, Park & Gardens: A£6.50 C£3.25 Family Ticket (A2+C2)£16.25

Concessions£4.75. Group rates on application. Special charges may operate for major events.
discount offer: 20% Discount Off Normal Admission. Valid Until 24 Sep 2000

↓*special events*

▶ **Grimsthorpe Game Fair**
3/6/00-4/6/00
10.00-18.00

▶ **Grimsthorpe Time Machine**
18/6/00-18/6/00
Travel back to 1540, will Henry VIII return? Open 10.00-18.00

▶ **Antiques Fair**
1/7/00-2/7/00
Open 09.00-18.00

▶ **Open Air Classical Concert**
8/7/00-8/7/00
An evening event with special guest and fireworks

▶ **Fun Day in aid of St. John**
28/8/00-28/8/00
Always a great family day, open 10.00-18.00

▶ **Farmers Weekly 4X4 and Country Car Show**
9/9/00-10/9/00
The latest off-road vehicles, crafts, antiques, fashion show and numerous countryside activities. 10.00-18.00

Historical

Belton House

Grantham Lincolnshire NG32 2LS
[3m NE of Grantham on A607 Grantham / Lincoln road easily reached and signposted from A1 BR: Grantham]
Tel: 01476 566116 Fax: 01476 579071

Built 1685-88 for Sir John Brownlow. The rooms contain portraits, furniture, tapestries, oriental porcelain, family silver and Speaker Cust's silver. Formal gardens, an Orangery and a magnificent landscaped park with a lakeside walk and the Bellmount Tower. Adventure playground and miniature train rides. Presentation of Queen's bedroom and Staircase Hall. Braille, audio guides and Hearing Scheme. Children's guide. Front baby slings on loan. Dogs on leads only in parkland.

House: 1 Apr-29 Oct Wed-Sun & Bank Hol Mon 13.00-17.30
Last Admission: 17.00
House & Garden: A£5.30 C(under 5)Free C(5-16)C£2.60

↓*special events*

▶ **Horse Trials**
8/4/00-8/4/00
Entrance via Belton Village. Charge per car. Tel: Charles Harrison (01775) 680333

▶ **Easter Egg Trail**
23/4/00-23/4/00
£1.50 per entrant. Children must be accompanied by an adult. Usual admission. 11.00-16.00

▶ **Garden Guided Tour**
26/4/00-26/4/00
With Head Gardener, followed by a glass of wine and nibbles. 18.30. £6. Booking essential

▶ **National Gardens Scheme Open Day**
6/5/00-6/5/00

▶ **Plant Fair**
7/5/00-7/5/00
Rare and unusual plants. 10.00-17.30. House and Fair £5.30. Gardens and Fair £3.80. NT members free

▶ **Paint in the Garden**
21/5/00-21/5/00
Basic materials will be provided and no experience is necessary. All ages are welcome. Usual admission. 11.00-16.00

▶ **Family Day**
4/6/00-4/6/00
Extra family attractions. Usual admission

▶ **National Gardens Scheme Open Day**
8/7/00-8/7/00

▶ **Backstairs Tour**
13/7/00-13/7/00
See entry for 8 June

▶ **Dance and Music Festival**
14/7/00-16/7/00
Call for further details

▶ **Treasure Hunt**
2/7/00-2/7/00
A seafaring theme. 11.00-16.00. £1.50. Normal admission charges

Belvoir Castle

Belvoir Grantham Lincolnshire NG32 1PD
[between A52 and A607]
Tel: 01476 870262 Fax: 01476 870443

Home of the Dukes of Rutland for many centuries, the turrets, battlements, towers and pinnacles of the house are a 19th century fantasy. Featuring paintings by Van Dyck, Murillo, Holbein and others. Includes the museum of the Queens Royal Lancers. The terraced gardens feature sculptures. Regular jousting tournaments. Member of the Historic Houses Association.

Apr-Oct Tue-Thur & Sat-Sun & Bank Hol 11.00-17.00
Last Admission: 16.00
A£5.25 C£3.00 Family Ticket (A2+C2)£14.50 OAPs£4.00

↓*special events*

▶ **Melton Archery Club**
16/7/00-16/7/00
Call for details

▶ **Medieval Jousting Tournament**
23/7/00-23/7/00

▶ **Proms Concert**

2/9/00-2/9/00
Call for details

▶ **Spring Gardens Opening**
22/10/00-22/10/00
See entry for 24 April

Burghley House

Stamford Lincolnshire PE9 3JY
[1m from A1, signposted]
Tel: 01780 752451 Fax: 01780 480125
www.stamford.co.uk/burghley

Built by William Cecil, the 1st Lord Burghley (1520-1598), Lord High Treasurer to Queen Elizabeth I, Burghley House is famous for its remarkable collection of works of art and paintings, including masterpieces by Brueghel, Gainsborough, Veronese and Dolci. The 17th century painted decoration, by Verrio, of many of the rooms at Burghley is one of the glories of the house. An immense project of cleaning and restoration has taken place in recent years. Conservator Michael Cowell completed work of the dramatic Hell Staircase in 1997 and is now engaged in cleaning the Heaven Room, Verrio's masterpiece. Visitors will now be fully able to appreciate Verrio's original dramatic concept. Member of the Historic Houses Association.

visitor comments: An amazing display of art and architecture, where you can see restoration in process.

1 Apr-8 Oct daily 11.00-16.30
Last Admission: 16.30
A£6.50 One C(5-12) free with each paying adult, otherwise C(5-12)£3.20 OAPs£6.10

↓*special events*

▶ **Rainbow Craft Fair**
27/5/00-29/5/00
Huge Craft Fair in the beautiful grounds of Burghley House. Call 01529 414793 for details

▶ **Close Encounters of a Classical Kind**
24/6/00-24/6/00
Gala concert in the park with firework finale. Booking office 01625 560000

▶ **Gala Concert in the Park**
29/7/00-29/7/00
Symphony Orchestra, lasers and fireworks. Booking office 01625 560000

▶ **Burghley Pedigree Chum Horse Trials**
31/8/00-3/9/00
Horse Trials enquiries: 01780 752131

Gainsborough Old Hall

Parnell Street Gainsborough Lincolnshire DN21 2NB
[in Gainsborough town centre, 20m W of Lincoln, 30m E of Sheffield]
Tel: 01427 612669 Fax: 01427 612779

A complete medieval manor house dating back to 1460-80 and containing a remarkable Great Hall and original kitchen with room settings. Richard III, Henry VIII, the Mayflower Pilgrims and John Wesley all in their day visited the Old Hall.

All year Mon-Sat 10.00-17.00, Easter-Oct Sun 14.00-17.30. Closed Good Friday, 24-26 Dec & 1 Jan
A£2.50 C£1.00 OAPs£1.50. Please pre-book guided tours

discount offer: Two For The Price Of One

↓*special events*

▶ **Spring Craft Fair**
26/3/00-26/3/00
The fair promises a wonderful range of over 50 stalls selling high quality handmade crafts and gifts with something for everyone. £0.75 admission

▶ **The Glory of the Gardens**
1/4/00-28/6/00
This inspiring exhibition celebrating one of Britain's favourite pastimes, traces the fascinating history of gardens from prehistoric to modern times

▶ **Easter Egg Hunt**
23/4/00-29/4/00
Search every nook and cranny of the Hall to find eggs hidden in the most surprising places

▶ **Living History Weekend**
30/4/00-1/5/00
At home with Lady Botreaux in 1475. The event features men and women's dress, cookery, arms and armour, archery, children's toys and games, food and drink. A£2.95 C/OAPs£1.95

▶ **Christmas Craft Fair**
25/11/00-26/11/00
Christmas starts here! High quality, locally made crafts for sale and seasonal celebrations in the Medieval kitchen. Christmas shopping, carols and mince pies too!

▶ **A Medieval Christmas**
9/12/00-9/12/00
Lord Burgh's Retinue recreate the magic of a Medieval Christmas. How did people decorate their homes? What did they eat for Christmas dinner? Games and activities for children of all ages!

Military & Defence Museums

Battle of Britain Memorial Flight Visitor Centre
Coningsby Lincolnshire LN4 4SY
[on A153]
Tel: 01526 344041 Fax: 01526 342330
View the aircraft of the Battle of Britain Memorial Flight, comprising the only flying Lancaster in Europe, five Spitfires, one Hurricane, Dakota and a Chipmunk. Because of the operational commitments specific aircraft may not be available. Call before planning a visit.
All year Mon-Fri conducted tours 10.00-15.30. Closed Bank Hol & 2 weeks Christmas
A£2.50 C&OAPs£1.25

Lincolnshire Aviation Heritage Centre
The Airfield East Kirkby Spilsby Lincolnshire PE23 4DE
[on A155. Plenty of on site parking available]
Tel: 01790 763207 Fax: 01790 763677
An aircraft museum based on a 1940's bomber airfield. Displays include: AVRO Lancaster Bomber, Barnes Wallis original bouncing bomb, original Control Tower, RAF Escaping Society, War-time blast shelter, Air-raid shelter, military vehicles and much more.
All year Summer Mon-Sat 10.00-17.00. Winter Mon-Sat 10.00-16.00
Last Admission: Summer 16.00 Winter 15.00
A£3.90 C(0-5)£Free C(5-16)£1.50 OAPs£3.40
discount offer: Two For The Price Of One

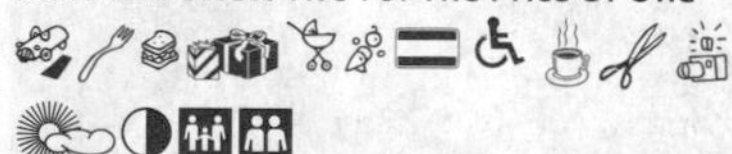

Social History Museums

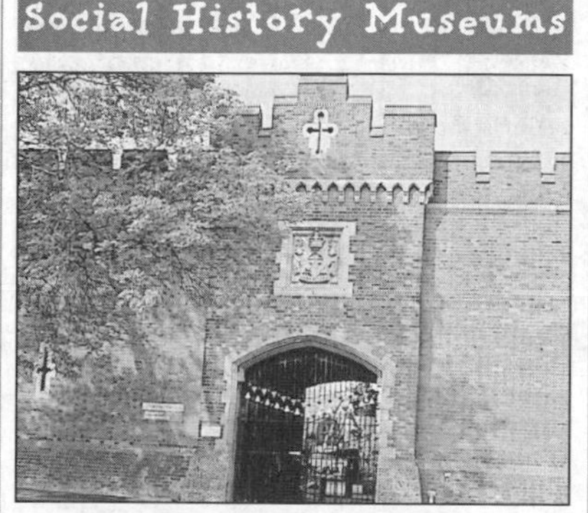

Museum of Lincolnshire Life
Burton Road Lincoln Lincolnshire LN1 3LY
[off the B1398, the A1102, situated near Lincoln Castle. Plenty of on site parking available]
Tel: 01522 528448 Fax: 01522 521264
The region's largest and most varied social history museum where the past two centuries of Lincolnshire life are illustrated by exciting displays. In April 2000, the newly refurbished Royal Licolnshire Regiment Galleries will re-open. From Steam Traction Engines and Tractors to the Chemist's shop and Co-operative Store; from the Schoolroom and Chapel to a WWI War Tank and Trench display; from an Edwardian Nursery and Parlour to a Lincolnshire Wagon and Wheelwright's workshop... we have it all and more... a very special treat for everyone. Special activities for children in school holidays. Please telephone for further details.
All year daily May-Sept 10.00-17.30. Oct-Apr Mon-Sat 10.00-17.30, Sun 14.00-17.30. Closed Good Fri, 24-27 Dec & 1 Jan
Last Admission: 1hr before closing
A£2.00 C£0.60
discount offer: 20% Discount For Groups Of 12+ AND 1 Child Free With Paying Adult

↓*special events*

▶ **Gallery Opening**
7/4/00-7/4/00
The opening day of the Regimental Gallery

▶ **Made In Lincoln Lectures**
14/4/00-14/4/00

▶ **Stamp Lincs 2000**
17/4/00-7/5/00

▶ **Evening Talk**
19/4/00-19/4/00
Join us in an evening talk and a tour of the new Regimental Gallery

▶ **Victorian Day**
22/9/00-22/9/00

▶ **Mini Steam Day**
21/10/00-21/10/00

▶ **Autumn Half-Term Activities**
24/10/00-26/10/00

▶ **Hands-On**
27/1/01-15/4/01

Theme & Adventure Parks

Butlin's Family Entertainment Resort
Butlins Skegness Lincolnshire PE31 7NQ
Tel: 01754 762311 Fax: 01754 767833
Plenty of activities in this fun adventure theme park, including a giant Kiddies Kingdom and amusement park (open during the summer months). The main current feature is the swimming pool, complete with water shoots and a wave-making machine.
Apr-Nov daily 10.00-18.00 Sat & Sun 10.00-

23.00
A&C£3.00 (until 18.00) A&C£5.00 (until 23.00)

Magic World of Fantasy Island
Sea Lane Ingoldmells Skegness Lincolnshire PE25 1RH
[just off the A52 Skegness / Mablethorpe road]
Tel: 01754 872030 Fax: 01754 874146
www.fantasyisland.co.uk
Britain's first themed indoor family resort with traditional family fun to theme park thrills... entertainment, architecture. High Street catering names: Burger King, KFC, Pizza Hut Express and the Nescafé Coffee Shop. New for 1998 the hottest ride on the coast Eruption the Ride, encounter the unimaginable, the uncontrollable volcanic forces of an erupting volcano, dare you experience it? Coming soon: The Millennium Roller Coaster in June 1999. There is also an Imax cinema where your seat moves in sync with the action on screen.
visitor comments: Great day out for all the family. Can be expensive.
7 Mar-26 April weekends only. Easter week daily. 2 May-1 Nov daily 10.00-closing times vary according to season
Admission Free, ride charges from £0.50. Free coach parking

Wildlife & Safari Parks

Butterfly and Wildlife Park
Long Sutton Spalding Lincolnshire PE12 9LE
[A17 off Long Sutton by-pass. Plenty of free on site parking.]
Tel: 01406 363833 Fax: 01406 363182
The Butterfly and Wildlife Park houses so much for the family to see including: a huge walk-through tropical butterfly and bird house, the NEW Reptile Land - from crocodiles to chameleons. Ant Room, Insectarium and Furry Friends House. Also NEW is Liberty, the American Bald Eagle in the Birds of Prey Centre housing the worlds largest owl, the worlds fastest bird of prey. Meet and greet Fred the vulture, the only known trained vulture in the East of England. In the natural and attractive setting of the 20 acre park the Falconer presents Birds of Prey displays at 12.00 & 15.00 daily. When the children have exhausted their eyes, a visit to the Adventure Playground with a mini assault course with rugged climbing frames, rope ladders, scramble nets and swing bridge for the more adventurous, will exhaust the rest of them! Parents can then relax in the licensed tea-rooms and tea-garden. There are free educational packs and nature trail leaflets for schools, which are National Curriculum recommended.
visitor comments: A magical and educational blend of birds, animals, insects and reptiles. Excellent catering facilities at reasonable prices.
18 Mar-29 Oct daily from 10.00
A£4.80 C(3-16)£3.20 Family Tickets (A2+C2)£15.00 (A2+C3)£17.00 OAPs£4.50.
Group rates and guided tours are available by prior booking.
discount offer: Two for the Price Of One

Abbeys

Chapter House And Pyx Chamber of Westminster Abbey
East Cloisters Westminster Abbey London SW1P 3PE
[Tube: Westminster, east side of the Abbey cloister]
Tel: 020 7222 5897 Fax: 020 7222 0960
www.english-heritage.org.uk
The Chapter House was built in 1250 by Royal Masons. It contains some of the finest

medieval sculpture to be seen and still has its original floor of glazed tiles. The tiled floor can now be seen in its former glory due to recent specialist cleaning.
1 Apr-30 Sept daily 09.30-17.00. 1-31 Oct daily 10.00-17.00. 1 Nov-31 Mar daily 10.00-16.00. Closed 24-26 Dec. May be closed at short notice on state occasions
A£2.50 C(0-5)£Free C(5-16)£1.30 Concessions£1.90. EH Members £Free

↓*special events*

▶ **Medieval Life**
20/5/00-21/5/00
From Noon. Calligraphy, spinning and weaving, games and crafts

▶ **Medieval Life**
17/6/00-18/6/00
See entry for 20 May

▶ **Music of the Normans and Angevins**
30/9/00-1/10/00
From Noon. Music played on authentic copies of period instruments by this ever-popular duo

Agriculture / Working Farms

Freightliners Farm

Sheringham Road London N7 8PF
[Holloway Road (A1), off Liverpool Road. BR/Tube: Highbury / Islington. Tube: Caledonian / Holloway Road]
Tel: 020 7609 0467 Fax: 020 7609 9934
Freightliners Farm is a model of a working farm in the heart of Islington. It's a great place to get away from the bustle of city life and make contact with the farming world. Take the opportunity to buy one of our many delicious eggs, honey and healthy produce. We also sell compost, hay, straw and animal feed. With many different types of animal from old and rare breeds to newly born chicks, piglets or lambs there is much to see for all the family. We have an education worker who runs school programmes relating to the National Curriculum. Classroom is available for hire for meetings and children's parties, call for details.
All year Tue-Sun 09.00-13.00 then 14.00-17.00
Admission Free

↓*special events*

▶ **Freightliners Farm Open Day**
29/5/00-29/5/00
Sheep shearing, pony and donkey rides and lots of other activities. 11.00-17.00

Hackney City Farm

1a Goldsmiths Row London E2 8QA
[junction of Hackney Road / Goldsmiths Row BR: Cambridge Heath]
Tel: 020 7729 6381
A thriving city farm with sheep, pigs, calves, chickens, ducks, geese etc... Farm café, gardens, textile classes, pottery classes, play schemes, film and tv. Feeding times 08.30 and 16.30.
All year Tue-Sun 10.00-16.30. Closed Mon
Last Admission: 16.00
Admission Free

Vauxhall City Farm

24 St Oswald's Place (entrance in Tyers Street) London SE11 5JE
[BR/Tube: Vauxhall]
Tel: 020 7582 4204
Two thirds of an acre of derelict land, transformed in 1977 by volunteers into a working farm. The animals are all friendly and used to being petted by visitors large and small. Bella the pig and Jacko the donkey are the favourites. A wide range of talks on Vauxhall City Farm is offered, plus lots of hands-on-work with the animals. Donkey rides, pony-care classes and milking demonstrations are also available on request. Registered Charity No. 281512. Many events are organised for fundraising, call for further programme details.
All year Sat, Sun, Tue, Wed, Thur 10.30-17.00
Admission Free - donations welcome. Guided Tours: Schools & Groups Talk Tour: C£1.00. Milking Demonstrations: C£0.50. Spinning Demonstrations: C£0.50. Min charge per group £5.00. Classroom available

Animal Attractions

Battersea Dogs' Home and Bell Mead Kennels
4 Battersea Park Road London SW8 4AA
[BR: Battersea Park. Tube: Vauxhall. Bus: 137]
Tel: 020 7622 3626 Fax: 020 7622 6451
www.dogshome.org
In 1860, Mrs Tealby, concerned by the number of animals roaming the streets of London, opened the Temporary Home for Lost and Starving Dogs' in Holloway. In 1871, the Home moved to its present site in Battersea, and was renamed Battersea Dogs' Home. The Home has remained here ever since, carrying out the same high ideals set by the Founder. Taking in stray and lost dogs, they are held for the statutory 7 days, to give their original owners a chance to claim them. Battersea then goes about finding new loving homes for any of the unclaimed dogs.
All year 6 days a week. Mon, Tue, Wed & Fri 10.30-16.15, Sat & Sun 10.30-15.15. Closed Thur. Bell Mead: all year Mon-Sat 10.00-12.00 & 14.00-16.00, Sun 09.30-12.00
Admission £0.50

College Farm
45 Fitzalan Road Finchley London N3 3PG
[North Circular/Finchley Road intersection. M1 J2, A1 North Circular intersection. Tube: Finchley Central]
Tel: 020 8349 0690 Fax: 020 8346 9988
College farm has a variety of farm animals housed in historic farm buildings. Art Gallery and cream teas on Sunday afternoons.
All year daily, Summer: 10.00-18.00, Winter 10.00-17.00
A£1.50 C(0-3)£Free C£0.75 OAPs£1.25

Kentish Town City Farm
1 Cressfield Close Grafton Road London NW5 4BN
[Tube: Chalk Farm / Kentish Town. BR: Kentish Town / Gospel Oak]
Tel: 0171 916 5421
Lots of pigs and sheep to see, as well as a wide range of farm activities for children and plenty of hands-on-demonstrations
All year Tue-Sun 09.00-18.00
Admission Free

Mudchute Community Farm
151 Manchester Road Isle of Dogs London E14
[DLR: Crossharbour Station, 5min walk]
Tel: 020 7515 5901 Fax: 020 7538 9530
Mudchute Community Farm boasts 17 acres of farmland housing pigs, sheep, goats, rabbits, chickens, geese and ducks, plus a llama! Lots of hands-on activities are on offer, in addition to an education centre for children, containing all the information on animal care. The riding stables have special facilities for those with disabilities.
All year Mon-Sun 09.00-17.00
Admission Free

Newham City Farm
King George Avenue Custom House London E16 3HR
[end of A406 intersection with A13, turn R to City, turn L into Tollgate Rd, bear R into Stansfeld Rd, Farm is on the right. BR: DLR Royal Albert Tube: Plaistow]
Tel: 020 7476 1170 Fax: 020 7474 4960
We are an inner city farm and visitor centre enabling visitors to get close to animals and the environment and find out information about them. Guided tours are available but need to be pre-booked. We also have special event days and activities. Animals include rare and minority breeds of cattle, sheep, pigs, goats and poultry. We also have a shire horse.
All year Tue-Sun Summer: 10.00-17.00. Winter: 10.00-16.00
Last Admission: 10mins before closing
Admission Free. School groups must pre-book £0.50 per head in Borough, £0.75 per head outside Borough

Spitalfields Farm
Weaver Street London E1 6HJ
[Tube: Whitechapel / Aldgate East]
Tel: 020 7247 8762
This farm houses a range of farm animals, including pigs, ducks and sheep. The farm offers a range of activities during school holidays, including drama workshops, animal care, painting, drawing and pottery classes for all ages with a qualified expert.
All year Tue-Sun 10.30-17.00
Admission Free but donations welcome

Stepney Stepping Stones Farm
Stepney Way London E1 3DG
[Tube: Stepney Green]
Tel: 020 7790 8204
An urban farm with educational and recreational facilities. Cows, sheep, goats, pigs, donkeys. Smaller animals that can be seen and enjoyed by the children. Scraps of food are welcome please ask before feeding to the animals. Tuck shop, wide selection of home produced jams, chutneys, pickles, honey and souvenirs. Classroom have games and books for visiting children to enjoy whilst parents have a cup of tea. Most of the site is wheelchair and pushchair accessible and dogs must be kept on a lead, no bicycles, limited on site parking.

London

Impromptu special events throughout the year call for details.
All year Summer: Tue-Sun & Bank Hol 09.30-18.00. Winter Tue-Sun & Bank Hol 09.30-dusk
Admission Free - donations welcome. Pre-booked guided tours for groups £0.45 each

Surrey Docks Farm
Rotherhithe Street Rotherhithe London SE16 1EY
[S end of Rotherhithe. Bus: P11, 10min walk from Surrey Quays Shopping Centre]
Tel: 020 7231 1010 Fax: 020 7237 6525
Surrey Docks farm is a special place for schools to visit, children are always really inspired to learn at first hand and experience the direct contact with the animals. The farm aims to use the direct experiences as a basis for delivering many elements of the national curriculum. Special talks and demonstrations can be booked at extra cost, on topics such as Goats and Milk, Bees and Honey, Eggs and Feathers and Sheep and Wool. Sample packs are available, as well as a Sensory Trail and other trails. The farm has a central animal yard, where visitors can meet the animals; goats, sheep, a cow, pigs and poultry. The farm has lovely gardens, including vegetable, herb, dye garden and orchard.
All year Tue-Sun 10.00-17.00. Closed for lunch 13.00-14.00 weekends & School Hol. Closed Fri during School Hol
Last Admission: 17.00
School parties £1.50 per head. Bookings: Daphne Ferrigan

Vauxhall City Farm
24 St Oswald's Place (entrance in Tyers Street) London SE11 5JE
[BR/Tube: Vauxhall]
Tel: 020 7582 4204
Two thirds of an acre of derelict land, transformed in 1977 by volunteers into a working farm. The animals are all friendly and used to being petted by visitors large and small. Bella the pig and Jacko the donkey are the favourites. A wide range of talks on Vauxhall City Farm is offered, plus lots of hands-on-work with the animals. Donkey rides, pony-care classes and milking demonstrations are also available on request. Registered Charity No. 281512. Many events are organised for fundraising, call for further programme details.
All year Sat, Sun, Tue, Wed, Thur 10.30-17.00
Admission Free - donations welcome. Guided Tours: Schools & Groups Talk Tour: C£1.00. Milking Demonstrations: C£0.50. Spinning Demonstrations: C£0.50. Min charge per group £5.00. Classroom available

Arts, Crafts & Textiles

Apsley House, The Wellington Museum
Hyde Park Corner London W1V 9AF
[Tube: Hyde Park Corner]
Tel: 020 7499 5676 Fax: 020 7493 6576
The refurbished London residence of the Duke of Wellington; the Iron Duke's palace which houses his famous collection of paintings, porcelain, silver, order and decorations. Paintings by artists including Goya, Velasquez, Rubens and Brueghel. In the Basement see the two new displays: the Duke's Death and Funeral and Medals and Memorabilia; also see the new video of a personal tour of the House and collections by the eighth Duke who lives there with his family in private apartments.
All year Tue-Sun & Bank Hol Mon 11.00-17.00. Closed Good Fri, May Day, 24-26 Dec & 1 Jan
Last Admission: 16.30
A£4.50 Concessions£3.00 C£Free. Pre-booked Group rates £2.50. Price includes sound guide
discount offer: Two For The Price Of One

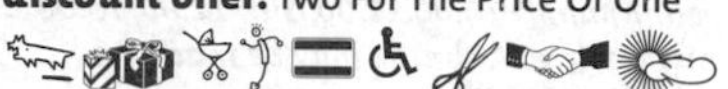

Barbican Art Gallery
Level 3 Gallery Floor Barbican Centre Silk Street London EC2Y 8DS
[the Barbican Centre is well signposted & has 4 car parks, 2 off Beech Street & 2 off Silk Street. Call Box Office for Disabled Parking Permit. Tube: Barbican / Moorgate / St. Paul's / Liverpool Street / Bank / Mansion House. BR: Liverpool Street / Farringdon / Blackfriars / City Thameslink / Barbican / Moorgate. Rail savings available through the Theatre and Concert Travel Club call 01727 841115]
Tel: 020 7588 9023 24hr info Fax: 020 7628 0364
www.barbican.org.uk
One of Britain's leading art venues, the Gallery offers a diverse program of temporary shows. Call for current details. NCP paying car park in Barbican Centre & Aldersgate Street. Free parking for people with disabilities.
All year Mon, Thur-Sat 10.00-18.45, Tue 10.00-17.45, Wed 10.00-19.45, Sun & Bank Hol 12.00-18.45
A£5.00 Concessions£3.00 Family Ticket (A2+C3)£12.00. Reduced admission after 17.00 Mon-Fri inclusive £3.00. Season tickets for each exhibition available. Group bookings: (10+) should be made at least 2 weeks in advance on 0181 638 8891. Education programme information call 0171 638 4141 x7640

British Museum
Great Russell Street London WC1B 3DG

[Tube: Holborn / Tottenham Court Road / Russell Square]
Tel: 020 7636 1555 Fax: 020 7323 8118
www.british-museum.ac.uk
Founded in 1753, this is the world's oldest museum. Two and a half miles of galleries display the national collection of antiquities, prints and drawings. The Museum departments are: Greek and Roman, Egyptian, Prehistoric and Romano-British, Western Asiatic, Oriental, Japanese, Coins, Medals and Bank Notes, Medieval and Later, Prints and Drawings and Ethnography. The Mexican Gallery from Olmec to Aztec: Prehispanic Art and Culture from Mexico. Among the famous exhibits are the Elgin Marbles, Lindow Man, the Rosetta Stone, and Egyptian Mummies. The British Library Reading Rooms have moved to St Pancras. As part of the Millennium Commission for development projects the renovation of the Great Court will be open to the public for the first time in 150 years creating a dramatic new public space. People will be able to meet and enjoy themselves close to one of the world's greatest cultural resources.
All year Mon-Fri 10.00.17.00, Sun 12.00-18.00
Admission Free. A charge may be made for Temporary Exhibitions

↓*special events*

▶ **Japanese Clocks, Zodiac and Calendar Prints**
1/12/99-1/3/00
▶ **Prints and Drawings Exhibitions**
1/12/99-1/4/00
▶ **Divine Rule**
1/12/99-1/5/00
▶ **Prints and Drawings Exhibitions**
1/6/00-1/9/00
▶ **Prints and Drawings Exhibitions**
1/10/00-1/12/00
▶ **Inaugural Exhibition**
1/11/00-30/11/00
▶ **Prints and Drawings Exhibition**
1/12/00-1/3/01
▶ **Prints and Drawings Exhibition**
1/6/01-1/9/01
▶ **Exhibition for Japan Festival**
1/9/01-1/12/01
▶ **Prints and Drawings Exhibition**
1/10/01-1/11/01

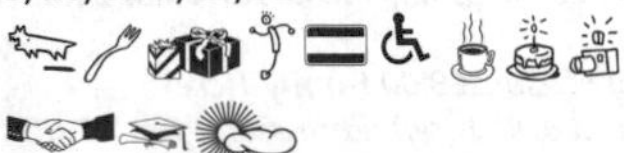

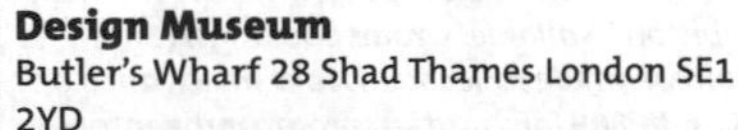

Design Museum

Butler's Wharf 28 Shad Thames London SE1 2YD
[Tube: London Bridge / Tower Hill]
Tel: 020 7403 6933 Fax: 020 7378 6540
www.designmuseum.org
The world's first museum dedicated to the study of 20th-century design. This stylish museum enables visitors of all ages to rediscover one hundred years of design, view state-of-the-art innovations from around the world and enjoy an extensive programme of special exhibitions on design and architecture.
All year daily 11.30-18.00. Closed Christmas Day
Last Admission: 17.30
Queuing Times: minimal
A£5.50 C&Concessions£4.00 Family Ticket (2A+2C) £12.00 Students £4.50
discount offer: One Child Free With Each Full Paying Adult

↓*special events*

▶ **Bauhaus Dessau**
10/2/00-4/6/00
The Bauhaus has profoundly influenced the architecture, design and craftmanship of modern times
▶ **Buckminster Fuller**
1/6/00-1/10/00
This exhibition will provide the first opportunity in this country to assess the vast range of his creative output.
▶ **Five Designs of Mr Brunel**
1/10/00-1/4/01
A look at a selection of the work of Isambard Kingdom Brunel
▶ **Luis Barragan**
1/3/01-1/7/01
The celebrated architect whose work has stretched far beyond his native Mexico

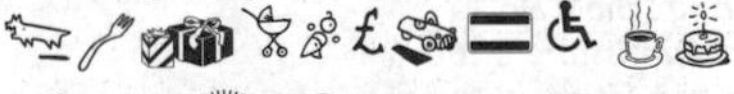

Dulwich Picture Gallery

College Road Dulwich London SE21 7AD
[just off A205 South Circular. BR: Victoria / West Dulwich]
Tel: 020 8693 5254 Fax: 020 8766 0090
The oldest public picture gallery in England is also one of the most beautiful. Housed in a building designed by Sir John Soane in 1811, displaying a fine cross-section of Old Masters. The Gallery will be closed from 1st Jan 1999 to May 2000 this is due to the award of a £5 million grant from the Heritage Lottery Fund. The money will go towards restoring and refurbishing the original gallery and a new building is to be constructed which will house lecture theatres, workshops and a café. England's oldest public art gallery reopens following a £9m refurbishment and extension.
Development project includes facilities such as a lecture hall, practical art room and cafe. Reopens with an exhibition entitled 'Soane's Favourite Subject: The Story of the Dulwich Picture Gallery'.
All year Tue-Fri 10.00-17.00, Sat 11.00-17.00, Sun 14.00-17.00, Bank Hol Mon 11.00-17.00. Closed Mon. Guided tours Sat & Sun 15.00. The

Gallery will be closed in 1999 for refurbishment and new building
Last Admission: 16.45
A£3.00 C(0-16)&Disabled&UB40s£Free OAPs&Students£1.50. Free to all on Fridays.
Guided Tours: £4.00 per head

↓*special events*

▶ **'Soane's Favourite Subject: The Story of the Dulwich Picture Gallery'.**
1/5/00-31/5/00

Estorick Collection of Modern Italian Art
39a Canonbury Square London N1 2AN
[Buses: 271 to door. 4, 19, 30, 48 to Upper Street / Canonbury Lane. Tube: Highbury / Islington. Limited parking on site]
Tel: 020 7704 9522 Fax: 020 7704 9531
The permanent collection shows powerful images by early 20th century Italian Futurists including Balla, Boccioni, Carrà, Severini and Russolo. There are also works by such figurative artists as Modigliani, Sironi and Campigli and the metaphysical painter de Chirico. An exciting programme of temporary exhibitions and events is scheduled for 2000. Credit cards are only accepted for shop purchases. Disabled access is limited to two floors and we have limited Orange Badge holders parking on site.
All year Wed-Sat 11.00-18.00. Sun 12.00-17.00. Closed Good Fri. Shop & Café: Gallery hours.
Library: By appointment only, call for details.
Guided Tours available for groups of 10+
Last Admission: Wes-Sat 17.30, Sun 16.30
A£3.50 C(under 16)£Free Concessions£2.50 includes exhibition and permanent collection. Café shop and garden free
discount offer: Two For The Price Of One

↓*special events*

▶ **The Art of Noises featuring Derek Shiel**
2/2/00-5/3/00
An exhilarating exhibition featuring twelve sound sculptures. Derek will be in Gallery 1, Wed-Fri 11.00-18.00, Sat 14.00-18.00 and Sun 13.00-17.00

▶ **Sculpted Sound**
1/3/00-1/3/00
Flautist Nicky Heinen and percussionist Trevor Taylor in concert with Derek Shiel

▶ **Primo Conti: A Futurist Prodigy (1900-1988)**
15/3/00-21/5/00
Exhibition of 15 paintings, 34 drawings and related archive material. A rare opportunity to see the work of the only 'child Futurist'.

▶ **Fortunato Depero (1892-1960)**
4/10/00-22/12/00
A leading figure in Italian Futurism, Depero celebrated technology and sought to break down traditional divisions between the arts.

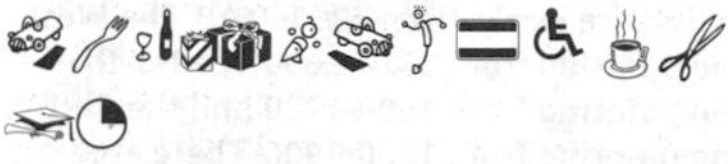

Flowers East
199-205 Richmond Road London E8 3NJ
[BR: Hackney Central. Tube: Bethnal Green. Bus: 106 / 253. Limited parking on site]
Tel: 020 8985 3333 Fax: 020 8985 0067
Angela Flowers Gallery opened in Soho in 1970 with the aim of introducing young contemporary British artists and promoting established artists whose excellence deserved greater recognition. In 1988 the gallery moved to Hackney, in London's East End, and became Flowers East. Since then it has acquired PLC status and expanded into one of the biggest and most important commercial galleries in the country. Flowers East has two large gallery spaces (as well as several smaller ones) and represents more than thirty-five artists, from young newcomers to major international figures. There is also a separate graphics department which publishes and sells limited edition prints by a wide range of contemporary artists. In February 1998 expansion continued overseas with the opening of Flowers West in Santa Monica, California, thus helping to further its artists' careers on the international stage.
All year Tue-Sat 10.00-18.00
Admission Free

National Gallery
Trafalgar Square London WC2N 5DN
[Tube/BR: Charing Cross. Tube: Leicester Sq / Embankment / Piccadilly Circus. Buses: 3 / 6 / 11 / 11 / 12 / 13 / 15 / 23 / 24 / 29 / 53 / x53 / 77a / 88 / 91 / 94 / 109 / 139 / 159 / 176. A public car park is in Whitcomb St. One parking

space for disabled badge holders can be booked through the Chief Warder's Office on 0171 747 2854]

Tel: 020 7839 3321 Fax: 020 7930 4764

www.nationalgallery.org.uk

A neo-classical building opened in 1838. All the great periods of European paintings are represented here although only a selection of British works are included. Particular treasures include Van Dyck's Arnolfini Marriage, Van Gogh's Sunflowers and Constable's Haywain. The Sainsbury Wing houses the early Renaissance works from 1260-1510. The West Wing painting from 1510-1600, the North Wing painting from 1600-1700 and the East Wing painting from 1700-1900. There are exhibitions throughout the year.

visitor comments: Beautiful, an incredible collection.

All year Mon-Sat 10.00-18.00, Sun 14.00-18.00, June-Aug Wed until 20.00. Closed Good Fri, 24-26 Dec & 1 Jan. Guided Tours: Mon-Fri 11.30 & 14.30, Sat 14.00 & 15.30, Wed evenings 18.30. Signed tours for the deaf on the first Sat of each month 11.30. Lunchtime Lectures: Tue-Fri 13.00, Sat 12.00. Films & Special Lectures: Mon 13.00 Admission Free - some major exhibitions charged for. Group bookings of adult parties can be made with special lectures or tours provided.

↓*special events*

▶ **Primary Pick: Watch this Place**
5/1/00-5/5/00
This display explores how artists have painted places, from real views of towns and buildings to imaginary countryside settings for stories.

▶ **Family Events**
8/1/00-29/4/00
Starting from 8 January 2000, there will be regular Saturday morning talks, introducing the Collection in a lively and interactive way. Talks will begin at 11.30am in the Education Centre foyer, and last approximately one hour. The sessions are aimed at families with children aged 5 to 11 years, and include a free badge.

▶ **Painted Illusions**
2/2/00-1/5/00
The Art of Cornelius Gijsbrechts.

▶ **Seeing Salvation: The Image of Christ**
26/2/00-7/5/00
Sainsbury wing. The exhibition explores how the figure of Christ has been represented in the Western tradition.

▶ **Encounters: New Art from Old**
14/6/00-17/9/00
Contemporary artists show work inspired by Old Masters. Admission charged.

▶ **Telling Time**
18/10/00-14/1/01
The exhibition Telling Time will be a Gallery-wide event focusing on the fascinating relationships between time and painting. Admission free.

▶ **Impression: Painting Quickly in France**
1/11/00-28/1/01
The first exhibition ever to examine how the Impressionists revolutionised the practice of the oil sketch, making it central to their work. Sainsbury Wing, admission charged.

National Portrait Gallery

2 St. Martins Place London WC2H 0HE

[Tube: Charing Cross / Leicester Square. Opposite Church of St Martin-in-the-Fields to the N of Trafalgar Square. Disabled access found at the Orange Street entrance]

Tel: 020 7306 0055 Fax: 020 7306 0056

www.npg.org.uk

A collection of portraits illustrating British history which was first housed in its present accommodation in 1896. The building was designed in the style of an Italian palazzo with a further wing added in 1933. Also displayed are sculptures, miniatures, engravings, photographs and cartoons. Gift shop and Book shop selling a unique range from books to posters and cards. Portrait Café now open.

All year 10.00-18.00, Sun 12.00-18.00. Closed Good Fri, May Day, 24-26 Dec & 1 Jan Admission Free, some exhibitions are charged.

↓*special events*

▶ **BP Portrait Award 2000**
1/1/00-24/3/00
Further information: BP Portrait Award Tel 0171 306 0055 Ext 274/245. CLOSING DATE FOR ENTRIES Friday 24 March 2000.

▶ **Recent Acquisitions**
15/1/00-31/5/00
Porter Gallery (Room 35) Exciting new commissions and acquisitions for the contemporary collection.

▶ **Princes of Victorian Bohemia**
28/1/00-14/5/00
Photography Gallery. In the 1860s the painter David Wilkie Wynfield produced a series of strikingly original photographic portraits of his artist contemporaries.

▶ **Photographs by Snowden**
25/2/00-4/6/00
Wolfson Gallery. The first complete retrospective of Snowdon's photographic work.

▶ **Defining Features**
14/4/00-17/9/00
Studio Gallery. This wide-ranging and innovative exhibition will include portraits, in all media, of scientists, doctors and technologists from the foundation of the Royal Society to the present day.

Queen's Gallery

Buckingham Palace Buckingham Palace Road London SW1A 1AA
[Tube: Victoria / St James Park]
Tel: 020 7839 1377 Fax: 020 7839 8168
www.royal.gov.uk

The Queen's Gallery at Buckingham Palace holds a diverse range of exhibitions from the Royal Collection, one of the finest art collections in the world. The Royal Collection has been amassed over the past 300 years by succeeding sovereigns, consorts and other members of the Royal Family, the majority of items were acquired before the end of the reign of King George V. Private Evening Tours at The Queen's Gallery are available exclusively for groups to enjoy these exhibitions. The tours can be arranged for groups (minimum of 15 persons), by appointment and subject to availability, after normal opening hours, between 16.30-17.30. Groups may provide their own speaker or guide if required. Permission is given by the Director of the Royal Collection for arts orientated groups and charities with Royal Patronage to hold private views of these exhibitions at The Queen's Gallery. Regrettably, due to architectural limitations, The Queen's Gallery is inaccessible for wheelchair users.

All year daily 09.30-16.30, during exhibitions except 2 Apr. Closed between exhibitions, see special events. Gallery Shop: 09.30-17.00. Closing in the autumn for major remodelling and extension and re-open in 2002, the year of The Queen's Golden Jubilee
Last Admission: 16.00
A£4.00 C(0-17)£2.00 OAPs£3.00. Group Private Evening Tours: surcharge of £0.50 per person on standard admission

Royal Academy of Arts

Burlington House Piccadilly London W1V 0DS
[Tube: Piccadilly Circus / Green Park. Buses: 9 / 14 / 19 / 22 / 38]
Tel: 020 7300 8000 Fax: 020 7300 8011
www.royalacademy.org.uk

The Royal Academy, in the heart of London's West End, is world famous for its exhibition programme. Founded in 1768, the Royal Academy is the oldest fine arts institution in Britain. Their exhibitions attract more than a million people each year, putting the Academy among the top ten attractions for paying visitors in London. The shop, café and restaurant are open to all, whether visiting an exhibition or not.

Daily 10.00-18.00, Fri until 20.30, except Sun in June-Aug. Closed Good Fri, 25-26 Dec
Last Admission: 17.30
Depends on Exhibition, call 020 7413 1717 for details and to book.

↓special events

▶ 1900: Art at the Crossroads
16/1/00-3/4/00
Art at the Cross-roads will bring together about 250 paintings and a selection of sculptures. Those artists who in 1900 were thought of as avant-garde, or were entirely disregarded but are now seen as great masters will be seen alongside those who were acclaimed at the time. Works by Cezanne, Degas, Gauguin, Munch, Klimt, Rodin and Toulouse-Lautrec will be shown.

▶ Chardin: 1699 - 1779
9/3/00-28/5/00
Sackler Wing. His paintings are incomparable in their control of tonal harmony, glimmering light and in the vitality of his use of paint. Visitors to the exhibition will have the rare pleasure of seeing a large group of his masterpieces and scholars will have the opportunity to re-assess his work.

▶ Alive
30/3/00-12/5/00
An exhibition of work by students from schools across the UK who have taken part in dynamic life drawing workshops organised by the Outreach Programme. This unique scheme is now celebrating its tenth year.

▶ Summer Exhibition 2000
29/5/00-7/8/00
The Summer Exhibition was first held in 1769, the year after the Royal Academy was founded, and is the oldest, largest and most popular open exhibition in the world. Any artist may enter work for selection and talented newcomers can find their work hung alongside that of artists with an international reputation, including Royal Academicians.

▶ Scottish Colourists
29/6/00-24/9/00
This exhibition, which will open at the Royal Academy of Arts and then travel to the Scottish National Gallery of Modern Art (Autumn/Winter 2000), will bring together for the first time up to one hundred of the Colourists' most important paintings from private and public collections.

▶ Terry Frost RA
12/10/00-12/11/00
The Royal Academy exhibition promises, like Frost himself, to be full of a celebratory enthusiasm for life itself.

▶ The Great Watercolours of JMW Turner
2/12/00-11/2/01
This exhibition will concentrate upon the large, set-piece drawings, from early works such as the Lambeth view to the final Swiss scenes.

▶ Premiums
11/2/01-24/2/01
These exhibitions provide an excellent platform from which the students can launch their pro-

fessional careers.

▶ **French Master Paintings from Baltimore**
1/6/01-1/9/01
This exhibition will bring together 50 masterpieces of the 19th and early 20th century, drawn from two highly important art collections that reflect the exceptional level of taste in Baltimore during this period.

Tate Britain
Millbank London SW1P 4RG
[Tube: Pimlico]
Tel: 020 7887 8000 Fax: 020 7887 8007
www.tate.org.uk
On 24 March 2000, the Tate Gallery at Millbank will be relaunched as Tate Britain as part of the Tate's ambitious programme of expansion and development. The Tate holds the greatest collection of British art in the world. The new Gallery will show British art from the sixteenth century to the present day in a dynamic series of new displays and exhibitions.
In 2000 Tate Britain will celebrate the extraordinary range and quality of the Tate's British collection by displaying its many masterpieces in new, theme-based galleries. In this special year, historic and modern works will hang together in challenging juxtaposition, drawing out new meanings from famous and familiar images.
All year daily 10.00-17.50. Closed 24-26 Dec
Admission Free (excluding special exhibitions)

↓*special events*

▶ **The Age of Reynolds and Gainsborough**
1/1/99-1/4/00

▶ **Hogarth and his Contemporaries**
1/1/99-1/4/00
Focuses on England's first great native painter who dominated British art in the first hald of the 18th century.

▶ **Ruskin, Turner and the Pre-Raphaelites**
9/3/00-29/5/00
A major exhibition marking the centenary of John Ruskin's death in 1900, and launches a year of international celebrations of his life and work. Admission: £6.50 (concessions £4.50)

▶ **New Acquisitions in British Art**
23/3/00-28/5/00
In 2000, a suite of rooms will be devoted to showing acquisitions of British art made over the last ten years by artists as diverse as William Hogarth, Thomas Gainsborough, Barbara Hepworth, Damien Hirst and Gillian Wearing.

▶ **Mona Hatoum**
24/3/00-9/7/00
The celebrated British artist Mona Hatoum has created a spectacular new group of works for the Tate's Duveen Galleries in the first of a new series of annual sculpture exhibitions.

▶ **Romantic Landscape: The Norwich School of Painters 1803(1833**
24/3/00-17/9/00
Paintings by John Sell Cotman, John Crome, and a host of exceptional works by lesser-known figures. Together with special displays of Turner and Constable, Romantic Landscape will offer the richest display of the great period of British landscape painting seen in London for many years.

▶ **New British Art 2000**
6/7/00-24/9/00
New British Art 2000 is the first in a series of major exhibitions of contemporary art, to be held every three years at Tate Britain.
Admission: £5.50 (concessions £4.00)

▶ **Turner Prize 2000**
20/10/00-23/1/01
The Turner Prize is awarded to a British artist under 50, for an outstanding presentation of their work in the last year.

▶ **William Blake**
9/11/00-11/2/01
This exhibition will take a fresh, bold look at the unique and innovative Romantic British artist and poet, William Blake (1757(1827).
Admission: £7.50 (concessions £5.00)

Tate Modern
25 Sumner Street London SE1
[Tude: Southwark]
Tel: 020 7887 8000 Fax: 020 7887 8007
www.tate.org.uk
Tate Modern will open to the public in the transformed Bankside Power Station on 12 May 2000. It is one of the most significant of all the projects being created for the new Millennium in Britain. Standing at the heart of London, beside the Thames and linked to St Paulis Cathedral by the first new bridge to be built in central London since 1894, Tate Modern will become a symbol of London in the twenty-first century. The new Gallery will take its place among the great modern art museums of the world. It will display the Tate Collection of international twentieth-century art, widely acknowledged to be one of the three or four most important in the world, featuring major works by the most influential

artists of this century including Bourgeois, Picasso, Matisse, Mondrian, Duchamp, Dalì, Bacon, Giacometti, Pollock, Rothko and Warhol. It will also be a Gallery for the twenty-first century exhibiting new art as it is created and drawing in new audiences.

Opens 12th May 2000 Sun-Thurs 10.00-18.00 Fri-Sat 10.00-22.00
Admission Free (excluding special exhibitions)

↓*special events*

▶ **The Unilever Series- Louise Bourgeois**
12/5/00-31/10/00
The French-born American sculptor Louise Bourgeois will create the inaugural work which will be unveiled in May 2000 when Tate Modern opens.

▶ **Herzog & de Meuron**
12/5/00-31/12/00
Herzog & de Meuronís work will be celebrated through an exciting new form of exhibition. Their relationship with the building of Sir Giles Gilbert Scott, the original architect of Bankside Power Station, will be explored at ten locations situated throughout the building.

Victoria and Albert Museum

Cromwell Road South Kensington London SW7 2RL

[Tube: South Kensington. There are two car parks in the area, charges vary but approx £5.00 for up to 2 hours & £9.00 up to 4 hours. Limited meter parking]

Tel: 020 7942 2000 Fax: 020 7942 2266
www.vam.ac.uk

The Victoria and Albert museum holds one of the world's largest and most diverse collections of decorative arts. 146 galleries contain unrivalled collections dating from 3,000 BC to the present day. Furniture, fashion, textiles, paintings, silver, glass, ceramics, sculpture, jewellery, books, prints and photographs illustrate the artistic life of many different cultures from around the world. Superb highlights for any visit should include: the V&A's collection of Italian Renaissance sculpture, the largest outside Italy; paintings and drawings by the 19th-century artist John Constable; the superb Canon Photography Gallery; and the Dress Gallery, covering over four hundred years of European fashionable dress from the mid-16th century to the present day. Re-opening in Feb 2000, The Silver Galleries: Phase Two, showcasing over 1000 extraordinary pieces from the National Collection of Silver. Free family activities on selected days. Guided tours, disabled access, shop, restaurant, Friends society, galleries and rooms available for hire.

visitor comments: Immense. Incredible. You need a whole day. Nice to relax in the Garden.

All year daily 10.00-17.45, Wed (Late View - seasonal) 18.30-21.30. Closed 24-26 Dec
A£5.00 C(0-18)£Free OAPs£3.00. Free Entry between 16.30-17.45. Free admission for: Disabled and carer, UB40 holders, full time students, Patrons and Friends of the V&A American and International Friends of the V&A. *Senior Citizens will be admitted FREE to the V&A as of the 1 April 2000. Some exhibitions may carry a separate charge in addition to the standard Museum entry.*

discount offer: Two For The Price Of One. Valid on Standard Museum Admission (£5) Only. Not Valid for Exhibitions

↓*special events*

▶ **Mao Zedong at the V and A**
13/10/99-23/4/00
Mao: From Icon to Irony and Fashioning Mao chart the impact of Mao Zedong's 'cult of personality' on Chinese Art and Culture.

▶ **Breathless! Photography and Time**
10/2/00-17/9/00
Exhibition exploring the notion of time and its associated themes of movement, speed, growth and reflection

▶ **Art Nouveau 1890-1914**
6/4/00-30/7/00
A timely reappraisal of this extraordinary style with masterpieces drawn from private and public collections throughout Europe and North America.

▶ **Brand New**
19/10/00-14/1/01
Exhibition examining how brands are constructed and their values communicated in the context of global consumerism

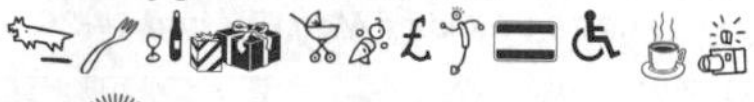

Birds, Butterflies & Bees

London Butterfly House

Syon Park Brentford Middlesex TW8 8JF

[Tube: Gunnersbury then bus 237 or 267. By road off A310]

Tel: 020 8560 0378 Fax: 020 8560 7272
www.butterflies.org.uk
The first live walk through butterfly exhibition situated in the middle of Syon Park - one of London's most popular parks and Stately Homes. An exotic indoor garden full of colourful, free-flying tropical butterflies. Separate displays of leaf cutting ants, spiders, lizards and other creepy crawlies. A wildlife themed gift shop is the perfect place to end your visit.
All year, Apr-Oct daily 10.00-17.30, Oct-Mar daily 10.00-15.30. Closed 25 & 26 Dec
Last Admission: 30mins before closing
A£3.30 C&OAPs£2.00 Family Ticket £7.75. School parties C£1.75

Caverns & Caves

Chislehurst Caves
Old Hill Chislehurst Kent BR7 5NB
[off A222]
Tel: 020 84673264 Fax: 020 82950407
This labyrinth of caves has been called the enigma of Kent. Miles of mysterious caverns and passages hewn out of the chalk over some 4,000 years can be explored with experienced guides to tell the history and legends of the caves.
Daily during school holidays including half terms. All other times Wed-Sun. Tours: hourly from 10.00-16.00. Closed Mon, Tue and 24-25 Dec
Last Admission: 16.00
A£3.00 C&OAPs£1.50. Longer tours Sun & Bank Hol only: A£5.00 C&OAPs£2.50
discount offer: One Free Admission When A Second Admission Of Equal Or Greater Value Is Purchased

Communication Museums

BBC Experience
Broadcasting House Portland Place London W1A 1AA
[Tube: Oxford Circus / Great Portland St]
Tel: 0870 60 30 304 Booking
www.bbc.co.uk/experience
BBC Experience allows the visitor a unique opportunity to view the corporations' heritage including the central role it has played in the nation's history and culture. A series of interactive displays will allow you to have fun trying out a range of broadcasting activities. You can become a sports commentator, direct Eastenders, create a radio play and of course read the weather. Education officer available for schools.
All year daily - opening hours vary call for details
Last Admission: Last Tour: 16.30
Queuing Times: Timed admission
A£6.95 C£4.95 Concessions£5.95 Family Ticket(2A+2C) £19.95. Ticket will provide entry for specific times. Pre-booking recommended during holidays. Groups rates available

↓*special events*

▶ **The Amazing Art of Gormenghast**
1/1/00-31/12/00
Behind the scenes to the making of BBC's Gormenghast, an ambitious adaptation of Mervyn Peake's classic trilogy. Costumes, scenery, special effects, lighting, props and secrets of the cast and characters will be on display

▶ **School Workshops**
1/1/00-31/12/00
Workshops are presented by our Education Officer or a specialist guest presenter on the following themes: Sounds in the Air, Key Stage 2 (7-11); The Radio and TV Age, Key Stages 2 & 3 (7-14); The BBC - Voice of the Nation, Key Stages 3 & 4; How to Make Radio Drama, Key Stages 2-4 & post 16 (7-18), Duration 2.5 hours, Cost £75.00 and Make a Radio Magazine Production. Average duration is 60mins, Max Group size for each workshop is 30, the cost £45.00 (unless otherwise stated). To book any of the above

Workshops call 0870 603 0304

Folk & Local History Museums

Bromley Museum and Priory Gardens
The Priory Church Hill Orpington BR6 0HH
[J4 M25, A224]
Tel: 01689 873826
www.bromley.gov.uk
The museum is housed in an impressive medieval / post medieval building set in attractive gardens. Find out about the archaeology of the London Borough of Bromley. Learn about Sir John Lubbock, 1st Lord Avebury, the eminent Victorian responsible for giving this country its Bank Holidays. See how people lived before World War II. Guided tours by arrangement. Throughout the year there are changing exhibitions by the Museum and local groups. Gardens and ground floor of museum only is suitable for wheelchairs. Enabling dogs are admitted. For details of the following events, call the venue.
Bromley Museum: All year Mon Fri 13.00-17.00, Sat 10.00-17.00. 1 Apr-31 Oct Sun 13.00-17.00, Bank Hol 13.00-17.00 Mornings Mon-Fri for educational purposes only. Priory Gardens: All year Mon-Fri 07.30-dusk, Sat Sun & Bank Hol 09.00-dusk
Admission Free

↓*special events*

▶ **"Simply Dinosaurs"**
8/1/00-16/3/00
A touring exhibition by the Dinosaur Society
▶ **Orpington Photographic Society**
18/3/00-25/3/00
▶ **"In and Around Bromley a Century Ago"**
27/3/00-9/4/00
▶ **"Commemoratives"**
11/4/00-26/4/00
With school collaboration
▶ **Orpington Sketch Club Open Exhibition**
28/4/00-6/5/00
▶ **Museums and Galleries North**
1/5/00-4/6/00
▶ **"The Borough's Churches"**
8/5/00-22/6/00
▶ **Botanical Illustration**
12/6/00-9/7/00
▶ **"What is a Museum?"**
10/7/00-26/7/00
▶ **2000 years of settlement in the Cray Valley**
29/7/00-28/8/00
▶ **St Mary Cray Action Group display**
30/8/00-27/9/00
▶ **Bromley's Hall of Fame**
29/9/00-29/10/00
▶ **Orpington Sketch Club Members Exhibition**
3/11/00-11/11/00

Honeywood Heritage Centre
Honeywood Walk Carshalton Surrey SM5 3NX
[by Carshalton Ponds off A232. BR: Carshalton]
Tel: 020 8770 4297 Fax: 020 8770 4777
www.sutton.gov.uk
The history of the borough and its people plus a programme of exhibitions, presented in a 17th century listed building. Features include Edwardian Billiard Room, Tudor Gallery and Art Gallery.
All year Wed-Fri 10.00-17.00, Sat Sun & Bank Hol Mon 10.00-17.30
A£1.20 £0.50
discount offer: Two For The Price Of One

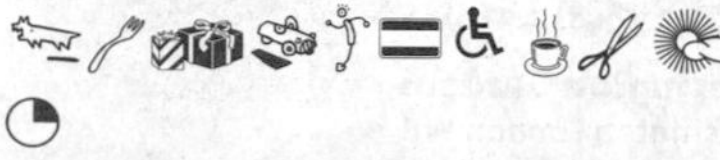

Gardens & Horticulture

Chelsea Physic Garden
66 Royal Hospital Road London SW3 4HS
[entrance in Swan Walk. Tube: Sloane Square]
Tel: 0207 352 5646 Fax: 0207 376 3910
www.cpgarden.demon.co.uk
The second oldest botanic garden in England

was begun in 1673 for the study of plants used in medicine by the Society of Apothecaries. By the late 18th century it was famous throughout Europe for is rare and unusual plants, and it is still used for botanical and medicinal research.
Apr-Oct Wed 12.00-17.00, Sun 14.00-18.00. Also opening during Chelsea Flower Show week & Chelsea Festival week. Groups at other times, by appointment
A&OAPs£4.00 C(5-15)
Students&Unemployed£2.00
discount offer: Two For The Price Of One. Valid Until 29 Oct 2000

↓*special events*

▶ **Timely Cures - Pharmaceutical Plants**
9/7/00-3/9/00
Photographic exhibition matched with the launch of a planted pharmaceutical garden

▶ **Summer School - Medicinal Plants**
7/8/00-11/8/00
Collections of herbal, pharmaceutical and essential oil plants, talks and demonstrations. Strictly limited numbers, please book in advance. Recreational course

▶ **Summer School in Medicinal Plants**
14/8/00-18/8/00
Herbal, pharmaceutical and essential oil plants, talks and demonstrations. Strictly limited numbers, please book in advance. Professional course

Kensington Gardens
Kensington London W8
[Tube: Queensway / Lancaster Gate]
This was part of Hyde Park until William III enclosed his palace gardens and even today the two areas are not physically divided. the 'invisible' boundary runs from north to south across the Serpentine Bridge. Kensington Gardens are noted for their tranquility and formality.
All year, any reasonable time
Admission Free

Kew Gardens Royal Botanic Gardens
Kew Richmond Surrey TW9 3AB
[Tube: Kew Gardens. BR: Kew Bridge]
Tel: 020 8940 1171 Fax: 020 8332 5197
www.rbgkew.org.uk
World-famous gardens at Kew began as a 9 acre site laid out by George III's mother Princess Augusta in 1759. Given to the state in 1841 the gardens covered 300 acres by 1904 - their present size. Famous landmarks are the Chinese Pagoda and the Palm House with plants from the tropics. Construction is under way for a Millennium Seed Bank to be completed by October 1999. The Royal Botanic Gardens aims to collect seeds of all British flora by the end of the year 2000 and ten per cent of the world's flowering plants by the year 2010, 25,000 species in all. They will be stored in freezers inside the research and exhibition centre, near Haywards Heath. Visitors will watch scientists at work, descending in glassed lifts to the vaults protecting the seeds. The bank will make its stocks available for research into the potential medical and industrial properties of plants that are disappearing in the wild.
All year daily Garden: from 09.30 closing times vary according to season, from 16.00 in Winter up to 19.30 in Summer. Conservatories close earlier. Closed 25 Dec & 1 Jan
A£5.00 C(5-16)£2.50 C(0-5)£Free Family Ticket £13.00 Concessions&OAPs££3.50

Heritage & Industrial

Bank of England Museum
Threadneedle Street London EC2R 8AH
[entrance in Bartholomew Lane. Tube: Bank]
Tel: 020 7601 5545 Fax: 020 7601 5808
www.bankofengland.co.uk
A fascinating insight into the world of banking and money from the Bank of England's foundation in 1694 to the present day. Unique displays of banknotes and gold bars. Experience the worlds of modern technology with the exciting interactive videos, and foreign exchange dealing games.
All year Mon-Fri 10.00-17.00. Closed weekends & Bank Hol
Admission Free

Guide Heritage Centre
17-19 Buckingham Palace Road London SW1W 0PT
[Tube: Victoria. Located in Palace Place on the corner of Palace Street]
Tel: 020 7834 6242 Fax: 020 7630 9052
Experience the interactive world of Guiding. Meet Brown Owl in the roots of her tree, experience life under canvas in Base Camp, find out

how the Brownies got their name. Who started Guiding for girls? What is Guiding all about? And what are the challenges in the global world of Guiding today. The answers to all these questions and more can be found at The Guide Heritage Centre.
All year Mon-Sat 09.30-17.00. Closed Bank Hol
£2.50 per person

Kew Bridge Steam Museum
Green Dragon Lane Brentford Middlesex TW8 0EN
[100 yards from the N side of Kew Bridge, next to the tall Victorian Tower. Bus: 65, 237, 267, 391. BR: Kew Bridge. Tube: Gunnersbury / Kew Gardens]
Tel: 020 8568 4757 Fax: 020 8569 9978
www.cre.canon.co.uk/~davide/kbsm
Housed in massive Victorian pumping station. Unique collection of water pumping engines including world's largest working Beam Engine. In steam every weekend. New 'Water for Life' gallery explores the story of London's water. Train rides on many weekends. Waterwheel and diesel engine house.
All year daily 11.00-17.00. Closed Good Fri & Christmas week
Weekdays: A£2.80 C(5-15)£1.00
OAPs&Concessions£1.50 Family Ticket £7.00.
Weekends: A£3.80 C(5-15)£2.00
OAPs&Concessions£2.50 Family Ticket £10.50

Markfield Beam Engine and Museum
Markfield Road South Tottenham London N15 4RB
[BR/Tube: Seven Sisters / Tottenham Hale]
Tel: 020 8800 7061
1886 Beam Pumping Engine restored to working order in original building. Steaming certain weekends and by arrangement. Small exhibition to illustrate aspects of public health engineering for which the large pumping engine was developed. Parking on site is limited.
28 Mar-1 Nov Sun only except Easter Sun by prior arrangement on 01763 287331 if venue is unattended
A£3.00 Concessions£2.00 on steam days otherwise voluntary donation

Royal Mint Sovereign Gallery
7 Grosvenor Gardens London SW1W OBH
[4mins walk from BR: Victoria and 10mins walk from Victoria Coach Station]
Tel: 020 7592 8601 Fax: 020 7592 8634
www.royalmint.com
The new Royal Mint Sovereign Gallery relates the 500-year old history of the famous Gold coin. A unique exhibition incorporating rare and priceless displays. The Gallery also offers for sale souvenir coin sets in gold and silver a perfect memento of your visit to the U.K. or as a gift for a very special occasion such as a Christening, Birthday or Wedding. During 1999 two special commemorative crowns will be issued for the Princess Diana Memorial and for the Millennium.
Mon-Fri 10.00-16.00. Closed Bank Hol Mon
Admission Free
discount offer: 10% off ANY product displayed

Historical

Alexandra Palace Trading Limited
Alexandra Palace Way Wood Green London N22 7AY
[M25 signposted. Tube: Wood Green. Bus: W3. Plenty of parking on site]
Tel: 020 8365 2121 Fax: 020 8883 3999
www.alexandrapalace.com
Opened in 1873, this majestic building is one of London's most famous landmarks, renowned as the birthplace of television. Set in 200 acres of parkland, it offers spectacular views of London's skyline. Attractions include a boating lake, pitch and putt golf course, Children's Playground, animal enclosure, conservation area, ice-skating and ice hockey, a café and the Phoenix Bar.
visitor comments: Great fun! The ice-skating is particularly enjoyable, and the stewards are a great help for first-timers.
Palm Court: All year daily 10.00-23.00.
Alexandra Park: All year daily 10.00-23.00
Admission Free
discount offer: Two For The Price Of One For Ice Rink

↓*special events*

► **Sailboat and Windsurf Show 2000**
4/3/00-5/3/00
Call the organiser, the Royal Yachting Association, on 01703 627425 for details

► **Alexander Palace Antique and Collectors Fair**
12/3/00-12/3/00
For more information please call the organisers, Pig and Whistle Promotions on 020 8883 7061

► **Antique and Collectors Fair**
12/3/00-19/11/00
Held on Mar 12, May 14, Sept 24 and Nov 19 only. London's largest Antiques Fair with over 700 stands plus furniture selling wide range of quality items

► **The London Classic Motor Show**
18/3/00-19/3/00
Commences 10.00-18.00. A£7.50 C(5-16)£3.00 OAPs£6.50

▶ **Spring Craft Fair**

22/4/00-24/4/00

Please call Marathon Event Management on 01273 833884 for more details

▶ **Afro Hair & Beauty 2000**

28/5/00-29/5/00

The latest hair and beauty ideas for black women, including fashion shows.

▶ **Children's Summer Fun Fair**

10/6/00-10/9/00

Family fun held on the boating lake car park, with a selection of rides and stalls themed for children and parents. Open weekends only up to July 16, 12.00-19.00 and then daily 12.00-20.00

▶ **The Evening Standard Hot Tickets Theme World Experience Show '99**

16/6/00-18/6/00

A show for all the family featuring theme parks, visitor attractions and fun days out!

▶ **Cyprus Wine Festival**

1/7/00-2/7/00

Promoting Cypriot products, especially the wine, and bringing the Cypriot Community together

▶ **4th Mind Sports Olympiad**

19/8/00-28/8/00

Call MSO Worldwide Ltd on 01707 659080 for further details

▶ **Iftex 2000**

2/9/00-3/9/00

Please call the organisers, Nexus Media Ltd/Nexus Horticulture on 01322 660070 for details

▶ **The National Self Build Homes Show**

14/9/00-17/9/00

▶ **The Knitting and Stitching Show**

12/10/00-15/10/00

For further details, please call Creative Exhibitions Ltd on 020 8690 8888

▶ **Dolls House Fair and Teddy Bear Fair 'The Event of 2000**

25/11/00-26/11/00

Open 10.00-17.00 daily. Sat: Collector's day tickets £8.00-£10.00 in advance by calling 01903 244900... One of the largest fairs of its type anywhere in the world, with hundreds and hundreds of stands to see, with stalls for everyone from the fascinated newcomer to the avid collector

▶ **Christmas Craft Fair and Festive Table**

1/12/00-3/12/00

Please call Marathon Event Management on 01273 833884 for more information

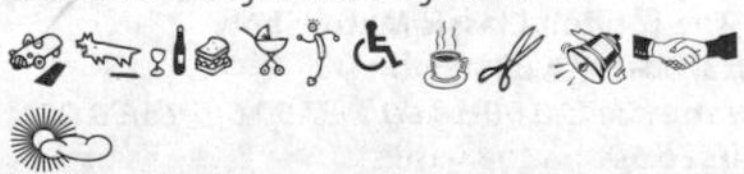

London

Chiswick House

Burlington Lane Chiswick London W4 2RD

[signposted off A4. Tube: Turnham Green. BR: Chiswick, 0.25m]

Tel: 020 8995 0508 Fax: 020 8742 3104

Lord Burlington's masterpiece built circa 1728 is one of England's first and finest Palladian villas. The ornately decorated interior includes the dazzling Blue Velvet Room. Beautifully laid out classical gardens with statues, urns and obelisks surround the House, as well as the newly restored water cascade. It has been said that a ghost of one of the past cooks prepares a full English Breakfast in the last afternoon. Such visitations are few and far between, and, when you consider that smell eminates from kitchens which have not existed for over 100 years it is rather spooky!

1Apr-30 Sept daily 10.00-18.00. 1 Oct-31 Oct daily 10.00-17.00. 1 Nov-31 Mar Wed-Sun 10.00-16.00. Closed 24-26 Dec

A£3.00 C(0-5)£Free C(5-16)£1.50 Concessions£2.30. EH Members £Free

↓*special events*

▶ **May Day, 1740**

30/4/00-1/5/00

From Noon. Celebrate May Day in period style! Make garlands and see the crowning of the May Queen

▶ **The Soprano In Pink**

10/6/00-11/6/00

From 13.00. Delightful Georgian song and spinet music, with gossip and talks about period fashion

▶ **Jurassic Giants!**

17/6/00-18/6/00

From Noon. Meet two 17th century comic archaeologists and help them reconstruct dinosaur skeletons

▶ **Tea and Scandal!**

27/8/00-28/8/00

From Noon. Enjoy the latest scandalous London gossip with Lady Devonshire!

▶ **Georgian Christmas Fun**

9/12/00-10/12/00

From Noon. Meet Lady Burlington and make an 18th century mask. Fun for all the family!

Down House - Home of Charles Darwin

Down House - Home of Charles Darwin
Luxted Road Downe Orpington Kent BR6 7JT
[off A233 signposted]
Tel: 01689 859119 Fax: 01689 862755
www.english-heritage.org.uk
See the home of one of the world's greatest scientists, Charles Darwin. It was from his study in Down House that Darwin worked on his most famous and controversial work, 'On the Origins of Species.' The ground floor has been recreated to its appearance in Darwin's time. The first floor contains an interactive exhibition detailing Darwin's life and work. Down House operates a timed ticket system (12 July-10 Sept if travelling by car).
1 Apr-31 Oct Wed-Sun 10.00-18.00 dusk if sooner in Oct. 1 Nov-31 Jan Wed-Sun 10.00-16.00. 1-31 Mar Wed-Sun 10.00-16.00. Closed 24-26 Dec & Feb. Alternative telephone number: 01689 859119.
Last Admission: 30mins before closing
A£5.50 C(0-5)£Free C(5-16)£2.80
Concessions£4.10. EH Members £Free

Geffrye Museum
Kingsland Road London E2 8EA
[Buses: 149 / 242 / 243 or 67. Tube: Liverpool Street then bus 149 or 242 / Old Street (exit 2), then bus 243, situated on A10 Kingsland Road. Meter parking in surrounding streets]
Tel: 020 7739 9893 Fax: 020 7729 5647
www.geffrye-museum.org.uk
One of London's most friendly and enjoyable museums, the Geffrye specialises in the domestic interiors of the urban middle class. Its displays span from 1600 to 2000, forming a sequence of period rooms which capture the quintessential nature of English interior style. The museum is set in elegant, 18th century buildings, just north of the City. It is surrounded by beautiful gardens including an award-winning walled herb garden and a series of historical garden rooms which highlight the key changes in urban middle-class gardens from the 17th to the 20th centuries (open April to October). The museum and gardens are regularly brought to life through an innovative programme of special exhibitions, seminars, workshops, drama and music. New for this year is the 70 seater restaurant.
visitor comments: Interesting period gardens. The herb garden is particularly fascinating, as it shows the uses for each herb. One of London's best kept secrets! A great place to take visitors.
All year Tue-Sat 10.00-17.00, Sun & Bank Hol Mon 12.00-17.00. Closed Mon, Good Fri, 24-26, 31 Dec & 1 Jan
Admission Free

↓special events

▶ **Matthew Hilton - Furniture for our time**
15/2/00-9/7/00
Exhibition will feature some of the most successful designs of Matthew Hilton, one of the UK's leading furniture designers

▶ **Contemporary Furniture 1 & 2**
23/2/00-2/7/00
Show #1, 23 Feb -30 Apr 2000. Show #2, 3 May-2 July. Two consecutive shows highlight the fine quality and innovative work of selected furniture designers from East London

▶ **Contemporary Furniture 1 and 2**
23/2/00-2/7/00
Show 1 Feb 23-Apr 30 and Show 2 May 3-July 2. Shows featuring recent work by five East London furniture designers

▶ **Eco Furniture: Workshop for Adults**
4/3/00-4/3/00

▶ **Heavy Metal: Workshop for Adults**
25/3/00-1/4/00
Two-day workshop in which participants have the opportunity to explore casting with metal. Tickets £36.00 (inc materials but not lunch) 11.00-16.00

▶ **Easter Workshop: Material World**
25/4/00-28/4/00
For ages 6-15, 10.30-12.45 and 14.00-16.00. Design with plastics, metals and wood. Children under 8 must be accompanied. First served basis 30 mins in advance

▶ **Easter Workshops: Making a Mirror Frame**
29/4/00-29/4/00
For children aged 3-5. 14.00 and 15.15. Children must be accompanied. First served basis 30 mins in advance

Ham House
Ham Street Richmond Surrey TW10 7RS
[on S bank of Thames W of A307 at Petersham. Tube/BR: Richmond, then Bus: 371]
Tel: 020 8940 1950 Fax: 020 8332 6903
A National Trust Property. Outstanding Stuart house built on the banks of the River Thames

in 1610 and enlarged in the 1670's. Contains rare survivals of the 17th century, including exquisite closets, fine furniture, textiles and pictures. Garden returned to its 17th century framework with continuing work to reinstate it to its former glory. South Terrace borders replanted in formal late 17th-century style; kitchen restored to early 18th-century original appearance.

House: 1 Apr-29 Oct Sat-Wed 13.00-17.00. Garden: Sat-Wed 10.30-18.00 or dusk if sooner. Orangery tea-room, tea garden & shop: Mar, Nov & Dec Sat & Sun 11.00-16.30. Apr-Oct Sat-Wed 11.00-17.30. Closed 25-26 Dec & 1 Jan

Last Admission: 30mins before closing

House: A£5.00 Family Ticket £12.50. Garden: £1.50 Pre-booked Groups 15+ A£4.00 C£2.00. Parking: £Free not NT

↓*special events*

▶ **Spring Plant Fair**

14/5/00-14/5/00

Buy plants and enjoy a walk around Ham House. Telephone 020 8940 1950 for information, 11.00-15.00, usual admission

▶ **Last Night of the Summer Proms**

25/6/00-25/6/00

British Concert Orchestra. Bring a picnic and seating. Send a SAE and cheque to Princess Alice Hospice, West End Lane, Esher, KT10 8NA or phone 01372 461855, A£16.00 C£8.00, 18.00 for 19.00

Horse Guards

Whitehall London SW1

[Tube: Westminster]

Tel: 0891 505452

Once Henry VIII's tiltyard (tournament ground), the Changing of the Guard still takes place here every day. The elegant buildings, completed in 1755, were designed by William Kent. On the left, as you pass on to the parade ground, is the Old Treasury, also by Kent.

Changing of the Guard & Dismounting Ceremonies: All year daily, please see special events for details

Admission Free

↓*special events*

▶ **Changing The Guard Ceremonies**

1/1/00-31/12/00

Mon-Sat 11.00, Sun 10.00 at Tilt Yard, forecourt of Horse Guards building.

Jewel Tower

Abingdon Street Westminster London SW1 3JY

[Tube: Westminster, opposite South end of Houses of Parliament. No parking except public car parks]

Tel: 020 7222 2219

www.english-heritage.org.uk

The Jewel Tower is one of two surviving buildings of the original Palace of Westminster. It was built circa 1365 to house the personal treasure of Edward III. The Jewel Tower is currently home to the 'Parliament Past and Present' exhibition and a new touch screen computer gives a virtual reality tour of both Houses of Parliament.

1Apr-30 Sept daily 10.00-18.00. 1-31 Oct daily 10.00-17.00. 1 Nov-31 Mar 2001 daily 10.00-16.00. Closed 24-26 Dec

A£1.50 C(0-5)£Free C(5-16)£0.80 Concessions£1.10. EH Members £Free

Iveagh Bequest, Kenwood House

Hampstead Lane London NW3 7JR

[Bus: 210 from; Tube: Golders Green / Archway

or Hampstead (then 20 min walk)]
Tel: 020 8348 1286 Fax: 020 7973 3891
www.english-heritage.org.uk
Visit the idyllic country retreat of Kenwood, remodelled by Robert Adam in the 1760s including the magnificent library. The house is home to the world famous Iveagh Bequest collection of paintings, which includes masterpieces by Rembrandt, Vermeer, Turner and Gainsborough. Outside, enjoy over a hundred acres of landscaped parkland with ornamental lakes and amazing views over London. Wheelchair access to ground floor only. Enjoy a season of summer concerts at the Kenwood Lakeside.
1 Apr-30 Sept daily 10.00-18.00. 1-31 Oct daily 10.00-17.00. 1 Nov-31 Mar daily 10.00-16.00. Closed 24-25 Dec
House & Grounds: Admission Free. Some Special Events are charged

↓special events

▶ **East, Drink and be Merry!**
27/6/00-24/9/00
A fascinating exhibition of food which explores the history and habits of the British at table, 1600-2000.

▶ **Victorian Vittles!**
9/7/00-9/7/00
Visit the 1900 kitchen, learn about Mrs Beeton, household management and recipes to try at home

▶ **Georgian Grub!**
16/7/00-16/7/00
The fad for French food in 1800 Britain, with salads, jellies and crystallised fruit. Plus the history of tea

▶ **Tudor Tucker!**
24/9/00-24/9/00
See entry for 23 July

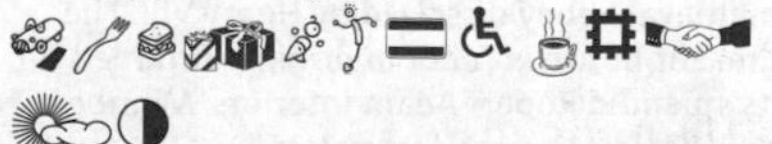

Marble Hill House and Park
Richmond Road Twickenham London TW1 2NL
[Tube: Richmond. BR: St Margaret's]
Tel: 020 8892 5115 Fax: 020 8607 9976
www.english-heritage.org.uk
This perfect English Palladian villa, set beside the River Thames, was built in 1724 for Henrietta Howard, Countess of Suffolk and mistress of King George II. The house contains important early Georgian paintings and furniture and the lavishly gilded Great Room. There are a range of sports facilities to be enjoyed in the park and concerts through the summer. Limited disabled access.
1 Apr-30 Sept daily 10.00-18.00. 1-21 Oct daily 10.00-17.00. 22 Oct-31 Mar Wed-Sun 10.00-16.00. Closed 24-26 Dec & 1-16 Jan
A£3.30 C(0-5)£Free C(5-16)£1.70 Concessions£2.50. EH Members £Free

↓special events

▶ **Easter Fun**
23/4/00-24/4/00
From 12.00 with Beaux Stratagems. Enjoy an Easter Egg Hunt and make your own Easter hat

▶ **A Regency Tea-Break**
13/5/00-14/5/00
From 12.00 with Hogarth's Heroes Comic Georgian decorators bravely recreating the Battle of Waterloo using everyday objects!

▶ **The Soprano in Pink**
28/5/00-29/5/00
With Rhiannon Gayle, from 13.00. Delightful Georgian song and spinet music, with gossip and talks about period fashion

▶ **Ghostly Goings On**
28/10/00-29/10/00
From 12.00 with Beaux Stratagems. Wear your scariest Halloween costume, join the footman for a ghostly tour of the house and listen to chilling tales

▶ **Georgian Christmas Fun**
16/12/00-17/12/00
Fun for all the family at 12.00 with Beaux Stratagems. Meet Lady Suffolk and make an 18th century mask

Queen Elizabeth's Hunting Lodge
Ranger's Road Chingford London E4 7QH
[A1069, Tube: Walthamstow Central. BR: Chingford. Limited on site parking]
Tel: 020 8529 6681
The royal hunting grandstand was built for Henry VIII in 1543. It is one of the finest examples of timber framed architecture in the UK. It houses displays about timber-framed architecture and Royal hunting in Epping Forest.
All year Wed-Sun 14.00-17.00 or dusk if sooner
Last Admission: 16.45
A£0.50 C(accompanied)£Free
discount offer: Two Adults For The Price Of One

Rose Theatre Exhibition
56 Park Street London SE1 9AR
[BR: Waterloo/London Bridge. Tube: Mansion House, Cannon Street or London Bridge. Buses: 45, 63, 172 to Blackfriars Bridge; 15, 17 to Cannon Street; 11, 15, 23, 26, 76 to Mansion House; 149, 344, P11 to Southwark Street]
Tel: 020 7593 0026 Fax: 020 7633 0367
www.rdg.ac.uk/Rose
The first purpose-built theatre on Bankside, the Rose is the only Elizabethan theatre site with remains completely available for modern exploration. Its covered remains are tucked into the basement of an office block, submerged beneath a protective pool of water. This atmospheric site not only provides an insight into Shakespeare and Marlowe's London, it offers the opportunity to 'tread the boards' in their footsteps. The exhibition, which unfolds the fascinating story behind this unique fragment of history, centres around a multi-media presentation narrated by Sir Ian McKellen, and designed by award winning theatre designer William Dudley.
All year daily 10.00-17.00
Last Admission: 16.30
A£3.00 C(under 5)£Free C(5-16)£2.00 Family Ticket (A2+C3)£8.00 Concessions£2.50
Registered Disabled £2.50 + escort £Free
discount offer: Two For The Price Of One

Shakespeare's Globe
21 New Globe Walk Bankside London SE1 9DT
[Tube: London Bridge / Mansion House]
Tel: 020 7902 1500 Fax: 020 7902 1515
www.shakespeares-globe.org
The biggest exhibition of its kind devoted to the world of Shakespeare, from Elizabethan times to the present day - situated beneath the Globe Theatre itself. Explore Bankside, the Soho of Elizabethan London, follow Sam Wanamaker's struggle to recreate an authentic Globe for the twentieth century and beyond, and take a fascinating guided tour of today's working theatre. Globe Education provide workshops, lectures and courses for students of all ages and nationalities. For further information please call (020) 7902 1433. GlobeLink is the Globe's association for schools and colleges and provides a range of services including a designated website, examination hotline, regular newsletters and priority booking. Globe Performances 12 May - 24 September 2000. Box Office (020) 7401 9919. The Globe Café offers light refreshments and main dishes from £6.00. The Globe Restaurant offers main dishes starting at £9.00. Two courses with coffee from £15.00.
visitor comments: Tour guides are "performing actors" adding new and fascinating dimensions to the visit.
Shakespeare's Globe Exhibition: May-Sept daily 09.00-12.00. Oct-Apr daily 10.00-17.00. Performance season: May-Sept. Globe Café: daily 10.00-23.00. Globe Restaurant: daily 12.00-23.00 (reservations 020 7928 9444)
A£7.50 Concessions£6.00 C£5.00 Family Ticket £23.00. Admission includes a guided tour of the Theatre. Group rates 10+ available
↓special events
▶ **Child's Play**
1/5/00-30/9/00
An active introduction for 8-11 year olds exploring Shakespeare's work.

Syon House and Gardens
Syon Park London Road Brentford Middlesex TW8 8JF
[approach via A310 Twickenham Road into Park Road]
Tel: 020 8560 0883 Fax: 020 8568 0936
Syon House is the London home of the Duke of Northumberland. It is built on the site of a medieval abbey dissolved by Henry VIII. The present house is Tudor in origin but famed for its splendid Robert Adam interiors. Member of the Historic Houses Association.
15 Mar-29 Oct Wed, Thur, Sun & Bank Hol 11.00-17.00
Last Admission: 16.45
Gardens: A£3.00 Concessions£2.50. Combined ticket for House & Gardens: A£6.00 Concessions£4.50 Family Ticket £15.00
discount offer: Two For The Price Of One Full Paying Adult For Combined Ticket Only
↓special events
▶ **Spit and Polish**
22/4/00-24/4/00
Come and see a Victorian dishwasher in action! Experience live demonstrations of 19th century gadgets, housework techniques and recipes
▶ **Absolutely Georgian**
30/4/00-1/5/00
Rhiannon Gayle gives a lively performance with music, song and gossip on the most controver-

sial women of the 18th century

▶ **Countryside Live**
19/5/00-21/5/00
A new event with demonstrations and displays about our rural heritage

▶ **The 1900 House Guests**
28/5/00-29/5/00
Hoi Polloi demonstrate what it was like to be a Syon House Guest at the turn of the century. For the first time, the nursery wing will be on view

▶ **Start of the London to Brighton Classic Car Run**
4/6/00-4/6/00

▶ **Craft Fair**
27/7/00-30/7/00

▶ **Death by Chocolate**
27/8/00-28/8/00
Baroque 'n' Roll present music and dance reflecting the gossip and intrigues of Chocolate, the drink introduced to Europe in the 17th and 18th centuries

Tower of London
Tower Hill London EC3N 4AB
[Tube: Tower Hill]
Tel: 020 7709 0765 Fax: 020 7480 5350
www.hrp.org.uk

Perhaps the most famous tower in the world, it was used as the State Prison where King Henry VIII had two wives executed, Sir Walter Raleigh was imprisoned for 13 years and during both World Wars German spies were incarcerated here. It is home to the Crown Jewels and famous ravens. Includes the Royal Fusiliers Museum. The Jewel House was refurbished in 1994 and is now accessible for Wheelchairs. Wheelchairs available Free. Free Beefeater Tours and talks throughout the year. During school holidays free Family Trails. The armoury display in the White Tower opened in 1998. The Tower of London is the worst haunted places in Britain with the ghost of Thomas a Becket who appeared in the mid 13th century during the building of the inner curtain wall. He apparently reduced the work to rubble by striking it with his cross. The ghosts of the Little Princes (12 year old King Edward V and his 9 year old brother Richard, Duke of York) have occasionally been seen in the Bloody Tower dressed in white nightgowns. The grisliest haunting of the Tower if that of the 70 year old Countess of Salisbury - 'The last of the Plantagenets' - executed by Henry VIII (to awful to describe ask at the Tower!) The most persistent ghost if that of Queen Anne Boleyn drifting from Queen's House to the Chapel of St Peter ad Vincula where she floats down the aisle to the site of her final resting place under the chapels's alter. And finally, the most haunted part of the Tower is the Salt Tower, not only do dogs refuse to enter but Yeoman Warders are unwilling to visit after nightfall. The following events are free to Tower ticket holders.

visitor comments: Long queues during Summer, get there early. Beefeater tour has some wonderful stories to tell and really involves the children. Expensive, but there's lots to see.

All year Mar-Oct Mon-Sat 09.00-17.00, Sun 10.00-17.00. Nov-Feb Tue-Sat 09.00-16.00, Mon & Sun 10.00-16.00. Closed 24-25 Dec & 1 Jan
Last Admission: Closes 30 mins after last admission
A£10.50 C(under 5)£Free C(5-16)£6.90 Family Ticket (A2+C3/A1+C4) £31.00 OAPs&Students&Disabled£7.90. Wheelchair pushers £Free

↓*special events*

▶ **The Tower Menagerie**
27/10/99-31/3/00
The fascinating development of the Tower's collection of exotic animals prior to their removal to form London Zoo.

▶ **Opening of Thomas More's Cell**
10/1/00-10/12/00
St Thomas More was imprisoned in the Bell Tower in 1534 for refusing to acknowledge Henry VIII as head of the English Church. Entrance by guided tour only.

▶ **Gun Salutes 2000**
7/2/00-4/8/00
Actual Dates: Feb 7, Apr 21, June 2, 10, Aug 4. Gun salutes have been fired on important state and royal events since Tudor times

▶ **The Rise and Fall of Anne Boleyn**
19/2/00-27/2/00

▶ **The Ceremony of the Constable's Dues**
24/3/00-14/10/00
To be held on Mar 24, May 12, June 24, Sept 9 and Oct 14 only. Celebrates the ancient custom of paying dues if moored in the Pool of London.

▶ **The Royal Armouries' Millennium Exhibition**
15/4/00-31/12/00
Celebration of 2000 years of Tower history. Exhibits to include a volume of the Domesday Book

▶ **King Richard III: Man and Myth**
22/4/00-30/4/00
Was Richard III responsible for the deaths of the Princes in the Tower or was it malicious gossip?

▶ **State Parades**
23/4/00-17/12/00
Apr 23, May 28 and Dec 17 only. Yeoman Warders in State Dress escort Resident Governor from Queen's House to Chapel Royal St Peter ad Vincula.

▶ **Shakespeare at the Tower**
27/5/00-4/6/00
Scenes from Shakespeare will be performed alongside presentations of the historical events

portrayed

▶ **The Great Crown Jewels Robbery**
21/10/00-29/10/00
Follow Captain Blood through the unsuccessful 1671 attempt to steal the Crown Jewels

▶ **The King's Medieval Christmas**
27/12/00-31/12/00
Period musicians, music and merriment fill the Medieval Palace for a Christmas celebration

Whitehall

1 Malden Road Cheam Sutton Surrey SM3 8QD
[on A2043 just N of junction with A232. BR: Cheam]
Tel: 020 8643 1236 Fax: 020 8770 4777
www.sutton.gov.uk
A unique timber-framed house built 1500. Displays include medieval Cheam pottery; Nonsuch Palace; timber-framed buildings and Cheam School.
Apr-Sept Tue-Fri Sun 14.00-17.30, Sat 10.00-17.30. Oct-Mar Wed, Thur, Sun 14.00-17.30, Sat 10.00-17.30, also Bank Hol Mon. Closed 24 Dec-2 Jan
A£1.20 C£0.50
discount offer: Two For The Price Of One

Landmarks

British Airways London Eye

Jubilee Gardens The Southbank London SE1 7SW
[Tube: Embankment, Waterloo, Charing Cross & Westminster. Access will be via the river utilising the new Waterloo Millennium Pier to be built adjacent to the London Eye.]
Tel: 020 77074159 Fax: 020 7465 0923
www.ba-londoneye.com
Sweeping one of the world's most famous skylines at 135m (450ft) high, British Airways London Eye is London's fourth tallest structure. Its gradual 30 minute 360 degree rotation will give passengers totally new perspectives of some of the Capital's most famous landmarks and provide a birds-eye view usually accessible only by helicopter or aircraft. Unrivalled views from 32 fully enclosed, high tech capsules, each accommodating up to 25 people, will be enhanced by commentary designed to enable visitors to get the most out of the experience.
All year daily, 1 Nov-31 Mar 10.00-18.00, 1 Apr-31 Oct 09.00-late evening. Call 0870 5000 600 Advance ticket hotline. Group bookings 0870 400 3005
A£7.45 C£4.95 Concessions£5.95. Tickets can be booked in advance on 0870 5000 600

Thames Barrier Visitors Centre

1 Unity Way Woolwich London SE18 5NJ
[BR: Charlton, in Charlton signposted from Greenwich]
Tel: 020 8305 4188 Fax: 020 8855 2146
Built to prevent the possibility of flooding, the Thames Barrier is the world's largest moveable flood barrier. The Visitor Centre explains the flood threat and the construction of this £480 million project, now valued at £1 billion. All 10 gates are tested each month for two hours with full day closure in the autumn. See special events for some closure times, they may vary as a result of testing or weather conditions, please call on the day to check.
visitor comments: Interesting and reasonably entertaining.
All year Mon-Fri 10.00-17.00, Sat & Sun 10.30-17.30. Evening opening by special arrangements for groups, call for details
Last Admission: 1hr before closing
A£3.40 C&OAPs£2.00 Family Ticket £7.50. Car park £1.00. Coach park £Free

Tower Bridge Experience

Tower Bridge London SE1 2UP
[in centre of London signposted. Bus: 15 / 25 / 40 / 42 / 27 / 78 / 100 / D1 / P11. Tube: Tower Hill / London Bridge. Car Parking in: Tooley Street & Lower Thames Street]
Tel: 020 7378 1928 Fax: 020 7357 7935

www.towerbridge.org.uk

One of London's most unusual and exciting exhibitions is situated inside Tower Bridge. Animatronic characters from the bridge's past guide you through a series of audio-visual presentations, telling the story of this world famous landmark. From the high-level walkways above the Thames, you'll also enjoy one of the memorable panoramic views of London. The Tower Bridge Experience has won the 'England for Excellence' award for London: All areas of The Tower Bridge Experience are accessible to disabled visitors, including those in wheelchairs. Ramps and wheelchair accessible toilets are provided, and if any of the party are unable to climb stairs, a guide will be happy to arrange for use of the lift.

All year Apr-Oct daily 10.00-18.30. Nov-Mar daily 09.30-18.00. Closed Good Fri, 24-25 Dec, 19 Jan

Last Admission: 75mins before closing

Queuing Times: 10mins max

A£6.15 C(5-15) & OAPs&Students £4.15 Family Ticket (A1+C2)£13.95 (A2+C2)£15.50 (A2+C3)£17.50 (A2+C4)£19.50. Group rates: A£5.55 C(5-15) & OAPs&Students £3.75. Prices expire 31 Mar 2000

↓*special events*

► **Tower Bridge Lifts**

1/1/00-31/12/00

Tower Bridge lifts around 500 times a year and as many as 10 times a day during the summer months. Visitors to London can find out when the bridge will be opening by phoning a 24 hour dedicated phone line. 020 7378 7700.

Literature & Libraries

Dickens House Museum

48 Doughty Street London WC1N 2LF

[Tube: Russell Square]

Tel: 020 7405 2127 Fax: 020 7831 5175

www.dickensmuseum.com

Charles Dickens lived in Doughty Street in his twenties and it was here that he worked on his first full-length novel, The Pickwick Papers, Oliver Twist and Nicholas Nickelby. Pages of the original manuscript are on view. Dickens' drawing room has been reconstructed.

All year Mon-Sat 10.00-17.00 incl 24-26 Dec 10.30-18.00

Last Admission: 16.30

A£4.00 C(5-15)£2.00 Family Ticket £9.00 OAPs&Students£3.00

discount offer: Two For The Price Of One

Living History Museums

Sir Winston Churchill's Britain at War Experience

64-66 Tooley Street London Bridge London SE1 2TF

[close to London Bridge]

Tel: 020 7403 3171 Fax: 020 7403 5104

www.britain-at-war.co.uk

Take an unforgettable journey back in time to the dark days of the Second World War and experience the fury and danger of war torn Britain and life on the Home Front. Special effects recreate the gihts and sounds of the London Blitz. Special children's activities during school holidays.

All year Mar-Oct daily 10.00-17.30, Oct-Mar daily 10.00-16.30. Closed 24-26 Dec & Jan 1

Last Admission: Summer 17.30, Winter 16.30

A£5.95 C£2.95 Family Ticket £14.00 Concessions£3.95

discount offer: One Child Free When Accompanied By A Full Paying Adult

Maritime

Cutty Sark Clipper Ship
Greenwich Pier King William Walk Greenwich London SE10 9HT
[A2 / A102(M), off A206 signposted to Greenwich. Tube: Island Gardens BR: Greenwich]
Tel: 020 8858 3445 Fax: 020 8853 3589
www.cuttysark.org.uk
The fastest tea clipper to be built once sailed 363 miles in a single day. She has been preserved in dry dock since 1957 and her graceful lines dominate the riverside at Greenwich. Exhibitions and video presentation on board tell the story of the ship and there is a magnificent collections of ships' figureheads.
All year daily 10.00-17.00. Closed 24-26 Dec
Last Admission: 30mins before closing
A£3.50 Family Ticket £8.50 Concessions£2.50. Passport Ticket (including National Maritime Museum & Royal Observatory) A£12.00 Concessions£9.60
discount offer: Two For The Price Of One

National Maritime Museum
Romney Road Greenwich London SE10 9NF
[J2 M25 then A2 and A206, follow signposts into central Greenwich. BR: Maze Hill DLR: Cutty Sark]
Tel: 020 8858 4422/312 6565 Fax: 020 8312 6521
www.nmm.ac.uk
See how the sea affects our daily lives in this impressive modern museum. Themes include exploration and discovery, Nelson, 20th century seapower, trade and empire, passenger shipping and luxury liners, maritime London, costume, art and the sea, the future of the sea and the global garden. Exhibition will take place in the Queen's House in the year 2000. This definitive exhibition will tell the 'Story of Time' with over 300 exhibits from around the world, with a unique mix of the arts and sciences, the works of mankind, and the natural world.
visitor comments: The newly refurbished museum is fantastic and employs the latest technology. Definitely worth a visit.
All year daily 10.00-17.00. Closed 24-26 Dec
Last Admission: 16.30
A£7.50 C(Under16)£Free Concessions£6.00
Group rates available. Story of Time extra charge
discount offer: One Free Ticket When An Adult Ticket Is Purchased. Ref: DOG

↓*special events*

► **Story of Time**
1/12/99-26/9/00
Exhibition of Man's Study of Time with world famous exhibits.

Medical Museums

The Old Operating Theatre, Museum and Herb Garret
9a St Thomas Street Southwark London SE1 9RY
[Tube: London Bridge]
Tel: 020 7955 4791 Fax: 020 7378 8383
Climb up a steep spiral staircase and into the roof of a church, which houses the oldest surviving operating theatre in Britain dating back to 1821 before the advent of antiseptic surgery or anaesthetic. Complete with wooden operating table, blood box and tiered stands from which spectators witnessed the ordeal of surgery. Pill making equipment, surgical paraphernalia and specimens, lurk amidst a cornucopia of medicinal herbs in the 300 year old apothecary's garret of Old St. Thomas Hospital.

All year Tue-Sun 10.00-17.00. Open most Mon - call to check. Closed 25 Dec
A£2.90 C£1.50 Family Ticket £7.25 Concessions£2.00
discount offer: Two For The Price Of One

Military & Defence Museums

HMS Belfast (Imperial War Museum)

Morgan's Lane Tooley Street London SE1 2JH
[BR/Tube: London Bridge. Tube: Tower Hill / London Bridge. DLR: Tower Gateway]
Tel: 020 7940 6328 Fax: 020 7403 0719
www.iwm.org.uk

HMS Belfast - the last of the Royal Navy's big-gun armoured warships from the Second World War. With nine huge decks, you can see for yourself where 850 men lived, worked and fought. Visitors can explore from the captain's bridge all the way down to the massive six inch gun turrets, boiler rooms, hammock-slung messdecks, galley, sick bay, punishment cells and more. Leave at least two hours for whole visit. Free Birthday Party facilities on board for pre-booked groups. In dry dock from 1 June-8 July 1999 therefore closed, but why not come to the Welcome Home Fun Day on the 17 July 99 - includes music, children's entertainment and rum punch!
Mar-Oct daily 10.00-18.00. Nov-Feb daily 10.00-17.00. Closed 24-26 Dec. 1 June-8 July 1999 HMS Belfast will be in dry dock and therefore closed
Last Admission: Mar-Oct 17.15, Nov-Feb 16.15
Queuing Times: Minimal
A£4.70 C(0-16)£Free Concessions£3.60. Group bookings £3.40 £2.60 & £1.70. Group bookings call for details. Additional discounts to pre-booked schools: One Teacher Admitted Free Per Ten Pupils

National Army Museum

Royal Hospital Road Chelsea London SW3 4HT
[BR: Victoria, Tube: Sloane Square, Bus: 11 / 19 / 22 & 211 along King's Road; 137 to Pimlico Road; 239 (Mon-Sat) stops immediately outside the Museum]
Tel: 020 7730 0717 Fax: 020 7823 6573
www.national-army-museum.ac.uk

Discover some of Britain's finest military treasures. Displays include weapons, paintings, equipment, uniforms, models, medals, reconstructions. Exhibits include nine Victoria Crosses, a model of the Battle of Waterloo, Florence Nightingale's jewellery, and the skeleton of Napoleon's horse. A new permanent exhibition, The Modern Army, is now open.
All year daily 10.00-17.30. Closed Good Fri, May Day, 24-26 Dec & 1 Jan
Admission Free

↓special events

► **String of Pearls Activities**
5/2/00-3/12/00
A series of events and activities in Chelsea on the first weekend of every month throughout 2000. Call for date confirmation and details

► **2000 Soldiers' Lives and Soldiers' Wives**
4/3/00-5/3/00

Royal Air Force Museum

Grahame Park Way Hendon London NW9 5LL
[signposted from A1 / A5 M1 N Circular. BR: Mill Hill. Tube: Colindale. Bus: 303]
Tel: 020 8205 2266 Fax: 020 8205 8044
www.rafmuseum.org.uk

There's something to entertain everyone with over 70 legendary planes, fascinating exhibits and an art gallery telling the story of aviation from the Wright Brothers to the RAF Eurofighter of the 21st century. Free return visit within six months of issue of individual tickets, ask for details. Please check info line for possible changes. Major new interactive gallery opens in the Spring - 'fun 'n' flight.'
All year daily 10.00-18.00. Closed 24-26 Dec & 1 Jan. Info line: 0891 600 5633 24hr
Last Admission: 17.30
A£6.50 C(0-5)£Free C(5-16)£3.25 Family Ticket (A2+C2)£16.60 Additional C£1.65 OAPs£4.90 Students&UB40s£2.25. Groups of 10+ 20% discount. School discounts: £1.50 1 Adult leader Free per 5 Children.
discount offer: Two For The Price Of One (based on highest priced ticket)

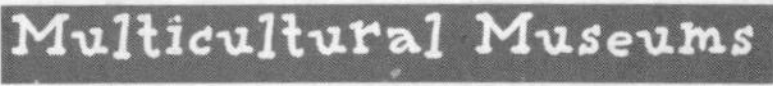

Horniman Museum and Gardens
100 London Road Forest Hill London SE23 3PQ
[situated on the South Circular. BR: Forest Hill, Bus: 176 / 185 / 312]
Tel: 020 8699 1872 Fax: 020 8291 5506
www.horniman.demon.co.uk
Situated in 16 acres of gardens, with displays about world cultures, natural history collection and an extensive exhibition of musical instruments from all over the world which can be experienced through computers in the Music Room. Hands-on talks for children are held throughout the year at no extra charge, however places are limited and must be allocated on a first-come-first-serve basis. The museum has recently been awarded a £9 million Lottery grant to improve its galleries and build a new extension. There will be more exhibition space, better public facilities and a conservation studio.
All year Mon-Sat 10.30-17.30, Sun 14.00-17.30. Closed 25 Dec. Gardens close at sunset
Last Admission: 17.20
Admission Free

Jewish Museum - Finchley, London's Museum of Jewish Life
80 East End Road London N3 2SY
[on A504. Tube: Finchley Central. 12mins walk via Station Road / Manor View]
Tel: 020 8349 1143 Fax: 020 8343 2162
www.jewmusm.ort.org
Social history displays tracing Jewish immigration and settlement in London including reconstructions of East End tailoring and cabinet-making workshops. Mezzanine gallery has special exhibition on Leon Greenman, British citizen and Holocaust survivor. Education programmes and group visits by prior arrangement. Guided walks of Jewish London also available.
All year Mon-Thur 10.30-17.00, Sun 10.30-16.30. Closed Jewish Festivals, Public & Bank Hol, 24 Dec-4 Jan. Also closed Sun in Aug and Bank Holiday Weekends
Last Admission: 30mins before closing
A£2.00 C£Free Concessions£1.00
discount offer: Two For The Price Of One Full Paying Adult

↓*special events*

▶ **Taxi!**
10/2/00-29/10/00
An exhibition about Jewish taxi drivers and the London cab trade. Call 020 8349 1143 for further details.

Music & Theatre Museums

British Library National Sound Archive
29 Exhibition Road London SW7
[Tube: South Kensington]
Tel: 020 7412 7440
Library and listening facilities by appointment only. Holds one million discs of all kinds and more than 80,000 hours of recorded tape. Collection of music, wildlife sounds, drama, spoken literature and sound effects.
Admission Free

Cabaret Mechanical Theatre
33-34 The Market Covent Garden London WC2E 8RE
[Tube: Covent Garden]
Tel: 020 7379 7961 Fax: 020 7497 5445
www.cabaret.co.uk/
The museum offers entertainment for the whole family with an impressive collection of Automata. Buy a ticket in the foyer area, get it stamped by the mechanical stamping man

and enter the magical world of Cabaret, where at the touch of a button or the insertion of a coin, machines are set in motion.
All year Mon-Sat 10.00-18.30, Sun 11.00-18.30. School holidays daily 10.00-19.00. Closed 25-26 Dec & 1 Jan
Last Admission: 18.15
A£1.95 Family Ticket £4.95 C&Concessions£1.20
discount offer: £1.00 Off Family Ticket

Musical Museum
368 High Street Brentford Middlesex TW8 0BD
Tel: 020 8560 8108
This museum will take you back to a bygone age to hear and see a marvellous working collection of automatic musical instruments from small music boxes to a mighty Wurlitzer theatre organ. Working demonstrations. Tour lasts 90mins. Registered Charity No. 802011.
Apr-Oct Sat & Sun 14.00-17.0. July-Aug Wed 14.00-16.00, Sat & Sun 14.00-17.00
A£3.20 C&OAPs£2.50 Family Ticket £10.00
discount offer: Two For The Price Of One. Not Valid For Special Events. Valid Until 31 Oct 2000

Rock Circus
The London Pavilion 1 Piccadilly Circus London W1V 9LA
[Tube: Piccadilly Circus]
Tel: 020 7734 7203 Fax: 020 7734 8023
www.madame-tussauds.com
London's Rock Circus is where the spirit of rock speaks to you, sings to you, plays for you, moves and touches you. Audio-animatronic moving and static wax figures, lasers, authentic memorabilia, videos, archive film and personal stereo sound surround you and astound you. There's a change of pace at every pace, a new rock turn at every turn. Rock Circus' award winning exhibition and show is the ultimate rock experience and will take you 90mins to see.
All year Sun-Thur 11.00-21.00, Tue 12.00-21.00, Fri & Sat 11.00-22.00. Rocking for Easter 1999, after transformations
A£8.25 C(0-16)£6.25 Concessions£6.95. Groups Rates of 10+: A£6.95 C(0-16)£5.10 Concessions£5.90

Natural History Museums

Natural History Museum
Cromwell Road London SW7 5BD
[Tube: South Kensington]
Tel: 020 7942 5000 Fax: 020 7942 5536
www.nhm.ac.uk
A day out for all the family. Highlights include 'Dinosaurs,' 'Creepy Crawlies,' 'Human biology' and 'The power within' where you can experience an earthquake and investigate the causes and devastating effects of volcanoes. Opening in July 2000 'Rhythms of life' will take a quirky look at the roles of rhythm and time in nature. Ideal for all age groups - closes Spring 2001. October 2000 - February 2001 BG Wildlife Photographer of the Year 2000, internationally famous exhibition of stunning wildlife photography.
visitor comments: Terrific value. Very Interesting displays and lots of touch screens. Wide variety of refreshments with quick service and pleasant surroundings. The Earth Gallery is fabulous!
All year Mon-Sat 10.00-17.50, Sun 11.00-17.50. Closed 23-26 Dec
Last Admission: 17.30
A£6.50 C£Free Concessions£3.50. Groups call for details.
↓*special events*

▶ Voyages of Discovery
4/7/99-1/3/00
▶ BG Wildlife Photographer of the Year Exhibition
23/10/99-29/2/00

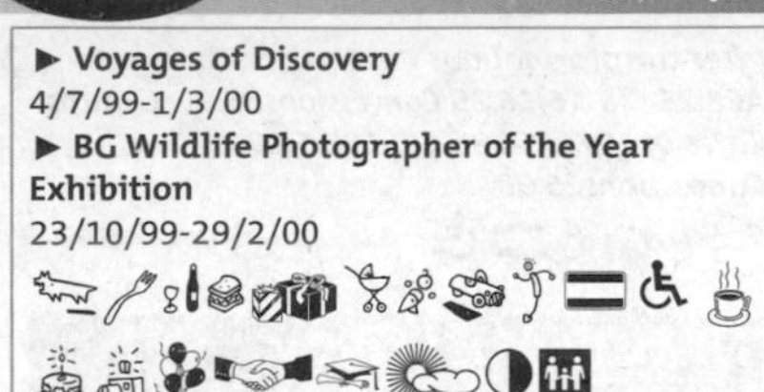

On the Water

Canal Cruises - Jenny Wren
250 Camden High Street London NW1 8QS
[Tube: Camden Town]
Tel: 020 7485 4433/6210 Fax: 020 7485 9098
Cruise along the picturesque Regent's Canal aboard the Jenny Wren, a traditionally designed and decorated canal boat. 90mins going through a lock, past London Zoo, Regent's Park to Little Venice and return with an interesting commentary on the canal's history. Evening buffet cruises for groups of 20/40. Call for details.
Mar-Oct daily all day
A£5.40 C&OAPs£3.25. School Groups each £2.00. Groups rates call for details

Canal Cruises - My Fair Lady
250 Camden High Street London NW1 8QS
[Tube: Camden Town]
Tel: 020 7485 4433/6210 Fax: 020 7485 9098
Enjoy a leisurely cruise along the Regent's Canal aboard the My Fair Lady, a luxury cruising restaurant. Whilst cruising an excellent three-course meal is served freshly cooked in the galley. My Fair Lady is also available for hire throughout the year for luncheon or dinner for a maximum of 80 guests.
All year, public cruise for lunch of Sunday, public cruise for dinner Tue & Sun
A£16.95-£29.85

Catamaran Cruisers
Charing Cross Pier Victoria Embankment London WC2N 6NU
[Tube: Embankment]
Tel: 020 7987 1185 Fax: 020 7839 1034
See the heart of London from the Thames. Daily sightseeing journey including commentary, from Charing Cross Pier to Tower Pier to Greenwich.
All year daily 09.30-16.30. Please telephone for departure times.
Last Admission: 16.30
A£7.00 C£3.80. Group Rates and School Parties available

Puppet Theatre Barge
Little Venice Blomfield Road London W9 2PF
[Tube: WarwickAvenue. All buses on the Edgware Rd]
Tel: 020 7249 6876 Box Office Fax: 020 7683 0741
The Hare and the Tortoise and other tales from Aesop are brought to life with drama and humour. Staged with beautiful lighting and carved marionettes, enchantment is guaranteed. Brer Rabbit visits Africa - This specially written play tells of Brer Rabbit arriving in Africa, in his new waistcoat, feeling rather proud of himself. He is staying with his old grandmother when he finds himself in trouble. All the animals including the elephant, the lion and the tortoise gather together to help. Brer Rabbit returns home much the wiser. A Shipful of Verse matinees for the family, inspired by R L Stevensons A Childs' Garden of Verses and Macbeth, evenings for adults, a new production. Full details from the box office.
All year weekends and School Hols.
Last Admission: Latecomers admitted in performance break
Matinees: A£6.00 C&Concessions£5.5 Evenings: A£7.50 C&Concessions£6.00. Apply to Box Office for Group Rates and School Parties. Seats can be booked in advance.
discount offer: One Ticket Free With Every Four Seats Booked

Palaces

Banqueting House
Whitehall London SW1A2ER
[Tube: Westminster / Embankment / Charing Cross]
Tel: 020 7930 4179 Fax: 020 7930 8268
www.hrp.org.uk
This fascinating building offers a haven of tranquility amidst the bustle of Westminster. Designed by Inigo Jones in 1619, the Banqueting House is all that survives of the

Palace of Whitehall, that was destroyed by fire in 1698. It has been the scene of many historic events including the execution of Charles I and restoration of Charles II. Features include magnificent ceilings painted by Rubens in 1635 and the Undercroft, where James I used to retreat from the commotion of court life.
All year Mon-Sat 10.00-17.00. Closed Good Fri, 24 Dec-2 Jan, Bank Hol & Government Functions
Last Admission: 16.30
A£3.80 C£2.30 Concessions£3.00

↓special events

▶ **The Faerie Queen (Purcell)**
6/3/00-6/3/00
▶ **Performed by Alibas**
3/4/00-3/4/00
▶ **Mistresse Musicke**
8/5/00-8/5/00
▶ **Court Dance**
5/6/00-5/6/00
▶ **Restoration London**
3/7/00-3/7/00
▶ **The Merrie Monarch**
7/8/00-7/8/00
▶ **Performance to be confirmed**
11/9/00-11/9/00
▶ **Mistresse Musicke**
9/10/00-9/10/00
▶ **The Merrie Monarch**
13/11/00-13/11/00

Buckingham Palace

Buckingham Palace Road London SW1 1AA
[Tube: Victoria / Green Park]
Tel: 020 7839 1377 Fax: 020 7930 9625
www.royal.gov.uk
Here among some of the finest pictures and works of art in the world, visitors can see where The Queen and Members of the Royal Family receive and entertain their guests on State, ceremonial and Official occasions. From the pomp and ceremony of a State Visit, when the Guard of Honour is mounted in the Quadrangle and The Queen entertains the visiting Head of State at a ceremonial banquet, to ministerial and diplomatic audiences, receptions and other events, the State Rooms provide a majestic backdrop to the on going work of the Monarchy. Masterpieces by Vermeer, van Dyck, Rubens, de Hooch, Zuccarelli and Rembrandt are among the forty or so paintings which hang in the Picture Gallery. Fine sculpture, including two groups by Antonio Canova, line the Marble Hall and, in the splendour of the White Drawing Room visitors can see the secret door used by The Queen and the Royal Family. To help visitors enjoy their visit fully, a comprehensive Official Guide is available for purchase in English, German, Italian, French, Spanish and Japanese languages. Wheelchair users are required to pre-book for the Summer Opening of the State Rooms. Regrettably, due to architectural limitations, The Queen's Gallery is inaccessible to wheelchair users. The Royal Mews, however is fully accessible.
6 Aug-3 Oct daily 09.30-16.30. Ticket Office: 31 July-3 Oct daily 09.00-16.00. The Changing of the Guard takes place at 11.30 daily from 1 Apr-early July and on alternate days thereafter. 24 hour information line: 0171 799 2331
Last Admission: 16.00
Queuing Times: 15-20mins
A£10.00 C£5.00. Over 60's £7.50. Advance Purchase via Credit Card (0171 321 2233) or from the Ticket Office in Green Park. Groups discounts to Summer Opening (min 15): 15-250 people £9.50 per person; 251-1000 £9.25 per person; 1001-2000 £9.00 per person; 2001-3500 £8.50 per person; 3501+ to be negotiated, please telephone

↓special events

▶ **Changing of the Guard Ceremonies**
2/1/00-31/12/00

Eltham Palace

Court Yard Eltham London SE9 5QE
[1m N of A20 off Court Yard. BR: Eltham or Mottingham 0.50m. Plenty of on site parking available]
Tel: 020 8294 2548
www.english-heritage.org.uk
Recently opened. Discover this unique site - home to a spectacular 1930s Art Deco country house and a magnificent medieval Great Hall. Scene of many society parties, the home of

millionaire Stephen Courtauld evokes the style and glamour of the 1930s era. Then step back in time and marvel at the 15th century Great Hall which stood at the heart of the medieval palace, the boyhood home of Henry VIII.
All year. 1 Apr-30 Sept Wed-Fri & Sun 10.00-18.00. 1-31 Oct Wed-Fri & Sun 10.00-17.00. 1 Nov-31 Mar Wed-Fri & Sun 10.00-16.00. Also open Bank Hol Mon. Closed 24-26 Dec
House & Grounds: A£5.90 C£3.00
Concessions£4.40. Grounds only: A£3.50 C£1.80 Concessions£2.60. Group rates 11+ 15%

Kensington Palace State Apartments
Kensington Gardens Palace Green London W8 4PX
[Tube: High Street Kensington]
Tel: 020 7376 2858 Fax: 020 7376 0198
www.hrp.org.uk
Designed by Sir Christopher Wren for William III and Mary II, this peaceful royal retreat was the childhood home of Queen Victoria. Features include the magnificent State Apartments and 'Dressing for Royalty', a stunning presentation of Royal Court and Ceremonial Dress dating from the 18th century. Multi language sound guides are available to lead visitors around the magnificent State Apartments. Highlights include the splendid Cupola Room, the most lavishly decorated State Room in the palace where Queen Victoria was baptised, and the beautifully restored King's Gallery. 'Dressing for Royalty' allows visitors to participate in the excitement of dressing for court - from invitation to presentation. There is also a selection of 16 dresses owned and worn by HM Queen Elizabeth II.
Mid Mar-mid Oct daily 10.00-18.00, mid Oct-mid Mar daily 10.00-17.00
Last Admission: 60mins before closing
A£8.50 C£6.10 Family Ticket £26.10
Concessions£6.70 (Entrance prices increase by £1.00 between 1 Oct 1999 - 31 March 2000)

↓special events

▶ **Diana, Princess of Wales - a Collection of her Dresses**
1/10/99-31/3/00
14 dresses that belonged to Diana, Princess of Wales and show her approach to dressing for royal occasions, are on display

Police, Prisons & Dungeons

London Dungeon
28-34 Tooley Street London SE1 2SZ
[Tube: London Bridge]
Tel: 020 0891 6000 666 Fax: 020 7378 1529
www.dungeons.com
Deep in the heart of London, buried beneath the paving stone lies the world's most chillingly famous museum of horror. The London Dungeon brings more than 2,000 years of gruesomely authentic history vividly back to life - and death. Visit the carnage and stench of a recently ransacked medieval village or wander through into the horrors committed under the name of God and the King before coming face to face with your own 'Judgement Day.' This recent £3.5million addition will take you on the ride of your death through the sewers of London. Finally find out more than you would really care to know about Jack the Ripper. A warning - in the Dungeons dark catacombs it always pays to keep your wits about you ... some of the exhibits have an unnerving habit of coming back to life! New for Easter 2000: Firestorm - new £1m feature.
visitor comments: Fantastical horror museum - but it may frighten younger children.
All year daily Apr-Sept 10.00-17.30 Oct-Mar 10.30-17.00
Last Admission: Mar-Oct 17.30, Nov-Feb 16.30
Queuing Times: 1-2 hours in Summer
A£9.50 C&OAPs£6.50 Students£8.50 Group rates available

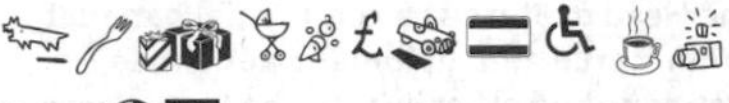

Science - Earth & Planetary

London Planetarium
Marylebone Road London NW1 5LR
[Tube: Baker Street]
Tel: 020 7935 6861 Fax: 020 7465 0862
www.madame-tussauds.com
Star shows are performed throughout the day

and visitors can experience a 3 dimensional journal through space. Interactive "Space Zone" exhibition areas provide up-to-date information about the stars and planets through touch-sensitive screens. Not recommended for the under 5's.
visitor comments: Queued for ages in boring surroundings. But the boys loved it once we got in.
All year daily, shows every 40 minutes from 12.20. Closed 25 Dec
Last Admission: 16.30
Queuing Times: 15mins
A£6.00 C£4.00 OAPs£4.60. Combined ticket with Madame Tussaud's A£12.25 C£8.00 OAPs£9.30

Royal Observatory Greenwich

Greenwich Park Greenwich London SE10 9NF
[off the A2. BR: Maze Hill DLR: Cutty Sark]
Tel: 020 8312 6565 Fax: 020 8312 6521
www.rog.nmm.ac.uk
Stand on the longitude zero, the Greenwich Meridian, the home of time. Explore the history of time and astronomy in this charming Wren building. see the Astronomer Royal's apartments. Watch the time-ball fall at 1 o'clock. Admire Harrison's amazing time-keepers and other historic clocks. Climb to the giant refracting telescope.
visitor comments: Very popular. Many visitors. Interesting and pleasing experience.
All year daily 10.00-17.00. Closed 24-26 Dec
Last Admission: 16.30
A£6.00 C£Free OAPs&Students£4.80. Combined Admission with National Maritime Museum also available
discount offer: One Free Ticket When An Adult Ticket Is Purchased. Ref: DOG

Science Museum

Exhibition Road South Kensington London SW7 2DD
[Buses: 9 / 10 / 14 / 345 / 49 / 52 / 74 / C1. Tube: South Kensington]
Tel: 020 7942 4354
www.nmsi.ac.uk
When the Wellcome Wing at the Science Museum opens in the summer of 2000, it will be the world's leading centre for the presentation of contemporary science and technology open to the public. The wing will be a breathtaking theatre of science. The exhibition spaces in the Wellcome Wing will feature interactive exhibitions devoted to some of the most important areas of modern science and technology - notably genetics, brain science, artificial intelligence and digital technology. The latest ideas and issues in science and technology will be presented using the most innovative, fast changing displays ever undertaken in the Science Museum. The Wellcome Wing marks a new era, enabling the Museum to do justice not only to the past work of the scientists and technologists but also the work they are doing today. The Wellcome Wing will house the state-of-the-art IMAX (large screen) 3D film theatre and catering and retail facilities.
visitor comments: Children loved the interactive parts. The 'Basement' really graps your attention! Excellent water play.
All year daily 10.00-18.00. Closed 24-26 Dec
A£6.50 C£Free Concessions£3.50, all visitors to the Museum after 16.30 £Free

↓special events

▶ **It's About Time**
1/3/99-1/3/00
▶ **The Art of Invention**
15/10/99-24/4/00
Exhibition bringing to life the incredible engineering projects which revolutionised design and architecture in Renaissance Italy. Open daily, 10.00-18.00. Closed 24-26, 31 Dec, 1 Jan.

The Dome

Greenwich Peninsular London SE10 OBB
[Tube: North Greenwich, by river: shuttle boats between historic Greenwich and the Dome; by foot and by bike, new walkways and cycle routes; by rail, new Millennium Transit link to the rail network; by tube, the largest underground station in Europe has been built at the heart of the Dome to serve the new Jubilee line extension, 12 mins from Central London]
Tel: 0870 606 2000 ticket line
www.dome2000.co.uk
Opened on time by the Queen on 31st Dec 1999 The Sixteen Zones are: 1 Central Show - Tells the story of a tragic larger-then-life family, played by a cast of 70 aerial acrobats. 2a Work- Discover the skills you need in the workplace of the future, 2b Learn - Test yourself in the orchard of learning and access the Tesco SchoolNet 2000 project. 3 Money - The walls

are lined with £1million of legal tender! experience spending this much money and see what impact it has. 4 Our Town Stage - More than 200 performances by local communities and international visitors in the World Stage Season. 5 Rest - There is nothing at all here, just a soothing light and sound show. 6 Mind - An exploration of the power of thought. 7 Faith, 7 Talk - Everything communication is here, create a web site send an email or leave a message for the future. 9 Self Portrait - A national portrait of how we see Britain. 10 Home Planet - Take a British Spaceways flight to future spacetravel. 11 Living Island - Virtual seaside resort made from recycled household waste. 12 Journey - Explores the history and future of motion from horses to sci-fi machines. 13 Shared Ground - The world's largest recycled cardboard structure created with items collected by Blue Peter Viewers. 14 Play - Video arcade for the future. 15 Body - Take a trip through the human body.

visitor comments: A simply superb day out, the Body Zone - it's not as good as the other zones... which are highly entertaining. So much to see, well worth the money, the building is amazing with much more than just the Dome. NO picnic areas! But you can eat picnics at food outlets. Lost Children: make sure you tell your child to ASK for help, then YOU ASK too, you will be reunited, NO tannoy system. Make sure you see the SHOW and the Black Adder Film... they're great. In all the Dome does not deserve the bad press it has had, I whole-hearted recommend a visit - Editor (I paid for my tickets)

All year daily from 1st Jan 2000 for 366 days till 31 Dec 2000. Daily 10.00-18.00 with late opening till 23.00 planned from Apr
Last Admission: Timed Tickets
Tickets must normally be purchased in advance, however, if available they can be be purchased at the Dome. A£20.00 C(0-5)£Free C(5-15) & Students£16.50 OAPs£18.00 ES40£12.00 Family Ticket (either A2+C3 or A1+C4)£57.00; Group rates 15+ A£17.50 OAPs£12.00 Students£14.50 Schools£8.00

↓*special events*

▶ **Daily Shows**
1/1/00-31/12/00

Sealife Centres & Aquariums

London Aquarium
County Hall Riverside Building Westminster Bridge Road London SE1 7PB
[Tube: Westminster, across Westminster Bridge from the Houses of Parliament]
Tel: 020 7967 8000 Fax: 020 7967 8029
www.londonaquarium.co.uk

The London Aquarium, housed within County Hall on the Thames, is three levels of exciting and educational exhibits, featuring hundreds of varieties of fish and marine life, many of which have not been seen before on these shores. The main attraction will give visitors the chance to enjoy an uninterrupted view of marine life via a huge twin tank display. Also included are some hands-on and interactive displays, where you can touch the starfish, crabs, mussels and rays. Additional tanks display aspects of sea and marine life from different regions and habitats around the world. There is a new interactive Coral display and our new exhibits include The Bizarre Nautilus.

visitor comments: Feel really close to fish and sharks. Good opportunity to touch some fish. The kids loved the day.

All year daily 10.00-18.00
Last Admission: 17.00
Queuing Times: Up to 3 hours
A£8.00 C(3-14)£5.00 Family Ticket (A2+C2)£22.00 Concessions£6.50

discount offer: £2.00 Off Published Admission Price

Social History Museums

Gunnersbury Park Museum
Popes Lane Acton London W3 8LQ
[J of A4, M4, North Circular. Bus: E3 Tube: Acton Town]
Tel: 020 8992 1612 Fax: 020 8752 0686

Set in 186 acres of parkland the Mansion was built circa1802 by architect owner Alexander Copland. Later enlarged by Sidney Smirke for N M Rothschild. Now a museum with constantly changing exhibitions, our collections represent social and local history, fashion and childhood. Special group tours can be arranged of Gunnersbury Mansion, phone for details.

Museum: Apr-Oct Mon-Fri 13.00-17.00, Sat, Sun & Bank Hol 13.00-18.00. Nov-Mar Mon-Fri 13.00-16.00. Closed 25-26 Dec & 1 Jan. House: Group tours by arrangement
Last Admission: 15min before closure
Admission Free

discount offer: Any Three Postcards Free

Imperial War Museum
Lambeth Road London SE1 6HZ
[Tube: Lambeth North, Waterloo, Elephant & Castle, well signposted]
Tel: 020 7416 5320 Fax: 020 7416 5374
www.iwm.org.uk

Features all aspects, of all wars involving Britain and the Commonwealth since 1914. Modern exhibitions using the latest technology. Includes special exhibitions and an extensive programme of events, as well as an art gallery. As part of the Millennium Commission for development, a new Holocaust and Total War gallery is due to open in June 2000. A major new exhibition runs to 30 May 2000, "From the Bomb to the Beatles: 1945 - 1965." Sir Terence Conran designed this special exhibition, which will chronicle the changing face of Britain in the post war years. Special features include a 1940's prefab. home, a 1950s coffee bar with a jukebox.

visitor comments: Very interesting - we all learnt a lot, and there's no charge for kids.

All year daily 10.00-18.00. Closed 24-26 Dec
A£5.20 C£Free Concessions£4.20. Group rates 10+ on application. Admission Free from 16.30 daily

↓*special events*

▶ **Do Touch the Exhibits**
19/2/00-27/2/00

▶ **Signs of the Times**
24/2/00-7/5/00
An exhibition of over 100 superb examples of graphic design from Eastern Europe

▶ **Go To It!**
1/3/00-1/12/00
Actual dates to be announced (call for details) A display to mark the contribution made by the many people who worked on the Home Front during WWII, often in dangerous and difficult conditions.

▶ **Recent Acquisitions**
1/3/00-1/1/01
A chance to see some of the latest acquisitions made by the museum, including objects, film, photographs and works of art

▶ **Korea**
14/4/00-1/12/00
Fifty years ago British and Commonwealth troops went off to fight in Korea. This exhibition looks at the experiences of those who were involved. End date not confirmed - please call for details

▶ **Spitfire Summer FIlms**
16/4/00-31/5/00
Angles One Five (1952) (98mins) 16 Apr only at 14.00. This Week: from Gaumont British News (1939-1940). (30mins) 3-28 Apr, 1-26 & 30-31 May weekdays at 16.00

▶ **Spitfire Scramble Easter Egg Hunt**
20/4/00-30/4/00
Free mini chocolate eggs for all those taking part

▶ **The Holocaust**
1/6/00-1/6/00
A major permanent exhibition about one of the most chilling events of the 20th century. Opens mid 2000 this date is to be confirmed

Spectator Sports

Arsenal Football Stadium Tour

Avenell Road Highbury London N5 1BU
[Tube: Arsenal]
Tel: 020 7704 4000 Fax: 020 7704 4101
www.arsenal.co.uk

Stadium tour of Marbel Hall, dressing rooms, trophy cabinet, manager's dugout and museum. Tours by arrangement, call for details.

By appointment only. Please telephone for details
A£4.00 C&OAPs£2.00

Chelsea Football Club

Stamford Bridge Fulham Road London SW6 1HS
[Tube: Fulham Broadway]
Tel: 0870 603 0005 Booking
www.chelseafc.co.uk

Sit on the seat of your favourite player, in the Manager's seat in the dugout. Walk up the players tunnel and hear the crowd roar. Find out how Chelsea Football Club are preparing for the 21st Century, how security and technology provide safety for the supporters, discover the secrets of the hallowed turf. Tour duration is 1.5hrs. For disabled visitors the tour will be specially arranged.

All year daily except Match and Event days, tour times 11.00, 13.00 & 15.00. Booking essential Hotline No: 0870 603 0005
Last Admission: 15.00
A£7.00 C&OAPs£4.50 Family Ticket (A2+C3)£23.00 - 3rd C goes FREE. Group rates 15+ 10% discount. Birthday Parties (ages 6-12) 15+ £15.00 per head to book call 020 7915 1924

discount offer: 4th Child Free When Family Ticket Purchased

M.C.C. Museum and Tour of Lord's

Lord's Ground St John's Wood London NW8 8QN
[Tube: St John's Wood]
Tel: 020 7432 1033 Fax: 020 7266 3825
www.lords.org

Lord's was established in 1787 and is the home of the MCC and cricket. When you tour this famous arena you follow in the footsteps of the 'great's' of the game, from W G Grace to

London

Ian Botham. Daily guided tours take you behind the scenes at this venue. You will visit the Members' Pavilion including the hallowed Long Room and the Players' Dressing Room, the MCC Museum where the Ashes Urn is on display and many other places of interest including the newly constructed Grand Stand and futuristic Natwest Media Centre.
All year Tours normally 12.00 & 14.00, vary on cricket days, call to book
A£6.00 C&OAPs&Students£4.40 Family Ticket £18.00
discount offer: Two For The Price Of One

Wembley Stadium Tours
Empire Way Wembley Middlesex HA9 0WS
[M1, M4, M40, A406, well signposted from all major approach roads. Tube: Wembley Park / Wembley Stadium]
Tel: 020 8795 5733 Fax: 020 8900 1045
www.wembleynationalstadium.com
World famous stadium and unique in the history of sport and entertainment. Many millions of people have experienced the magic of Wembley Stadium. On your tour you will visit behind the scenes areas not generally seen, and explore Wembley's unique history. The Stadium is scheduled to close for redevelopment in August 2000.
visitor comments: A surprisingly good time
All year daily: Summer 10.00-16.00, Winter 10.00-15.00. Closed for major special events & 25-26 Dec. Due to redevelopment scheduled August 2000 please call to check availability before making a special journey
Last Admission: Summer 16.00 Winter 15.00
Available on request

↓*special events*

▶ **England v Hungary**
25/3/00-25/3/00
Schools International Football

▶ **The F.A. Cup Semi Finals**
8/4/00-9/4/00
Sponsored by AXA

▶ **The Auto Windscreens Shield Final**
16/4/00-16/4/00

▶ **The F.A. Carlsberg Vase Final**
6/5/00-6/5/00

▶ **The F.A. Umbro Trophy Final**
13/5/00-13/5/00

▶ **The F.A. Cup Final**
20/5/00-20/5/00
Sponsored by AXA

▶ **The Nationwide Football League Playoffs**
27/5/00-29/5/00
May 27 Division 3, May 28 Division 2 and May 29 Division 1

▶ **Tina Turner in Concert**
15/7/00-15/7/00

▶ **Oasis in Concert**
22/7/00-22/7/00

▶ **The One-2-One F.A. Charity Shield**
30/7/00-30/7/00

Sporting History Museums

FA Hall of Fame
County Hall Riverside Building Westminster Bridge Road London SE1 7PB
[Tube: Westminster]
Tel: 0870 8488484/0171 9283636 Fax: 020 7928 3939
www.hall-of-fame.co.uk
The F.A. Premier League Hall of Fame is a multi-themed new visitor centre. It is an entertaining celebration of English football from the past to the present day. The main entrance is located on Westminster Bridge, adjacent to the magnificent Member's Carriageway gate. There are five themed areas. The Hall of Legends featuring a spectacular stroll through the history of English football. The F.A. Premier League Hall of Fame, a living history of the Premier League. The Hall of Fans, a unique tribute to the heritage and culture of football fanaticism. Hope and Glory, a special film depicting the dreams of a young boy inspired by the stars of today's Premier League. Virtual Stadium, offers visitors the chance to test their skills on interactive football games.
visitor comments: Well-presented new attraction. Very clean, very new - my son loved it.
Opened 12th June 1999. All year10.00-18.00 closed Christmas day.
Last Admission: 17.00
Queuing Times: 10 min
£9.95 C(4-15)£6.50 Student rate £7.50 Group 15+ Group & Corporate booking 0171 928 1800

Museum of Rugby and Twickenham Stadium Tours
Rugby Football Union Rugby Road Twickenham Middlesex TW1 1DZ
[follow A316 from Central London and Richmond then turn R at the Currie Motors roundabout onto Whitton road, at mini roundabout turn R into Rugby Road. Keep stadium to your L, turn L at the Tesco Roundabout into Whitton Dene Road. Entrance to the North Car Park is on the L, approximately 25 metres. BR: Twickenham 10mins walk from the ground]
Tel: 020 8892 2000 Fax: 020 8892 2817
www.rfu.com
A fascinating behind the scenes Guided Tour. Includes breathtaking views from the top of the North Stand, and a visit to the players tunnel and the famous changing rooms with their 60 year old baths. The new multi-media Museum of Rugby appeals to enthusiasts of all ages and charts the history and world-wide growth of rugby, using touchscreens, video clips and film.
All year, Non-Match Days: Tue-Sat & Bank Hol 10.00-17.00, Sun 14.00-17.00. Closed Mon, Good Fri & 24-26 Dec. Match Days: 11.00-1 hour prior to kick-off. Match ticket holders only. Open for 1 hour after Match.
Last Admission: 16.30
Museum/Tour: A£3.00 C&Concessions£2.00. Museum & Tour: A£5.00 C&Concessions£3.00 Family Ticket (A2&C3)£15.00. Groups of 15+ 10% discount, for Group Catering Requirements, please pre-book on 0181 891 4565. School Parties Welcome, call for details. Identification is required for Students & Senior Citizens for concession price
discount offer: One Child Free When Accompanied By A Full Paying Adult
↓*special events*
▶ **Tetleys Bitter Cup Final**
13/5/00-13/5/00

Wimbledon Lawn Tennis Museum
All England Lawn Tennis & Croquet Club Church Road Wimbledon London SW19 5AE
[Tube: Wimbledon Park / Southfields. Car: from central London take the A3 Portsmouth Road to Tibbet's Corner, at the underpass turn L towards Wimbledoon, down Parkside. Entrance is in Church Road, ample free parking from Aug-May - drive in the Museum gates]
Tel: 020 8946 6131 Fax: 020 8944 6497
Wimbledon is synonymous with lawn tennis and the museum in the grounds of the All England Lawn Tennis Club is the only one of its kind in the world. Trophies, pictures, equipment, displays and memorabilia trace the development of the game over the last century. See the famous Centre Court and the enjoyable interactive quizzes and data banks for all ages. New for this year is the Costume Gallery where 100 years of changing Ladies' Fashions at Wimbledon are depicted. The Library containing the finest collection in the world of books and periodicals relating to Lawn Tennis is open by appointment.
All year daily 10.30-17.00. Tea Room: As Museum but 10.00-17.00. Call for Christmas, New Year and Tournament opening details A£4.00 C&OAPs&Students£3.00. Group rates 20+ on application
discount offer: £1.00 Off Adult Admission
↓*special events*
▶ **Wimbledon Lawn Tennis Championships**
26/6/00-9/7/00
Note their is no play on Sun 2nd July. Call 020 8946 2244 for information.

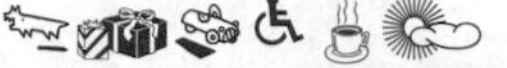

Toy & Childhood Museums

Bethnal Green Museum of Childhood
Cambridge Heath Road London E2 9PA
[Tube: Bethnal Green 500yds. Buses 106 / 253 / 309 / D6 (Cambridge Heath Road) 8 (Roman Road / 26 / 48 / 55 (Hackney Road). Meter parking 500 yards from the tube station free on Sat, Sun & Bank Hol at other times £3.00 for 2 hours]
Tel: 020 8983 5200 Switchboar Fax: 020 8983 5225
The National Museum of Childhood at Bethnal Green is a fascinating blend of toys and other nursery objects that belong to the experience of childhood. The ground floor is packed full of playthings, ranging from dolls' houses, dolls and games to teddy bears, toy soldiers and trains, dating from the 17th century to the present day. The upper gallery explores the process of growing up from birth through to the teenage years, including baby equipment, nursery furniture and children's dress, from working smock to party dresses. Education: The child-friendly atmosphere of the Museum also makes it an excellent resource for schools, while the familiar world of toys and childhood allows children to access the collections easily and quickly. Ring for a copy of the Education leaflet, offering: free direct teaching sessions related to the National Curriculum, free group visits, free use of picnic room and Resource Pack for Teachers. Guided Tours: For adult groups, the Museum has a rare nostalgic appeal; book a guided tour, focusing on some of the showstoppers in the collections, and reminisce over your old favourite toys. Access:

The Museum has steps throughout. Help is available but must be arranged in advance. There is a wheelchair accessible toilet, two steps down from the Museum's main floor and three steps up from the entrance. Shop: The Museum Shop sells souvenirs, books, postcards and toys. Café: The licensed Café serves salads, sandwiches, cakes, children's lunch boxes and hot and cold drinks, also offers children's birthday parties.

visitor comments: Wonderful, big airy building, helpful staff, much to see. Exhibitions & events are brilliant!

All year Mon-Thur & Sat-Sun 10.00-17.50. Closed Fri, 24-26 Dec & 1 Jan. Recorded information line: 0181 980 2415

Admission Free. Education & Group booking and access help: 0181 983 5205. Recorded Information: 0181 980 2415

London Toy and Model Museum

21-23 Craven Hill London W2 3EN

[Tube: Bayswater / Paddington / Lancaster Gate]

Tel: 020 7706 8000 Fax: 020 7706 8823

Reopened in 1995 after being extensively redeveloped, the museum has 21 themed galleries all with sounds and smells to create the atmosphere. A fascinating display of over 7000 exhibits including detailed working models, villages, railways and funfairs. There are vintage roundabout and train rides for children.

visitor comments: Not very "hands-on" for younger visitors. Basic train ride and roundabout do not operate in wet weather.

All year daily 09.00-17.30

Last Admission: 16.30

A£5.50 C(0-4)£Free C£3.50 Family Ticket £15.00 Concessions£4.50. Group 10+: A£4.00 C£2.50. Schools: A£5.50 C£3.20 (1 Free adult for every 10 children). Wheelchair users and visually impaired visitors £Free

Pollock's Toy Museum

1 Scala Street London W1P 1LT

[Tube: Goodge Street]

Tel: 020 7636 3452

Displays include teddy bears, wax and china dolls, dolls' houses, board games, toy theatres, tin toys, mechanical and optical toys, folk toys and nursery furniture. Items from all over the world and all periods are here in two small interconnecting houses. Toy theatre performances available for school visits and during school holidays. Pushchairs need to be left downstairs.

All year Mon-Sat 10.00-17.00. Closed Public Hol

Last Admission: 16.30

A£2.50 C£1.00

Transport Museums

London Canal Museum

12-13 New Wharf Road London N1 9RT

[Buses: 10 / 17 / 30 / 45 / 46 / 63 / 73 / 91 / 214 / 259 / A2 / C12. Tube: Kings Cross 5 mins walks]

Tel: 020 7713 0836 Fax: 020 7713 0836

www.charitynet.org/~LCanalMus

The museum tells the story of the development of London's Canals. Visitors can learn about the people who strove to make a meagre livelihood by living and working on them, the horses which pulled their boats, and the cargoes they carried. Housed in a former ice warehouse built in the 1860s for Carlo Gatti, the famous ice cream maker, this Museum also features the history of the almost forgotten trade in natural ice. Visitors can peer down into a huge ice well, where the ice was once stored. Temporary exhibitions, book and gift shop.

All year Tue-Sun & Bank Hol Mon 10.00-16.30. Closed 24-26 & 31 Dec 1 Jan

Last Admission: 15.45

A£2.50 C&Concessions£1.25

↓*special events*

▶ **The Croydon Canal**

29/12/99-26/3/00

A tape-slide presentation about the canal will be the centrepiece of the exhibition

▶ **Lecture Working and Living on the Cut**

2/3/00-2/3/00

Experiences of hotel boating in the 1999s

▶ **Science Engineering and Technology Week**

21/3/00-24/3/00

A series of workshops for schools

▶ **Posters of the Canals**

28/3/00-26/6/00

London Transport Museum

Covent Garden Piazza Covent Garden London WC2E 7BB

[Tube: Covent Garden / Leicester Square / Holborn. Bus: to Strand or Aldwych 1, 4, 6, 9, 11, 13, 15, 23, 26, 68, 77A, 188, 501, 171 and 171A]

Tel: 020 7836 8557/565 7299 Fax: 020 7836 4118

www.ltmuseum.co.uk

Travel through time at the London Transport Museum. It's London history. It's London people. It's trams, trains, buses, and more. It's a hands-on moving experience right in the heart of Covent Garden. As well as the stunning collection, actors, working models and videos plus special Fun Bus for the Under 5's. There are special exhibitions, talks and family activities, all bringing the Museum's story to life. For details of school visits and educational material contact the Education Service 0171 379 6344. A lift and ramps give access throughout the Museum. Disabled toilets. From December 1997 the Museum launches "Kid Zones" - fifteen hands-on zones marking an easy-to-follow route around the Museum. Each zone will feature a fun activity to help kids and families learn a different part of the Museum's story.

visitor comments: Excellent. Friendly staff and helpers. Attractively and interestingly presented. Plenty of activities for older children. Definitely worth another visit.

All year Sat-Thur 10.00-18.00, Fri 11.00-18.00. Closed 24-26 Dec

Last Admission: 17.15

A£5.50 C&Concessions£2.95 C(0-5)£Free Family Ticket(A2+C2)£13.95

discount offer: £1.00 Off Adult, 50p Off Child Admissions & £2.00 Off Family Ticket(A2+C2)

↓*special events*

▶ **Fast Forward. Rewind. Londoners' Future Transport 1900-2026AD**
20/9/99-31/7/00

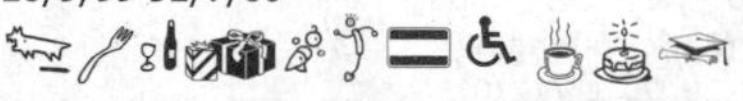

Wax Works

Madame Tussaud's

Marylebone Road London NW1 5LR
[Tube: Baker Street]
Tel: 020 7935 6861 Fax: 020 7465 0862
www.madame-tussauds.com

Madame Tussaud's world-famous waxwork collection was founded in Paris in 1170. It was moved to England in 1802 and to London's Marylebone Road in 1884. A star studded cast of sportsmen, world leaders and movie actors will make a visit to London's premier attraction a real winner. Mingle with the stars and meet the likes of Kate Winslet and Robert Carlyle; part of the brand new 'Superstars and Legends' in 1999. Our new infamous Chamber of Horrors is sure to give you a fright. Dare you enter? As a finale to Madame Tussaud's you will take a spectacular moving journey through London's extraordinary past. Visit the Planetarium, where you will enter the magnificent space age dome to be taken on Planetary Quest, a breathtaking cosmic journey through the splendours of our Universe!

visitor comments: Quite amazing - lovely watching the kids faces light up.

All year daily 10.00-17.30 (earlier opening throughout the summer). Groups can book a guaranteed timed admission between 09.30-16.30 daily, please telephone for details.

Last Admission: 17.30

A£10.00 C(under 16)£6.50 OAPs£4.60. Combined ticket with Planetarium A£12.25 C£8.00 OAPs£9.30

Zoos

Battersea Park Children's Zoo

Battersea London SW11
[Tube: Sloane Square BR: Battersea Park then Bus: 137]
Tel: 020 8871 7540 Fax: 020 7350 0477

Small zoo housing domestic farm and non domestic animals including monkeys, otters, birds, wallabies, pot bellied pigs, cows, reptile house. Animal contact area where children can touch, feel and feed the animals, pony rides and carousel rides.

visitor comments: Excellent value for money. Interesting with lots to see and do. Educational features a must for older children.

Mar-Sept Mon-Sun 10.00-17.00. Oct-Feb weekends only 11.00-15.00. Closed 25 Dec, 1 Jan

Last Admission: 16.30

A£1.20 C£0.60 OAPs£0.60. School groups £0.40 per pupil

London Zoo

Regents Park London NW1 4RY
[Tube: Camden Town / Great Portland Street / Regents Park]
Tel: 020 7722 3333 Fax: 202 7586 5743
www.weboflife.co.uk

Home to over 12,000 animals, insects, reptiles and fish. Opened in 1827 and claims the world's finest aquarium, insect and reptile house. Rare and exotic animals, many participating in captive breeding programmes. Daily events give visitors an insight to animal behaviour. Children's Zoo and whole range of educational programmes for schools. The new Web of Life biodiversity exhibition, a Millennium Commission project, opened in April 99. It uses a unique combination of 61 live animal exhibits, interactive displays and on-show breeding habitats to astonish the visitor with the complexity of nature and its myriad habitats.

visitor comments: Plenty to see. Opportunity to see animals being fed. Possibly more suitable for older children. The guide leaflet is very helpful.

All year daily Summer: 10.00-17.30 Winter: 10.00-16.00. Closed 25 Dec

Queuing Times: 10mins

A£9.00 C(3-14)£7.00 OAPs&Students£8.00 Saver Ticket £28.00 (2A+2C or 1A+3C) Group rates 15+

discount offer: One Child Free With A Full Paying Adult

↓*special events*

▶ **Daily Events**

1/1/00-31/12/00

11.30-12.30 - DIscovering Reptiles in the Reptile House. 12.30 - Feeding the Pigs in the Children's Zoo. 13.00 - Feeding the Pelicans near the Fountain Court. 13.30 - Animals in Action in the Lifewatch Centre not suitable for very young children. 14.00 - Wonders of the Web in the Web of Life. 14.30 - Feeding the Fish in the Aquarium. NB: Please note that different fish are fed on different days. Check the noticeboard at the Aquarium entrance for details. 15.00 - Elephant Time (Weekends and school holidays only) in the Elephant House. NB: All events are subject to the availability of animals and suitable weather conditions.

Arts, Crafts & Textiles

Tate Gallery Liverpool

Albert Dock Liverpool Merseyside L3 4BB

[BR: Lime Street]

Tel: 0151 702 7400 Fax: 0151 709 7401

www.tate.org.uk

Reopened in May 98 after a £7 million refurbishment, Tate Liverpool is housed in a converted Victorian warehouse with stunning views across the Mersey. It offers visitors a unique opportunity to see the best of the national collections of modern art. The Gallery has a changing programme of exhibitions drawing upon works by internationally renowned artists.

All year Tue-Sun & Bank Hol Mon 10.00-17.50. Closed 24-26 Dec & 1 Jan. Open Bank Hol Mon Admission Free to Tate Collection. Charges for certain exhibitions - A£3.00 Concessions£2.00

↓*special events*

▶ **Victor Pasmore - Changing the Process of Painting**

1/5/99-1/3/00

▶ **Heaven - An Exhibition That Will Break Your Heart**

11/12/99-27/2/00

▶ **Modern British Art**

12/2/00-1/2/01

▶ **The Other Side of Zero**

4/3/00-1/5/00

Video positive 2000.

▶ **Tony Cragg**

17/3/00-4/6/00

One of Britain's leading sculptors. This exhibition is exclusive to Tate Liverpool and several new sculptures have been created especially for this exhibition. A£3.00 Concessions £2.00

▶ **Shirazeh Houshiary and Anish Kapoor**

17/3/00-28/8/00

Sculpture, Drawings and Prints.

▶ **Peter Blake About Collage**

7/4/00-1/3/01

▶ **American Abstraction**

20/5/00-1/4/01

Work from the 1960's

▶ **Mark Wallinger**

23/10/00-17/12/01

This mid-career retrospective exhibition of the work of Mark Wallinger is the most comprehensive to date, and brings together a selection of his art in all media from the past 15 years. A£3.00 Concessions £2.00

Walker Art Gallery

William Brown Street Liverpool Merseyside L3 8EL

[Liverpool City centre, signposted, 2mins from BR Station]

Tel: 0151 478 4199 Fax: 0151 478 4190

www.nmgm.org.uk

An outstanding collection of European paintings, and sculpture. Especially notable are the Italian, Netherlands, and Pre-Raphaelite and Victorian paintings. There is an award-winning sculpture gallery and temporary exhibitions are held throughout the year.

All year Mon-Sat 10.00-17.00, Sun 12.00-17.00. Closed 23-26 Dec & 1 Jan

A£3.00 C£Free Concessions£1.50 Family Ticket (A2+C3)£7.50 Groups of 20+ 25% discount, special rates for educational parties please call for details. Charge allows unlimited re-entry for 1 year to all NMGM venues

↓*special events*

▶ **Adrian Henri**

1/1/00-1/5/00

▶ **Constable's Clouds**

1/5/00-1/7/00

▶ **Death in Victorian And Edwardian Art**
1/9/00-1/12/00
▶ **George Romney 1734-1802**
1/1/02-1/6/02
▶ **Liverpool Pre-Raphaelites**
1/7/02-1/9/02

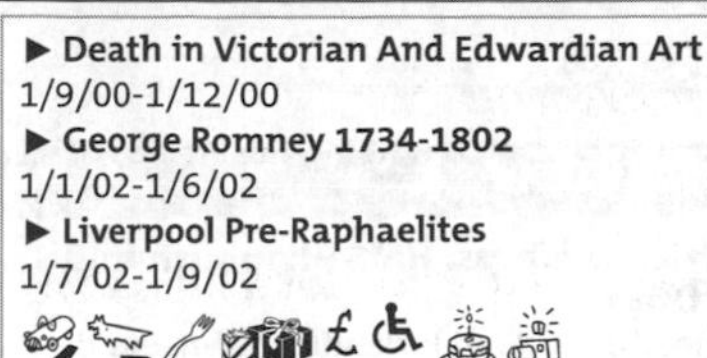

Heritage & Industrial

Port Sunlight Village and Heritage Centre
95 Greendale Road Wirral Merseyside CH62 4XE
[J5 M53 A41 Birkenhead]
Tel: 0151 644 6466 Fax: 0151 645 8973
Picturesque 19th century village built by William Hesketh Lever for his soap factory workers, now a unique architectural and social history attraction. The Heritage Centre tells the fascinating story of the Village and its community. Guided walking tours of the Village, Sundays and Bank Holiday Mondays (April-September). Pre booked group tours (all year), also features magnificent Lady Lever Art Gallery.
All year 10.00-16.00 Apr-Oct Sat & Sun 10.00-16.00; Nov-Mar Sat & Sun 11.00-16.00
A£0.60 C£0.30 Concessions £0.50
discount offer: Two For The Price Of One

Historical

Liverpool Town Hall
High Street Liverpool Merseyside L2 3SW
[City Centre location. 5mins walks from amin shopping centre]
Tel: 0151 707 2391 Fax: 0151 709 2252
Marvel at the ornate decoration, the grand staircase, the beautiful furniture and the precious silverware. Visit the Hall of Remembrance, then have some light refreshments in the café. Guided tours available throughout the day.
22 Mar-9 Apr Mon-Sat 11.00-16.00. Closed Bank Hol
Last Admission: 15.30
Admission Free. Charge for guided tours.

Meols Hall
Botanic Road Churchtown Southport Merseyside PR9 7LZ
[3m N of Southport 16m SW of Preston 20m N of Liverpool nr A565 & A570]
Tel: 01704 228326 Fax: 01704 507185
www.meolshall.freeserve.co.uk
A 17th century house, with subsequent additions, containing an interesting collection of pictures, furniture, china etc. Member of the Historic Houses Association.
14 Aug-14 Sept 14.00-17.00
Last Admission: 16.30
A£3.00 Accompanied C(0-10)£Free C(10+)£1.00. Coach parties by appointment with afternoon tea available at £8.50 per person
↓special events
▶ **Southport Spring Gardening Festival**
22/4/00-24/4/00
*A£5.50 *£7.00 OAPs£4.50 *£6.00 Wheelchair £3.00 *£3.00 (*on the gate). A feast of horticultural entertainment for everyone, from the amateur to the professional gardener, 09.30-18.00*
▶ **Wedding Evening**
5/7/00-5/7/00
Call for details
▶ **House Open-Group Afternoon Teas**
14/8/00-14/9/00
Call for details
▶ **Churchtown Country Show**
23/9/00-24/9/00
Arena events, rural crafts and handicraft, floral art and much more. Gates open 10.30. Call for further details
▶ **Bonfire and Grand Firework Display**
4/11/00-4/11/00
Side shows, fairground, barbecue, 17.00 for 19.30. A£2.00 C£1.00. Pedestrians via the main gate, free car parking - Moss Lane entrance

Sir Paul McCartney's Birthplace
20 Forthlin Road Allerton Liverpool Merseyside L18 9TN
[access by minibus from Speke Hall]
Tel: 0870 900 0256
The McCartney family lived in the house from 1955-1964 - the vital Beatles years. It became their meeting place because during the day it was empty with Paul's widowed father being out at work. It was here that early Beatles songs such as Love Me Do and I Saw Her Standing There were created. Each visitor will

hear an audio tape about the house, to which members of the McCartney family are contributing. The Trust's main object is to offer a space which can be experienced, where you can stand, breathe in and imagine that yup, this is where those Beatles all began. Only 14 visitors at a time will be allowed in.
29 July-31 Oct Wed-Sat, 7 Nov-12 Dec Sat only A£4.50 C£2.50 NT Members£1.50 (to cover minibus). For bookings please ring 0870 900 0256

Speke Hall
The Walk Speke Liverpool Merseyside L24 1XD
[8m SE of Liverpool city centre, S of A561. Signposted]
Tel: 0345 585702 info line Fax: 0151 427 9860
One of the most famous half-timbered houses in the country set in varied gardens and an attractive woodland estate. The Great Hall, Oak Parlour and priest holes evoke Tudor times while the small rooms, some with original William Morris wallpapers, show the Victorian desire for privacy and comfort. Fine plasterwork and tapestries, plus a fully equipped Victorian Kitchen and Servants' Hall. The restored garden has spring bulbs, rose garden, Summer border and stream garden; bluebell walks in the ancient Clough Woodland, rhododendrons, spectacular views of the grounds and Mersey Basin from a high embankment - the Bund. Peaceful walks in the wildlife oasis of Stocktons Wood. 1998 was the 400th anniversary of Speke Hall and this marks the four hundred years since the date of 1598 was carved over the front door during the time of Edward Norris, the first owner of Speke Hall, to mark the completion of the North Range and the building we see today. Events and activities will reflect the different eras of the history of Speke, its estate and the families who lived and worked there, including open air theatre, children's activities, a special musical evening and much more. Picnics may be taken in the Orchard only. Guided tours must be pre-booked. Partial disabled access please call before visit, 0151 427 7231.
Hall open as Garden 28 Mar-31 Oct; then 6 Nov-12 Dec Sat & Sun 130--16.30. Garden: 28 Mar-31 Oct Tue-Sun & Bank Hol Mon 12.00-17.30; Nov-Mar 2000 Tue-Sun 12.00-16.00. Closed 1 Jan, 24-26 Dec, 31 Dec & Good Fri
Last Admission: 30 mins before closing
Hall & Gardens: A£4.20 C£2.10 Family Ticket £10.50. Garden & Grounds: A£1.60 C£0.80
discount offer: Two For The price Of One. Valid On Tuesdays-Fridays

Maritime

Historic Warships: HMS Plymouth and HMS Onyx
East Float Dock Road Birkenhead Merseyside CH41 1DJ
[J1 M53 to All Docks then follow signs to Historic Warships, Wallesey Tunnel 1st Exit off]
Tel: 0151 650 1573 Fax: 0151 650 1473
www.warships.freeserve.co.uk
Here is a chance to see the Falklands frigate, HMS Plymouth battered by the Argentine Air Force but home safely. Also here is HMS Onyx, a submarine which conducted a 117-Day patrol during the conflict; see how her men and the SAS lived in this unique attraction. Come and explore whatever the weather. NEW: A German U Boat now open to the public.
All year Summer: daily 10.00-17.00, Winter: daily 10.00-16.00
Last Admission: 16.00
A£5.00 C£3.00 Family Ticket £14.00 OAPs£4.00. Does not include U534 tour. Bookings only for this £12.50 Combined Ticket
discount offer: One Child Free With Full Paying Adult

Military & Defence Museums

Western Approaches
1-3 Rumford Street Liverpool Merseyside L2 8SZ
[town centre from M62 A5038]
Tel: 0151 227 2008 Fax: 0151 236 6913
Set beneath the streets of Liverpool, re-live the times of 1940s Britain. See the life and work of Wrens and Waafs working under constant pressure in the original area command headquarters for the battle of the Atlantic. Now open to the public, visit the 50,000 sq.ft. labyrinth of audio linked original rooms including main operations room, Admirals office,Teleprinter station and also a re-constructed Educational centre, with Anderson shelter, and Bombed-out room.
1 Mar-31 Oct Mon-Thur & Sat 10.30-16.30
Last Admission: 15.30
A£4.75 Family Ticket £9.95 Concessions£3.45 Group 10+ £2.99
discount offer: 50p Off Full Adult Admission Price

On the Water

Mersey Ferries Ltd
Victoria Place Wallasey Merseyside CH44 6QY
[Pier Head via M62 & Liverpool city centre Wirral via M56 / M53 or A41. Limited parking on site]
Tel: 0151 630 1030 Fax: 0151 639 0578
www.merseyworld.com/ferries/
Mersey Ferries 50 minute Heritage cruises trace their 800 year history. Stop at Seacombe to visit Aquarium and Pirate's Paradise play area or Woodside Restaurant for lunch or afternoon tea. Retail and catering services available. Various children's events held in school holidays, Family Fun Days and Evening Theme Cruises, please call for further information.
All year daily Mon-Fri 07.30-19.30, Sat & Sun: 09.00-19.20. Cruise Timetable: See special events guide or call venue
Last Admission: 19.00
A£3.40 C£1.75 Family Ticket £8.70 Concessions £2.40. Group Rates 10% discount, School Parties Special discount. Small price increase due in April 2000
discount offer: One Child Free With Every Full Fare Paying Adult On River Cruise

Sport & Recreation

Awesome Walls Climbing Centre
St Albans Church Athol Street off Great Howard Street Liverpool Merseyside L5 9XT
[M57 / M58 - A5036 (head S), church on the left after 2m, by large Chinese Restaurant called Tai Pan]
Tel: 0151 298 2422 Fax: 0151 922 3431
Awesome Walls is situated in an 150 year old church. Here we have walls to suit everyone, from small top-rope walls to massive overhanging walls, plus we have a totally unique free standing 12m featured pinnacle, hence our slogan - 'Little Angels To Rock Gods'. Come to us for an action packed fun-filled time. It's the ideal birthday party location and all our instructors are fully qualified and experienced rock climbers. The centre, one of the largest in Europe, is able to suit everyone's capabilities.
All year Mon-Fri 12.00-22.00, Sat & Sun 10.00-21.00
A£4.50 Concessions£4.00. Taster sessions and group bookings available, please call
discount offer: One Adult Admission (per card) At £4.00

Sporting History Museums

Liverpool Football Club and Stadium Tour
Anfield Road Liverpool Merseyside L4 0TH
Tel: 0151 260 6677
This new interactive museum is now open - Britain's greatest football club now has the newest and finest football museum. Cups, trophies, interactives and a unique film show, plus much more. Stadium tours around 'Fortress Anfield' - pre-booking essential.
visitor comments: Terrific value, great tour, well conducted and friendly staff.
All year daily 10.00-17.00. Match Days: 10.00-1 hr before kick-off. No tours on Match days
Last Admission: 16.00
Visitor Centre: A£5.00 C&OAPs£3.00 Family Ticket £13.00. Visitor Centre & Tours: A£8.00 C&OAPs£5.00 Family Ticket £20.00
discount offer: Two For The Price Of One

Theme & Adventure Parks

National Discovery Park
Chavasse Park Liverpool Merseyside **Tel: 0161 907 3366**
The concept is built around the rapid growth in IT, broadcasting and multi-media linked with public discovery, training, education and leisure. The Commission's grant will be for a visitor attraction - the Discovery Centre, a glass covered park and a new bridge. The centre houses the Space Time Machine which will educate and entertain on the history of time. A pedestrian footbridge will link the project with the Albert Dock development.

Pleasure Island
International Festival Park Riverside Drive Liverpool Merseyside *[2m S of Liverpool City Centre]*
Tel: 0151 728 7766
A great value family day out. Liverpool's Fun Capital has something for everyone. Pay once only for unlimited use of Quasar, 10 Pin Bowling, Rollerskating and 'The Works', which includes 120 foot hair raising tube slides and drop slides.
All year daily, Mon-Fri 16.00-24.00, weekends, School Hol & Bank Hol 10.00-24.00
From £1.00

Pleasureland
Marine Drive Southport Merseyside PR8 1RX
[10min walk from Southport BR. From the north M6 J31 A59 to Preston then A565 to Southport. From the south M6 J26 M58 to Ormskirk then A570 to Southport]
Tel: 01704 532 717 Fax: 01704 537 936
www.pleasureland.uk.com
The home of TRAUMAtizer; a mix of corkscrew, sidewinder, loops, rolls, inversions and flipovers. Other high tech rides include the Himalaya and Chaos. The Pleasureland Grand Prix has three go-kart race circuits. For the younger visitor the Big Apple kiddies coaster provides plenty of screams and new for 99 is the Flying Elephant ride. There are also mini-dodgems, a building site with operational cranes and various train trips and slides. Water rides include the Viking Boats and River Caves that take you on a journey through ancient Egypt. The Cyclone wooden roller coaster was voted third best in Europe by the American Coaster Enthusiasts in 1996 and there is also a Sky Ride cable car that allows you to survey the whole park.
Easter to 7th Nov 10.00-21.00 hours vary call for details
Free admission then access to rides by wrist-bands under 1m £5.00 under 1.2m £7.50 over 1.2m £12.99 Family Ticket £36.00 for any four bands.

Wildlife & Safari Parks

Knowsley Safari Park
Prescot Merseyside L34 4AN
[J6 M62 J2 M57 A57 follow signs. Plenty parking on site]
Tel: 0151 430 9009 Fax: 0151 426 3677
www.knowsley.com
A five-mile drive through the reserves enables visitors to see lions, tigers, elephants, rhinos, baboons, and many other animals in spacious natural surroundings. Includes reptile house, children's farm, otters, meerkats, plus a parrot and sealion show. Extra attractiions include amusement park and miniature railway. There is also a souvenir centre and fast food restaurant.
visitor comments: Safari drive was excellent.
Mar-Oct daily 10.00-16.00
Last Admission: 16.00
A£7.00 C(3-16)£5.00 OAPs£5.00

Zoos

Southport Zoo and Conservation Trust
Esplanade Princes Park Southport Merseyside PR8 1RX
[next to Pleasureland signposted throughout town area]
Tel: 01704 538102 Fax: 01704 538102
www.southportzoo.f9.co.uk
Visit this wonderful wildlife collection including lions, leopards, lynx, servals, chimpanzees, monkeys, lemur, tamarins, mara, capybara, tapir, parrots, porcupine, binturong, penguins, flamingo, giant tortoise and mandrills, situated in landscaped gardens. Visit the reptile house, aquarium and pets corner - no extra charges. Children's play area, as well as educational talks. Low cost entrance fee. Don't Delay, Come Today!
visitor comments: Lots of slopes. Good variety of animals. Car park not close to venue
All year Summer 10.00-18.00, Winter 10.00-16.00. Closed 25 Dec
A£3.80 C£2.80 OAPs£3.20. Group rates 20+ available
discount offer: One Free Zoo Pack Per Family (not valid for Bank Holidays)

Animal Attractions

Park Farm
Snettisham King's Lynn Norfolk PE31 7NQ
[signposted on A149]
Tel: 01485 542425 Fax: 01485 543503
Lambing in action here in the spring. Sheep shearing in May and deer calving in June and July. Sheep, goats, lambs rabbits, turkeys, ducks, chickens, ponies and piglets. Tractor and trailer safaris to the deer park, where the animals will eat from your hand.
All year Spring & Summer & Autumn daily 10.00-17.30, call for Winter opening times
A£3.95 C£2.75 OAPs£3.50 Family Ticket £13.00. Deer safaris extra A£3.95 C£2.75 Concessions£3.50

Redwings Horse Sanctuary
Hall Lane Frettenham Norwich Norfolk NR12 7RW
[7m from Norwich on the B1150]
Tel: 01603 737432 Fax: 01603 738286
www.redwings.co.uk
Redwings Horse Sanctuary was founded in 1984 and rescues horses, ponies, donkeys and mules from neglect and slaughter. There is plenty to keep the whole family occupied. You can meet the horses, visit the information centre, stroll along the farm walks or simply enjoy the tranquillity of the Pets Remembrance Garden. The Gift Shop has a wide range of souvenirs to appeal to all ages, and suit all pockets. The Sanctuary also holds Humane Horse Handling Demonstrations on the first Sunday of every month at 2.30pm and 2pm following the end of British Summer Time.
visitor comments: A chance to spot some of the animals featured on 'Pet Rescue'
Easter-6 Dec Sun and Bank Holidays 12.30-17.00 (16.00 in Winter). Also Mon July & Aug
A£2.00 C&Concessions£1.00

Birds, Butterflies & Bees

Pensthorpe Waterfowl Park and Nature Reserve
Pensthorpe Fakenham Norfolk NR21 0LN
[signposted off A1067 Norwich to Fakenham road]
Tel: 01328 851465 Fax: 01328 855905
Pensthorpe Waterfowl Park is situated in the valley of the River Wensum and covers 200 acres of beautiful Norfolk countryside. Our lakes are home to the largest collection of waterfowl and waders in Europe. With spacious walkthrough enclosures, a network of hardsurfaced pathways ensures close contact with birds at the water's edge. Peaceful nature trails, new Millennium Perennial Garden, excellent gift shop, play area and Courtyard Restaurant.
27 Mar 00-8 Jan 01 daily, Spring & Summer 10.00-17.00, Winter 10.00-16.00, 4 Jan 99-mid Mar weekends only 10.00-16.00
A£4.80 C£2.25 OAPs£4.20 Family Ticket £12.00. Group rates 15+ £3.85

↓*special events*

- **Gardens Fair**
3/6/00-4/6/00
- **Millennium Perennial Garden**
8/8/00-8/8/00
Official opening
- **National Wildlife Carving Exhibition**
25/8/00-3/9/00

Folk & Local History Museums

Lynn Museum
Market Street King's Lynn Norfolk PE30 1NL
[on A47 Peterborough-Norfolk road, A17 from NE and A10 from the SE]
Tel: 01553 775001 Fax: 01553 775001
Displays illustrate the lives of West Norfolk people from prehistoric times to be 20th century. Range of hands-on activities from trying on a Roman toga and handling real fossils to visiting the Victorian Ironmongers shops. Also varied programme of events and temporary exhibitions.

Norfolk

All year Tue-Sat 10.00-17.00. Closed Public Holidays
A£1.00 C£0.80 Concessions£0.60

↓*special events*

▶ **Gressley Green**
1/1/00-26/2/00

▶ **Time for Tea**
4/3/00-10/6/00
The story of tea and tea drinking. Also features the Norwich Castle Museum's teapot collection

▶ **The Holme Timber Circle**
22/3/00-22/3/00
What has been discovered about the Bronze Age circle since the excavation? 19.30, £3.00 entry.

▶ **Five Thousand Years of Tea**
12/4/00-12/4/00
Ever wondered how tea came into being? This talk will explain. Doors open 19.15, £3.00 entry.

▶ **Tea Tasting**
8/5/00-8/5/00
Taste the subtle and refreshing flavours of Twinings teas. Doors open 19.15, £3.00.

▶ **Paintings from the Collections: Walter Dexter and Henry Baines**
17/6/00-9/9/00
Fine oil and watercolour paintings from Walter Dexter (1876-1958) and Henry Baines (1823-1894)

Norfolk Rural Life Museum and Union Farm

Beech House Gressenhall Dereham Norfolk NR20 4DR
[3m NW of Dereham. Follow the brown signs from A47 from Dereham centre to the B1146. Bus: 0500 626116. Plenty of on site parking available]
Tel: 01362 860563 Fax: 01362 860385
www.norfolk.gov.uk/museums

Housed in what used to be a workhouse, it has special emphasis on agriculture, rural crafts and village life, with working reconstructions. Union Farm is a typical small mixed farm of the 1920's with heavy horses and rare breeds of sheep, cattle, pigs and poultry. There is a nature trail around the farm.

1 Apr-29 Oct 2000 Mon-Sat 10.00-17.00
Last Admission: 16.30
A£3.90 C£1.80 Family Ticket £9.80 Concessions £2.90 Groups 10+ £2.90

↓*special events*

▶ **All Fools Weekend**
1/4/00-2/4/00
Entertainment for the whole family

▶ **Doing What Comes Naturally**
16/4/00-16/4/00
Have a go at pond dipping, be a nature detective, make casts of footprints and more

▶ **Tastes of Anglia Easter Monday 'Eggs'-travaganza**
24/4/00-24/4/00
Local food producers with their unusual, traditional and interesting fayre

▶ **Day Schools**
29/4/00-20/10/00
Apr 29 and Sept 30, The Ins and Outs of the Workhouse, May 13-14, Handling Heavy Horses and Oct 20 Cleft Gate Hurdle Making

▶ **Norfolk Mini Owners Club Annual Gressenhall Rally**
7/5/00-7/5/00
Minis old and new, original and remodeled

▶ **Skeletons in the Closet**
14/5/00-14/5/00
Experts provide advice on how to find out about your village, home or ancestors

▶ **Animal Magic**
28/5/00-29/5/00
Two days devoted to all that is four legged on the farm

Gardens & Horticulture

Mannington Gardens and Countryside

Mannington Hall Norwich Norfolk NR11 7BB
[2m N of Saxthorpe near B1149, 18m NW of Norwich, 9m from coast. Plenty of on site parking]
Tel: 01263 584175 Fax: 01263 761214

This moated manor house was built in 1460. Gardens to view and lovely countryside.

Gardens: 27 May-28 Aug Wed-Fri 11.00-17.00. May-Sept Sun 12.00-17.00. Hall: open only by appointment for special interest groups. Walks & Car Park: daily 09.00-dusk
Last Admission: 16.55
Gardens: A£3.00 Accompanied C(0-16)£Free Students&OAPs£2.50. Walks Car Park £1.00 (free for garden visitors)

discount offer: Two For The Price Of One Full Paying Adult Or 50p Discount. Not Valid On Special Event Days

↓*special events*

▶ **Gardens open first day**
30/4/00-30/4/00

In aid of National Gardens Scheme
▶ **Dawn Chorus Walk**
6/5/00-6/5/00
▶ **Family Nature Day**
7/5/00-7/5/00
▶ **Tent Exhibition and Sale**
26/5/00-29/5/00
▶ **Gardens Open**
15/6/00-15/6/00
In aid of the British Heart Foundation
▶ **Donizetti's L'Elisir d'Amore**
4/8/00-4/8/00
Garden Opera
▶ **Sheringham Little Theatre**
13/8/00-13/8/00
Open Air Concert
▶ **Charities Day**
3/9/00-3/9/00
▶ **Gardens Open**
29/10/00-29/10/00
In support of National Gardens Scheme

Heritage & Industrial

Bressingham Steam Museum and Gardens

Bressingham Diss Norfolk IP22 2AB
[2.5m W of Diss 14m E of Thetford on A1066, follow brown tourist signs]
Tel: 01379 687386/687382 Fax: 01379 688085
Alan Bloom is an internationally recognised nurseryman and a steam enthusiast, and has combined his interests to great effect at Bressingham. There are three steam-hauled trains including a garden railway, and a 15in gauge running through two and a half miles of the wooded glades.
visitor comments: A good value for money attraction. Very interesting, with lovely gardens. Lots to entertain families of all ages.
Steam Museum & Dell Garden: Apr-Oct daily 10.30-17.30
Last Admission: 16.30
A£4.50/£5.00 C£2.50/£3.00 Passport Ticket £17.00/£23.00 OAPs£4.00/£4.00. Rides are extra
discount offer: One Child Free With Each Paying Adult. For Admission Only. Valid Until 31 Oct 99

Historical

Blickling Hall

Blickling Norwich Norfolk NR11 6NF
[1.5m NW of Aylsham on N side of B1354 which is 15m N of Norwich on A140]
Tel: 01263 738030 Fax: 01263 731660
www.ukindex.co.uk
Flanked by dark yew hedges and topped by pinnacles, the warm red brick front of Blickling makes a memorable sight. The house was built in the early 17th century, but the hedges may be earlier. The centrepiece of the houses is the carved oak staircase which winds up in double flights from the hall.
Hall: 8 Apr-30 July Wed-Sun, 1-31 Aug Tues-Sun, 1 Sept-29 Oct Wed-Sun 13.00-17.00. Garden, Shop, Restaurant & Plant Centre: dates same as hall 10.30-17.30, plus 2 Nov-17 Dec Thurs-Sun 6 Jan-Mar Sat-Sun 11.00-16.00 (Plant Centre closed Nov-Mar)
Last Admission: Hall: 16.30
Hall & Garden: A£6.50 C£3.25. Gardens: A£3.70 C£1.85. Group rates available. Taster Tour of Hall £2.50 additional charge
discount offer: Two Adults For The Price Of One

Sandringham House Grounds Museum and Country Park

Sandringham Norfolk PE35 6EN
[8m NE of King's Lynn off A148]
Tel: 01553 772675 Fax: 01485 541571
The private country retreat of HM The Queen, Sandringham House is at the heart of beautiful estate. The house was built in 1870. Portraits of the Royal Family, collections of porcelain, jade, quartz, enamelled Russian silver, gold and bronzes can be seen. The museum contains displays of Royal memorabilia. Housed in a former stable block is a collection of 15 cars run by the royal family.
Easter-8 Oct daily 11.00-16.45. House closed 18 July-3 Aug
Last Admission: 16.45
A£5.50 C£3.50 OAPs£4.50 Family Ticket £14.50

↓*special events*
▶ **Sandringham Craft Fair**
14/4/00-24/9/00
Held on Apr 14-16 and Sept 22-24 only
▶ **Sandringham Country Weekend**
1/7/00-2/7/00
▶ **Firework Concert**
8/7/00-8/7/00
▶ **Flower Show**
26/7/00-26/7/00

Thetford Priory

Thetford Norfolk
[on W side of Thetford near station]
Tel: 01604 730320

Norfolk

The 14th century gatehouse is the best preserved part of this Cluniac priory built in 1103. The extensive remains include the plan of the cloisters.
Any reasonable time
Admission Free

Wolterton Park
Erpingham Aylsham Norfolk NR11 7LY
[nr Erpingham signposted from A140 Norwich to Cromer road. BR: Gunton. Plenty of one site parking]
Tel: 01263 584175 Fax: 01263 761214
Extensive historic park with lake, Orienteering, Adventure playground, Walks. The 18th century mansion house open on Fridays and some Sundays, is recommended for adults. For the following special events, please call the venue for details.
Park all year daily 09.00-17.00 or dusk if sooner. Hall: 14.00-17.00
Last Admission: Hall: 16.00
£2.00 per car. House: £5.00
discount offer: Two For The Price Of One Full Paying Adult

↓*special events*

▶ **Jane Austen Society Plays**
4/3/00-5/3/00

▶ **History 2000 Lecture**
9/3/00-2/11/00
Held on Mar 9, 30, Sept 21, Oct 5 and Nov 2 only, at the Hall

▶ **Days Out in North Norfolk**
8/4/00-8/4/00

▶ **An Evening with Fanny Burney**
13/5/00-13/5/00

▶ **Beautiful Country Homes and Gardens 2000**
15/6/00-17/6/00
Held in the Hall and Park

▶ **Themed Hall Tours**
18/6/00-18/6/00
Tours with a Georgian feel

▶ **Eton Musical Concert**
1/7/00-1/7/00

▶ **Bygones Day**
9/7/00-9/7/00

▶ **Themed Hall Tours**
16/7/00-16/7/00
Tours with a Victorian feel

▶ **Special Norfolk Concert**
21/7/00-21/7/00
(EDP We Care Appeal)

▶ **Themed Hall Tours**
10/9/00-10/9/00
Tours with an Edwardian feel

▶ **Organic Gardening Day**
24/9/00-24/9/00

▶ **Carol Concert**
15/12/00-15/12/00
Held at the Hall

Mining

Grime's Graves
Lynford Thetford Norfolk IP26 5DE
[7m NW of Thetford off A134]
Tel: 01842 810656
www.english-heritage.org.uk
These remarkable Neolithic flint mines, unique in England, comprise over 300 pits and shafts. The visitor can descend some 10m (30ft) by ladder into one excavated shaft, and look along the radiating galleries, from where the flint for making axes and knives was extracted.
1 Apr-31 Oct daily 10.00-18.00, 17.00 in Oct. 1 Nov-31 Mar Wed-Sun 10.00-16.00. Closed 13.00-14.00. Closed 24-26 Dec
Last Admission: 20 mins before closing
A£2.00 C£1.00 Concessions£1.50. 15% discount for groups (11+)

↓*special events*

▶ **2000 Years BC**
30/4/00-26/8/00
Stone Age man demonstrates how he made flint tools, axes and arrowheads on 30 Apr, 4 June, 23 July & 26 Aug

▶ **Guided Tours**
14/5/00-13/8/00
At 11.30, 14.00 & 15.30 on 14 May & 13 Aug ONLY. Authors of the first national staudy of Neolithic flint mines guide visitors around this fascinating site and describe previous excavations and new interpretations

Nature & Conservation Parks

Blakeney Point
Warden's Address 35 The Cornfield Langham

Holt Norfolk NR25 7DQ
[Morston Quay Blakeney & Cley are all off A149 Cromer-Hunstanton road. Access on foot from Clay Beach or by ferry from Morston or Balkeney BR: Sheringham]
Tel: 01263 740480 Apr-Sept Fax: 01263 740241
One of Britain's foremost bird sanctuaries, the Point is a 3.5 mile-long sand a shingle spit noted in particular for its colonies of breeding terns and for the rare migrants that pass through in spring and autumn. Both common and grey seals can be seen, as well as an interesting range of seaside plants. An information centre at Morston Quay provides further details on the area's attractions. Oct-Mar Tel 01328 830401. Dogs on leads only. No dogs west of Old Lifeboat House on Blakeney Point, Apr-Sept.
All year any reasonable time. Apr-Sept light refreshments in the Old Lifeboat House subject to tide times
Car Park at Blakeney quay and Morston Quay £1.50 NT members free. No landing fee. Small charge for booked school parties and special interest groups

Brancaster
National Trust Dial House Brancaster Staithe King's Lynn Norfolk PE31 8BW
[Brancaster Staithe is halfway between Wells and Hunstanton on A149 coast road. Bus Eastern Counties Coastliner. BR King's Lynn]
Tel: 01485 210719
Here you can find a large beach with 4 miles of tidal foreshore, sand dunes and saltmarsh, as well as the site of the Roman Fort of Branodunum. Brancaster Millennium Activity Centre offers courses for schools, from Key Stage 2 to A Level, with cutting-edge environmental technology. Also field studies and outdoor pursuits, including birdwatching, coastal processes, orienteering, sailing and cycling; send sae for details of adult courses. Dogs to be kept under control at all times on the beach; not on Scolt Head Island mid Apr-mid Aug. Dog-free area on Brancaster Beach, west of golf clubhouse May-Sept.
All year any reasonable time. Information at Dial House Barn and Shop, open subject to staff availability
Admission Free. Golf Club car park at Brancaster Beach, parking charge (inc. NT members)

Norfolk Broads
The Broads Authority Thomas Harvey House 18 Colgate Norwich Norfolk NR3 1BQ
Tel: 01603 782281
A huge wetland area including six rivers and forty Broads. The Broads themselves are the remains of medieval peat diggings. The earth was dug up and used for fuel leaving gaping holes which were later flooded by changing sea levels: these formed the Broads as we know them today. An area perfect for boating, walking and cycling. Cycles are available for hire. A more detailed events programme runs in the better weather including guided walks, activity days for children, puppet shows and Wherry tours on the old sailing crafts. Contact information centre for details.

Norfolk Wildlife Trust
72 Cathedral Close Norwich Norfolk NR1 4DF
Tel: 01603 625540 Fax: 01603 630593

RSPB Titchwell Marsh Nature Reserve
Main Road Titchwell King's Lynn Norfolk PE31 8BB
[6m E of Hunstanton on A419. Limited on site parking available]
Tel: 01485 210779 Fax: 01485 210779
Facilities at this popular reserve include two birdwatching hides, a visitor centre and a gift shop, a servery and picnic area and toilets. Avoid arriving by car at weekends, the car park can often be full. Please telephone 0500 626 116 for bus service information. All birds on the reserve are wild, visitors might hope to see a selection of wading birds and wildfowl including avocets and shelducks.
Open at all times, Visitor Centre daily 10.00-17.00, Nov-Mar 10.00-16.00
Admission Free. Car park to Non-Memebers £3.00

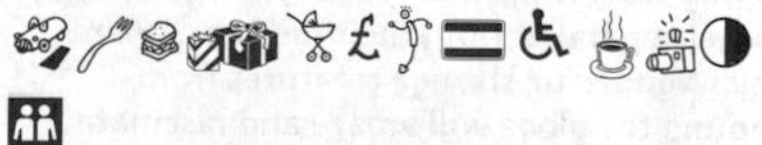

Railways

Bure Valley Railway
Bure Valley Railway Aylsham Norfolk NR11 6BW
[Aylsham Station is situated mid-way between Norwich and Cromer on the A140]
Tel: 01263 733858
www.bvrw.co.uk
Travel through the Norfolk countryside on the 9 mile long 15 inch Bure Valley Steam Railway. The Boat Train connects with cruises on the Broads - inclusive fares available. Regular services from Easter to End of September. Steam Locomotive Driving Courses are also available in off peak periods.
visitor comments: Beautifully kept trains, with reasonably priced restaurant and friendly staff.
Easter to Sept 30 call for timetable
Sample fares from A£4.00 C(5-15)£2.50 OAPs£3.60

Sealife Centres & Aquariums

Great Yarmouth Sea Life Centre

Marine Parade Great Yarmouth Norfolk NR30 3AH

[A47 or A12 to Great Yarmouth, then head towards Sea Front]

Tel: 01493 330631 Fax: 01493 330442

One of the country's biggest Sea Life Centres, Great Yarmouth is home to a spectacular tropical sharp display...and Britain's largest shark Nobby the nurse shark. Travel back to the dawn of time and discover how life on Earth first developed in Living Fossils. Come face to face with the oceans' living dinosaurs - completely unchanged for millions of years.

All year Mon-Sun 10.00-17.30, later closing times during July & Aug

A£4.95 C(3-15)£3.50

Hunstanton Sea Life Centre

Southern Promade Hunstanton Norfolk PE36 5BH

[on seafront, signposted]

Tel: 01485 533576 Fax: 01485 533531

Hunstanton Sea Life Centre overlooks The Wash...home to England's biggest colony of common seals, and is a vital rescue centre for young seals which fall foul of stormy weather or get separated from their mothers. Wierd and Wonderful, strange creatures from around the globe will amaze and fascinate you. Daily talks & seal feedings call for times.

All year Summer daily10.00-17.30. Winter daily 11.00-15.00

Last Admission: 15.00

A£5.25 C£3.75 OAPs£4.45. Group 10+ discounts

Social History Museums

Sheringham Museum

22-26 Station Road Sheringham Norfolk NR26 8RE

Tel: 01263 821871 Fax: 01263 825741

Displays on Fishing Industry, lifeboats, with models, War Years, geology with local fossils, local families, growth of town with photographic records, tourism, boat building with original tools from 1800's, Japanese POW camps with original diaries. Flint picking and a prehistoric elephant.

Easter-Oct Tue-Sat 10.00-16.00, Sun 14.00-16.30. Weekends in Nov & Dec

A£1.00 Concessions£0.50. Groups 10+ £0.35

discount offer: Two For The Price Of One

Theme & Adventure Parks

Great Yarmouth Pleasure Beach

South Beach Parade Great Yarmouth Norfolk NR30 3EH

[on the seafront at the southern end of Great Yarmouth's Golden Mile]

Tel: 01493 844585

www.pleasure-beach.co.uk

The Pleasure Beach is situated on the seafront at the southern end of Great Yarmouth's Golden Mile and covers 9 acres. Apart from the main ride area, we have two water based rides in the boating lakes and the Pleasure Beach Gardens which consists of two Crazy Golf courses and a traditional seafront tea-room pavilion. The main attraction is the famous old wooden Roller Coaster, which has been operating here since 1932. In addition, there are several white knuckle thrillers, 'family' rides and children's rides. There are three amusement arcades, many sidestalls and a number of catering outlets, including a large fast-food eatery, Ice Cream Parlour, Doughnut - Popcorn - Hot Dog - Candy Floss stalls and the Pleasure Beach Inn Public House. The Ejector Seat is the only ride of its kind outside the USA. It has been thrilling riders and audiences alike at the Pleasure Beach since mid June 1998, by hurling its victims
from 0 to 60 mph in less than one second vertically to a height of 150 feet.

visitor comments: Wristbands prove good value if you stay the whole day.

Daily from May 23rd to September 13th 11.00-22.00

Admission free: Wristbands £8.00 valid till 18.00 Ejector seat £16.50, riders must be 48 inches high to the shoulder.

Joyland

Marine Parade Great Yarmouth Norfolk NR30

[Marine Parade on the sea front Great Yarmouth]

Tel: 01493 844094

Children's pleasure park with super rides including; Snails; Tubs; Cars; Neptune's Kingdom; The Wheel; Major Orbit; and Pirate Ship. New for 1998 - Toytown and Spook Express Ride.

visitor comments: Staff a bit grumpy. Nice rides for children of all ages.

All year daily from 10.00-early evening

£0.25 per token. Rides: 4 tokens per person

Norfolk Dinosaur Park
Weston Park Lenwade Norwich Norfolk NR9 5JW
[9m from Norwich off A1067]
Tel: 01603 870245 Fax: 01603 873040
www.dinosaurpark.co.uk
Our unique tourist and leisure attraction has provided family entertainment for many years, set amongst acres of woodland in Norfolk's scenic countryside. Follow the dinosaur trail, housing one of the largest collections of lifesize dinosaurs, meet Dippy the Dinosaur, visit the new Climb-a-Saurus, The Lost World Maze and lots, lots more.
visitor comments: Excellent educational experience. Wonderful play areas and children's farm. Lots of fun!
March 27-May 2 Fri-Sun 10.00-16.00, May 3-Sept 5 daily 10.00-17.00, Sept 6-Oct 31 Fri-Sun 10.00-16.00
A£4.50 C(3-14)£3.50 OAPs£4.00

Zoos

Banham Zoo
Kenninghall Road Banham Norwich Norfolk NR16 2HE
[situated between Attleborough and Diss on the B1114 Norwich to Bury St Edmunds road, follow the brown tourist signs]
Tel: 01953 887773 Fax: 01953 887445
www.banham-zoo.co.uk
Banham Zoo is East Anglia's premier wildlife attraction. Located in the heart of Norfolk amongst beautiful parkland, it's simply purrrfect for that family day out. Where else can you enjoy over 150 individual species of animals including many rare and endangered breeds. You will soon be immersed in our animal experience with tigers, snow leopards, magnificent shire horses and many, many others. Listen and learn at a feeding talk, ride the roadtrain, run amok in the adventure play area or simply relax and enjoy a picnic or ice cream in one of the many gardens.
All year daily from 10.00 Jan-end Mar closes 16.00, end Mar-end June closes 17.00, July-end Sept closes 17.30, Oct-end Dec closes 16.00. Closed 25-26 Dec
Last Admission: 60mins before closing
A£6.95 C£4.95 C(under 3)£Free
discount offer: One Child Free When Accompanied By Two Full Paying Adults. Not To Be Used In Conjunction With Any Other Offer

Thrigby Hall Wildlife Gardens
Filby Road Thrigby Great Yarmouth Norfolk NR29 3DR
[on unclass road off A1064]
Tel: 01493 369477 Fax: 01493 368256
www.optipoint.co.uk/thrigby
The 250-year old park of Thrigby Hall is now the home of animals and birds from Asia, and the lake has ornamental wildfowl. There are tropical and bird houses, a unique blue willow pattern garden and tree walk and a summer house as old as the park.
visitor comments: Beautiful walkways and gardens through the trees and over lakes. Large selection of animals - amazing to be so close!
All year daily from 10.00
Last Admission: Summer 16.00 Winter 15.30
A£5.50 C(4-14)£3.90 OAPs£4.90. Pre-booked Group rates A£5.00 C£3.50 OAPs£4.50
discount offer: 50p Off Standard Rates. Valid Until 31 Dec 2000

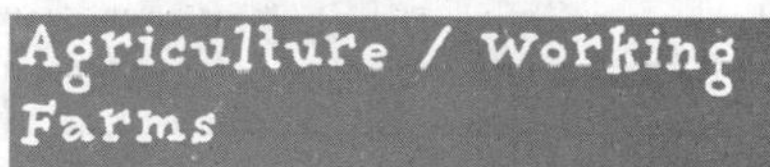

Agriculture / Working Farms

Manvell Farm and Animal Sanctuary
Kettering Road Walgrave Northamptonshire NN6 9PY
[off the main A43 between Kettering & Northampton nr the village of Broughton]
Tel: 01604 781775
Small farm and animal sanctuary. See. touch and enjoy the animals which include, pigs, horses, donkeys, sheep, lambs, goats, kids, rabbits, chickens, chicks, ducks and ducklings. Many of the animals have been rescued.
visitor comments: Some animals roam free. Children need supervision at all times.
All year Apr-Sept 10.00-17.00 Oct-March 11.00-15.00 closed Christmas
A£1.75 C&Concessions £1.25

Animal Attractions

West Lodge Rural Centre
Back Lane Desborough Kettering
Northamptonshire NN14 2SH
[signposted off A6 N of Desborough]
Tel: 01536 763762/760552 Fax: 01536 762937
www.members.tripod.com/~west_lodge
One of the most spacious open Family Farms with over 100 acres and 3.5m of walks to explore. Encompassing rare breeds, cuddle corner, falconry centre, display barn, tractor rides, fantasy sculpture trail, nature trails, play areas, play barn. Many special events held throughout the year.
visitor comments: Good adventure playground. Mainly small animals good for younger children. Good farmhouse cooking.
Mar-Sept daily 10.00-17.00
A£3.75 C£2.00 Concessions£3.00 School Groups £2.35. Groups 20+ 10% discount

Arts, Crafts & Textiles

Northampton Central Museum and Art Gallery
Guildhall Road Northampton
Northamptonshire NN1 1DP
[J15 M1, signposted town centre]
Tel: 01604 238548 Fax: 01604 238720
The Central Museum and Art Gallery reflects Northampton's proud standing as Britain's boot and shoe capital by housing a collection of boots and shoes considered one of the finest in the world. Also on display are Northampton's history, decorative arts, the Art Gallery and the Leathercraft Gallery.
All year Mon-Sat 10.00-17.00, Sun 14.00-17.00. Closed 25 Dec & 1 Jan
Admission Free

↓*special events*

▶ **Northampton Scribes Calligraphy Exhibition**
11/3/00-9/4/00
Also, Fashioned by Stitch, an exhibition by the Embroiderers Guild

▶ **Northants Guild of Designer Craftsmen**
15/4/00-14/5/00
Pottery, jewellery, wood turning and other crafts. Paintings by John Lockett also featured

▶ **Painting and Photographic Exhibition**
20/5/00-18/6/00
Work by local artists Sarah Bament and Adrian Pinkard

▶ **Models and Miniaturists for the Millennium**
24/6/00-23/7/00

▶ **Exhibition by Local Artists**
29/7/00-3/9/00
Contemporary and experimental prints by Ian McCulloch and Sarah Hyde.

▶ **Computer Generated Psychic Art**
9/9/00-8/10/00
By Sue and Paul Hopgood with paintings by Clifford Knight

▶ **"Strangely Familiar"**
14/10/00-12/11/00
Humourous life size papier mache sculptures by Philip Cox

▶ **Photographic Exhibition by Gerry Broughton**
18/11/00-10/12/00
Northamptonshire photographs old and new

▶ **Town and County Art Society**
10/12/00-15/1/01

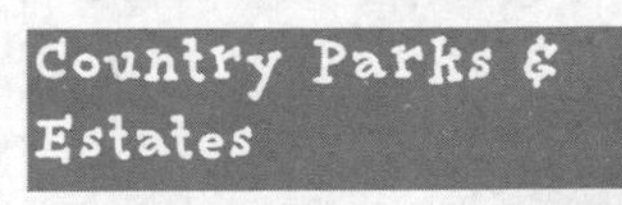

Country Parks & Estates

Billing Aquadrome Limited
Crow Lane Great Billing Northampton
Northamptonshire NN3 9DA
[follow the distinctive Billing Aquadrome signs from J15 M1 - just 15mins away via dual carriageway - or pick up the signed routes from Northampton which is just 10 minutes away]
Tel: 01604 784948 Fax: 01604 784412
www.aquadrome.co.uk

The park is renowned for a wide range of leisure facilities, including a swimming pool and licensed bars offering tempting meals and a variety of amusements. For youngster there are plenty of free play areas, a safe paddling pool, interesting walks and bicycle rides, and an exciting range of family amusements. Anglers can try their luck on the one mile of river on the nine lakes which lie within our natural wildlife environment. For your convenience within the Park complex we have a funfair, jet-ski's, a supermarket, a wide variety of fast-food outlets, a caravan / camping accessory shop, a launderette, public telephones. Many sites have electrical hook-up points and are all within easy reach of modern and fully equipped toilet blocks. For further details on any of the following special events, please call 01604 408181.

visitor comments: Good facilities. Good value for money.

Mar-Nov

Day Visitor Charges: at all times £5.00 per car, Pedestrians £1.00 at all times, motorcycles £1.00 at all times, additional cars will be charged at £5.00. Caravan charges vary according to duration etc.

↓*special events*

▶ **Bargain Weekend One**
14/4/00-16/4/00
£15.00

▶ **Granada MKII Collection**
14/4/00-16/4/00

▶ **Olympic C.C.**
21/4/00-24/4/00

▶ **American Auto Club Springnationals**
21/4/00-24/4/00

▶ **Ely and District C.C.**
21/4/00-24/4/00

▶ **Trailer C.C. Vale of Trent Section**
21/4/00-1/5/00
20 hook ups and 30 non-hook up spaces plus a marquee space. No charge at gate

▶ **Billing Country Horse Drive**
19/5/00-21/5/00

▶ **Vauxhall Bedford Opel Association**
14/7/00-16/7/00

▶ **Volkswagen Type II O.C.**
15/7/00-21/7/00

▶ **Land Rover Off Road Events**
21/7/00-23/7/00

▶ **Granada MKI and MKII Drivers Guild**
29/7/00-28/7/00

▶ **Toyota Enthusiasts Club**
29/7/00-30/7/00

▶ **International Koi Show**
5/8/00-6/8/00

▶ **Monkey Bike Rally**
5/8/00-6/8/00

▶ **Performance Car Club**
11/8/00-13/8/00

▶ **Granada MKII Collection**
11/8/00-13/8/00

▶ **Mrs Pitts and Friends**
25/8/00-28/8/00

▶ **Bargain Weekend Three**
8/9/00-10/9/00

▶ **Barclays C.C.**
3/11/00-5/11/00

▶ **Peugeot C.C.C.**
3/11/00-5/11/00

▶ **Land Rover Workers C.C.**
3/11/00-5/11/00

▶ **Coventry Morris Engines**
3/11/00-5/11/00

▶ **Bargain Weekend Four with Fireworks**
3/11/00-5/11/00

Festivals & Shows

Northampton Balloon Festival

Race Course Park Northampton
Northamptonshire NN2 7BL
[1m N of town on the Kettering Rd. Park & Ride Scheme available. Parking on site charged]
Tel: 01604 238791 Fax: 01604 238796

Over 250,000 people visited the 1999 festival making it one of the most successful ever held. Three days of balloon glows, flights (daily at 6AM and 6PM), fireworks and festival fun. A fun-filled day out for the whole family.

visitor comments: A fun filled day out for the whole family. Night balloon glow to music was great.

Aug 18-20 2000

Admission Free

↓*special events*

▶ **Northampton Balloon Festival**
18/8/00-20/8/00

Northampton Festival of Music and Arts

Various Northampton Northamptonshire
[Various locations across Northampton.]
Tel: 01604 238791 Fax: 01604 238796

Northampton Borough Council is pleased to present the third music and arts festival. The initiative aims to highlight music and arts in a wide variety of styles such as theatre, photography and dance. In various venues throughout the town it provides a platform for performers and local organisations promoting "The Arts". Programme available late April/May

June 9-25 2000

Vary according to the event, some free

Northampton Town Show

Kingsley Road Northampton
Northamptonshire *[Signposted on all major*

routes into Northampton.]
Tel: 01604 238791 Fax: 01604 238796
Established favourites such as the art exhibition, dog show, food hall, horticulture and National Farmers Union. Learn about different sports and activities, listen to local bands, wonder at the agility of the arena entertainments, enjoy evening concerts and top bands. Finish off a memorable evening with a fireworks display
July 21-23 2000, Fri 13.00-22.00 Sat 10.00-22.00 Sun 10.00-18.00
Admission Free

↓special events
▶ **Northampton Show**
21/7/00-23/7/00

Folk & Local History Museums

Abington Museum
Abington Park Northampton
Northamptonshire NN1 5LW
[in Abington Park]
Tel: 01604 631454
A 15th century manor house, once the home of Shakespeare's granddaughter Elizabeth Barnard, who is buried in the nearby church grounds. It is now a museum showing the social history of the house including Victorian Cabinet of Curiosities, a 19th-century fashion gallery too. Also here is the Northamptonshire Regiment museum and Northamptonshire Yeomanry.
All year Bank Hol Mon & Tue-Sun 13.00-17.00
Admission Free

↓special events
▶ **Mirror, Bead and Thread**
8/2/00-14/5/00
An exhibition by Moti and Kanchan Malde

Manor House Museum
Sheep Street Kettering Northamptonshire
NN16 0AN
[in the town centre]
Tel: 01536 534219 Fax: 01536 534370
The Museum invites the historical re-enactment group, Time Travellers, to run educational weeks at the Museum for school visits. In addition the Museum runs activity days for children on every day during school holidays, including half terms. There are always based on the principal of making and taking home a museum-inspired object.
All year Mon-Sat 09.30-17.00, Wed 10.00-17.00. Closed Sun & Bank Hol
Last Admission: 16.45
Admission Free

Historical

Althorp House and Park
Althorp Northampton Northamptonshire NN7 4HG
[J16 M1, A45 to Northampton, A428 Northampton / Coventry Road, approx 5m NW of Northampton]
Tel: 01604 592020 tickets Fax: 01604 770042
www.althorp-house.co.uk/
Althorp House, the final resting place of Diana, Princess of Wales, has been the home of the Spencer Family since 1508. The house was built in the 16th century, but has been changed since, most notably by Henry Holland in the 18th century. Recently restored by the present Earl, the house is in immaculate condition. Open only from Diana, Princess of Wales' birthday to the eve of the anniversary of her death by prior ticket purchase only by calling the above number. A former stable block in Althorp Park has been transformed into a classical temple as a permanent memorial to Diana, Princess of Wales. Included is a marble silhouette of Diana and a simple wooden cross on top of the facade. Visitors are not allowed on the ornamental island where she is buried, but a stone urn on a plinth is visible from the lake-side temple. Inscriptions highlighting Diana's life's work are featured on the memorial. Guides direct you through the house and the memorial museum.
visitor comments: Take flowers and sit by the island where Diana is buried. Staff helpful and friendly.
Open only from Diana, Princess of Wales' birthday to the eve of the anniversary of her death for those wishing to pay their respects. 1 July-30 Aug 2000

Boughton House
Living Landscape Trust Kettering
Northamptonshire NN14 1BJ
[3m N of Kettering on A43 access from A14]
Tel: 01536 515731 Fax: 01536 417255
www.boughtonhouse.org.uk
Northamptonshire home of the Dukes of Buccleuch and their Montagu ancestors since 1528. 500-year-old Tudor monastic building enlarged around seven courtyards until the French-style addition of 1695. Many art treasures, Armoury, park with lake. Member of the Historic Houses Association.
House: 1 Aug-1 Sept 14.00-17.00, Grounds: 1 May-15 Sept Sun-Thur 13.00-17.00. Staterooms strictly by prior appointment by telephone

Last Admission: 16.30
House: A£4.00 C&OAPs£3.00 Grounds: A£1.50 C&OAPs£1.00

Canons Ashby House
Canons Ashby Daventry Northamptonshire NN11 3SD
[J11 M40, A422 exit then left along unclassified road or J16 M1 signposted from A5, 2m S of Weedon crossroads. Plenty of parking on site]
Tel: 01327 860044
Home of the Dryden family since the 16th century, this manor house was built circa 1550, added to in the 1590's and altered in the 1630's and circa 1710; largely unaltered since. Within the house, Elizabethan wall-paintings and outstanding Jacobean plasterwork are of particular interest. A formal garden includes terraces, walls and gate piers of 1710. There is also a mediaeval priory church and a 28-ha park.
visitor comments: One of the finest Tudor homes in the East Midlands.
House & Garden: Easter-Oct Sat-Wed 13.00-17.30 or dusk if sooner. Closed Thur & Fri
Last Admission: 17.00
A£4.00 C£2.00 Family Ticket £10.00

↓*special events*

▶ **Spring Plant Fair**
14/5/00-14/5/00
Commences 11.00

▶ **Paint in the Garden**
21/5/00-21/5/00
Basic materials will be provided and no experience is necessary. All ages are welcome. Usual admission. 12.00-16.00

▶ **Bat Walk**
10/6/00-10/6/00
Meet in car park at 20.00

▶ **Herbs, Hives and History Day**
18/6/00-18/6/00
Family activities from 13.00

▶ **Paint in the Garden**
25/6/00-25/6/00
See entry for 21 May

▶ **Flower Festival**
22/7/00-2/8/00

▶ **Embroidery Exhibition**
5/8/00-16/8/00

▶ **Paint in the Garden**
10/9/00-10/9/00
See entry for 21 May

Holdenby House, Gardens and Falconry Centre
Holdenby Northampton Northamptonshire NN6 8DJ
[6m NW of Northampton off A428 & A5199 approx 7m from J15a/16/J18 M1]
Tel: 01604 770074 Fax: 01604 770962
Just across the fields from Althrop, this former palace and prison of Charles I provides a stately backdrop to a beautiful garden and host of attractions. Falconry, 17th Century Farmstead, children's amusements, shop and teas.
Gardens & Falconry Centre: Apr-end Sept Sun 13.00-17.00, July & Aug Mon-Fri 13.00-17.00, House: Bank Hol Mon 24 Apr 29 May & 28 Aug 13.00-17.00. Closed Sat
House & Gardens (Bank Hol Mon only): A£4.00 C£2.00 OAPs£3.75. Garden: A£3.75 C£1.75 OAPs£2.25

Kirby Hall
Deene Corby Northamptonshire NN17 5EN
[on unclassified road off A43 4m NE of Corby]
Tel: 01536 203230
Begun in 1570 this beautiful Elizabethan manor house boasts an unusual richness and variety of architectural detail in the Renaissance style. The extensive gardens - currently being restored - were among the finest in England at their peak during the 17th century.
1 Apr-31 Oct daily 10.00-18.00, 17.00 in Oct. 1 Nov-31 Mar Wed-Sun 10.00-16.00. Closed 13.00-14.00. Closed 24-26 Dec & 1 Jan
A£2.70 C£1.40 OAPs£2.00

↓*special events*

▶ **Meet the Custodian**
8/4/00-9/4/00
Tours by the people who know them best

▶ **Meet the Custodian**
15/4/00-16/4/00
See entry for 8 April

▶ **Mansfield Park Tours**

22/4/00-24/4/00
Hear how the hall became a film set for "Mansfield Park"
▶ **Mansfield Park Tours**
30/4/00-1/5/00
See entry for 22 April
▶ **Captain Hook!**
13/5/00-14/5/00
The magical adventures of Peter Pan, Captain Hook and of course, the crocodile
▶ **Civil War Battle Spectacular**
28/5/00-29/5/00
Exciting battle action as Roundheads and Cavaliers clash
▶ **Archaeology Tours**
23/7/00-23/7/00
Archaeology made simple!
▶ **History in Action**
12/8/00-13/8/00
Spectacular action from Romans to D-Day! The biggest event of its kind in the world
▶ **Apple Days**
30/9/00-1/10/00
Apple Days Apple varieties identified, a fascinating talk on the ancient origins of apples, stalls and entertainments

On the Water

Blisworth Tunnel Boats
Gayton Road Blisworth Northampton
Northamptonshire NN7 3BN
[off the A43 in the village of Blisworth]
Tel: 01604 858868
Enjoy a relaxing day out with your family and friends aboard one of our self-steer narrow boats. Navigate the Blisworth Tunnel and Stoke Bruerne locks, or just potter gently through the Northamptonshire countryside.
Mar-Oct 9.30-18.00
£100.00 inclusive for a whole day for a max of 12 on each boat. Weekdays £85.00 per day. Half day £50.00: 09.30-13.15 or 14.15-18.00

Indian Chief Cruises
The Boat Inn Stoke Bruerne Towcester
Northamptonshire NN12 7SB
[in village centre just off A508]
Tel: 01604 862428
Take a leisurely cruise along the picturesque Grand Union Canal in the hospitable narrow boat Indian Chief. Trips avaliable from 25 mins to 6hrs. Light buffet meals and teas by arrangement.
Easter-Sept and Santa Cruises in Dec, for public trips call for daily schedule
Prices vary, please call for details

Linda Cruising Company
Cosgrove Wharf Lock Lane Cosgrove
Northamptonshire *[A5 or J15 M1 onto A508. In Cosgrove follow signs to Caravan Park then R into Lock Lane]*
Tel: 01604 862107 Box Office
www.lindacruising.co.uk
Come and enjoy the countryside at the slow pace of canal life, and immerse yourself in the history and heritage of Britain's inland waterways. We offer cruises on the Grand Union Canal from one hour to a day trip, in the veteran ex-working narrowboat 'Linda' (built 1912). Cosy, well-stocked on-board bar and souvenir shop, offering hand-pumped real ale on many trips. Regular public trips at weekends, and weekdays during the summer holidays - please call for current timetable either 01604 862107 or 0973 915652. We also offer private charter cruises, educational trips and corporate entertainment.
All year, call for timetable
Prices vary according to type and length of trips. Concessions for children, family groups & educational trips

Railways

Northampton and Lamport Railway
Pitsford & Brampton Station Pitsford Road
Chapel Brampton Northampton
Northamptonshire NN6 8BA
[J15a / J15 M1, between A50 / A508]
Tel: 01604 847318 Fax: 01604 670953
www.nlr.org.uk
In 1981 a group was formed with the intention of reopening the branch from Northampton to Market Harborough which was designed by George Bidder and George R Stephenson and opened in 1859. In 1984 the Society started to rebuild the railway in the old goods yard at Pitsford and Brampton station. Phase 1 (now complete) consists of a station, two signal boxes, 3/4 mile of running lime and sidings. When completed to Lamport, the line will be approximately 6.5 miles long. The line was formally opened on 31st March 1996. Further work was started in early 1997. The current rolling stock consists of steam and diesel locomotives with further stock in various stages of restoration. Other stock: carriages, guards vans and wagons are held, ready for use. The railway can offer private hire of trains for birthday parties, receptions or corporate entertainment. School parties, youth groups and society bookings are also welcome. For further information call our 24 hour line on 01604 820327 - manned on oper-

ating days.
Trains run every Sun and Bank Hol Mon. Low Season: Mar & Nov - Diesel Multiple service, Off Peak Season: Apr & Oct - Steam and Diesel service 11.30, 12.30, 13.30, 14.30 & 13.30. Peak Service: May-Sept - Steam and Diesel Service 11.00, 11.45, 12.30, 13.15, 14.00, 14.45, 15.30 & 16.15
Last Admission: 16.30
A£2.80 C(4-15)&OAPs£1.80 Family Ticket £8.00, special events rates may differ

Spectator Sports

Silverstone Circuit
Towcester Northamptonshire NN12 8TN
[600yds from Silverstone between Towcester and Brackley on A43]
Tel: 01327 857271 Fax: 01327 857663
www.silverstone-circuit.co.uk
Britain's premier motor racing circuit. Hosts the British Grand Prix.
Book in Advance : Lines open 08.00-19.00 Mon-Fri & 10.00-14.00 Weekends & Bank Hol (excl. Christmas) By Phone: 01327 857273. By Fax: 01327 320300
See special events for details

↓*special events*

▶ **RAC British Grand Prix**
21/4/00-23/4/00
This sensational sporting event is as popular as it is spectacular - it never fails to sell out... featuring Round 4 of the FIA Formula One World Championship & F3000. Fri 21 Apr: from A£35.00 C£8.00 Centre Transfer, all £17.00. Sat 22 Apr: from A£75.00-£50.00 C£30.00-£10.00 Centre Transfer all £20.00. Sun 23 Apr: from A£90.00-160.00 C£15.00-£50.00 Centre Transfer all £25.00 3 Day A£375.00

Sport & Recreation

Santa Pod Raceway
Airfield Road Podington Wellingborough Northamptonshire NN29 7XA
[M1 J14. Plenty of on site parking available]
Tel: 01234 782828 Fax: 01234 782818
'The Home of European Drag Racing' Santa Pod Raceway established for over 30 years in North Bedfordshire is the home of European Drag Racing - the fastest motorsport on earth! Sited on what was once an American airbase, Santa Pod attracts over 200,000 visitors each season (February to November) to watch one of America's great motor sports. This is motor racing at it's fastest and the season's calendar comprises over 35 different car/bike related events. Free kids admission, free events calendar, free camping for weekend ticket holders, children's activities, corporate hospitality and track hire and testing.
Feb-Nov weekend race meetings 10.00-21.00
Prices vary according to the event, please call to clarify prices. All children £Free

↓*special events*

▶ **Easter Thunderball**
22/4/00-24/4/00
National event

▶ **Big Bang**
6/5/00-7/5/00
VW Beetle Festival

▶ **FIA Main Event**
27/5/00-29/5/00
European Championship event with Top Fuel Cars & Bikes

▶ **The Cannonball Weekend**
1/7/00-2/7/00
International Funny Car Festival

▶ **Bug Jam**
21/7/00-23/7/00
Europe's largest Volkswagen Beetle event

▶ **Ultimate Street Car Festival**
18/8/00-20/8/00
Public participation weekend

▶ **FIA European Finals**
8/9/00-10/9/00
European Championship Finals with Top Fuel Cars and Bikes

▶ **The October Meet**
7/10/00-8/10/00
National Drag Racing Championship Finals

▶ **Flame and Thunder Show**
4/11/00-4/11/00
End of season drag racing plus firework spectacular with stunts and displays

Birds, Butterflies & Bees

Chain Bridge Honey Farm
Horncliffe Berwick-upon-Tweed Northumberland *[signposted from A698, Berwick to Coldstream rd, 1m from A1]*
Tel: 01289 386362

The Chain Bridge Honey Farm, established 30 years ago lies on the banks of the River Tweed in the beautiful border countryside. There are over 1000 colonies of bees belonging to the honey farm which are kept in out-apiaries throughout the Scottish borders and North Northumberland. The honey, beeswax and propolis from the bees is used in the many products we make.

visitor comments: Fascinating displays and lots to buy. Chain Bridge is 5 minutes down the road, with beautiful walks along banks of river.

Good Fri-end Oct Mon-Sat 10.30-17.00, Sun 14.00-17.00. Nov-Apr Mon-Fri only
Visitor Centre: Admission Free

Forests & Woods

Kielder Castle Forest Park Centre

Forest Enterprise Keilder Castle Keilder Hexham Northumberland NE48 1ER
[situated at the N end of Keilder Water follow brown tourist signs for Keilder Water and Forest]
Tel: 01434 250209/220242 Fax: 01434 250209

Built in 1775 as a hunting lodge for the Duke of Northumberland Keilder Castle today houses the Forestry Commission Visitor Centre for Keilder Forest Park. A free exhibition over two floors explores the history, wildlife, landscape and recreation of the area. Starting point for many forest trails, cycle routes and 'What's On' events. At the heart of the forest lies the seven mile long Kielder Water reservoir.

Easter-31 Oct daily 10.00-17.00, Aug 10.00-18.00. Winter weekends 10.00-16.00
Last Admission: 30mins before closing
Admission Free. £1.00 car parking

↓*special events*

▶ **Kielder Reiver Trail Quest**
6/5/00-6/5/00
A mountain bike event at the Castle

▶ **Historic Cars Pre 1974**
20/5/00-21/5/00

▶ **Kielder Festival**
6/8/00-6/8/00
A not-to-be-missed day out with family entertainment, folk music and craft displays

▶ **Kielder Millennium Arts Festival**
23/9/00-24/9/00

Historical

Alnwick Castle

Alnwick Northumberland NE66 2NO
[just off the town centre on the N side of Alnwick. Free Coachpark]
Tel: 01665 510777 / 603942 Fax: 01665 510876

Alnwick Castle is the second largest inhabited castle in England and home of the Percy family since 1309. The magnificent state rooms are furnished in Renaissance style with paintings by Titian, Canaletto and Van Dyck, fine furniture and exquisite china collection. Constable's Tower remains untouched since the 14th century and now houses the history of the Tenantry from the early 19th century. Postern Tower houses a collection of early British and Roman objects from various periods, many of which were found in Northumberland. Abbot's Tower features state-of-the-art video and interactive displays evoking the history of this famous Regiment from 1674 to the Gulf War and Bosnia. There are woodland walks with peaceful views over landscape designed by Capability Brown. Please note that the Guest Hall is not open to Castle visitors. There is wheelchair access to the Tea Room, Shop and Grounds, but unfortunately not to the Castle. Member of the Historic Houses Association.

Maundy Thur-end Sept daily 11.00-17.00. Open all Bank Hol & Good Fri. Private Tours and functions by arrangement
Last Admission: 16.15
A£5.95 C(5-16)£3.50 Family Ticket(A2+C2) £15.00 OAPs&Students£5.45. Grounds only £4.00. Group rates on request

Bamburgh Castle

Bamburgh Northumberland NE69 7DF
[on the coast 16m N of Alnwick 6m from Belford 3m from Seahouses]
Tel: 01668 214208/214515 Fax: 01668 214060

Rising up dramatically on a rocky outcrop, Bamburgh Castle is a huge, square Norman castle. Restored in the 19th century by Lord Armstrong, it has an impressive hall and armoury. Member of the Historic Houses Association.

22 Mar-Oct daily11.00-variable closing times
A£3.50 C£1.50 OAPs£2.50. Party 12+ by arrangement

Cherryburn

Station Bank Cherryburn Cottages Mickley Stocksfield Northumberland NE43 7DB
[11m W of Newcastle 11m E of Hexham 0.25m N of Mickley Square leave A695 & follow signposts]
Tel: 01661 843276

The birthplace of Thomas Bewick, Northumbria's greatest artist, wood engraver

and naturalist. The 19th farmhouse houses a small exhibition on Bewisk's life and works. Also farmyard animals and beautiful views of Tyne Valley.
House: 1 Apr-30 OctThurs-Mon & Bank Hol Mon 13.00-17.30
Last Admission: House: 16.45 Gardens: 17.00
A£3.00 NT Members Free. Morning coffee for pre-booked groups only

↓*special events*

▶ **May Day Celebratons**
1/5/00-1/5/00
Traditional Northumbria music, clog dancing and Maypole dancing. Prize for best dressed May King or Queen. Bewick Whistling Competition (with or without penny whistle) - trophy for winner. National Trust Members £1.00 Non Members A£4.00 C£2.00

▶ **Sunday Folk in the Farmyard 2000**
4/6/00-27/8/00
Traditional music, dance and song in the farmyard. Folkworks ceilidh bands, concert bands, folk groups, clog dancers, flutes, guitars, whistles etc. SAE to Cherryburn for Sunday afternoon programme. Usual admission charges apply

Cragside House Garden and Grounds

Cragside Morpeth Northumberland NE65 7PX
[0.5m E of Rothbury 20m N of Newcastle-upon-Tyne entrance off Rothbury / Alnwick road B6341]
Tel: 01669 620333

This splendid Victorian masterpiece was built for Sir William (later the first Lord) Armstrong in stages, between 1864 and 1895. It was designed for him by the architect Richard Norman Shaw and the interior of the house reflects the taste and style of both its architect and its owner. Usual admission charges apply against any walks held during normal property opening times where the walk is free.
House: 1 Apr-29 Oct Tue-Sun & Bank Hol Mon 13.00-17.30. Estate & Garden: As House 10.30-19.00. Restaurant & Shop: As House 10.30-17.30. Winter Opening: Estate, Gardens and Visitor Centre 1 Nov-17 Dec Wed-Sun 11.00-16.00. House Closed
Last Admission: House: 16.30, Estate & Garden 17.00
House, Garden & Estate: A£6.50 Group rates 15+ £5.70. Garden & Estate: A£4.00 Group rates 15+ £3.50. Family Ticket(A2+C3) for House, Garden & Estate £16.00, £10.00 Garden & Estate

↓*special events*

▶ **Spring Arrives**
16/4/00-16/4/00
A walk through the Rock Garden and Formal Garden

▶ **Easter Egg Trail**
23/4/00-23/4/00
11.00-15.30. Enjoy woodland and river walks following the clues to the Easter Eggs, C£1.50

▶ **Blooming Bulbs**
7/5/00-7/5/00
A gentle walk. Meet in the Formal Garden Car Park

▶ **Riotous Rhododendrons**
8/6/00-8/6/00
An evening wander around the Mansion and Rock Gardens concluding with a walk to the formal gardens, at 19.00 A£2.00 C£Free

▶ **The History of Cragside Gardens**
16/7/00-16/7/00
National Gardens Scheme Day. A walk looking at the design of the gardens

▶ **Summer Splendor in the Formal Garden**
13/8/00-13/8/00
A gentle walk. Meet in the Formal Garden Car Park

▶ **September Stroll in the Formal Garden**
17/9/00-17/9/00
See entry for 13 August

▶ **Autumnal Tips at Cragside Garden**
15/10/00-15/10/00
See entry for 16 April

▶ **Putting the House to Bed**
11/11/00-12/11/00
A behind the scenes tour of the house, 13.00, £7.00, booking essential

▶ **The Winter Landscape**
19/11/00-19/11/00
A wander through the Pinetum, Rock Gardens and Valley Garden. Meet in the Formal Garden Car Park

Lindisfarne Castle

Holy Island Berwick-Upon-Tweed Northumberland TD15 2SH
[5m E of Beal across causeway]
Tel: 01289 389244

The 16th-century castle was restored by Sir Edwin Lutyens in 1903 for the owner of Country Life magazine. The austere outside walls belie the Edwardian comfort within, and there is a little garden deisgned by Gertrude Jekyll.
1 Apr-31 Oct Sat-Thur & Good Fri 13.00-17.30. Tide & Staff levels permitting open 12.00-15.00. Island not accessible two hours before & four hours after high tide. Other times by arrangement with Administrator.
Last Admission: 17.00
A£4.00 family Ticket (2A+2C) £10.00

Norham Castle

Berwick-Upon-Tweed Northumberland TD15 2JY
[off A1, on A1167]

Tel: 01289 382329
One of the strongest border fortresses, this castle has one of the finest Norman keeps in the country and overlooks the River Tweed.
27 Mar-31 Oct daily 10.00-18.00 or dusk if sooner
A£1.70 C£0.90 Concessions£1.30

↓*special events*

▶ **Medieval Entertainers**
10/6/00-11/6/00
Authentic medieval games, cures, folklore and early machinery, plus a children's play about the formative years of Parliament

▶ **The History Man**
1/7/00-2/7/00
Enjoy unusual guided tours with the presenter of the BBC's History Man programmes

▶ **Border Rievers!**
15/7/00-16/7/00
Superb equestrian skills of the dreaded Border Reivers recreated. Plus 16th century music

▶ **Medieval Living History**
12/8/00-13/8/00
15th century living hisotry, medieval music, artillery and combat displays with skirmish

▶ **Medieval Dance**
27/8/00-28/8/00
Join in with 14th century formal court and exuberant folk dances

▶ **Captain Hook!**
9/9/00-10/9/00
The magical adventures of Peter Pan, Captain Hook and of course, the crocodile!

Paxton House
Berwick-Upon-Tweed Northumberland TD15 1SZ
[5m from Berwick on Tweed on B6461, signposted from A1. BR: Berwick-on-Tweed 5m]
Tel: 01289 386291 Fax: 01289 386660
www.natgalscot.ac.uk
Highly commended by Scottish Tourist Board 1998. Scotland's most perfect Palladian country mansion. Built for a daughter of Frederick the Great. Designed by the Adam family and furnished by Chippendale and Trotter. Restored Regency picture gallery the largest in a Scottish country house (outstation of National Gallery). Gardens. Riverside Walks. Adventure Playground. Tearoom. Gift Shop.
1 Apr-Oct. House: daily 11.00-17.30. Grounds daily 10.00-sunset
Last Admission: House 16.15
House: A£4.50. Grounds only: A£2.25 Family Ticket £12.00
discount offer: One Child Free With Each Full Paying Adult. Valid until 1 Oct 1999

Prudhoe Castle
Prudhoe Northumberland NE42 6NA
[in Prudhoe off A695]
Tel: 01661 833459
www.english-heritage.org.uk
Standing on the River Tyne, this 12th-to14th century castle was the stronghold of the d'Umfravelles and Percys. The keep stands in the inner bailey. Access is to the Pele Yard only.
27 Mar-31 Oct daily 10.00-18.00 or dusk if sooner
Last Admission: 30mins before closing
A£1.70 C£0.90 Concessions£1.30

↓*special events*

▶ **Medieval Combat**
30/4/00-1/5/00
Archery, dance and children's activities, with 13th century combat at 15.00

▶ **Watercolours by Dr Lewis Walker Hanna**
12/5/00-26/5/00

▶ **Medieval Music**
28/5/00-29/5/00
Lively medieval music and song

▶ **Wind in the Willows**
9/6/00-11/6/00
Meet Toad, Ratty, Mole and Badger in this enchanting children's fantasy at 12.30 & 15.00

Nature & Conservation Parks

Farne Islands
Farne Islands Northumberland *[2-5m off the Northumberland coast opposite Bamburgh, trips every day weather permitting]*
Tel: 01665 721099
The islands provide a summer home for over 17 kinds of seabirds. There is a chapel built in memory of St Cuthbert who died here. Certain areas may not be accessible for wheelchairs. Refreshments in Seahouse not on islands.
Breeding season: 1 May-31 July daily. Access limited to Staple Island 10.30-13.30 and Inner Farne 13.30-18.00 Out of Season: 1-30 Apr & 1Aug-30 Sept 10.30-18.00
Per Island: May-end July A£4.00. Pre-booked school groups £2.00 all other times £3.00. Pre-booked school groups £1.70

Northumberland Wildlife Trust - Hauxley Nature Reserve and Visitor Centre
Low Hauxley Amble-by-the-Sea Northumberland NE65 0JR
[S of Amble directly off the A1068 coast road]
Tel: 01665 711578
Created following open cast mining on the site, this picturesque lake sprinkled with

islands is home to a wide variety of breeding birds, especially terns, and is a popular spot for migrating waders. There are excellent on-site facilities including a visitor centre with displays showing the history of Druridge Bay.
All year daily 08.00-Dusk
A£1.50 C&Concessions£0.75. Groups rates £1.00

Roman Era

Chesters Roman Fort
Chollerford Humshaugh Hexham
Northumberland NE46 4EP
[0.5m SW of Chollerford on B6318]
Tel: 01434 681379
www.english-heritage.org.uk
One of the Roman forts on Hadrian's Wall is now in the park of Chesters, an 18th-century mansion. The fort names Cilurnum housed 500 soldiers and covered nearly 6 acres. The excavations were started in the 19th century by the owner of Chesters, and have revealed a great deal about life in a Roman fort.
27 Mar-31 Oct daily 10.00-18.00 dusk if sooner. Apr-Sept daily 09.30-18.00. 1 Nov-26 Mar daily 10.00-16.00
Last Admission: 1 hour before closing
A£2.70 C£1.40 Concessions£2.00

↓special events

▶ **The Roman Army Returns to Hadrian's Wall**
28/5/00-29/5/00

▶ **Meet a Roman Soldier**
2/7/00-2/7/00

▶ **Classical Cuisine**
9/7/00-9/7/00
From Noon. Cooking demonstrations and recipies

▶ **Roman Storytelling**
16/7/00-16/7/00
From Noon. Enthralling Roman stories to enjoy

▶ **Music of the Border Reivers**
23/7/00-23/7/00

▶ **Arthurian Antics**
30/7/00-30/7/00
From Noon. Stories of brave knights and daring dragons, told by King Arthur

▶ **Fort Pila and Pots**
6/8/00-6/8/00
From Noon. Meet a Roman soldier and watch a Roman potter in action

▶ **Guided Tours**
13/8/00-13/8/00
Discover the Fort's fascinating history

▶ **Meet a Roman Soldier**
20/8/00-20/8/00
See entry for 2 July

▶ **Roman Fun!**
28/8/00-28/8/00
Cooking demonstrations, recipies and mosaics wokshop

Corbridge Roman Site
Corbridge Northumberland NE45 5NT
[off A69, 1.5m NW of Corbridge signposted]
Tel: 01434 632349
www.english-heritage.org.uk
The remains of a Roman 'Corstopitum', built around AD210, include granaries, portico columns and the probable site of legionary headquarters. Finds from excavations of the site are displayed in a museum on the site.
27 Mar-31 Oct daily 10.00-18.00 or dusk if sooner. 1 Nov-26 Mar Wed-Sun 10.00-16.00
A£2.70 C£1.40 Concessions£2.00

↓special events

▶ **The Roman Army Returns to Hadrian's Wall**
28/5/00-28/5/00

▶ **Meet A Roman Soldier**
1/7/00-1/7/00
From Noon. Younger visitors can dress up in armour

▶ **Classical Cuisine**
8/7/00-8/7/00
From Noon. Cooking demonstrations and recipies

▶ **Roman Storytelling**
15/7/00-15/7/00
From Noon. Enthralling Roman stories to enjoy

▶ **Roman Site Music**
22/7/00-22/7/00
From Noon. Of the Border Reivers

▶ **Arthurian Antics**
29/7/00-29/7/00
From Noon. Stories of brave knights and daring dragons, told by King Arthur

▶ **Pila and Pots**
5/8/00-5/8/00
From Noon. Meet a Roman soldier and watch a Roman potter in action

▶ **Guided Tours**
12/8/00-12/8/00
Discover the Fort's fascinating history

▶ **Meet A Roman Soldier**
19/8/00-19/8/00
See entry for 1 July

▶ **Roman Fun!**
27/8/00-27/8/00
Cooking demonstrations, recipes and mosaics workshop

Housesteads Roman Fort
Bardon Mills Haydon Bridge Hexham
Northumberland NE47 6NN
[2.5m NE of Bardon Mill on B6318]
Tel: 01434 344363
Housesteads was the Roman fort of Vercovicium. It has a spectacular site on Hadrian's Wall, and is also one of the best preserved Roman forts. It covers five acres, includ-

ing the only know Roman hospital in Britain, and a 24-seater latrine with a flushing tank. There is also a museum.
1 Apr-1 Nov daily 10.00-18.00 or dusk if sooner. 2 Nov-31 Mar Wed-Sun 10.00-16.00
Last Admission: 1 hour before closing
A£2.70 £1.40 Concessions£2.00

↓special events

▶ **The Roman Army Returns to Hadrian's Wall**
28/5/00-28/5/00

Roman Vindolanda

Chesterholm Museum Bardon Mill Hexham Northumberland NE47 7JN
[signposted from A69 or B6318]
Tel: 01434 344277 Fax: 01434 344060
Visit the fascinating Roman Fort and town excavations and follow the archaeological site trails. Reconstructions of a Roman shop, house and temple, set in charming gardens. Souvenirs and refreshments within the superb museum.
visitor comments: We enjoyed the reconstructed buildings - brings remains to life.
All year daily from 10.00 to seasonally variable closing times call for details
Last Admission: 30mins before variable closing
A£3.50 C£2.50 OAPs&Students£2.90

Wildlife & Safari Parks

Chillingham Wild Cattle Park

Chillingham Alnwick Northumberland NE66 5NW
[off B6348]
Tel: 01668 215250
The park at Chillingham boasts an extraordinary survival: a herd of wild white cattle descended from animals trapped in the park when the wall was built in the 13th century; they are the sole surviving pure-bred examples of their breed in the world. Binoculars are recommended for a close view.
Apr-Oct daily 10.00-12.00 & 14.00-17.00, Sun 14.00-17.00. Closed Tue
A£3.00 C£1.00 OAPs£2.50. Group rates 20+. School trips £0.50 per child

Animal Attractions

Sherwood Forest Farm Park

Lamb Pens Farm Edwinstowe Mansfield Nottinghamshire NG21 9HL
[just off A6075 between Edwinstowe and Mansfield Woodhouse. Carry straight on at the traffic lights in Edwinstowe and travel for approximately 3m]
Tel: 01623 823558 Fax: 01623 825998
At Sherwood Forest Farm Park the lovely rare breeds of farm animals, horses, wallabies, fallow deer, water buffalo and Kune Kune pigs are waiting to give a friendly welcome to visitors of all ages. With indoor and outdoor play areas, pets corners, a tea room and a gift shop the Farm Park guarantees 'A great day out for young and old alike!' NEW for 2000: narrow gauge Steam Railway - opening in the Spring.
Apr-mid Oct daily 10.30-17.15
Last Admission: 16.45
A£4.00 C£2.50 C(under 3s)£Free OAPs£3.50. Group rates - excellent reductions call for details
discount offer: One Person Free With A Full Paying Adult

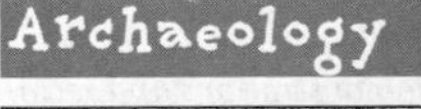

Archaeology

Creswell Crags

Crags Road Welbeck Worksop Nottinghamshire S80 3LH
[between A616 / A60, 1m E of Creswell village, 5m SE of J30 M1]
Tel: 01909 720378 Fax: 01909 724726

www.creswell-crags.org.uk

The deep narrow gorge of Creswell Crags is honeycombed with caves and rock shelters used as seasonal camps by Ice Age hunters who preyed on mammoth, reindeer and bison that roamed nearby. The most northerly place on earth inhabited during the Ice Age. A visitor centre with audio-visual programme and museum display tells the story of life at Creswell Craggs in the Ice Age. Lakeside trail through the gorge. Regular cave tours (booking advised) and other events.

visitor comments: Pleasant walks through the woods. Tours of caves take approximately 1 hour.

All year Feb-Oct daily 10.30-16.30, Nov-Jan Sun only 10.30-16.30

Cave tour: A£2.25 C£1.60 (booking advised)

Caverns & Caves

Caves of Nottingham

Drury Walk Broad Marsh Centre Nottingham Nottinghamshire NG1 7LS

[situated beneath Broadmarsh Shopping centre]

Tel: 0115 924 1424 Fax: 0115 924 1430

Over 300,000 visitors have descended into this 700 year old man-made cave system, since it opened in 1994. Featuring the latest digital audio technology, explore this unique subterrainean attraction which includes: A World War II air raid shelter, Pub Cellars, the remains of a Victorian Slum and the only remaining underground medieval tannery in the UK. Experience a glimpse of Nottingham's fascinating past.

All year Mon-Sat 10.00-17.00, Sun 11.00-17.00. Closed 25-26 Dec

Last Admission: 1 hour before closing

A£3.25 Family Ticket £9.50 Concessions £2.25

discount offer: 50p Off Adult and 25p Off Concessionary Admissions

Country Parks & Estates

Rufford Abbey and Country Park

Rufford Abbey Ollerton Newark Nottinghamshire NG22 9DF

[just off A614, 2m S of Ollerton roundabout]

Tel: 01623 822944 Fax: 01623 824840

www.ruffordcraftcentre.org.uk

Tour the remains of the 12th century Abbey set in beautiful parklands, including a new Exhibition on Cistercian life in the undercroft. Visit our renowned gallery, craft shops and new ceramics centre. Enjoy the restored Orangery, formal gardens, Savile Restaurant, Lakeside Garden Shop and Outdoor Living Shop. Various special events throughout the year, telephone for details.

visitor comments: A haven of peace in a mad world! Have a picnic, feed the ducks. Inexpensive. The Garden Shop is great for garden supplies.

Park: All year 09.00-17.30. Craft Centre, Gallery, Ceramics Centre, Abbey and Shops: Easter-end Sept daily 10.30-17.00; Oct-Easter 11.00-16.00. Savile Restaurant: Mar-Dec daily 10.30-16.00; Jan & Feb - closed. Coach House Coffee Shop: Mar-Nov daily 10.00-17.00; Dec-Mar daily 10.00-16.00. Facilities close pm on 24 Dec & re-open 26 Dec

Admission £Free. Car Park charge at various times throughout the year

Sherwood Forest Country Park and Visitor Centre
Edwinstowe Mansfield Nottinghamshire NG21 9HN
[situated on the B6034, N of Edwinstowe between the A6075 and the A616. For Public transport details to the Park call 0115 924 0000]
Tel: 01623 823202/824490 Fax: 01623 823202
Visit the legendary home of England's most famous outlaw - Robin Hood. Over 450 acres of ancient oak woodland, including the famous Major Oak. Enjoy the hands on exhibition, video on the history of the former Royal Hunting Forest, heritage and gift shops and restaurant. Explore woodland paths, picnic in forest glades and enjoy a year-round programme of events and activities including the Annual Robin Hood Festival 31 July-6 August.
visitor comments: Wonderful peaceful walks, lovely for picnics. A great historical site, whatever time of year. The craft centre is worth a visit.
Country Park: all year daily dawn-dusk. Visitor Centre: Apr-Oct daily 10.30-17.00, Nov-Mar daily 10.30-16.30
Admission Free, Car Park charge at various times throughout the year

↓*special events*

▶ **Annual Robin Hood Festival**
31/7/00-6/8/00
A week of medieval merriment in the home of the world's most famous outlaw

Folk & Local History Museums

Brewhouse Yard Museum
Castle Boulevard Nottingham Nottinghamshire NG7 1FB
Tel: 0115 915 3600
17th century cottages on two acre site. Museum depicts everday life in Nottingham over 300 years. Period rooms with local objects displayed. Re-created shops, including between the wars shopping street. Displays of past and present life in Nottingham. A school room and toyshop of the thirties. Caves behind used as air raid shelters.
visitor comments: Interesting collection of everyday items through the ages.
All year daily 10.00-16.30. Closed Fri from the beg Nov-Feb 18 (except for booked school groups). Closed 24, 25, 26, 31 Dec & 1 Jan. Last Admission: 16.45
Mon-Fri: Free, Weekends & Bank Hol A£1.50 C&Concessions£0.80 Family Ticket (A2+C4)£3.80. Concessions for City Card holders.

↓*special events*

▶ **Nottinghamshire People of Vision**
6/1/00-26/3/00
The story of people including The Pilgrim Fathers and William Booth who helped to improve the world

▶ **Nottinghamshire Women's History Group Talks**
26/1/00-26/4/00
A£1.50 Concessions£1.00. Talks at 19.30 on Jan 26, Feb 23, Mar 29 and Apr 26. Call for details

▶ **Out of the Kitchen - Brampton Saltglaze Pots from the 19th Century**
15/4/00-30/5/00
Brown salt-glazed pottery produced around Chesterfield in Derbyshire

▶ **The Great Easter Egg Hunt**
17/4/00-21/4/00
10.00-16.00, £0.50. Traditional egg hunt followed by drawing competition with prizes.

▶ **Victorian May Day**
7/5/00-7/5/00
11.00-16.00 A£2.00 Concessions£1.00. Celebrate a traditional May Day with dancing, games and more

Castle Museum and Art Gallery
Castle Place Nottingham Nottinghamshire NG1 6EL
Tel: 0115 915 3700
17th century building with much restored 13th century gateway. Now a Museum and Art Gallery, guided tour of underground passages is conducted every afternoon. A 'Story of Nottingham' interactive display brings to life the history of the city. Collections of Silver, glass, ceramics, paintings and jewellery. Automated car for disabled.
All year daily 10.00-17.00. Grounds: 08.00-dusk (09.00 Sun). Closed Fri from the beg Nov- Feb 18 (except for booked school groups). Closed 24, 25, 26, 31 Dec & 1 Jan
Mon-Fri £Free. Weekends & Bank Hol: A£2.00

C(5-15)&Concessions£1.00 Family Ticket (A2+C4) £5.00. Concessions for City Card Holders. Free admission for disabled visitors. Tickets valid all day.

↓*special events*

▶ **Diary of a Victorian Dandy**
23/12/99-2/4/00
Life-size, photographs portray a young Victorian gentleman at five moments in his day

▶ **Fried Eggs and Jam**
1/1/00-31/7/00
Interactive gallery space for children and grown ups. Call to confirm closing dates

▶ **Dancing the Old Fashioned Way**
11/1/00-11/4/00
Jan 11, 25, Feb 8, Mar 7, 21 and Apr 11 only. Participate or just watch. £2.00 inc. tea and cake

▶ **Flower Show**
11/3/00-1/5/00
13 well known artists who are concerned with the depiction or use of flowers in their work

▶ **You are a Work of Art**
11/3/00-1/5/00
Artist Judy Lieberts and several young people have explored ideas around pregnancy, birth and babies

▶ **The Winchcombe Pottery 1926 to Today**
15/3/00-15/3/00
Talk about the history, pots and potters. Book on 0115 915 3648. 14.00-15.00, £2.00/£1.00

▶ **Character Studies: Artemisia Gentileschi to Freud**
21/3/00-23/3/00
Mar 21 and 23 only, 10.30-12.00, £3.00

▶ **Nottingham Castle: A Ducal Residence**
29/3/00-29/3/00
Visual and documentary evidence for Nottingham Castle. £3.00, 14.00-15.00, book on 0115 915 3600

▶ **A Medieval City**
26/4/00-26/4/00
The mysteries of the archaeological collections. £3.00, 14.00-15.00, book on 0115 915 3600

Tales of Robin Hood

30-38 Maid Marian Way Nottingham
Nottinghamshire NG1 6GF
[J25 M1 Southbound, J26 M1 Northbound, follow signs for the City]
Tel: 0115 948 3284 Fax: 0115 950 1536
www.robinhood.uk.com

Enter the world's greatest medieval adventure, to a world of mystery and merriment. Be an outlaw for the day and flee through the forest to escape the evil sheriff. Jump on the magical 'Travel back in time' adventure ride and join in the search for Robin.

visitor comments: The ride was well paced, plenty of time to take in the detailed scenes. Restuarant was extremely reasonable in cost.

All year daily 10.00-18.00
Last Admission: 90mins before closing
A£4.75 C£3.75 Family Ticket (A2+C2)£14.95 OAPs&Students£4.25

discount offer: Two For The Price Of One.

Heritage & Industrial

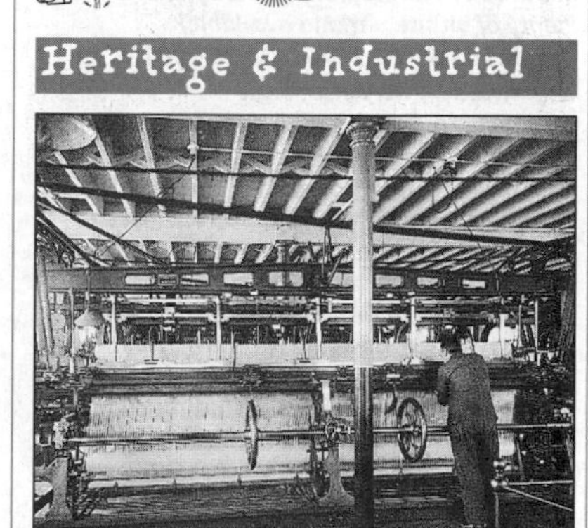

The Museum of Nottingham Lace

3-5 High Pavement The Lace Market
Nottingham Nottinghamshire NG1 1HF
[follow all main roads to city centre]
Tel: 0115 9897365 Fax: 0115 9897301
www.nottinghamlace.org

Discover the industry that made Nottingham great. Hear how the cottage craft was transformed in the Industrial Revolution from the workers, inventors and entrepreneurs. Experience the atmosphere of our lace machines in action and see costumes and videos. Alternatively, take the trail around The Lace Market area. Browse around the extensive range of lace on offer in the shop and rest in the "Coffee Corner."

All year daily 10.00-17.00. Closed 25-26 Dec & 1 Jan. Please call for Sunday Winter openings
Last Admission: Exhibition: 16.00 Trail 15.30
A£2.95 C£1.95 Concessions£2.50 Trail: £1.95 (ref deposit required for Trail only)

↓*special events*

▶ **laCeD 2000**
15/4/00-12/7/00
A global collection of hand-made lace designed to mark the new Millennium. This exhibition challenges the commonly-held perceptions of bobbin lace

▶ **Made in Long Eaton: The Industry of Nottingham Lace**
13/7/00-20/9/00
The reality of the manufacture of Nottingham Lace, this exhibition takes a working town and examines the effects that the lace industry has

had on it

Historical

Clumber Park
Clumber Gardens Clumber Park Worksop Nottinghamshire S80 3AZ
[4.5m SE of Worksop, signposted from A1. Plenty of on site parking available]
Tel: 01909 476592 Fax: 01909 500721
www.nationaltrust.org.uk
1538 hectares of parkland, farmland, lake and woodlands. The mansion was demolished in 1938, but the fine Gothic Revival Chapel, built 1886-89 for the 7th Duke of Newcastle, survives. Park includes the longest double lime avenue in Europe and a superb 32 hectare lake. Also Classical bridge, temples, lawned Lincoln Terrace, pleasure grounds and the stable block with restaurant, shop and information room. Walled Garden including Victorian Apiary, Vineries and Tools exhibition. Clumber Conservation Centre near Cricket Ground. Guided walks may be booked for groups throughout the summer. *NB: prior booking for all Clumber Park walks is essential, £1.50, and meet at Conservation Centre unless otherwise stated.
Park: All year daily during daylight hours. Walled Garden, Victorian Apiary, Fig House, Vineries, Garden Tools Exhibition & Conservation Centre: Apr-Oct Weekends & Bank Hol Mon, also Wed & Thur in July & Aug 10.30-17.00 (except Conservation Centre). Chapel: Apr-Oct daily 10.30-18.00, Nov-Mar 2000 daily 10.30-16.00. Closed 15 July, 19 Aug & 25 Dec
Pedestrians Free, Car motorbikes £3.00 (with the exception of NT members) Individual attractions charged, call for details

↓*special events*

▶ **Clumber Seasons with Warden**
4/3/00-4/3/00
** Meet at 10.00*

▶ **Pancake Fun Day**
5/3/00-5/3/00
Pre-pancake day fun and games. 11.00-15.00, £1 per person

▶ **Orienteering Workshops**
11/3/00-12/3/00
Expert help for beginners.10.30-15.30, £5.00 per day. Booking essential

▶ **Birds in Spring**
12/3/00-12/3/00
**Meet at the main car park near Chapel grounds entrance at 09.30*

▶ **Sherlock Holmes Murder Mystery Dinner**
18/3/00-18/3/00
Assist Holmes in solving Indian Intrigue. 19.00, £25 (incl 3 course dinner). Booking essential

▶ **The Year 2000**
25/3/00-25/3/00
**Find out what is happening at Clumber this year. Join the Property Manager on a guided walk through the Park. 10.00*

▶ **Spring Concert**
1/4/00-1/4/00
With Sempre Ensemble. 19.00, £5.00. Booking essential.

▶ **The Historic Manor of Hardwick**
9/4/00-9/4/00
**Explore Hardwick village in the company of historian, John Fletcher. Meet: Hardwick village car park, 10.00*

▶ **Dukeries Cycle Ride**
16/4/00-16/4/00
25 mile guided cycle ride, includes full day mountain bike hire and Sunday lunch. Start: 10.00, £15.00. Booking essential

▶ **Easter Egg Trail**
23/4/00-24/4/00
£1.50 per entrant. Children must be accompanied by an adult. Usual admission. 10.30-17.00

▶ **A Warden's View**
1/8/00-1/8/00
**Find out about the Park with warden, Roy Turner. 14.00 or 18.30*

▶ **South Peak Estate - Children's Nature Day**
4/8/00-4/8/00
Environmental activities for C5-10. 11.00 onwards, C£1.50

▶ **Teddy Bear Fun Day**
6/8/00-6/8/00
Children's entertainment, stories and music. 14.00-16.00. C£1.00, accompanying adults and Teddy Bears free.

▶ **History and Renovation of the Walled Garden**
27/8/00-27/8/00
With Head Gardener. Meet: main car park, 14.30

▶ **Bug Hunting (day) & Bats! (evening)**
5/8/00-5/8/00
**Fun for all the family. Children must be accompanied by an adult. 10.00, 13.00 or 14.00. Evening Walk: Bats. An evening with the North Nottinghamshire Bat Group. 19.00. Bring a torch!*

D H Lawrence Birthplace Museum
8a Victoria Street Eastwood Nottinghamshire NG16 3AW
[J26 M1 then A610 or 27 M1 then A608 towards Derby]
Tel: 01773 717353 Fax: 01773 713509
More than a museum - the Birthplace is a home. The home of the Lawrence's and their growing family. Soak up the atmosphere, as a time capsule of Victorian life unfolds before your eyes.

All year daily Apr-Oct 10.00-17.00, Nov-Mar 10.00-16.00. Closed 24 Dec-1 Jan
From April 2000 A£2.00 Concessions£1.20 Joint Family Ticket £8.00. Group rates £1.75 School parties £0.75

Nottingham Castle Museum and Art Gallery
Nottingham Nottinghamshire NG1 6EL
[near city centre on A52]
Tel: 0115 915 3700 Fax: 0115 915 3653
Nottingham Castle commands spectacular views over the city and once rivalled the great Castles of Windsor and the Tower of London. Totally destroyed after the Civil War, it was replaced by a magnificent Ducal mansion in 1674 and in 1875 was converted into the first municipal museum and art gallery outside London. Cave tours tell this history taking you down into the tunnels. The museum contains spectacular fine and decorative arts galleries, as well as telling the story of Nottingham, the Sherwood Foresters Regimental Museum. Shop, an award-winning café and a medieval playground within its grounds.
All year daily 10.00-17.00. Museum 13.00-17.00. Closed 24-26 Dec, 1 Jan & Fri 1 Nov-18 Feb
Mon-Fri £Free, Weekends & Bank Hol A£2.00 C&Concessions£1.00
discount offer: One Child Free With Two Full Paying Adults For Weekends & Bank Holidays

Living History Museums

Galleries of Justice
Shire Hall High Pavement Lace Market Nottingham Nottinghamshire NG1 1HN
[city centre, signposted both traffic and pedestrian, multi-story parking signposted, 5-10mins walk]
Tel: 0115 952 0555 Fax: 0115 993 9828
Based in and around an original Victorian courtroom and county gaol, this award-winning museum will show you everything you could wish to know about justice in England through the ages. The lives and crimes of the unfortunate men, women and children who once occupied these very buildings are brought vividly to life by stunning authentic detail. A visit can take a whole day or you can split your visit over 2 or 3 days (no extra cost). Tickets are valid for one visit to each exhibition over 12 months.
All year Tue-Sun & Bank Hol 10.00-17.00
Last Admission: 16.00, allow approx 4 hours
A£7.95 C£4.95 Family Ticket (A2+C2)£23.95
Concessions£5.95 Wheelchair access 85%
discount offer: Two For The Price Of One

Military & Defence Museums

Newark Air Museum
Winthorpe Showground Lincoln Road Newark Nottinghamshire NG24 2NY
[off the A1 then A46 next to the Showground. Plenty of parking on site]
Tel: 01636 707170 Fax: 01636 707170
The museum's collection of more than forty five aircraft and helicopters covers all aspects of aviation: jet fighters; bombers; transport; trainers; civilian; and light aircraft. In the recently published National Aviation Heritage Register the airframes in the museum's care were classified as follows: 11 National Benchmark (the top listing possible); 25 Significant; and 15 Noteworthy. Large under-cover Display Hall, Engine Hall, Artefact Displays, large shop and café. Anyone wishing to fly-in to the Museum should call in advance for Briefing Sheets and approval contacts.
All year Apr-Sept Mon-Fri 10.00-17.00 Sat, Sun & Bank Hol 10.00-18.00. Oct & Mar daily 10.00-17.00. Nov-Feb daily 10.00-16.00. Closed 24-26 Dec
Last Admission: 30mins before closing
A£4.00 C£2.50 Family Ticket (A2+C2)£10.00 OAPs£3.25. Special rates for concessions and Groups 10+ available. Pre-booked guided tours available
discount offer: 50p Per Person Discount Off Normal Admission

↓*special events*

▶ **Bomber Command Days**
27/5/00-28/5/00
Cockpits of the Vulcan, Canberras and Shackleton will be open to the public with many other displays. AEROBOOT avionics and aviation sale on May 27

▶ **Cockpit Meet**
17/6/00-18/6/00

A variety of visiting aircraft cockpit sections. Please call to confirm dates

▶ **"Bravo 2000"**
22/7/00-23/7/00
An event to follow a Maritime Patrol, Search and Rescue theme

▶ **"Tribute to a Test Pilot"**
27/8/00-28/8/00
Celebrate the 80th Birthday of Wg.Cdr. R.P. (BEE) Beamont, CBE, DSO, DFC, DL, FRAeS. An exhibition about the life and aircraft of a Legend of British Aviation

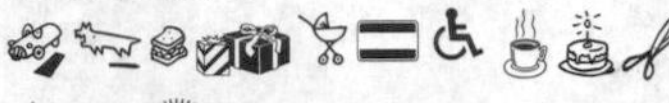

Theme & Adventure Parks

Sundown Kiddies Adventureland
Sundown Pets Garden Treswell Road Rampton Retford Nottinghamshire DN22 0HX
[3m off A57 at Dunham crossroads]
Tel: 01777 248274 Fax: 01777 248967
'The children's story book theme park'. Magical fairy tales come to life, nursery rhymes, castles, wizards and dragons are just part of the attractions, with Smuggler's Cove and the Boozey Barrel Boat Ride. Indoors a jungle and musical pet shop, and a mini farm with live animals. Also a new story book village. Events throughout year. Special Christmas Weekends.
visitor comments: Excellent value for money.
All year daily from 10.00. Closed 25-26 Dec & weekdays during Jan, except for New Year Day; Christmas opening times: Mon-Fri 10.00-16.00, Sat & Sun 10.00-19.00
All £4.50 C(0-2)£Free

Animal Attractions

Royal Oak Farm
Islip Road Beckley Oxfordshire OX3 9TY
[J8 M40 Off A40 towards Headington]
Tel: 01865 351246
Animal garden with friendly goats, pigs, sheep, chickens and ducks. All animals can be fed, and you can bottlefeed lambs and kids. Relax in the tearoom serving light lunches and teas.
Good Friday-Aug 31
Admission Free

Wellplace Zoo
Ipsden Oxfordshire OX9 6OZ
[off A423 or B4074 on unclassified road]
Tel: 01491 680473/680092
A large and varied collection of birds and animals from all over the world can be seen. The zoo is set in beautiful Oxfordshire countryside. Also has: Museum, wishing well, children's pay area, shrubs and plants, bird feeding, educational packs. Don't forget to bring your camera.
visitor comments: Lovely little zoo with lots to see. Very reasonably priced. Nice play area.
Easter-end Sept daily 10.00-17.00, Oct-Easter Weekends only 10.00-16.00
A£2.00 C£0.50

Arts, Crafts & Textiles

Ashmolean Museum of Art and Archaeology
Beaumont Street Oxford Oxfordshire OX1 2PH
[centre of Oxford opposite The Randolph Hotel. Bus: 5mins. BR: 10mins]
Tel: 01865 278000 / 278015 Fax: 01865 278018
www.ashmol.ox.ac.uk
The Ashmolean is Oxford University's Museum of Art and Archaeology housing world famous collections of fine and applied art from Europe, Japan, India and China, as well as historic coins and medals and artefacts from Ancient Egypt, Greece and Rome. Disabled Access: There is a lift to all floors; a wheel chair is available on application to the staff. The Museum has a new Shop and Café. Evening concerts, tours and lectures - information available by calling 01865 278015.
All year Tue-Sat 10.00-17.00 Sun 14.00-17.00, Bank Hol Mon 14.00-17.00 (until 20.00 on Wed in May, June & July) Closed 25 & 26 Dec, 1 Jan & 2-4 Apr re-opening 5 Apr 14.00. Also closed during St Giles Fair
Admission Free: Guided tours by arrangement

↓*special events*

▶ **In the Red: An Exhibition of the History of Debt**
11/1/00-30/4/00

▶ **Ginso Severini: From Futurism to Classicism**
18/1/00-5/3/00
Traces Severini's development from his early post-impressionist canvases of the Paris cityscape

▶ **Facing Forward Looking Back: Millennium Lecture Series**
28/1/00-4/3/00
The Ashmolean Museum, in association with the Oxford Playhouse presents a series of six lectures during 2000. Call: 01865 798600

▶ **Golden Pages**
3/2/00-2/4/00
Qurans and prayer books from the H E Shaik Ghasan I. Shaker collection

▶ **Eighteenth Century Venetian Drawings**
14/3/00-4/6/00

From the Ashmolean's collection

Birds, Butterflies & Bees

Waterfowl Sanctuary and Children's Farm
Wiggington Heath between Bloxham & Hook Norton Banbury Oxfordshire OX15 4LB
[off the A361 Banbury / Chipping Norton road]
Tel: 01608 730252
www.visitbritain.com
Hundreds of friendly animals waiting to meet you at this family-run sanctuary - including a large selection of birds and rare farm breeds. It serves as a conservation breeding centre for endangered species. Children are encouraged to handle chicks, ducklings and baby rabbits etc. under supervision. Arranged school parties are welcomed, video available. Refreshments available from Easter-October.
visitor comments: Magical & enchanting for all ages. Wellyboots on wet days. Caring staff. Go in the area with children it's a must.
All year daily 10.30-18.00 or dusk if sooner
A£3.00 Accompanied C(1-15)£2.00 OAPs£2.90

Exhibition & Visitor Centres

The Oxford Story Exhibition
6 Broad Street Oxford Oxfordshire OX1 3AJ
[town centre, 0.5 mile from Oxford Station]
Tel: 01865 790055 Fax: 01865 791716
www.heritageattractions.co.uk
An excellent introduction to Oxford - 800 years of University history in one hour! Step aboard our amazing 'ride' and enjoy our enlightening commentary along your fascinating journey of discovery. Child and multi-language commentaries available. At the beginning of The Oxford Story there is a new film,"The Student Life".
All year Apr-Oct daily 09.30-17.00, July-Aug daily 09.00-18.00, Nov-Mar Mon-Fri 10.00-16.30 Sat & Sun 10.00-17.00. Closed 25 Dec
A£5.70 C(4-16),OAPs&Students(17+)£4.70
Family Ticket (A2+C2)£17.50. Group rates available
discount offer: £1.00 Off Normal Admission Prices (offer does not apply to groups)

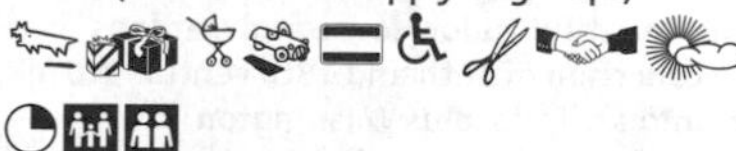

Historical

Broughton Castle
Banbury Oxfordshire OX15 5EB
[2m W of Banbury on the B4035 Shipston on Stour road]
Tel: 01295 276070 Fax: 01295 276070
www.broughtoncastle.demon.co.uk
Historic 14th and 16th century moated house, with Civil War connections. Home of the family of Lord Saye and Sele for 600 years, Broughton has fine walled gardens and is often the location for many T.V. programmes and films, most recently Emma and Noel's House Party.
visitor comments: The gardens are lovely - you can view the grounds from the roof, and the church is worth going in to.
Easter & 21 May-13 Sept Wed & Sun, July & Aug Thur, Bank Hol Sun & Mon 14.00-17.00.
Groups welcome anytime by arrangement
Last Admission: 25min before closing
A£4.00 C£2.00 OAPs&Students£3.50
discount offer: Two Adults For The Price Of One Full Paying Adult

Sulgrave Manor
Manor Road Sulgrave Banbury Oxfordshire OX17 2SD
[situated in the village of Sulgrave just off B4525 Banbury to Northampton road. 7m NE

of Banbury. 6m NW of Brackley and the A43. 19m W of Towcester and the A5. Oxford and Stratford are approximately 30m distant and London via either the M1 or M40, 70m. BR: Banbury. Plenty of free on site parking.]

Tel: 01295 760205 Fax: 01295 768056

www.stratford.co.uk/sulgrave

Sulgrave Manor was bought in 1539 by Lawrence Washington, wool merchant and twice Mayor of Northampton. It was here that George Washington's ancestors lived until 1656. Beautiful Tudor House and Gardens. Fine collection of 16th and 18th century furniture and artifacts, plus Washington Memorabilia. Educational Visits: A children's guide book and schools pack are available. A new Courtyard Range of visitor facilities now open. George Washington Exhibition, Brewhouse Buttery Restaurant and Brass Rubbing Centre. A superb, traditionally timbered and galleried function hall - an ideal venue for weddings, conferences, society dinners, family celebrations or other events. Picnic facilities for both in and outdoors available.

1st Apr-31 Oct Thur-Tue 14.00-17.30, Weekends & Bank Hol 10.30-13.00 & 14.00-17.30, Nov Dec & Mar 10.30-13.00 & 14.00-16.30. Closed 25-26 Dec. Outside normal opening hours for pre-booked schools and groups only, including evenings

Last Admission: 60mins before closing

A3.75 C£2.00. Group rates for 12+

discount offer: Two For The Price Of One

↓*special events*

▶ **The Three Musketeers - Outdoor Theatre Production**

28/7/00-30/7/00

Alexander Dumas' famous play. 19.00 on Friday and Saturday, 15.00 matinee on Sunday. A£7.50 C&OAPs£5.00. Please write or phone to book 01295 760205

▶ **Stars, Stripes and Stitches**

12/8/00-20/8/00

Sulgrave's superb annual needlework festival. Exhibitions, displays, workshops. 10.30-17.00. Closed 16th

▶ **Seven Years War - 1756-1763**

26/8/00-28/8/00

Re-enactment of George Washington's first major experience as a soldier fighting in the French-Indian wars. 10.30-17.00. A£4.50 C£2.25

▶ **The Siege of Sulgrave**

16/9/00-17/9/00

A re-enactment of an actual event that took place at Sulgrave in 1644 during the English Civil War. A£4.50 C£2.25

▶ **Chamber Music Concert**

30/9/00-30/9/00

A buffet supper with wine will follow the concert. Booking essential. Commences 19.30. Tickets: £17.50

▶ **Apple Day**

21/10/00-22/10/00

A theme of the apple. Displays, demonstrations, stalls, food, drink, crafts and more. 10.30-17.00

▶ **Chamber Music Concert**

4/11/00-4/11/00

A buffet supper with wine will follow the concert. Booking essential. Commences 19.30. Tickets: £17.50

▶ **Embroiders Casket**

11/11/00-12/11/00

Aweekend festival based on historic embroidery and textiles. Demonstrations, stalls and more. 10.30-16.30

▶ **Chamber Music Concert**

2/12/00-2/12/00

A buffet supper with wine will follow the concert. Booking essential. Commences 19.30. Tickets: £17.50

▶ **A Tudor Christmas**

2/12/00-30/12/00

The Great Hall bedecked with seasonal greenery, log fire burning and beeswax candles glowing. Each weekend during Dec except 23 & 24. Commences: 10.30-13.00 & 14.00-16.30.

Railways

Didcot Railway Centre

Didcot Oxfordshire OX11 7NJ

[on A4130 at Didcot Parkway Station signed from J13 M4 and A34]

Tel: 01235 817200 Fax: 01235 510621

www.didcotrailwaycentre.org.uk

The biggest collection anywhere of Great Western Railway trains is housed in the GWR engine shed, including 20 steam locomotives, a diesel railcar, and a large amount of passenger and freight rolling stock. A typical GWR station and Brunel's original broad gauge track have been recreated.

All year Sat & Sun, 1 Apr-1 Oct daily 10.00-17.00, Nov-Feb 10.00-16.00, Steamdays first & last Sun of each month from Mar, Bank Hol, all

Sun July-Aug, Wed 12 July- 30 Aug
Last Admission: 30mins before closing
A£4.00-£8.00 C£3.00-£6.50 OAPs£3.50-£5.50 depending on event
discount offer: One Adult or Child Free With Full Paying Adult

↓*special events*

▶ **Didcot Steam 2000**
27/5/00-4/6/00
The Great Western steam event of the millennium

▶ **Thomas Santa Specials**
15/12/00-24/12/00
Let Thomas take you to see Santa in his Grotto, advanced booking essential dates 15-17 and 23 & 24 Dec

Social History Museums

River and Rowing Museum

Mill Meadows Henley-on-Thames Oxfordshire RG9 1BF
[follow signs for Mill Meadows off the A4130]
Tel: 01491 415600 Fax: 01491 415601
www.rrm.co.uk

The National Heritage NPI Museum Of The Year is housed in a specially commissioned building on the River Thames, at Henley. The Thames displays trace the flow of the river, its role in history and conservation of the river. The rowing displays illustrate the history of rowing, with interactives on the art of rowing. Exhibits include Steve Redgrave and Mathew Pinsent's boat used to win Britain's only gold medal in the Olympic Games in Atlanta, and the world's oldest known competitive rowing boat. Excellent meals and refreshments available at the museum Riverside Café.

Easter-Sept Open daily 10.00-18.00 (Mon-Fri), 10.30-18.00 (Sat & Sun) Oct-Easter closes 17.00. Closed 24, 25 & 31 Dec, 1 Jan
Last Admission: 17.00
A£4.95 C&Concessions£3.75 Family Ticket £13.25 Groups 10+ and season tickets
discount offer: Two For The Price Of One

↓*special events*

▶ **John Piper (1902-1992)- Master of Diversity**
18/3/00-10/7/00
An exhibition of John Piper's art work

▶ **Five Ring Circus**
15/6/00-15/10/00
Celebration of rowing in the Olympics. Please call to confirm finishing dates

▶ **Looking for Alice**
15/7/00-30/10/00
The work of Lewis Carroll

Sport & Recreation

Funtasia

9-15 Warwick Road Banbury Oxfordshire OX16 9AB
[from Banbury Cross along North Bar Street head towards Southam A423. At the Box Junction traffic lights turn left into A41 Warwick Road. We are located approx 100 yards on left with a visitors car park in forecourt and a large public car park is adjacent]
Tel: 01295 250866

Indoor Adventure Play Centre for Children. Facilities include Giant Adventure Climbing Maze, Daredevil Drop Slide, Swinging Punch Bags, Rope Swings, Monkey Swings, Trapeze Bars and Twizzler, Inflatable Obstacle Pirate Ship with Slide, Scramble Net, Wobblers and Tunnels and lots more.

All year Mon-Thur 13.00-18.00, Fri 13.00-19.00, Sat & Sun 10.00-19.00. During school holidays from 10.00. Closed 24-26 Dec
A£Free C(0-5)£2.50 C(5-12)£3.00, possible price increase

Go Bananas

34-36 Market Square Witney Oxfordshire OX8 6AD
Tel: 01993 779877

A safe, stimulating environment, where children can let off steam, learn co-ordination skills, and stimulate both their mind and body. Fun and Fitness for them, whilst you just relax. Share the smiles on their faces and watch them 'Go Bananas!'

visitor comments: We will certainly be returning again and again.

All year daily, Mon-Fri 10.00-19.00, Sat & Sun 10.00-18.00
C(under 4)£1.50 C(4-11)£2.50. Discounts available for large groups, schools, nurseries and playgroups. Children's Parties: £5.50 per child to include food, drink & balloon

Stately Homes

Blenheim Palace
Woodstock Oxfordshire OX20 1PX
[on A44 Oxford / Evesham road. BR: Oxford - local bus from there]
Tel: 01993 811325 Fax: 01993 813527
Blenheim Palace, home of the 11th Duke of Marlborough and birthplace of Sir Winston Churchill, was built for John Churchill 1st Duke of Marlborough by Vanbrugh, with a magnificent collection of paintings, tapestries and furniture. It is set in a Capability Brown landscaped park, with lake and formal gardens by Wise, Brown and Duchêne. An inclusive ticket covers Palace tour, Churchill exhibition, motor launch, park and pleasure gardens, train and butterfly house. Optional extras: rowing boat hire and Marlborough Maze, the world's largest symbolic hedge maze. Disabled access. Average visit time 3 hours. Member of the Historic Houses Association.
Palace: mid Mar-Oct daily 10.30-17.30. Park: All year daily 09.00-17.00
Last Admission: 16.45
A£8.50 C(5-15)£4.50 Family Ticket £22.00 OAPs&Students £6.50. Coach & Minibus rates on application

Kingston Bagpuize House
Kingston Bagpuize Abingdon Oxfordshire OX13 5AX
[5.5m W of Abingdon A415 just S of A420 interchange]
Tel: 01865 820259 Fax: 01865 821659
Beautiful Family owned Manor House originally dating from 1660's but remodelled in early 1700's. Cantilevered staircase, well proportioned panelled rooms with some good furniture and pictures. Surrounded by mature parkland the Gardens, including shrub borders and woodland garden, contain a notable collection of unusual trees, shrubs, perennials and bulbs. House is not suitable for wheelchairs but Garden is. Member of the Historic Houses Association.
Mar-Oct selected dates 14.00-17.30: 12, 26 Mar; 8, 9, 22, 23, 24, 29, 30 Apr; 1, 13, 14, 27-29 May; 10, 11, 25 June; 8, 9, 22, 23 July; 9, 12, 13, 26-28 Aug; 6, 9, 10, 23, 24 Sept & 8, 22 Oct. All Bank Hol weekends (Sat-Mon) from Easter. Groups (20+) open by appointment throughout year. House tours: 14.30 & 16.45
Last Admission: Garden: 17.00
House and Garden: A£3.50 C£2.50 OAPs£3.00. Gardens only: A£1.50. C(under 5) not admitted to the House but £Free to Garden. Groups welcome by written appointment. Feb-Nov rates on request

↓*special events*

► **Classic Motor Show**
16/7/00-16/7/00
New event for 2000. Opens: 10.00-17.00 daily. A£5.00 C(5-16)£1.00 OAPs£4.00. Tel: 01296 631181. Sorry NO dogs

Upton House
Upton Banbury Oxfordshire OX15 6HT
[on A422]
Tel: 01295 670266
The house, built of mellow local stone, dates from 1695, but the chief attractions are the outstanding collections in the house itself. They include paintings by English and Continental Old Masters, Brussels tapestries, Sevres porcelain, Chelsea figures and 18th-century furniture. The gardens have terraces, herbaceous borders, fruit, vegetable and water gardens and lakes.
House, Shop & Tearoom: 27 Mar-31 Oct Sat-Wed 14.00-18.00. Entry to House by timed tickets at peak times on Sun in holiday periods & Bank Hol Mon
Last Admission: 17.30, 17.00 after 24 Oct
A£5.20 C£2.60 Family Ticket £13.00, Garden only: A£2.60 C£1.30

↓*special events*

► **Just Dixie Picnic Jazz Concert**
1/7/00-1/7/00
Commences: 19.30-22.00. Tickets £8.50. Gates open 19.00. Call 01985 843601 for tickets

► **The Pete Lay Jazzers Picnic Concert**
15/7/00-15/7/00
Commences: 19.30-22.00. Tickets £8.50. Gates open 19.00. Call 01985 843601 for tickets

Victorian Era

Cogges Manor Farm Museum
Church Lane Witney Oxfordshire OX8 6LA
[0.5m SE of Witney off A40. Plenty of parking on site]
Tel: 01993 772602 Fax: 01993 703056
Farm museum with breeds of animals typical of the Victorian period, historic site and buildings including Manor House, dairy and walled garden. Daily cookery on the Victorian kitchen range, an historic trail, and riverside walk. The first floor of the Manor house has reopened following extensive restoration, and features 17th- and 19th century interiors.
26 Mar-29 Oct Tue-Fri & Bank Hol Mon 10.30-17.30, Sat & Sun 12.00-17.30. Closed Good Fri
Last Admission: 60mins before closing
A£4.00 C(3-16)£2.00 Family Ticket (A2+C2)£11.00 Concessions£2.50. Pre-booked

groups discounted
discount offer: Two For The Price Of One

Zoos

Cotswold Wildlife Park
Bradwell Grove Burford Oxfordshire OX18 4JW
[2.5m S of A40 on A361. Plenty of parking on site]
Tel: 01993 823006 Fax: 01993 823807
The 160 acre landscaped zoological park, surrounding a Gothic-style Manor House, has a varied collection of animals from ants to white rhinos, bats to the big cats, plus large reptile collection and children's farmyard. Other attractions include an adventure playground, animal brass-rubbing centre in the Manor House and train rides during the summer months. Large cafeteria and picnic areas. Heart of England Tourist Board - commended in Attraction of the Year category 1999.
visitor comments: Editor's Choice. Enjoyable day out in pleasant surroundings. Oozes animal care and conservation. Staff friendly and helpful. Plenty of picnic sites. Narrow-gauge railway in summer, included in price.
All year daily from 10.00. Closed Christmas Day
Last Admission: Mar-Sept 17.00, Oct 16.00, Nov-Feb 15.30
A£6.00 C(3-16incl)&OAPs£4.00 Pre-booked groups 20+: A£5.00 C£3.00 OAPs£3.50 Disabled £3.00
discount offer: One Child Free With Two Full Paying Adults

↓*special events*

► **Bird of Prey Demonstrations**
22/4/00-3/9/00
See the Birds of Prey in flight on the following days: Easter 22-24 Apr, May Day Weekend 29 & 30 Apr & 1 May, Whitsun 27-29 May, Weekends & Bank Hol Mon from 15 July-3 Sept. Approximately 13.00 and 15.30 weather permitting

Agriculture / Working Farms

Acton Scott Historic Working Farm
Wenlock Lodge Acton Scott Church Stretton Shropshire SY6 6QN
[signposted off the A49, approximately 17m S of Shrewsbury, 14m N of Ludlow]
Tel: 01694 781306/7 Fax: 01694 781569
www.go2.co.uk/for/actonscott.html
Living history in the Shropshire Hills. Experience daily life on an upland farm at the turn of the century. The waggoner and his team of heavy horses work the land with vintage farm machines. In the cottage the farmer's wife goes about her chores. This working farm museum gives a vivid introduction to traditional rural life. Children will love the cows, pigs, poultry and sheep in the farmyard and fields. There are Tamworth pigs and Shropshire sheep amongst the rarer breeds. Daily demonstrations of rural crafts complete the picture of estate-life a hundred years ago. Guided tours of the farm are available, as well as a cartwheel maze play area and holiday activities. NO DOGS
31 Mar-1 Nov Tue-Sun 10.00-17.00. Closed Mon except Bank Hol
Last Admission: 16.30
A£3.25 C(0-5)£Free C£1.50 Family Ticket £10.00 OAPs£2.75 UB40s£Free. Group Rate: A£3.00 C£1.25 OAPs£2.50. Season Ticket (To the Farm, Ludlow and Much Wenlock Museums) A£8.00 C£4.00. Guide: A£7.50 per 20 Adults C£5.50 per 20 C/Tots. One A£Free for every 10 paying Children. £Free admission to helpers of disabled groups where a one to one, or a wheelchair pusher is required.

Rays Farm Country Matters
Billingsley Bridgnorth Shropshire WV16 6PF
[off B4363]
Tel: 01299 841255 Fax: 01299 841455
Enjoy a warm welcome at Rays Farm Country Matters. Set in the heart of unspoilt Shropshire countryside, a perfect way to spend a relaxing day. While ambling round the farm you will meet friendly, unusual animals and birds in charming, tranquil settings. Shropshire's longest Bridleway - The Jack Mytton Way starts here.
visitor comments: Excellent for younger children. Good selection of animals. Wellies advised!
1 Mar-24 Dec daily, weekends & School Hol from 27 Dec-end Feb 10.00-17.30 or dusk in winter
A£3.00 C(1-16)£1.75 C(under 1)£Free OAPs£2.50. Groups 20+ 10% discount

Animal Attractions

Hoo Farm Animal Kingdom and Christmas Tree Farm
Preston-on-the-Weald Moors Telford
Shropshire TF6 6DJ
[follow brown signs from A442 at Leegomery or A518 at Donnington]
Tel: 01952 677917 Fax: 01952 677944
www.telford.gov.uk/tourism/hoofarm/
Life on the Farm steps up a gear this year, with the introduction of Quad Bikes for the 6-9 year olds. The daily New Egg Experience will take egg collecting into a new dimension, with the journey from egg to chicken or which came first. Also New for this year are several workshops run by the R.S.P.B, this, with a new bird feeding area and squirrel walks will enhance the wildlife at Hoo Farm. For the first time 1999 sees the introduction of 'The Potting Shed' where you can throw your own pot. The famous Sheep Steeplechase season which starts on Easter Monday and continues until Sunday 31 October adds fun throughout the season.
visitor comments: The children loved the sheep racing. Animal "hands-on" experiences on quiet days.
20 Mar-5 Sept 10.00-18.00 daily. 7 Sept-12 Nov Tue-Sun 10.00-17.00
Last Admission: 17.00
A£3.95 (includes a FREE bag of animal food), C(under 2)£Free C(2-14)£2.75 (includes FREE return visit), Family Ticket (A2+C3)£13.50 OAPs£3.25 (includes a FREE bag of animal food). Season Tickets: A£15.00 C&OAPs£12.00 (unlimited visits 21 Mar-24 Dec

Country Parks & Estates

Hawkstone Park
Weston-under-Redcastle Shrewsbury
Shropshire SY4 5UY
[off A49 towards Whitchurch then M54. Follow brown tourist signs. BR: Stafford & Crewe (approx. 45mins taxi ride); Shrewsbury & Telford (30mins drive). Air: Birmingham & Manchester airports approx. 1 hour drive. Helicopter: By prior arrangement]
Tel: 01939 200300 Fax: 01939 200332
www.hawkstone.co.uk
Created in the 18th century by the Hill family, Hawkstone was once one of the greatest historic parklands in history. After almost one hundred years of neglect it has been restored and designated a Grade I historic park. Visitors can experience this magical world of intricate pathways, arches and bridges, towering cliffs and follies, and an awesome grotto. Covering nearly 100 acres of hilly terrain it is advised that visitors wear sensible walking shoes and clothing. The tour is well signposted. Allow 3-4 hours for the complete circuit. Dogs must be kept on leads at all times.
visitor comments: Be prepared for a lot of walking, part of route strenuous. Take along a pocket torch, for some of the tunnels. Lots of picnic places, a very memorable day out.
1 Apr-31 Oct daily 10.00-18.00 then every Sat & Sun 7 Nov-end Feb 2000. Also Father Christmas visits in Dec. Limited access to Cleft, Grotto & Caves: 23 Oct-1 Nov, No access 1 Nov 99-end Feb 2000
A£4.75 C£2.50 Family Ticket(A2+C3)£12.50 OAPs£3.75. Bank Hol & Special Events: A£5.00 Family Ticket(A2+C3)£14.00. Special reductions for groups of 12+ and at any time providing they are pre-booked and paid for in advance
discount offer: Half Price Family Ticket (A2+C3)£6.25 (Normal Price £12.50). Valid Until 31 Oct 99. Not Valid on Sun Or Bank Holidays

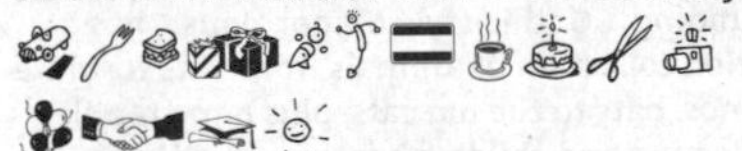

Heritage & Industrial

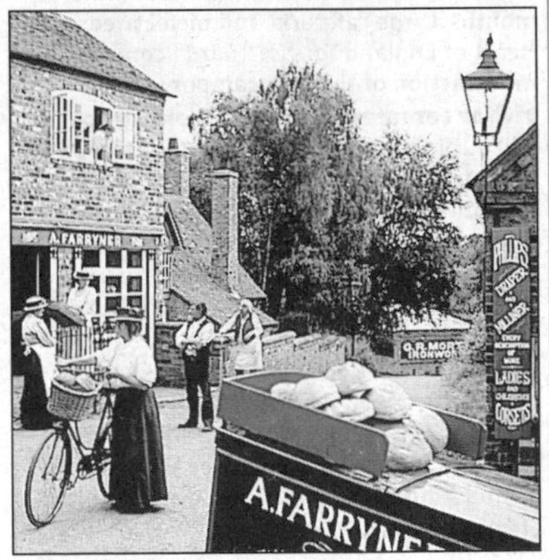

The Ironbridge Gorge Museums
Ironbridge Telford Shropshire TF8 7AW
[J4 M54, signposted. Plenty of on site parking available.]
Tel: 01952 432166/433522 Fax: 01952 432204
www.ironbridge.org.uk
It has taken us over 200 years to create the perfect day out. The Iron Bridge Gorge is one of Britain's great World Heritage sites and is home to nine superb attractions set within six

square miles of beautiful scenery. These include the world famous Iron Bridge, Blists Hill Victorian working town - where you can change your money into token Victorian coins to spend in the shops, Coalport China Museum - once one of the country's finest porcelain manufacturers, and Jackfield Tile Museum - where you can now see a unique collection from the former world centre of the decorative tile industry. A great family day out.
Main sites: All year daily 10.00-17.00. Closed 24,25 & 31 Dec & 1 Jan. Some sites close in winter, please call for details Freephone 01952 432166
A£9.50 Passport Ticket to all Museums C&Students£5.50 Family Ticket (A2+C5)£29.00 OAPs£8.50. Valid until you have visited all nine attractions. Prices valid until Easter 2000

Historical

Attingham Park
Attingham Park Shrewsbury Shropshire SY4 4TP
[4m SE of Shrewsbury on B4380]
Tel: 01743 708123 Fax: 01743 708150
An elegant Neo-classical mansion of the late 18th century with magnificent state rooms, built for the 1st Lord Berwick. His eldest son added a top-lit picture gallery by Nash to display his Grand Tour collection. The 3rd Lord Berwick contributed splendid Regency Silver, Italian Neo-classical furniture and more pictures, making this one of the richest displays of Regency taste to survive. The park was landscaped by Humphrey Repton; there are attractive walks along the river and through the deer park. Prior notice of wheelchair visitors is appreciated as access to house is by rear lift with staff assistance. No dogs in deer park, on leads in the immediate vicinity of the house.
visitor comments: There are fine works of art, and lovely ceilings, however needs some renovation.
House: 4 Apr - 1 Nov Sat-Wed & Good Fri 13.30-17.00, Bank Hol Mon 11.00-17.00. Deer Park & Grounds: Mar Oct daily 08.00-21.00, Nov-Feb daily 08.00-17.00 Tearoom & Shop: 4 Apr - 1 Nov Sat-Wed & Good Fri 12.30-17.00, daily in Aug, Nov & Dec Sat & Sun 12.30-16.00. Closed 25 Dec
Last Admission: House 16.30
House & Park: £4.00 Family Ticket £10.00, Park and Grounds only: £1.50, pre-booked parties £3.00
discount offer: Free Entry For Children Under 16 To The Park Only

Boscobel House
Boscobel Lane Bishop's Wood Shropshire ST19 9AR
[on unclassified road between A41 / A5, 8m NW of Wolverhampton]
Tel: 01902 850244
www.english-heritage.org.uk
Fully refurbished and restored the panelled rooms, secret hiding places and pretty gardens lend this seventeenth century timber-framed hunting lodge a truly romantic character. King Charles II hid in the house and in the nearby oak after the battle of Worcester in 1651. House not suitable for wheelchairs, access to gardens only.
1 Apr-31 Oct daily 10.00-18.00, 17.00 in Oct
Admission by guided tour. Tearooms: 1 Apr - 31 Oct Tues-Sun 11.00-17.00
Last Admission: 45mins before closing
A£4.30 C£2.20 Concessions£3.20

↓*special events*

► **Traditional Song**
15/7/00-16/7/00
From Noon. A performance of delightful unaccompanied song.

► **A Civil War Surgeon**
22/7/00-23/7/00
From Noon. A fascinating and gruesome insight into 17th century medical care. Not for the faint-hearted!

► **Meet a Musketeer**
29/7/00-30/7/00

► **Victorian Farming**
16/9/00-17/9/00
From Noon. Meet a late 19th century farm worker and his wife and find out about their everyday lives

► **Halloween Tours**
21/10/00-31/10/00
At 11.00 & 14.30. Dark tales about Boscobel House for Halloween

Buildwas Abbey
Iron Bridge Telford Shropshire TF8 7BW
[on S bank of River Severn on B4378 2m W of Iron Bridge]
Tel: 01952 433274 Fax:
The beautiful, ruined, Cistercian abbey was founded in 1135, and stands in a picturesque setting. The church with its stout round pillars is roofless but otherwise almost complete.
1 Apr-31 Oct daily 10.00-18.00, 17.00 in Oct
A£1.95 C£1.00 Concessions£1.50

↓*special events*

► **Medieval Living History**
17/6/00-18/6/00
Encampment, drill, archery, mumming plays and dancing

▶ **Family Entertainment**
19/8/00-20/8/00
Have-a-go archery, juggling and face-painting

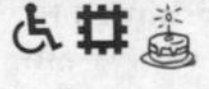

Stokesay Castle

Stokesay Craven Arms Shropshire SY7 9AH
[7m NW of Ludlow off A49]
Tel: 01588 672544
www.english-heritage.org.uk
Wonderfully preserved and little altered, this 13th century manor house has a romantic setting in peaceful countryside. Special features are the timber-framed Jacobean gatehouse, the great hall and, reached by an outside staircase, a solar with 17th century panelling. Parish church nearby.
visitor comments: Very interesting. The stereo guide is well worth using.
1 Apr-31 Oct daily 10.00-18.00, 17.00 in Oct. 1 Nov-31 Mar Wed-Sun 10.00-16.00 (closed 13.00-14.00). Closed 24-26 Dec & 1 Jan
A£3.50 C£1.80 Concessions£2.60. Personal stereo included in admission price

↓*special events*

▶ **Carry on Piping!**
5/8/00-6/8/00
Lively, humorous, have-a-go family show with 16th century rock 'n' roll!

▶ **A Regency Murder Mystery**
12/8/00-13/8/00
A murder to solve, plots, sword fights and tight breeches!

▶ **Soldiers of George III**
19/8/00-20/8/00
Redcoats, encampment, drill, musket and cannon firing of 1776

▶ **The Bard and the Blade**
27/8/00-28/8/00
Shakespearean dialogue and dramatic duels with sword and dagger

▶ **Medieval Entertainers**
28/10/00-29/10/00
Authentic medieval games, cures, folklore and early machinery, plus a children's play about the formative years of Parliament

Walcot Hall

Nr Bishops Castle Lydbury North Shropshire SY7 8AZ
[3m E of Bishops Castle on B4385, 0.5m outside Lydbury North. BR: Craven Arms]
Tel: 020 7581 2782 Fax: 020 7589 0195
Built by Sir William Chambers for Lord Clive of India, Walcot Hall possesses a free-standing ballroom; stable yard with twin clock towers; extensive walled garden and wonderful arboretum noted for its rhododendrons, azaleas and specimen trees.
Arboretum: 1 Apr-31 Oct Fri, Sat & Sun 12.00-16.30. House: by appointment except National Garden Scheme Open Day 28-29 May 2000 14.00-18.00
A£3.00 C(0-15)£Free. Collect tickets from Powis Arms, beside main gate

Weston Park

Weston-under-Lizard Shifnal Shropshire TF11 8LE
[7m W of J12 M6, 3m N of J3 M54]
Tel: 01952 850207 Fax: 01952 850430
Built in 1671, this fine house stands in elegant gardens and a vast park designed by Capability Brown. Three lakes, a miniature railway and a woodland adventure playground are to be found in the grounds. The house is open to the public for special gourmet dinner evenings. Call for details. Member of the Historic Houses Association.
visitor comments: The children enjoyed the play areas. Definitely a dry day venue.
Park & House: 3-5 Apr. Then 2 May-19 Sept: every weekend in May and June incl Bank Hol Mon (closed 1 May), 28 June-3 Sept daily (closed 17 July, 14-15 Aug), then every weekend in Sept until 19
Last Admission: Park 17.00, House 16.30
Park & Gardens: A£3.80 C£2.20 OAPs£2.80. House, Park & Gardens: A£5.50 C£3.40 OAPs£4.30
discount offer: Two For The Price Of One. Not Valid On Special Event Days. Valid Until 19 Sept 99

Military & Defence Museums

Royal Air Force Museum, Cosford

Cosford Shifnal Shropshire TF11 8UP
[on the A41, only 1m from J3 on the M54]
Tel: 01902 376200 Fax: 01902 376211
www.rafmuseum.org.uk
One of Britain's largest and best kept aviation collections with extensive displays: over 50 rockets and missiles from the deadly experimental types to current state-of-the-art technology; aero engines include power plants from early piston engined aircraft to the modern jet. Exhibitions include British, German, Japanese and American war planes including the Spitfire, Hurricane, Mosquito, Liberator and Lincoln, along with the mighty post-war bombers and fighters such as Vulcan, Victor and Lightning. Research and development aircraft from the early days of 1941 when the first British jet aircraft made its maiden flight,

through the post-war years, the advancement of aviation technology made thrilling and fascinating strides. The Royal Airforce Museum is the home to many huge retired civil and military transport aircraft which tell the story of passenger carrying by air from the early days to the present time. All of this in three fully heated hangers. The Royal Airforce Museum provides a unique venue for corporate entertaining and private parties. A range of events can be accommodated. Call for further information.
All year daily 10.00-18.00. Closed 24-26 Dec & 1 Jan
Last Admission: 16.00
A£5.00 C£3.00 Family Ticket £13.00 OAPs£4.00 Group rates 20+ and educational groups available on application
discount offer: £1.00 Off Adult/OAPs & 50p Off Child Admissions

Victorian Era

Blists Hill Victorian Town

Legges Way Madeley Telford Shropshire TF8 7EF
[on the A442 from Telford, signposted]
Tel: 01952 432166 Fax: 01952 432204
www.vtel.co.uk
Recreated working Victorian town, staff in Victorian costume, working exhibits, pub, restaurant, even Victorian 'token' currency. See our main listing under Museum- Industrial - Ironbridge Gorge Museums.
visitor comments: Extremely well put together, with helpful staff and plenty to see.
Mar-Nov daily 10.00-17.00, Nov-Mar daily 10.00-16.00. Closed 24-25 Dec & 1 Jan
Last Admission: 15.30
A£6.80. Passport tickets to all attractions A£9.00 C&Students£5.50 Family Ticket (A2+C5)£29.00 OAPs£8.50

Agriculture / Working Farms

Home Farm

Blue Anchor Minehead Somerset TA24 6JS
[2m off A39 at Washford, on E end of Blue Anchor seafront,]
Tel: 01984 640817
A small working farm where you can learn how your food is produced and meet traditional farm animals. A wonderful 'hands on experience' for young and old. Traditional farmhouse cream teas served. During your visit, you can also wander through woodland, see the wild flowers and relax in the quiet of a garden which enjoys views of the Brendon Hills and the occasional hoot of a steam train. Blue Anchor Station is only 10 minutes walk away, so why not combine a nostalgic journey on the West Somerset Railway with a visit to Home Farm.
Apr-Sept daily 10.30-17.00, closed Sat. Cream Teas until 17.30. Groups by prior arrangement at any time
Last Admission: 17.00
A£2.50 C£1.75 Family Ticket (A2+C2)£8.00 Season Ticket Family of Four £25.00, Groups 10+ 10% discount, School parties welcome price on application

Animal Attractions

Bee World and Animal Centre

Lower Stream Farm Stogumber Station Stogumber Taunton Somerset TA4 3TR
[A358, signposted to Williton Road, 1.5m from Main Road, or alight from train at Stogumber Station]
Tel: 01984 656545
Watch working honey bees - all behind glass, see honey extracted and wax candles produced. Hands-on experience with the animals, lamb and calf feeding, milking the cow, and Shetland pony rides. Play areas, sand pit, swings and wild flower walk to enjoy. You won't bee disappointed.
Easter-31 Oct daily 10.00-18.00 or dusk if sooner
Last Admission: 16.30
A£3.00 C(5-16)£2.00 OAPs£2.65 Concessions£2.50

Bridgewater Camel Company

Orchard Farm Plainsfield Over Stowey Bridgwater Somerset TA5 1HH
[based at the foot of the Quantoch Hills]
Tel: 01278 733186 Fax: 01278 733186
Camels brought over from Tenerife in December 1996, giving rides for all the family. Called Teifet (boy), Atakor (boy), Tazruk (boy) and Seita (girl) all very gentle. Rides available range from minimum of one hour to a day and overnight trek.
Please call to make booking
One hour ride: £12.00 per person. Half day trek with meal: A£36.00 C£18.00. One day trek with meal: A£69.00 C£35.00. One day and overnight trek with 3 meals: A£99.00 C£50.00

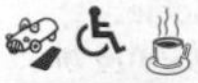

Arts, Crafts & Textiles

Holbourne Museum of Art
Great Pulteney Street Bath Somerset BA2 4DB
[Central Bath. BR: Bath Spa 15mins walk or Bus: No 4]
Tel: 01225 466669 Fax: 01225 333121
www.bath.ac.uk/holbourne
This jewel in Bath's crown, originally the 18th century Sydney Hotel, takes its name from Sir William Holburne (1793-1874) whose collections of national importance include superb English and continental silver, porcelain, maiolica, glass and portrait miniatures. Among the many fine paintings are works by Gainsborough, Stubbs, Turner and Guardi, complemented by the marble sculpture by Plura of "Diana & Endymion" and the famous Susini bronze once owned by Louis XIV. There is also a lively programme of lectures and events. Licensed Tea House in garden setting. Book Shop. Guided tours by prior arrangement.
Mid Feb-Mid Dec Mon-Sat 11.00-17.00, Sun 14.30-17.30
A£3.50 C£1.50 Family Ticket £7.00 OAPs£3.00 Students£2.00. Group rates 20-50 discounted, except for guided tours £2.00 exhibitions only
discount offer: 10% Discount On Admission Prices

↓*special events*

▶ **Thomas Hartley Cromek - A Classical Vision**
1/3/00-2/5/00
Vibrant Victorian Watercolours of Rome, Florence, Venice and Athens

▶ **17th Century Raised Needlework Exhibition**
18/5/00-3/9/00
"Stumpwork" from the Holburne Collection

▶ **And Miss Carter Wore Pink**
9/9/00-29/10/00
Illustrations from an Edwardian Childhood by Helen Bradley

▶ **A Child Is Born**
8/11/00-16/12/00
Paintings and Sculpture celebrating the Millennium

Royal Photographic Society
The Octagon Milsom Street Bath Somerset BA1 1DN
[Central Bath. BR: Bath Spa 10mins walk]
Tel: 01225 462841 Fax: 01225 448688
www.rps.org
The Museum tells the story of the history of photography from its earliest inception to the 20th century. Illustrated with many items of equipment and pictures from the Society's world-famous Collection, including some of the earliest and rarest photographic items. Also a full programme of contemporary exhibitions and holographic display.
All year daily 09.30-17.30. Closed 24 Dec-2 Jan
Last Admission: 16.45
A£2.50 C&Concessions£1.75 C(0-7)&Disabled£Free Family Ticket £5.00. Party 12+ call for details
discount offer: Two For The Price Of One

↓*special events*

▶ **Retouching & Restoration**
11/3/00-11/3/00
09.30-17.00 at City of Bath College, £95.00. A range of popular restoration and retouching techniques

▶ **Nature Photography**
12/3/00-12/3/00
10.00-17.00, £40.00. Practical workshop with Heather Angel looks at how you can improve your nature photographs

▶ **Members Gallery - Israel Members**
16/3/00-29/3/00

▶ **Members Gallery - Visual Journalism Group**
30/3/00-12/4/00

▶ **Faces Of The Century**
15/4/00-2/7/00
Significant images of the last 100 years of British history.

▶ **143 International Print Exhibition**
8/7/00-1/10/00
An annual event, which aims to produce an exhibition reflecting the wide diversity of modern photography.

▶ **RPS Collection Show**
7/10/00-1/1/01
The largest and most definitive exhibition ever drawn from its own collection.

Birds, Butterflies & Bees

Exmoor Falconry and Animal Farm
West Lynch Farm Allerford Porlock Somerset

TA24 8HJ
[J23 M5 into Bridgwater, follow A39 to Minehead, and on towards Porlock. 5m W of Minehead on a sharp left hand bend at Allerford, turn right, through the village, just along on the left hand side, past a small 15th century chapel]
Tel: 01643 862816
www.exmoor-holidays.co.uk/bossington
Set in the heart of Exmoor National Park, you may have a memorable day experiencing a range of birds of prey, handling, manning, and flying at the bird of prey centre, followed by half a day hawking over the woods, combes and farms on Lorna Doone's Exmoor. Hawking Days: After a little elementary tuition on handling the hawks you will be taken onto the wild side of Exmoor to fly the birds over specially selected farmland, and wooded coombes to immerse yourself in the art, skill and science of flying hawks in their own environment, listening for the sound of the kicking buck rabbit, or the whisper of the pheasant through the undergrowth, using rising thermals, playing in the wind, always watchful and alert. Please wear sensible clothes and shoes. There is also a Summer Hawk Walk, Personal Wildlife Safaris, Horse Riding, Walking & Birdwatching and the Farm Park. Bed and Breakfast available
1 Mar-31 Oct Daily 10.30-16.30
Hawk Walk: A£10.00 per person for 1 hour, A£25.00 for 2.5hrs including light meal and wine. Special rates for children. Maximum number 6. Hawking Weekend: A£60.00 per day, A£150.00 3 days, £240.00 5 days. Rates negotiable for those wishing to bring their own birds. Horse Riding: hire £10.00 per hour; Horseback guide £5.00 per hour. Please telephone for B&B prices. All costs payable at time of booking

Rode Tropical Bird Gardens
Rode Bath Somerset BA3 6QW
[off A36 between Bath and Warminster]
Tel: 01373 830326 Fax: 01373 831288
www.openworld.co.uk/britain/
17 acres planted with trees, shrubs and flowers. The bird collections consists of around 1200 birds of 200 species. There is also a clematis collection, ornamental lake, Pet's Corner, children's play area, information centre and woodland steam railway.
visitor comments: A 'whole day' attraction, but make sure the weather is good.
All year Summer daily 10.00-18.00, Winter 10.00-dusk. Closed 25 Dec
Last Admission: 60mins before closing
A£5.00 C(3-15)£2.50 Family Ticket (A2+C2)£14.50 OAPs£4.50. Group rates: A£4.50 C£2.20 OAPs£4.00 School £2.00 Hospital £2.50. Season Ticket £28.00 (includes 1 child). Train rates: A£1.10 C£0.90 Group £0.70 Rover £2.50 Season Ticket £0.80

Caverns & Caves

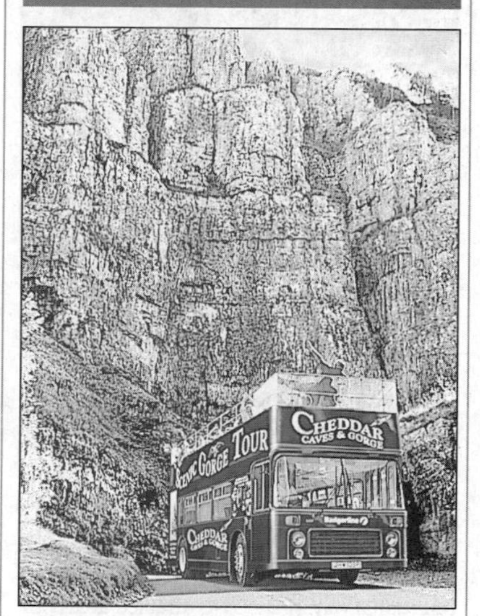

Cheddar Caves and Gorge
Cheddar Gorge Cheddar Somerset BS27 3QF
[on A371 between Wells and Weston-Super-Mare, or J22 on M5 then follow A38. Plenty of free on site parking.]
Tel: 01934 742343 Fax: 01934 744637
Britain's two most beautifully illuminated showcaves - Gough's Cave and the stunning colours of Cox's Cave - plus 'The Crystal Quest', a dark walk fantasy adventure underground. Visit 'Cheddar Man', Britain's oldest complete skeleton. Climb Jacob's Ladder to Pavey's Lookout Tower and clifftop walks. Open-top gorge tours in Summer. Partial disabled access.
visitor comments: Absolutely fantastic views of the gorge. Caves were brilliant. Well worth the entrance fee. Staff are friendly and helpful.
All year Easter-Sept daily 10.00-17.00 rest of year daily 10.30-16.30
Last Admission: Summer 17.00, Winter 16.30
'Caves and Gorge Explorer' ticket A£7.50 C£5.00
discount offer: 50p Per Person (maximum of 6 persons) Off The Cost Of The 'Caves and Gorge Explorer Ticket'

Somerset

Wookey Hole Caves and Papermill
Wookey Hole Wells Somerset BA5 1BB
[J22 M5, A39, A38, A371. Plenty of on site parking]
Tel: 01749 672243 Fax: 01749 677749
www.wookey.co.uk
The caves are the main feature of Wookey Hole. Visitors are guided through the Chambers seeing the amazing stalagmites and stalactites including the famous Witch of Wookey. There is also a Victorian Papermill where handmade paper is still made in the traditional way. There is NO disabled access to the caves.
visitor comments: The best caves I've seen, absolutely amazing. Kids loved the paper making.
All year Mar-Oct 10.00-17.00, Nov-Feb 10.30-16.30. Closed 17-25 Dec inclusive
Last Admission: Summer 17.00, Winter 16.30
A£7.20 C£4.20
discount offer: £1.00 Off Full Admission Price For A Maximum Of 6 People, Not With Family Tickets

Folk & Local History Museums

Chard and District Museum
High Street Chard Somerset TA20 1QL
Tel: 01460 65091
Margaret Bondfield first woman Cabinet Minister. Displays on the History of Chard, John Stringfellow pioneer of powered flight, early artificial limbs made in Chard, cider making and agriculture, with a complete blacksmith's forge, carpenter's and plumber's workshop.
May-End Oct Mon-Sat 10.30-16.30, additionally Sun mid July & Aug
A£2.00 C£0.80 Family Ticket £5.00 OAPs£1.50
discount offer: Two For The Price Of One. Valid Until 31 Oct 99

The Time Machine Museum
Burlington Street Weston-super-Mare Somerset BS23 1PR
[signposted from the high street. Limited on site parking]
Tel: 01934 621028 Fax: 01934 612526
www.n-somerset.gov.uk/museum
This family museum is set around a central courtyard with a Chemist Shop, Dairy, fountain and seaside gallery. Adjoining the museum is Clara's Cottage, an authentic Westonian home of the 1900's, with a display of Peggy Nisbet dolls. Displays of local archaeology, natural history and mining, plus its own Art Gallery and People's Collections. Along with the shop and café, making this a very entertaining visit for all the family. Conference/Function room available.
visitor comments: Staff are friendly and helpful. Let your children explore, whilst you enjoy a cup of tea.
Mar-Oct daily 10.00-17.00, Nov-Feb daily 10.00-16.00. Closed 25-26 Dec & 1 Jan
Last Admission: 30mins before closing
A£3.10 C(0-16)£1.25 Family Ticket (A2+C3/A1+4C))£8.00 OAPs£2.10, which permits unlimited free return visits for rest of year.
Group rates available on request
discount offer: Two Adults For The Price Of One

Food & Drink

Harveys Wine Cellars
12 Denmark Street Bristol Somerset BS1 5DQ
[Central Bristol. BR: Temple Meads]
Tel: 0117 927 5036 Fax: 0117 927 5001
www.harveysbc.com
Enjoy a world of wine at Harveys wonderful 13th century wine cellars. An exciting range of Wine Tasting Events are provided by an experienced team. Choose from classical or unusual wine tastings, diverse tastings of sherry or port, buffet suppers, gourmet dinners and much more. Please call for further details.
All year Mon-Sat 10.00-17.00. Closed Sun & Bank Hol. Occasionally closed for Private Events, please call before making a special journey
A£4.00 Family Ticket £8.00
OAPs&Students£3.00

Historical

Forde Abbey
Chard Somerset TA20 4LU
[A358, B3167 follow the brown signs from Chard to Forde Abbey]
Tel: 01460 221290 Fax: 01460 220296
This 12th-century Cistercian monastery was converted into a private dwelling in the mid-17th century by Cromwell's attorney general. In the house there are good pictures and furniture and an outstanding set of Mortlake tapestries. The large gardens are some of the finest in Dorset and include an historic kitchen garden, rock garden and bog garden.
Gardens: All year daily 10.00-16.30. House: 1 Apr-31 Oct Tue, Wed, Thur, Sun & Bank Holiday afternoons 13.00-16.30
Last Admission: 16.30
House & Gardens: A£5.20 C(0-15)£Free OAPs£5.00. Gardens: A£4.00 C(0-15)£Free OAPs£3.80. Discounts for pre-book groups 20+ can be arranged for any day of the week during the season. Please tel: 01460 220 231 for details
discount offer: 50p Off Full Admission Prices
↓*special events*
▶ **Wonderful Flowers**
29/4/00-1/5/00
▶ **Jazz in the Garden**
28/5/00-28/5/00

Gaulden Manor
Tolland Lydeard St. Lawrence Taunton Somerset TA4 3PN
[9m NW of Taunton signposted from A358 and B3224]
Tel: 01984 667213
Small historic manor of great charm, a real lived in home. Guided tours by owner. Fine plasterwork, antique furniture, hand embroideries and extensive and fascinating gardens.
Garden: June 8-28 August on Sun and Thurs 2-5 A£3.00 C£1.00. House and Garden: 2 July-28 Aug on Sun and Thur 14.00-17.00. Teas on Sundays when House is open
Last Admission: 16.30
House and Garden: A£4.20 C£1.00 C(0-4)£Free. Garden only: All £3.00
discount offer: Two Children Free With Two Full Paying Adults. Valid 8 June-28 Aug 2000

Maritime

SS Great Britain
Great Western Dock Gas Ferry Road Bristol Somerset BS1 6TY
[off Cumberland Road located in City well signed. BR: Temple Meads]
Tel: 0117 926 0680 Fax: 0117 925 5788
Brunel's great ship, the SS Great Britain was launched in Bristol in 1843 and was the largest ever iron ship to be steam driven by a screw propeller. As the forerunner of all the great passenger liners, the SS Great Britain is of great historical importance. She served first as a luxury transatlantic liner, then carried emigrants to Australia, troops to the Crimea, and ultimately became a cargo ship. Abandoned in the Falkland Islands, her wreck was used as storage until, in 1970, her rusting hull was towed 9000 miles back to Bristol. Restoration is now well under way and visitors can see what life would have been like on a passenger ship in the Victorian days with the assistance of the audio-visual introduction. Also on site

you will find a Maritime Heritage Centre and Bristol Blue Glass Blowing. Now also fully restored and open to the public is the Ladies Boudoir. Disabled access is limited, please call venue for further details.
Summer: daily 10.00-17.30, Winter: daily 10.00-16.30. Guided Tours by prior arrangement. Closed 24-25 Dec
Last Admission: 30mins before closing
A£6.25 C£3.75 Family Ticket(A2+C2)£17.00 OAPs£5.25. Coaches welcome.

Military & Defence Museums

Fleet Air Arm Museum
Royal Naval Air Station Yeovilton Yeovil Somerset BA22 8HT
[J25 M5, on B3151 just off A37 / A303]
Tel: 01935 840565 Fax: 01935 840181
www.faam.org.uk
Experience the exciting development of Britain's Flying Navy. Step back in time and follow the paths of the people, ships and aircraft that made history. 'Fly aboard' our Aircraft Carrier, see how sailors live and work at sea. Based at the Royal Naval Air Station, the museum houses a collection of 40 historic aircraft. Special exhibitions include World War I, the Inter-war Years, WRENS, recent conflicts and more. Climb aboard Concorde 002 and watch aircraft taking off and landing. Children's areas and the Ultimate Aircraft Carrier Experience.
Apr-Oct daily 10.00-17.30, Nov-Mar daily 10.00-16.30. Closed 24-26 Dec
Last Admission: 90mins before closing
A£6.50 C£4.00 Family Ticket £18.00 OAPs£5.50

↓*special events*

▶ **Model Show 2000**
26/2/00-26/2/00

▶ **Easter Egg Hunt**
21/4/00-23/4/00
Come and join in the fun, meet Flopsy the bunny, get a free creme ege for completing the hunt.

▶ **Wartime Weekend**
16/9/00-17/9/00

▶ **Pirate's Treasure Hunt**
29/10/00-29/10/00

Multicultural Museums

Helicopter Museum
The Heliport Locking Moor Road Weston-Super-Mare Somerset BS22 8PL
[Weston Airport A371 near J21 M5 - signposted]
Tel: 01934 635227 Fax: 01934 822400
www.helicoptermuseum.freeserve.co.uk
A unique collection of helicopters and autogyros - over 50 on display - with exhibits of models, photographs and components to illustrate how the aircraft work. Restoration Hangar, Pleasure Flights plus Special Events...including Open Cockpit Days and Restoration Open Days. Please ring for further information.
Nov-Mar Wed-Sun 10.00-16.00. Apr-Oct daily 10.00-18.00. Closed 25-26 Dec & 1 Jan
Last Admission: 60mins before closing
A£3.50 C(0-4)£Free C(5-16)£2.50 Family Ticket £10.00 OAPs£3.00
discount offer: One Child Admitted Free When Accompanied By A Full Paying Adult

↓*special events*

▶ **Helicopter Pleasure Flights**
12/3/00-8/10/00
Normally take place in conjunction with Open Cockpit Days and on additional days during the peak summer period July-Aug and Bank Holidays. Further details, including prices, Sight-Seeing Specials and Trial Lessons can be obtained from the Museum

▶ **Open Cockpit Days**
12/3/00-8/10/00
The public are given access to selected Helicopters with an experienced guide to explain the cockpit operation and mechanical working, normal admission prices apply. 2000 dates are: 12 Mar, 9 Apr, 14 May, 11 June, 9 July, 13 Aug, 10 Sept and 8 Oct

▶ **Remote Helicopters**
19/3/00-19/3/00
Fly a Helicopter by Remote Control! For All the Budding Pilots out There. To celebrate SET Week 2000 (Science, Engineering & Technology). Local enthusiasts demonstrate the skills involved in flying Remote control model helicopters. There will also be a Trainer Helicopter available for you to practice your flying skills

▶ **Easter Sunday**
23/4/00-23/4/00
Includes the Fast and Furious Sports Car Display and Kids Easter Egg Painting Competition.

▶ **Museums and Galleries Month**
1/5/00-31/5/00
Various exhibitions to show the importance of the helicopter within our emergency services. Careers information on hand for all budding Air Ambulance Pilots

▶ **Weston-Super-Helidays (3 days)**
28/7/00-30/7/00
Helicopter Fly-in & Fun Spectacular on the Sea Front at Weston super Mare. Gates 10.00 daily, includes static displays of over 50 Military & Civil helicopters and autogyros

▶ **Family Fun Day**

20/8/00-20/8/00
Come along and join in with the various games and entertainment with music, refreshments, children's rides and hopefully wonderful sunshine! Reduced admission charges apply

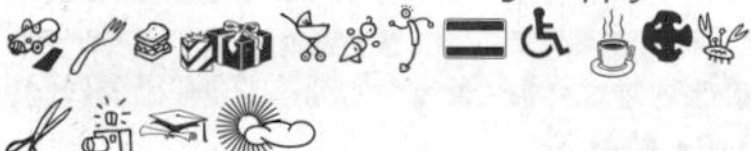

Nature & Conservation Parks

Secret World-Badger and Wildlife Rescue Centre
New Road East Huntspill Highbridge Somerset TA9 3PZ
[J22 Southbound or J23 Northbound M5, signposted off A38 1m S of Highbridge]
Tel: 01278 783250 Fax: 01278 793109
www.secretworld.co.uk
Don't miss this unique centre which is an all weather attraction. Exciting things to see and do for the whole family. The home of the Bluebell Sett. Adventure playground, wildlife displays and talks, Nocturnal House, Hedgehog Room, Observation Hive, Yesteryear's Farming, Badger Observation Sett, Badger Cub Rearing Centre, Play areas, animals, animals, animals, you'll love it. Dogs allowed on leads.
visitor comments: Staff are really friendly and the tea room is good value. Allow about 5 hours for a visit. Suited for older chidren.
Mar-Nov daily 10.00-18.00, Nov-Mar daily 10.00-17.00. Closed in jan
Last Admission: 16.00
A£4.95 C£3.50 Family Ticket (A2+C2)£15.00 OAPs£4.50. Group rates available. Reduced prices and facilities during winter months.
Season tickets available
discount offer: Two For The Price Of One

↓special events

▶ **Tortoise and Turtle Weekend**
15/7/00-16/7/00
The British Chelonia Group will be with us with many different species of tortoise and turtle and advice on how to keep these creatures

▶ **Bat Weekend**
12/8/00-13/8/00
A unique chance to see live British bats. Bat groups will be on hand to expel some of the myths surrounding these nocturnal creatures

▶ **Care for the Wild, World-Wide Weekend**
23/9/00-24/9/00
Care for the Wild International will talk about the many animals they are involved with such as tigers, rhinos, elephants and orangutans

▶ **National Badger Day**
28/10/00-28/10/00
Badger group members will be on hand to give advice on how you can help badgers across the country

Railways

East Somerset Railway
Cranmore Railway Station Shepton Mallet Somerset BA4 4QP
[signposted off A361 Frome / Shepton Mallet road]
Tel: 01749 880417 Fax: 01749 880764
Steam locomotives and rolling stock can be seen here along with an engine shed and workshops. The art gallery displays David Shepherd's and other artists' work. Steam train services include Santa Specials in December here also is a wildlife information centre, restaurant and play area. Guided tours for schools.
All year daily from 10.00, Steam trains run: Mar & Nov Sun, Apr-May & Oct Weekends, June-Sept Wed-Sun, July & Aug daily call for timetable
A£5.50 C£3.50 OAPs£4.50, Non-steam days A£2.00 C£1.00 OAPs£1.25

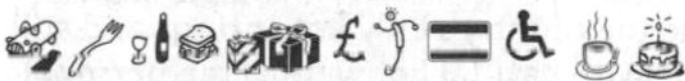

West Somerset Railway
The Railway Station Station Terrace Minehead Somerset TA24 5BG
[M5, A358, signposted]
Tel: 01643 704996 Fax: 01643 706349
Britain's longest heritage railway operating steam and diesel trains through the Quantock Hills and along the Somerset coast. There are usually about seven or eight trains a day along the 22 mile route from Minehead to Bishops

Lydeard and back, which stop at places such as Washford and Watchet on the way.
visitor comments: Get off at the little stations along the route and explore before getting back on the next train
Mar-Dec daily, times vary
Queuing Times: 10mins
A£1.70-£8.90 C(5-15)£4.10, Family fares available with very generous discounts, 20% discount for OAPs, half fares for local residents with Starcards

Roman Era

Roman Baths
Pump Room Stall Street Bath Somerset BA1 1LZ
[J18 M4 then take A46, situated in Bath City centre]
Tel: 01225 477785 Fax: 01225 477743
www.romanbaths.co.uk
This Great Roman Temple and bathing complex is one of Britain's most spectacular ancient monuments, built 2000 years ago around the country's only hot springs and still flowing with natural hot water. Free personal audio-guided tours of the Baths and Temple of Sulis Minerva, Goddess of Wisdom and Healing.
visitor comments: Very informative - the audio tours are great. Worth the entrance fee.
All year Apr-Sept daily 09.00-18.00, Aug daily 09.00-21.30, Oct-Mar daily 09.30-17.00. Closed 25-26 Dec
Last Admission: 30mins before closing
A£6.90 C£4.00 Family Ticket £17.50. Group A£5.30 C£2.50/£2.90

Stately Homes

Forde Abbey
Chard Somerset TA20 4LU
[A358, B3167 follow the brown signs from Chard to Forde Abbey]
Tel: 01460 221290 Fax: 01460 220296
This 12th-century Cistercian monastery was converted into a private dwelling in the mid-17th century by Cromwell's attorney general. In the house there are good pictures and furniture and an outstanding set of Mortlake tapestries. The large gardens are some of the finest in Dorset and include an historic kitchen garden, rock garden and bog garden.
Gardens: All year daily 10.00-16.30. House: 1 Apr-31 Oct Tue, Wed, Thur, Sun & Bank Holiday afternoons 13.00-16.30
Last Admission: 16.30
House & Gardens: A£5.20 C(0-15)£Free OAPs£5.00. Gardens: A£4.00 C(0-15)£Free OAPs£3.80. Discounts for pre-book groups 20+ can be arranged for any day of the week during the season. Please tel: 01460 220 231 for details
discount offer: 50p Off Full Admission Prices
↓*special events*
▶ **Wonderful Flowers**
29/4/00-1/5/00
▶ **Jazz in the Garden**
28/5/00-28/5/00

Theme & Adventure Parks

Butlin's Family Entertainment Resort
The Seafront Minehead Somerset TA24 5SH
[off the A39 in Minehead, signposted off all major motorways and roads]
Tel: 01643 703331 x5123 Fax: 01643 705264
Butlin's Somerwest World is open to all visitors! Traditional funfair, waterworlds, shows and entertainment, restaurants, bars, shops and much more! Where else can you get up to 14 hours of non-stop fun and entertainment?
Apr-Oct daily 10.00-24.00
Last Admission: 21.00
A£8.50 C(4-14)£7.50 Family Ticket £27.00 Concessions£5.50. Group and school rates 20+ A&C£5.00 1 teacher free with every 10 students. Admission includes Butlin's Funfair but

not Sussex Amusement Rides or Big Fun Extras

Transport Museums

Haynes Motor Museum
Sparkford Yeovil Somerset BA22 7LH
[from A303 follow A359]
Tel: 01963 440804 Fax: 01963 441004
Experience the thrill of 100 smiles per hour... Travel through motoring history at Britain's most spectacular collection of historic cars, motorcycles and motoring memorabilia. Breath-taking displays include the $1.5million Duesenberg, red collection, Dawn of Motoring street scene and Hall of Motor Sport and the new Millennium Exhibition Hall to feature modern supercars and future classics. Working exhibits and demonstrations, military vehicles, peddle cars, Motorland play park, the Motorists book and souvenir shop, outdoor picnic facilities and much more, all adds up to the thrill of .... 100 smiles per hour at the Haynes Motor Museum. Registered Charity No: 292048.
visitor comments: Excellent facilities. Children's menu and large play area for all ages.
All year Mar-Oct 09.30-17.30, open until 19.30 during School Hol. Nov-Feb 10.00-16.30. Closed 25-26 Dec & 1 Jan
A£4.95 C(5-16)£2.95 Concessions£3.95 Family Ticket £12.80
discount offer: One Adult Or Child Free With Every Two Full Paying Adults

↓*special events*

▶ **Italian Tour by Air and Coach**
1/9/00-30/9/00
Specific dates have yet to be confirmed. The coach tour will visit 9 car museums in 4 Mediterranean countries including Maranello, the home of Ferrari

▶ **Falling Leaves Classic Tour**
24/9/00-24/9/00
A relaxed atmosphere, beginning with a party on Saturday night and followed by enjoyable roads and fascinating places to visit on Sunday

▶ **Boxing Day Treasure Hunt**
26/12/00-26/12/00
Get the family together and work off those Christmas day excesses cracking the cryptic clues whilst exploring the countryside

Wildlife & Safari Parks

Wildlife Park at Cricket St. Thomas
Chard Somerset TA20 4DD
[on the A30, 2m E of Chard, follow brown signs]
Tel: 01460 30111 Fax: 01460 30817
www.cricketwildlifepark.co.uk
The Wildlife Park has over 400 animals and birds from around the world and is home to more than 70 different species, many at risk from extinction. The walk-through lemur wood is sanctuary for three different species of lemurs - a unique setting amongst the largest of its kind in the world. Amur leopards, pets corner, safari train, 1000 acres in scenic and peaceful countryside.
visitor comments: Great for under 5's, well worth the entry fee. Beautiful grounds.
All year 10.00-18.00. Closed 25 Dec
Last Admission: Summer 16.00, Winter 15.00
A£4.95 C(under 3)£Free C(4-14)£3.75 Family Tickets £16.00

Zoos

Bristol Zoo Gardens
Clifton Bristol Somerset BS8 3HA
[follow brown tourist signs from J17 M5 or J18 or the city centre. From Bristol Temple Meads take the No. 8 or 9 bus to the Zoo gates. Limited on site parking.]
Tel: 0117 973 8951 info line Fax: 0117 973 6814
www.bristolzoo.org.uk
Enjoy an exciting real life experience and see over 300 species of wildlife in beautiful gardens. Seal and Penguin Coasts with fantastic underwater viewing now join favourites such as Gorilla Island, Bug World, Twilight World, the Aquarium, the Reptile House and the children's play area. The popular 'hands-on' Activity Centre, the interactive Zoolympics trial, special events and feeding time talks make it an educational as well as enjoyable day out. Your visit will also help to fund our important conservation work. Registered

Charity no. 203695. Sorry - dogs are not admitted to the Zoo.
visitor comments: Allow plenty of time - there's loads to see. Indoor attractions are great if the weather is bad.
All year Summer daily 09.00-17.30, Winter daily 09.00-16.30. Closed 25 Dec
Queuing Times: during Easter and Bank Hol
A£8.20 C(3-13)£4.60 Concessions£7.20

↓*special events*

▶ **Toddler's Weeks**
26/6/00-21/7/00
Mon-Fri you can get your 3-5 year olds in for £3.20

▶ **Summer Activities**
29/7/00-3/9/00
Summer has arrived and the kids need something to do... special activities in the Conservation Education Centre. Please call for further details

▶ **Christmas Events**
1/12/00-31/12/00
Revive your spirits and get in the festive mood with our Christmas carol evenings. Please call for details

Tropiquaria

Washford Cross Watchet Somerset TA23 0JX
[on A39]
Tel: 01984 640688 Fax: 01984 640688
Housed in a 1930's BBC transmitting station, the main hall has been converted into an indoor jungle with a 15 foot waterfall with a newly modernised Aquarium, tropical plants and free flying birds. Downstairs is the submarine crypt. Other features include landscaped gardens, outdoor aviaries, a children's playground with adventure fort and the Shadowstring Puppet Theatre.
Apr-Sept daily 10.00-17.00, Oct daily 11.00-16.00, Nov & Mar Weekends & school Hol daily 11.00-16.00, 28 Dec-4 Jan daily 11.00-16.00
Last Admission: Summer 16.40 Winter 15.30
A£4.40 C£2.95 OAPs/Students£3.95
discount offer: One Child Free With A Full Paying Adult (up to 2 per card)

Animal Attractions

Ash End House Children's Farm

Middleton Lane Middleton Tamworth Staffordshire B78 2BL
[travelling along A4091 from either direction follow our signs. Coaches must approach via the A4091 and are by appointment only. All coaches must stay on the property for the duration on this visit]
Tel: 0121 329 3240 Fax: 0121 329 3240
Small family owned farm with lots of friendly animals to feed and stroke. Play areas, picnic barns, lots of undercover activities for the children during school holidays and weekends including "make a memento" to take home, ie. Friendship bands, colouring cards etc.
Bookings also taken from schools, playgroups, clubs and Birthday Parties on the farm. Every Sunday from March to November there are wool spinning demonstrations and "Have-A-Go" yourself on the spinning wheel. Each Christmas we put on a special Nativity for all visitors to take part in, why not visit Father Christmas too!
All year daily 10.00-17.00 dusk in Winter. Closed 25-27 Dec, 1 Jan
Last Admission: 60mins before closing
A£1.80 C£3.60
discount offer: One Adult Free When A Child Pays Full Price

Blackbrook Zoological Park

Blackbrook Winkhill Nr Leek Staffordshire ST13 7QR
[from Leek take the Leek - Ashbourne Road (A523) until your reach Little Chef on your R. Take 1st R (signposted for Alton Towers) and Blackbrook is the 1st entrance on the R.]
Tel: 01538 308293/387159 Fax: 01565 308293
Enjoy a day with a difference at the Zoological park of the Moorlands. Birds, animals, aquarium, insects, reptiles, children's farm and pet and play areas, picnic facilities, talks, displays, shop, tea rooms and accessible for all.
All year daily 10.30-17.30. Closed 25 Dec & 1 Jan
A£4.95 C£2.95 OAPs£2.95 Family Ticket(2A+2C)£13.50

Arts, Crafts & Textiles

Gladstone Working Pottery Museum

Uttoxeter Road Longton Stoke-On-Trent Staffordshire ST3 1PQ
[on A50 signposted from A500 link with M6. Plenty of free on site parking.]
Tel: 01782 319232 Fax: 01782 598640
www.stoke.gov.uk/museums/gladstone
Discover the story of the Potteries at the last Victorian Pottery Factory from the days of coal fired bottle ovens. A visit to the Potteries is not

complete without a tour of the Gladstone's famous bottle ovens. Plenty of opportunities to have a go at Pottery making which you can take home as the ultimate in souvenirs: throw a pot on a potters wheel, try your hand at making pottery flowers or decorate your own unique piece of pottery. Gladstone is a great day out for all ages.
All year daily 10.00-17.00. Limited opening Christmas & New Year
Last Admission: 16.00
A£3.95 C(5-16)£2.50 Family Ticket (A2+C2)£10.00 Concessions£2.95
discount offer: One Child Free With Every Full Paying Adult

Factory Outlets & Tours

Royal Doulton Visitor Centre
Nile Street Burslem Stoke-On-Trent
Staffordshire ST6 2AJ
[J15/16 M6, follow A500 to junction with A527, Royal Doulton is then signposted. Parking on site is limited.]
Tel: 01782 292434 Fax: 01782 292424
www.royal-doulton.com/rd/visitors
Visit the home of the Royal Doulton Figure, featuring the world's largest public display, live demonstration area showing how figures are made, museum, restaurant and retail shop. Factory tours are available Mon-Fri (except factory holidays), prior booking is advised for tours (allow half a day for a tour).
All year Mon-Sat 09.30-17.00, Sun 10.30-16.30. Factory tours by appointment, Closed Christmas and New Year
Last Admission: 16.00
Visitor Centre: A£3.00 Concessions£2.25, Visitor Centre & Factory Tour: A£6.50 Concessions£5.00
discount offer: Two For The Price Of One With One Full Paying Adult For The Visitor Centre Only

↓*special events*

► **Bunnykins Millennium Exhibition**
15/4/00-31/5/00
Exhibition featuring the world's favourite nurseryware. Call for details on demonstrations and talks

Food & Drink

Bass Museum
Horninglow Street Burton-On-Trent
Staffordshire DE14 1YQ
[A511 from Stoke-on-Trent to Leicester]
Tel: 01283 511000 Fax: 01283 513613
www.bass-museum.com
In the heart of England, in Britain's brewing capital of Burton-On-Trent, The Bass Museum brings together a unique collection of artifacts and memorabilia tracing the fascinating history of both the brewing industry and the family of William Bass, one of the world's most famous brewing dynasties. Using a mixture of audio-visual presentations and original brewing apparatus, we explain the fascinating history of brewing. The art of coopering is kept alive in an authentic reconstruction. Wandering through these historic buildings you come across four of the most famous horses in the land. This history collection is presented on three floors of the Old Joiners's Shop and includes many beautiful models, interac-

tive displays and reconstructions. And So Much More...

visitor comments: Very informative. Our entry was discounted even on a "special event day" - a real days out treat!

All year Mon-Fri 10.00-17.00, Weekends 10.00-17.00

Last Admission: 16.00

A£4.75 C£2.00 OAPs £3.00 Family Ticket £12.50, call for details on Educational Visits, hiring the venue for special occassions, Children's parties, pre-booked group tours, function rooms etc

discount offer: Two For The Price Of One

↓*special events*

▶ **Neales Antique Valuation Day**
1/3/00-6/12/00
Mar 1, Apr 5, May 3, June 7, July 5, Aug 2, Sept 6, Oct 4, Nov 1 and Dec 6 only. Have your objects valued, 14.30-17.00 in reception

▶ **Agricultural Horse Show**
20/8/00-20/8/00
Decorated Harness, Brood Mare and Best Agricultural Turnout are some of the classes judged

▶ **Start of the Burton Festival**
21/9/00-1/10/00

▶ **CAMRA National Breweriana Auction and Collector's Fair**
23/9/00-23/9/00
Brewery related items from yesteryear and today

▶ **Umpah Evening**
23/9/00-29/12/00
Sept 23 and Dec 29 only. Enjoy a Traditional Beirkellar Night with The Heinz Miller Umpah Band

▶ **World Barrel Rolling Championship**
24/9/00-24/9/00
Fancy footwork, strength and teamwork all help towards a good fun day out

▶ **Cooking with Beer**
27/9/00-27/9/00

▶ **Coachman Owners Club Caravan Rally**
13/10/00-15/10/00
Over 20 caravans and club members will visit

▶ **International Gold Cup Record Breakers**
14/10/00-14/10/00

Gardens & Horticulture

Biddulph Grange Garden
Biddulph Grange Biddulph Stoke-On-Trent Staffordshire ST8 7SD
[off A527 0.5m N of Biddulph]
Tel: 01782 517999

An exciting and rare survival of a high-Victorian garden, acquired by the Trust in 1988 and focus of an extensive restoration project. Conceived by James Bateman, the 6ha are divided into a number of small gardens designed to house specimens from his extensive and wide-ranging plant collection. An Egyptian Court, Chinese Pagoda, Joss House, Bridge and Pinetum, together with many other settings, all combine to make the garden a miniature tour of the world. Picnics in the car park only.

27 Mar-31 Oct Wed-Fri 12.00-18.00, Weekends 11.00-18.00, 6 Nov-19 Dec Weekends 12.00-16.00 or dusk if sooner. Closed Good Fri

Last Admission: 17.30 or dusk

Mar-Oct: A£4.20 C£2.10 Family Ticket £10.50. Pre-booked Guided Tours A£5.50, Group rates 15+ A£3.00. Nov-Dec: A£2.00 C£1.00 Family Ticket £5.00. Pre-booked groups or educational visits welcome. Joint ticket with Little Moreton Hall A£6.00 C£3.00 Family Ticket £15.00

Historical

Ford Green Hall
Ford Green Road Smallthorne Stoke-on-Trent Staffordshire ST6 1NG
[NE of Stoke-on-Trent on B551 between Burslem / Endon]
Tel: 01782 233195 Fax: 01782 233194
www.stoke.gov.uk/fordgreenhall

This timber-framed farmhouse was built in 1624 for the Ford family and extended in the early 1700's. Furnished with items and utensils used by a farming family from the 16th-19th centuries. 17th century style period gardens in grounds. Wheelchair access limited to ground floor only.

All year Sun-Thur 13.00-17.00. Closed Christmas-New Year

Last Admission: 16.45

A£1.50 Concessions£1.00. Wheelchair users & C(0-4)£Free. Groups & coaches by appointment

discount offer: Two For The Price Of One

↓*special events*

▶ **Gardening Masterclass**
8/4/00-8/4/00
Meet the Head Gardner of Bridgmere Gardens.

Please book, call for further details

▶ **Easter Fun**
23/4/00-23/4/00
Come on kids, eat your carrots and bring those eyes to seek out the Easter Eggs hidden all around. 13.00-16.30

▶ **Selling Crafts Exhibition**
26/11/00-26/11/00
Presented by the North Staffordshire Guild of Craftsmen. 13.00-16.30. Call for further details

Shugborough Estate
Shugborough Milford Stafford Staffordshire ST17 0XB
[6m E of Stafford off A513. J13 M6 on A513 Stafford / Lichfield Road]
Tel: 01889 881388 Fax: 01889 881323
www.staffordshire.gov.uk/shugboro/shugpark.htm
The magnificent 900 acre seat of the Earls of Litchfield. The 18th century Mansion House contains fine collections of ceramics, silver, paintings and French furniture. Grade I listed garden with terraces and an Edwardian rose garden. Unique neo-classical monuments. County Museum including working laundry, kitchens and brewhouse. Georgian Park Farm with rare breeds and restored working corn mill. Children's birthday parties catered for at Park Farm.
25 Mar-1 Oct 11.00-17.00 Daily except Mon. Open Bank Holiday Mondays. Open all year to pre-booked parties
Last Admission: 16.15
A£4.00 Concessions£3.00 Family Voyager (all 3 sites) £18.00. NT Members £Free to all sites. £2.00 entry per vehicle

↓*special events*

▶ **Gamekeepers Fair**
15/4/00-16/4/00

▶ **Classic Car Show**
30/4/00-1/5/00
Displays of cars, bikes, buses and agricultural vehicles from 1905 onwards. Separate charge for this event

▶ **Staffordshire Garden & Leisure Show**
6/5/00-7/5/00
Everything for the home and garden and something of interest for all the family

▶ **Dressage Festival**
21/5/00-21/5/00
Staffordshire's only national dressage competition. Separate charge

▶ **Spring Craft Show**
27/5/00-29/5/00
See skilled craft people at work. Fun for all the family. Separate charge for this event

▶ **Close Encounters...**
17/6/00-17/6/00
...of the classical kind. Music and glorious fireworks. Gates open from 17.00. Separate charge.

▶ **Gardeners Weekend**
1/7/00-2/7/00
Floral displays, gardening exhibits and experts on hand to answer any horticultural queries. 10.00-18.00. Separate charge for show

▶ **Midland Studio Pottery & Ceramic Festival**
8/7/00-9/7/00
Pick up a pot from the hundreds to choose at this new event focusing on the art of pottery

▶ **Goose Fair**
16/7/00-16/7/00
Riotous characters, entertainers and colourful market sellers, all the fun of the 1820 village fair.

▶ **Fireworks and Laser Symphony Concert**
22/7/00-22/7/00
Live music, magnificent fireworks, brilliant lasers and dancing water fountains. Separate charge. Book early to avoid disappointment

▶ **6th National Collectible World Studios**
29/7/00-30/7/00
Collectors from all over the UK will converge at Shugborough to view fascinating collectibles

Tamworth Castle
The Holloway Tamworth Staffordshire B79 7LR
[J10 M42, signposted off A51/A5]
Tel: 01827 709626 Fax: 01827 709630
www.tamworthcastle.co.uk
Dramatic Norman motte and bailey castle set in attractive town centre park with floral terraces. Fifteen authentically furnished rooms open to the public, including Great Hall, Dungeon and Haunted Bedroom. Living Images of Baron Marmion, the Black Lady ghost and a Victorian prisoner. "The Tamworth Story" is a fascinating interactive exhibition telling the market town's history from Roman times to the present day using exhibits from the Museum Collection. "Tamworth on the Move" illustrates how transport has evolved from the time of the Norman Conquest. Battlement wall-walks and giftshop.
All year Mon-Sat 10.00-17.30, Sun 14.00-17.30. Please check opening details after 1 Nov
Last Admission: 16.30
A£4.20 Concessions£2.10 Family Ticket £11.60 Disabled £1.60 NB: Wheelchair users confined to ground floor
discount offer: Two For The Price Of One

Roman Era

Wall Roman Site (Letocetum)
Watling Street Wall Lichfield Staffordshire WS14 0AW
[off A5 at Wall Nr. Lichfield]
Tel: 01543 480768
Originally the Roman fort of Letocetum situated at the crossroads of Watling Street and Rykneild Street. 19th century excavations revealed the most complete bath house ever found in Britain. Three baths: cold, tepid and hot as well as a furnace room and an exercise hall. Museum of finds on site.
1 Apr-31 Oct daily 10.00-18.00 or dusk. Closed 13.00-14.00
A£2.25 C£1.10 Concessions£1.70

↓*special events*

▶ **Meet the Custodian**
8/4/00-9/4/00
Tours by the people who know them best

▶ **Meet a Roman Soldier**
20/5/00-21/5/00
Talks about armour and military skills, plus guided tours

▶ **End of the Roman Empire**
19/8/00-20/8/00
Military and civilian life in the last days of Roman Britain, together with a taste of the future in the form of the Saxon invader

Theme & Adventure Parks

Alton Towers
Alton Stoke-On-Trent Staffordshire ST10 4DB
[travelling N J23A M1 or J15 M6 travelling S J28 M1 or J16 M6 clearly signposted. Plenty of on site parking available]
Tel: 08705 204060 24hr Fax: 01538 704097
www.alton-towers.co.uk
Britain's number one theme park welcomes in the new millennium with Hex - The Legend of the Towers, a brand new spine-tingling experience guaranteed to enthral and exhilarate all the family. When it comes to nail biting, white knuckle rides, Alton Towers' "Big Five" are enough to leave even the most hardened thrill seekers begging for mercy! And for the little ones, there's a whole host of family fun including Riverbank Eye Spy and the live action Peter Rabbit and Friend On Ice. Situated in 500 acres of beautiful Staffordshire countryside there are rides and attractions for everyone. For further details call 08705 20 40 60.
visitor comments: Beautiful garden valley. Very little shelter in bad weather and on site rain wear expensive.
1 Apr-29 Oct daily
Peak: A£19.95 C(under 4)£Free C(4-13)£15.95 Family Ticket £59.00 Off Peak: A£14.95 C£11.95 Family Ticket £49.00. Please call 08705 20 40 60 for enquiries

↓*special events*

▶ **Barney, BJ and Baby Bop**
1/4/00-29/10/00
Barney the purple dinosaur and his friends will be performing their all-singing, all-dancing live shows up to three times a day. Book in advance and guarantee a seat

▶ **Science Alive**
4/4/00-6/4/00
Johnny Ball is the celebrity lecturer as school kids test scientific theories such as gravity and speed by riding and viewing the rides. School parties only

▶ **Jellikins Jelly Challenge**
17/4/00-21/4/00
The six cute Jellikins characters, stars of their own TV show, will be calling all tots to ride six little 'pink knuckle' rides to win a t-shirt and maybe a cuddle!
▶ **Fearsome Five Fortnight - Approach with Caution!**
5/6/00-16/6/00
Ride the five scariest white knuckle rides in Britain - Oblivion, Nemesis, Corkscrew, Black Hole and Ripsaw to claim a free limited edition t-shirt!
▶ **Summer Spectacular -Boom!**
5/8/00-28/8/00
Starring the Royal Marines Commando Display Team, this is an awe-inspiring live action event complete with explosions, mock battles and special effects
▶ **Halloween Spooktacular**
14/10/00-26/10/00
Held on Oct 14-20 and 23-26 only. Witness the re-creation of the true spirit of Halloween with music and dance, illusions, special effects and much more! Dare you ride Oblivion in the dark?
▶ **UK's Largest Firework and Laser Spectacular**
21/10/00-29/10/00
Held on Oct 21, 22, 27, 28, 29 only. World record-breaking fireworks, earth shaking explosions, spectacular lasers and lighting. Could the mystery of Hex finally be revealed?
▶ **Christmas Craft Fayre**
24/11/00-26/11/00
Quality seasonal crafts to suit every pocket, 10.00-18.00. Tickets: £1.00-£5.00

Drayton Manor Park
Tamworth Staffordshire B78 3TW
[J9 or 10 M42 on A4091 near Tamworth. 10m N of Birmingham, signposted A5/A38]
Tel: 01827 287979 Fax: 01827 288916
www.drayton-manor.co.uk
250 acre theme park and zoo, with over 50 rides and attractions to suit all ages. Extensive catering from fast food, bars, corporate banqueting and restaurants. Garden centre, shops, walks and a 15 acre zoo. Ride the new "Storm Force 10" - a ride set in a Cornish fishing village, where you are launched in a lifeboat that speeds through rapids and over spectacular drops along the route. Please allow at least 6 hours to obtain maximum enjoyment from your visit.
visitor comments: A good day out. Rides suitable for everyone. Expect long queues.
27 Mar-31 Oct daily 10.30-19.00
A£3.00 C(0-4)£Free C(4-13)&OAPs£2.00 Wheelchair visitor £2.00. Wristband: A£11.00 C(under 900mm)£Free C(900mm-13yrs) £8.00 Wheelchair & helper & OAPs£5.00 each, or pay as you go tickets @ £0.70 each (1,2 or 3 tickets for most rides). Group Rates: 27+ A£9.00 C(900mm-13yrs) £7.00 Wheelchair & helper & OAPs£4.50 each; 12-26 people: A£9.50 C(900mm-13yrs)£7.50 Wheelchair & helper & OAPs£5.00 each. School groups 12+: Apr-June & Sept-Oct £6.00 per pupil, July £7.00, Teachers 1 FREE per 10 pupils, group rates apply to extra adults. Student groups 12+ aged 17-21 Apr-June & Sept-Oct £7.00 per student, July £8.00, Lecturers 1 FREE per 10 students. School & Student group prices apply Mon-Fri during Term Time only. Standard group rates apply at weekends

Waterworld
Festival Park Stoke-on-Trent Staffordshire ST1 5PU
[on the Festival Park Site at Etruria. 5mins from M6 J15 & 16]
Tel: 01782 283838 24hr Fax: 01782 201815
Waterworld is home to the UK's first indoor roller coaster, Nucleus a 375 foot water roller coaster in which you can jet around in special rafts for a thrilling ride, dare you ride it? Waterworld also houses a further 17 water attractions which thrill and entertain everyone in a safe, constantly maintained 86 degrees tropical envirnoment.
All year daily
A£4.50 C(under 5)£0.50 C(under 15)£3.75 OAPs&Students£3.50. Spectators: A£1.00 C£0.50

Animal Attractions

Baylham House Rare Breeds Farm
Mill Lane Baylham Suffolk IP6 8LG
[off B113]
Tel: 01473 830264 Fax: 01473 830264
On the site of Combretovium Roman settlement. Breeding groups of rare cattle, pigs, sheep, goats and poultry. Children's paddock with animals to feed. Picnic area. Riverside Walk. Visitor's Centre with shop, refreshments and Roman remains.
visitor comments: Excellent for young children, very friendly.
Easter-end Sept Tue-Sun & Bank Hol Mon 11.00-17.00. Other times by arrangement
Last Admission: 17.00
A£2.75

Easton Farm Park
Pound Corner Easton Woodbridge Suffolk IP13

0EQ
[signposted of the A12 at Wickham Market Framlingham turn off]
Tel: 01728 746475 Fax: 01728 747861
Victorian model farm setting situated in the picturesque Deben River Valley. Numerous breeds of farm animals, some of which are rare, to be seen here. A purpose built dairy centre allows visitors to watch cows being milked and in contrast, an original Victorian Dairy that houses a collection of dairy bygones. Something for everyone.
visitor comments: Very interesting, with variety of rare animals. Good value for money. Some surfaces difficult for pushchairs and wheelchairs.
22 Mar-30 Sept Tue-Sun & Bank Hol & Mon in July & Aug 10.30-18.00
Last Admission: 16.30
A£4.10 C(3-16)£2.60 OAPs£3.60

Pets Corner
Nicholas Everitt Park Oulton Broad Lowestoft Suffolk NR33 9JU
Tel: 01502 563533
Lots of children's favourites. Pot bellied pigs, snakes, rabbits, monkeys, turkeys, geese, ducks, exotic birds, goats, sheep, pygmy goats. Buy food and enjoy feeding some of the animals. Free bouncy castle.
visitor comments: No toilets, go before you visit! My husband was "mugged" by a pygmy goat! A lovely day.
All year daily 10.00-17.00
A£1.60 C(0-2)£Free C(2+)£1.10

Rede Hall Farm Park
Rede Bury St Edmunds Suffolk IP29 4UG
[6m from Bury St Edmunds on A143 (do NOT go to Rede village). Towards Haverhill. Plenty of parking on site]
Tel: 01284 850695 Fax: 01284 850345
Rede Hall is a working farm based on the agricultural life and practice of the 1930-1950 period. It includes working Suffolk and Shire horses being trained to farm work and forestry. Rare and minority East Anglian breeds can also be seen. The use of old farm implements, the growing of crops and the husbandry of livestock are employed in the traditional way. Coach and school groups are welcome. A full range of educational activities are being developed giving invaluable source material for topics within the National Curriculum. Feed the animals, picnic/ play area and small museum.
1 Apr-30 Sept daily 10.00-17.00
Last Admission: 16.00
A£4.00 C£2.50 OAPs£2.50

↓special events

► **Lamb and Spring Working**
23/4/00-23/4/00
Spring lambs and old farm machinery preparing for crops. Free cart rides

► **Heavy Horse and Vintage Tractor Day**
30/4/00-30/4/00
Demonstrations from tractors and horses. Feed the animals and enjoy a cart ride

► **Sheep Shearing Day**
28/5/00-28/5/00

► **Heavy Horse Extravaganza**
11/6/00-11/6/00
Suffolk, Shire and Percheron horses at work and play

► **Harvest Day**
30/7/00-30/7/00
Harvesting with the old fashioned binder and vintage Massey Harris 726 combine (weather permitting)

► **Children's Countryside Day**
27/8/00-27/8/00
Feed the animals and have free cart and pony rides

► **Threshing and Working Day**
17/9/00-17/9/00
Threshing the corn the old fashioned way with a threshing drum.

► **Vintage Plough Sunday**
8/10/00-8/10/00
Heavy horses and vintage tractors preparing for the new crops

Archaeology

West Stow Anglo Saxon Village
West Stow Country Park Icklingham Road West Stow Bury St Edmunds Suffolk IP28 6HG
[off A1101]
Tel: 01284 728718 Fax: 01284 728277
The village is a reconstruction of a pagan Anglo-Saxon settlement dated 420-650 AD. Seven buildings have been reconstructed on the site of the excavated settlement, using the same techniques, tools and building material used in the original village. Early Anglo-Saxon Centre housing the finds from the site and Café opening 21st July 1999.
All year daily 10.00-16.00. Closed Christmas
Last Admission: 16.00
A£4.50 Concessions£3.50 Family Ticket £13.00. Events A£5.00 Concessions£4.00 Family Ticket £15.00
discount offer: Two For The Price Of One. Does Not Apply To Family Ticket

Costume & Jewellery Museums

Manor House Museum
Honey Hill Bury St Edmunds Suffolk IP33 1HF
[close to A14]
Tel: 01284 757076/757072 Fax: 01284 757079
www.stedmundsbury.gov.uk/manorhse.htm
This Georgian building specialises in costume, horology and fine and decorative art. It has an extensive collection of costumes from the Victorian period to the present day and stunning collections of longcase clocks and watches. Also a 'Friendly Ghost.'
All year Tue-Sun 10.00-17.00. Closed Mon except Bank Hol, also closed Good Fri & 25-26 Dec. Closed Jan 2000
Last Admission: 16.30
A£3.00 C&Concessions£2.00 Family Ticket £9.00
discount offer: Two For The Price Of One

Folk & Local History Museums

Moyse's Hall Museum
Cornhill Bury St Edmunds Suffolk IP33 1DX
[A14]
Tel: 01284 757488 Fax: 01284 757079
www.stedmundsbury.gov.uk
This rare 12th century house of flint and stone is now a museum of Suffolk history, archaeology and natural history. Collection includes the famous William Corder "Murder in the Red Barn" relics. Two temporary exhibition galleries ensure there is always something new to view. Events, workshops and themed days all year round.
All year Mon-Sat 10.00-17.00, Sun 14.00-17.00. Closed 25-26 Dec & Good Fri
Last Admission: 17.00
A£1.70 Concessions£1.10 Family Ticket £5.20. Group rates A£1.50 Concessions£0.95
discount offer: Two For The Price Of One

National Horseracing Museum
99 High Street Newmarket Suffolk CB8 8JL
[centre of Newmarket off A14]
Tel: 01638 667333/560622 Fax: 01638 665600
Special Millennium Exhibition: The Essential Horse - the horse in agriculture, sport, art & literature, entertainment, transport and war. Five galleries of loans from major museums and private collections.
Museum: 18 Apr-31 Oct Tue-Sun 10.00-17.00. Also open Bank Hol & Mon in July & Aug. Stud & Yard Minibus Tours: Apr-end Oct. Depart: 09.25. Café & Shop: Nov-2 Mar Mon-Sat. Apr-Oct daily
Last Admission: 16.30
Museum: A£3.50 C£1.50 OAPs£2.50, Tours: A£15.00 C&OAPs£12.50. Groups 10% discount
discount offer: 10% Discount On Admissions And Tours

↓*special events*

▶ **An Afternoon with Neil Cawthorne**
30/6/00-30/6/00
Meet the artist at Newmarket races as he demonstrates how he structures a painting from the beginning.

▶ **Neil Cawthorne**
21/7/00-21/7/00
A follow-up with Neil on the progress of his painting, 11.00-15.00, £15.00

▶ **Art Class**
16/8/00-16/8/00
A class with Neil Cawthorne from 10.00-15.00, bring your own work. Tickets £15.00

Guided Tours

Newmarket Equine Tours
99 High Street Newmarket Suffolk CB8 8JL
[centre of Newmarket off A14]
Tel: 01638 560622 Fax: 01638 665600
Minibus tours of historic Newmarket, visiting people and places that you would never find on your own. Our tour guides are steeped in racing, and will introduce you to stable staff and their horses. View the equine swimming pool and the majestic sight of horses working out on the gallops and entry to the Museum. Telephone for details of our special tours - an introduction to the races (including entry to the Members' Enclosure), bloodstock (including Tattersalls famous sales), and afternoon tours visiting the British Racing School.
Stud & Yard Minibus Tours: 11 Apr-end Oct Mon Sat when the museum is open. Depart 09.25. Booking is strongly advised as numbers are limited. Cafe & Shop: 1 Jan - 2 Mar Mon-Sat, Apr-Oct daily
Museum: A£3.50 C£1.50 OAPs£2.50. Town tour A£15.00, C&OAPs£12.50 includes entry to the National Horseracing Museum. Booking Agent for National Stud
discount offer: 10% Discount Off Tour Prices. Valid Until 31 Oct 2000

Historical

Framlingham Castle
Castle Street Framlingham Woodbridge Suffolk IP8 9BP
[in Framlingham on B1116]
Tel: 01728 724189
Built between 1177 and 1215, the castle has full height curtain walls, 13 towers and an array of Tudor chimneys. Queen Mary was told here that she was Queen of England and Mary I awaited for news of whether she was to be queen. At different times the castle has been a fortress, an Elizabethan prison, a poor house and a school.
All year 1 Apr-30 Sept daily 10.00-18.00 (17.00 in Oct). 1 Nov-31 Mar daily 10.00-16.00. Closed 24-26 Dec & 1 Jan
A£3.10 C£1.60 Concessions£2.30

↓*special events*

► **Traditional Song**
23/4/00-24/4/00
A performance of delightful unaccompanied song

► **The Norman Army**
30/4/00-1/5/00
Mounted knights and men-at-arms demonstrate the ruthless efficiency of the Norman army

► **The Bard and the Blade**
8/7/00-9/7/00
Shakespearean dialogue and dramatic duels with sword and dagger

► **Nosher The Pig and The Black-hearted Baron**
9/9/00-10/9/00
At 12.30 & 15.00. A fantastic tale of a besieged town and crazy puppet characters

► **A Medieval Christmas**
2/12/00-3/12/00

► **Seasonal Period Dance**
10/12/00-10/12/00
Relive the dance scenes from "Pride and Prejudice" and "Wives and Daughters"

Ickworth House Park and Gardens
The Rotunda Ickworth Bury St Edmunds Suffolk IP29 5QE
[2.5m S of Bury St Edmunds]
Tel: 01284 735270 Fax: 01284 735175
Much to interest visitors with a wonderful collection of paintings including works by Titian, Gainsborough and Velasquez. Set in magnificent Italianate garden and parklands created by Capability Brown with many rare species of plants and trees. Deer enclosure, waymarked walks and an adventure playground. New for 1999: 'House Opening' and 'Putting to Bed' tours; vineyard open days; family and special needs activity trail and exploration packs; handling collection and replica costumes for children. Dogs on leads and only in park.
visitor comments: Breathtakingly beautiful house. Good adventure play area. Lovely woodland and country walks.
House & Garden: 20 Mar-31 Oct Tue, Wed, Fri , Sat, Sun, Bank Hol Mon & Good Fri 13.00-17.00. Gardens only: 1 Nov-end Mar 2000 Mon-Fri 10.00-16.00; . Park: daily 07.00-19.00. Garden & Park closed 25 Dec. Shop: same as house 12.00-17.00, Nov-19 Dec 11.00-16.00
House, Park & Garden: A£5.20 C&Concessions£2.20. Park & Garden only: A£2.20 C£0.70. Pre-booked groups A£4.20 C£1.70, no group rates Sun & Bank Hol Mon

Kentwell Hall
Long Melford Sudbury Suffolk CO10 9BA
[off A134 between Sudbury / Bury St Edmunds]
Tel: 01787 310207 Fax: 01787 379318
www.kentwell.co.uk
Kentwell Hall is a mellow red-brick Tudor Mansion House, surrounded by a broad, fish filled moat, extensive gardens, woodland walks and Rare Breeds farm. The house and grounds are open to the public at various times throughout the year. Re-creations of Tudor domestic life take place each Bank Holiday weekend and 1940s events on other selected weekends. Member of the Historic Houses Association.
Mid Mar-end Oct Sun 12.00-17.00. 12 July-24 Sept daily 12.00-17.00.
Last Admission: 16.30
A£5.50 C(5-15)£3.30 Concessions£4.75, Special charges for Re-creation events, call for details
discount offer: One Child Free With Two Or More Full Paying Adults. Valid Until 31 Oct 2000

↓*special events*

► **Land Girls on the Farm**
8/4/00-9/4/00
The Women's Land Army are portrayed working on a wartime farm. 11.00-18.00, A£6.70 C£4.55 OAPs£5.75

► **Recreation of Tudor Life at Eastertide**

21/4/00-24/4/00
Life at Kentwell in 1521. 11.00-18.00, A£6.50 C£4.40 OAPs£5.60

▶ **Tudor Hirelings Week**
25/4/00-28/4/00
Tudor crafts, cookery and other hands-on activities for children to have a go. Open 11.00-18.00, A£6.70 C£4.55 and OAPs£5.75

▶ **Recreation of Tudor Life at May Day**
29/4/00-1/5/00
May Day celebrations,11.00-18.00, A£7.95 C£5.35 OAPs£6.90. Pre-booked group discounts available

▶ **Recreation of Tudor Life at Whitsuntide**
27/5/00-29/5/00
Life at Kentwell in the 16th century,11.00-18.00, A£7.95 C£5.35 OAPs£6.90. Pre-booked group discounts available

▶ **Great Annual Recreation of Tudor Life**
18/6/00-9/7/00
Life at Kentwell in the year 1578. Each weekend and Fri 7 July, 11.00-17.00, A£11.60 C£8.25 OAPs£9.95

▶ **Recreation of Tudor Life at Michaelmas**
23/9/00-24/9/00
Life at Kentwell in the year 1578, 11.00-17.00, A£7.95 C£5.35 OAPs£6.90

▶ **World War II Recreation**
14/10/00-15/10/00
Life at Kentwell during WWII, 11.00-17.00, A£7.95 C£5.35 OAPs£6.90

Orford Castle
Castle Terrace Orford Woodbridge Suffolk IP12 2ND
[in Orford on B1084, 20m NE of Ipswich]
Tel: 01394 450472
www.english-heritage.org.uk
Built by Henry II circa 1165 as a Royal castle and coastal defence in the twelfth century. A magnificent keep survives almost intact with three immense towers reaching to 30 metres (90 feet).
1 Apr-31 Oct daily 10.00-18.00, Oct 10.00-17.00. 1 Nov-31 Mar Wed-Sun 10.00-16.00. Closed 24-26 Dec. Closed 13.00-14.00 in winter A£2.50 C£1.30 Concessions£1.90

↓*special events*

▶ **Illustration and Calligraphy**
22/7/00-23/7/00
Create a page of manuscript using a real quill pen

▶ **Puppet Making Workshops**
29/7/00-30/7/00
The opportunity for younger visitors to make a puppet and take part in a puppet show

▶ **Medieval Music**
5/8/00-6/8/00
Enjoy melodies and dance tunes dating back to the 12th century

▶ **Carry On Piping!**
12/8/00-13/8/00
Lively, humorous, have-a-go family show with 16th century rock 'n' roll!

▶ **Stories & Mask-making**
19/8/00-20/8/00
See entry for 15 July

▶ **Recruiting for Wellington**
27/8/00-28/8/00
Meet Regency soldiers and civilians and learn about life in Wellington's army

▶ **Medieval Entertainers**
21/10/00-22/10/00
Authentic medieval games, cures, folklore and early machinery, plus a children's play about the formative years of Parliament

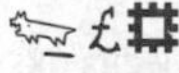

Museum- Textiles

Manor House Museum
Honey Hill Bury St Edmunds Suffolk IP33 1HF
[close to A14]
Tel: 01284 757076/757072 Fax: 01284 757079
www.stedmundsbury.gov.uk/manorhse.htm
This Georgian building specialises in costume, horology and fine and decorative art. It has an extensive collection of costumes from the Victorian period to the present day and stunning collections of longcase clocks and watches. Also a 'Friendly Ghost.'
All year Tue-Sun 10.00-17.00. Closed Mon except Bank Hol, also closed Good Fri & 25-26 Dec. Closed Jan 2000
Last Admission: 16.30
A£3.00 C&Concessions£2.00 Family Ticket £9.00
discount offer: Two For The Price Of One

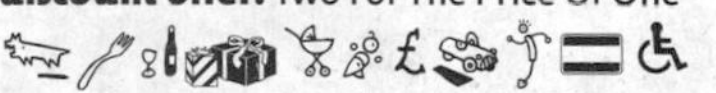

Sport & Recreation

Discoverig
East Point Pavilion Royal Plain Lowestoft Suffolk NR33 0AP
[in Lowestoft seafront off Marine Parade in the East Point Pavilion Visitor Centre]
Tel: 01502 523000
Themed on a North Sea Gas Exploration Rig, this brightly coloured multi-level Play Platform offers unlimited scope for fun and games in a safe and exhilarating play environment. Discoverig is designed for children and includes Ropes, Scramble Nets, Tubes, Ball Pond, Giant Slide and lots more. Its a great place for children to let off steam for an hour

or so, and will give Mum and Dad or Granny and Grandad a welcome break! Our team of trained and enthusiastic Rig Crew patrols all levels of the platform to ensure that a high level of safety and enjoyment is experienced by all the children. We also offer a special Birthday Party package which includes a Birthday meal and "goody bags" for the children, but we recommend that you book these parties early.

visitor comments: Nice seating for parents to sit a watch from! Some items a little scary. More for the 3+ age group.

All year daily

C(0-3)£1.70 per hour C(3+)£2.20 per hour

The National Stud

The National Stud Newmarket Suffolk CB8 0XE

Tel: 01638 666789 Fax: 01638 665173

Guided tour by appointment only of high class stud with racing superstars of the past and future. Breeding mares and foals.

visitor comments: A must for horse lovers, excellent value for money.

Mar-Sept: Mon-Sat 11.15 & 14.30, Sun 14.30 only

A£4.00 C&Concessions£3.00 Family Ticket £12.00. Group rates & School Parties 10% reduction

Sporting History Museums

National Horseracing Museum and Tours

99 High Street Newmarket Suffolk CB8 8JL

[centre of Newmarket off A14]

Tel: 01638 667333/560622 Fax: 01638 665600

Special Millennium Exhibition: The Essential Horse - the horse in agriculture, sport, art & literature, entertainment, transport and war. Five galleries of loans from major museums and private collections. Then ask our staff of retired jockeys and trainers about racing today - why do horses have passports? How dangerous is horse racing? How do horses and jockeys prepare for the races? Is it easy to be a racing commentator? Let our staff teach you how to tack up a model horse before you dress in silks and ride our horse simulator - racing at the equivalent of 35 miles per hour. Or join minibus tour to meet the stable and stud staff with their horses - see our entry under Guided Tours. Groups can be accommodated during the closed season, depending on gallery redisplay plans. The Practical Gallery may be booked for private parties at any time of the year. Hold a birthday party at the Museum and entertain your children's friends in the Museum's Practical Gallery under the watchful eye of retired jockeys and trainers. They can dress up in jockey silks, ride the horse simulator and learn how to tack-up and bandage horses legs. Award for The Best Visitor Attraction in The East of England under 100 000 visitors in 1999.

visitor comments: Horse simulator definitely worth the experience. Very informative and helpful curators

Museum: 18 Apr-31 Oct Tue-Sun 10.00-17.00. Also open Bank Hol & Mon in July & Aug. Stud & Yard Minibus Tours: Apr-end Oct. Depart: 09.25. Café & Shop: Nov-2 Mar Mon-Sat. Apr-Oct daily

Last Admission: 16.30

Museum: A£3.50 C£1.50 OAPs£2.50, Tours: A£15.00 C&OAPs£12.50. Groups 10% discount

discount offer: 10% Discount On Admissions And Tours

↓*special events*

▶ **Daily Newmarket Tours**

11/4/00-29/10/00

See horses training on the gallops, the horses' swimming pool and a training yard as well as a town tour. Tours are conducted by expert staff. A£15.00 Concessions£12.50.

▶ **Luca Cumani Tour**

13/6/00-13/6/00

Visit Luca Cumani's large public stable, one of the largest in Newmarket, with a 'Who's Who' of owners and a fascinating history. Departs 09.20, tickets £15.00

▶ **Behind the Scenes at Huntingdon Racecourse**

6/10/00-6/10/00

Minibus tour which combines a behind the scenes tour with a great days racing. Departs 09.30, tickets £25.00 including Members Enclosure badge

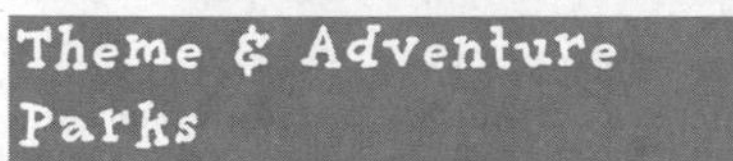

Theme & Adventure Parks

Pleasurewood Hills Leisure Park
Leisure Way Corton Lowestoft Suffolk NR32 5DZ
[off A12 at Lowestoft. Plenty of on site parking available]
Tel: 01502 586000 Fax: 01502 567393
Pleasurewood Hills is an action packed day out with new thrill rides and family shows, as well as Woody's Little Big Park specially for the under 9's. There are over 40 rides to choose from including the Cannonball Express Rollercoaster providing thrills as you thunder around tight corners, through tunnels and along bottomless mine shafts. Make sure you grip tight as you ride through the raging waters of the Tidal Wave and Log Flume. The Horror Dome, Rattlesnake, Pirate Ship and much, much more, come back and see the changes. A range of shops and games and a wide choice fo food menus including a fully licensed bar, will complete your day. East Anglia's No. 1 Attraction.
visitor comments: Really good day out for the family. Lots of things to do. Excellent 'show' in the Castle.
Easter-31 Oct from 10.00
£11.95 (over 1m in height) Admission Free (under 1m in height)
discount offer: £2.00 Discount Off Standard Admission. Valid Until 31 Oct 2000

Wildlife & Safari Parks

Suffolk Wildlife Park - The African Adventure
Whites Lane Kessingland Lowestoft Suffolk NR33 7SL
[situated on the A12 near Lowestoft, just 20mins S of Great Yarmouth]
Tel: 01502 740291 Fax: 01502 741104
There is much to see here, African lions, cheetahs, giraffes, chimpanzees, sitatunga, bontebok, Arabian oryx, zebra, giant Poitou donkeys, striped hyenas and colonies of lemur at liberty amongst the trees on their new Islands. The only aardvarks in the country, porcupines in their new purpose built house, and bats in the new Bat House. There is a Free safari road train, explorer trails, crazy golf, bouncy castle and children's play area. Bird of Prey flying displays throughout the day on Tuesdays and Wednesdays (weather permitting) from mid July to 1st week in September.
All year daily from 10.00, Jan-end Mar closes 16.00, end Mar-end June closes 17.00, July-end Sept closes 17.30, Oct-end Dec closes 16.00. Closed 25 & 26 Dec
Last Admission: 16.00
A£6.80 C£4.50 C(under 3)£Free. Prices subject to seasonal variation.
discount offer: One Child Free When Accompanied By Two Full Paying Adults. Not To Be Used In Conjunction With Any Other Offer

Animal Attractions

Godstone Farm
Tilburstow Hill Road Godstone Surrey RH9 8LX
[J6 M25, follow signs to Godstone Village]
Tel: 01883 742546 Fax: 01883 740380
The most popular children's farm in the south east. The animals are very friendly and children are encouraged to stroke and cuddle the smaller ones. The play areas are enormous and great fun. There is also a large indoor play barn, making it worthwhile for a winter visit.

The views are superb and the tea cakes legendary!

visitor comments: A large number of animals, hands-on experience. Well worth paying 50p for the large indoor play area with tea shop and picnic area close by. Educational and good value.

Daily Summer 10.00-18.00, Winter 10.00-17.00
Last Admission: 1 hour before closing
£3.80 per person aged 2+. One adult free with each paying child. OAPs£2.80

Horton Park Children's Farm
Horton Lane Epsom Surrey KT19 8PT
[J9 M25 between Epsom and Chessington]
Tel: 01372 743984 Fax: 01372 749069
Friendly and informal, ideal for 2-8 year olds. Staff encourage children to pet and enjoy the animals. The adventure playgrounds are expanding each year with specially designed mazes. Food is simple, but good and excellent value for money.
Summer daily 10.00-18.00, Winter 10.00-17.00
A£3.65 C£3.65 OAPs£2.65 One Adult Free With Each Paying Child

Birds, Butterflies & Bees

Birdworld and Underwater World
Holt Pound Farnham Road Holt Pound Farnham Surrey GU10 4LD
[3m S on A325]
Tel: 01420 22140 Fax: 01420 23715
28 acres of garden and parkland are home to a wide variety of birds including many rare and unusual species. Rare baby birds can be seen at the Incubation Research Station during breeding times. Shop and café, special penguin feeding times and animal handling sessions.

visitor comments: Excellent value. Brilliant entertainment for under 5's. Very easy access for prams. Extremely friendly staff.

5 Jan-11 Feb weekends only, 12 Feb-ealy Nov daily, early Nov-early Dec weekends only, early Dec-24 Dec daily. Summer 09.30-18.00, Winter 09.30-16.40
Last Admission: Summer 17.00 Winter 15.30
A£7.95 C(3-14)£4.75 Family Ticket (A2+C2)£22.95 Extra C£4.25 Concessions£6.50

↓*special events*

▶ **Craft Fair**
20/5/00-21/5/00

▶ **Old Macdonald's Farm Fun Day**
1/6/00-1/6/00
Rustic fun and games for the whole family

▶ **Treasure Island Fun Day**
17/8/00-17/8/00
Yo-ho-ho and a big bottle of fun on this great day out with a swashbuckling pirate theme!

▶ **Mad Hatters Party**
31/8/00-31/8/00
Alice and her friends will all be there to greet you at this mad fun day out

▶ **Santa Specials**
30/11/00-24/12/00
A magical train ride for children to Santa's Grotto to meet Santa

Country Parks & Estates

Box Hill - The Old Fort
Box Hill Road Box Hill Tadworth Surrey KT20 7LB
[1m N of Dorking, 2.5m S of Leatherhead on A24. Bus: London & Country 516. BR: Boxhill & Westhumble 0.5m]
Tel: 01306 885502 Fax: 01306 875030
On the edge of the North Downs rising some 130 metres above the River Mole this Country Park consists of acres of woods and chalk downland, with magnificent views to the South Downs. Dogs under strict control.
All year any reasonable time
Admission Free

↓*special events*

▶ **Pre-Spring Walk**
19/3/00-19/3/00
Meet in the main car park (TQ179514) for this 2-mile walk, £1.00, 10.30-12.00

▶ **Easter Egg Trail**
23/4/00-24/4/00
Follow a trail, answer clues and win a prize, £1.50, 11.00-15.00

▶ **Children's Activity Afternoon**
8/8/00-22/8/00
Environmental games and activities with the Wardens on Box Hill. Tickets in advance from the North Downs Office. Telephone 01306 742809 for information, C£2.50 incl refreshments, 14.00-16.00 on 8, 15 and 22 Aug

▶ **Plants: Poison or Medicines?**
16/9/00-16/9/00
Meet in the main car park (TQ179514) for this 2-mile walk, £1.00, 14.00-16.00

▶ **Woodland Discovery Day**
25/10/00-25/10/00
Create and explore in a superb natural setting. Suitable for all over 5 years old! Tickets in advance from North Downs office. Telephone 01306 742809 for information, A£2.00 C£4.00, 10.00-16.00

Gardens & Horticulture

Claremont Landscape Garden

Portsmouth Road Esher Surrey KT10 9JG
[S edge of Esher, E side of A307. BR: Esher 2m, Hersham 2m, Claygate 2m]
Tel: 01372 467806 Fax: 01372 464394
One of the earliest surviving English landscape gardens, restored to its former glory. Features include a lake, island with pavilion, grotto and turf amphitheatre. Dogs on leads Nov to Mar and not admitted Apr to Oct. Coach parties by arrangement only.
All year, Jan-end Mar Tue-Sun 10.00-17.00 or sunset if sooner. Apr-end Oct Mon-Fri 10.00-18.00, Sat Sun & Bank Hol Mon 10.00-19.00. Nov-end Mar Tue-Sun 10.00-17.00 or sunset if sooner. Closed 25 Dec
Last Admission: 30mins before closing
A£3.20 C£1.60 Family Ticket £8.00. £0.50 discount if arriving on public transport please present valid ticket. Guided Tours 15+ £1.00 extra. All coach parties must book

↓*special events*

▶ **Walk Through the History and Beauty of Claremont**
1/4/00-30/4/00
Guided tours on the 1, 12, 15 & 30 April, looking at the history and beauty of Claremont. Meet at entrance kiosk. Sorry, no dogs, A£1.00 C£0.50p plus usual admission, 14.00-15.30

▶ **Easter Egg Trail**
22/4/00-22/4/00
Fun for the family, C£1.50 plus usual admission, 11.00-16.00

▶ **Walk Through the History and Beauty of Claremont**
6/5/00-28/5/00
See entry for 1 April except tours are on the 6, 10, 20, 27 & 28 May

▶ **Spring Plant Fair**
14/5/00-14/5/00
Volunteer-grown plants, garden bric-a-brac, etc., all for sale, 11.00-16.00

▶ **Walk Through the History and Beauty of Claremont**
3/6/00-30/7/00
See entry for 1 April except tours on 3, 14, 17, 24 & 25 June, 1, 19, 22, 29 & 30 July

▶ **Claremont Carnival & Millennium Fete**
13/7/00-16/7/00
A spectacular open air, fancy dress extravaganza, offering non-stop entertainment culminating in a fantastic fireworks finale over the lake. Prizes for the best themed fancy dress. Thur A£17.00 C£10.00, Fri A£20.00 C£14.00, Sat A£22.00, Sun A£18.00 (No child prices Sat & Sun). 10% discountfor groups 15+ on Thur & Fri, 19.00-23.00

▶ **Treasure Hunts**
31/7/00-4/8/00
Call 01372 467806 for full details

▶ **Walk Through the History and Beauty of Claremont**
5/8/00-29/10/00
See entry for 1 April except tours on the 5, 9, 19, 26 & 27 Aug, 2, 13, 16, 23 & 24 Sept, 7, 11, 21 & 29 Oct

RHS Garden Wisley

RHS Garden Wisley Woking Surrey GU23 6QB
[J10 M25 on A3, London 22m, Guildford 7m. Plenty of on site parking available.]
Tel: 01483 224234 Fax: 01483 211750
www.rhs.org.uk
Voted Visitor Attractions of the Year 1999 in the English Tourism Council's England for Excellence Awards, Wisely demonstrates British gardening at it's best in all aspects. Covering over 240 acres, highlights include the Alpine Meadow carpeted with daffodils in Spring, Battleston Hill, brilliant with rhododendrons in early Summer, the heathers and Autumnal tints. New for this year is the Daily Telegraph 'Reflective Garden,' winner of Best Garden Award and Gold Medal at the 1999 Chelsea Flower Show. For the following walks and demonstrations, tickets are £5.00 for Members and £10.00 for non-members. Send a cheque made payable to RHS, enclosing a SAE and daytime telephone number to the Administration Dept., RHS Garden, Wisley, Woking, GU23 6QB.
Garden: Mon-Fri 10.00-18.00 or sunset if sooner, Sat-Sun 09.00-18.00 or sunset if sooner. RHS Members only on Sun
A£5.00 C(0-6)£Free C(6-16)£2.00. Groups 10+ £4.00 if booked 21 days in advance
discount offer: Two For The Price Of One. Valid Oct 2000-Mar 2001, Mon-Sat only

↓*special events*

▶ **Rose Pruning**
1/3/00-5/3/00
Demonstrations on Mar 1 at 14.00 and Mar 5 at 10.30

▶ **Two-day Botanical Art Courses with Niki Simpson**
29/3/00-21/11/00
Workshops at beginners/intermediate level held on Mar 29-30 and Nov 20-21 at 10.00-16.30. Call for details

▶ **Alpine Specialist Day**
5/4/00-5/4/00
From 10.00-16.00. Please call for further information

▶ **Photographic Workshop Weekends**
8/4/00-26/11/00
Workshops for beginners on Apr 8-9, Nov 25-26 and for intermediates on Sept 16-17. Please call for details

▶ **The Rock Garden, Alpine Meadow and Alpine House**
9/4/00-12/4/00
A walk at 10.30 on Apr 9 and 12 only

▶ **Drought-Resistant Plants**
9/8/00-9/8/00
Walk to be held at 10.30

▶ **Sculpture Trail**
1/9/00-27/9/00
The garden trail will feature work created from a range of materials and covering a diversity of subject matter

▶ **Soil Management for Gardeners**
25/10/00-25/10/00
Demonstration commencing at 14.00

Loseley Park
Estate Offices Loseley Park Guildford Surrey GU3 1HS
[leave A3 at Compton on B3000 signposted. BR: Guildford 2m. Bus: 1.25m. Plenty of parking on site]
Tel: 01483 304440 Fax: 01483 302036
Loseley Park has been the home of the More-Molyneux family for over 400 years. The Elizabethan Mansion is set amid 1,400 acres of glorious parkland and rolling pastures grazed by the famous Jersey herd. Built in 1562 by an ancestor of the present owner, the House features many fine works of art, including paintings, tapestries and panelling from Henry VIII's Nonsuch Palace. The Walled Garden has been carefully restored over the past six years and includes an award winning rose garden, as well as herb, flower, vegetable and fountain gardens, and an idyllic moat walk. Member of the Historic Houses Association.
Garden, Gift Shop & Courtyard Tea Room: beginning May-end Sept Wed-Sat & Bank Hol. Sun in June, July & Aug 11.00-17.00. House: end May-end Aug Wed-Sun & Bank Hol 14.00-17.00. At other times by arrangement.
Last Admission: Last Tour: 16.30
House & Gardens: A£5.00 C£3.00 Concessions£4.00. Gardens only:A£2.50 C£1.50 Concessions£2.00. Discounted Group rates available

↓*special events*

▶ **Home Design Exhibition**
25/2/00-27/2/00
Ideas for the Home and Garden

▶ **Surrey Advertiser Motor Show**
6/5/00-7/5/00
Stands displaying and selling new cars and hands-on 4x4

▶ **Craft Fair**
25/5/00-28/5/00
Stalls selling and demonstrating Arts and Crafts

▶ **Open Air Opera**
23/6/00-23/6/00

▶ **WI Flower Show**
27/6/00-28/6/00
Stalls selling W1 produce and a display of flower arrangements

▶ **Great Gardening Show**
21/7/00-23/7/00
Show gardens, demonstrations, plants and garden accessories for sale

▶ **Open Air Concert and Fireworks**
13/8/00-13/8/00
Classical music and magnificent fireworks, call for further details and how to book

Historical

Hatchlands Park
East Clandon Guildford Surrey GU4 7RT
[E of E Clandon, N of A246 Guildford to Leatherhead Road, 5m E of Guildford. Plenty of on site parking available]
Tel: 01483 222482 Fax: 01483 223176
A handsome House built in 1758 by Stiff Leadbetter for Admiral Boscawen, and set in a beautiful Repton park offering a variety of park and woodland walks. Hatchlands contains splendid interiors by Robert Adam. It

houses the Cobbe collection, the world's largest group of early keyboard instruments associated with famous composers e.g. Purcell, JC Bach, Chopin, Mahler and Elgar. Audio Guide. There is a small garden by Gertrude Jekyll (flowering late May to early June). Licenced restaurant, for lunches and teas open same days as house (booking advisable tel: 01483 211120). Wheelchair access to show rooms, restaurant, shop and part of the garden.

House & Grounds: 2 Apr-31 Oct Tue, Wed, Thur, Sun. Also Fri in Aug & Bank Hol Mon 14.00-17.30. Park walks: Apr-Oct daily 11.30-18.00
Last Admission: 30mins before closing
House & Grounds: A£4.40 C(5-18)£2.20. Family Ticket £11.00. Combined Ticket with Clandon Park £6.40. Park Walks & Garden only: A£1.80 C£0.90. Special group rate weekdays only: £3.60

↓*special events*

► **Hatchlands Hat Trick - #1 Rhythm and Blues Night**
7/7/00-7/7/00
The Blues Band plus local support band 'The Skidmarks'. Bring a picnic and enjoy this open air concert. Tickets from Southern Region Box Office on 01372 451596, £12.50, 18.30 for 19.30. Hat Trick savings: Book for 2 or 3 productions at reduced rates: 2 = £22.50, 3 = £34.00

Loseley Park

Estate Offices Loseley Park Guildford Surrey GU3 1HS
[leave A3 at Compton on B3000 signposted. BR: Guildford 2m. Bus: 1.25m. Plenty of parking on site]
Tel: 01483 304440 Fax: 01483 302036

Loseley Park has been the home of the More-Molyneux family for over 400 years. The Elizabethan Mansion is set amid 1,400 acres of glorious parkland and rolling pastures grazed by the famous Jersey herd. Built in 1562 by an ancestor of the present owner, the House features many fine works of art, including paintings, tapestries and panelling from Henry VIII's Nonsuch Palace. The Walled Garden has been carefully restored over the past six years and includes an award winning rose garden, as well as herb, flower, vegetable and fountain gardens, and an idyllic moat walk. Member of the Historic Houses Association.

Garden, Gift Shop & Courtyard Tea Room: beginning May-end Sept Wed-Sat & Bank Hol. Sun in June, July & Aug 11.00-17.00. House: end May-end Aug Wed-Sun & Bank Hol 14.00-17.00. At other times by arrangement.
Last Admission: Last Tour: 16.30
House & Gardens: A£5.00 C£3.00 Concessions£4.00. Gardens only:A£2.50 C£1.50 Concessions£2.00. Discounted Group rates available

↓*special events*

► **Home Design Exhibition**
25/2/00-27/2/00
Ideas for the Home and Garden

► **Great Gardening Show**
21/7/00-23/7/00
Show gardens, demonstrations, plants and garden accessories for sale

► **Open Air Concert and Fireworks**
13/8/00-13/8/00
Classical music and magnificent fireworks, call for further details and how to book

Nature & Conservation Parks

Bockett's Farm Park

Young Street Fetcham Surrey KT22 9BS
[A246 south of Leatherhead]
Tel: 01372 363764 Fax: 01372 361764

Bockett's is a working farm with more than 500 sheep. They also have water buffalo, Llamas and all the usual farm animals. There is a big childrens play area with swings, slides and a straw bale mountain.

visitor comments: Thoroughly recommended for under 5's. Fantastically educational, good weather trip preferable.

All year daily 10.00-18.00 closed 25-27 Dec 31-1 2000
A£3.45 (3-17)C£2.95 OAPs £2.95 2yrs £2.05 under 2 free

Palaces

Hampton Court Palace and Gardens

Hampton Court Palace East Molesey Surrey KT8 9AU
[M25 exit J12 M3 towards central London exit at J1 Sunbury signposts follow for 4m. A308 towards Kingston. From Central London take A4

Surrey

W towards Hammersmith then A316 / M3 then exit at J1 Sunbury as above. Tube: Richmond, then R68 bus. Rail: Hampton Court Station]
Tel: 020 8781 9500 Fax: 020 8781 9669
www.hrp.org.uk
With its 500 years of royal history Hampton Court Palace has something to offer everyone. Set in sixty acres of world famous gardens the palace is a living tapestry of history from Henry VIII to George II. From the elegance of the recently restored Privy Garden to the domestic reality of the Tudor Kitchens, visitors are taken back throughout the centuries to experience the palace as it was when royalty was in residence. Enjoy the splendour of the royal apartments, and look out for the ghost of Catherine Howard in the Haunted Gallery. Costumed guides and audio tours bring the palace to life and provide an insight into how life in the palace would have been in the time of Henry VIII and William III, and free family trails encourage a closer look at the Palace with the chance to win a prize. The Palace also has an exciting programme of holiday and half-term activities to entertain all the family.
Mid Mar-mid Oct Mon 10.15-18.00, Tue-Sun 09.30-18.00. Mid Oct-mid Mar Mon 10.15-16.30, Tue-Sun 09.30-16.30. Gardens: all year daily 07.00-dusk
Last Admission: 60mins before closing (Palace)
A£10.50 C(5-16)£7.00 Family Ticket (A2+C3)£31.40 Concessions£8.00. Season Tickets available

↓special events

▶ **All the King's Creatures**
19/2/00-27/2/00
Discover the creatures of the royal court past and present. Visitors can enjoy beastly family trails and explore the theme of animals and heraldry

▶ **Florimania - The Queen's Flowers**
31/3/00-4/4/00
The scent of flowers is in the air as Queen Mary II's Apartments are adorned with 17th century floral bouquets and arrangements.

▶ **Royal Sport at Hampton Court**
22/4/00-30/4/00
Discover the sports and games enjoyed by the royal residents. Costumed tours and demonstrations

▶ **The Rise and Fall of Catherine Howard**
27/5/00-4/6/00
A week of activities reveals the life of Henry VIII's fifth wife

▶ **Lantern Lit Tours**
20/11/00-20/12/00
Lantern lit tours of Henry VIII's vast kitchens and apartments with tales of rich history and famous inhabitants. Booking essential on 020 8781 9540. Not suitable for young children. Dates to be confirmed

▶ **A Tudor Christmas**
27/12/00-3/1/01
Combine history with festivities and discover the very essence of a Tudor Christmas including entertainment and festive food. Dates to be confirmed

Spectator Sports

Epsom Racecourse
Epsom Downs Epsom Surrey KT18 5LQ
[2m S of Epsom on B290, J8 & J9 M25. BR: Epsom Downs or Tattenham Corner]
Tel: 01372 726311 Fax: 01372 748253
www.demon.co.uk/racenews.epsom
Major races run: The Vodafone Derby; The Vodafone Oaks; Vodafone Diomed S; Vodafone Coronation Cup; Moet & Chandon Silver Magnum
Call for fixture list
Dependent on event

↓special events

▶ **Derby Day**
10/6/00-10/6/00

Theme & Adventure Parks

Chessington World of Adventures
Leatherhead Road Chessington Surrey KT9 2NE
[situated on the A243. Approximately 2m from both the A3 and J9/10 M25. BR: 30mins from Waterloo to Chessington Station on South West trains]
Tel: 01372 727227 Info Line Fax: 01372 725050
www.chessington.co.uk
Chessington World of Adventures, the South's No. 1 theme park and animal experience is filled with fantastic family adventures. Watch out for amazing new crazy cartoon land, opening in April 2000 featuring a world famous cartoon character in a multi-million pound

investment. Also at Chessington the mighty Samurai ride, the swirling Rameses Revenge, plunging Dragon falls and wild encounters with exotic animals, you'll have an unbeatable day out.

visitor comments: All rides are free - you can ride as many times as you want. Good quality gifts. Staff are polite and friendly. Limited rides for very young children, but there's still loads to see and do, making it a great day.

5 April-29 Oct 10.00-17.00. 15 July-3 Sept Extra Happy Hours (open till 21.00). Family Fright Nights (open till 21.00) 21, 22, 27, 28 & 29 Oct

Last Admission: 15.00

Queuing Times: Possible in peak season and weekends

A£19.50 C(under 4)£Free C(4-13)£15.50 OAPs£10.50 Disabled£9.50

Family Ticket £59.00 Group rates available for 12+ for details call: 01372 729560 (prices subject to change)

Thorpe Park

Staines Lane Chertsey Surrey KT16 8PN

[J11 or 13 M25 on A320 between Chertsy / Staines]

Tel: 01932 562633 Fax: 01932 566367

www.thorpepark.co.uk

The Great Thorpe Park offers thrills, excitement and a great day out for all the family. New for 1999 Pirates 4-D: you may have experienced 3-D and you may have been stunned by the visual effects, but for the first time in the UK and only at Thorpe Park you can expereince the 'fourth dimension', an experenice so new, so intense you'll never trust your senses again! Recoil as the edvanture comes alive before your eyes and not only see and hear, but also feel the action. Thorpe Park is also the UK's wettest theme park, you'll get Wet Wet Wet! whatever the weather on the 3 torpedo tubes that twist and turn in all directions before spilling you out into the pool below, or take the plunge on an inflatable raft down a 40ft slide as you Depth Charge. If you want to get wetter still, try white water rafting on Thunder River, or the world famous Loggers Leap, a water flume that's wet, wild, wonderful and the highest in the UK! And don't forget the little ones who have a water ride of their very own, Dino Bumper Boats, where they can get bumper to bumper in motorised rubber tyres in this watery version of dodgems. Of course Thorpe Park still has everything you could need for a perfect day out, whatever your age or shoe size! Adrenaline-seekers can scream in fear as they realise there is X:\ No Way Out - the world's first and only pitch-black backwards rollercoaster - whilst younger 'pink knuckle' riders will enjoy the Flying Fish rollercoaster. Little ones can make friends with the animals on Thorpe Farm, climb aboard one of the rides in Octopus Garden, enjoy the lives shows and music or explore Slides by SLides, a slide and climb playground in a tropical setting. And with the excellent catering facilities on park you need never run out of energy!

visitor comments: Editor's Choice. Great for children of all ages (and adults!). Plenty of space to run around. Beach area with waterslides. An excellent day out!

Feb-Nov daily. Midnight weekend & Bank Holiday opening in August

Queuing Times: varies

A£16.50 C(0.9m)£Free C(1.4m)£13.00 C(1.4m+)£15.95 OAPs&Disabled£13.00 Carers/Helpers£15.95. New this year the Family Ticket (valid for 4 people, minimum 1 adult) for only £52.00. All you have to do is call the credit card hotline on 0990 880 880 before 17.00 on the day prior to your visit. Alternatively buy one on the day for £56.00.

↓*special events*

▶ **Christmas Craft Festival**

10/11/00-12/11/00

Ideal for those unusual Christmas gift ideas. Commences 10.00-18.00. Tickets £1.00-£5.00

Transport Museums

Brooklands Museum

Brooklands Road Weybridge Surrey KT13 7QN

[J10/11 A3 & M25]

Tel: 01932 857381 Fax: 01932 855465

www.motor-software.co.uk

Brooklands racing circuit was the birthplace of British motorsport and of British aviation. From 1907, when it opened to 1987 when the British Aerospace factory closed, it was a world-renowned centre of engineering excellence. The Museum opened in 1991 on 30 acres of the original 1907 motor racing circuit and features Brookland racing cars and vintage aircraft as well as historic buildings. Home to John Cobb's 24 litre Napier-Railton. The Campell Shed in the restored motoring village opens at the end of June with a new display telling the story of Brooklands Track from 1907. 'Percy' is supposed to haunt the Banking by the Members Bridge, he died on Hallowe'en!

All year Tue-Sun, Summer: 10.00-17.00. Winter: 10.00-16.00, closed Good Fri & Christmas week

Last Admission: 16.00

A£6.00 OAPs&Students£5.00 C(5-16)£4.00

discount offer: One Child Free With Each Adult Paying Full Admission

Dapdune Wharf
Wharf Road Guildford Surrey GU1 4RR
[just off A320 in Guildford Town centre behind Surrey Sports Ground]
Tel: 01483 561389 Fax: 01483 561389
The Wey was one of the first British rivers to be made navigable, and opened to barge traffic in 1653. This 15.5 mile waterway linked Guildford to Weybridge on the Thames, and thence to London. The Godalming Navigation, opened in 1764, enabled barges to work a further 4 mile up river. Dapdune Wharf in Guildford is the home of Reliance, a restored Wey barge, as well as models and an interactive exhibition telling the story of the waterway, the people who lived and worked on it, and the barges built there. New for 1998 is a tea room and ice-creams normally available at Dapdune Wharf and electric launch river bus service - from Dapdune Wharf to Guildford, operating during opening hours; additional charge (including NT members).
1 Apr-1 Nov Wed 12.00-17.00, Weekends & Bank Hol 11.00-17.00. Pre-booked groups and school parties welcome throughout the year.
A£2.50 Family Ticket £6.00. Pre-booked groups £1.50

↓*special events*

▶ **Working Waterways Week**
15/4/00-16/4/00
A weekend of guided walks along the towpath, with demonstrations, displays and boat trips to mark the start of Woking Waterways Week. Call for details. Donations welcome

▶ **Easter Egg Hunts**
20/4/00-24/4/00
Follow a trail around Dapdune Wharf and Island. Two trails available, suitable for 3-6 and 7-13 year olds, C£1.00 plus usual admission, 11.00-17.00

▶ **Lock Up Your Kids!**
27/5/00-4/6/00
A week of activities including boat trips to the lock, £2 per boat trip plus usual admission, 11.00-17.00 on 27-29 May, 1-3 June

▶ **Down Your Wey**
18/6/00-18/6/00
Pond dipping, hurdle making, nature trails, river walks and boat trips are just some of the things you can see and do on this family day out, usual admission, 11.00-17.00

▶ **Coracle Making**
24/6/00-25/6/00
Discover how these unique boats are made and see how they are handled in the water, usual admission, 11.00-17.00

▶ **Guildford Boat Gathering**
1/7/00-1/7/00
Annual gathering of boats. Follow the Raft Race from Millmead Lock at 14.30 and watch the Decorated Boat Pageant in the Meadows at 18.00, donations welcome

▶ **Get Knotted**
1/7/00-2/7/00
Try your hand at tying up a boat or learn how to make a rope fender or keyring. Cost of materials plus usual admission, 11.00-17.00

▶ **Guided Walk**
10/9/00-10/9/00
This walk will look at the clues to the Wey's industrial past which still survive today. Meet the Lengthsman at Stoke Lock (TQ002516) for this 3.5-mile walk, £1.00 donation, 14.00-15.30

▶ **Pirate Party / Treasure Trail**
30/7/00-30/7/00
Fancy dress competition for best dressed pirate, treasure hunts and other activities, £1.00 plus usual admission, 11.00-17.00

Zoos

Gatwick Zoo
Russ Hill Glovers Road Charlwood Horley Surrey RH6 0EG
[Signposted off A23]
Tel: 01293 862312 Fax: 01293 862550
The zoo covers almost 10 acres and has hundreds of birds and mammals. The monkey island has spider and squirrel monkeys and other animals and birds can be seen in large naturalised settings.
visitor comments: The Zoo is nicely set out around Monkey Island - take along a picnic. Wonderful for small children.
All year daily Mar-Oct 10.30-18.00 Nov-Feb 10.30-dusk
Last Admission: 60 mins before closing
A£3.95 C(3-14)£2.95 C(0-3)£Free OAPs£3.45

Animal Attractions

Fishers Farm Park
Newpound Lane Wisborough Green Billingshurst West Sussex RH14 0EG
[off A272]
Tel: 01403 700063 Fax: 01403 700823
www.fishersfarmpark.co.uk
Fishers Farm Park is a unique place to visit, mixing rural activities with up front fun and gives the whole family a wonderful day out. There is so much to do whatever the weather. The Farmyard and barns give children and adults the opportunity to see animals well cared for in a happy environment, close enough to touch - you can even enter some of the pens to say hello to the goats and lambs. The play areas are designed for varying age groups, ideally suited for toddlers to 9 year olds, with everything from toddlers swings to

a giant zip slide. Have an ice-cream on the Beach, while the children paddle, then meander through the woods to the Fun-karts, tractor track and toddlers race circuit! While the grown-ups can enjoy tea and home-made cakes, the children can burn off their remaining energy racing around the 3-level playzone and drop slide.
visitor comments: Good facilities for children. Excellent playground. Plenty of farm animals and hands-on experience.
All year daily 10.00-17.00. Closed 25 & 26 Dec Mid Season: A£5.00 C&OAPs£4.50 Family Tickets (A2+C2)£17.00, (A2+C3)£21.25, (A3+C3)£25.50. High Season: A£6.00 C&OAPs£5.50 Family Tickets (A2+C2)£21.00, (A2+C3)£26.25, (A3+C3)£31.50. Nov & Jan: Low Season special weekday prices

Gumber Bothy Gumber Farm
Slindon Estate Nr Arundel Warden Arundel West Sussex BN18 0RG
[No vehicular access 1m to S of South Downs Way BR: Amberley 4m via South Downs Way]
Tel: 01243 814554/814484
Traditional West Sussex farm buildings in this peaceful and unspoilt area of the South Downs. The Bothy is one mile from the South Downs Way and 5 minutes walk from Stane Street, the old Roman road. Set in the heart of the 1417-ha Slindon Estate, the Bothy makes an ideal base for exploring the many rights-of-way.
31 Mar-end Oct. Please phone for details A£5.00 C£2.50. Reduction for parties of 12 or more Mon-Fri only. Possible price increase

Seven Sisters Sheep Centre
The Fridays East Dean Eastbourne Sussex BN20 0DG
[4m W of Eastbourne off A259. Plenty of on site parking available]
Tel: 01323 423207 Fax: 01323 423302
A family run farm for animal lovers of all ages, with over 45 British breeds of sheep and all the other farm favourites, tame enough to touch and feed. Daily bottle feeding sessions. Lambing time 4 March until 1 May then closed until 20 May. 20 May until 3 September, come and see daily shearing and sheep milking demonstrations. Tractor trailer rides, tea room, gift shop and picnic area.
visitor comments: Good value. Lambing time is a delight.
4 Mar-1 May & 20 May-3 Sept Mon-Fri 14.00-17.00. Sat & Sun and East Sussex school hol 11.00-17.00
Last Admission: 16.00
A£3.00 C(2-15)£2.00 Concessions£2.50
discount offer: Two For The Price Of One. Valid Until 3 Sept 2000

Birds, Butterflies & Bees

Bentley Wildfowl and Motor Museum
Harveys Lane Halland Lewes East Sussex BN8 5AF
[7m NE of Lewes signposted on A22, A26 & B2192]
Tel: 01825 840573 Fax: 01825 841322
Hundreds of swans, geese and ducks from all over the world can be seen on lakes and ponds along with flamingoes and peacocks. Fine array of Veteran, Edwardian and Vintage vehicles, house has splendid antiques and wildfowl paintings. Woodland walks, nature-trail, audio-visual in the education centre, adventure playground, and miniature train running during Summer weekends and Bank Holiday Mondays. Guild of Sussex Craftsmen. Dogs only in parking area.
Grounds, Wildfowl Reserve & Motor Museum: 20 Mar-31 Oct daily 10.30-16.30 (17.00 in July & Aug) Nov & Feb & 1-19 Mar weekends only 10.30-16.00. Closed Dec-Jan. House: 1 Apr-31 Oct 12.00-17.00 closed in winter
Last Admission: 16.30
A£4.80 C(under 3)£Free C(4-15)£3.00 Family Ticket (A2+C4)£14.50 OAPs&Students£3.80. Group rates 11+ 10% discount. Special rates for pre-booked school parties and the disabled
discount offer: Two For The Price Of One

Festivals & Shows

Airbourne 2000
Seafront and Western Lawns Eastbourne

Sussex *[A22 from London, A259 from Hastings, A27 from Brighton. BR: Trains from London & Gatwick hourly]*
Fax: 01323 638686
www.eastbourne.org/events
Four day airshow. Vast range of flying displays, arena displays, trade stands, Red Arrows, RAF exhibition, helicopter rides and grand finale fireworks.
Aug 17-20 2000 10.00-18.00
Admission Free

↓special events
▶ **Airbourne 2000**
17/8/00-20/8/00

Brighton Festival 2000
Brighton Sussex BN1 1EL
[events take place at various venues throughout Brighton]
Tel: 01273 700747 Fax: 01273 707505
www.brighton-festival.org.uk
England's biggest arts festival takes place every May in Brighton. Families will enjoy our opening Children's Parade, circus, funfair and special children's theatre shows. With some 900 events over 3 weeks, there is plenty to see and do in Brighton at Festival time. Our free festival programme will be available in March.
May 6-28 2000
Prices are dependant on the choice of event

↓special events
▶ **Brighton Festival**
6/5/00-28/5/00

Direct Line International Ladies Tennis Championships 2000
International Lawn Tennis Centre Devonshire Park College Road Eastbourne Sussex BN21 4JJ
[A22 from London, A259 from Hastings, A27 from Brighton. Trains from London & Gatwick hourly]
Tel: 01323 415442 Fax: 01323 638686
www.eastbourne.org/events
A Wimbledon warm-up featuring professional players from all over the world. Traditional English Garden Party atmosphere and surroundings.
June 17-24 2000 09.00-close of play
Prices range from £2.00 for ground tickets and £22.00 for centre court tickets. Call box office 01323 412000

↓special events
▶ **Direct Line Insurance International Ladies Tennis Championships**
17/6/00-24/6/00

Goodwood Motor Racing Circuit
Goodwood Chichester West Sussex PO18 0PX
[from: J10 M25, take A3 to Milford, then A283 to Petworth, from Petworth take the A285 to Halnaker then follow signs to Goodwood. From: Southampton, Portsmouth, Worthing and Brighton take the A27 to Chichester and follow signs to Goodwood from the by-pass. From: Petersfield, Haslemere and A3 take A286 to Singleton. From: Pulborough and Horsham, take A29 to meet A27, then as from Brighton]
Tel: 01243 755055 Fax: 01243 755058
www.goodwood.co.uk
Goodwood Circuit is the only completely original racetrack to have survived the pressures of the modern world, a classic circuit in the great tradition of post-war motor sport. The Goodwood Motor circuit first opened for racing in 1948. The brainchild of the ninth Duke of Richmond, better known to the motor racing fraternity as Freddie March. An integral part of Britain's post-war sporting heritage, Goodwood became the battle ground for such motor racing legends as Stirling Moss, Mike Hawthorn, Jim Clark and Graham Hill. Even today the lap record stands to Jim Clark and Jackie Stewart after an epic battle in 1965. Raised viewing platform for those in wheelchairs available. Access by disabled parking pass which must be applied for in advance.
Goodwood Revival Meeting: 15-17 Sept Fri 15th Sept: Advance £10.00 On the Day £15.00 Sat 16th Sept: Advance £20.00 On the Day £25.00 Sun 17st Sept Advance £30.00 On the Day £35.00. Circuit Weekend (Fri, Sat & Sun) Advance Only £50.00. Grandstands (per seat) Fri Advance £10.00 On the Day £15.00 Sat Advance £15.00 On the Day £20.00 Sun Advance £25.00 On the Day £30.00

↓special events
▶ **Goodwood Festival Of Speed**
23/6/00-25/6/00
World's biggest historic motor racing festival. Star drivers and rare cars. From 06.00-18.00

Herstmonceux Castle Medieval Festival
Herstmonceux Castle Hailsham Sussex BN27 1RP
[Rail: Polegate, bus every 30mins. Off the A271 signposted]
Tel: 01273 723249 Fax: 01273 723249
www.herstmonceux.com
Herstmonceux Castle Medieval Festival, now in its eighth year is Britain's largest three-day celebration of the colourful Middle Ages. In this magical setting, history will come to life. Hundreds of combatants with cannon support will siege the castle walls. Mounted Knights

*Please use a ball-point pen when filling in these forms

Would you like to have your say on the attractions you have visited in 2000 and have your comments printed in the guide? Now is your chance, just fill in your details below and pop this card in the post and we will send you full information. As a thank you, we will give you a free copy of the regional guide (2001) that covers the area where you live. Please register by 30th September 2000.

→ MrΔ MrsΔ MissΔ MsΔ DrΔ

First name________________________

Surname________________________

Address________________________

____

Postcode__________ Country__________

Tel__________ Email__________

- - - - - - - - - - - - - - - - - - - -

Please use this form to order copies of next year's guide books. Published at the end of Feburary 2001. **Days Out UK** will cost £9.99 and we charge £1 postage and packing. A total of £10.99. Dispatch is normally the same day (when published) or on publication when ordered beforehand. **To Order** please fill in your details below and post, or, if you prefer to send a cheque, make it payable to: **Days Out UK** and enclose it, with this completed form, in an envelope quoting the address on the reverse of this card for free postage.

→ MrΔ MrsΔ MissΔ MsΔ DrΔ

First name________________________

Surname________________________

Address________________________

____

Postcode__________ Country__________

Card no________________________

Expiry date__________

Card Visa Δ Delta Δ Mastercard Δ Switch Δ

Free Phone order line 0800 316 8900

BUSINESS REPLY SERVICE
Licence No. MID17765
1
DAYS OUT UK
The Leading Days Out Guide
Days Out UK
PO Box 427
NORTHAMPTON
NN2 7BR

will joust and Europe's finest archers will compete. Activities and entertainment for the whole family, fire-eaters, falconrym puppeteers, strolling minstrels, period craft stalls, living history village and kid's kingdom. 24hr recorded information: 0891 172902.
Aug 26-28 2000 10.00-18.00
A£10.00 C(3-13)£5.00 Concessions£9.00 Family Ticket £20.00 Group rates and advance tickets available: 01273 723249. 24hr recorded information 0891 172902.

↓*special events*

▶ **Herstmonceux Castle Medieval Festival**
26/8/00-28/8/00

Folk & Local History Museums

Battle and District Historical Society Museum Trust

Memorial Hall High Street Battle Sussex TN33 0AQ
[opposite Abbey Green car park in Battle]
Tel: 01424 775955

The focal point is a diorama of the Battle of Hastings and a reproduction of the Bayeux Tapestry. There are also local history exhibits. A Summer Arts Festival is held, and the Battle Festival takes place in June/July. Special displays of old photographs, toys etc. are arranged throughout the season.
Easter-Sept Mon-Sat 10.00-16.30, Sun 14.00-17.00
Last Admission: 15mins before closing
A£1.00 C(accompanied)£Free otherwise £0.20
discount offer: Two For The Price Of One.

Weald and Downland Open Air Museum

Singleton Chichester West Sussex PO18 0EU
[on A286 between Midhurst and Chichester. Discounted combined ticket on Stagecoach Coastline Bus. Plenty of parking on site]
Tel: 01243 811348 Fax: 01243 811475
www.wealddown.co.uk

Situated in a beautiful downland setting, this museum displays more than 40 rescued historic buildings from south-east England. The buildings range from early medieval houses to a 19th-century schoolhouse and Victorian labourers cottages. There is a medieval farmstead complete with animals, gardens and fields, a lakeside cafe, a working watermill and lots more of interest.
All year Mar-Oct daily 10.30-18.00 Nov-Feb Wed Sat & Sun 10.30-16.00 26 Dec-1 Jan 10.30-16.00
Last Admission: Main Season 18.00 Winter 16.00
A£6.00 C(5+)&Students£3.00 Family Ticket (A2+C3)£15.00
discount offer: One Child Free With Two Full Paying Adults. Valid Until 31 Oct 2000

↓*special events*

▶ **Heavy Horse Summer Spectacular**
4/6/00-4/6/00
A wonderful and continuous display of the grace, skill and power of these magnificent beasts

▶ **The Copper Family...**
19/7/00-19/7/00
... perform songs and tell tales of Sussex past by candlelight in one of the medieval hall houses of the museum. Commencing at 20.00, separate charge

▶ **Rare and Traditional Breeds Show**
23/7/00-23/7/00
Over 500 farmyard animals. Busy rural show loved for its personal and friendly atmosphere.

▶ **South Downs Harness Club Show**
6/8/00-6/8/00
Horses and ponies showing off their driving skills in full show finery. Classes for beginners through to experienced whips and grooms.

▶ **Romeo and Juliet**
10/8/00-10/8/00
Open air Shakespeare performed by Illyria. Recall the delighted of being young and in love. Tickets and details available on 01243 811348

▶ **Children's Activity Weekend**
12/8/00-13/8/00
Children, (and their parents and carers!) can try their hand at an astonishing range of things.. far too many to mention

▶ **Emperor's New Clothes**
18/8/00-18/8/00
Hans Christian Anderson's well loved tale performed by Illyria. Rollicking good fun for all

▶ **Rural History Re-enactment**
24/8/00-29/8/00
An authentic reconstruction of English domestic history.

▶ **Autumn Countryside Collection**
21/10/00-22/10/00
A celebration of how the countryside used to be

▶ **Half Term Activities**
23/10/00-27/10/00
Many and various activities for children including music, storytelling and lots to make and do.

▶ **Tree Dressing**
3/12/00-3/12/00
A festival of trees rooted in the Green Man legends of ancient times and the importance of natural objects to man

Gardens & Horticulture

Borde Hill Garden

Balcombe Road Haywards Heath Sussex RH16 1XP

[1.5m N of Haywards Heath, 3m from M23, , signposted from Cuckfield / Haywards Heath]

Tel: 01444 450326 Fax: 01444 440427

www.bordehill.co.uk

A botanical garden of contrasts established in the 19th century. Set in 200 acres of parkland, the garden contains a phenomenal range of rare trees, shrubs and perennials. All year colour. Recent Garden Rennaissance with Lootery grant includes Rose and Italian Gardens and Victorian Greenhouses.

All year daily 10.00-18.00 (or dusk if earlier)
Last Admission: 17.00
A£4.50 C£1.75 OAPs £3.75 Family Day Ticket £11.00 Family Season Ticket £27.50. Pre-booked groups of 20+ £4.00. Guided tours available

↓*special events*

▶ **Special Camellia Days**
18/3/00-31/3/00
58th Anniversary of Camellia 'Donation' created at Borde Hill Garden. View the other 33 varieties of Camellias on show also. Talks and tours by Camellia specialists by prior arrangement

▶ **Children's Activities**
1/8/00-31/8/00
Held every weekday afternoon in the parkland - face painting, juggling, pond dipping, children's trail and fishing. Please call to confirm dates

▶ **Fuchsia Show**
6/8/00-6/8/00
Fuchsia displays and sales from specialist nurseries plus information and talks on the growing and care of your fuchsias

▶ **L'Elisir d'Amore (The Love Potion)**
12/8/00-12/8/00
Garden Opera returns after their great success last year, with Donizetti's hilarious rustic comedy. 19.00-22.00, A£18.50 Concessions£16.50

▶ **Rare Plants Fair**
3/9/00-3/9/00
A feast for plant hunters - specialist nurseries selling unusual plants

▶ **Children's Fun Days**
23/10/00-27/10/00
Activities for children every afternoon in the adventure playground, 14.00-17.00

Denmans Garden

Clockhouse Denmans Lane Fontwell Arundel West Sussex BN18 0SU

[5m E of Chichester on A27. Limited on site parking]

Tel: 01243 542808 Fax: 01243 544064

This garden has been created from land which was part of an estate owned by Lord Denman in the 19th century. The present three-and-a-half acre garden was begun in the 1940's by the late Mrs J H Robinson and has gradually developed over the last 50 years. A school of Garden Design is housed in the Clock House. Since 1980 the garden has been run by John Brookes and from Clock House, within the property he runs his School of Garden Design. The garden is unique in its domestic scale, and in its combination of a strong organic design which is overlaid by generous planting. Having a dry, gravelly soil - both Mediterranean and native plants are grown in profusion. There are areas of glass, for plant sales and a garden cafe for coffee, light lunches and tea.

1 Mar-31 Oct daily 09.00-17.00
A£2.90 C(4+)£1.60 C(0-4)Free OAPs£2.60

discount offer: Two Full Paying Adults For The Price Of One. Excluding Weekends and Bank Holidays. Valid 1 Mar-31 Oct 2000

↓*special events*

▶ **Garden Design Course**
24/3/00-25/3/00
The Gravel Garden. Programme: 09.15-16.30, coffee, lunch and tea included in the £51.75 per person incl vat. Call for booking details

Holly Gate Cactus Garden and Nursery

Billingshurst Road Ashington Sussex RH20 3BB

[10m equidistant between Horsham and Worthing on A24 0.5m off on the B2133. Plenty of on site parking available.]

Tel: 01903 892930

www.users.globalnet.co.uk/~tmh

A mecca for the cactus enthusiast, with more than 30,000 succulent cactus plants, including many rare types. They come from both arid and tropical parts of the world, and are housed in over 10,000 square feet of greenhouses.

All year daily 09.00-17.00. Closed 25-26 Dec
A£2.00 C&OAPs£1.50. Group rates 20+ A£1.50 C£1.00

discount offer: Two For The Price Of One

Nymans Garden

Handcross Haywards Heath Sussex RH17 6EB
[B2114]
Tel: 01444 400321 Fax: 01444 400253
www.nationaltrust.org.uk

Set in the Sussex Weald, Nymans has flowering shrubs and roses, a flower garden in the old walled orchard, and a secret sunken garden. Lady Rosse's drawing room, library and walled gardens, now open, provide an insight into the Messel family's creative character. There are some fine and rare trees and wonderful woodland walks.

Gardens: 1 Mar-29 Oct Wed-Sun & Bank Hol Mon 11.00-18.00 or sunset if sooner. House: 29 Mar-29 Oct Wed-Sun & Bank Hol Mon 12.00-16.00. For details about new winter weekend opening and special events, call 01444 400321
Last Admission: Garden: 17.30
A£5.00 C£2.50 Family Ticket £12.50 RHS members free

discount offer: Two For The Price Of One. Not Valid on Bank Holidays

↓special events

▶ **Teddy Bears' Picnic**
22/7/00-22/7/00
Pirate-themed fancy-dress teddy bears' picnic, Punch & Judy, side shows, story-telling. Call for prices, 12.00-17.00

▶ **Craft Fair**
5/8/00-6/8/00
Local craftspeople, usual admission, 11.00-17.00

▶ **Opera in the Garden**
11/8/00-11/8/00
Opera Brava perform popular classics, from Mozart to Gilbert & Sullivan. Tickets: Southern Region Box Office on 01372 451596, £17.50, 18.30 for 19.30

▶ **Barber of Seville**
12/8/00-12/8/00
Rossini's masterpiece performed by Opera Brava. Tickets from Southern Region box office on 01372 451596, £17.50, 18.30 for 19.00

▶ **Guided Woodland Walk**
26/10/00-26/10/00
See entry for 26 April

Pashley Manor Gardens

Pashley Road Ticehurst Wadhurst Sussex TN5 7HE
[on B2099 off A21 follow brown signposts]
Tel: 01580 200692 Fax: 01580 200102

Pashley Manor Gardens, dating from 1550, stands in a well timbered park with magnificent views across to Brightling Beacon. A garden of great age, steeped in romance where all you can hear is the sound of splashing water and bird-song. A wide selection of plants, herbs and shrubs are on sale. Guided Tours of 10+ by arrangement. Picnics and dogs in the Car Park only. Member of the Historic Houses Association.

Garden & Tea Rooms: 12 Apr-30 Sept Tue, Wed, Thur, Sat and Bank Hol Mon 11.00-17.00. Gardens also open Oct Tue, Wed, Thur, Sat 11.00-17.00
A£4.50 C&OAPs£4.00

discount offer: Children Under 16 Free With Full Paying Adults. Valid Until 30 Oct 99

Wakehurst Place

Selsfield Road Ardingly Haywards Heath Sussex RH17 6TN
[J10 M23, A264 towards East Grinstead. 1.5m NW on B2028. BR: Haywards Heath. Bus Nos: 482 / 772 on Sundays. Plenty of on site parking available]
Tel: 01444 894066 Fax: 01444 894069
www.rbgkew.org.uk

Managed by the Royal Botanic Gardens, Kew; Wakehurst Place is set in over 180 acres. Vibrant ornamental plantings, providing year round colour and interest, blend into the beautiful natural landscape. Footpaths lead through sweeping woodlands of native and exotic trees. Set around a striking Elizabethan mansion containing a gift shop and a nearby restaurant.

visitor comments: Excellent gardens, well worth a long visit, particularly long walk to lower ponds.

All year daily from 10.00, closing times vary according to season, please call if making a special journey. Closed 25 Dec & 1 Jan
Last Admission: 30mins before closing
A£5.00 C(0-5)£Free C(5+)£2.50 Family Ticket (A2+C4)£13.00 Concessions£3.50

↓special events

▶ **Spring Weekend**
6/5/00-7/5/00
Guided walks and vehicular tours departing throughout the day, usual admission, 10.00

▶ **Woodland Skills**
9/7/00-9/7/00
Traditional woodland skills, usual admission, 10.00

▶ **Countryside Craft Fayre**
26/8/00-28/8/00
A fair with a theme of 100 years ago with over 150 crafts stands, A£4.00 C£1.50 OAPs£3.50, 10.00-18.00

▶ **West Sussex Millennium Cycle Ride**

17/9/00-17/9/00
One of four cycle rides - from 9-36 miles. Visit the new Millennium Seed Bank project at Wakehurst Place - the start and finish point for the cycle rides, open free to cyclists participating. Cycling Support Services on 01273 230822, £5.00 discounts available for early bookers and family groups. (Times to be confirmed).

▶ **Autumn Colour Weekend**
14/10/00-15/10/00
See entry for 6 May

Heritage & Industrial

Story of Rye
Rye Heritage Centre Strand Quay Rye East Sussex TN31 7AY
[at the Strand Quay in Rye, follow TIC signposts]
Tel: 01797 226696 Fax: 01797 223460
A complete sound and light show bringing the history of Rye alive! Follow the smugglers' footsteps and experience the medieval life and times of Rye as it was in bygone ages.
Mar-Oct daily 09.00-17.30. Nov-Feb daily 10.00-16.00
Last Admission: 15mins before closing
Centre or Personal Stereo Tour: A£2.00 C£1.00 Concessions£1.50. Group rates 10+ £1.00. All leaders and drivers £Free
discount offer: Two For The Price Of One For Either The Story of Rye Or The Personal Stereo Tour

Historical

1066 Story in Hastings Castle
Castle Hill Road West Hill Hastings Sussex TN34 3RG
[A259 or A21 into Hastings signposted]
Tel: 01424 781111 Fax: 01424 781186
Visit Britain's first Norman Castle built by William the Conqueror in 1067, after the Battle of Hastings. Enter the medieval siege tent and enjoy an exciting audio-visual experience 'The 1066 Story' which covers the Conquest and the history of the Castle through the centuries.
Easter-Sept daily 10.00-17.00, Oct-Easter daily 11.00-last show 15.30
A£3.00 C£2.00
discount offer: Two For The Price Of One

↓*special events*

▶ **Hastings & St Leonards Millennium Festival**
20/4/00-1/5/00
Featuring Jack in the Green Morris Dancing Festival, a dinosaur day, opera South East, jazz breakfasts, millennium ceilidh and a Mayday marathon walk

Battle Abbey
High Street Battle Sussex TN33 0AD
[leave A21 onto A2100 abbey at end of Battle High Street]
Tel: 01424 773792
www.english-heritage.org.uk
One date in English history that everyone can remember is 1066, the Battle of Hastings, when the Anglo Saxon army was defeated by the invading troops of William the Conqueror. Visit this famous site and experience the height of the battle at it's fiercest, through unique interactive displays. Also see the atmospheric ruins of the Abbey.
All year daily 1 Apr-30 Sept 10.00-18.00. 1 Oct-

31 Oct 10.00-17.00. 1 Nov-31 Mar 10.00-16.00. Closed 24-26 Dec & 1 Jan
A£4.00 C£2.00 Family Ticket (A2+C3) £10.00 Concessions£3.00 All prices include introductory video and interactive battlefield audio tour

↓special events

▶ **Warriors of Hastings**
22/7/00-8/10/00
Meet a mounted Norman knight and a Saxon warrior fron noon on 22/23, 29/30 July, 5/6, 12/13, 19/20 27/28 Aug, 2/3, 9/10, 16/17, 23/24 30 Sept/1 Oct, 7/8 Oct

▶ **The French and Indian Wars**
19/8/00-20/8/00
From Noon. 1750's Indian encampment, colonial living history and savage skirmish.

▶ **The Battle of Hastings Spectacular**
14/10/00-15/10/00
From Noon. Re-enactment of the most famous battle in English history, on the original site.

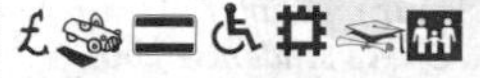

Bodiam Castle

Bodiam Robertsbrigde Sussex TN32 5UA
[3m S of Hawkhurst, 2m E of A21 Hurst Green. BR: Robertsbridge 5m]
Tel: 01580 830436 Fax: 01580 830398

Built in 1385 against a French invasion which never came, and as a comfortable dwelling for a rich nobleman. Voted one of the most popular and exciting castles for children to explore with spiral staircases and battlements. There is an audio-visual presentation on life in a medieval castle, and a small museum.

All year 13 Feb-31 Oct daily 10.00-18.00. Nov-3 Jan Tue-Sun 10.00-16.00. Closed 24-26 Dec. Last Admission : Feb-Oct 17.00 or dusk. Nov-Jan dusk Last Admission: Feb-Nov 17.00 or dusk. Nov-Jan dusk
A£3.50 C£1.75 Family Ticket £8.75 Group rates £3.00. Car Parking £1.00.

↓special events

▶ **The Emperor's New Clothes**
25/6/00-25/6/00
Open air theatre for families. Starts 18.30, tickets A£8.00 C£4.00

▶ **Romeo and Juliet**
16/7/00-16/7/00
Open air theatre starting at 18.30, tickets £9.00.

▶ **Magic**
22/7/00-22/7/00
A tribute to Freddie Mercury and Queen, 19.30, tickets £13.00

▶ **Book Day and Family Fun**
9/8/00-9/8/00

▶ **Treasure Hunt**
27/10/00-29/10/00
Normal opening times, £2.00 extra charge

Charleston

Firle Lewes East Sussex BN8 6LL
[6m E of Lewes on A27 between Firle and Selmeston]
Tel: 01323 811626 Fax: 01323 811628

The home of Vanessa Bell and Duncan Grant (painters), which became the country retreat of the group known as Bloomsbury. Decorated walls, furniture, textiles and ceramics, influenced by the post-impressionists, fresco painting and Italian and French interior decoration.
visitor comments: The guided tour is worthwhile.

23 Mar-30 June & 1 Sep-31 Oct Wed-Sun & Bank Hol Mon 14.00-17.00, 1 July-31 Aug Wed Sun 11.00-17.00
Last Admission: 17.00
A£5.00 C£3.00 Connoisseur Days £6.00 S&OAP&UB40&Concessions Wed & Thur

Goodwood House

Goodwood Chichester West Sussex PO18 0PX
[3 miles north east of Chichester, signposted from the A27]
Tel: 01243 755000 Fax: 01243 755005

Goodwood House has taken on new life. After two years of intensive restoration the Regency splendor of the Egyptian State Dining Room is guaranteed to make visitors catch their breath. The grand Yellow Drawing Room forms a glowing heart to the house with it's ottomans, sofas and chairs. The richness of the state rooms provides a perfect setting for the magnificent art collections including paintings by Canaletto, Stubbs, Reynolds and Van Dyck, porcelain, furniture and tapestries. Goodwood is also the home of the famous Goodwood motor racing circuit and racecourse. Many special events are held throughout the year. Member of the Historic Houses Association.

12 Apr-27 Sept Sun & Mon,Aug Sun-Thur 13.00-17.00. Closed event days, 9-10 May, All of June and 19 Sept.
A£6.00 C12-18£3.00 C(Under 12)£Free Groups 25+ £4.50

Hammerwood Park

Hammerwood East Grinstead Sussex RH19 3QE
[3.5m E of East Grinstead on A264 Tunbridge Wells 1m W of Holtye. BR: East Grinstead then by taxi for £6.00. plenty of on site parking available]
Tel: 01342 850594 Fax: 01342 850864
www.name.is/hammerwood

Said by visitors to be the most interesting house in Sussex. Built in 1792 as a temple of Apollo, the house was the first work of

Latrobex, the architect of the White House and The Capitol Building in Washington DC, USA. Family members conduct visitors on a colourful tour of the building and its grounds, ending in tea with a fine collection of lucious cakes and scones, served beneath a replica of the Parthenon frieze in the Elgin Room.
Easter Mon-end Sept Wed, Sat & Bank Hol Mon 14.00-17.30. Guided tour starts 14.05. Coach (21 seats or more) only by appointment. School groups welcome
A£4.50 C£1.50
discount offer: Three For The Price of Two

Herstmonceux Castle, Gardens and Grounds

Herstmonceux Hailsham Sussex BN27 1RN
[located just outside the village of Herstmonceux on the A271, the entrance is on Wartling road. Plenty of free on site parking]
Tel: 01323 833816 Fax: 01323 834499
www.seetb.org.uk/herstmonceux
Experience the peace and tranquility of 550 acres of glorious woodland and Elizabethan gardens surrounding a 15th century moated castle. Visitor's Centre, Children's Woodland play area, Tearoom and Nature trail.
15 Apr-29 Oct daily 10.00-18.00
Last Admission: 17.00 (16.00 in Oct)
A£3.50 C&Concessions£2.70. Joint ticket available with the Science Centre. Group booking rates for 15+ call 01323 834457

↓*special events*

▶ **Easter Egg Hunt**
23/4/00-23/4/00
Find the eggs hidden in the grounds of the Castle

▶ **Summer Proms**
24/6/00-24/6/00
Popular classics and firework finalé with Royal Philharmonic Orchestra. Commences 20.00, grounds open 16.00. Tickets from White Rock Theatre 01242 78100

▶ **Kite Festival and Fun Day**
30/7/00-30/7/00
A day out for all the family

▶ **Medieval Festival**
26/8/00-26/8/00
300 men and women in period costume attacking and counter-attacking will full cannon support in an effort to storm the castle and lay siege

Lewes Castle and Barbican House Museum

169 High Street Lewes East Sussex BN7 1YE
[Lewes Castle is located centrally in Lewes off the High Street, a few minutes walk from the bus and railway stations. Lewes is accessed from A27, A26 and A275, drivers using the A27 should enter the town from the eastern end of the Lewes by-pass via Guilfail Tunnel, Lewes.]
Tel: 01273 486290
The Lewes properties provide a wide range of possibilities for educational activities including artifact handling sessions, gallery tours activity sheet and practical workshops. The Museum at Barbican House traces the development of local people and features the Normans and their Castles, Medieval Realms and the history of Lewes, complimented by the Lewes Town Model.
visitor comments: Excellent video history. Opportunity to study the scale model making view from the top more relevant. Bookshop is well worth a visit.
All year Mon-Sat 10.00-17.30, Sun & Bank Hol 11.00-17.30. Closed 25-26 Dec. Castle closes at dusk in winter
Last Admission: Dusk during Winter
A£3.50 C(5-15)£1.80 OAPs&Students£3.00 Family Ticket (A2+C2)£10.00. Group: A£3.10 C£1.50 OAPs&Students£2.70 (min 20). Combined ticket with Anne of Cleves House: A£4.80 C£2.50 OAPs&Students£4.00 Family ticket(A2+C2)£12.00

Living History Museums

Buckleys Yesterdays' World

Next to Battle Abbey 80-90 High Street Battle East Sussex TN33 0AQ
[J5 M25, A2100 off A21]
Tel: 01424 775378 Fax: 01424 775174
www.yesterdaysworld.co.uk
Experience a 'day in a bygone age' at one of the most unusual attractions in South East England. In a charming medieval house you'll see over thirty shop and room displays with thousands of authentic exhibits dating from 1850-1950. A new Kitchen Exhibition details kitchen equipment from 1900s-1960s. To help you discover the past there are push button commentaries, moving figures and evocative

smells.
visitor comments: Highly recommended! A brilliant day out, with lovely gardens and a tea garden to relax in. Nice shop with bits and bobs!
All year daily Mar-Oct 10.00-18.00, Oct-Mar daily, hours vary call for details. Closed 25-26 Dec & 1 Jan
Last Admission: Summer: 16.45 Winter: 16.00
A£4.50 C(under 4)£Free C£2.99 OAPs£3.99 Disabled £2.00 Family Ticket(2A+2C) £13.95
discount offer: Two For The Price of One

Military & Defence Museums

Tangmere Military Aviation Museum Trust

Tangmere Chichester West Sussex PO20 6ES
[off A27. Plenty of parking on site]
Tel: 01243 775223 Fax: 01243 789490
Based at a former airfield, which played an important role during World War II, this museum spans 80 years of military aviation and has a wide-ranging collection of relics relating to Tangmere and air warfare in the south-east of England. A hangar houses record breaking aircraft Meteor and Hunter, plus a rare Supermarine Swift. Actual size replicas of Spitfire MK5, Hurricane and Spitfire prototype K5054. There are various simulators including one of a Spitfire for young visitors to 'fly'.
Mar-Oct daily 10.00-17.30. Feb & Nov daily 10.00-16.30
Last Admission: 1 hour before closure
A£3.00 C£1.50 OAPs£2.50
discount offer: Two For The Price Of One

↓*special events*

▶ **D Day Luncheon**
10/6/00-10/6/00
With a Guest Speaker, call for further details

▶ **Battle of Britain Luncheon**
16/9/00-16/9/00
A special day celebrating 60th anniversary

▶ **Armistice Day Service**
11/11/00-11/11/00

▶ **Open Day**
28/11/00-28/11/00

Railways

Bluebell Railway

Sheffield Park Station Uckfield East Sussex TN22 3QL
[4.5m E of Haywards Heath, off A272 on A275 BR: Haywards Heath, East Grinstead]
Tel: 01825 722370/723777 Fax: 01825 724139
The Bluebell Railway operates steam trains through nine miles of Sussex countryside. Sheffield Park is the main station. Here you will find the locomotive sheds, shop, museum and restaurant. Trains run between Sheffield Park, Horsted Keynes and Kingscote. Due to planning restrictions, there is no parking at Kingscote station. Passengers wishing to board here must catch the bus (service 473) which connects Kingscote and East Grinstead. Pullman dining trains run Saturday evenings and Sunday lunchtimes, and can be chartered - please call 01825 722008 for details. In December 'Santa Special' Christmas trains operate.
visitor comments: In a lovely setting. My 2 year old loved the train journey!
Open every weekend, daily May-Sept & during School Hol. Call 01825 722370 for Talking Timetable
3rd Class Return Fare: A£7.40 C(3-15)£3.70 Family Ticket £19.90. Museum & Locomotive sheds only: A£1.60 C£0.80. Discounts for pre-booked groups of 20+

Sealife Centres & Aquariums

Brighton Sea Life Centre

Marine Parade Brighton East Sussex BN2 1TB
[A23, M23]
Tel: 01273 604233/604234 Fax: 01273 681840
www.sealife.co.uk
The magnificent Brighton Sea Life centre combines the timeless elegance of fantastic Victorian architecture with the most up-to-date marine life habitats. The spectacular underwater tunnel - the longest in England - winds its way through an enormous seabed, alive with sharks, rays and conger eels. Newly

restored Victorian displays are now home to over 60 varieties of marine wildlife - including many unusual native and tropical species, and the mystical Kingdom of the Seahorse lets you discover all about these beautiful creatures and their complex behaviour.

visitor comments: Experienced some difficulty with parking. Suitable for all ages - quite spectacular.

All year daily 10.00-18.00. Additionally later in summer and school hol. Closed 25 Dec
Last Admission: 17.00
A£5.95 C(0-3)£Free C(4-14)£3.95 Students&UB40s£4.25 Concessions available

Hastings Sea Life Centre

Rock-A-Nore Road Hastings East Sussex TN34 3DW
[A21 from London A259 from Eastbourne and Folkestone signposted in Hastings]
Tel: 01424 718776 Fax: 01424 718757

Steeped in maritime history, Hastings provides the ideal setting for a Sea Life Centre...and ancient Rock-A-Nore Road, with its curious fishermen's huts and pebbly beach, is the ideal location within the resort. New in '97 - Neptune's Nursery - follow the incredible early life-cycles of sharks, rays, cuttlefish, seahorses and other mini-marine marvels from newly-hatched eggs and larvae to tiny babies and half-grown juveniles.

All year daily 10.00-18.00
Last Admission: 17.00
Queuing Times: Max 20mins
A£4.95 C£3.50 OAPs£3.75

Weald and Downland Open Air Museum

Singleton Chichester West Sussex PO18 0EU
[on A286 between Midhurst and Chichester. Discounted combined ticket on Stagecoach Coastline Bus. Plenty of parking on site]
Tel: 01243 811348 Fax: 01243 811475
www.wealddown.co.uk

Situated in a beautiful downland setting, this museum displays more than 40 rescued historic buildings from south-east England. The buildings range from early medieval houses to a 19th-century schoolhouse and Victorian labourers cottages. There is a medieval farmstead complete with animals, gardens and fields, a lakeside cafe, a working watermill and lots more of interest.

All year Mar-Oct daily 10.30-18.00 Nov-Feb Wed Sat & Sun 10.30-16.00 26 Dec-1 Jan 10.30-16.00
Last Admission: Main Season 18.00 Winter 16.00
A£6.00 C(5+)&Students£3.00 Family Ticket (A2+C3)£15.00

discount offer: One Child Free With Two Full Paying Adults. Valid Until 31 Oct 2000

↓*special events*

▶ **Rare and Traditional Breeds Show**
23/7/00-23/7/00
Over 500 farmyard animals. Busy rural show loved for its personal and friendly atmosphere.

▶ **South Downs Harness Club Show**
6/8/00-6/8/00
Horses and ponies showing off their driving skills in full show finery. Classes for beginners through to experienced whips and grooms.

▶ **Romeo and Juliet**
10/8/00-10/8/00
Open air Shakespeare performed by Illyria. Recall the delighted of being young and in love. Tickets and details available on 01243 811348

▶ **Children's Activity Weekend**
12/8/00-13/8/00
Children, (and their parents and carers!) can try their hand at an astonishing range of things.. far too many to mention

▶ **Half Term Activities**
23/10/00-27/10/00
Many and various activities for children including music, storytelling and lots to make and do.

▶ **Tree Dressing**
3/12/00-3/12/00
A festival of trees rooted in the Green Man legends of ancient times and the importance of natural objects to man

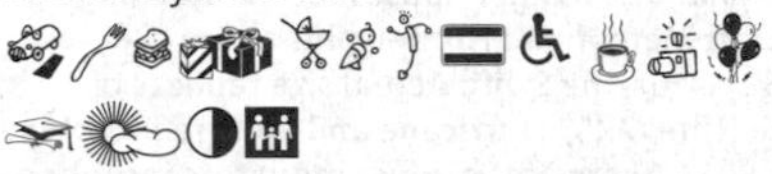

Sport & Recreation

Knockhatch Adventure Park

Hempstead Lane Hailsham Sussex BN27 3PR
[A22 at Hailsham. 9m N of Eastbourne]
Tel: 01323 442051 Fax: 01323 843878

Exciting, yet relaxing - the most varied day out around. Bird of prey centre, children's farm, crazy golf, boating lake, soft play, an indoor play area of 2000 sq ft, adventure playground, nature trail, free fall slides, grass karting, laser game, laser clays, picnic areas and restaurant, and for groups/corporate events: archery,

paintball, clay shooting and karting.
1 Apr-30 Sept weekends and school holidays 10.00-17.30. At other times (except Jan) open to pre-booked groups
A£5.25 C£4.25 Family Ticket £16.95 OAPs&Concessions£3.45

Theme & Adventure Parks

Paradise Park
Avis Road Newhaven East Sussex BN9 0DH
[signposted off A26 & A259. Just 30mins from Brighton and 20mins from Eastbourne. Plenty of on site parking available]
Tel: 01273 512123 Fax: 01273 616005
www.paradisepark.co.uk
Discover one of Britain's best Indoor Botanic Gardens and Paradise Water Gardens, an inspiration for garden lovers. Situated in 9 acres of grounds all of which are flat and disabled friendly. The gardens are designed with themed areas illustrating different habitats from around the world. Attractions include an extensive Planet Earth Exhibition, Garden Centre and Pleasure Gardens with children's rides and amusements, an extensive coffee shop offering delicious meals all adding up to the perfect day out for everyone.
visitor comments: Editors Choice: Children enjoyed every aspect. A thoroughly excellent day out. Easy to get round for little legs, plenty of animals to pet, no indoor picnic area.
All year daily 10.00-18.00. Closed 25-26 Dec. Alternative phone number 01273 616006
Combined Ticket to all 3 attractions: A£4.25 C&OAPs£3.99 Family Ticket (A2+C2)£15.99
discount offer: Two For The Price Of One

Stade Family Fun Park
East Beach Street Hastings Sussex TN34 3AR
[located on A259, Hastings seafront]
Tel: 01424 716068 Fax: 01424 719609
The Stade is a unique amusement park offering excellent family value. Super kids rides, dodgems, ghost train, roller coaster and boating lake. NEW for Easter 2000: The Oh!Zone indoor entertainment centre offering ten pin bowling, dodgems, interactive venture play area, Big Screen Sport, amuseuments and a range of catering.
Oh!Zone: daily from 15 April 2000. Park: 15 Apr-4 Sept, 19-27 Feb & 21-29 Oct daily, Mar-Oct weekends only from 10.00
Ride tokens: £0.50p each; Wristbands from £5.00

Zoos

Drusillas Park
Alfriston Sussex BN26 5QS
[off A27 between Brighton / Eastbourne, 7m from Seaford beach]
Tel: 01323 870234 Fax: 01323 870846
www.drusillas.co.uk
Drusillas Park is widely regarded as the Best Small Zoo in England with a wide variety of animals along the pretty, well planned zoo walk. Beautiful gardens, Explorers Restaurant, Playland, Indoor Toddler Village, Petworld, Train, Panning for Gold, Wacky Workshop, Maasai exhibition, Animal Encounter sessions and five shops including Teddy's Jungle Safari. New for 2000: Millennium Bugs and the mysterious Saki Monkeys. Wheelchair access throughout. Situated near historic Alfriston and next door to the English Wine Centre. Indoor and Outdoor picnic areas. Our Challenge Days for Beaver Scouts, Brownies, Cubs and Rainbows consist of a simple, informative Quiz which helps children to observe and understand their environment. Dates follow in the special events section.
visitor comments: A complete day out at reasonable cost. Very informative and educational. Excellent play area.
All year Summer: daily 10.00-18.00, Winter: daily 10.00-17.00. Closed 24-26 Dec
Last Admission: 60mins before closing
A£7.60 C(0-3)£Free C(3-12)£6.50 OAPs, Long Term Disabled & Carers £6.00 Groups 15+: A£6.60 C(3-12)£5.50 C(0-3)£Free OAPs, Long Term Disabled & Carers £5.00. Please enquire for winter discount prices

↓*special events*

▶ **Adopter Day**
25/3/00-7/10/00
Held on Mar 25 and Oct 7 only

▶ **Brownie Challenge Days**
15/4/00-16/12/00
Held on Apr 15, May 20, June 24, July 8, Sept 16, 30 and Dec 16 only
▶ **Julian Ford and his Birds of Prey**
19/4/00-30/8/00
Fabulous display of these majestic birds with talks and small flying displays. Held on Apr 19, 26, July 26, Aug 2, 9, 16, 23 and 30 only
▶ **Charlie the Clown**
20/4/00-31/8/00
Held on April 20, 27, June 1, Aug 3, 10, 17, 24 and 31 only
▶ **Easter Egg Challenge**
21/4/00-24/4/00
▶ **Waterworld**
25/7/00-15/8/00
Held on July 25 and Aug 15 only
▶ **Clowns Day**
27/7/00-27/7/00
▶ **Fur, Feathers and Fins**
1/8/00-22/8/00
Held on Aug 1 and 22 only
▶ **Santa's Christmas Cottage**
1/12/00-23/12/00
▶ **What does Santa do after Christmas?**
27/12/00-7/1/01
Come along and you might just see Santa relaxing in his secret Drusillas hide away

Country Parks & Estates

Derwent Walk Country Park
Thornley Lane Rowlands Gill Tyne And Wear NE39 1AU
Tel: 01207 545212 Fax: 01207 549835
11 mile track bed of the old Derwent Valley Railway between Swalwell and Consett suitable for walking, cycling, horses and wheelchairs. The Walkis part of the C2C cross England cycle route. It contains woodlands, meadows, ponds and riverside walks. New feature is the reclaimed Derwentthaugh Cokeworks site with extensive riverside disabled access. Visitor centres at Rowlands Gill and Swalwell.
All year

Exhibition & Visitor Centres

National Glass Centre
Liberty Way Sunderland SR6 0GL
[From A194, off A1231. Plenty of on site parking available]
Tel: 0191 515 5555 Fax: 0191 515 5556
Once inside visitors of all ages and interests can take in some amazing experiences. The Kaleidoscope Gallery where every aspect is explored, witness spectacular glass-making demonstrations where you may even get to try it yourself, plus our fantastic Glass Gallery with exhibitions from around the world. Excellent shop and riverside restaurant.
All year 10.00-17.00
Last Admission: 16.00
A£5.00 C£3.00
discount offer: One Person Free With Every Full Paying Adult
↓*special events*
▶ **Artist Talks: Jane Charles**
28/3/00-28/3/00
Jane has a piece of commissioned artwork in the Centre and work in the shop. The talk at 14.00 is followed by a demonstration at 15.30
▶ **Frog Wine: Bring a Bottle**
1/4/00-1/4/00
No April Fool! Workshop in glass painting using recycled bottles. 10.00-12.00, tickets £8.00
▶ **Light Catchers**
8/4/00-8/4/00
From 10.00-13.00, make your own lightcatcher in stained glass. Tickets £10.00
▶ **Spring Open Winner**
11/4/00-11/4/00
A talk at 14.30 by the prize-winner of the Open
▶ **Spring Flowers**
22/4/00-22/4/00
£7.00, from 10.00-12.00, make enamelled pendants for spring
▶ **Blooming Marvellous**
29/4/00-29/4/00
Paperweights for spring - learn to create a flower inside a paperweight using hot glass. 10.00-12.00, £10.00 per person

Festivals & Shows

Window On The World International Music Festival
Northumberland Square North Shields Tyne & Wear NE30 1QQ
[off A1 10 E of Newcastle Upon Tyne in Fishquay town centre and Harbour]
Tel: 0191 200 8909 Fax: 0191 200 8910
Britains biggest Free Music Festival. Contemporary music from World to Blues Roots & Pop. Street Theatre, Pageant Parade, International Food, Funfair, Boat Trips. The vessel made famous by the 'Hornblower' series will be berthed alongside the Western Quay and will be open for visitors. A children's village with activities, workshops and entertainments will be open all weekend also. See special events diary for fuller details.
May 27-29 2000 10.00-23.00 Sat/Sun 10.00-20.00 Mon
Admission Free
↓*special events*
▶ **Celtic Dance Stage**
27/5/00-27/5/00
Held at the Low Lights Fish Quay from 12.00-23.00. Featuring Flook, Wildcats of Kilkenny, Peatbog Faeries, Tartan Amoebas and The Popes.
▶ **WOW2000 Carnival Parade**
27/5/00-27/5/00
Parade begins at 10.00 from Northumberland Square, North Shields and travels to the World Stage for the finale and official opening at 12.00
▶ **Festival Fireworks Display**
27/5/00-27/5/00
Held at 22.15 on the river off North Shields Fish Quay
▶ **Emerging Talent Stage**
27/5/00-29/5/00
May 27 12.00-23.00, May 28 13.00-23.00 and May 29 13.00-20.00, in the Dolphin area. Features The Nexus Busker of the Year finals and a programme of new bands.
▶ **Jumpin' 'n' Hot Club Stage**
27/5/00-29/5/00
Norfolk Street, May 27 14.00-23.00, May 28 13.00-23.00 and May 29 14.00-20.00. Programme includes Blues, Roots, Swing and Soul music from around the world. Louisiana Red headline
▶ **Galaxy Dance Stage**
28/5/00-28/5/00
From 13.00-23.00 at the Low Lights Fish Quay and featuring a mix of DJ's and live artists
▶ **Street Performance on the Quayside**
29/5/00-29/5/00
12.00-13.00, a premiere of 'The Big Bang', a musical and dance piece inspired by the industrial history of Tyneside and the carnival traditions of North East Brazil

Historical

Washington Old Hall
The Avenue District 4 Washington Tyne & Wear NE38 7LE
[2m from A1 in Washington on E side of Ave 5m W of Sunderland S of Tyne Tunnel follow signs for Washington District 4 & then village]
Tel: 0191 416 6879/529 3161
The home of George Washington's ancestors from 1183 to 1613, the Old Hall was originally an early medieval manor, but was rebuilt in the 17th century. The house has been restored and filled with period furniture and a NEW Jacobean Garden. The property was given to the National Trust in 1956.
2 Apr-31 Oct Sun-Wed & Good Fri 11.00-17.00. Groups by appointment only
Last Admission: 16.30
A£2.80. Pre-booked Groups £2.30 Family Ticket(2A+3C) £7.00

Maritime

Newcastle Discovery Museum
Blandford House Blandford Square Newcastle Upon Tyne Tyne & Wear NE1 4JA
[off A6115 A6125]
Tel: 0191 232 6789 Fax: 0191 230 2614
A multi-museum housing Fashion Works, A Soldier's Life, Great City and Science Factory. All hands-on, bodies-in permanent displays giving a fun packed day out for all ages. The

centre-piece of the museum is the new Turbinia Gallery housing the world's first ever steam driven vessel, once the fastest ship afloat.
All year Mon-Sat 10.00-17.00, Sun 14.00-17.00. Closed 25-26 Dec & 1 Jan & Good Fri
Last Admission: 16.30
Admission Free

St Mary's Lighthouse and Visitor Centre
St. Mary's Island Whitley Bay Tyne & Wear **Tel: 0191 200 8650**
Three buildings open to the public, lighthouse, bird watching hide and visitor centre. Exhibition, shop, cafe. Events include rockpool rambles, geology jaunts, treasure hunts.
Nov-Mar Sat-Sun Wed and School holidays
A£1.50 C/OAPs£0.75 Family ticket £3.50

Nature & Conservation Parks

Wildfowl and Wetlands Trust Washington
District 15 Washington Tyne & Wear NE38 8LE
[E of Washington 4m from A1(M) 1m from A19 signposted off A195 & A1231]
Tel: 0191 416 5454 Fax: 0191 416 5801
www.washington.co.uk
Our 3 newest attractions will give everyone an insight into the wonder of wetlands and the vital need for their conservation. Glaxo Wellcome Wetland Discovery Centre; packed full of things to do for all ages, Spring Gill Wood; delightful walk carefully designed to provide access for people with disabilities, James Steel Waterfowl Nursery; watch fluffy ducklings and goslings take their first wobbly steps.
All Year daily 09.30-17.00. Closed 25 Dec
A£4.75 C(0-4)£Free C(4-16)£2.75 Family Ticket (2A&2C) £12.00 Concessions£3.75
discount offer: One Admission Free With A Full Paying Adult

Places of Worship

St. Nicholas Cathedral
St. Nicholas Churchyard Newcastle Upon Tyne Tyne & Wear NE1 1PF
Tel: 0191 232 1939 Fax: 0191 230 0735
Mainly 14th-15th century. Norman arch circa 1175. Unique lantern tower. Guided tours by prior arrangement.
All year Mon-Fri 07.00-18.00, Sat 08.00-16.00, Sun 07.00-12.00 16.00-19.30
Admission Free

Tynemouth Castle
East Street Tynemouth North Shields Tyne & Wear NE30 4BZ
[near North Pier in Tynemouth]
Tel: 0191 257 1090
www.english-heritage.org.uk
The castle, fortifications and priory are a testament to the vital strategic importance of the site and its great religious significance. The soaring arches of the presbytery testify to a time when the priory was one of the richest in England and the Percy Chantry at the east end of the church is virtually complete.
27 Mar-31 Oct daily 10.00-18.00 or dusk if sooner. 1 Nov-26 Mar Wed-Sun 10.00-16.00
Last Admission: 1 hour before closing
A£1.70 C£0.90 Concessions£1.30

↓*special events*

▶ **Children's Seaside Entertainment**
27/5/00-29/5/00
Punch & Judy, local dancing

▶ **Medieval Knight prepares for War**
15/7/00-16/7/00
Meet mounted knights and their retinue from the time of the Wars of the Roses
▶ **Medieval Jousting Spectacular**
27/8/00-28/8/00
Armoured knights from the 11th to 14th centuries battle for supremacy!
▶ **Viking Encampment**
23/9/00-24/9/00
Viking living history, crafts and skills-at-arms

Railways

Tanfield Railway
Old Marley Hill Nr Stanley Newcastle Upon Tyne Tyne & Wear NE16 5ET
[off the A6076 4m from the Metro Centre, 3m N of Stanley]
Tel: 0191 388 7545 Fax: 0191 387 4784
www.tanfield-railway.freeserve.co.uk
The world's oldest existing railway, originally opened in 1725. Three mile steam passenger railway between Sunniside, Causey Arch and East Tanfield. Collection of 40 locos including Wellington of 1873, Victorian carriages and vintage workshop at Britain's oldest engine shed, built in 1854.
All year daily 10.00-17.00. Train times: all year Sun, PLUS Summer School Holidays Wed and Thur 11.00-16.00. Winter Sun 11.30-15.15. Admission Free. Train Fares: A£3.50 C(under 5's)£Free C&OAPS£2.00
discount offer: One Child Free With Every Full Paying Adult. Excluding December 1999.

Roman Era

Arbeia Roman Fort and Museum
Baring Street South Shields Tyne And Wear NE33 2BB
[via the A185/A194 from Gateshead. Approaching South Shields up the A194, watch for a roundabout exit to the B1303 that skirts round the N of South Shields by the Tyne and turn right down Baring Street. The Fort is on your left]
Tel: 0191 456 1369 Fax: 0191 427 6862
The most exciting archaeological site in the region. South Shields is one of the few places in Britain where you can see almost the whole layout of a Roman Fort. See the latest finds and explore the ruins. Visit the reconstructed Gateway and the exhibition 'Gateway to the Past' tracing the rich history of Arbeia from 8,000BC to the present day. Visit 'Time Quest' the hands-on Archaeology Gallery.
visitor comments: A marvellous place to take children.
All year Tue-Fri 10.00—17.30, Sat 10.00-16.30, Sun Easter Sept only 14.00-17.00 also Bank Hol Mon. 1999 Yimes: Easter-30 Sept Mon-Sat 10.00-17.30, Sun 13.00-17.00
Oct-Easter Mon-Sat 10.00-16.00
A£1.00 C&Concessions£0.50

Sealife Centres & Aquariums

Tynemouth Sea Life Centre
Grand Parade Tynemouth Tyne & Wear NE30 4JF
[signposted from A19 & A1058]
Tel: 0191 258 1031 Fax: 0191 257 2116
A historic town with a famously rugged coastline...and a Sea Life Centre which takes visitors beyond the tide edge to explore the many diverse marine habitats which lie unseen beneath the waves. Look out for the amazing Underwater Tunnel where many strange creatures will silently glide just inches above your head.
All year Mon-Sun daily 10.00-17.00
Last Admission: 17.00
A£4.50 C£2.95 OAPs£3.25

Theme & Adventure Parks

New Metroland
39 Garden Walk Metrocentre Gateshead Tyne & Wear NE11 9XY
[signposted for MetroCentre from A1/M]
Tel: 0191 493 2048 Fax: 0191 493 2904
Europe's largest indoor funfair theme park. Completely refurbished in 1998. Ride the New Rollercoaster, Wonderful Waveswinger, Swashbuckling Ship, Beautiful Balloons ferris wheel and fabulous Whirling Waltzer, plus much more. Have fun in Monty Zoomers children's adventure play area and see the amazing talking clocks. Children's parties and full catering at Barnaby's Deli-Diner.
School holidays: Mon-Wed 10.00-20.00, Thur & Fri 10.00-21.00, Sat 09.00-21.00, Sun 11.00-19.00. Term Time: Mon-Fri from 12.00
All Day ride pass A&C£6.30 Evening ride pass after 18.00 A&C£4.20

Animal Attractions

Broomey Croft Children's Farm
Bodymoor Heath Lane Bodymoor Heath Nr

Tamworth Warwickshire B76 0EE
[10mins from J9 M42. Follow A4091 towards Drayton Manor and pickup the brown tourism signs]
Tel: 01827 873844
Lots of friendly farm animals, traditional and rare breeds. A place where children and animals come first and the seasons are respected. The farm has been created with children in mind but with something for everyone. Family fun in a safe, clean and pleasant environment.
1 Apr-10 Sept daily 10.00-17.00, mid Sept-end Mar weekends and half-term 10.00-16.00
Last Admission: 30mins before closing
A£2.80 C£2.00

Hatton Country World
Dark Lane Hatton Warwick Warwickshire CV35 8XA
[5 min from J15 off M40 via A46 (towards Coventry) signed off A4177 Warwick to Solihull Road. Plenty of on site parking available]
Tel: 01926 843411 Fax: 01926 842023
www.hattonworld.com
Hatton is a totally unique blend of Shopping and Leisure carved out of 19th Century Farm Buildings set in the heart of the Warwickshire Countryside. Hatton Shopping village is home to England's biggest Craft Centre, or you can stroll around the farm park and enjoy the animals and pets.
visitor comments: Indoor and outdoor play areas and hands-on farm animals.
Daily 10.00-17.00. Closed 25-26 Dec & 1 Jan (from 14.00 on 24 & 31 Dec)
Last Admission: 17.00
Shopping Village: £Free. Farm Park: A£4.25 C£4.25 OAPs&Concessions£4.25. Group Rates Available.

↓*special events*

▶ **February Frolics**
19/2/00-27/2/00

▶ **Mothers Day Specials**
2/4/00-2/4/00

▶ **10-Day Easter Special**
21/4/00-30/4/00

▶ **Whitsun Wonder Week**
27/5/00-4/6/00

Stratford Shire Horse Centre
Clifford Road Stratford on Avon Warwickshire CV37 8HW
[1m from Stratford - follow signs for Broadway]
Tel: 01789 415274
Enjoy a new attraction - The Shire World Theatre where displays and a cinema introduction tell you the story of the Shire Horse past and present. Enjoy the 'up-close' experience of the Gentle Giants, a wagon ride will help you understand real horse-power! Visit us in late April to see our new foals. Numerous rare breed farm animals including friendly goats and sheep; Pat-a-Pet; lambing January to Easter; hyperslides, in and outdoor play areas.
Mar-Oct daily 10.00-17.00, Nov-Feb Sat-Wed 10.00-17.00
A£4.95 C£3.95 OAPs£4.25 Concessions, Group Rates & School Parties £2.70

Birds, Butterflies & Bees

Stratford-Upon-Avon Butterfly Farm
Tramway Walk Swan's Nest Lane Stratford-Upon-Avon Warwickshire CV37 7LS
[south bank of River Avon opposite RSC]
Tel: 01789 299288 Fax: 01789 415878
www.butterflyfarm.co.uk
Europe's largest live Butterfly and Insect Exhibit. Hundreds of the world's most spectacular and colourful butterflies. Insect City has a huge collection of strange and fascinating animals. Arachnoland features the 'dealers in death.' There is also an outdoor British butterfly garden in the summer.
Summer daily 10.00-18.00. Winter 10.00-dusk. Closed 25 Dec
1999 Prices: A£3.75 C£2.75 Family Ticket £10.75 Concessions£3.25 Special school tours can be arranged

Country Parks & Estates

Coombe Country Park
Brinklow Road Binley Coventry Warwickshire CV3 2AB
[on B4027 between Coventry / Rugby, follow brown tourist signs]
Tel: 024 76453720 Fax: 024 76635350
400 acres of historic parkland offer a memorable countryside experience. Plant, bird and animal life reside in abundance with each change of season offering it's own natural focus. There are two children's adventure playgrounds, Discovery Centre, souvenir shop and picnic areas. The Visitor Centre offers guided walks, lectures, workshops and demonstrations all which need to be booked in advance. There is also a Young Rangers Club with sessions designed to be hands on and lots of fun! Under 8's must be accompanied by an adult. Wherever possible, the facilities and activities within the Country Park have been designed to allow access for all. These include a network of all weather pathways, Easirider vehicles available for use free of charge to wheel chair users (please book 24 hours in advance); large bird hide with large ramped access and views of Warwickshire's largest heronry and bird feeding station; accessible trail in the Duck Decoy with tap rail and board walk; play equipment designed for disabled children; wheel chair accessible pond dipping stages; sensory themes on the Walk and Talk programme and sensory games in the Discovery Centre; accessible toilet facilities at the Visitors Centre and Top Pool Lodge. Most of the parkland is classified as a Site of Special Scientific Interest. Follow the paths to the 12th century Coombe Abbey set in 550 acres of Capability Brown designed parkland with lakes and magnificent Redwood trees. Guided tours of Coombe Abbey and its grounds are available throughout the season. Join the "No Ordinary Hotel" team for a Mediaeval delight.
visitor comments: Very picturesque; lovely place for a picnic. Excellent play park for children.
All year daily dawn-dusk
Admission Free. Car park charge

Ryton Pools Country Park
Ryton Road Bubbenhall Coventry Warwickshire
[off the A445 S of Ryton-on-Dunsmore, near Coventry]
Tel: 024 76305592 Fax: 01827 872660
www.warwickshire.gov.uk
The new 100 acre Country Park was opened on 16 August 1996 by the Chairman of the County Council and represented the culmination of 5 years work to transform the former landfill site into a new and exciting Country Park. During that time two million tonnes of rubbish from Rugby, Warwick and Leamington Spa have been covered in clay and top soil and over 2,500 trees and shrubs have been planted. Over the coming years the site's character will change as the trees and shrubs grow and the site develops into both a haven for wildlife and an ideal place to walk or picnic.
visitor comments: A delightful piece of countryside. Great for picnics. Good small play area.
All year daily, hours according to season
Admission Free

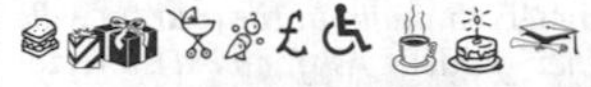

Gardens & Horticulture

Ryton Organic Gardens
Wolston Lane Coventry Warwickshire CV8 3LG
Tel: 024 7630 3517 Fax: 024 7663 9229
www.hdra.org.uk
Ten acres of glorious gardens show how to grow in harmony with nature. Award winning organic restaurant on site. Large shop, conference facilities. Coaches and groups welcome by prior arrangement. Events shown below, for further details or to book please call 024 7630 8211, specific leaflets are available, see below for course prices. (G) = the course is part of Grow Your Own Organic Fruit and Vegetables Campaign.
All year 09.00-17.00. 1 Nov-Good Fri 10.00-dusk. Closed Christmas week
Last Admission: 16.30
A£3.00 C(accompanied)£Free. HDRA/RHS members free. Course Fees: unless stated otherwise are: Half Day £15.00 (HDRA £12.00), Full Day £30.00 (HDRA £25.00). Courses marked with RHS are offered to RHS Members at HDRA Member rates
discount offer: Two For The Price Of One Full Paying Adult

↓*special events*

► **Willow Structures**
27/5/00-28/5/00
See entry for 25 March

► **National Gardens Scheme**
3/6/00-3/6/00

In support of the National Gardens Scheme charity, 100.00-17.00, A£3.00 C£Free. HDRA/RHS/ North Hort Soc Free

▶ **(G) Organic Vegetable Growing Day**
11/6/00-11/6/00
A day devoted to vegetable growing, talks, demos and activities for everyone, 10.00-16.00, usual admission

▶ **HDRA at the BBC Gardeners' World Live Show**
14/6/00-18/6/00
At the NEC in Birmingham

▶ **National Organic Gardening Weekend**
17/6/00-18/6/00
Organic gardeners throughout the country will be opening their gardens. Ask for a FREE directory

▶ **(G) Summer Care of Soft Fruit**
21/6/00-21/6/00
This course will cover early and midsummer management of summer fruits, 10.00-12.30

▶ **Watercolour Painting**
2/7/00-2/7/00
See entry for 30 April

▶ **Ryton at Hampton Court Flower Show**
4/7/00-9/7/00
Come and see our Stand at the Hampton Court Flower Show

▶ **Ryton at Tatton Park**
19/7/00-23/7/00
See our stand at RHS's Tatton Park Show, Cheshire

▶ **Butterfly Tours**
29/7/00-29/7/00
Join the British Butterfly Society, call 024 7630 8211 for further information

▶ **National Organic Gardening Weekend**
5/8/00-6/8/00
See entry for 17 June

▶ **(G) Summer Pruning of Top Fruit**
8/8/00-8/8/00
The course will cover the annual pruning of plums and cherries and summer work on restricted forms of apples and pears, 10.00-12.30

▶ **Hands on Energy Saving**
2/9/00-2/9/00
How to install energy savers in your own home, 09.30-17.30

▶ **Tortoise Day**
3/9/00-3/9/00
If you are thinking about adopting a tortoise, already have one and would like to join BATK or simply would like to come along and socialise, you and your tortoise would be most welcome to attend! 12.00-16.00, usual admission

The Cottage Tea Garden
Cottage Lane Shottery Stratford on Avon Warwickshire CV37 9HH
[J15 M40 to Stratford, follow signs to Anne Hathaways Cottage, Tea Garden is opposite the Cottage]
Tel: 01789 293122 Fax: 01789 298056
The Cottage Tea Garden is opposite the world famous Anne Hathaway's Cottage. Enjoy delicious home made cream teas, cakes and lunches. Ice creams, soft drinks, ice cold beer and wince. Stroll through the traditional English Cottage Garden. Buy plants and herbs grown by the Trust's gardeners. See the famous Hathaway Bed. Retrace the steps William Shakespeare might have taken when courting Anne Hathaway along Shottery Brook and Jubilee Walks. Coach parties can be catered for please call for details. Seating for both smoking and non-smoking.
Mar-Oct daily 09.30-17.30

Historical

Arbury Hall
Arbury Nuneaton Warwickshire CV10 7PT
[5M SW of Nuneaton off B4102 Meriden road. Plenty of on site parking]
Tel: 02476 382804 Fax: 02476 641147
The 16th century Elizabethan house, Gothicised in the 18th century, has been the home of the Newdegate family for over 450 years. The finest complete example of Gothic revival architecture in the country. Fine furniture, glassware and portraits. Spectacular plaster work ceilings. Member of the Historic Houses Association.
House: Easter-Sept 14.00-17.30 Sun & Mon Bank Holiday Weekends, Sun & Mon. Gardens as House
Last Admission: 17.00
A£4.50 C£2.50 Gardens only A£3.00 C£2.00
Family Ticket £10.00

↓*special events*

▶ **Theatre in the Garden**
15/7/00-15/7/00
Sheridan's The Rivals. Call for full details

▶ **Warwickshire Home, Garden and Leisure SHow**
24/7/00-25/7/00
Call for details
▶ **Motor Transport Spectacular**
20/8/00-20/8/00
Vintage Car Rally with displays of cars, bikes, buses and agricultural vehicles, call for details
▶ **Fireworks in the Park**
2/9/00-2/9/00
The night sky above Arbury Hall will be bright with the colours of fireworks, call for full details

Coughton Court

Coughton Alcester Warwickshire B49 5JA
[2m N of Alcester, on E side of A435. Plenty of on site parking available.]
Tel: 01789 762435 Fax: 01789 765544
www.coughtoncourt.co.uk

An impressive central gatehouse dating from 1530. During the Civil War this formerly moated and mainly Elizabethan house was attacked by both sides. Also has strong connections with the Gun Powder Plot. Featuring some notable furniture, porcelain, portraits and memorabilia of the Throckmorton family resident since 1409. Two churches, tranquil lake, riverside walk and newly created formal gardens. Photography allowed in grounds only. Member of the Historic Houses Association.

visitor comments: House and history very interesting. Very well laid out with just the right amount of supporting information. Expensive cup of tea!

18-31 Mar Sat-Sun 11.30-17.00, Easter Mon-Wed 11.30-17.00, Apr-Sept Wed-Sun 11.30-17.00, July-Aug Tue-Sun 11.30-17.00, 1-29 Oct Sat-Sun 11.30-17.00. Grounds: 11.00-17.30 also Bank Hol Mon & Tue
Last Admission: 30mins before closing
Queuing Times: Timed tickets for House on busy days
House & Gardens: A£6.40 C(5-15)£3.20 Family Ticket (A2+C4)£19.50. Gardens only: A£4.60 C(5-15)£2.30 C(under 5)£Free Family Ticket (A2+C4)£14.40. Groups (15+ pre-booked) House and Gardens £5.15 per person, Gardens only £3.70 per person. No concessions. Free entry for essential helpers for disabled. NT Members: Free admission to house only with membership passes during normal opening hours (£2.00 entry charge to Walled Garden)

discount offer: Two Adults (@ £6.25) For The Price Of One. Not Valid Saturdays, Sundays Or Bank Holiday Mondays. Valid Until 29 Oct 2000

↓*special events*

▶ **Vintage and Classic Car Rally**
11/6/00-11/6/00
▶ **Garden Festival**
15/7/00-16/7/00
▶ **Fireworks Concert**
22/7/00-22/7/00
▶ **Food Festival**
29/7/00-30/7/00
▶ **Craft Fair**
12/8/00-13/8/00
▶ **Home Design and Interiors Exhibition**
3/11/00-5/11/00

Mary Arden's House and the Shakespeare Countryside Museum

Station Road Wilmcote Stratford-Upon-Avon Warwickshire CV37 9UN
[3m NW off A34]
Tel: 01789 204016 Fax: 01789 296083

Mary Arden was William Shakespeare's mother, and this picturesque, half-timbered Tudor house was her childhood home. The house is the main historic feature of an extensive complex of farm buildings which house displays of farming and country life, including a remarkable dovecote, a smithy and cooper's workshop.

All year 20-Mar 19 Oct Mon-Sat 09.30-17.00, Sun 10.00-17.00, 1 20 Oct-19 Mar Mon-Sat 10.00-16.00, Sun 10.30-16.00. Closed 23-26 Dec A£4.40 C£2.20 FamilyTicket £11.00 Parties 20+ 10% discount

Warwick Castle

Castle Hill Warwick Warwickshire CV34 4QU
[J15 M40 then A429 into Warwick]
Tel: 01926 406600 Fax: 01926 401692
www.warwick-castle.co.uk

Over a thousand years of secrets hide in the shadows of Warwick castle. Murder, mystery, intrigue and scandal: the Castle has witnessed it all, and now you too can discover the secret life of England. From the days of William the Conqueror to the reign of Queen Victoria, the Castle has provided a backdrop for many turbulent times. Here you can join a mediaeval household in our Kingmaker attraction, watching them prepare for the final battle of the Earl of Warwick. Enter the eerie Ghost Tower, where it is said that the unquiet spirit of Sir Fulke Greville, murdered most foully by a manservant, still roams. Descend into the gloomy depths of the Dungeon and Torture Chamber, then step forward in time and marvel at the grandeur of the State Rooms and the 14th century Great Hall. Witness the perfect manners and hidden indiscretions of Daisy, Countess of Warwick and her friends and the Royal Weekend Party 1898. Stroll through the 60 acres of grounds and gardens, landscaped by Capability Brown, which surround the Castle today of for the really energetic a climb up the Castle towers to the ramparts provides stunning views of the Warwickshire countryside. There is an exciting programme of special events throughout the year, including daily entertainment in June, July and August. The story of Warwick Castle is best told first hand, so come and hear it for yourself.

visitor comments: Editor's Choice. Don't miss the jousting tournaments, the kids loved it! Wonderful Medieval village. Lots to see, but expect queues.

All year daily 10.00-18.00, Nov-Mar 10.00-17.00. Closed 25 Dec
Last Admission: 30mins before closing
1/3/99-31/5/99 & 1/9/99-29/2/2000: Individuals A£9.50 C(4-16)£5.80 Family Ticket (A2+C2)£27.00 OAPs£6.85 Students£7.25. Pre-booked Groups 20+ A£7.75 C£5.00 OAPs£6.15 Students£6.70 1/6/99-31/8/99: A£10.50 C(4-16)£6.25 Family Ticket (A2+C2)£28.00 OAPs£7.50 Students£7.80. Pre-booked Groups 20+ A£8.50 C£5.25 OAPs£6.75 Students£7.25. Guide Book £3.25. Audio tour hire £2.00 per person

Performing Arts

Royal Shakespeare Company

Waterside Stratford-Upon-Avon Warwickshire CV37 6BB

[A3400 J15 M40 Theatre signed within Stratford. There are a limited number of parking space outside the RST, but numerous spaces in the Recreation Car Park on the South Side of the River Avon and Church St. Car Park (Mon-Fri 18.00-midnight. Sat & Bank Hol all day.) All Pay and Display]

Tel: 01789 403 403 Fax: 01789 294810

www.rsc.org.uk

At the Royal Shakespeare Theatre, the Swan Theatre and The Other Place, the Company performs plays by Shakespeare and other great playwrights including contemporary work. There are two restaurants. Tours of the RST are available, enquiries by telephone 01789 412602. The RSC Swan Gallery is housed in the original Victorian building which opened in 1879. Comprising Theatre, Paintings and Sculpture Gallery, and Reading Room, the latter were not destroyed when the Theatre was burnt down in 1926. On The Edge: pre performance and after show events which compliment the repertoire and put the RSC's work in context. For bookings contact the Box Office on 01789 403403

Swan Gallery: All year Mon-Sat 09.15-end evening, Sun 12.00-16.30, Nov-Mar Sun 11.00-15.30. Closed 24 & 25 Dec.
Dinner/theatre/overnight stay packages availabe all year round. Closed 24 & 25 Dec
Exhibition: A£1.50 C&OAPs&Students £1.00.
Theatre Tours: A£4.00 C&OAPs&Students £3.00

↓*special events*

► **The Lion, The Witch and the Wardrobe - venue: RST**
24/11/99-5/3/00

► **King Lear - venue: RST**
3/12/99-26/2/00

► **Macbeth**
1/3/00-18/3/00

► **As You Like It**
15/3/00-5/10/00
Performed at the Royal Shakespeare Theatre

► **Richard II**
20/3/00-5/10/00
Performed at The Other Place

► **The Rivals**
23/3/00-7/10/00
Performed in the Swan Theatre

► **Henry IV Part 1**
10/4/00-6/10/00
Performed at the Swan Theatre great stuff

► **Romeo and Juliet**
23/6/00-7/10/00
Performed at the Royal Shakespeare Theatre

► **Henry V**
24/8/00-7/10/00
Performed in the Royal Shakespeare Theatre

► **Back to Methuselah**
24/8/00-7/10/00
Performed at The Other Place

£

Places of Worship

Coventry Cathedral and Visitors Centre

7 Priory Row Coventry Warwickshire CV1 5ES

[signposted from M6 M69 A45 & A46]

Tel: 024 7622 7597 Fax: 024 7663 1448

www.coventrycathedral.org

Coventry's former Cathedral was bombed during an air raid in November 1940 which devastated the city. It's remains have been carefully preserved. The new Cathedral was designed by Sir Basil Spence and consecrated in May 1962. It contains many pieces of artwork. The Visitors Centre displays Cathedral treasures, old and new and houses an award-winning audio-visual display, telling the story of the

city and Cathedral.
All year daily Easter-Sept 08.30-18.00, Oct-Easter 09.30-17.30. Visitors Centre: Summer 10.00-16.00. Restricted Winter opening
Cathedral: Free, requested donation of £2.00. Visitor Centre: A£2.00 C(0-6)£Free C(6-16)Students & OAPs£1.00 Camera charge £1.00. Video charge £3.00
discount offer: Two For The Price Of One For Visitors Centre

↓*special events*

▶ **Elgar: Dream of Gerontius**
8/4/00-8/4/00
Performed by St Michael's Singers

▶ **Vaughan Williams' Sea Symphony**
20/5/00-20/5/00
Performed by the Warwickshire Symphony Orchestra

▶ **Special Exhibition**
1/6/00-30/6/00
A display of the new Coventry Cathedral Millennium Vestments

▶ **Benjamin Britten's War Requiem**
14/11/00-14/11/00
A performance by the Cambridge University Music Societyl on the 60th Anniversary of the bombing of Coventry Cathedral

Toy & Childhood Museums

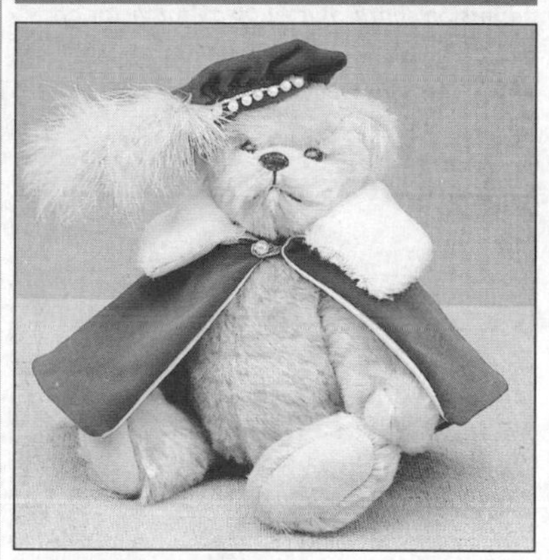

Teddy Bear Museum
19 Greenhill Street Stratford-Upon-Avon Warwickshire CV37 6LF
[J15 M40, off the A46, in the centre of Stratford]
Tel: 01789 293160
www.teddybearmuseum.uk.com
Ten settings, in a house which dates from Shakespeare's time, are devoted to bears of all shapes and sizes. Many very old bears are displayed and there are also mechanical and musical bears. Some of the bears belong to famous people, for example, Jeffrey Archer and Barbara Cartland. Pushchairs are required to be left at reception. Air conditioned.
Mar-Dec daily 09.30-18.00, Jan & Feb daily 09.30-17.00. Closed 25-26 Dec
A£2.25 C£1.00 Family Ticket (A2+C3)£5.95, Groups rates of 20+ A£1.95 C£0.90
discount offer: One Child Free With One Full Paying Adult

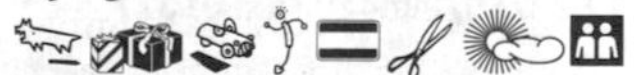

Warwick Doll Museum
Oken's House Castle Street Warwick Warwickshire CV34 4BP
[next to Warwick Castle]
Tel: 01926 495546
Displays on dolls and their houses, puzzles and games. A timber framed house famed for it's collection of 100's of dolls and toys from days gone by also a video showing how the mechanical toys work in the collection.
visitor comments: My 4 year old enjoyed playing hopscotch on the specially marked floor.
Easter-end Oct Mon-Sat 10.00-17.00, Sun 11.00-17.00, Nov-Easter Sat only 10.00-16.00 or dusk if earlier
A£1.00 Family ticket £3.00 Concessions£0.70

Transport Museums

Heritage Motor Centre
Banbury Road Gaydon Warwickshire CV35 0BJ
[J12 M40, 2-3mins away on the B4100, follow signs. Plenty of on site parking available]
Tel: 01926 641188 Fax: 01926 641555
www.stratford.co.uk/bmiht
Heritage Motor Centre, home of the Great British Car Collection has around 200 vehicles on display. The Exhibition Hall features themed displays including the Time Road, 1930s garage and Corgi and Lucas Collections. Outside visitors can enjoy the 4x4 Off Road Circuit, children's roadway, adventure playground, small nature trail and picnic area. The Heritage Motor Centre is ideal for a family day out.
Apr-Oct daily 10.00-17.00, Nov-Mar daily 10.00-17.00. Closed 24, 25-26 Dec & 1 Jan
A£6.00 C(0-4)£Free C(5+)£4.00 Family Ticket (A2+C3)£17.00 OAPs£5.00
discount offer: Two For The Price Of One

↓*special events*

▶ **Christmas Craft Fayre**
1/12/00-3/12/00
Plenty of gift ideas for last minute shopping,

10.00-18.00. Tickets: £1.00.£3.00

Zoos

Twycross Zoo Park
Atherstone Warwickshire CV9 3PX
[A444 near Market Bosworth on the Burton to Nuneaton Road, J11 M42]
Tel: 01827 880250/880440 Fax: 01827 880700
Specialises in primates, and also includes gibbons, gorillas, orang-utangs and chimpanzees. There is a huge range of monkeys from the tiny tamarins and spider monkeys to the large howler monkeys. Also various other animals such as lions, tigers, elephants and giraffes, with a pets' corner for younger children.
visitor comments: Allow a whole day, lots to see. Avoid school holidays. Take a picnic, café very popular. My children love it - particularly the monkeys and the donkey rides. Buy Zoo guide - really helps. Great play area.
All year daily 10.00-18.00. Winter closing 16.00. Closed 25 Dec
A£6.00 C(3-14)£4.00 OAPs£4.50. Group rates 25+ A£4.50 C(3-14)£3.50 C(1-3)£0.50. Special rates for school, college, university parties and physically handicapped/special needs
discount offer: One Child Free With Two Adults Paying Full Price
Expires 31/8/99

Animal Attractions

Cholderton Rare Breeds Farm
Amesbury Road Cholderton Salisbury Wiltshire SP4 0EW
[just off the A338, signposted from the A303, 9m W of Andover & 9m N of Salisbury. Free car and coach parking on site]
Tel: 01980 629438 Fax: 01980 629438
www.farm-animals.co.uk
Set in beautiful countryside and winner of The Best Family Attraction Award 1998, this superb collection of rare farm animals delights everyone. Touch and feed the friendly creatures. Rabbit World is probably the worlds largest collection with over 50 breeds. During peak periods watch the famous pig races. Adventure and toddlers play areas, gardens, water gardens, nature trails, café and shop. A covered Picnic area for wet weather days. A special Learning Centre depicts the history of British Livestock. Bags of animal feed are available for sale in the gift shop. Tractor & Trailer, Pony & Cart rides during peak times (small additional charge). A great day out. No unaccompanied children admitted. Well behaved dogs on leads in the Park only.
1 April-Nov daily 10.00-18.00
Last Admission: 16.45
A£4.25 C(2-14)£2.75 Family Ticket (A2+C2)£13.00 OAPs£3.75. Group rates A£3.25 C£2.00 OAPs£3.00. School parties: A&C£2.50 1 Adult Free per 10 Children
discount offer: 50p Off Normal Admission Charges Per Person. Valid Until 5 Nov 2000

↓special events

▶ **The Pork Stakes Pig Race**
20/4/00-5/9/00
Seven piglets race over hurdles, twice daily at 12.30 and 15.30. Every weekend until September, and every day in school holidays

▶ **Old England Days**
23/4/00-24/4/00
Everything old fashioned in aid of charity. There will be heavy horse displays, hog roast, stalls, pig racing and children's entertainment. Normal admission charge but £1.00 off for Victorian costume

Farmer Giles Farmstead Ltd
Teffont Salisbury Wiltshire SP3 5QY
[Just off A303 London-Exeter road at Teffont, 11m W of Salisbury and 12m from Stonehenge]
Tel: 01722 716338 Fax: 01722 716993
www.farmergiles.co.uk
Family Leisure Farm. Watch 150 cows milked with "hands-on" our large selection of animals

and birds. Beech Belt Walk, Panoramic views, Ponds, Windpump. Rare Breeds, Indoor and Outdoor picnic areas. Gift shop, Exhibition Areas and Licenced Restaurant serving home cooked food.
18 Mar-12 Nov daily 10.00-18.00. Weekends during Winter. Group bookings all year. Closed 25 Dec
A£3.95 C£2.85 Family Ticket (A2+C2)£13.00 OAPs£3.50. Group rates on application
discount offer: One Adult Free With Two Or More Full Paying Children

↓*special events*

▶ **Kite Flying Competition**
2/4/00-2/4/00
Let's go fly a kite...

▶ **Easter Egg Hunt**
23/4/00-24/4/00
Where are they, check the bushes, the nooks and crannies

▶ **Fluffy Chick Weekend**
13/5/00-14/5/00
See chicks hatching

▶ **Keep a Lid on It**
27/5/00-28/5/00
Thatching demonstration

▶ **Cowboy Weekend**
1/7/00-2/7/00
In association with Portsmouth Wild West Association. Barn Dance Fun

▶ **Children's Fun Weekend**
29/7/00-30/7/00
Come on, bring the kids to us this weekend, we'll entertain them, and YOU

▶ **Children's Balloon Race**
26/8/00-27/8/00
Up, up and away for Spire FM

▶ **Toy Tractor Meet**
5/11/00-5/11/00
Chug chug!

Roves Farm Visitor Centre
Sevenhampton Nr Highworth Swindon Wiltshire SN6 7QG
[2m E of Swindon, off the B4000 Highworth / Shrivenham road in Sevenhampton, or the A361]
Tel: 01793 763939
Bottle-feed the lambs, pets corner and other farm animals. Bouncy castle and ball pond, adventure playground, lots of lovely walks, toddlers soft play area. Bring your wellies this is a working farm although there is a lot undercover for rainy day fun. Children's parties catered for, farmhouse bed and breakfast available, large comfortable rooms available all year.
visitor comments: Indoor and outdoor picnic space. Great homemade cakes. Bottle feeding the young animals is great. So much to see and do. Brilliant value for money. I can't stress how good this farm is!
7 Mar-Sept Wed-Sun and Bank Hol 11.00-17.00
A£4.00 C(0-3)£Free C(3+)£3.00 Concessions£3.50. Group discounts and Season tickets available

Archaeology

Devizes Museum
41 Long Street Devizes Wiltshire SN10 1NS
[in Devizes, signposted in town]
Tel: 01380 727369 Fax: 01380 722150
World-famous collections from the Neolithic, Bronze and Iron Age are on display. There is a Bronze Age gallery, an art gallery with a John Piper window, displays of natural history, and a Wiltshire research library. A local history gallery. Wheelchair and pushchair access limited.
All year Mon-Sat 10.00-17.00. Closed Bank Hol with the exception of May 1 & 29
Free on Mondays, A£2.00 C£0.50 Concessions£1.50
discount offer: Two For The Price Of One

↓*special events*

▶ **Wiltshire Ceramics 2000**
15/1/00-20/5/00
An exciting display of contemporary ceramics by seven local ceramicists

▶ **A Wiltshire Lad**
22/2/00-6/5/00
The etchings of Robin Tanner - full of charm and skill and continue to delight all ages

▶ **Chippenham before the Camera**

27/5/00-19/7/00

A Victorian artist's view of Chippenham - the pictures show a fascinating view of Chippenham over 100 years ago

▶ **Extinction 2000**

27/5/00-30/9/00

This exhibition looks at the vanished, the threatened, the new introductions and, as the new millennium dawns, the few lucky species that are planning their comeback in Wiltshire

▶ **Visions of Stonehenge**

22/7/00-30/9/00

This exhibition will include pictures and items from the museum's collections

▶ **Cheque this Out! (provisional)**

7/10/00-30/12/00

The History of Wiltshire Banks - venue may not be available, please call before making a special journey

▶ **Fragmentations**

14/10/00-16/12/00

Paintings, Prints and Mosaics - dealing with the themes of breakage and loss and the renewing power of the creative energy symbolised by the Green Man

Salisbury and South Wiltshire Museum

The King's House 65 The Close Salisbury Wiltshire SP1 2EN

[close to Salisbury cathedral follow signposts]

Tel: 01722 332151 Fax: 01722 325611

Home of the Stonehenge gallery and winner of 6 awards including 'England for Excellence.' Great archaeology - Early Man, Pitt Rivers collection, Romans & Saxons. History of Salisbury (with the famous Giant and Hob Nob), Turner watercolours, ceramics, costume, lace and embroidery are some of the many popular displays.

All year Mon-Sat 10.00-17.00. Also Sun July & Aug 14.00-17.00. Closed Christmas

A£3.00 C£0.75 C(0-5)£Free Concessions£2.00. Saver tickets available

discount offer: Two For The Price Of One Full Paying Adult

↓*special events*

▶ **The 20th Century Community Show**

27/11/99-25/3/00

▶ **A walk around Westminster Abbey**

23/3/00-23/3/00

▶ **Textiles 2000**

1/7/00-21/10/00

Gardens & Horticulture

Courts Garden

Holt Trowbridge Wiltshire BA14 6RR

[3m N of Trowbridge on B3107]

Tel: 01225 782340

A 3 acre garden full of charm and an imaginative blend of colour, surrounds the topiary, water features and garden ornaments. Arboretum containing many fine species of trees. An 18th century house (not open to the public) where weavers came to have their disputes settled.

2 Apri-15 Oct daily 13.30-17.30. Closed Sat. Out of season by appointment

A£3.10 C£1.50

↓*special events*

▶ **Conservatory Care**

27/4/00-27/4/00

Planting pots for garden display, 11.00

▶ **Staking and Supporting**

25/5/00-25/5/00

Pea stick material preparation techniques, 11.00

▶ **Evening Exploration**

8/6/00-8/6/00

Evening in the garden with drinks, 19.00, £3.10, booking essential

▶ **Common Pests and Diseases**

27/6/00-27/6/00

Identification with discussion on control measures, 11.00

▶ **Autumn Lawn Maintenance**

24/10/00-24/10/00

How to achieve that perfect lawn, 11.00

▶ **Waking up the Borders**

2/11/00-2/11/00

Renovation of tired border, 11.0o

Larmer Tree Gardens

Rushmore Estate Tollard Royal Salisbury Wiltshire SP5 5PT

[Heart of Cranborne Chase, off A354 Blandford-Salisbury Road, off B3081 Shaftesbury Road, signposted]

Tel: 01725 516 228 Fax: 01725 516 449

Historical Gardens of General Pitt Rivers laid out in 1880. Acres of interesting gardens to explore. Water features, Open Air Theatre, Roman Temple, Free Flying Macaws, Nepalese Carved Buildings. Entertainment on Sundays.

Easter-Oct daily except Sat 11.00-18.00. Closed 3-12 July & 1-9 Aug

Last Admission: 17.00

A£3.50 C5+£1.50 Concessions £3.00 Groups 15+ A£3.25 C£1.35 OAPs£2.75

Luckington Court Gardens
Chippenham Wiltshire SN14 6PQ
[6m W of Malmesbury on B4040 Bristol Road, suitable parking next to the Church adjacent to Luckington Court]
Tel: 01666 840205
Mainly Queen Anne with magnificent group of ancient buildings. Beautiful mainly formal garden with fine collection of ornamental trees and shrubs. Refreshments available by arrangement with The Old Royal Ship (01666 840222). Famous for the filming of Pride & Prejudice.
Garden Only: All year Wed 14.00-17.00
Gardens only: A£1.00

Stourhead House and Garden
Stourton Warminster Wiltshire BA12 6QD
[3m NW of Mere off B3092. Please telephone for details of how to reach us by public transport]
Tel: 01747 841152 Fax: 01747 841152
www.nationaltrust.org.uk
Magnificent 18th century landscape garden with lakes, temples, grotto and rare trees. Changing scene of colour and fragrance throughout the seasons. Fine Palladium house, designed in 1721 for Henry Hoare, with outstanding library, works of art and furniture by the younger Chippendale. King Alfred's Tower, an intriguing red-brick folly built in 1772 is almost 50m high and gives breathtaking views over the estate. Tours by arrangement. Dogs on leads in garden from Nov-end Feb. Photography allowed in the garden only.
Garden: all year daily 09.00-19.00 or sunset if earlier. (Garden closes at 17.00 on 20-23 July (last admission 16.00). House 1 Apr-29 Oct Sat-Wed 12.00-17.30, or dusk if earlier. King Alfred's Tower: 1 Apr-29 Oct Tue-Fri 14.00-17.30 (or dusk if earlier), Sat & Sun 11.30-17.30, also open Bank Hol Mon
Last Admission: House: 30mins before closing
Garden: Peak Season A£4.60 C£2.60 Family Ticket (A2+C3)£10.00. Groups 15+ £4.10, Low Season A£3.60 C£1.50 Family Ticket (A2+C3)£8.00. House: A£4.60 C£2.60 Family Ticket (A2+C3)£10.00. Groups 15+ £4.10. House & Garden: Peak Season A£8.00 C£3.80 Family Ticket (A2+C3)£20.00, Groups 15+ £7.70. King Alfred's Tower: A£1.50 C£0.70

↓*special events*

▶ **Gardening the Past - Preserving the Future**
9/3/00-9/3/00
How the world famous landscape garden is maintained. £10.00 to incl lunch at The Spread Eagle. Meet at 10.30 at visitor reception

▶ **A Peek in the Archives**
13/4/00-13/4/00
A journey of discovery through the fascinating facts and details. £8.50 incl afternoon tea, 15.00

▶ **Tall Trees Trail**
27/4/00-27/4/00
Tree facts for Children 5-11. C£3.50 C£4.00, meet at 10.30 at visitor reception

▶ **Pelargoniums, Plant Pots & Pastries**
6/7/00-6/7/00
Discover the secrets of successful pest control, feeding and watering. Meet at 15.00 at visitor reception, £8.50 to incl afternoon tea

▶ **Attics and Cellar Tours**
11/7/00-11/7/00
See entry for 15 May

▶ **Stourhead - A Journey Through Time**
20/7/00-23/7/00
Breathtaking spectacle of music, song and dance in the garden. Evening picnic concert with fireworks.Breathtaking spectacle of music, song and dance in the garden. Evening picnic concert with fireworks. Gates from 17.30 for 19.30 start. Thur: A£17.00 C£11.00, Fri: A19.00 C£13.00, Sat: A£22.00 C£16.00 on the gate if available, advance booking recommended (discounted). Book bt 31 March and save an extra £1.00 per ticket

▶ **A Community Celebrates**
23/7/00-23/7/00
Parish Community Millennium event. From 14.00, 18.30 - Music of the Night

▶ **A Midsummer Night's Dream**
5/8/00-5/8/00
Theatre Set-Up. Gates from 18.00 for 19.30 start. Bring picnics and rugs. A£8.00 C£6.00

▶ **Stourhead at Dawn**
10/8/00-10/8/00
Meet Head Gardener at 05.30 at visitor reception for an early morning walk. NT members £6.00, non-members £10.00, incl drink

▶ **Attics and Cellar Tours**
6/9/00-6/9/00
See entry for 5 May

▶ **Talking Trees**
25/9/00-25/9/00
Illustrated talk on the extensive tree collection. Meet at 10.30 at The Spread Eagle Inn. £10.00

to incl lunch

▶ **Woodland Den Building**
7/10/00-7/10/00
Join in a morning of fun building a woodland den. No unaccompanied children please, wellies and old clothes essential. Meet at 10.30 at King Alfred's Tower car park

▶ **Tree Day**
21/10/00-21/10/00
Demonstrations of tree climbing and aspects of tree maintenance, 10.00-17.00

▶ **Winter Warmer**
17/12/00-17/12/00
Garden walk

Historical

Lacock Abbey, Fox Talbot Museum and Village
High Street Lacock Chippenham Wiltshire SN15 2LG
[3m S of Chippenham off A350. Bus: Badgerline 234/7 Tel 01225 46446. Fosseway 234, 72 Tel 01249 444444. BR: Chippenham 3.5m]
Tel: 01249 730227/730459
The Abbey was founded in 1232 and converted into a country house in 1540. A fine example of medieval cloisters, sacristy, chapter house and monastic rooms. The museum of photography commemorates the achievements of William Fox Talbot, inventor of the modern photographic negative. The village has featured in many TV dramas: Pride and Prejudice; Emma and Moll Flanders and dates back to the 13th century.
Museum Cloisters & Gardens: 26 Feb-29 Oct daily 11.00-17.30, closed Good Fri. Abbey: 28 Mar-31 Oct daily 13.00-17.30 closed Tue. Closed Good Fri Museum: Also open some winter weekends tel. for details
Last Admission: 17.00
Museum, Cloisters & Grounds: A£3.70 C£2.20 Family Ticket £10.60. Abbey, Grounds, Cloisters & Museum: A£5.80 C£3.20 Family Ticket £15.90 Groups A£5.30 C£2.70. Museum A£2.10
discount offer: One Child Free With A Full Paying Adult

↓*special events*

▶ **Celebration Walks**
1/3/00-29/3/00
Walk Fox Talbot's woodland and botanic gardens, every other Wed in Mar at 14.30, £3.50 to incl afternoon tea, booking essential

▶ **Easter Concert**
22/4/00-22/4/00
19.30, £8.00, booking on 01249 730042

▶ **Easter Egg Hunt & Quiz**
24/4/00-24/4/00
At 10.30... usual admission

▶ **Spring Plant Fair**
14/5/00-14/5/00
11.00-17.00... usual admission

▶ **Children's Woodland Trail**
30/5/00-30/5/00
Great fun for children, 14.00, C£Free

▶ **A Midsummer Night's Dream**
13/6/00-13/6/00
Presented by Theatre Set-up. Gates open at 18.00 for 19.00 start, bring a picnic and a rug or chair. A£7.50 C£3.75 in advance, £2.00 extra if available on the gate, book early to avoid disappointment

▶ **The Complete Millennium Musical**
16/7/00-16/7/00
Presented by The Reduced Shakespeare Company. Gates open at 18.00 for 19.00 start, bring a picnic and a rug or chair. A£13.00 in advance, book early to avoid disappointment

▶ **The Importance of Being Ernest**
30/7/00-30/7/00
Presented by Illyria. Gates open at 18.00 for 19.00 start, bring a picnic and a rug or chair. A£8.00 C£4.00 in advance, £2.00 extra on the gate if available, book early to avoid disappointment

▶ **Colouring Competition**
12/8/00-13/8/00
13.00-16.00... no extra charge

▶ **Spooky Tales and Mask-Making**
24/10/00-24/10/00
Great fun for children, 14.00, C£Free

▶ **Christmas Concerts**
15/12/00-16/12/00
19.30 at Lacock Abbey, £8.00 to incl wine, book on 01249 730042

▶ **Carols at Lacock Abbey**
17/12/00-17/12/00
At 15.00 and 19.00... £5.00 to incl wine book on 01249 730042

Lydiard Park
Lydiard Tregoze Swindon Wiltshire SN5 9PA
[J16 M4, follow Brown Tourist Signs]
Tel: 01793 770401 Fax: 01793 877909
www.swindon.gov.uk
Set in beatiful parkland, this fine Georgian house belonged to the Viscounts Bolingbroke for 500 years until 1943, when it was purchased by Swindon Corporation. Since then the sadly delapidated house has been gradually restored and refurbished with much of the original family furnishings and protraits. Character figures and audio guides bring the story of Lydiard Park to life.
House: All year Mon-Fri 10.00-13.00 & 14.00-17.00, Sat 10.00-17.00, Sun 14.00-17.00. Closed Good Fri & Christmas. Nov-Feb closing 16.00. Park: all year daily closing at dusk each day
Last Admission: 16.30 15.30 (winter)

A£1.25 Concessions£0.60
discount offer: Free Guide Book on Lydiard House worth £1.50

Old Sarum Castle
Castle Road Salisbury Wiltshire SP1 3SD
[2m N of Salisbury on A345. Plenty of parking on site]
Tel: 01722 335398 Fax: 01722 416037
www.english-heritage.org.uk
The story of Old Sarum began in pre-history; it was once the location for an Iron Age camp. What the visitor sees today, however, are the remains of a thriving community that grew up around a Norman cathedral and castle.
visitor comments: Fascinating if you are interested in ancient history.
1 Apr-31 Oct daily 10.00-18.00, 17.00 in Oct1 Nov-31 Mar daily 10.00-16.00. Closed 24-26 Dec & 1 Jan
A£2.00 C£1.00 Concessions£1.50
↓*special events*
▶ **Mini Event**
8/7/00-9/7/00
▶ **Iron Age Pottery**
15/7/00-16/7/00
Iron age craft demonstrations including pottery making using a Romano-British kiln
▶ **A Roman and his British Wife**
22/7/00-23/7/00
Fascinating talks and displays of Romano-British life
▶ **Old Sarum Through the Ages**
29/7/00-30/7/00
Walk through time and meet the soldiers of Sarum from the Romans to D-Day!
▶ **Medieval Life**
5/8/00-6/8/00
15th century military and domestic life, with crafts, men-at-arms and period games
▶ **Life in the Age of Chivalry**
12/8/00-13/8/00
Weapons, skills-at-arms, have-a-go archery, crafts and 14th century living history
▶ **The Bard and the Blade**
19/8/00-20/8/00
Shakespearean dialogue and dramatic duels with sword and dagger
▶ **King Arthur's Greatest Victory**
27/8/00-28/8/00
Find out the facts behind Arthurian fiction at this recreation of the Battle of Baden Hill

Wilton House
The Estate Office Wilton Salisbury Wiltshire SP2 0BJ
[3m W of Salisbury on the A30. Plenty of on site parking available]
Tel: 01722 746729 Fax: 01722 744447
450 year old stately home to the Earls of Pembroke and the present family home of the 17th Earl. Magnificent Inigo Jones State Rooms, Palladian architecture and world famous art collection. Visitor Centre with dynamic introductory film, Tudor Kitchen, Victorian Laundry and the Wareham Bears. Huge adventure playground. Exhibition for 2000 is a selection of photographs dating back over 150 years
10 Apr-29 Oct daily 10.30-17.30. Please pre-book guided tours
Last Admission: 16.30
A£6.75 C(5-15)£4.00 C(0-5)£Free Family Ticket(A2+C2)£17.50 Students&OAPs£5.75
discount offer: Two For The Price Of One
↓*special events*
▶ **Wilton House Antiques Fair**
3/3/00-5/3/00
The 23rd annual fair in the Cloisters/Indoor Riding School. 10.30-17.00, A£3.50
▶ **Medieval Weekend**
20/5/00-21/5/00
Come and see court dancing, archery, knights in combat, servants and peasants dancing, heraldry, armour making and the recreation of falconry. Grounds entry ticket price applies
▶ **BBC Gardeners' World Subscribers' Day**
10/6/00-10/6/00
▶ **Millennium Garden Party**
11/6/00-11/6/00
Special afternoon for the people of Wilton, including an open air Church service for the Mayor. Free grounds only entry after 14.00
▶ **Wilton Horse Trials**
24/6/00-25/6/00
Traditional country horse trial event. Separate access and admission charges apply, please call 01749 812994
▶ **Open Air Musical Concert with Fireworks**
15/7/00-15/7/00
With the Bournemouth Symphony Orchestra. Gates open at 18.00, call 01202 669925 for tickets
▶ **A Russian Festival**
15/7/00-15/7/00
Bournemouth Symphony Orchestra with Christopher Bell as conductor. Call for further

details on 01202 669925. Tickets: From £14.00-19.00 C&Students half price

▶ **Hamdon Craft Fairs**

28/7/00-30/7/00

Separate entrance fees and access. Palladian Bridge open to the craft fair for House/Grounds visitors with a small price supplement

▶ **Children's Fun Day**

6/8/00-6/8/00

Meet the Crazy Bears, enjoy the huge adventure playground and Crazy Cottage. Special effects and pyrotechnics. Grounds only admission prices apply, free to season holders on production of ticket

▶ **Chef's Challenge**

23/9/00-24/9/00

Come and enjoy samples of food and drink from the various regional exhibitors and watch regular cookery demonstrations. Ground entry rates apply

Landmarks

Stonehenge

Amesbury Salisbury Wiltshire SP4 7DE

[Monument 2m W of Amesbury at J of A303 & A344/A360. Bus: Wilts & Dorset 3 BR: Salisbury-Stonehenge Tel: 01722 336855 BR: Salisbury 9.5m]

Tel: 01980 624715 info line Fax: 01980 623465

www.english-heritage.org.uk

Stonehenge is a prehistoric monument of unique importance, which has been designated a World Heritage Site. Known throughout the world, for over 5,000 years these enigmatic stones have engendered a sense of reverence in the millions of people who have visited them. Why they were put there remains a mystery.

visitor comments: Excellent view of stones with a helpful audio guide, which is free. Small overcrowded shop. Refreshments are just an open-air stall. No real picnic area.

16 Mar-31 May daily 09.30-18.00. 1 June-31 Aug daily 09.00-19.00. 1 Sept-15 Oct daily 09.30-18.00. 16 Oct-23 Oct daily 09.30-17.00. 24 Oct-15 Mar daily 09.30-16.00. Closed 24-26 Dec

Last Admission: 20mins before closing

A£4.00 C(5-15)£2.00 Family Ticket(A2+C3)£10.00 Concessions£3.00

↓*special events*

▶ **John Aubrey at Stonehenge**

27/5/00-28/5/00

17th century antiquarian explains his theories as to why Stonehenge was built

▶ **Morris Dancing**

9/7/00-9/7/00

▶ **John Aubrey at Stonehenge**

23/9/00-24/9/00

See entry for 27 May

Places of Worship

Salisbury Cathedral

33 The Close Salisbury Wiltshire SP1 2EJ

[A30, M3, M27 signposted locally]

Tel: 01722 555120 Fax: 01722 555116

www.salisburycathedral.org.uk

Built between 1220 and 1258 Salisbury Cathedral is a masterpiece of medieval architecture. Its elegant spire at 123 meters (404 feet) is the tallest in England. Cathedral treasures include Europe's oldest working clock and an original Magna Carta.

All year Sept-May 07.00-18.30, June-Aug 07.00-20.15

Guidelines for donations: A£3.00 C£1.00 OAPs & Students £2.00 Family Ticket £6.00

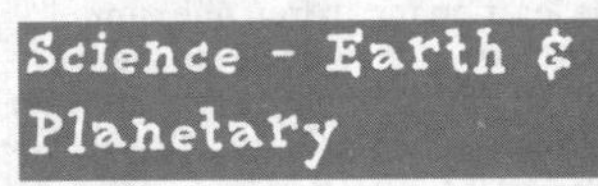

Science - Earth & Planetary

Science Museum Wroughton

Red Barn Gate Wroughton Airfield Swindon Wiltshire SN4 9NS

[Wroughton Airfield is situated on the A4361 Swindon to Devizes Road, 4m S of Swindon, 1m S of Wroughton Village. Access is normally via Red Barn Gate from A4361 and M4J16. On special occasions alternative routes may be used and these are then signposted]

Tel: 01793 814466 Fax: 01793 813569

www.nmsi.ac.uk/wroughton

The Science Museum Wroughton is the large object storage facility for the National Museum of Science and Industry and house a diverse range of aircraft, road transport and heavy vehicles, medical equipment, civil engineering and experimental objects from the national collections

May-Sept Sat & Sun for a variety of special weekend events or by appointment throughout the year for groups of 30+. Leaflet available from Feb 2000 for events

Last Admission: 17.00

A£3.00 C£Free

Transport Museums

Atwell-Wilson Motor Museum

Downside Stockley Road Calne Wiltshire SN11 0NF

[off A4 at Quemerford, off J16 on M4]
Tel: 01249 813119 Fax: 01249 813119
The museum contains over 70 exhibits with a number of new donations to the Museum including a Vauxhall Victor DeLux with 370,000 miles, which compliments classic cars from 1924-1983, classic motorbikes, lawn mowers and memorabilia. The 45-acre site also includes a 17th Century water-meadow walk and a very nice children's play area.
All year Apr-Oct Mon-Thur 11.00-17.00, Sun 11.00-17.00, Nov-Mar Mon-Thur 11.00-16.00, Sun 11.00-16.00
A£2.50 C£1.00 OAPs£2.00
discount offer: Two For The Price Of One

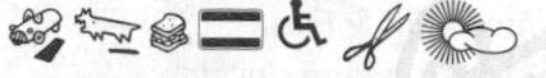

Wildlife & Safari Parks

Longleat
The Estate Office Longleat Warminster Wiltshire BA12 7NW
[A36 between Bath & Sailisbury, A362 Warminster to Frome. Plenty of on site parking]
Tel: 01985 844400 Fax: 01985 844885
www.longleat.co.uk
Longleat offers a great day out for all the family... From lions to tigers and monkeys to giraffe, discover many of the world's most majestic and endangered creatures as they roam within the magnificent Safari Park. Get lost in the 'World's Longest Hedge Maze,' let of steam in the Adventure Castle, travel on the Safari Boats, get close to the animals in Pets Corner and marvel at the historic treasures and heirlooms within Longleat House... Your day at Longleat will never be long enough!
visitor comments: Possibly the best Safari Park I have visited so far, especially the walkabout amongst the giraffes and zebras. Excellent value, with something for all ages. Use the Safari Bus Service! The boats get really busy, so go first thing, and allow for queueing time.
Longleat House: 1 Apr-31 Dec daily. Closed 25 Dec. Pre-booked groups only Jan-Mar. Easter-Sept 11.00-18.00 rest of year 11.00-16.00. Safari Park: 1 Apr-29 Oct daily 10.00-17.00 (sunset if earlier). Other attractions: 1 Apr-29 Oct daily 11.00-17.30
Last Admission: 17.30 or sunset if sooner
Longleat Passport Ticket: A£13.00 C&OAPs£11.00 - includes entry to all of Longleat's attractions with ability to return before end of season to visit attractions not visited before
discount offer: £2.00 Off Per Person For Up To Six People (limited to Passport Ticket sales only). One coupon per party. Valid 1 Apr-29 Oct 2000 excluding Bank Holidays

↓*special events*

▶ **'Great Paw Trek'**
21/5/00-21/5/00
A sponsored walk on behalf of the Guide Dogs for the Blind with Dog Show. Please call: 01985 216187

▶ **Longleat Canada Life Horse Trials**
2/6/00-4/6/00
Eventing at its best with both British and International eventing stars taking on dressage, show-jumping and cross-country. Please call 01747 838807

▶ **Radio Rally**
25/6/00-25/6/00
An event for the amateur radio enthusiast or those just fascinated by technology! Please call: 0117 985 6253

▶ **Celebrity Family Fun Day**
22/8/00-22/8/00
Live entertainment, top bands, favourite Soap Stars and fun fair. Please call: 01985 844400

▶ **Dog Agility Stakes**
8/9/00-10/9/00
Dog agility show. Please call: 01255 765078

▶ **Tipadel Hill Climb**
23/9/00-24/9/00
Speed hill climb for cars. Please call: 01305 774611

▶ **Santa Special Trains**
26/11/00-23/12/00
A chance to ride the train to meet Father Christmas in his Log Cabin Grotto and receive an early Christmas present! Please call: 01985 845408 (pre-booking essential) Sat & Sun only from 26 Nov

Factory Outlets & Tours

Royal Worcester Visitor Centre
Severn Street Worcester Worcestershire WR1 2NE
[J7 M5 follow signs for City Centre, turn left at 5th set of traffic lights near the Cathedral]
Tel: 01905 21247 Fax: 01905 23601
Whether you shop for bargains in the Bestware or Seconds Shop, take a Factory Tour, paint a plate, visit the Museum of Worcester

Porcelain or browse in Wigornia Court where interesting household items abound, a day at Royal Worcester's Visitor Centre offers something for everyone. Guided Factory Tour (1hr): Join Royal Worcester's experienced Tour Guides for an informative tour of the working factory, includes several flights of steep stairs, not available for under 11 due to the safety regulations. Manufactory & Film Tour: Experience the industrial past, watch an artist at work, take a behind the scenes look at Royal Worcester's Design Department and compare the techniques of today. The Museum of Worcester Porcelain Tour: Travel on a design journey through time to see rare porcelain sumptuously displayed in period settings. Special All in One: Guided Factory Tours, entrance to Manufactory, Film and Museum Tour (45mins).

All year Mon-Sat 09.00-17.30, Sun 11.00-17.00. Guided Tours available daily

Museum: A£3.00 Concessions£2.25. Guided Factory Tour: All £5.00. Manufactory and Film Tour: A2.25 C(under 5)£Free Concessions£1.75. The Museum of Worcester Porcelain Tour: A£3.00 C(under 5)£Free Concessions£2.25. Special All in One Tour: A£8.00 Concessions£6.75. Guided Tour of Museum and Manufactory: A£4.50 Concessions£3.75

discount offer: Two For The Price Of One Admission To The Museum

Folk & Local History Museums

Avoncroft Museum of Historic Buildings

Redditch Road Stoke Heath Bromsgrove Worcestershire B60 4JR

[2m S of Bromsgrove off the A38 Bromsgrove by-pass 400 yards N of its junction with B4091 3m N of J5 M5. 3.5m S of J1 M42]

Tel: 01527 831363 Fax: 01527 876934

www.avoncroft.org.uk

A visit to Avoncroft takes you through nearly 700 years of history. You can see 25 buildings rescued from destruction and authentically restored on a 15 acre rural site. The magnificent timbered roof of Worcester Cathedral's original Guest Hall dates from 1330 and now crowns a modern hall in which a wide variety of functions, including civil weddings, are held.

visitor comments: The collection of telephone kiosks is fantastic. Best visited in fair weather.

July-Aug & Bank Hol daily 10.30-17.00 (weekend 17.30) Apr-June & Sept-Oct 10.30-16.30 (weekends 17.00). Closed Mon. Mar & Nov 10.30-16.00. Closed Mon & Fri

Last Admission: 1 hour before closing

A£4.60 C£2.30 Family Ticket £12.50 OAPs£3.70

discount offer: One Child Free With A Full Paying Adult OR £2.00 Off a 2nd Full Paying Adult

↓special events

▶ United States Civil War

8/4/00-9/4/00

A living history weekend celebrating the US Civil War

▶ Easter Extravaganza Weekend

22/4/00-24/4/00

Come celebrate with us this Easter with plenty to do for all the family

▶ May Day Festival

1/5/00-1/5/00

All the usual fun and more

▶ Living History Event

13/5/00-13/5/00

History comes alive with re enactments of over 600 years of English Life

▶ Living History Event

28/5/00-29/5/00

See history come to life in front of your own eyes

▶ Re-enactors Market and Fayre

23/9/00-24/9/00

Enjoy the fun, sounds and smells of an historic Market and Fayre

▶ Harvest Home

21/10/00-22/10/00

Demonstrations of ancient harvesting, traditional games, song and dance celebrating Autumn

▶ Annual Craft Show

25/11/00-26/11/00

Just in the nick of time for those Christmas gifts

Museum of Local Life
Friar Street Worcester Worcestershire WR1 2NA
[Central Worcester 5mins walk from the Cathedral]
Tel: 01905 722349
This interesting 500-year timber-framed house has a squint and an ornate plaster ceiling. It is now a museum of local life featuring a children's room, an Edwardian bathroom and displays of the Home Front of World War II. There is a changing programme of temporary exhibitions and events.
All year Mon-Wed & Fri-Sat 10.30-17.00. Open Bank Hol Mon. Closed Good Fri, Easter Sun, 25-26 Dec & 1 Jan
Admission Free

Gardens & Horticulture

Burford House Gardens
Tenbury Wells Worcestershire WR15 8HQ
[off A456, 1m W of Tenbury Wells, 8m from Ludlow]
Tel: 01584 810777 Fax: 01584 810673
The sweeping lawns and plantsman's paradise of Burford House Gardens are set in the picturesque valleys of the River Teme and Ledwych Brook. The late Georgian bridge over the Ledwych has been restored, leading to a new wildflower gardens down to the heavenly spot where the two rivers meet. The grass garden has been redesigned, a bamboo collection planted, and the National Collection of Clematis of over 200 varieties continues to grow. The nursery of Treasures of Tenbury grows over 300 varieties of clematis and many of the unusual plants that can be seen in the gardens, which are also on sale in the Plant Centre. Also on site is the Burford House Gallery: contemporary and botanical art shows; Burford Buttery: serving a wide selection of homemade cakes, hot and cold meals; Evening Bistro (Thurs, Fri & Sat); Gift Shop; Mulu exotic plants; Jungle Giants bamboos.
visitor comments: Wonderful wild meadow field. Nearby church worth a visit. Excellent service and good choice in restaurant.
All year daily 10.00-17.00 or dusk if sooner
A£3.50 C£1.00. Group rate 10+ £3.00
discount offer: Two For The Price Of One Into The Gardens

Stone House Cottage Gardens
Stone Kidderminster Worcestershire DY10 4BG
[2m SE on A448]
Tel: 01562 69902
A beautiful walled garden with towers provides a sheltered area of about one acre for rare shrubs, climbers and interesting herbaceous plants. Adjacent to the garden is a nursery with a large selection of unusual plants.
Gardens & Nursery: Mar-Sept Wed-Sat 10.00-17.30
A£2.00 C£Free
discount offer: Two For The Price Of One. Valid Until 30 Sept 99

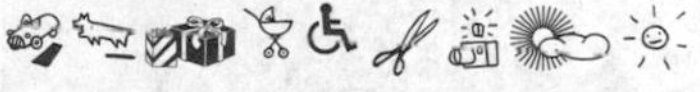

Historical

Goodrich Castle
Goodrich Ross-on-Wye Worcestershire HR9 6HY
[5m S of Ross-on-Wye off A40]
Tel: 01600 890538
www.english-heritage.org.uk
Goodrich Castle towers majestically over an ancient crossing of the River Wye. The castle was built here in medieval times and saw much action during the Civil War, when a locally made cannon called 'Roaring Meg' was used to bombard the Royalist garrison ending a long siege. The cannon can still be seen at Hereford Cathedral.
1 Apr-31 Oct daily 10.00-18.00, 17.00 in Oct. 1 Nov-31 Mar 10.00-16.00. Closed 24-26 Dec & 1 Jan
A£3.20 C£1.60 OAPs£2.40
↓*special events*
► **Medieval Entertainers**
23/4/00-24/4/00

Play authentic medieval games, cures, folklore and early machinery, plus a children's play about the formative years of Parliament

▶ **Civial War Living History**
29/4/00-1/5/00

▶ **Medieval Living History**
28/5/00-29/5/00
A 15th century household with military displays, artillery, encampment and dancing

▶ **A Civil War Surgeon**
1/7/00-2/7/00
A fascinating and gruesome insight into 17th century medical care. Not for the faint-hearted!

▶ **Medieval Living History**
8/7/00-9/7/00
Crafts, archery, weaponry and a mummers' play

▶ **Carry on Piping!**
15/7/00-16/7/00
Lively, humorous, have-a-go family show with 16th century rock 'n' roll!

▶ **Merry Men?**
22/7/00-23/7/00
Hoodwinked Robin and Marian return to Sherwood to sort out truth from legend, with hilarious results!

▶ **Medieval Falconry**
9/9/00-10/9/00
Medieval falconry demonstrations

▶ **Hallowe'en Tours**
21/10/00-29/10/00
At 11.00 & 14.30. Chilling tales about our haunted heritage - a little light exorcise! on 21, 22, 28 & 29 Oct

Hanbury Hall

School Road Hanbury Droitwich
Worcestershire WR9 7EA
[4.5m E of Droitwich, 1m N of B4090, 6m S of Bromsgrove, 1.5m W of B4091. BR: Droitwich. Plenty of on site parking]
Tel: 01527 821214 Fax: 01527 821251
www.ntrustsevern.org.uk

William & Mary-style red-brick house, completed in 1701. Hanbury is an outstanding example of an English country house built by a prosperous local family, with painted ceilings and staircase by Thornhill. The Watney Collection of porcelain is also on display in the house. No dogs in garden, allowed on leads in park.

visitor comments: Interesting house and gardens. Pleasant for both the "NT Diehards" and for those wanting to just wander around house and gardens!

2 Apr-29 Oct Hall 14.00-18.00. Gardens, tearoom and shop now open from 12.30. Evening guided tours for pre-booked parties
Last Admission: 17.30 or dusk if sooner
House & Garden: A£4.60 C£2.30 Family Ticket (A2+C3)£11.50, Garden only: A£2.90 C£1.45

↓*special events*

▶ **Gardener's Tours**
5/4/00-6/9/00
Held on Apr 5, May 3, June 7, July 5, Aug 2 and Sept 6 only. Commence at 15.00, normal admission rates apply

▶ **Easter Trail**
25/4/00-25/4/00
Starts at 13.00, £2.25 for garden and kiosk trail

▶ **Estate Walk**
14/5/00-14/5/00
Begins at 15.00, normal admission charges apply

▶ **Jazz and BBQ Night**
12/8/00-12/8/00
Held in the Marquee at 20.00. £8.00 per person, not including food

▶ **Craft Fair**
27/8/00-28/8/00
Held in the West Courtyard from 10.00-16.00. £1.50 in addition to normal admission

▶ **Free Entry Day**
13/9/00-13/9/00
Free entry for all from 12.30!

▶ **Book Fair**
24/9/00-24/9/00
Held in the Marquee from 12.30, normal admission charges apply

Lower Brockhampton

Brockhampton Bringsty Worcester
Worcestershire WR6 5UH
[2m E of Bromyard on Worcester road A44 reached by a narrow road through 1.5m of woods and farmland]
Tel: 01885 488099

A late 14th century moated manor house, with an attractive detached half-timbered 15th century gatehouse, a rare example of this type of structure. Also, the ruins of a 12th century chapel. Gatehouse and upper floor not accessi-

ble to wheelchairs, Braille guide. Car park for cars and coaches with information panels and facilities: woodland walks, including access for all and sculpture trails.
visitor comments: Not to be missed. Viewing the property takes about 15 minutes.
Medieval hall, parlour, minstrels gallery & chapel: 1 Apr-end Sept Wed-Sun & Bank Hol Mon 10.00-17.00. Closed Good Fri. Oct-1 Nov Wed-Sun 10.00-16.00
A£2.00 C£1.00 Family Ticket £5.00. Car Park £1.50

The Commandery
Sidbury Worcester Worcestershire WR1 2HU
[Worcester city centre 3mins walk from the Cathedral. A44 from J7 M5]
Tel: 01905 361821 Fax: 01905 361822
This delightful 15th century timber-framed building was the headquarters of Charles II's army during the Battle of Worcester in 1651. It has an impressive Great Hall with fine examples of 15th century stained glass. The building contains fascinating Civil War displays including audio-visuals. A varied events programme all year.
All year Mon-Sat 10.00-17.00, Sun 13.30-17.00. Closed 24-28 Dec & 1 Jan
Last Admission: 16.30
A£3.60 C£2.50 Family Ticket £9.60, a small price increase likely 1/4/2000
discount offer: Two For The Price Of One. One Free Child With Every Full Paying Adult
↓*special events*
▶ **Millennium Exhibition Opens**
6/5/00-31/12/00
Plotting the Past, Planning the Future
▶ **Oak Apple Festival**
27/5/00-28/5/00
Join our Oak Apple Celebrations with Charles II
▶ **Medieval Pagent**
9/9/00-10/9/00
Come and experience all things medieval at this exciting two day event

Places of Worship

Worcester Cathedral
College Green Worcester Worcestershire WR1 2LH
Tel: 01905 28854/21004 Fax: 01905 611139
Worcester Cathedral with its 200 foot tower stands majestically beside the River Severn. The Crypt, built by St. Wulstan in 1084, is a classic example of Norman architecture. The 12th century Chapter House and Clositers are a reminder of the cathedral's monastic past. King John and Prince Arthur are buried near the High Altar.
visitor comments: A beautiful, large Cathedral. Purchase a permit before taking photos or videos.
All year daily 7.30-18.00
Admission Free: Invite donation of A£2.00.
Groups essential to book in advance

Railways

Severn Valley Railway
The Railway Station Bewdley Worcestershire DY12 1BG
[Kidderminster Town station is adjacent to BR station. This in on Comberton Hill on the A448. Plenty of free on site parking available.]
Tel: 01299 403816 Fax: 01299 400839
www.svr.co.uk
The leading standard gauge steam railway, with one of the largest collections of locomotives and rolling stock in the country. Services operate from Kidderminster and Bewdley to Bridgnorth through 16 miles of picturesque scenery along the River Severn. 'Day Out With Thomas' events take place during the year.
visitor comments: Very interesting and entertaining for all age groups. Toilets and Buffet cars clean and tidy. Allow a whole day.

Try make it onto the steam trains - worthwhile. A "Thomas" special event weekend is fabulous!
Weekends throughout year, daily 13 May-24 Sept plus school holidays
Prices depend on journey undertaken, call for details

↓*special events*

▶ **Branch Line Gala Weekend**
18/3/00-19/3/00
An intensive service of trains re-creating the branch line scene of a bygone era

▶ **"Day out with Thomas" Events**
13/5/00-10/9/00
Held on May 13-14 and 20-21 only. Two weekends of fun and games with Thomas, Percy, Duck and their many friends

▶ **Heavy Horse Weekend**
10/6/00-11/6/00
Many shire and other heavy horses in action at various points along the line

▶ **1940's Weekend**
1/7/00-2/7/00
A nostalgic look at Britain in wartime

▶ **Autumn Steam Gala**
22/9/00-24/9/00
Still the UK's premier steam railway event including all-night train services. Something for all the family to enjoy.

▶ **Diesel Gala**
29/9/00-1/10/00
An intensive service of trains using some of our historic diesel locomotives, on Sept 29 all trains will be diesel hauled

▶ **Classic Vehicle Day**
8/10/00-8/10/00
A comprehensive gathering of classic road vehicles

▶ **Santa Steam Specials**
2/12/00-24/12/00
To be held on Dec 2/3, 9/10, 16/17 and 23/24 only. Further details and booking forms available from late Aug 2000

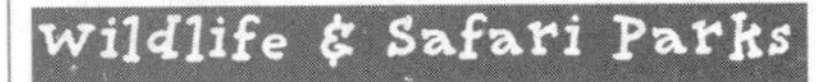

Wildlife & Safari Parks

West Midland Safari and Leisure Park

Spring Grove Bewdley Worcestershire DY12 1LF
[on the A456 between Kidderminster and Bewdley. From Birmingham: main Hagley road to the Quinton Expressway A456 through Hagley and Blakedown following Safari Park signs. From Wolverhampton: take the A449 to Kidderminster then the A456 to Bewdley. From the North: M^ S J8 to M5 J3, follow the A456 through Kidderminster to Bewdley. From the South: take the M5 N J6, follow the A449 to Kidderminster then A456 to Bewdley. From the East: take the M42 W then the M5 NW, leave J4, follow Safari Park signs]
Tel: 01299 402114 Fax: 01299 404519
www.wmsp.co.uk

A 200 acre site incorporating drive through safari park, pets corner, reptile house, hippo lakes, tiger world, goat walk, live shows and train ride to amusement area with over 25 rides and amusements including the Wall's Twister coaster and the new Flying Lion Kings ride. A variety of souvenir and catering outlets, ice cream and fast food kiosks, cafeterias together with indoor and outdoor picnics areas and cover shopping plaza. Dogs are welcome - please ensure they are on a lead and booked into our kennels on arrival as pets are not allowed in the reserve.

visitor comments: Go early to avoid queues. Helpful, expert and friendly staff. Pocket money priced gifts. Great value. Leisure area is expensive. Excellent log flume.
20 Mar-end Oct daily 10.00-16.00
Last Admission: 16.00
A&C£5.25 C(0-4)£Free. Ride Tickets 5-£4.00 10-£8.00 or 20-£14.50. Unlimited ride wristband £6.25. Group rates available for minimum of 12 paying persons arriving by coach or minibus. 1999 prices under review.

Abbeys

Rievaulx Abbey

Rievaulx Yorkshire YO6 5LB
[2.25m W of Helmsley on minor road of B1257]
Tel: 01439 798228
www.english-heritage.org.uk

The site for this magnificent abbey was given to a band of 12 Cistercian monks in 1131. Building began in about 1132 and most was completed by the end of the 12th century. The Abbey was extremely prosperous, and under its third abbot, Aelred there were 140 monks and over 500 lay brothers. Experience the unrivalled peace and serenity of this 12th century site in the beautiful valley of the River Rye. Trace the past glories and splendours of the thriving community of monks who lived and worked here. Take an audio tour of the magnificent soaring ruins, available in French, Swedish and Japanese.

visitor comments: Extensive and magnificent Abbey ruins. Beautiful location in wooded valley.
1 Apr-30 Sept daily 10.00-18.00, Oct 10.00-17.00, 1 Nov-31 Mar daily 10.00-16.00
A£3.40 C£1.70 Concessions£2.60

↓*special events*

▶ **Bilsdale Band Concert**

28/5/00-28/5/00
▶ **Medieval Monastic Entertainers**
22/8/00-23/8/00
Authentic medieval games, cures, folklore and early machinery, plus a unique guided tour
▶ **Bilsdale Band Concert**
10/9/00-10/9/00

Whitby Abbey
Whitby Yorkshire YO22 4JT
[on clifftop E of Whitby town centre]
Tel: 01947 603568
www.english-heritage.org.uk
One of the most spectacular historic sites in the country. The ruins of the 13th-century Benedictine abbey Whitby Abbey dominates the skyline above the fishing port to Whitby. The stone abbey was erected on the site of the wooden abbey of St Hilda, which was built in 657. The present building was badly damaged by shellfire during World War I. A recent grant of £5 million is to be used to construct a permanent visitor centre, re roof the building and restore the recently discovered stone garden. The works are scheduled to be completed by the year 2000.
1 Apr-30 Sept daily 10.00-18.00, Oct 10.00-17.00, 1 Nov-31 Mar daily 10.00-16.00
A£1.70 C£0.90 Concessions£1.30
↓*special events*
▶ **Music of the First Millennium**
30/4/00-1/5/00
▶ **Medieval Music**
1/7/00-2/7/00
Lively medieval music and song
▶ **Have-a-go Archery**
8/7/00-9/7/00
Archers introduce visitors to the art of archery
▶ **Wind in the Willows**
15/7/00-16/7/00
Meet Toad, Ratty, Mole and Badger in this enchanting children's fantasy
▶ **Stories & Mask-making**
22/7/00-23/7/00
Traditional folk tales, myths, legends and mask-making
▶ **Medieval Music**
29/7/00-30/7/00
Lively music and song from the 11th to 16th centuries
▶ **Mini Event**
5/8/00-6/8/00
▶ **More Skulduggery!**
12/8/00-13/8/00
Captain Darke, Liza and Cora the Crow are back with more tales of fearsome pirates and buried treasure
▶ **Medieval Monastic Entertainers**
19/8/00-20/8/00
Authentic medieval games, cures, folklore and early machinery, plus a unique guided tour
▶ **Flashing Blades**
27/8/00-28/8/00
Deulling from the 13th to 19th centuries brought to life in this demonstration of European martial arts

Animal Attractions

Big Sheep and The Little Cow
The Old Watermill Aiskew Bedale North Yorkshire DL8 1AW
[off A1 on B6285 or B6268]
Tel: 01677 422125
On Bedale's old water meadows is a small dairy farm where both sheep and cows (Dexters, Britain's smallest breed) are milked. During a friendly and informative guided tour visitors are invited to bottle feed lambs, inspect the calves, feed the pigs etc. Farm quiz, pony rides and light refreshments.
visitor comments: A great experience, as you get to interact with the animals. Lovely speciality ice-creams!
Mar-Sept daily 10.30-17.00. No guided tours in winter except by special arrangement
A£2.50 C&OAPs£2.00 Parties of over 20 all £2.00

Cannon Hall Open Farm
Cawthorne Barnsley South Yorkshire S75 4AT
[Signposted off A635, Barnsley Manchester Road. Plenty of parking on site]
Tel: 01226 790427 Fax: 01226 792511
www.cannonhallfarm.co.uk
A world of animal magic with plenty of baby animals displayed all year round. Adventure playground, tearoom and gift shop. Feed the animals and then enjoy our excellent home-made cakes and scones. One of Yorkshire's busiest farm attractions.
Open daily 10.30-16.30, except Christmas Day
A£2.10 C & OAPs£1.60

Hazel Brow Farm
Low Row Richmond North Yorkshire DL11 6NE
[15m W of Richmond on B6270]
Tel: 01748 886224
You may be lucky enough actually to see some of the Swaledale lambs being born at this working farm in the Yorkshire Dales. As well as feeding some of the orphans, you can stroke the ponies, hold a day old chick, look for wildlife along the riverside trail, and help to bottle milk from the Friesian cows-putting a green top on your own pint to take home with

you.
23 Mar-30 Sept Sun-Thurs 14.00-18.00
A£2.00 C£1.50

Major Bridge Park
Selby Road Holme On Spalding Moor Yorkshire
[2m through Holme On Spalding Moor on the A163 to Selby]
Tel: 01430 860992
Have a nostalgic look at farm and horticultural machinery including threshing machines, stationary engines, vintage tractors and a rack saw bench. There are regular working demonstrations. There are Victorian fairground rides, a nature trail walk, beautiful gardens and small farm animals.
visitor comments: Set in lovely tranquil woodland, with lots of picnic areas.
May-July & Sept Thur & Sun 10.00-17.00. Aug Mon-Fri & Sun 10.00-17.00
A£1.50 AccompaniedC(0-16)£Free OAPs£1.00.

Ponderosa Rural Therapeutic Centre
Off Smithies Lane Heckmondwike West Yorkshire WF16 0PL
[2 mins drive from Heckmondwike town centre and 10 mins from all major motorways]
Tel: 01924 235276
Ponderosa is a non-profit making association incorporating a rare breeds farm, where the animals and nature walkways give therapeutic value to all its visitors and workers. People with learning difficulties, the physically disabled, blind, deaf and those suffering from depression are all PEOPLE FIRST and disadvantaged second. At Ponderosa people can work together, gaining experience in a number of skills. A unique range of rare breeds and reptile room housing snakes, iguanas, lizards and many more. Pregnant women are advised not to go near sheep during the lambing season.
visitor comments: A wonderful visit - the animals are friendly and are used to children.
All year daily 10.00-16.00
A£1.50 C&OAPs£1.00. Educational Guided Tours - Prices on Applicaion

St Leonard's Farm Park
Chapel Lane Esholt Bradford West Yorkshire BD17 7RB
[off the A6038 Bradford / Otley & Ilkley road]
Tel: 01274 598795
A working dairy farm set in the picturesque village of Esholt in Bradford; Home of T.V's Emmerdale. The farm keeps a variety of rare and modern breeds of farm animals some of which you can feed. Facilities on the farm include outdoor paddocks, large covered areas, nature footpaths, listed barns and buildings, picnic and play areas, straw play barn, tractor, miniature caravan display and gift shop. Food is available on site. Schools always welcome, educational facilities available, special needs catered for. No dogs allowed, children must be supervised at all time. Strictly NO smoking.
visitor comments: Absolutely excellent. Great play areas. Limited menu. Two minute walk from the 'Woolpack'.
Easter-end Oct Tue-Sun 10.00-18.00. Nov & Dec closed. Jan-Easter Sat & Sun 10.00-16.00. All Bank Hol Mon and Mon throughout Bradford School Summer Holidays (otherwise closed Mon)
A£1.75 C90-2)£Free C&OAPs£1.25. Group rates 12+. School parties: Pre-visit for teachers £Free A£Free (1:5 ratio) C£1.00 Guided Tour £Free Books for follow up work £Free. Birthday Party £5.99 per head (all inclusive call for details)

Staintondale Shire Horse Farm
Staintondale Scarborough North Yorkshire YO13 0EY
[on the North York Moors National Park coastline, signposted from the A171 Scarborough to Whitby Road]
Tel: 01723 870458
Award winning, all weather and well loved family attraction. Live shows on most open days with shire horses, Shetland ponies and a very special palomino in full Western roping rig. Picnic and play areas in idyllic surroundings. Beautiful trails with cliff top and countryside paths. Excellent facilities with gift shop and café.
26 May-17 Sept 2000 Sun, Tue, Wed, Fri & Bank Hol Mon 10.30-16.30. Closed Mid Sept-mid May
A£3.50 C£2.50 Third child in family £1.50 OAPs£3.00

Archaeology

Jorvik Viking Centre
Coppergate York North Yorkshire YO1 9WT
[close to centre of York can be reached from the A1 via A64 or A19 or A1079 Park and Ride service call 01904 613161]
Tel: 01904 643211 Fax: 01904 627097
Step aboard a time car and drift back through the centuries to the Viking city of Jorvik. The atmosphere, sounds and smells of Viking age York are accurately recreated from archaeological evidence displayed in the centre. Enjoyed by over 11 million people Jorvik Viking Centre

is the first and best journey through time.
visitor comments: The detail is astonishing
All year May-Oct daily 09.00-17.30, Nov-Dec daily 09.00-16.30. Closed 25 Dec
Last Admission: Timed tickets possible in high season
A£5.35 C£3.99 Infant£Free Family Ticket (A2+C2)£17.00 Student&OAP£4.60

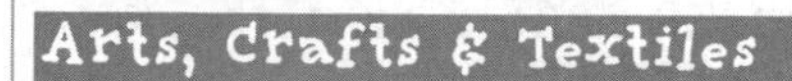

Arts, Crafts & Textiles

1853 Gallery Salt's Mill

Victoria Road Shipley West Yorkshire BD18 3LA
[Saltaire village]
Tel: 01274 531163 Fax: 01274 531184
www.clanvis.com/loc/hock.htm
On the ground floor of a magnificent former textile mill there is a permanent exhibition of more than 300 pieces of David Hockney's work. On the second floor there is a working space for the artist's use. The second gallery is next to Salts Diner which has an exhibition of his holiday snaps. There is a third gallery above the diner. David Hockney's painting of Salt's Mill in memory of the owner Jonathan Silver along with other Yorkshire landscapes are now on show.
All year 10.00-18.00. Closed Christmas
Admission Free

Colour Museum

Perkin House PO Box 244 1 Providence Street Bradford West Yorkshire BD1 2PW
[City centre]
Tel: 01274 390955 Fax: 01274 392888
Britain's only Museum of Colour run by the Society of Dyers and Colourists, comprises two galleries packed with visitor-operated exhibits demonstrating the effects of light and colour, including optical illusions and the story of dyeing and textile printing. Features computer aided exterior and interior design.
All year Tue-Fri 14.00-17.00, Sat 10.00-16.00
Last Admission: 30mins before closing
A£1.50 C&Concessions£1.00 Family Ticket £3.75 Season Ticket £6.00

Henry Moore Institute

74 The Headrow Leeds Yorkshire LS1 3AH
Tel: 0113 246 7467
www.henry-moore-fdn.co.uk
The Henry Moore Institute, and award-winning building house four gallery spaces for temporary sculpture exhibitions of all periods and nationalities. It includes a bookshop, audio-visual facilities, sculpture reference library, slide library and archive.
All year daily 10.00-17.30, Wed 10.00-21.00
Admission Free

↓special events

► **Andrea Blum 'Mobile Institute'**
12/1/00-31/3/00
The Mobile Institute is designed to travel from one institution to another and will mirror in microcosm the range of the Henry Moore Institute facilities

► **Eternal Return**
19/1/00-5/1/01
An exhibition of six consecutive displays of sculptural works that represent different conceptions of the cycles of time

► **Belvedere**
5/2/00-30/4/00
An exhibition of contemporary work exploring the circular viewing experience associated with architecture as manifested in sculpture, drawing and film

Leeds City Art Gallery

The Headrow Leeds Yorkshire LS1 3AA
[Leeds City Centre]
Tel: 0113 247 8248 Fax: 0113 244 9689
www.leeds.gov.uk
Collection of Victorian Paintings, early English Watercolours, 20th century British paintings and sculpture; Henry Moore Study Centre. Temporary exhibition programme. Wheelchair access restricted to upper floor.
Mon-Sat 10.00-17.00, Wed 10.00-20.00, Sun 13.00-17.00. Closed Bank Hol Mon
Admission Free

↓special events

▶ **Leeds: Shaping a Century**
12/1/00-31/3/00
A new display of the Gallery's permanent collection which highlights key moments when Leeds had a significant bearing on the course of 20th century

▶ **Vital**
12/1/00-31/3/00
Artist-led Saturday afternoon workshops for 13-16 year olds which take the environment as their theme. £2.50 per session.

▶ **Cafe Zone Shows**
12/1/00-31/3/00
Continuing the ongoing programme of exhibitions which showcase new work by artists from our region. Work usually for sale

▶ **Lunchtime Chamber Music**
8/3/00-19/4/00
Concerts held at 13.05 on Mar 8, 15, 22, 29 and Apr 5, 12 and 19 only. Free admission

York City Art Gallery
Exhibition Square York North Yorkshire YO1 2EW
[A64 A59 centre of York 2mins walk from York Minster]
Tel: 01904 551861 Fax: 01904 551866
www.york.gov.uk
700 years of European painting, from early Italian gold-ground panels to the art of the 20th century. Exceptional in its range and interest, the collection includes works by Parmigianino and Bellotto, Lely and Reynolds, Frith and Boudin, Lowry and Nash and nudes by York born Etty. Outstanding collection of studio pottery.
All year Mon-Sat 10.00-17.00, Sun 14.30-17.00. Closed Good Fri, 25-26 Dec & 1 Jan
Last Admission: 16.30
Admission Free

Yorkshire Sculpture Park
Bretton Hall West Bretton Wakefield West Yorkshire WF4 4LG
[J38 M1 off A637 Huddersfield road signposted from M1]
Tel: 01924 830302 Fax: 01924 830044
One of Europe's leading sculpture parks, Yorkshire Sculpture Park has pioneered the siting of sculpture in the open air, organising temporary exhibitions of modern and contemporary sculpture by national and international artists in over 200 acres of beautiful 18th century parkland. Café, craft shop, galleries, specialist bookshop and free scooters for elderly/disabled. Sculptors include Sir Anthony Caro, and from July, Joel Shapiro and Shaun Pickard.
Grounds: Summer daily 10.00-18.00, Winter daily 10.00-16.00 Shops/Galleries/Cafe: Summer daily 11.00-17.00 Winter daily 11.00-16.00 Closed 25-26 Dec & 31 Dec
Last Admission: Summer 17.00 Winter 15.00
Admission Free. Car Parking £1.50

Birds, Butterflies & Bees

Falconry U.K. Limited Bird of Prey and Conservation Centre
Sion Hill Hall Kirby Wiske Thirsk North Yorkshire YO7 4EU
[off A167 6m S of Northallerton follow brown tourist signs]
Tel: 01845 587522 Fax: 01845 523735
Enjoy the thrills and excitement of falconry at the Bird of Prey Centre in the picturesque grounds of Sion Hill Hall with 80 birds of 34 species. Eagles, Hawks and Owls will swoop and dive around you as you sit in a beautiful English Garden. Skilled handlers will explain why the birds hunt and fly as they do, where they come from in the wild and how they are trained. Owls, Hawks, Falcons, Eagle, Buzzards and Vulture flying demonstrations daily at 11.30, 13.30 and 15.30.
1 Mar-31 Oct daily 10.30-17.30
Last Admission: 17.00
Provisional prices A£4.00 C£2.00 Family Ticket £10.00 Concessions£3.00

Honey Farm Park
Racecourse Road East Ayton Scarborough North Yorkshire YO13 9HT
[from Scarborough take the A170 road to Pickering. The Honey Farm is just 10mins out of Scarborough on this road]
Tel: 01723 864001
www.beehealth.co.uk
An amazing exhibition on the Honey Bee. Also an adventure playground, children's animal farm, crafts and tearoom.
All year daily 10.00-17.00
Last Admission: 16.15
Queuing Times: max 20mins
A£2.95 accompanied C(under 15)£Free OAPs£1.50

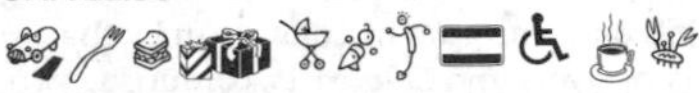

Yorkshire Dales Falconry and Conservation Centre
Crows Nest nr. Giggleswick Settle North Yorkshire LA2 8AS
[A65 bypass from Settle to Kendal, 2nd left after Giggleswick railway station]
Tel: 01729 822832/825164 Fax: 01729

825160
The centre aims to educate and raise awareness about world's birds of prey, and the threat of extinction facing some of them.
Most of the year, daily 10.00-17.00, call for Winter opening. Closed Christmas Day
A£4.95 C£2.95 Family Ticket (A2+C2)£13.95 Concessions£2.95. Group Rates 15+ A£3.50 C(0-14) £2.50

Caverns & Caves

Blue-John Cavern and Mine
Buxton Road Castleton Sheffield Yorkshire S30 2WP
[on the A625 at the foot of Mam-Tor]
Tel: 01433 620638 Fax: 01433 621586
www.bluejohn.gemsoft.co.uk
The cavern is a remarkable example of a water-worn cave, and measures over a third of a mile long, with chambers 200ft high. It contains 8 of the 14 veins of Blue John stone and has been the major source of this unique form of fluorspar for nearly 300 years.
All year daily 09.30-18.00 or dusk if sooner. Winter: weather permitting
A£5.00 C(5-15)£3.00 Family Ticket (A2+C2)£15.00 Students&OAPs£4.00. Group rates on application
discount offer: One Child Free With Every Full Paying Adult

Mother Shipton's Cave and the Petrifying Well
High Bridge Knaresborough North Yorkshire HG5 8DD
[on A59 4m W of A1(M)]
Tel: 01423 864600 Fax: 01423 868888
Features to enjoy using your all inclusive ticket: Guided tour of Mother Shipton's Cave, the Petrifying Well and the Wishing Well; Historia Museum; adventure playground; picnic areas; Sir Henry Slingsby's Walk; woodland walks; Mother Shipton's Kitchen serving tasty Yorkshire dishes; historic tour of Knaresborough from Sir Henry Slingsby's Walk.
visitor comments: The tour is amazing and very informative. The Museum is small but ideal for lovers of local trivia.
All year daily Easter-Oct 09.30-17.45, Nov-Easter 10.00-16.45
Last Admission: 45 mins before closing
A£4.25 C£3.25 OAPs£3.95 Family Ticket£11.75

Communication Museums

National Museum of Photography Film and Television
Pictureville Bradford West Yorkshire BD1 1NQ
[J26 M62, joining M606 follow into Bradford city centre, follow city centre/museum signs]
Tel: 01274 202030 Fax: 01274 394540
www.nmpft.org.uk/
Discover the World of photography, film and television through six floors of hands-on exhibits including the giant IMAX Cinema - now in 3D! Fly on a mgaic carpet, read the news and revisit the classics of British television in our growing archive TV Heaven. Brand new galleries take you to the digital frontier, explain how Wallis and Gromit were created and how advertisers persuade us to buy. Also, with a new simulator ride, the museum offers something for the whole family.
visitor comments: The interactive displays are really good, especially for children. Prebook for Imax theatre.
All year Tue-Sun & Bank Hol 10.00-18.00
Admission Free. IMAX Cinema: A£5.80 C&Concessions£4.00

↓special events

▶ **Make Your Own TV Programme**
1/2/00-31/12/00
Each Sunday: mornings 10.30-13.00, afternoons 14.00-16.30

▶ **Saturday Film Club (The SFC)**
1/2/00-31/12/00
Saturday Film Club for children aged 8-12, during term time, hands-on workshop followed by a film. Booking essential.

▶ **3D Days - Spring Half Term**
19/2/00-27/2/00

Country Parks & Estates

Marsden Moor Estate Office
The Old Goods Yard Station Road Marsden Huddersfield Yorkshire HD7 6DH
[6m SW of Huddersfield on the A62 BR: Marsden]
Tel: 01484 847016 Fax: 01484 847071
Get on your walking boots, explore some wonderful scenic countryside and fill your lungs with fresh country air. Many Special events and guided walks see Guide, codes for walks and events F=Families ND=No Dogs DOLO=Dogs On Leads Only LWA=Limited Wheelchair Access WA= Wheelchair Access

PL=Packed Lunch Required B= Bookings SAE to Estate Office
Any reasonable time
Admission Free

↓*special events*

▶ **Discovering Wessenden - Walk**
12/3/00-12/3/00
Meet Ruth at Marsden Railway Station at 13.30 for a 4/5 mile walk with some climbs

▶ **Clean Up Day**
25/3/00-25/3/00
Meet at Estate Office at 10.00-14.00 to help clean up

▶ **Hunt the Cookoo Walk**
14/4/00-14/4/00
Meet David at Mechanics Hall at 19.00 for a 2 mile medium stroll followed by a folk evening at the Riverhead Brewery Tap

▶ **Building of Huddersfield - Walk**
22/6/00-22/6/00
Meet David at 19.00 outside Huddersfiedl Central Library, call for details

▶ **Moorland Revegetation**
25/6/00-25/6/00
Meet Ruth at Standedge car park on the A62 for a 3-4 mile walk, call for details

▶ **Yet Moor Mince Pies - Walk**
17/12/00-17/12/00
Explore Marsden Moor in winter time and stop for mince pies on the way. Meet Ruth at Marsden Railway Station for a 7 mile medium walk

▶ **Boxing Day Breather - Walk**
26/12/00-26/12/00
Meet David at 10.00 at Marsden Railway Station for a 10 mile hard walk

Factory Outlets & Tours

Freeport Hornsea Retail and Leisure Village

Rolston Road Hornsea East Yorkshire HU18 1UT
[travel towards Hornsea and follow brown directional signs for Freeport Hornsea]
Tel: 01964 534211 Fax: 01964 536363
A unique shopping village offering both retail and leisure facilities. Famous High Street brand names selling their merchandise at huge discounted prices. Restaurant and take-away facilities available. Adventureland leisure attraction includes Model Village, Butterfly World, Outdoor adventure play, Fun Golf, Bouncy Castles and Picnic Areas.
All year daily 09.30-18.00
Admission £Free
discount offer: Two For The Price Of One To Butterfly World & Adventureland

Wensleydale Creamery

Gayle Lane Hawes North Yorkshire DL8 3RN
[A684 from A1 Leeming Bar junction, J36 / 37 M6 on A684]
Tel: 01969 667664 Fax: 01969 667638
Do come and enjoy 'The Cheese Experience' (tour 30 minutes to 1 hour 30 minutes) as offered by our Visitor Centre. Please note that the optimum time for viewing cheesemaking is between 10.30 and 15.00. Do come and enjoy 'The Cheese Experience' (tour 30 minutes to 1 hour 30 minutes) as offered by our Visitor Centre. Please note that the optimum time for viewing cheesemaking is between 10.30 and 15.00.
Mar-Nov Mon-Fri 09.00-17.00, Sat & Sun 09.30-16.30, Dec-Feb daily 10.00-16.00. The rest of the Visitor Centre is open during the following times: Mon-Sat 09.30-17.00 Sun 10.00-16.30. Closed 25 Dec
Last Admission: 15.30
Queuing Times: 20mins
A£2.00 C£1.50 Family Ticket £6.50 Schools £1.50 Guided Tours £2.50. Coach Party Booking essential

Festivals & Shows

Great Yorkshire Show 2000

Great Yorkshire Showground Harrogate North Yorkshire HG2 8PW
[off A661 follow AA signs]
Tel: 01423 541000 Fax: 01423 541414
www.yas.co.uk
The largest agricultural show in the region. Hundreds of stands for shopping everything from handbags to tractors. Military bands, hundreds of things to see and do, including a flower show and ferrets!
July 11-13 2000. 08.00-19.30. Closes 18.00 on 13 July
Last Admission: 17.00
Queuing Times: 5mins
A£12.00 C£6.00 OAPs£9.00 Family Ticket (in advance only) £25.00 School parties £3.50. Pre-

booking discounts available please call for details

↓*special events*

► Great Yorkshire Show 2000
11/7/00-13/7/00

Harrogate International Festival 2000
(Festival Office) 1 Victoria Avenue Harrogate Yorkshire HG1 1EQ
[the Festival uses several venues in Harrogate and Ripon. Harrogate can be accessed easily from the M1 via the A61 from Leeds, or from the A1 via the A661]
Tel: 01423 562303 Fax: 01423 521264
www.harrogate-festival.org.uk
Come and celebrate the 35th Harrogate International Festival. Visit Yorkshire's floral resort, set in some of Britain's most breathtaking countryside, and enjoy a feast of international performers in a world class line-up. We promise to inspire, provoke, delight and entertain you with an unrivalled programme of classical music, dance, stand-up comedy, jazz, world music and street theatre. Family events include our free outdoor Fiesta of World Music, street theatre and children's activities. Why not join us?
July 20-Aug 5 2000
Prices vary according to chosen venue, call the booking office in May for details. Free festival programme

↓*special events*

► Paul Watkins, cello and Huw Watkins, piano
27/2/00-27/2/00

► International Sunday Series
5/3/00-30/4/00
Held at 11.00 in the Old Swan Hotel. Features Japanese pianist Momo Kodama on Mar 3, the British Gould Piano Trio on Mar 26 and the Vellinger Quartet on Apr 30. Call 01423 537230 for tickets

► Harrogate International Festival 2000
20/7/00-5/8/00

Folk & Local History Museums

Millennium
Harbourside Scarborough Yorkshire YO11 1PG
[follow the signs for South Bay and brown signs for Millennium]
Tel: 01723 365272
www.eclipse.co.uk/scarmill
Millennium is a time-travel adventure through 1,000 years of Scarborough' turbulent past. You visit the Viking Settlement of Skarthaborg, trudge through the building of the Castle and see all the fun of Scarborough Fair.
All year, High Season: daily 10.00-22.00, Low Season: weekends only 10.00-16.00
A£2.95 C£2.45
discount offer: Two For The Price Of One

Scarborough Museums and Gallery
c/o Londesborough Lodge The Crescent Scarborough North Yorkshire YO11 2PW
[central Scarborough]
Tel: 01723 232323 Fax: 01723 376941
Visit three magical buildings and explore 200 million years of Scarborough life at Wood End Museum, Scarborough Art Gallery and the Rotunda Museum. All located centrally, displays include dinosaur footprints, paintings of the moonlit sea at Scarborough and flint and bone tools from the world famous Star Carr and Scarborough's original pancake bell. We offer changing exhibitions, activities for children and special events throughout the year.
Spring Bank Hol-mid Oct Tue-Sun 10.00-17.00. Mid Oct-Spring Bank Hol reduced opening, check before your visit
Visit all 3 sites: as often as you like for A£3.00 Concessions£1.50 Family Ticket £7.00. One site, one visit A£2.00 Concessions£1.00

World of James Herriot
Skeldale House 23 Kirkgate Thirsk Yorkshire YO7 1PL
[in Thirsk town centre]
Tel: 01845 524234 Fax: 01845 525333
www.hambleton.gov.uk
This £1.4 million development combines history, humour, nostalgia, science and education in a unique tribute to Alf Wright, the author of the James Herriot novels. Hambleton District Council's millennium project explores the veterinary science, take visitors on a journey back to the 1940s and even allows you to take part in your own TV series! To ensure every visitor enjoys the atmosphere of the original surgery, visitors may have an advanced admission time with their ticket, allowing time for a relaxed stroll through Thirsk Market Place where shops, restaurants and cafés abound.
visitor comments: Informative, interactive and interesting throughout (even for non-Herriot fans!). Tour takes about two hours.
All year daily
A£4.00 C(under 4)£Free C(4-16)&OAPs£3.00 Family Tickets (A2+C2)£12.00 (A2+C3)£14.00 Students£3.50. Pre-booked Group rates 10+: A£3.50 Organiser/Coach Driver £Free, School £2.50 1A £Free, OAPs£3.00
discount offer: Two For The Price Of One Adult Admission

Yorkshire Museum and Gardens
Museum Gardens York Yorkshire YO1 7FR
[A1 M1 running N/S M62 E/W provide easy access from the port of Hull, and from Manchester, Leeds, Bradford, Newcastle & Teeside Airport via A19, the A59 or the A64]
Tel: 01904 629745 Fax: 01904 651221
www.york.gov.uk
Set in 10 acres of botanical gardens in the heart of the historic city of York, the museum displays some of the finest Roman, Anglo-Saxon, Viking and Medieval treasures ever discovered in Britain. The Middleham jewel, a fine example of English Gothic jewellery, is on display in the Medieval Gallery.
visitor comments: The gardens are a great place for kids, as is the Exploration Gallery. The jewel is beathtaking!
All year daily 10.00-17.00
Last Admission: 16.30
A£3.75 C£2.40 (subject to change0

Gardens & Horticulture

Harlow Carr Botanical Gardens
Crag Lane Beckwithshaw Harrogate North Yorkshire HG3 1QB
[off B6162]
Tel: 01423 565418 Fax: 01423 530663
www.stressweb.com/harlow
The gardens celebrate 50 years of welcoming visitors in 2000. In the 68 acres of ornamental and woodland gardens you will find flowers, attractive barks, fragrances, magnificent colours and harmonious displays of plants - every season offers new discoveries.
All year Mar-Oct daily 09.30-18.00, Nov-Feb daily 09.30-17.00 or dusk if sooner
A£4.00 C(0-16)£Free OAPs£3.00. Group rates for 20+. RHS members free

Stillingfleet Lodge
Stillingfleet York North Yorkshire YO19 6HP
[6m S of York A19 York-Selby road B1222 signposted Sherburn in Elmet in Stillingfleet turn opposite church garden is at end of lane]
Tel: 01904 728506 Fax: 01904 728506
A garden of about 1 acre constructed by the owner's since 1977 and subdivided into small gardens each with a colour theme. There is a national collection of pulmonaria. Also wildflower meadow, pond and herbaceous borders. Partial access for wheelchairs.
16 Apr 13.30-17.30, May & June Wed & Fri 13.00-16.00, 14 May & 25 June 13.30-17.30 for NGS
A£2.00 C£Free
discount offer: Two For The Price Of One

Heritage & Industrial

Armley Mills Industrial Museum
Canal Road Armley Leeds Yorkshire LS12 2QF
[2m W of city centre off A65]
Tel: 0113 263 7861
Once the world's largest woollen mill, Armley Mills evokes memories of the 18th century showing the progress of wool from the sheep to knitted clothing. The museum has its own 1920s cinema illustrating the history of projection including the first moving pictures taken in Leeds. Demonstrations of static engines and steam locomotives and a unique exhibition of underground haulage.
All Year Tue-Sat 10.00-17.00, Sun 13.00-16.00
Last Admission: 1 hour before closing
A£2.00 C(0-5)£Free C(accompanied)£0.50 C(unaccompanied)£1.00 Concessions£1.00
discount offer: Two For The Price Of One

↓*special events*

► **Leeds Tapestry**
12/1/00-31/3/00
Come and see the embroidery in progress at an open day or workshop. (Free to view, £8.00 for the workshops)

Kelham Island Museum
Kelham Island Alma Street Sheffield Yorkshire S3 8RY
[0.5m NW take A61 N to West Bar]
Tel: 0114 272 2106 Fax: 0114 275 7847
Housed in a former generating station, this lively museum tells the story of Sheffield's industrial development over the last 400 years. Features displays of working machinery, traditional cutlery craftsmen at work, exhibitions of a wide variety of goods made in Sheffield, both past and present, film and slide shows and the most powerful working steam engine in the world 'in steam.'
All year Mon-Thur 10.00-16.00, Sun 11.00-

16.45. Closed Christmas & New Year
Last Admission: 60mins before closing
A£3.50 C£2.00 Family Ticket £8.00 Concessions £2.50
discount offer: Two For The Price Of One (Limited To One Offer Per Card)

Historical

Bramham Park

The Estate Office Bramham Wetherby Yorkshire LS23 6ND
[on A1 4m S of Wetherby. Plenty of on site parking available]
Tel: 01937 846005 Fax: 01937 846006
18th century French-style park and gardens designed in the style of André Le Notre, now almost unique in England. Fabulous ornamental ponds, cascades, templed and almost 2 miles of monumental Beech avenues. "One of the best wildflower gardens in the country."
2 Feb-30 Sept 10.30-17.30
Last Admission: 17.00
A£2.95 C&OAPs£1.95 C(0-5)£Free
discount offer: Two For The Price Of One. Valid Until 30 Sept 2000

Castle Howard

Castle Howard York North Yorkshire YO60 7DA
[15m from York, off A64. Plenty of on site parking available]
Tel: 01653 648444 Fax: 01653 648501
www.castlehoward.co.uk
One of Britain's finest and most spectacular historic houses. This 18th century castle provides pleasure and enjoyment for visitors of all ages. Superb rooms and galleries filled with family treasures. Principal location for 'Brideshead Revisited.' Rose gardens, lakes, fountains, woodland garden and an adventure playground for the children.
Castle, Grounds & Gardens: 17 Mar-5 Nov daily. Castle: from 11.00, Grounds & Gardens from: 10.00. Guided Tours: Pre-booked ONLY please call for details
Last Admission: 16.30
A£7.50 C£4.50 Students&OAPs£6.75. Family Ticket and Group rates available
discount offer: Two Children Free When Accompanied By Two Full Paying Adults To The House & Grounds. Valid Until 17 Mar-5 Nov 2000

East Riddlesden Hall

Bradford Road Keighley Yorkshire BD21 4EA
[1.5m N of Keighley]
Tel: 01535 607075 Fax: 01535 691462
17th century manor house with oak furniture and embroideries. A small secluded garden with colourful herbaceous borders and herbs. Large tithe barn.
1 Apr-1 Nov Sun-Wed & Good Fri 12.00-17.00, Sat 13.00-17.00. Also July-Aug Thur 12.00-17.00
Last Admission: 16.30
A3.30 C£1.80 Family Ticket £8.50. Pre-booked Groups 15+ £2.80, 40+ £2.50

↓special events

▶ **Mothering Sunday**
2/4/00-2/4/00
Lunches and afternoon teas

▶ **A Look at 17th Century Life**
10/7/00-30/8/00
Costumed tour every Sun, Mon & Tue excluding Bank Hol Mon and Sun in Sept. Also a tour for children at 14.00 and Sun 3, 10, 17 and 24 Sept

▶ **Through the Port Hole**
9/8/00-9/8/00
14.00-16.00,,, storytelling in the garden and children's activities

▶ **Anchor's Away**
16/8/00-16/8/00
14.00-16.00... Treasure trail for children in the garden

▶ **Aire Valley YFC Country Show**
27/8/00-27/8/00
All the fun of a Country Show and more. On the field. £1.00 admission or admission by House ticket. 13.00-17.00

▶ **Walk the Plank**
28/8/00-28/8/00
Learn to juggle and stilt walk. Join in the magic of the Curious Eyebrows family show at 15.00. Fun starts 12.00-16.00

▶ **Christmas Concert**
16/12/00-16/12/00
Booking essential, commences 20.00, £8.50

Harewood House and Bird Garden

Harewood Leeds Yorkshire LS17 9LQ
[A61 / A659 Leeds / Harrogate road]

Tel: 0113 2181010 Fax: 0113 2181002
www.harewood.org/
The 18th century home of the Earl and Countess of Harewood is renowned for it's stunning architecture, furniture, paintings and porcelain. 'Capability' Brown landscaped grounds offer woodland and lakeside walks, plus the hugely popular Bird Garden, Adventure Playground and regular special events. Special 'Behind the Scenes' tours available by appointment.
visitor comments: Fascinating bird garden. Worth admission cost if you make a day of it. A great children's playground. Take along walking shoes and walk to the church - lovely!
1 Apr-29 Oct daily. Bird Garden & Grounds: 10.00-18.00, House: 11.00-16.30. Nov-Dec Grounds only Sat-Sun only
Last Admission: 16.30
All attractions: A£7.95 C£5.00 OAPs£6.50 Family Ticket £25.00. Grounds & Bird Garden: A£6.00 C£3.50 Family Ticket £18.00 OAPs£5.00. Group rates available
discount offer: One Adult 'Freedom' Ticket At Child Rate, If Accompanied By One Other Adult Paying For A Full Price 'Freedom' Ticket. Not Available For Group Visits

Lotherton Hall
Lotherton Lane Aberford Leeds Yorkshire LS25 3EB
[off the A1 0.75m E of junction with B1217]
Tel: 0113 2813 259
www.leeds.gov.uk
Visit beautiful Lotherton Hall and you could be forgiven for thinking that you've travelled back to Edwardian times. The Hall was the home of the great Colliery owning family, the Gascoignes, who created a charming home during the halcyon days before the First War and filled it with a wonderful array of furniture, paintings and opulent trophies. Experience a taste of the East as you explore the new Oriental Gallery, a ravishing display of over 1,000 items dating from the Neolithic period to the 18th century. Outside there is a chance to enjoy the formal Edwardian garden and one of the finest Bird Gardens in the country - home to over 200 species. Visit the Stables Courtyard - for a shop, café, toilets.
visitor comments: Excellent value for money. Step back in time. Nice, open grassed picnic areas - very peaceful.
1 Apr-31 Oct Tue-Sat 10.00-17.00, Sun 13.00-17.00. 1 Nov-31 Dec & Mar Tue-Sat 10.00-16.00, Sun 12.00-16.00. Closed Jan & Feb
Last Admission: 45mins before closing
A£2.00 C£0.50 Concessions£1.00 Season Ticket A£10.00 C£2.50 Concessions£5.00
discount offer: One Child Free With Every Full Paying Adult

Newby Hall and Gardens
Ripon North Yorkshire HG4 5AE
[4m SE of Ripon off B6265]
Tel: 01423 322583 Fax: 01423 324452
This late 17th-century house had its interior and additions designed by Robert Adam, and contains an important collection of classical sculptures and Gobelin tapestries. Twenty-five acres of award-winning gardens including a miniature railway, an adventure garden for children and a woodland discovery walk.
House & Gardens: Apr-30 Sept Tue-Sun & Bank Hol, Gardens: 11.00-17.30, House: 12.00-17.00
Last Admission: 16.30
House & Garden: A£6.30 C(under 4)£Free C£3.80 OAPs£5.20. Gardens only: A£4.50 C(under 4)£Free C£3.00 OAPs£3.80
discount offer: One Child Free When Accompanied By A Full Paying Adult. Valid until 30th September 1999

Sewerby Hall and Gardens
Church Lane Sewerby Bridlington Yorkshire YO15 1EA
[2m N of Bridlington in Sewerby Village, sign-posted. BR: Bridlington 3m. Limited on site parking]
Tel: 01262 673769 Fax: 01262 673090
www.bridlington.net/sewerby
Situated in a dramatic cliff-top position, forming the gateway to the Flamborough Heritage Coast, Sewerby Hall and Gardens, set in 50 acres of early 19th century parkland, enjoys the spectacular views over Bridlington Bay. The Hall contains the magnificent Orangery, art and photographic galleries, period rooms, an Amy Johnson room displaying a collection of her awards, trophies and mementoes, the History of East Yorkshire permanent display, Mayor's Parlour and Mayoral Regalia displays, Trevor Field Trust Art Gallery, Bridlington Promenade Art Gallery. The gardens are amongst the best in the region and include pleasure gardens, walled gardens, bandstand and Clock Tower Tea Rooms. Courtyard toilets with baby change facilities and craft units. There is also a children's zoo, 12 hole pitch and putt golf course, 18 hole putting green, Crown green bowling, Children's playground, Donkey rides and scenic cliff-top train ride to Limekiln Lane.
All year Gardens & Zoo daily. Hall: 19 Feb-18 Apr & 30 Oct-17 Dec Sat-Tue 11.00-16.00, 21 Apr-29 Oct daily 10.00-18.00
A3.00 C£1.00 OAPs£2.20. Pre-booked groups 10+ half price. Special events may be charged extra

Skipton Castle
Skipton Yorkshire BD23 1AQ
[located in Skipton centre]
Tel: 01756 792442 Fax: 01756 796100
www.skiptoncastle.co.uk
Skipton Castle is one of the best preserved, most complete medieval castles in England. Dating from Norman times with a charming Tudor Courtyard it withstood a three year siege in the Civil War. Explore this exciting castle and relax in the peaceful grounds.
All year daily Mar-Sept Mon-Sat 10.00-18.00, Sun 12.00-18.00, Oct-Feb Mon-Sat 10.00-16.00, Sun 12.00-16.00. Closed 25 Dec
Last Admission: 18.00 Mar-Sept, 16.00 Oct-Feb
A£4.20 inc illustrated tour sheet in choice of 8 languages (English, French, German, Dutch, Italian, Spanish, Japanese or Esperanto) C(0-5)£Free C(5+)£2.10 Family Ticket (A2+C3)£11.50 OAPs£3.60, Students£3.60 (must show ID)
discount offer: One Free With One Full Paying Adult. Valid to 31 Dec 2000

↓*special events*

▶ **Red Wyvern Society Re-enactment**
27/5/00-29/5/00
See Skipton Castle the way it was in the 15th century

▶ **Feudal Archers**
19/8/00-20/8/00
A demonstration of arms, armour and domestic life (1135-1216)

Temple Newsam House and Park
Temple Newsam Park Leeds Yorkshire LS15 0AE
[off A63]
Tel: 0113 264 7321/264 5535 Fax: 0113 260 2285
www.leeds.gov.uk
Described as 'the Hampton Court of the North' this Tudor and Jacobean mansion boasts extensive collections of decorative arts in their original room settings, including the incomparable Chippendale collection. The 1,200 acres of parkland landscaped 'Capability' Brown features the Rare Breeds Centre in the Home Farm which is a working Rare Breed Centre, the largest in Europe and home to over 400 ani-

mals, cattles, sheep, pigs, goats, chickens and ducks. A 300 year old barn provides the backdrop for displays of old agricultural equipment, horse drawn carts and wagons.
visitor comments: Fantastic adventure playgrounds - one for the under 5's. Extensive menu in tearoom, and nice and clean.
House: Apr-31 Oct Tue-Sat & 10.00-17.00, 1 Nov-28 Dec & Mar Tue-Sat 10.00-16.00, Sun 12.00-16.00. Home Farm: daily 10.00-17.00, 16.00 in winter, Gardens: 10.00-dusk, Estate: daily dawn-dusk
Last Admission: House 16.15. Farm: 30mins before closing
A£2.00 C£0.50 Concessions£1.00. Farm admission £Free
discount offer: One Child Free With Every Full Paying Adult

↓*special events*

▶ **Textiles at Temple Newsam: The Roger Warner Collection**
12/1/00-31/3/00
A selection of rare and beautiful textiles from the collection of Roger Warner acquired by him and his father over a period of 75 years

Military & Defence Museums

Green Howards Museum

Trinity Church Square Market Place Richmond Yorkshire DL10 4QN
Tel: 01748 822133
This award-winning museum traces the military history of the Green Howards from the late 17th century onwards. The exhibits include uniforms, weapons, medals and a special Victoria Cross exhibition. Regimental and civic plate is also displayed.
Feb, Mar & Nov Mon-Fri 10.00-16.30; Apr-mid May Mon-Sat 09.30-16.30; Mid May-Sept Mon-Sat 09.30-16.30 Sun 14.00-16.30; Oct Mon-Sat 09.30-16.30
£2.00 C£1.00 Family Ticket(2A+3C) £5.00
discount offer: Two For The Price Of One

Royal Armouries Museum

Armouries Drive Leeds West Yorkshire LS10 1LT
[off A61 close to city centre follow brown tourist signs]
Tel: 0990 1066 66 gen info Fax: 0113 220 1955
www.armouries.org.uk
The multi award-winning museum displaying the national collection of arms and armour. Objects from across the world dating back from 600 BC to the present day are displayed in five multi-media galleries. Live demonstrations, films and computer interactive programmes designed for the enjoyment of all ages and levels of knowledge offer unparalleled insights into the significance of arms and armour in mankind's development. Regular object handling and question and answer sessions provide an extra dimension to every visit. An all weather attraction the museum also has an outdoor tiltyard. craftcourt and menagerie of stables, mews and kennels for its own horses, dogs and hawks. An active education centre supported by the Halifax caters for many different aspects of the national curriculum from reception to graduate levels. The museum is recognised as one of the region's corporate hospitality venues for conferences, exhibitions, seminars and company promotions. Allow 3-4 hours for a visit.
visitor comments: Signs a little scarce. Parking is quickly taken. Indoor and outdoor picnic areas.
All year daily 10.30 except 24, 25 & 31 Dec & 1 Jan. Alternative telephone number: 0113 220 1999
Last Admission: 2hours before closing
A£4.90 Concessions£3.90 Family Ticket (A2+C3)£24.95. Concessions available for Leeds residents, groups, schools, the disabled and their carers
discount offer: Two For The Price Of One

Mills - Water & Wind

Thwaite Mills

Thwaite Lane Leeds Yorkshire LS10 1RP
[2m S of City centre off A61]
Tel: 0113 249 6453 Fax: 0113 277 6737
www.leeds.gov.uk
A fascinating tour of this water-powered mill which sits between the River Aire and the Aire and Calder Navigation. Two great swishing wheels continually drive a mass of cogs and

grinding wheels which crushed stone for putty and paint throughout the 19th century.
1 Apr-31 Oct Tue-Sat 10.00-17.00, Sun 13.00-17.00. 1 Nov-31 Dec & Mar Tue-Sun 10.00-16.00, Sun 12.00-16.00. Closed Jan & Feb
Last Admission: 16.00 last tour
A£2.00 C£0.50 Concessions£1.00 Season Ticket A£10.00 C£2.50 Concessions£5.00
discount offer: Two For The Price Of One

Nature & Conservation Parks

Earth Centre

Kilners Bridge Doncaster Road Denaby Main South Yorkshire DN12 4DY
[BR: Conisbrough 7 min from Doncaster main line station. M18 J2 A1M J A630 then A6023 signposted]
Tel: 01709 512000 Fax: 01709 512010
www.earthcentre.org.uk/
The largest environmental project to be built to commemorate the Millennium. It in April 99 and is based on the twin themes of the natural environment and sustainability, set in 350 acres it is overlooked by Conisbrough Castle. The first phase has four main areas, Planet Earth described as a hands on educational experience, Water Works which demonstrates how we handle water, Children's Theatre and a Nature Centre which includes a wharf on the river Don. There are acres of children's play areas.
All year daily 10.00-20.00
Last Admission: 17.00
A£8.95 C£6.95 Concessions£4.95 Coach or minibus passengers A£5.95 C£4.95 C(Under 5)£Free Rail passengers A£4.95 School pupils £3.99

Longshaw Estate

Peak District National Park Sheffield Yorkshire S11 7TZ
[7.5m from Sheffield next to A625 Sheffield / Hathersage road Woodcroft car park is off B6055 200mtr S of junction with A625. Car Park 200mtrs from Visitor Centre, access difficult for coaches, no coaches at Weekends of Bank Hol]
Tel: 01433 631757
688 hectares of open moorland and farms in the Peak District National Park, with dramatic views and varied walking. Stone for the Derwent and Howden Dams was quarried from Bolehill, and millstones may be seen in quarries on the estate. There is a quarry winding house above Grindleford station. No dogs in Visitor Centre, on leads on walks only. *NB: prior booking for all Peak District walks is essential unless otherwise stated. A donation of £2.00 per person towards the National Trust's Peak District Appeal would be much appreciated
Estate: all year. Visitor Centre: Jan-Mar & Nov-Dec weekends only, Apr, May & Oct Wed-Sun & Bank Hol Mon, June-Sept daily, 10.30-17.00. Pre-booked parties at other times, by arrangement
Admission Free

↓*special events*

▶ **Longshaw Estate - Wildflower Walk**
15/5/00-15/5/00
Meet at the Visitor Centre at 14.00

▶ **High Peak Estate - Guided Walk**
17/5/00-17/5/00
**Winnats Pass Ghost Walk. Meet: Mam Nick car park, 19.00*

▶ **High Peak Estate - Guided Walk**
21/5/00-21/5/00
**The Ridge with a Little Bit of History. Guided walk from Mam Tor to Losehill. Meet: Castleton Market Place, 10.30. Bring packed lunch*

▶ **High Peak Estate - Creatures for the Murky Depths**
21/5/00-21/5/00
Pond dipping at Blackden pond. Meet Blackden View lay-by on A57, 11.00. GR 132 895. £2.00 Booking essential

▶ **High Peak - Guided Walk**
10/6/00-10/6/00
**Over Kinder and Back. 9 mile strenuous hike from Edale to Kinder Downfall. Meet: Edale car park, 10.00. Bring packed lunch*

▶ **Longshaw Estate - Myths & Legends**
21/6/00-21/6/00
Storytelling walk with refreshements aftwerwards. Meet at the Visitor Centre at 19.00. £4.00

▶ **High Peak Estate - Guided Walk**
25/6/00-25/6/00
**Ashes Farm Walk and Tea. Easy walk around Ashes Farm- cream teas available. Details from estate office*

▶ **High Peak Estate - Guided Walk**
1/7/00-1/7/00
**Mid-Summer Moorland. Walk from Blackden Brook to Fairbrook. Meet: Blackden view lay-by on A57 GR: 132 895, 16.00*

▶ **Land Rover Safari**
24/8/00-24/8/00
See entry for 13 July

▶ **High Peak Estate - Guided Walk**
25/8/00-25/8/00
**Rocking Stones and Purple Haze. Meet: King's Tree bus stop. SK158938, 10.30. Bring packed lunch*

Places of Worship

York Minster
Deangate York Yorkshire YO1 2JN
[in the city centre]
Tel: 01904 624426/639347 Fax: 01904 654604
It is believed Edwin King of Northumbria built the first church on this site in 627: since then both Saxons and Normans built cathedrals here, and parts of the latter survive in many places in the present structure. From 1220 to 1472 the present church was built to replace the romanesque one. It is notable for its size - the largest medieval church north of the Alps - and for its wealth of stained glass, most of which is original to the building. Daily worship of God has thus been conducted on this site for thirteen centuries.
Mon-Sat daily 08.00-18.00 later in summer Sun after 13.00
Admission free but donation asked for except for Foundations & Treasury A£1.80 C£0.70 OAPs & Students £1.50 Chapter House A£0.70 C£0.30 Central Tower A£2.00 C£1.00 Crypt A£0.60 C£0.30

Railways

Keighley and Worth Valley Railway
Station Road Haworth Keighley West Yorkshire BD22 8NJ
[J24 M62, A629 to Keighley, A650, A65, A59]
Tel: 01535 645214/647777 Fax: 01535 647317
www.kwvr.co.uk
Take the branch line to the Brontës and beyond, to the days of gas lights and coal fires, steam engines and compartment carriages. Every weekend and daily in the summer you can take a memorable steam train journey back in time on the Keighley & Worth Valley Railway - Britain's last remaining complete branch line railway. Travel from delightfully restored stations through classic West Yorkshire scenery.
All year: Train services operate every weekend throughout the year and daily in the summer and during holiday periods. Call for a timetable.
Last Admission: Low Season 15.30 & High Season 17.00
A£6.00 Concessions£3.00 Family Ticket £16.00. Special fares may apply for special events call 01535 647777 for details

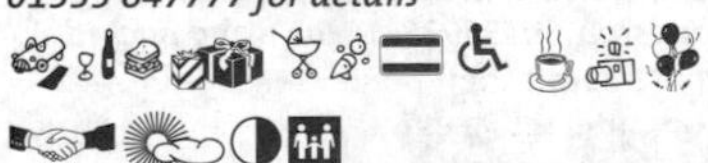

Kirklees Light Railway
Park Mill Way Clayton West Huddersfield West Yorkshire HD8 9XJ
[from north J39 M1& from south J38 M1 then on A636 Wakefield-Denby Dale road]
Tel: 01484 865727
Scenic ride on narrow gauge 15inch steam railway in enclosed carriages on old country branch line. Children's playground and miniature fairground rides. cosy café, ample free parking, discount for groups. New extension opened Easter 1997.
Spring Bank Hol-beg Sept daily hourly from 11.00, and most scheduled holidays. Every weekend Sept-May
A£4.50 C(3-4)£2.00 C(5-15)£3.25 OAPs&Students £4.00

Middleton Railway Leeds
Moor Road Hunslet Leeds West Yorkshire LS10 2JQ
[J5 M621 or follow signs from A61]
Tel: 0113 271 0320
www.middletonrailway.org.uk
The first railway authorised by an Act of Parliament (1758) and the first to succeed with steam locomotives (1812). Steam trains run each weekend in season from Tunstall Road roundabout to Middleton Park. A nature trail and playgrounds for children are amongst the other attractions.
Viewing all year. Trains run Mar-Dec Sat-Sun and Bank Hol, please call for timetable, special events are listed below, times and prices may apply please call for details
Last Admission: 14.20
Station Free. Return Fare: A£2.00 C(3-15)£1.00 Family Ticket (A2+C2)£5.00. Tickets valid for unlimited rides on day of purchase
discount offer: Two Adults For The Price Of One
↓*special events*
► **A Day out with Thomas**
25/3/00-12/11/00
Come and meet 'Thomas the Tank Engine' on the following dates: Mar 25, 26 & 31, Apr 1 & 2,

Nov 4, 5, 11 & 12

▶ **Easter Bunnies Weekend**
21/4/00-24/4/00
Wear your Easter bonnet, bring your Easter Bunny and receive a free Easter egg!

▶ **Postman Pat's Special**
13/5/00-14/5/00
Postman Pat arrives in full steam with all the mail. Treasure Hunt and competitions

▶ **40th Anniversary Gala**
17/6/00-18/6/00
Celebrate with us. See steam and diesel locomotives and some surprises in store

▶ **Volunteers' & Members' Open Day**
9/7/00-9/7/00
It takes alot to run a railway, come and find out

▶ **Teddy Bears' Picnic**
6/8/00-6/8/00
Take the train to the Park, munch on honey and marmalade sandwiches, and enter the 'Smartest Bear' competition

▶ **Steam Extravaganza**
23/9/00-24/9/00
Goods trains- Intensive timetable- Visiting engines.

▶ **Santa Train Services**
3/12/00-24/12/00
Book early! All children receive a gift from Santa. Booking forms from August onwards, please send SAE

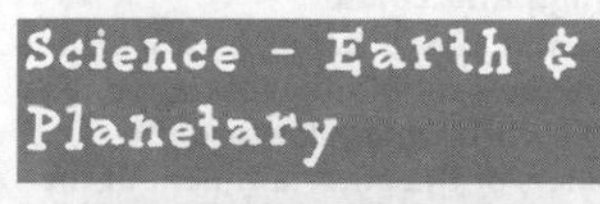

Science - Earth & Planetary

Elsecar - The PowerHouse

Elsecar Heritage Centre Wath Road Elsecar Barnsley South Yorkshire S74 8HJ
Tel: 01226 740203 Fax: 01226 350239

Elsecar is located in the beautiful South Yorkshire countryside. It is an historic working museum; a steam railway; an interactive science centre and an exciting day out for everyone.

visitor comments: Lots of hands-on experiments. Reasonably priced restaurant. The steam ride is great - but it doesn't run everyday.

All year daily 10.00-17.00. Closed 25 Dec-1 Jan
Passport Ticket to: Power House, Railway & Living History Exhibition A£5.25 C£3.00. Concessions and Groups 10+ £3.00. Power House: A£3.25 C&Concessions&Groups £2.00. Railway: A£2.50 C&Concessions&Groups £1.00. Site: Admission Free

discount offer: One Child Free With One Full Paying Adult

↓*special events*

▶ **Days out with Thomas**
11/3/00-22/10/00
Meet Thomas the Tank Engine, Sir Topham Hatt, the Fat Controller and many other friends at this spectacular family event held on the following days only, 11-12 Mar and 21-22 Oct

▶ **Elsecar Home and Garden Show**
9/4/00-9/4/00
Browse amongst the displays, stalls and demonstrations of everything for your house and garden

▶ **Model Engineering Gala**
5/8/00-6/8/00
Model railways, boats, planes, cars, and many displays from societies around the country

▶ **1940's Weekend**
19/8/00-20/8/00
A 1940's weekend extravaganza. Battle re-enactments, air raids, street party and a 1940's swing ball

▶ **Santa on the Steam Train**
2/12/00-24/12/00
Meet Father Christmas aboard the Elsecar Steam Railway. Presents and refreshments for all. Trains run weekends and pre-Christmas week. Booking essential

▶ **Elsecar Christmas Fayre**
9/12/00-10/12/00
Crafts galore, festive entertainment, refreshments and a chance to visit Father Christmas aboard the Steam Railway, 11.00-18.00

Eureka! The Museum for Children

Discovery Road Halifax West Yorkshire HX1 2NE
[next to the railway station]
Tel: 01422 330069 Fax: 01422 330275
www.eureka.org.uk

Eureka! is Britain's only hands-on museum designed specifically for children up to the age of 12. Four lively galleries, packed with larger than life exhibits encouraging visitors to find out more about their bodies and the world through interactive exploration. Children and adults can share in the adventure of learning,

from finding out what makes the toilet flush and how TV programmes are made to working on a factory production line and changing a car wheel.
visitor comments: A good family day out, with helpful, friendly staff. Well organised - interesting, fun and educational. Afterwards, take a stroll up the hill to Piece Hall - an architectural delight.
All year daily 10.00-17.00. Closed 24-26 Dec
A&C(12+)£5.75 C(3-12)£4.75 C(under 3)£Free
Family Saver Ticket (A2+C3-12x2)£15.75

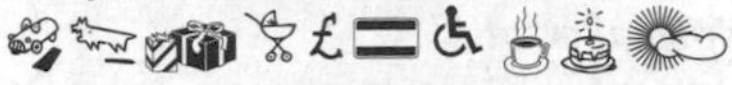

Sealife Centres & Aquariums

Scarborough Sea Life Centre

Scalby Mills Road Scarborough North Yorkshire YO12 6RP
[Scarborough North Bay]
Tel: 01723 376125 Fax: 01723 376285
Overlooking Scarborough's dramatic North Bay, the Sea Life Centre's famous three pyramids are home to thousands of incredible marine creatures. A firm favourite with all our visitors is the Seal Rescue & Rehabilitation Centre, a vital lifeline for injured and stray pups and a haven for resident adult grey seals.
visitor comments: The children loved watching the seals being fed! Quite pricey, but there's plenty to see.
All year Mon-Sun daily from 10.00. Closing times vary according to season
Queuing Times: variable
A£5.50 C(4-14)&OAPs&Students£3.95 C(0-4)&Wheelchair Users£Free. Groups 10+ A£4.50 C(4-14)&Students£3.25 OAPs£3.50, 1 in 10 free. School Groups £2.75 per person, 1 in 5 free

Stately Homes

Nostell Priory

Doncaster Road Nostell Wakefield West Yorkshire WF4 1QE
[on A638 Wakefield / Doncaster road]
Tel: 01924 863892 Fax: 01924 865282
Built by Paine in the middle of the 18th century, the priory has an additional wing built by Adam in 1766. It contains a notable saloon and tapestry room and displays pictures and Chippendale furniture. Credit Cards accepted in the shop and tearooms only, regret not for admission.
visitor comments: Annual country fair is worth a visit.
Now closed until Spring 2001
↓*special events*

▶ **Easter Craft Fair**
22/4/00-24/4/00
Call for details

▶ **Spring Plant Fair**
14/5/00-14/5/00
Plants of all varieties for sale

▶ **Balloon Event**
3/6/00-4/6/00
Call for further details

▶ **Nostell Priory Country Fair**
15/7/00-16/7/00
A fair steeped in tradition. Value for money fun for all the family. Music, merriment and country pursuits

▶ **Last Night At The Proms**
21/7/00-22/7/00
A spectacular outdoor concert with firework finale, call for further details

Theme & Adventure Parks

Flamingo Land Theme Park and Zoo

The Rectory Kirby Misperton Malton North Yorkshire YO17 6UX
[off the A64 by pass running between York and Scarborough off A169 Malton / Pickering road from N A19 then A170]
Tel: 01653 668287 Fax: 01653 668280
www.flamingoland.co.uk
At Flamingo Land, the UK's fourth most visited theme park, there's something for everyone, whether its the thrill of the dozen white-knuckled chillers or the entertainment of the eight fantastic family shows. We also boast the north's largest privately owned zoo and for the little ones, there's hours of fun in the Kiddies Kingdom. New Attractions for this year include Europe's only triple looping rollercoaster, as well as Little Monsters, a superb indoor themed attraction for all the family.
visitor comments: Great value for money. Nice picnic spots and something for chidren of all ages - a sufficient variety. Will definitely visit again.
9 Apr-29 Oct daily from 10.00. Closing times vary according to season
A&C£12.00 C(0-4)£Free OAPs£6.00 Family Ticket (4 people)£42.00

Hemsworth Waterpark and Playworld

Wakefield Yorkshire
Tel: 01977 617617
Facilities include gardens, lakes, inland play

beaches, miniature railway and pets corner. Speedboats and pedalos are available. Second lake reserved for fishing. Meals and refreshments at the Windsurfer family pub.
Any reasonable time
Admission Free

Lightwater Valley Theme Park
North Stainley Ripon Yorkshire HG4 3HT
[A61 off A1 then A6108 to Masham. Plenty of on site parking available]
Tel: 01765 635334/635368 Fax: 01765 635359
www.lightwatervalley.co.uk
Set in 175 acres of country park and lakeland, Lightwater Valley offers a selection of rides and attractions suitable for all the family. Enjoy the white-knuckle thrills of the world's longest roller coaster, the Ultimate, as well as the Rat and the Wave, or, for the less adventurous, there are the Ladybird, the steam train and boating lake.
15 Apr-1 May daily. 6,7,13,14, 20 & 21 May. 27 May-10 Sept daily. 16, 17, 23, 24, 30 Sept, 1, 7, 8, 14 & 15 Oct. 21-29 Oct daily. Gates open at 10.00, rides and attractions open at 10.30. Last Admission: 17.00 depending on time of year
Pay once and ride all day: Over 1.33m (4ft 4ins) £12.50, Under 1.33m (4ft 4ins) £9.95, Under 1m (3ft 3ins) £Free, Family Ticket (2A+2C)£39.00 additional family ticket member £9.75. OAPs £5.95. Group discounts available
discount offer: One Guest Admitted Free When Accompanied By Two Full Paying Guests. Excludes Bank Holidays and August. Excludes Family Ticket or Group Rates. Confirm Opening Times on 01765 635321

Transport Museums

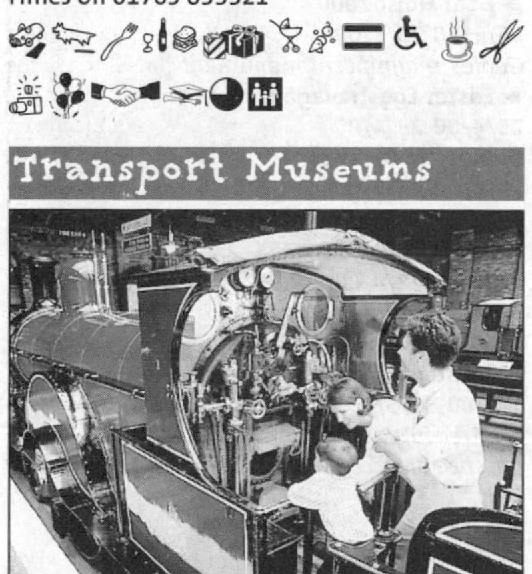

National Railway Museum
Leeman Road York Yorkshire YO26 4XJ
[A64 from Scarborough, Malton & Pickering. A64 from Tadcaster, Leeds, M62, M1 & A1. A19 from Selby. A19 from Teeside & Thirsk. A59 from Harrogate. Outer ring road A1237. On Leeman Road, just outside the City Centre, behind the Railway Station.]
Tel: 01904 621261 Fax: 01904 611112
www.nrm.org.uk
Nowhere tells the story of the train better than the National Railway Museum, now with a new £4 million wing. From Stephenson's Rocket and giant steam engines to Eurostar and miniature railway rides, rail travel is brought dramatically to life with interactive displays and lavish exhibitions. Discover it all in one fun-packed family day out where children get in free. Picnic facilities available both in and outdoors.
visitor comments: Plenty to see. The cafe is good value, clean and relaxing.
All year Mon-Sun 10.00-18.00. Pre-booked Guided Tours (prices on application).
A£6.50 C£Free OAPs£4.90 Concessions£4.00. Group rates A£5.50

↓special events
- **Worth a Thousand Words**
1/12/99-31/3/00
- **South For Sunshine**
6/12/99-27/2/00
- **Days Out with Thomas**
19/2/00-3/3/00

Sandtoft Transport Museum
Belton Road Sandtoft Doncaster South Yorkshire DN8 5SX
[J2 M180]
Tel: 01724 711391 24hr info
www.sandtoft.org.uk
The museum, Britain's first national trolleybus museum, boasts a collection of vehicles which date from 1927-1985 from both Britain and Europe. Attractions include Trollybus Rides, Miniature Railway, 1960s shop windows, children's adventure playground and 'Have-a-Go' trolleybus and motorbus simulators (ideal for children). Admission ticket entitles the holder to all trolleybus rides and first ride on the

miniature railway.
Various opening times throughout year, call info line for the next held, with details of bus and train operating days and free bus service from Doncaster. (SAE with postal enquiries).
12.00-17.00
Last Admission: 16.00
Museum: (Except Gathering, Railway Days, Santa Special) A3.50 C(under 5)£Free C&OAPs£2.00 Family Ticket (A2+C4)£10.00
discount offer: One Child Free With One Full Paying Adult Per Family Group

↓*special events*

▶ **North Lincolnshire Heritage Day**
25/6/00-25/6/00
Threshing Machine demonstration with displays of tractors and other local attractions

▶ **Sandtoft Gathering 2000**
30/7/00-30/7/00
Preview July 29 12.00-17.00 Main event July 30 10.00-18.00. Vintage and classic buses, motorcycles, lorries, cars etc. Trade stalls, CAMRA beer tent and many other attractions.

▶ **Special Railway Days**
9/8/00-16/8/00
Includes bus and rail rides, open 12.00-16.00. Unlimited rides on the miniature railway, ideal for children and adults

▶ **European Weekend**
27/8/00-28/8/00
Display and operation of trolleybuses from Europe. There are four resident European trolleybuses and others invited. If you have a European classic or vintage car to enter, please write to the museum

▶ **Yorkshire Day**
22/10/00-22/10/00
Includes the St Leger run from Doncaster. Many visiting buses and cars from the region. Vehicle Cavalcades old and new. Open 12.00-18.00 Write for trade and vehicle booking forms

▶ **Santa Specials**
10/12/00-17/12/00
Sun Dec 10 and 17 only, 11.00-17.00. Take a train and trolleybus ride to see Santa in his Grotto. Presents and Live festive music also

Vintage Carriages Trust - Vintage Railway Carriage Museum

Ingrow Railway Centr Ingrow Keighley West Yorkshire BD22 8NJ
[1m from Keighley town centre on the A629 Halifax road. BR: Keighley KWVR to Ingrow. Plenty of parking on site]
Tel: 01535 680425 Fax: 01535 646472
www.neotek.demon.co.uk/vct/
A fascinating display centred on a unique collection of beautifully restored elderly railway carriages telling the story of rail travel in fact and fiction.
All year daily Summer: 11.30-17.00 Winter: 11.30-16.00. Closed 25-26 Dec
Last Admission: Summer 16.30 Winter 15.45
A£1.00 C&OAPs & Students & unemployed £0.75
discount offer: Two For The Price Of One

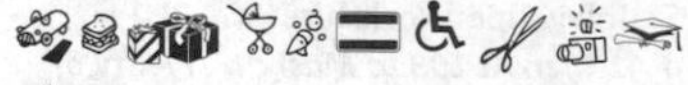

Waterways Museum and Adventure Centre

Dutch River Side Goole Yorkshire DN14 5TB
[area is signposted from J36 M62]
Tel: 01405 768730 Fax: 01405 769868
The Waterways museum contains interactive's, models, walk in displays, interchangeable photos and a contemporary art exhibition. There is also a café, gift shop, nature trail, weekend boat trips and a floating Art Gallery.
Mon-Fri 09.00-16.00, Weekends April-end Oct 12.00-17.00
Last Admission: 16.00
A£1.00 C&Concessions£0.50. Free admission to British Waterways Staff, Retired Staff, Museum/Gallery Staff, Teachers & English Heritage Members

↓*special events*

▶ **VHF Radio Course**
11/3/00-14/10/00
Held on Mar 11 and Oct 14 only

▶ **CBA Boat Handling Weekend**
18/3/00-17/9/00
Held on Mar 18-19, May 27-28, July 22-23 and Sept 16-17 only.

▶ **Boat Hoist 2000**
25/3/00-25/3/00
Goole's magnificent monument

▶ **Easter Eggstravaganza**
23/4/00-23/4/00

▶ **Bugs 'n' Beasties**
25/4/00-25/4/00
Pond dipping on a nature trail for children

▶ **Mad for Murals**
26/4/00-28/4/00
A mural painting workshop to keep children entertained in the holidays!

▶ **Museum Month**
1/5/00-31/5/00
Ten Treasures exhibition with Audrey 2000 send off, special prices and competitions throughout May

▶ **Stranded**
29/8/00-29/8/00
Holiday drama workshop for children

▶ **Hallowe'en Lanterns**
26/10/00-26/10/00
Lantern making workshops for children

Animal Attractions

Oban Rare Breeds Farm Park
New Barran Oban Argyll PA34 4QD
[2m from Oban on a bus route]
Tel: 01631 770608/604
Conservation centre breeding and exhibiting rare breeds of farm ainmals - cattle, sheep, pigs, goats and poultry. Pets Corner, tearoom for that special treat and try the tempting home-baking, gift shop, picnic areas, woodland walk, beautiful views of the Argyllshire countryside.
Apr-Oct daily 10.00-17.00
Last Admission: 17.00
A£5.00 C£3.00
discount offer: Two For The Price Of One When One Adult Pays

Archaeology

Archaeolink Prehistory Park
Oyne Insch Aberdeenshire AB52 6QT
[1m off A96 Aberdeen-Inverness road, 8m N of Inverurie]
Tel: 01464 851500 Fax: 01464 851544
www.archaeolink.co.uk
The fascinating world of ancient Aberdeenshire is brought vividly to life through a variety of interactive displays, a film presentation spanning 6000 years, a myths and legends gallery, a working Iron Age farm with costumed guides and plenty of hands on opportunities to ensure a great day out for all the family.
visitor comments: Excellent, family orientated introduction to early history of Scotland. Set amidst beautiful countryside.
3 Apr-31 Oct daily 09.30-17.00, Nov-Feb 10.00-17.00
Last Admission: Summer 16.00
A£3.90 C£2.35 Family Ticket £11.00
Concessions£2.35 School Parties £1.50 Group Rates 10% discount
discount offer: Two For The Price Of One

↓*special events*

▶ **Family Fun Day**
2/4/00-2/4/00

▶ **Beltaine/Celtic Fair**
29/4/00-1/5/00
Experience the hustle and bustle of a Celtic market day

▶ **Midsummer Stone Circles**
17/6/00-18/6/00
A celebration with magical fires and processions, storytelling and dance

▶ **Roman and Celtic Day**
23/7/00-23/7/00
Realistic combat displays, weapon demonstrations and marching drills

▶ **Samhain Celtic Halloween**
29/10/00-29/10/00

Arts, Crafts & Textiles

City Art Centre
2 Market Street Edinburgh Midlothian EH1 1DE
[A199]
Tel: 0131 529 3993 Fax: 0131 529 3977
www.cac.org.uk
The City Art Centre houses the city's permanent fine art collection and stages temporary exhibitions drawn from all over the world. It has six floors of display galleries (with escalators and lift), a shop, cafe and facilities for disabled visitors.
All year Mon-Sat 10.00-17.00
Admission generally free for exhibitions. For special exhibitions, charges are levied and opening times may vary

Fergusson Gallery
Marshall Place Perth PH2 8NU
[Adjacent to S Inch and large public car park]
Tel: 01738 441944
Based in an old waterworks dating from 1832. Now houses the most extensive collection of the work of J. D. Ferguson (1874-1961), one of the leading figures in 20th century Scottish art.
Mon-Sat 10.00-17.00
Admission Free

Paisley Museum and Art Galleries

High Street Paisley Renfrewshire PA1 2BA
[J27 M8, close to Paisley town centre]
Tel: 0141 889 3151 Fax: 0141 889 9240
www.renfrewshire.gov.uk
Pride of place here is given to a world-famous collection of Paisley shawls. Other collections illustrate local industrial and natural history, while the emphasis of the art gallery is on 19th-century Scottish artists and an important studio ceramics collection. There are various exhibitions throughout the year. On-site parking for disabled visitors only.
All year Tue-Sat 10.00-17.00, Sun 14.00-17.00. Public Hol 10.00-17.00. Closed Mon unless a Public Hol
Admission Free

↓special events

▶ **Rush on Paper**
5/2/00-26/3/00
3-D models made by Peter Rush, from wallpaper paste and kitchen rolls, life-size - depicting past and present celebrities

▶ **Jan Niedojadlo Soft Sculptures**
1/4/00-7/5/00
Come and get right into 'Chrysalis,' 'Shell' and 'Crystal' - literally!

▶ **112th Annual Exhibtion**
22/4/00-21/5/00
The Paisley Art Institute exhibition

▶ **81st Scottish Salon of Photography 2000**
13/5/00-3/6/00
An exhibition of work from the Scottish Photographic Federation

▶ **Scottish Drawing Competition**
27/9/00-29/9/00
Biennial exhibition of drawing from all over Scotland

▶ **Lochwinnoch Art Group Annual Exhibition**
4/10/00-4/11/00
Annual exhibition form a local art group

▶ **School's Out**
14/10/00-20/10/00
Half Term children's activities

▶ **Paisley Artists**
19/11/00-16/12/00
The 88th annual show from a local art group

▶ **Monumental Miniatures for the Millennium**
9/12/00-28/1/01
Architectural miniatures spans the new Millennium

Country Parks & Estates

Finlaystone Country Estate

Langbank Renfrewshire PA14 6TJ
[A8 10mins W of Glasgow Airport. Plenty of parking on site]
Tel: 01475 540505 Fax: 01475 540285
www.finlaystone.co.uk
Charming exhibitions of Victoriana, including an old kitchen, are displayed in this homely family house. There are beautiful gardens overlooking the Clyde, woodland walks and an adventure playground. Teas served in the walled garden. A private collection of dolls of all sorts, from many countries are located within the Visitor Centre. Ranger Service is also available.
Estate open all year daily 11.00-17.00. House: Tours by appointment. Doll Exhibition : daily 12.00-17.00. Visitor Centre: daily 12.00-17.00, Winter months: Sat & Sun
A£2.50 C&OAPs£1.50. Entry to Doll Exhibition: £0.50
discount offer: Two For The Price Of One

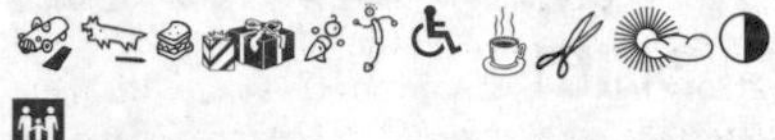

Hirsel Country Park

Hirsel Estate Coldstream Berwickshire TD12 4LP
[0.5m W on A697. Plenty of parking on site]
Tel: 01890 882834 Fax: 01890 882834
The Hirsel is the seat of the Home family and whilst the house is not open to the public, there is much to see in the Homestead Museum, Craft Centre and Workshops. There are various woodland walks which show bird life and flowers to the fullest extent. View the Snowdrops, Aconites and Daffodils in Spring and the fantastic Rhododendrons and Azaleas in May/June, in Dundock Wood and in the grounds. Herbaceous borders and roses in the Summer and a marvellous colour display in Autumn. A playground and picnic area are situated adjacent to the car park, which helps to make it a family day out. The Cottage Tearooms serve snacks and local produce. Coach parties must book prior to arrival.
All year daylight hours Garden & Grounds Museum 10.00-17.00 Craft Centre Mon-Fri

10.00-17.00 weekends noon-17.00
Easter-30 Sept £2.00 per car 1st Oct-Easter £1.00 per car Coaches/Minibuses £0.50 per person

↓*special events*

▶ **Hirsel May Fair**
29/4/00-1/5/00
Live entertainment, music, food and over 30 craft stalls

▶ **Craft Fair for Christmas**
11/12/00-12/11/00
Visiting and local craft stalls selling original Christmas gifts

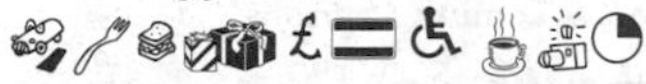

Kelburn Castle and Country Centre
South Offices Fairlie Largs Ayrshire KA29 0BE
[A78 2m S of Largs]
Tel: 01475 568685 Fax: 01475 568121
Home of the Earls of Glasgow, Kelburn enjoys spectacular views over the Firth of Clyde. Explore its historic gardens and romantic glen, waterfalls and unique trees. There is also a riding school and trekking, adventure playgrounds, craft shop, licensed cafè, exhibitions and Scotland's most unusual attraction - the 'Secret Forest'.
Apr-Oct daily 10.00-18.00. Nov-Mar 11.00-17.00. Castle open July and Aug for afternoon guided tours, (3 per day).
A£4.50 Concessions£3.00 Family tickets (A2+C3 or A1+C4)£13.00. (Family tickets may be used again, discounting the next visit to £10.00).

Factory Outlets & Tours

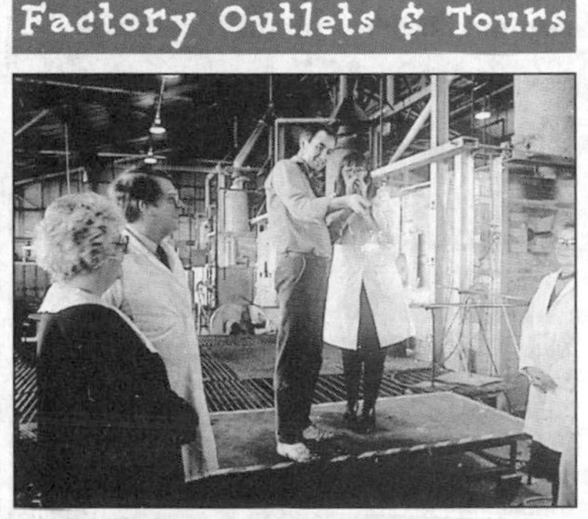

Edinburgh Crystal Visitor Centre
Eastfield Industrial Estate Penicuik Midlothian EH26 8HB
[on A701]
Tel: 01968 675128 Fax: 01968 674847
A tour around the factory shows the various stages of the art of glass making including glass blowing, cutting and engraving. New Exhibition and video "Capturing the Light". Factory shop with best prices ever.
All year Factory Tours Mon-Fri 09.00-15.30. Apr-Sept Sat & Sun 11.00-14.30. Visitor Centre Mon-Sat 09.00-17.00, Sun 11.00-17.00. Closed 25-27 Dec & 1-2 Jan
A£3.00 Family Ticket £7.50 Concessions£2.00
discount offer: Two For The Price Of One

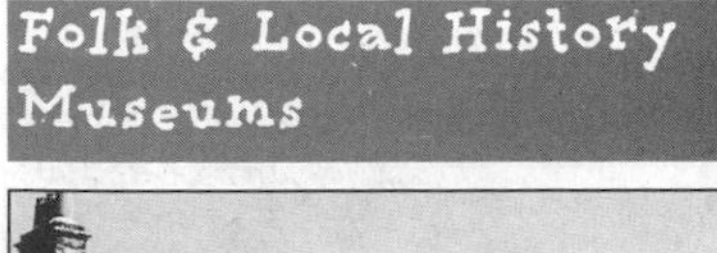

Folk & Local History Museums

Andrew Carnegie Birthplace Museum
Moodie Street Dunfermline Fife KY12 7PL
[400yds from Abbey. Limited parking on site]
Tel: 01383 724302
www.carnegiemuseum.co.uk
The museum tells the story of the humble handloom weaver's son who was born here in 1835. Andrew Carnegie created the biggest steel works in the USA then became a philanthropist on a huge scale. Weaving demonstrations are held on the first Friday of each month from May-Oct.
April-Oct 11.00-17.00 Mon-Sat, 14.00-17.00 Sun. Closed 1 Nov-31 March. Pre-booked groups outside these times
Last Admission: 30mins before closing
A£1.50 C(0-15)£Free Concessions£0.75

Perth Museum and Art Gallery
George Street Perth Perthshire PH1 5LB
[J10 or J11 M90. A9, A93, A85]
Tel: 01738 632488 Fax: 01738 443505

This purpose-built museum houses collections of fine and applied art, social and local history, natural history and archaeology. Temporary exhibitions are held throughout the year.
visitor comments: Helpful staff. Most changing displays suitable for the disabled.
All year Mon-Sat 10.00-17.00. Closed Christmas & New Year
Admission Free

Forests & Woods

Queen Elizabeth Forest Park Visitor Centre
Trossachs Road (Dukes Pass) Aberfoyle Stirling Stirlingshire FK8 3UX
[1m N of Aberfoyle on the A821. Plenty of parking on site]
Tel: 01877 382258 Fax: 01877 382120
The Visitor Centre has an Exhibition Wing, Forest Craft Shop, Cafe, Woodcarver, Baby Changing Room, Toilets and disabled toilets. Superb views from every window. Set in 50,000 acres of mountain and glen in the heart of the beautiful Trossachs, with walks, cycle routes, forest drives and orienteering. Guided walks are available by pre-booking.
Mar- Oct 10.00-18.00. Nov & Dec 11.00-16.00. Closed Jan-Feb
Admission Free. Parking charge

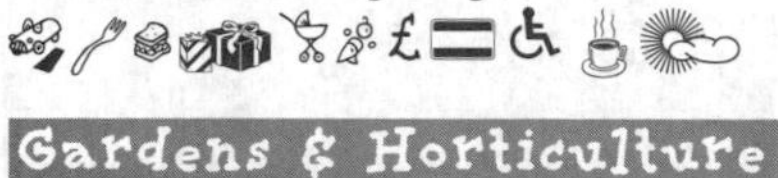

Gardens & Horticulture

Kailzie Gardens
Peebles Peeblesshire EH45 9HT
[A703]
Tel: 01721 720007
These extensive grounds with their fine old trees provide a Burnside walk flanked by bulbs, rhododendrons and azaleas. A walled garden contains herbaceous, shrub rose borders, greenhouses and a small formal rose garden. There is a waterfowl pond, an art gallery, and a children's play area. Stocked Trout pond.
Gardens Mid Mar-End Oct 11.00-17.30. End Oct-Mar Gardens only open dawn to dusk. Trout Pond Mar-Oct 08.00-dusk. Restaurant open as Gardens but please call for winter opening times.
Mid Oct-mid Mar: Honesty Box, recommended £1.00. 21 Apr-mid Oct: A£2.50 C(5-14)£0.75. Group rates available
discount offer: 21 Apr-mid Oct £1.00 discount per person. Maximum 2 persons

Torosay Castle and Gardens
Craignure Isle Of Mull Argyll PA65 6AY
[1.5m SE of Craignure by A849, by Forest Walk or by NG Steam Railway. BR: Oban]
Tel: 01680 812421 Fax: 01680 812470
www.holidaymull.org/members/torosay
Early Victorian house by David Bryce, still a family home, surrounded by 12 acres of terraced and contrasting informal gardens, all offset by dramatic West Highland scenery. Gardens and tea room only suitable for wheelchairs, dogs on leads in Gardens only.
Castle: mid Apr-mid Oct 10.30-17.30. Gardens: Summer 09.00-19.00, Winter sunrise-sunset
Last Admission: 17.00
Castle A£4.50 C£1.50 Family Ticket £10.00 Concessions£3.50. Honesty box when Castle closed
discount offer: Two For The Price Of One

Heritage & Industrial

New Lanark World Heritage Village
New Lanark Mills Lanark Strathclyde ML11 9DB
[1m S of Lanark]
Tel: 01555 661345 Fax: 01555 665738

www.newlanark.org
200 year old Cotton mill village, site of Robert Owen's social and educational experiments, now nominated as a World Heritage Site. Set in the Clyde Gorge, surrounded by beautiful woodlands and the Falls of Clyde, New Lanark is Europe's premier industrial heritage site. Award-winning Visitor Centre.
All year daily 11.00-17.00. Closed Dec 25 & 1-2 Jan
A£3.75 C£2.50 Family Ticket 1 A2+C2) £9.95 Family Ticket 2 (A2+C4) £12.50. Pre-booking advisable for groups, special rates for schools. Access to village free

Scotch Whisky Heritage Centre
354 Castlehill The Royal Mile Edinburgh Midlothian EH1 2NE
[the Centre is next to Edinburgh Castle]
Tel: 0131 220 0441 Fax: 0131 220 6288
www.whisky-heritage.co.uk
The Scottish Tourist Board Highly Commended, Scotch Whisky Heritage Centre, brings the story of whisky to life in an entertaining and informative way. Experience Scotland's turbulent past and learn the ancient traditions surrounding Scotch Whisky making. Journey through centuries of history on a whisky barrel ride and meet our 'ghostly' blender. Guided tours are available in eight different languages, and a free dram is offered to adults and a free balloon and soft drink for children. The Restaurant and Whisky Bond Bistro & Bar gives visitors the opportunity to try over 220 different whiskies, and the Gift and Whisky Shop to purchase those special souvenirs. Tutored Whisky Tastings can be arranged on and off-site, and two beautiful reception rooms are available for corporate hospitality, conferences and Scottish banquets.
visitor comments: Presentation is excellent, staff particularly helpful.
All year daily Summer: 09.30-17.30 Winter: 10.00-17.00. Closed 25 Dec
Last Admission: Last tour: Summer 17.30, Winter 16.30
A£5.50 C(5-17)£2.75 Family Ticket £13.50 Concessions£3.85

Historical

Blair Castle
Blair Atholl Pitlochry Perthshire PH18 5TL
[7m NW of Pitlochry off A9]
Tel: 01796 481207 Fax: 01796 481487
www.blair-castle.co.uk
Traditional home of the Dukes of Atholl and his unique private army, the Atholl Highlanders. The castle dates back to the 13th century but was altered in the 18th century and later given a castellated exterior. The oldest part is Cumming's Tower, built in about 1270.
1 Apr-29 Oct daily 10.00-18.00. During July & Aug we open at 09.30 and at other time by special arrangement
Last Admission: 17.00
House & Grounds: A£6.00 C(5-16)£4.00 Family Ticket £18.00 OAPs£5.00 Disabled £2.00. Grounds Only: A£2.00 C(5-16)£1.00 Family Ticket £5.00 Disabled £Free. Group Rates 12+; House & Grounds: A£5.00 C(5-16)£4.00 Primary School C£3.00 OAPs£4.50 Disabled £2.00. Grounds Only: A£2.00 C(5-16)£1.00 Primary School C£1.00 Disabled £Free. Group rates apply only when all tickets are bought by the Driver, Courier, Party Leader at one time

Bowhill House and Country Park
Bowhill Selkirk Scottish Borders TD7 5ET
[3m W of Selkirk on A708 Moffat St Marys Loch Road. Plenty of on site parking available]
Tel: 01750 22204 Fax: 01750 22204
Border Home of the Scotts of Buccleuch. Famous artists include Guardi, Canaletto, Claude, Gainsborough etc. Superb 17th/18th century French and 19th century British furni-

ture and porcelain. Monmouth, Sir Walter Scott and Queen Victoria relics. For details of our specialist art courses, please tel: Buccleuch Heritage Trust Selkirk (01750) 22204. Restored Victorian kitchen, Visitor Centre and Theatre.
House: July daily 13.00-16.30. Country Park (inc Adventure Woodland Play area and nature trails): 22 Apr-28 Aug Sat-Thur 12.00-17.00 Fri in July with house. Other times by appointment for education groups. 2000 Times: House: July daily 13.00-16.30. Country Park (inc Adventure Woodland Play area and nature trails): 22 Apr-28 Aug Sat-Thur 12.00-17.00 Fri in July with house. Other times by appointment for education groups.
Last Admission: 45mins before closing
House & Grounds: A£4.50 C£2.00 Wheelchair users £Free OAPs£4.00. Grounds only: £2.00.

↓special events

▶ **"My Borderland"**
24/3/00-24/3/00
With local historian Ian Landles at 19.30

▶ **"Billy Goats Gruff"**
10/4/00-10/4/00
From the Clydebuilt Puppet Theatre at 14.00

▶ **"Quelques Fleurs" by Liz Lochhead**
25/4/00-26/4/00
The Brunton Theatre Company. 19.30, A£6.00 Concessions£5.00, optional supper £8.50

▶ **"Inspirations" from The Edinburgh Jazz Quintet**
12/5/00-12/5/00
At 20.00, A£6.00 Concessions£5.00, optional supper £8.50

▶ **"Sex and Chocolate" from the MsFits Theatre Company**
23/6/00-23/6/00
19.30, tickets A£6.00 Concessions£5.00, optional supper £8.50

▶ **"French and Blues"**
7/7/00-7/7/00
Ian Louthian and Hilary Bell at 19.30. A£6.00 Concessions£5.00, optional supper £8.50

Culzean Castle and Country Park
Maybole Ayrshire KA19 8LE
[12m S of Ayr, on A719, 4m W of Maybole of A77]
Tel: 01655 884400 Fax: 01655 884503
www.nts.org.uk
18th century Castle on clifftop, designed by Robert Adam for David fourth Earl of Cassillis. Noted for oval staircase, circular drawing room and plasterwork. Scotland's first country park, woodland walks cover 563 acres to shoreline; pagoda, walled garden. Visitors centre and Ranger guided walks and information.
Castle, Visitor Centre, Licensed Restaurants & Shops: 1 Apr-31 Oct daily 10.30-17.30. Country Park: all year daily 09.30-sunset. Other times by appointment
Last Admission: 17.00
Castle & Country Park: A£7.00 C&Concessions£5.00. Group rates 20+ A£6.00 Concessons£5.00. Country Park only: A£3.50 C&Concessions£2.50. Group rates 20+ A£3.00. School per coach £20.00 BUT School Membership held £Free. All NT/NTS members £Free
discount offer: Children Free During 2000 (maximum 3 per adult)

↓special events

▶ **ACORN Mini Craft Fair**
22/4/00-25/6/00
Held on Apr 22-24, May 27-29 and June 24-25 only

▶ **Culzean Family Fun Run**
30/4/00-30/4/00
Up to 300 entrants negotiate their way over possibly the most scenic Fun Run course in Britain. Closing date for entries Apr 25. Run starts at 14.00, Band at Visitor Centre at 13.00

▶ **3D2D Craft and Design Fair**
29/6/00-30/6/00
Held on the events field 10.30-17.30 with around 50 crafts people. All under cover and several exhibitors will be demonstrating the making of their products

▶ **Scotlands Gardens Scheme**
7/7/00-7/7/00
'Culzean Vinery' - Evening talk and buffett supper. Date to be confirmed

▶ **Children's Weeks**
10/7/00-18/8/00
Held on July 10-14, July 31-Aug 4 and Aug 14-18. For children aged 6-12, meet at the Visitor Centre at 10.00

▶ **Romeo and Juliet**
11/7/00-11/7/00
Presented by ILLYRIA

▶ **The Emperor's New Clothes**
20/7/00-20/7/00
Presented by ILLYRIA

▶ **Culzean Classic Vehicle Show**
6/8/00-6/8/00

This well-established event attracts upwards of 500 entries with many supporting attractions. Organised with East Ayrshire Car Club. 10.00-17.00 on the events field.

▶ **Falconry Day**
13/8/00-13/8/00
Displays, demonstrations and other activities on the events field from 10.30-17.00

▶ **Festival of Scottish Music and Dance**
20/8/00-20/8/00
Held from 12.30-16.30 at Fountain Court. Music, dance and song in the Scottish tradition

▶ **Culzean Horse Trials**
17/9/00-17/9/00
From 10.00-17.00, novice and pre-novice trials organised jointly with the British Horse Society

▶ **Christmas Shopping**
2/12/00-2/12/00
Includes Acorn Craft Fair 11.00-17.00 in the Stone Barn.

▶ **Christmas at Culzean**
3/12/00-3/12/00
With Acorn Craft Fair 11.00-17.00 in the Stone Barn and Victorian Family Christmas in the Castle, 10.30-12.15 and 13.00-16.30

▶ **Christmas at Culzean**
9/12/00-9/12/00
Christmas Bazaar in Stone Barn, 11.00-1700 and Carol Concert in Castle 15.00 and 18.30 with the choir of Paisley Abbey. Call for details

▶ **Christmas at Culzean**
10/12/00-10/12/00
Christmas Bazaar 11.00-17.00 in the Stone Barn and Victorian Family Christmas in the Castle from 10.30-12.15 and 13.00-16.30

Cawdor Castle
Nairn Inverness-shire IV12 5RD
[SW of Nairn on B9090 between Inverness and Nairn. Plenty of on site parking]
Tel: 01667 404615 Fax: 01667 404674
The 14th century Keep, fortified in the 15th century and impressive additions mainly in the 17th century, form a massive fortress. Gardens, nature trails and splendid grounds. Shakespearian memories of Macbeth. The most romantic castle in the Highlands. It makes a super day out for the whole family; rain or shine; connoisseurs or kids. Disabled access limited.
1 May-8 Oct daily 10.00-17.30
Last Admission: House 17.00
A£5.60 C(5-15)£3.00 Family Ticket (A2&C5)£16.50 Concessions£4.60. Group 20+ A£5.10 C(5-15)£2.50. Gardens, grounds and nature trail only £2.90. Visually impaired £Free. Parking £Free

↓*special events*

▶ **Special Gardens Weekend**
3/6/00-4/6/00
Guided tours of Cawdor Gardens by Head Gardener and guided "Bluebell Walks" in wood by Estate Ranger - included in normal cost of admission

Duart Castle
Isle of Mull Argyll PA64 6AP
[Duart is 3m from Craignure off the A849 on the way to Iona. Plenty of free on site parking]
Tel: 01680 812309
Duart Castle stands on a cliff overlooking the Sound of Mull, home of the Chief of Clan Maclean. Burnt by the English in 1758 and restored by Sir Fitzroy Maclean in 1912. There are dungeons and state rooms in the 13th century keep, an exhibition of the shipwreck that sank below the castle in 1653 and fabulous views from the battlements. Dogs on leads in grounds only.
mid May-mid Oct daily 10.30-18.00
A£3.50 C£1.75 Family Ticket (A2+C2)£8.75 Concessions£3.00

Floors Castle
Kelso Roxburghshire TD5 7SF
[well signposted from all directions near Kelso. Plenty of parking on site]
Tel: 01573 223333 Fax: 01573 226056
www.roxburghe.bordernet.co.uk
Sir Walter Scott described this fairy-tale castle as 'altogether a kingdom for Oberon and Titania to dwell in.' Today it is the home of the 10th Duke of Roxburghe and its lived-in atmosphere enhances the superb collection of French furniture, tapestries and paintings contained inside.
Easter-Oct daily 10.30-16.30
Last Admission: 16.00
A£5.00 C£3.00 Family Ticket £14.00 OAPs£4.50
discount offer: Two For The Price Of One. Valid Until 29 Oct 2000. Excludes 27 August

Traquair House
Innerleithen Peeblesshire EH44 6PW
[on B709 off A72 at Peebles]
Tel: 01896 830323/830785 Fax: 01896 830639
www.traquair.co.uk
This is said to be Scotland's oldest inhabited and most romantic house. It dates back to the 12th century and 27 Scottish monarchs have stayed here. William, The Lion Heart held court at Traquair, and the house has rich association with Mary, Queen of Scots and the Jacobite risings. Also 18th century working brewery, maze and craft workshops.
22 Apr-31 Oct daily12.30-17.30. June-Aug 10.30-17.30. Grounds: Easter-Oct daily 10.30-17.30
Last Admission: 17.00
A£5.20 C£2.60 OAPs£4.20 Family Ticket £14.00 Group rates: A£4.60 C£2.00 Grounds only: A£2.00 C£1.00
discount offer: One Child Free With A Full Paying Adult. Valid Until 31 Oct 2000

Living History Museums

Callender House
Callender Park Falkirk Stirlingshire FK1 1YR
[E of Falkirk Town Centre on A803. BR: Falkirk High / Grahamstone. Plenty of parking on site]
Tel: 01324 503770 Fax: 01324 506171
www.falkirkmuseums.demon.co.uk
Imposing mansion within attractive parkland. Facilities include a working kitchen of 1825, where costumed interpreters carry out daily chores including cooking based on 1820's recipes. Exhibition area and "Story of Callendar House" plus two temporary galleries, regularly changing exhibitions, a history research centre, gift shop and Georgian tea-shop at the Stables. New, major permanent exhibition 'William Forbes Falkirk' and working 1820's garden, Store, Clockmaker and Printer.
All year Mon-Sat 10.00-17.00. Apr-Sept Sun 14.00-17.00 also all Bank Hol
Last Admission: 16.15
A£3.00 C£1.00 Family Ticket (A2+C2)£7.00
discount offer: Two Adults For The Price Of One

Buckie Drifter
Freuchny Road Buckie Banffshire AB56 1TT
Tel: 01542 834646 Fax: 01542 835995

www.moray.org

The Buckie Drifter is an exciting maritime heritage centre. You can discover what life was like in the fishing communities of Moray Coast during the herring boom years of the 1890's and 1930's. Sign-on as a crew member of a steam drifter and find out how to catch, gut and pack herring.

Apr-Oct Mon-Sat 10.00-17.00, Sun 12.00-17.00
A£2.75 C&OAPs£1.75 Family Ticket £8.00

discount offer: Two For The Price Of One. Valid Until 31 Oct 2000

Military & Defence Museums

Black Watch Regimental Museum

Balhousie Castle Hay Street Perth Perthshire PH1 5HR

[A9, M90, A85 to Perth]

Tel: 0131 310 8530 Fax: 01738 643245

The treasures of the 42nd/73rd Highland Regiment from 1739 to the present day are on show in this museum, together with paintings, silver, colours and uniforms.

All year May-Sept Mon-Sat 10.00-16.30. Oct-Apr Mon-Fri 10.00-15.30. Closed last Sat in June & 23 Dec-6 Jan. Other times & Groups 16+ by appointment
Last Admission: 30mins before closing
Queuing Times: occasionally
Admission Free, donations welcome

discount offer: 5% Discount On Gift Shop Purchases

Royal Scots Dragoon Guards Museum

The Castle Edinburgh EH1 2YT

[in Edinburgh Castle]

Tel: 0131 220 4387 Fax: 0131 310 5101

320 years of history and tradition of Scotland's Cavalry Regiment, including Royal Scots Greys and 3rd Carabiniers. Uniforms, medals, pictures, silver and flags, complemented by landscape displays and models of military action and cavalrymen. Archives and Guided Tours available by request.

Apr-Oct daily 09.30-17.30, Nov-Mar 09.30-16.30
Admission Free

Natural History Museums

Creetown Gem Rock Museum

Chain Road Creetown Newton Stewart Wigtownshire DG8 7HJ

[7m from Newton Stewart, 11m from Gatehouse-of-Fleet, just off the A75 Carlisle / Stranraer trunk road. Follow Gem Rock Museum signs on entering Creetown village]

Tel: 01671 820357/820554 Fax: 01671 820554

www.gemrock.net

The museum, completely refurbished in 1993, displays gemstones and minerals collected by the owners from around the world. The outstanding collection of Gold Nuggets includes the 'Maverick' nugget 23.8oz of Californian Gold. The beautiful collection also includes gemstone objects d'art. There are three large exhibition halls and a gemstone workshop. The Crystal Cave combines our years of experience and 'state of the art' techniques to create a dazzling display with audio-visual display and interactive computers. Your visit will be truly crowned at the sight of the secret treasures displayed in all their magnificence in hidden crevices and crystal lodes. Your breath will be taken away as our unique ultra-violet centrepiece display radiates its colours in fluorescent light. After you've taken it all in, why not visit The Prospector's Pantry, where you can sample our home-made cakes, biscuits, fresh cream delights, toasties, pies, tea, Rombouts coffee and soft drinks.

Mar-Easter daily 10.00-16.00. Easter-Sept daily 09.30-17.30. 1 Oct-30 Nov daily 10.00-16.00. 1 Dec-28 Feb weekends 10.00-16.00 or by appointment during the week. Closed from 23rd Dec for two weeks
Last Admission: 30mins before closing
A£2.90 C(under 5)£Free C(5-15)£1.75 Family Ticket £7.55 OAPs£2.40. Group rates 20+ available

discount offer: Two For The Price Of One Full Paying Adult

↓*special events*

▶ **Creetown Country & Western Music Festival**
15/9/00-17/9/00
Best of type of music festival in South Scotland. 15 top bands, great fun for all the family.
▶ **Country & Western Themed Weekend**
15/9/00-17/9/00

Nature & Conservation Parks

Kylerhea Otter Haven
Strathoich Fort Augustus Inverness PH32 4BT
Tel: 01320 366322 Fax: 01320 366581
www.forestry.gov.uk
A hide perched above the shore of Kyle Rhea (Skye) giving an excellent opportunity to watch a wide variety of coastal wildlife.
All year daily Summer 09.00-20.00. Winter 09.00-16.00
Admission Free

Palaces

Scone Palace
Scone Perth Perthshire PH2 6BD
[2m NE of Perth on A93. Plenty of parking on site]
Tel: 01738 552300 Fax: 01738 552588
www.scone-palace.co.uk
Family home of the Earl of Mansfield, Scone Palace houses a magnificent and varied collection of works of art. Scone Palace is set in mature and historic grounds, with an adventure playground and the Murray Star Maze. Once the crowning place of the Kings of Scotland, Scone offers a fascinating day out for all the family.
visitor comments: You really need a day to explore the Palace and Garden.
7 Apr-23 Oct daily 09.30-17.15. Special groups at other times and Winter by arrangement
Last Admission: 16.45
Palace & Grounds: A£5.60 C£3.30. Grounds only: A£2.80 C£1.70 Family Ticket £17.00. Group 20+ A£5.10 C£2.80.

Performing Arts

Waltzing Waters Aqua Theatre
Main Street Newtonmore Inverness-Shire PH20 1DR
Tel: 01540 673752 Fax: 01540 673752
A most elaborate water and light show. Thousands of dazzling patterns created by coloured lights and moving water in time to wonderful music. A unique show!
Feb-Dec daily including Bank Hols with limited opening during Christmas season. Shows: last approx 45mins every hour between 10.00-16.00. Evening Shows Mar-Oct at 17.00 & 20.30
A£4.00 C£1.50 Concessions£3.50. Group rates on appplication
discount offer: One Child Free With A Full Paying Adult

Railways

Isle of Mull Railway
Craignure (old pier) Station Craignure Isle Of Mull Argyll PA65 6AY
[near the old pier beyond the police station]

Tel: 01680 812494 Fax: 01680 300595
www.holidaymull.org/rail/Welcome
The first passenger railway on a Scottish island opened in 1984 runs to Torosay Castle and Gardens. Both steam and diesel trains 260mm gauge operate on the one-and-a-quarter mile long route, and there are extensive and dramatic woodland and mountain views. Limited disabled facilities on trains.
Easter-21 Oct daily. Call for a timetable
Return: A£3.30 C£2.20 Family Ticket Return (A2+C2)£8.75. Single: A£2.30 C£1.40 Family Ticket Single (A2+C2)£6.00. Group rates available
discount offer: 15% Discount On Normal Fares For Adults And Children

Science - Earth & Planetary

Hunterian Museum

University Avenue Glasgow Strathclyde G12 8QQ
[situated in the Hillhead district, 2m W of the city centre. BR: Underground station, Hillhead. Buses: Strathclyde Buses, Nos. 44, 59, from the city centre to University Avenue. By car : Signposted locally. Parking within the grounds is permit only. Free parking along KelvinWay; pay-and-display in University Avenue and adjoining streets; disabled drivers within University grounds by arrangement.]
Tel: 0141 330 4221 Fax: 0141 330 3617
www.gla.ac.uk/Museum
The museum is named after 18th century physician, Dr. William Hunter, who bequeathed his large and important collections of coins, medals, fossils, geological specimens and archaeological and ethnographic items to the university. The museum opened in 1807 and added to, the emphasis is now on Geology, Archeology, coins and Anthropology. Exhibitions including temporary ones held. Disabled Access - Museum: lift to main floor (prior notice). Art Gallery: ramp to ground floor, lift to basement and print gallery. No access to upper floors of the Mackintosh House. The University Visitors Centre provides tea, coffee and light snacks. It also has a range of interactive displays on Glasgow University. The Hub, adjacent to the Art Gallery, also contains a restaurant, together with a shop and bank, which visitors are welcome to use.
All year Mon-Sat 09.30-17.00 closed certain days, please telephone for details. The Mackintosh House is closed weekdays 12.30-13.30
The Museum and Art Gallery are maintained by the University of Glasgow as a service to the public. Donations towards the high costs involved are always welcome. Group bookings welcome. Both the Museum and Art Gallery may be hired for appropriate functions, please write to the Director.

Sealife Centres & Aquariums

Deep Sea World

Forthside Terrac North Queensferry Fife KY11 1JR
[J1 M90. Plenty of on site parking available]
Tel: 01383 411880 Fax: 01383 410514
www.deepseaworld.com
A moving walkway travels along the largest underwater transparent viewing tunnel and enables visitors to walk along the sea bed without getting their feet wet. Here visitors can get a diver's view of the spectacular underwater universe. 24hr information line, calls cost 50p per minute at all times. Service provider: Interloq Ltd, KY12 8NZ.
visitor comments: Great family day out, staff helpful and informative. Touch creatures in rock pools. Easily accessible for pushchairs. The tunnel is as good as Seaworld in the USA. A world class exhibit.
Mar-Oct daily 10.00-18.00. July-Aug 10.00-18.30. Nov-Mar Mon-Fri 11.00-17.00, Sat & Sun 10.00-18.00
A£6.25 C£3.95 C(0-3)£Free Family Ticket (A2+C4) £18.95 Concessions£4.50
discount offer: One Child Free With Each Full Paying Adult

Theme & Adventure Parks

Landmark Highland Heritage and Adventure Park

Carrbridge Inverness-Shire PH23 3AJ
[off A9 between Aviemore and Inverness]
Tel: 0800 7313446 Fax: 01479 841384
Don't miss the Watercoaster, a raft ride flume. Landmark is fun and discovery for all ages. NEW exhibition 'Microworld - a journey into innter space.' The Foresty Heritage Park has a 65 foot viewing tower. Demonstrations of timber sawing on a steam powered mill and log hauling by a Clydesdale Horse. Try your hand at forestry skills. Have fun in the Giant Adventure Play Area, maze, shop, restaurant with full menu and snack bar.

visitor comments: Everyone loved the water slide. Good choice of catering.
Apr & Oct daily 10.00-18.00. Mid July-mid Aug daily 09.30-19.00, Nov-Mar daily 10.00-17.00
Last Admission: 60mins before closing
Queuing Times: Watercoaster: 15mins at peak times only
Peak A£6.50 C£4.50

M & D's Scotland's Theme Park

Strathclyde Country Park Motherwell
Lanarkshire ML1 3RT
[9m S of Glasgow just off J5 M74. Located in Stratchclyde Country Park]
Tel: 01698 333999 Fax: 01698 303034

If you are looking for a fantastic day out, you'll find it here! Certainly something for everyone, M & D's is bursting with family theme park favourites, as well as boasting the largest collection of spine-chilling rides in the country. This includes Scotland's largest ever roller coaster - the awesome Tornado, it needs to be experienced to be believed. M & D's is an all weather venue, with a major section of the facility undercover and is packed with rides, amusement games, restaurants and bars - all to entertain you in good and inclement weather.
Indoor complex: All year daily 10.00-22.30. Theme Park Rides: Easter-end Oct peak days 12.00-22.00 Sat, Sun, Bank Hol & School Hol. Off peak times vary so please telephone
Admission Free. Car Park Free. Unlimited Ride Wristband: Under 1.3 metres: £7.95; over: £10.95 Family Ticket £32.00. Tokens £0.25 (rides start at just 2 tokens). Buy £10.00 of tokens and get £2.50 worth Free. Group discounts available. Price increase likely, please call for details
discount offer: Two Wristbands For The Price Of One. Ref BOGOF

Toy & Childhood Museums

Finlaystone Doll Collection

Finlaystone Langbank Inverclyde PA14 6TJ
[A8 10mins W of Glasgow Airport]
Tel: 01475 540285 Fax: 01475 540285
www.finlaystone.co.uk

A private collection of dolls of all sorts, from many countries located within the Visitor Centre. Wheelchairs only on ground floor. Tea room, formal Gardens and woodland walks.
1 Apr-30 Sept Estate: 11.00-17.00, Doll Exhibition: 12.00-17.00. Visitor Centre: 12.00-17.00 Sat & Sun in Winter
A£2.50 C&OAPs£1.50. Entry to Doll Exhibition: £0.50
discount offer: Two For The Price Of One

Transport Museums

Grampian Transport Museum

Main Street Alford Aberdeenshire AB33 8AE
[signposted on A944. Plenty of on site parking available]
Tel: 01975 562292 Fax: 01975 562180

There is a strong local theme to this road and rail museum. Its large collection of vintage vehicles includes cycles and motorcycles, horse-drawn and steam vehicles, cars and lorries. A new library and archive facility opened in March 1998 with the help of a Heritage Lottery Fund grant and can be viewed by appointment only.
2 Apr-31 Oct daily 10.00-17.00
Last Admission: 17.00
A£3.75 C£1.50 Family Ticket (A2+C3)£9.00 £OAPs£3.00. Membership: Individual £12.00 per annum, Family £18.00 per annum
discount offer: Two Adults For The Price Of One. Valid Apr-Oct 2000

↓*special events*

▶ **Grand Opening and Spring Autojumble**
2/4/00-2/4/00

▶ **Grampian Classic Sprint**
4/5/00-4/5/00
A half-mile sprint run under RAC regulations for classic cars - a unique speed spectacle. Time: 11.00-16.30

▶ **Children's Mega Party**
7/5/00-7/5/00
FREE entry for accompanied children. Games, competitions, performing artistes, music, magician, 'freebies' and a wide selection of vintage vehicle rides. Indoor and outdoor. Time: 12.00-16.30.

▶ **Commercial Vehicle Show**
21/5/00-21/5/00

▶ **Alford Cavalcade**

23/7/00-23/7/00
Over 200 entries, trade stands, arena acts. A really great family day out. Time: 11.00-17.00.

▶ **Eco Marathon**
20/8/00-20/8/00
A look at transport of the future - economy and ecologically friendly vehicles compete in an "Economy Marathon" on the sprint circuit. Time: 11.00-16.30

▶ **Grampian Motorcycle Convention**
3/9/00-3/9/00
Vintage, classic and modern machines. Demonstrations, stunts and arena displays. Marquee trade show. Famous Moped Marathon. Time: 11.00-17.00.

▶ **Alford Auction and Autojumble**
24/9/00-24/9/00
Ideal hunting ground for the restorer. Amazing bargains! Over 80 autojumble stalls. Licensed bar. Time: 11.00-17.00.

Wildlife & Safari Parks

Blair Drummond Safari and Leisure Park

Blair Drummond Stirling Scotland Central Region FK9 4UR
[J10 M9 4m along A84 towards Callander sign-posted on M9 & A84. Plenty of parking on site]
Tel: 01786 841456/841396 Fax: 01786 841491
Drive through the wild animal reserves and see, at close range a variety of wonderful animals. The monkeys, zebras, Rhino, North American bison, antelope, elephants, giraffes, lions, tigers and camels will all charm you. Pets' Farm is home to a wide variety of animals. Other attractions include the sea-lion show, a boat safari through the waterfowl sanctuary and around Chimpanzee Island, an adventure playground and amusements galore.
1 April-2 Oct daily 10.00-17.30
Last Admission: 16.30 Allow 3hrs for visit
Queuing Times: likely over Bank Hol
A£8.50 C(3-14)£4.50 C(0-3)£Free OAPs£4.50.
Free Kennels at entrance for dogs
discount offer: One Child Free With Two Full Paying Adults. One Card Per Vehicle. Valid Until 2 Oct 2000

Highland Wildlife Park

Kincraig Kingussie Inverness-Shire PH21 1NL
[7m S of Aviemore on B9152]
Tel: 01540 651270 Fax: 01540 651236
www.kincraig.com/wildlife
Discover Scottish wildlife, past and present at this unique attraction owned by the Royal Zoological Society of Scotland. Encounter native species then step back in time and meet those creatures long since extinct in the wild - the animals of your ancestors. Explore the main reserve by car for an exciting 'safari experience' with large herds of deer, bison, wild horses and Highland cattle roaming freely. Get eye to eye with a wonderful variety of creatures in the walk-around areas including lynx, wildcat, reindeer, arctic fox, otter, badger and owl. Venture into Wolf Territory where a raised walkway leads you into the heart of the enclosure above the Park's magnificent pack of wolves. Join in the fun at spe-

cial themed event weekends with activities such as talks, trails, arts and crafts, quizzes and face-painting. Join the wardens as they feed the Park's carnivores at the 'Food Chain' talk every afternoon (except Saturdays). You can also catch the 'Drive-in-Breakfast' every day at 10.00 (April-October) as the warden feeds the many animals in the main reserve. You can be sure of a wild day out in the heart of the Highlands.
Apr-Oct daily 10.00-18.00. June-Aug daily 10.00-19.00. Nov-Mar daily 10.00-16.00 weather permitting
Last Admission: 2hrs before closing
A£6.30 C£4.30 OAPs£5.25 including free guide book and Edinburgh Zoo voucher per car. Group discount available. Reduced rates apply Nov-Mar. Prices subject to change in 2000
discount offer: £1.00 Off Per Person Per Voucher (Not Valid For Family Ticket) April-October

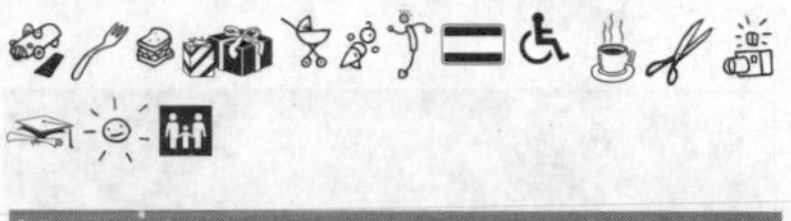

Zoos

Edinburgh Zoo
Corstorphine Road Edinburgh Midlothian EH12 6TS
[3m W of Edinburgh city centre on A8, towards Glasgow, signposted]
Tel: 0131 334 9171 Fax: 0131 316 4050
www.edinburghzoo.org.uk
Scotland's largest and most popular wildlife attraction! Discover over 1,000 animals - furry, feathery and scaly - from tiny blue poison arrow frogs to massive white rhinos. See over 150 penguins splashing about in Europe's largest penguin pool (complete with underwater viewing windows) and don't miss the penguins on their daily parade outside their enclosure (March to October weather permitting). Explore the fountain-filled evolution maze and the wonderful African Plains Experience, where a high level walkway takes you into the heart of the enclosure, overlooking ostrich, zebra and oryx. New for Summer 1999 is the spectacular lion enclosure with walkway and viewpoint. Join in the Animal Handling classes and enjoy brass rubbing, touch tables and talks during the Easter and Summer holidays. Pushchair hire, baby changing facilities, babyfood heating, highchairs and special children's menus available. Self-service restaurant, snack kiosks (in Summer), picnic area and lovely giftshop.
visitor comments: Restaurant clean and tidy, plenty of places to picnic. Steep in places for pushchairs. Excellent gift shop.
All year Apr-Sept Mon-Sat 09.00-18.00, Sun 09.30-18.00. Oct-Mar Mon-Sat 09.00-16.30, Sun 09.30-16.30
Queuing Times: 20mins, school hols & Easter
A6.80 C(3-14)£3.80 Family Ticket from £19.00. Small price increase possible from 1.4.99

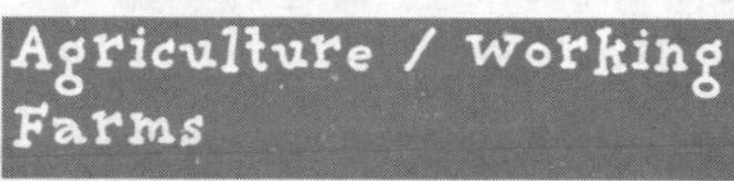

Agriculture / Working Farms

Greenmeadow Community Farm
Greenforge Way Cwmbran Gwent NP44 5AJ
[1m W of Cwmbran town centre, bus No 5 or No 6]
Tel: 01633 862202 Fax: 01633 489332
www.farmvisit.co.uk
Just four miles from the M4, this is one of Wales' leading farm attractions - milking demonstrations, tractor and trailer rides, dragon adventure play area, farm trail, nature trail and lots more. Phone for details of lambing weekends, shearing, country fair and agricultural shows, Halloween and Christmas events.
All year Summer: daily 10.00-18.00. Winter: daily 10.00-16.30. Closed 25 Dec
Last Admission: 1hour before closing
A£3.25 C&Concessions£2.50 Family Ticket (A2+C3)£11.00. Group rates available
discount offer: One Child Free With A Full Paying Adult, one discount per family

Arts, Crafts & Textiles

Aberystwyth Arts Centre
Penglais Aberystwyth Ceredigion SY23 3DE
[A487 from N and S and A44 meet at Aberystwyth, situated on University Campus. Plenty of parking on site]
Tel: 01970 623232 Fax: 01970 622883
www.aber.ac.uk/~arcwww/index.htm
The Arts Centre is situated on the university campus and has panoramic views over Cardigan Bay. Purpose built in 1970, and recently relaunched after a £3.6 million redevelopment project, it has steadily gained recognition as a major arts venue in Wales. The Centre offers busy year long programme of live events, cinema, exhibitions and courses. Also houses a bookshop, craftshop and a popular café.
All year Mon-Sat 10.00-20.00. Open later on Performance nights
Admission Free, events charges vary

Museum of the Welsh Woollen Industry
Dre-Fach Felindre Llandysul Ceredigion SA44 5UP
[4m E of Newcastle Emlyn and W of Carmarthen off A484]
Tel: 01559 370929 Fax: 01559 371592
www.cf.ac.uk/nmgw/oursites.html
The museum is housed in the former Cambrian Mills and has a comprehensive display tracing the evolution of the industry from its beginnings to the present day. Demonstrations of the fleece to fabric process are given on 19th-century textile machinery.
All year Apr-Sept Mon-Sat 10.00-17.00, Oct-Mar Mon-Fri 10.00-17.00. Closed 24-26 Dec & 1 Jan. Evening visits by prior arrangement
A£2.60 C£1.60

discount offer: 10% Discount On Admission Prices

National Museum and Gallery Cardiff
Cathays Park Cardiff Cardiff County CF1 3NP
[M4, A470 located in Cardiff city centre]
Tel: 029 20397951 Fax: 029 20373219
www.cf.ac.uk/nmgw/oursites.html
The National Museum and Gallery, Cardiff is sure to have something to spark your interest. Its unique amongst British museums and galleries in its range of art and science displays. The Art Galleries provide magnificent settings for works by some of the world's most famous artists, including the Impressionists in the outstanding Davies collection.
All year Tue-Sun & Bank Hol Mon 10.00-17.00
A£4.40 Concessions£3.00
discount offer: One Child Free When Accompanied By A Full Paying Adult

↓*special events*

▶ **2000 Things**
5/12/99-28/2/00

Birds, Butterflies & Bees

Felinwynt Rainforest and Butterfly Centre
Felinwynt Cardigan Ceredigion SA43 1RT
[from A487 turn onto B4333 at Airfield, follow Rainforest signposts. Plenty of on site parking]
Tel: 01239 810882 Fax: 01239 810882
Experience a rainforest atmosphere full of exotic plants and tropical butterflies with the sounds of the Perlivian Amazon. Relax in our

tearoom with hot or cold drinks and home-made cakes. Study the rainforest exhibition and watch a video about butterflies or rain-forests and browse in our gift shop. There is something for everyone including colouring for the children's gallery. Personal Guide available. Don't forget that butterflies are more active on sunny days. Picnic areas: both in and outdoor facilities.
Easter-end of Sept daily 10.30-17.00
Last Admission: 17.00
A£3.50 C(4-14)£1.50 OAPs£3.00
discount offer: Two For The Price Of One

Folk & Local History Museums

Celtica
Y Plas Machynlleth Powys SY20 8ER
[2 mins walk S of town clock. Car park entrance off Aberystwyth Road (A487)]
Tel: 01654 702702 Fax: 01654 703604
www.celtica.wales.com
Located in a restored mansion house, Celtica is an exciting exhibition introducing the history and culture of the Celtic people. The sights and sounds of Celtic life are brought alive as you go on an unforgettable journey portraying the Celtic spirit of the past, present and future.
All year daily 10.00-18.00
Last Admission: 16.40
A£4.95 C£3.80 Family Ticket £13.75
discount offer: One Child Free When Accompanied By A Full Paying Adult

Tenby Museum and Art Gallery
Castle Hill Tenby Pembrokeshire SA70 7BP
[on the A478]
Tel: 01834 842809 Fax: 01834 842809
This museum covers the local heritage from prehistory to the present in galleries devoted to archaeology, geology, maritime history, natural history, militaria and bygones. The art gallery concentrates on local associations with an important collection of works by Augustus and Gwen John. The new art gallery features temporary exhibitions. There is a museum shop.
1 Apr-Oct daily 10.00-17.00, Nov-Easter Mon-Fri 10.00-17.00
Last Admission: 16.30
A£2.00 C£1.00 Family Ticket £4.50
Concessions£1.50

Caldicot Castle and Country Park
Church Road Caldicot Monmouthshire NP6 4HU
[on B4245, between Chepstow and Newport. Plenty of parking on site]
Tel: 01291 420241 Fax: 01291 435094
Caldicot Castle's well preserved fortifications were founded by the Normans and fully developed, in royal hands, by the late 14th century. Restored as a family home by a wealthy Victorian, the castle offers the chance to explore medieval walls and towers in a setting of tranquil gardens and wooded Country Park. Disabled access limited to grounds only.
Mar-Oct Mon-Fri 10.30-17.00, Sat & Bank Hol 10.30-17.00, Sun 13.30-17.00
A£1.50 C£0.85
discount offer: One Child Free With Every Full Paying Adult. Valid Until 31 Oct 2000

↓*special events*

▶ **Easter Egg Hunt**
21/4/00-24/4/00
Please call for specific dates and times

▶ **Classic Car Rallies**
1/6/00-30/6/00
Please call for specific details

▶ **Lawnmower Racing**
15/7/00-16/7/00

▶ **A Midsummer Night's Dream**
8/8/00-8/8/00

An open air theatre performance

▶ **Merlins Child**
27/8/00-27/8/00
An open air theatre performance

▶ **Open Heritage Weekend**
9/9/00-10/9/00
Event to include medieval re-enactments and battles, medieval fayre and various demonstrations

Carew Castle and Tidal Mill

Carew Tenby Pembrokeshire SA70 8SL
[on A4705 5m E of Pembroke. Plenty of on site parking]
Tel: 01646 651657/651782 Fax: 01646 651782
www.pembrokeshirecoast.org.uk
This magnificent Norman castle - later an Elizabethan residence - has royal links with Henry Tudor and was the setting for the Great Tournament of 1507. Nearby is the Carew Cross an impressive 13ft Celtic cross dating from the 11th century. Carew Mill is one of only four restored tidal mills in Britain.
Easter-end Oct daily 10.00-17.00
Castle & Mill: A£2.65 C&OAPs£1.70 Family Ticket£7.00. Single ticket Castle or Mill A£1.80 C£1.30

Carreg Cennen Castle and Farm

Trapp Llandeilo Carmarthenshire SA19 6UA
[minor roads from A483 to Trapp. M4 J49 then signposted]
Tel: 01558 822291 Fax: 01558 823811
Wales' most dramatically situated castle. Explore its unique prehistoric cave dwelling and vaulted passageway. Enjoy the welcome of a working Welsh Hill Farm with its 17th century Longhouse and rare and unusual farm animals. View the Balwen Art Gallery or treat yourself to all homemade farmhouse cooking in the 18th century Barn and Restaurant Tea Room. Walk riverside and hill footpaths through the habitat of many of Britain's rarest birds of prey. This unique and most magical Welsh castles, once the bastion of Lord Rhys, is now under the care of CADW.
All year late Oct-late Mar daily 09.30-16.00, late Mar-late Oct daily 09.30-18.30, June & Aug 09.30-20.00. Closed Christmas Day only
Last Admission: 30 mins before closing
A£2.50 Family Ticket (A2&C3)£7.00 Concessions£2.00

Pembroke Castle

Castle Terrace Pembroke Dyfed SA71 4LA
[West end of Main St]
Tel: 01646 681510 Fax: 01646 622260
This 12th to 13th century fortress has an impressive 80ft high round keep. There is also a new Interpretative Centre with introductory video and Pembroke Yeomanry exhibition.
All year daily Apr-Sept 09.30-18.00, Mar & Oct 10.00-17.00, Nov-Feb 10.00-16.00. Closed 24-26 Dec
A£3.00 C(5-16) & OAPs£2.00 Family Ticket £8.00

Penhow Castle

Nr Newport Wales NP26 3AD
[on A48 midway between Newport / Chepstow]
Tel: 01633 400800/400900 Fax: 01633 400990
www.penhowcastle.com
Wales' oldest lived-in Castle, first home of the Seymour family. Cross the drawbridge to discover the most enchanting Knight's Castle on the Welsh border. Explore from battlements to kitchens with acclaimed walkman audio tours included in the admission. 8 Awards for restoration and interpretation.
Good Fri-Sept 30 Wed-Sun & Bank Hol 10.00-18.00, Aug open daily, Winter: Wed 10.00-16.00 & some Sun 13.00-16.00
Last Admission: 17.15
A£3.60 C£2.30 Family Ticket £9.50. Group rates 20+ 10% discounts by arrangement only
discount offer: Two For The Price Of One

Scolton Manor House

Spittal Haverfordwest Pembrokeshire SA62 5QL
[5m N of Haverfordwest on B4329]
Tel: 01437 731328 Fax: 01437 731743
The early Victorian mansion and stables illustrate some of the social history of Pembrokeshire. Within the mansion are period rooms on three floors. There are 60 acres of grounds and an environmentally friendly

Visitor Centre. Children's play areas and various Country Park events. All event enquiries should be directed to 01437 760460.
Museum Easter-Oct Tue-Sun & Bank Hol 10.30-17.00, Park all year Easter-Sept 10.00-19.00, Oct-Easter 10.00-16.30 Closed 25-26 Dec. Open all year for groups by prior arrangement
Last Admission: Museum 17.00
A£1.50 C&Concessions£0.75 (under revision). Car Park £1.00
discount offer: Two For The Price Of One

↓*special events*

▶ **Flower Festival**
4/3/00-5/3/00
Join the Pembrokeshire Horticultural Society at the Welsh Open Spring Show and Flower Festival

▶ **Children's Fun Day**
24/4/00-24/4/00
Come along and join in the fun, oh don't forget the children!

▶ **Welsh Festival of Gardening**
29/4/00-30/4/00

▶ **Wool Day**
29/5/00-29/5/00
A whole day with a 'wooly' theme

▶ **A Dig Day?**
22/7/00-22/7/00
Calling all Young Archaeologists everywhere, this is a day for you...

▶ **Sky Watching**
29/7/00-30/7/00
A model aircraft show, with lots to see and do

▶ **Champion Fruit, Veg & Flowers**
4/8/00-6/8/00
A treat for garden enthusiasts everywhere!

▶ **Pet Show**
12/8/00-12/8/00
If you can't have your own pet, come along a look at someone else's!

▶ **Family Fun Day**
28/8/00-28/8/00
FUN for all the family, all day long!

▶ **Michaelmas Plant Sale**
30/9/00-30/9/00

▶ **Video Games Week**
21/10/00-29/10/00

Smallest House

Quay Conwy North Wales LL32 8DE
[take the Conway road off the A55, signposted in the town]
Tel: 01492 593484
The 'Guinness Book of Records' lists this as the smallest house in Britain. Just 6ft wide by 10ft high, it is furnished in the style of a mid-Victorian Welsh cottage. The last person to live here was 6'3".
Apr-mid Oct daily 10.00-18.00, July & Aug 10.00-21.00, Winter by arrangement
Last Admission: 18.00 21.00 July & Aug
A£0.70 C£0.40

Historical

Abergavenny Museum and Castle

Castle Street Abergavenny Gwent NP7 5EE
[off A40 / A465 Abergavenny roundabout]
Tel: 01873 854282
Craft tools, a Welsh kitchen, a saddler's shop and local exhibits are displayed at the museum, and the remains of the castle's walls, towers and gateway can be seen. New for 1997 1940 grocers shop. There is limited access for wheelchairs and pushchairs, please ring for details.
All year Museum: Mar-Oct Mon-Sat 11.00-13.00 & 14.00-17.00, Sun 14.00-17.00, Nov-Feb Mon-Sat 11.00-13.00 & 14.00-16.00. Castle: daily 08.00-dusk
A£1.00 C£Free when accompanied by an adult, Concessions£0.75. Pre booked educational parties £Free

Cilgerran Castle

Cilgerran Pembrokeshire SA43 2SF
[on rock above left bank of the Teifil, 3m SE of Cardigan]
Tel: 01239 615007
This 13th century ruin is perched overlooking the spectacular Teifi gorge and has inspired many artists, including Turner.
All year daily. Late Mar-late Oct 09.30-18.30, late Oct-late Mar 09.30-16.00
Last Admission: 30mins before closing
A£2.00 C(0-5)£Free Concessions£1.50 Family Ticket (A2+C3)£5.50. NT Members £Free. Please call for current admission prices

Conwy Castle

Rosehill Street Conwy Conwy LL32 8LD
[by A55 or B5106]
Tel: 01492 592358 Fax: 01492 592358
The castle is a magnificent fortress, built from 1283-7 by Edward I. There is an exhibition on castle chapels on the ground floor of the Chapel Tower. The castle forms part of the same defensive system as the extensive town walls.
All year late Oct-late Mar Mon-Sat 09.30-16.00, Sun 11.00-16.00 late Mar-late Oct daily 09.30-18.30. Closed 24-26 Dec & 1 Jan
Last Admission: 30mins before closing
A£3.50 Family Ticket (A2+C3)£9.50 Concessions£2.50
discount offer: 10% For Parties of 15 Persons or More

Harlech Castle

Castle Square Harlech Gwynedd LL46 2YH

[from A496. Limited parking on site]

Tel: 01766 780552

Harlech Castle was built in 1283-89 by Edward I, with a sheer drop to the sea on one side. Owain Glyndwr starved the castle into submission in 1404 and made it his court and campaigning base. Later, the defence of the castle in the Wars of the Roses inspired the song Men of Harlech. Free parking is available at the bottom of the castle from June-August.

29 Mar-21 May & 4-31 Oct 09.30-17.00 22 May-3 Oct 09.00-18.00 1 Nov-28 Mar Mon-Sat 09.30-16.00 Sun 11.00-16.00. Closed 24-26 Dec & 1 Jan

Last Admission: 30mins before closing

A£3.00 FamilyTicket (A2+C3)£8.00 Concessions£2.00

Kidwelly Castle

Kidwelly Carmarthenshire SA17 5BQ

[via A484]

Tel: 01554 890104 Fax:

www.cadw.wales.gov.uk

This is an outstanding example of late-13th-century castle design, with its walls within walls defensive system. There were later additions made to the building, with the chapel dating from about 1300. Of particular interest are two vast circular ovens and the massive gatehouse.

All year late Oct-late Mar Mon-Sat 09.30-16.00 Sun 11.00-16.00 late Mar-late Oct daily 09.30-18.00 Closed 24-26 Dec & 1 Jan

Last Admission: 30mins before closing

A£2.20 Family Ticket (A2+C3)£6.10 Concessions£1.70

Penhow Castle

Nr Newport Wales NP26 3AD

[on A48 midway between Newport / Chepstow]

Tel: 01633 400800/400900 Fax: 01633 400990

www.penhowcastle.com

Wales' oldest lived-in Castle, first home of the Seymour family. Cross the drawbridge to discover the most enchanting Knight's Castle on the Welsh border. Explore from battlements to kitchens with acclaimed walkman audio tours included in the admission. 8 Awards for restoration and interpretation.

Good Fri-Sept 30 Wed-Sun & Bank Hol 10.00-18.00, Aug open daily, Winter: Wed 10.00-16.00 & some Sun 13.00-16.00

Last Admission: 17.15

A£3.60 C£2.30 Family Ticket £9.50. Group rates 20+ 10% discounts by arrangement only

discount offer: Two For The Price Of One

Smallest House

Quay Conwy North Wales LL32 8DE

[take the Conway road off the A55, signposted in the town]

Tel: 01492 593484

The 'Guinness Book of Records' lists this as the smallest house in Britain. Just 6ft wide by 10ft high, it is furnished in the style of a mid-Victorian Welsh cottage. The last person to live here was 6'3".

Apr-mid Oct daily 10.00-18.00, July & Aug 10.00-21.00, Winter by arrangement

Last Admission: 18.00 21.00 July & Aug

A£0.70 C£0.40

Literature & Libraries

National Library of Wales

Penglais Hill Aberystwyth Ceredigion SY23 3BU

[on A487 signposted]

Tel: 01970 632800 Fax: 01970 615709

www.llgc.org.uk

The huge library is one of Britain's six copyright libraries, and specialises in Welsh and Celtic literature. It has maps, manuscripts, prints and drawings, as well as books in all languages. A major permanent exhibition 'A Nation's Heritage' is on view and there is a programme of travelling exhibitions.

All year Library & Reading Rooms Mon-Fri 09.30-18.00 Sat until 17.00. Closed Bank Hol & First week Oct. Please telephone to check Bank Hol opening

Free Admission to reading rooms available by ticket, proof of identity required

Living History Museums

Llancaiach Fawr Manor
Nelson Treharris Mid Glamorgan CF46 6ER
[from M4 take A470 N turn off onto A472 signposted from this roundabout]
Tel: 01443 412248 Fax: 01443 412688
www.caerphilly.gov.uk
Step back in time to the exciting Civil War period at this fascinating living history museum. The year is 1645 and you are invited into the Manor to meet the servants of 'Colonel' Edward Prichard - from the puritanical to the gossipy. Please telephone for further details.
All year Mar-Oct Mon-Fri 10.00-17.00, Sat-Sun 10.00-18.00, Nov-Feb Tues-Fri 10.00-17.00, Sat-Sun 10.00-18.00 Call for Christmas opening
Last Admission: 90mins before closing
A£4.50 C&Concessions£3.00 Family Ticket £12.00
discount offer: One Child Free With A Full Paying Adult. Excludes bank Holidays

Mining

Welsh Slate Museum
Padarn Country Park Llanberis Gwynedd LL55 4TY
[on the A4086]
Tel: 01286 870630 Fax: 01286 871906
www.nmgw.ac.uk/wsm/wsmhome.html
See the story of slate come alive at this living working Museum. Visit the industrial workshops, UNA the steam engine, giant waterwheel and slate splitting and brass casting demonstrations. New attractions include a spectacular 3-D multi media presentation of life in the quarries; restored Chief Engineer's House, unique working slate carrying incline, gift shop and cafe. NEW for 1999 will be a terrace of quarrymen's houses re-located to the museum site and a children's educational play and discovery area.
Easter-Oct daily 10.00-17.00, Nov-Easter Sun-Fri 10.00-16.00
Last Admission: 60mins before closing
A£3.50 C&OAPs&Students£2.00 Family Ticket £7.90
discount offer: Two For The Price Of One

Places of Worship

St Davids Cathedral
The Close St Davids Pembrokeshire SA62 6RH
[A487]
Tel: 01437 720199 Fax: 01437 721885
www.stdavidscathedral.org.uk
Begun 1181 on the site reputed to be where St David founded a monastic settlement in the 6th century. The present building was altered during the 12th to the 14th centuries and again in the 6th. The architecture is varied. Organ recitals and Cathedral Music Festival. Special events see guide.
All year daily 08.30-18.00
Suggested donation of £2.00

↓*special events*

▶ **Pembrokeshire Craftsmen's Circle Craft Fairs**
18/4/00-28/10/00
To be held on Apr 18-29, May 26-June 10, July 18-29, Sept 9-20 and Oct 19-28. Crafts include jewellery, ceramics, pewterwork, glass engraving, silk-painting, woodturning, textile art and furniture.

▶ **St Davids Cathedral Festival**
27/5/00-4/6/00
A week of classical music concerts in the incomparable setting of Wales' National Shrine

▶ **St Davids Cathedral Festival**
26/5/01-3/6/01
A week of classical music concerts in the incomparable setting of Wales' National Shrine

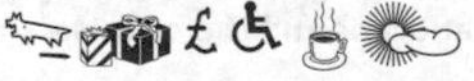

Railways

Ffestiniog Railway
Harbour Station Porthmadog Gwynedd LL49 9NF
[A487 station well signposted]
Tel: 01766 512340 Fax: 01766 514576
www.festrail.co.uk
The Ffestiniog Railway is the Oldest Independent Railway Company in the World. On our trains you can travel by steam through the spectacular scenery of the Snowdonia

National Park (narrow gauge steam railway running for 13.5 miles), between Porthmadog and Blaenau Ffestiniog. Breathtaking views, superb scenery. Buffet service on all trains including licensed bar. Comfortable seating, some trains heated, toilet facilities on corridor carriages.

visitor comments: Excellent views of the Welsh countryside.

Late Mar-early Nov daily service and also 26 Dec-1Jan. Limited service Feb & Mar

Last Admission: varies according to time of year

Full distance return: A£13.80 1 child free with each adult

↓special events

▶ **Ffestiniog Experience 2000**

15/4/00-15/4/00

An open weekend for prospective volunteers

▶ **A Day Out with Thomas**

29/4/00-1/5/00

Sir Topham Hatt, The Fat Controller, Thomas Bach and others will be visiting the railway for a day of family fun

▶ **Steam and Cuisine**

26/5/00-1/9/00

Fridays from May 26 to Sept 1. Travel on the Ffestiniog Railway accompanied by the finest cuisine. Book before 11.00 on day of travel, £39.95 per person, trains depart at 18.10.

▶ **Jazz on a Summer's Evening**

1/6/00-31/8/00

Held on June 1, July 20, Aug 3, 17 and 31 only. The Ffestiniog Railway's ever popular Jazz Special leaves Porthmadog Station at 19.15, £9.50 per person.

▶ **Welsh Highland Railway Open Day**

16/9/00-17/9/00

Held at Caernarfon

▶ **Vintage Trains on the Ffestiniog Railway**

7/10/00-8/10/00

The Ffestiniog Railway's own history comes to the fore with special trains and displays relating to the wonderful heritage of the Railway.

▶ **Santa Trains**

9/12/00-19/12/00

To be held on Dec 9, 17 and 19 only. Father Christmas visits with presents and Special Trains to Tan-y-Bylch

Llangollen Railway PLC

The Station Abbey Road Llangollen Denbighshire LL20 8SN

[all the stations on the open section of line are located on or near the A5. Ruabon station: leave the A483 on the A539 heading for Llangollen, and you will cross the Chester to Shrewsbury line. Llangollen station: is at the junction of the A5 and the A539. The railway station is by the bridge over the River Dee. Berwyn station: is on a bend in the A5, opposite the Chain Bridge Hotel. Glyndyfrdwy station: turn off the A5 in the village of Glyndyfrdwy towards Rhewl. Carrog station: turn off the A5 at Llidiart y Parc following the sign for Carrog; the car park is on the right just after the Railway bridge]

Tel: 01978 860951/860979 Fax: 01978 869247

www.joyces.demon.co.uk/

The restored Great Western Railway Station is situated in the town centre and beside the River Dee. Locomotives and rolling stock are displayed, and passenger trains run on a fifteen-and-a-half mile round trip between Llangollen and Carrog. A special coach for the disabled is sometimes available.

Station open every Weekend. Steam hauled trains: Feb-Oct Sun, May-Sept daily. Diesel railcars: Oct Mon-Sat, Feb-Apr Sat

A£7.00 C£3.50 OAPs£5.20 2nd class only

discount offer: One Child Travels Free With Each Full Fare Paying Adult. (Not valid on Berwyn Belle or Santa Specials)

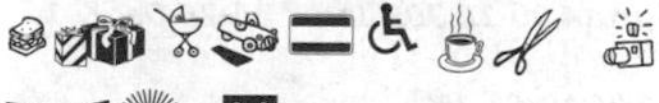

Snowdon Mountain Railway

Llanberis Caernarfon Gwynedd LL55 4TY

[on A4086 Caernarfon to Capel Curig road, 7.5m from Caernarfon]

Tel: 01286 870223 Fax: 01286 872518

Britain's only public rack-and-pinion railway is operated by five vintage steam and four modern diesel locomotives, and a three car diesel electric railcar set. The journey of just over four-and-a-half miles takes passengers more than 3000ft up to the summit of Snowdon with breathtaking views (when weather is fine).

15 Mar-1 Nov daily from 09.00 weather permitting

Last Admission: Last Departure Weekdays 17.00, Sat 15.30

Return: A£15.00 C£10.80, Single: A£10.80 C£7.70, Groups 15+ by prior arrangement

Roman Era

Caerleon Fortress Baths Amphitheatre and Barracks

High Street Caerleon Newport Gwent NP18 1AE

[on B4236]

Caerleon was an important Roman military base with accommodation for thousands of men. The foundations of barrack lines and parts of the ramparts can be seen, with remains of the cookhouse, latrines and baths.

The nearby amphitheatre is one of the best examples in Britain. The fortress baths were excavated in the 1970s.
Mar-Oct daily 09.30-17.15, Oct- Mar Mon-Sat 09.30-17.00, Sun 12.00-16.00. Closed 24-26 Dec & 1 Jan
Last Admission: 30mins before closing
A£2.00 C(0-5)£Free Concessions£1.50 Family Ticket (A2+C3)£5.50

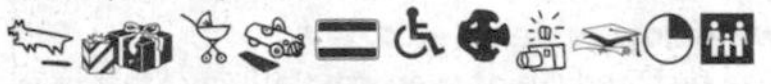

Roman Legionary Museum
High Street Caerleon Newport Gwent NP6 1AE
[2m N of M4 J25 or J26]
Tel: 01633 423134 Fax: 01633 422869
The museum illustrates the history of Roman Caerleon and the daily life of its garrison. On display are arms, armour and equipment, with a collection of engraved gemstones, a labyrinth mosaic and Roman finds from the legionary base at Usk. Please call for details of children's holiday activities.
All year 15 Mar-15 Oct Mon-Sat 10.00-18.00, Sun 14.00-18.00, 16 Oct-14 Mar Mon-Sat 10.00-16.30, Sun 14.00-16.30. Closed 24-26 Dec & 1 Jan
A£2.10 C&OAPs£1.25

Science - Earth & Planetary

Techniquest
Stuart Street Cardiff CF10 6BW
[J33 M4, follow A4232 until signposted]
Tel: 029 20475 475 Fax: 029 20482 517
www.tquest.org.uk
Located in the heart of the Cardiff Bay redevelopment area, here you will find science and technology made accessible - and fun - at Britain's leading hands-on science discovery centre, where visitors of all ages can participate in the activities and experiment with the exhibits. A fun-filled day for the whole family.

visitor comments: Great educational day out with fun thrown in for good measure. Good cafe and gift shop. Friendly, helpful and informed staff and bright displays. Ample parking.
All year Mon-Fri 09.30-16.30, Sat-Sun & Bank Hol 10.30-17.00
Last Admission: 45mins before closing
A£5.50 C(under 5)£Free C&Concessions£3.80 Family Ticket £15.75 Events in the Planetarium and Laboratory are chargeable in addition to main admission, call for details
discount offer: One Child Free With One Or More Full Paying Adult/s

special events

▶ **Blast Off! - Planetarium Show**
5/2/00-26/3/00
Feb 5, 6, 12, 13, 19-27 and Mar 4, 5, 11, 12, 18, 19, 25 and 26 only. Take a trip into space with friendly animated characters then take a tour of the night sky

▶ **Bubbles and Bangs - Science Theatre Show**
4/3/00-12/3/00
Performances on Mar 4, 5, 11 and 12 only. See exploding bubbles, giant bubbles and bubbles lighter than air in this brilliant interactive show!

▶ **National Science Week**
18/3/00-26/3/00
Join us on Mar 18, 19, 25 and 26. Spot ladybirds in a Wales-wide experiment, visit the Techicolour workshop, enjoy the science of the circus, 'Blast Off!' to explore space in the Planetarium and more!

▶ **Encounter with Colour - Laboratory workshop**
18/3/00-26/3/00
Mar 18, 19, 25, 26 only. Do we see the same colours as insects? How do doctors use colour to test if we are healthy? These questions and more will be answered

▶ **HealthQuest Show - Science Theatre Show**
1/4/00-9/4/00
Apr 1, 2, 8 and 9 only. Play the game show and improve your health knowledge. Build a skeleton and try on protective clothing.

▶ **Mars: The Red Planet - Planetarium Show**
1/4/00-4/6/00
Apr 1, 2, 8, 9, 15-30, May 6, 7, 13, 14, 20, 21, 27 and June 4 only. Using the latest video footage, take a guided tour around Mars

▶ **Amazing Eggsperiments - Science Theatre Show**
15/4/00-7/5/00
Apr 15-30 and May 6-7 only. What has man learned from the humble egg about chemistry, engineering and cookery? An eggsciting show especially for Easter!

▶ **The Great Egg Race**
17/4/00-28/4/00
Using junk from around the house, groups will be set a challenge to transport an egg in a mys-

tery challenge. Prizes for the winners!

▶ **Water Show - Science Theatre Show**
13/5/00-4/6/00
May 13, 14, 20, 21, 27 and June 4 only. A brand new show all about water. What is it? Why is it so important to us and what do we use it for?

▶ **Alternative Energy - Library**
13/5/00-4/6/00
May 13, 14, 20, 21, 27-June 4 only. Take a look at the alternatives to fossil fuels and nuclear power for use in energy production.

▶ **Solar Power Workshop - Laboratory**
29/5/00-2/6/00
Discover how our most important energy source, the Sun, helps us produce electricity

▶ **One Small Step**
16/9/00-15/10/00
Sept 16, 17, 23, 24, 30, Oct 1, 7, 8, 14 and 15 only. Celebrate man's first step on the moon with this Planetarium Show.

Social History Museums

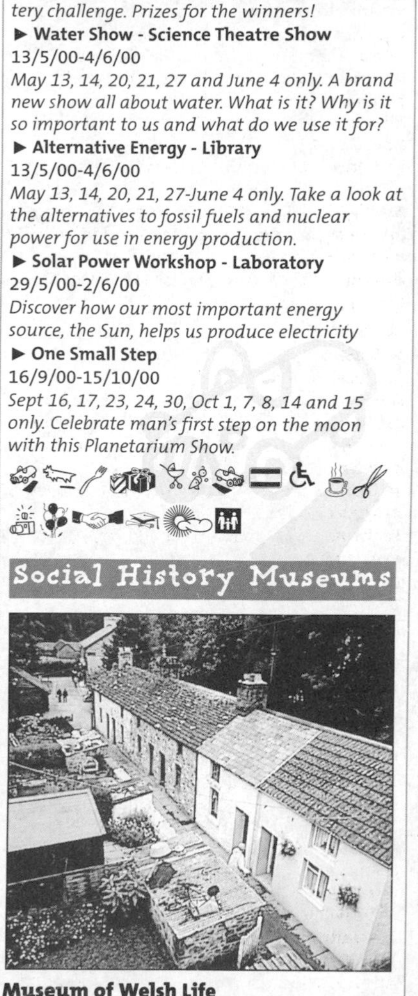

Museum of Welsh Life
St. Fagans Cardiff Vale of Glamorgan CF5 6XB
[on A4232, 3m W of Cardiff]
Tel: 02920 573500 Fax: 02920 573490
www.nmgw.ac.uk
The Museum of Welsh Life is a place where you can walk back in time. A stroll around the indoor galleries and one hundred acres of beautiful grounds is guaranteed to give you a fascinating insight into how people in Wales have lived, worked and spent their leisure hours since Celtic times.
All year July-Sept daily 10.00-18.00, Oct-June daily 10.00-17.00. Closed 24-25 Dec
A£5.50 C£3.20 Family Ticket (A2+C2)£14.00 OAPs£3.90
discount offer: 10% Discount On Admission Prices

Toy & Childhood Museums

Museum of Childhood Memories
1 Castle Street Beaumaris Anglesey LL58 8AP
[on A545 from A55]
Tel: 01248 712498
www.nwi.co.uk/museumofchildhood
Rare and valuable exhibits illustrate life and interests of families over 150 years. Exhibits include money boxes, dolls, educational toys and games, early clockwork trains, cars and aeroplanes, push toys and cycles. Also shown are things that were used by children such as pottery, glassware and furniture. Wheelchair access limited to ground floor only.
Easter-31 Oct 10.30-17.30, Sun 12.00-17.00
Last Admission: 60mins before closing
A£3.00 C£1.75 OAPs£2.50 Family Ticket £8.50
Wheelchairs Free
discount offer: One Child Free When Two Adults Pay Full Price. Valid Until 31 Oct 2000

Transport Museums

National Coracle Centre
Cenarth Falls Newcastle Emlyn

Carmarthenshire SA38 9JL

[A484 between Cardigan and Carmarthen]

Tel: 01239 710980/710507

www.coraclecentre.co.uk

The National Coracle Centre is situated beside the beautiful Cenarth Falls and Salmon Leap, housing a unique collection of coracles from all over Wales and many parts of the World: including Iraq, Tibet, India, Vietnam and North America. Coracles date from the ice-age and, these once skin-covered boats, are still in use and made for salmon fishing in West Wales today. During your visit you will see the 17th century Flour Mill overlooking the falls and salmon leap. Why not round your visit off by taking tea in the Tea Rooms. For that extra special visit why not book a guide tour.

Easter-31 Oct Sun-Fri 10.30-17.30 and at other times by appointment

A£2.50 C(0-5)£Free C(5+)£1.00 Concessions£2.00. Group rates for 20+ available on request

discount offer: One Child Free With Full Paying Adult. Valid Until 31 Oct 2000

Index

C

D

E

N

O

P

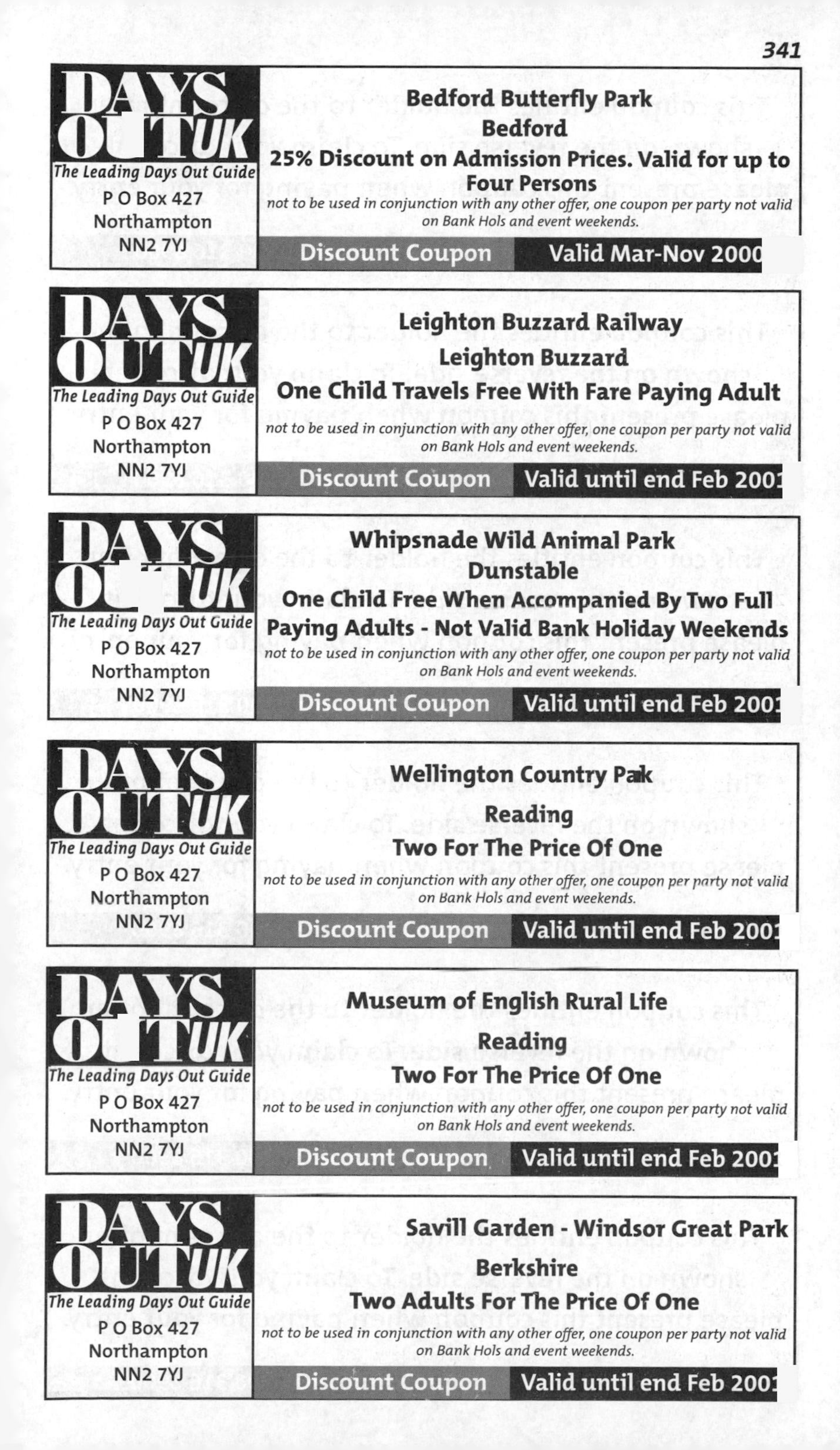

DAYS OUT UK
The Leading Days Out Guide
P O Box 427
Northampton
NN2 7YJ

Bedford Butterfly Park
Bedford
25% Discount on Admission Prices. Valid for up to Four Persons
not to be used in conjunction with any other offer, one coupon per party not valid on Bank Hols and event weekends.
Discount Coupon | Valid Mar-Nov 2000

DAYS OUT UK
The Leading Days Out Guide
P O Box 427
Northampton
NN2 7YJ

Leighton Buzzard Railway
Leighton Buzzard
One Child Travels Free With Fare Paying Adult
not to be used in conjunction with any other offer, one coupon per party not valid on Bank Hols and event weekends.
Discount Coupon | Valid until end Feb 2001

DAYS OUT UK
The Leading Days Out Guide
P O Box 427
Northampton
NN2 7YJ

Whipsnade Wild Animal Park
Dunstable
One Child Free When Accompanied By Two Full Paying Adults - Not Valid Bank Holiday Weekends
not to be used in conjunction with any other offer, one coupon per party not valid on Bank Hols and event weekends.
Discount Coupon | Valid until end Feb 2001

DAYS OUT UK
The Leading Days Out Guide
P O Box 427
Northampton
NN2 7YJ

Wellington Country Park
Reading
Two For The Price Of One
not to be used in conjunction with any other offer, one coupon per party not valid on Bank Hols and event weekends.
Discount Coupon | Valid until end Feb 2001

DAYS OUT UK
The Leading Days Out Guide
P O Box 427
Northampton
NN2 7YJ

Museum of English Rural Life
Reading
Two For The Price Of One
not to be used in conjunction with any other offer, one coupon per party not valid on Bank Hols and event weekends.
Discount Coupon | Valid until end Feb 2001

DAYS OUT UK
The Leading Days Out Guide
P O Box 427
Northampton
NN2 7YJ

Savill Garden - Windsor Great Park
Berkshire
Two Adults For The Price Of One
not to be used in conjunction with any other offer, one coupon per party not valid on Bank Hols and event weekends.
Discount Coupon | Valid until end Feb 2001

This coupon entitles the holder to the discount offer shown on the reverse side. To claim your discount please present this coupon when paying for your entry.

Customer care line number *free* phone 0800 316 8900

This coupon entitles the holder to the discount offer shown on the reverse side. To claim your discount please present this coupon when paying for your entry.

Customer care line number *free* phone 0800 316 8900

This coupon entitles the holder to the discount offer shown on the reverse side. To claim your discount please present this coupon when paying for your entry.

Customer care line number *free* phone 0800 316 8900

This coupon entitles the holder to the discount offer shown on the reverse side. To claim your discount please present this coupon when paying for your entry.

Customer care line number *free* phone 0800 316 8900

This coupon entitles the holder to the discount offer shown on the reverse side. To claim your discount please present this coupon when paying for your entry.

Customer care line number *free* phone 0800 316 8900

This coupon entitles the holder to the discount offer shown on the reverse side. To claim your discount please present this coupon when paying for your entry.

Customer care line number *free* phone 0800 316 8900

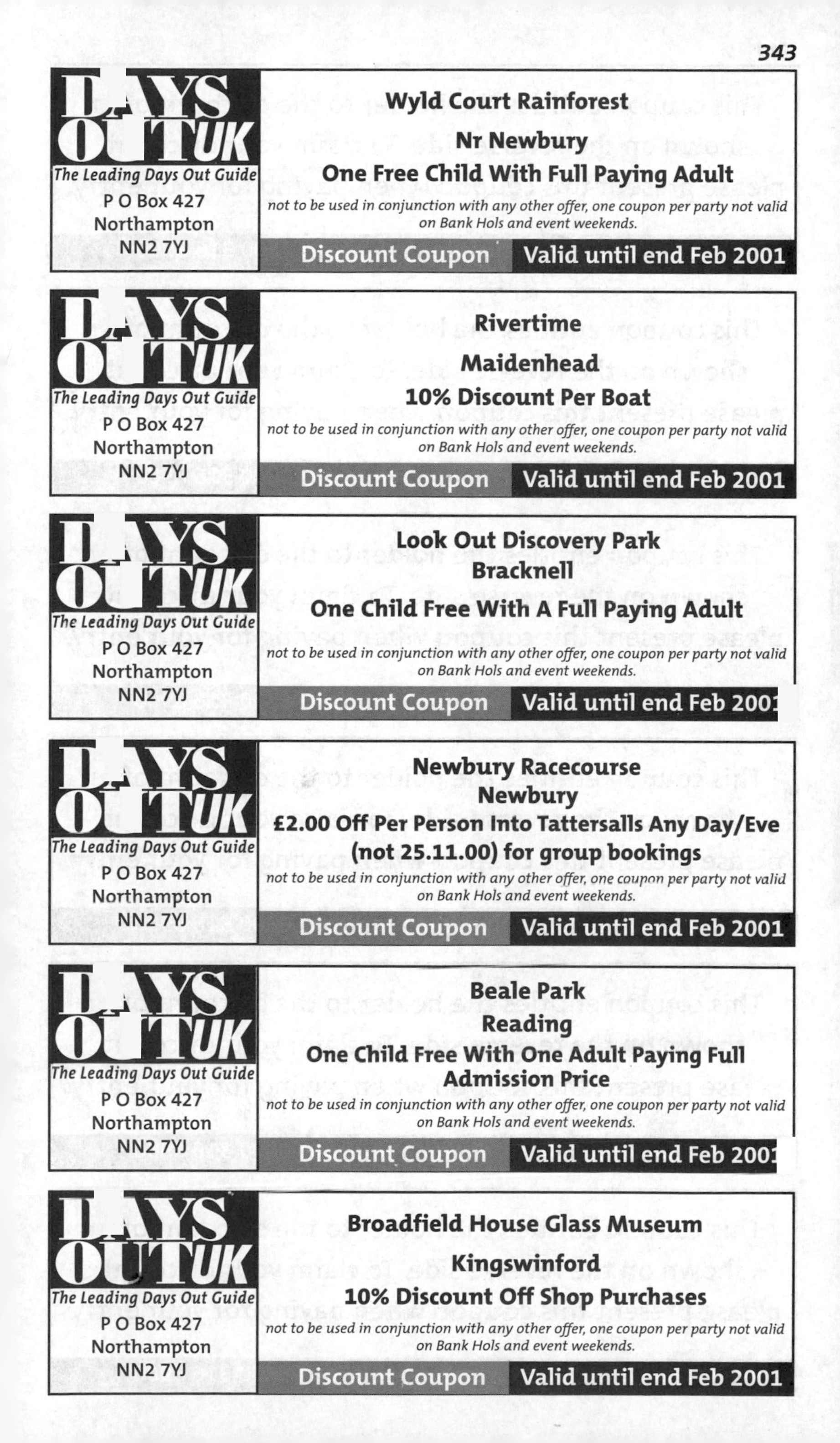
DAYS OUT UK
The Leading Days Out Guide
P O Box 427
Northampton
NN2 7YJ
Wyld Court Rainforest
Nr Newbury
One Free Child With Full Paying Adult
not to be used in conjunction with any other offer, one coupon per party not valid on Bank Hols and event weekends.
Discount Coupon
Valid until end Feb 2001
DAYS OUT UK
The Leading Days Out Guide
P O Box 427
Northampton
NN2 7YJ
Rivertime
Maidenhead
10% Discount Per Boat
not to be used in conjunction with any other offer, one coupon per party not valid on Bank Hols and event weekends.
Discount Coupon
Valid until end Feb 2001
DAYS OUT UK
The Leading Days Out Guide
P O Box 427
Northampton
NN2 7YJ
Look Out Discovery Park
Bracknell
One Child Free With A Full Paying Adult
not to be used in conjunction with any other offer, one coupon per party not valid on Bank Hols and event weekends.
Discount Coupon
Valid until end Feb 2001
DAYS OUT UK
The Leading Days Out Guide
P O Box 427
Northampton
NN2 7YJ
Newbury Racecourse
Newbury
£2.00 Off Per Person Into Tattersalls Any Day/Eve
(not 25.11.00) for group bookings
not to be used in conjunction with any other offer, one coupon per party not valid on Bank Hols and event weekends.
Discount Coupon
Valid until end Feb 2001
DAYS OUT UK
The Leading Days Out Guide
P O Box 427
Northampton
NN2 7YJ
Beale Park
Reading
One Child Free With One Adult Paying Full Admission Price
not to be used in conjunction with any other offer, one coupon per party not valid on Bank Hols and event weekends.
Discount Coupon
Valid until end Feb 2001
DAYS OUT UK
The Leading Days Out Guide
P O Box 427
Northampton
NN2 7YJ
Broadfield House Glass Museum
Kingswinford
10% Discount Off Shop Purchases
not to be used in conjunction with any other offer, one coupon per party not valid on Bank Hols and event weekends.
Discount Coupon
Valid until end Feb 2001

This coupon entitles the holder to the discount offer shown on the reverse side. To claim your discount please present this coupon when paying for your entry.

Customer care line number *free* phone 0800 316 8900

This coupon entitles the holder to the discount offer shown on the reverse side. To claim your discount please present this coupon when paying for your entry.

Customer care line number *free* phone 0800 316 8900

This coupon entitles the holder to the discount offer shown on the reverse side. To claim your discount please present this coupon when paying for your entry.

Customer care line number *free* phone 0800 316 8900

This coupon entitles the holder to the discount offer shown on the reverse side. To claim your discount please present this coupon when paying for your entry.

Customer care line number *free* phone 0800 316 8900

This coupon entitles the holder to the discount offer shown on the reverse side. To claim your discount please present this coupon when paying for your entry.

Customer care line number *free* phone 0800 316 8900

This coupon entitles the holder to the discount offer shown on the reverse side. To claim your discount please present this coupon when paying for your entry.

Customer care line number *free* phone 0800 316 8900

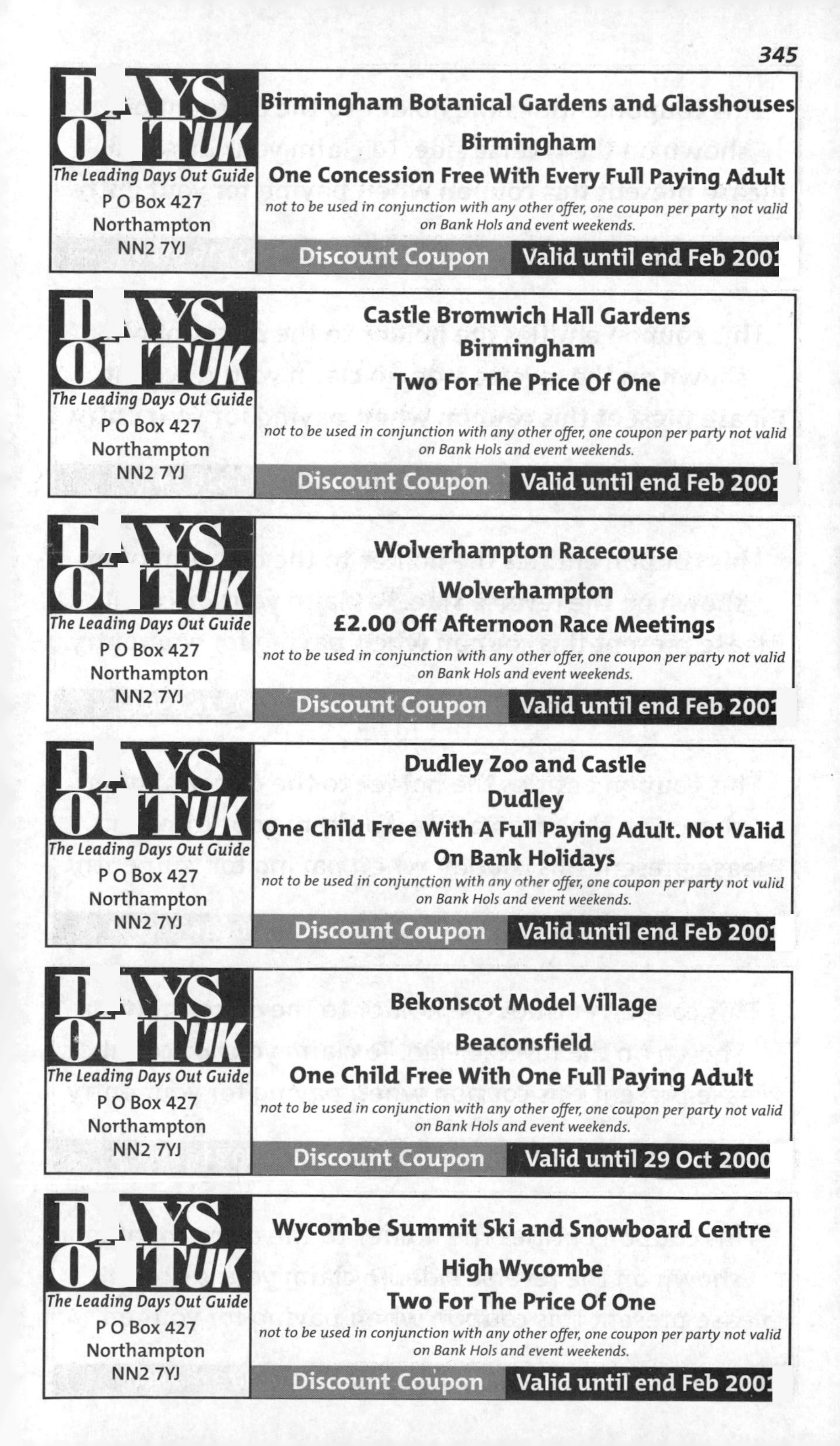
DAYS OUT UK
The Leading Days Out Guide
P O Box 427
Northampton
NN2 7YJ
Birmingham Botanical Gardens and Glasshouses
Birmingham
One Concession Free With Every Full Paying Adult
not to be used in conjunction with any other offer, one coupon per party not valid on Bank Hols and event weekends.
Discount Coupon
Valid until end Feb 2001
DAYS OUT UK
The Leading Days Out Guide
P O Box 427
Northampton
NN2 7YJ
Castle Bromwich Hall Gardens
Birmingham
Two For The Price Of One
not to be used in conjunction with any other offer, one coupon per party not valid on Bank Hols and event weekends.
Discount Coupon
Valid until end Feb 2001
DAYS OUT UK
The Leading Days Out Guide
P O Box 427
Northampton
NN2 7YJ
Wolverhampton Racecourse
Wolverhampton
£2.00 Off Afternoon Race Meetings
not to be used in conjunction with any other offer, one coupon per party not valid on Bank Hols and event weekends.
Discount Coupon
Valid until end Feb 2001
DAYS OUT UK
The Leading Days Out Guide
P O Box 427
Northampton
NN2 7YJ
Dudley Zoo and Castle
Dudley
One Child Free With A Full Paying Adult. Not Valid On Bank Holidays
not to be used in conjunction with any other offer, one coupon per party not valid on Bank Hols and event weekends.
Discount Coupon
Valid until end Feb 2001
DAYS OUT UK
The Leading Days Out Guide
P O Box 427
Northampton
NN2 7YJ
Bekonscot Model Village
Beaconsfield
One Child Free With One Full Paying Adult
not to be used in conjunction with any other offer, one coupon per party not valid on Bank Hols and event weekends.
Discount Coupon
Valid until 29 Oct 2000
DAYS OUT UK
The Leading Days Out Guide
P O Box 427
Northampton
NN2 7YJ
Wycombe Summit Ski and Snowboard Centre
High Wycombe
Two For The Price Of One
not to be used in conjunction with any other offer, one coupon per party not valid on Bank Hols and event weekends.
Discount Coupon
Valid until end Feb 2001

This coupon entitles the holder to the discount offer shown on the reverse side. To claim your discount please present this coupon when paying for your entry.

Customer care line number *free* phone 0800 316 8900

This coupon entitles the holder to the discount offer shown on the reverse side. To claim your discount please present this coupon when paying for your entry.

Customer care line number *free* phone 0800 316 8900

This coupon entitles the holder to the discount offer shown on the reverse side. To claim your discount please present this coupon when paying for your entry.

Customer care line number *free* phone 0800 316 8900

This coupon entitles the holder to the discount offer shown on the reverse side. To claim your discount please present this coupon when paying for your entry.

Customer care line number *free* phone 0800 316 8900

This coupon entitles the holder to the discount offer shown on the reverse side. To claim your discount please present this coupon when paying for your entry.

Customer care line number *free* phone 0800 316 8900

This coupon entitles the holder to the discount offer shown on the reverse side. To claim your discount please present this coupon when paying for your entry.

Customer care line number *free* phone 0800 316 8900

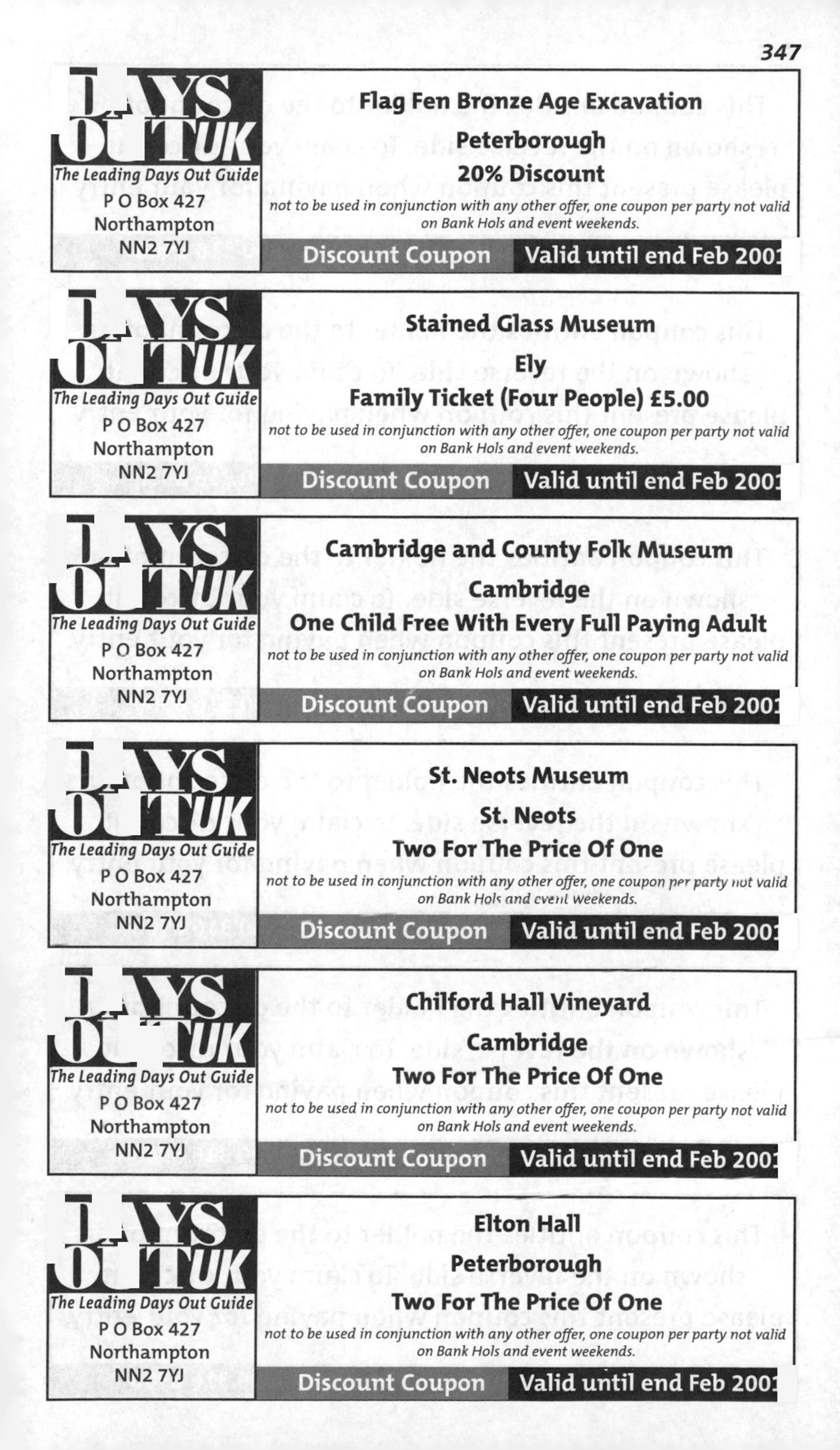
DAYS OUT UK
The Leading Days Out Guide
P O Box 427
Northampton
NN2 7YJ
Flag Fen Bronze Age Excavation
Peterborough
20% Discount
not to be used in conjunction with any other offer, one coupon per party not valid on Bank Hols and event weekends.
Discount Coupon
Valid until end Feb 2001
DAYS OUT UK
The Leading Days Out Guide
P O Box 427
Northampton
NN2 7YJ
Stained Glass Museum
Ely
Family Ticket (Four People) £5.00
not to be used in conjunction with any other offer, one coupon per party not valid on Bank Hols and event weekends.
Discount Coupon
Valid until end Feb 2001
DAYS OUT UK
The Leading Days Out Guide
P O Box 427
Northampton
NN2 7YJ
Cambridge and County Folk Museum
Cambridge
One Child Free With Every Full Paying Adult
not to be used in conjunction with any other offer, one coupon per party not valid on Bank Hols and event weekends.
Discount Coupon
Valid until end Feb 2001
DAYS OUT UK
The Leading Days Out Guide
P O Box 427
Northampton
NN2 7YJ
St. Neots Museum
St. Neots
Two For The Price Of One
not to be used in conjunction with any other offer, one coupon per party not valid on Bank Hols and event weekends.
Discount Coupon
Valid until end Feb 2001
DAYS OUT UK
The Leading Days Out Guide
P O Box 427
Northampton
NN2 7YJ
Chilford Hall Vineyard
Cambridge
Two For The Price Of One
not to be used in conjunction with any other offer, one coupon per party not valid on Bank Hols and event weekends.
Discount Coupon
Valid until end Feb 2001
DAYS OUT UK
The Leading Days Out Guide
P O Box 427
Northampton
NN2 7YJ
Elton Hall
Peterborough
Two For The Price Of One
not to be used in conjunction with any other offer, one coupon per party not valid on Bank Hols and event weekends.
Discount Coupon
Valid until end Feb 2001

This coupon entitles the holder to the discount offer shown on the reverse side. To claim your discount please present this coupon when paying for your entry.

Customer care line number *free* phone 0800 316 8900

This coupon entitles the holder to the discount offer shown on the reverse side. To claim your discount please present this coupon when paying for your entry.

Customer care line number *free* phone 0800 316 8900

This coupon entitles the holder to the discount offer shown on the reverse side. To claim your discount please present this coupon when paying for your entry.

Customer care line number *free* phone 0800 316 8900

This coupon entitles the holder to the discount offer shown on the reverse side. To claim your discount please present this coupon when paying for your entry.

Customer care line number *free* phone 0800 316 8900

This coupon entitles the holder to the discount offer shown on the reverse side. To claim your discount please present this coupon when paying for your entry.

Customer care line number *free* phone 0800 316 8900

This coupon entitles the holder to the discount offer shown on the reverse side. To claim your discount please present this coupon when paying for your entry.

Customer care line number *free* phone 0800 316 8900

DAYS OUT UK
The Leading Days Out Guide
P O Box 427
Northampton
NN2 7YJ
Guernsey Museum and Art Gallery
Guernsey
10% Discount On Full Admission Prices Only
not to be used in conjunction with any other offer, one coupon per party not valid on Bank Hols and event weekends.
Discount Coupon
Valid until end Feb 2001
DAYS OUT UK
The Leading Days Out Guide
P O Box 427
Northampton
NN2 7YJ
Flying Flowers
Jersey
Two For The Price Of One
not to be used in conjunction with any other offer, one coupon per party not valid on Bank Hols and event weekends.
Discount Coupon
Valid until 31 Oct 2000
DAYS OUT UK
The Leading Days Out Guide
P O Box 427
Northampton
NN2 7YJ
Castle Cornet
Guernsey
10% Discount, On Full Admission Prices Only
not to be used in conjunction with any other offer, one coupon per party not valid on Bank Hols and event weekends.
Discount Coupon
Valid until end Feb 2001
DAYS OUT UK
The Leading Days Out Guide
P O Box 427
Northampton
NN2 7YJ
Sausmarez Manor
Guernsey
Two For The price of One In Sculpture Park And Woodland Garden
not to be used in conjunction with any other offer, one coupon per party not valid on Bank Hols and event weekends.
Discount Coupon
Valid until end Feb 200
DAYS OUT UK
The Leading Days Out Guide
P O Box 427
Northampton
NN2 7YJ
Fort Grey Shipwreck Museum
Guernsey
10% Discount On Full Admission Prices
not to be used in conjunction with any other offer, one coupon per party not valid on Bank Hols and event weekends.
Discount Coupon
Valid until end Feb 2001
DAYS OUT UK
The Leading Days Out Guide
P O Box 427
Northampton
NN2 7YJ
On the Air: The Broadcasting Museum
Chester
Two For The Price Of One
not to be used in conjunction with any other offer, one coupon per party not valid on Bank Hols and event weekends.
Discount Coupon
Valid until end Feb 200

This coupon entitles the holder to the discount offer shown on the reverse side. To claim your discount please present this coupon when paying for your entry.

Customer care line number *free* phone 0800 316 8900

This coupon entitles the holder to the discount offer shown on the reverse side. To claim your discount please present this coupon when paying for your entry.

Customer care line number *free* phone 0800 316 8900

This coupon entitles the holder to the discount offer shown on the reverse side. To claim your discount please present this coupon when paying for your entry.

Customer care line number *free* phone 0800 316 8900

This coupon entitles the holder to the discount offer shown on the reverse side. To claim your discount please present this coupon when paying for your entry.

Customer care line number *free* phone 0800 316 8900

This coupon entitles the holder to the discount offer shown on the reverse side. To claim your discount please present this coupon when paying for your entry.

Customer care line number *free* phone 0800 316 8900

This coupon entitles the holder to the discount offer shown on the reverse side. To claim your discount please present this coupon when paying for your entry.

Customer care line number *free* phone 0800 316 8900

DAYS OUT UK
The Leading Days Out Guide
P O Box 427
Northampton
NN2 7YJ

Dunham Massey Hall, Garden and Park
Altrincham
Three Children Free With Two Full Paying Adults to House & Garden
not to be used in conjunction with any other offer, one coupon per party not valid on Bank Hols and event weekends.

Discount Coupon **Valid until 1 Nov 2000**

DAYS OUT UK
The Leading Days Out Guide
P O Box 427
Northampton
NN2 7YJ

Norton Priory Museum & Gardens
Runcorn
Two For The Price Of One Full Paying Adult. Not Valid On Public Holidays
not to be used in conjunction with any other offer, one coupon per party not valid on Bank Hols and event weekends.

Discount Coupon **Valid until end Feb 2001**

DAYS OUT UK
The Leading Days Out Guide
P O Box 427
Northampton
NN2 7YJ

Macclesfield Silk Museum and Paradise Mill
Macclesfield
Two Full Paying Adults For The Price Of One
not to be used in conjunction with any other offer, one coupon per party not valid on Bank Hols and event weekends.

Discount Coupon **Valid until end Feb 2001**

DAYS OUT UK
The Leading Days Out Guide
P O Box 427
Northampton
NN2 7YJ

Arley Hall and Gardens
Northwich
Two For The Price Of One to Garden only. NOT Valid For Special Events
not to be used in conjunction with any other offer, one coupon per party not valid on Bank Hols and event weekends.

Discount Coupon **Valid until end Feb 2001**

DAYS OUT UK
The Leading Days Out Guide
P O Box 427
Northampton
NN2 7YJ

Dorfold Hall
Nantwich
Two For The Price Of One
not to be used in conjunction with any other offer, one coupon per party not valid on Bank Hols and event weekends.

Discount Coupon **Valid until end Feb 2001**

DAYS OUT UK
The Leading Days Out Guide
P O Box 427
Northampton
NN2 7YJ

Tabley House
Knutsford
One Child Free With One Full Paying Adult
not to be used in conjunction with any other offer, one coupon per party not valid on Bank Hols and event weekends.

Discount Coupon **Valid until 31 Oct 2000**

This coupon entitles the holder to the discount offer shown on the reverse side. To claim your discount please present this coupon when paying for your entry.

Customer care line number *free* phone 0800 316 8900

This coupon entitles the holder to the discount offer shown on the reverse side. To claim your discount please present this coupon when paying for your entry.

Customer care line number *free* phone 0800 316 8900

This coupon entitles the holder to the discount offer shown on the reverse side. To claim your discount please present this coupon when paying for your entry.

Customer care line number *free* phone 0800 316 8900

This coupon entitles the holder to the discount offer shown on the reverse side. To claim your discount please present this coupon when paying for your entry.

Customer care line number *free* phone 0800 316 8900

This coupon entitles the holder to the discount offer shown on the reverse side. To claim your discount please present this coupon when paying for your entry.

Customer care line number *free* phone 0800 316 8900

This coupon entitles the holder to the discount offer shown on the reverse side. To claim your discount please present this coupon when paying for your entry.

Customer care line number *free* phone 0800 316 8900

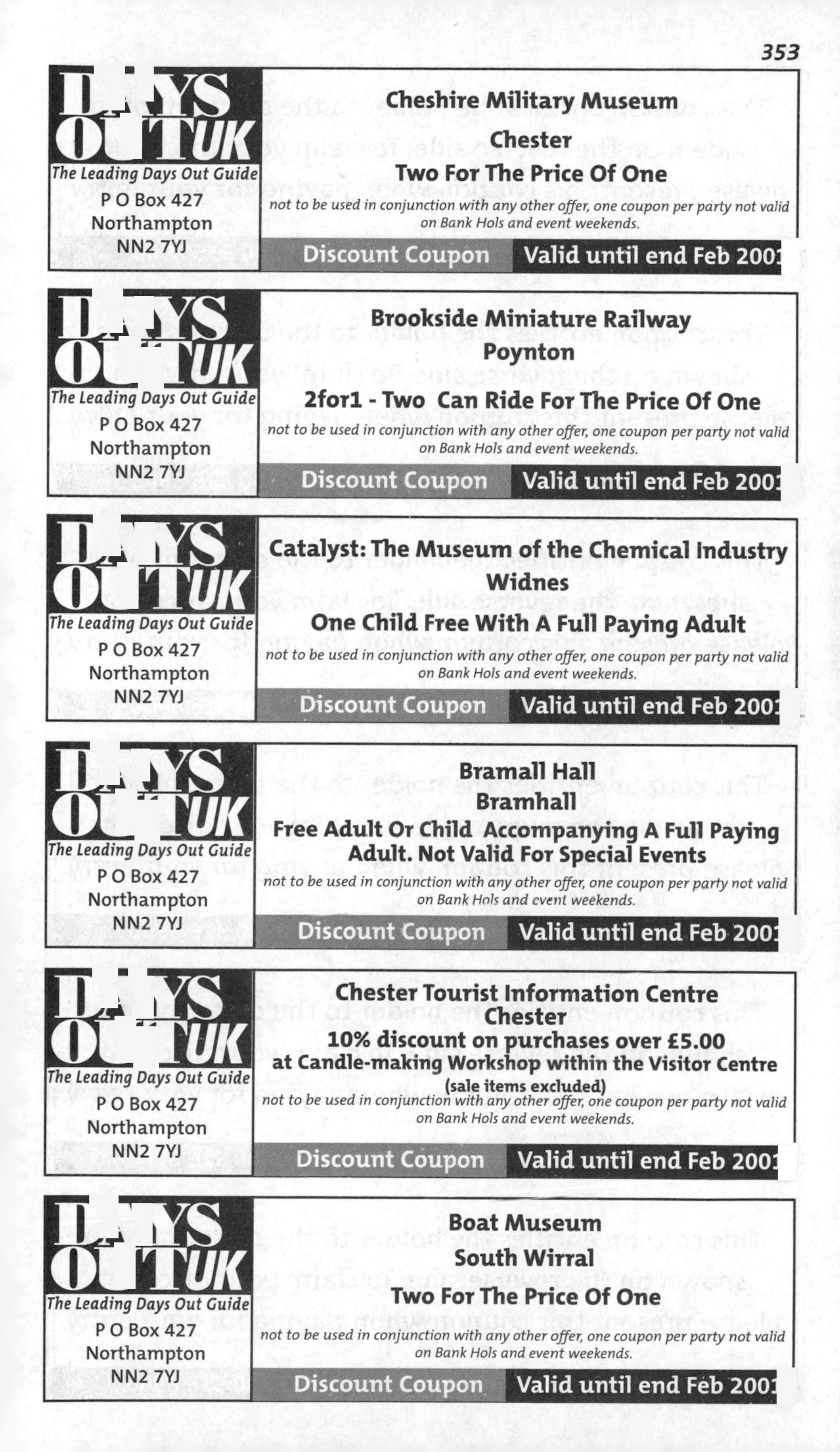
The Leading Days Out Guide
P O Box 427
Northampton
NN2 7YJ
Cheshire Military Museum
Chester
Two For The Price Of One
not to be used in conjunction with any other offer, one coupon per party not valid on Bank Hols and event weekends.
Discount Coupon
Valid until end Feb 2001
The Leading Days Out Guide
P O Box 427
Northampton
NN2 7YJ
Brookside Miniature Railway
Poynton
2for1 - Two Can Ride For The Price Of One
not to be used in conjunction with any other offer, one coupon per party not valid on Bank Hols and event weekends.
Discount Coupon
Valid until end Feb 2001
The Leading Days Out Guide
P O Box 427
Northampton
NN2 7YJ
Catalyst: The Museum of the Chemical Industry
Widnes
One Child Free With A Full Paying Adult
not to be used in conjunction with any other offer, one coupon per party not valid on Bank Hols and event weekends.
Discount Coupon
Valid until end Feb 2001
The Leading Days Out Guide
P O Box 427
Northampton
NN2 7YJ
Bramall Hall
Bramhall
Free Adult Or Child Accompanying A Full Paying Adult. Not Valid For Special Events
not to be used in conjunction with any other offer, one coupon per party not valid on Bank Hols and event weekends.
Discount Coupon
Valid until end Feb 2001
The Leading Days Out Guide
P O Box 427
Northampton
NN2 7YJ
Chester Tourist Information Centre
Chester
10% discount on purchases over £5.00
at Candle-making Workshop within the Visitor Centre
(sale items excluded)
not to be used in conjunction with any other offer, one coupon per party not valid on Bank Hols and event weekends.
Discount Coupon
Valid until end Feb 2001
The Leading Days Out Guide
P O Box 427
Northampton
NN2 7YJ
Boat Museum
South Wirral
Two For The Price Of One
not to be used in conjunction with any other offer, one coupon per party not valid on Bank Hols and event weekends.
Discount Coupon
Valid until end Feb 2001

This coupon entitles the holder to the discount offer shown on the reverse side. To claim your discount please present this coupon when paying for your entry.

Customer care line number *free* phone 0800 316 8900

This coupon entitles the holder to the discount offer shown on the reverse side. To claim your discount please present this coupon when paying for your entry.

Customer care line number *free* phone 0800 316 8900

This coupon entitles the holder to the discount offer shown on the reverse side. To claim your discount please present this coupon when paying for your entry.

Customer care line number *free* phone 0800 316 8900

This coupon entitles the holder to the discount offer shown on the reverse side. To claim your discount please present this coupon when paying for your entry.

Customer care line number *free* phone 0800 316 8900

This coupon entitles the holder to the discount offer shown on the reverse side. To claim your discount please present this coupon when paying for your entry.

Customer care line number *free* phone 0800 316 8900

This coupon entitles the holder to the discount offer shown on the reverse side. To claim your discount please present this coupon when paying for your entry.

Customer care line number *free* phone 0800 316 8900

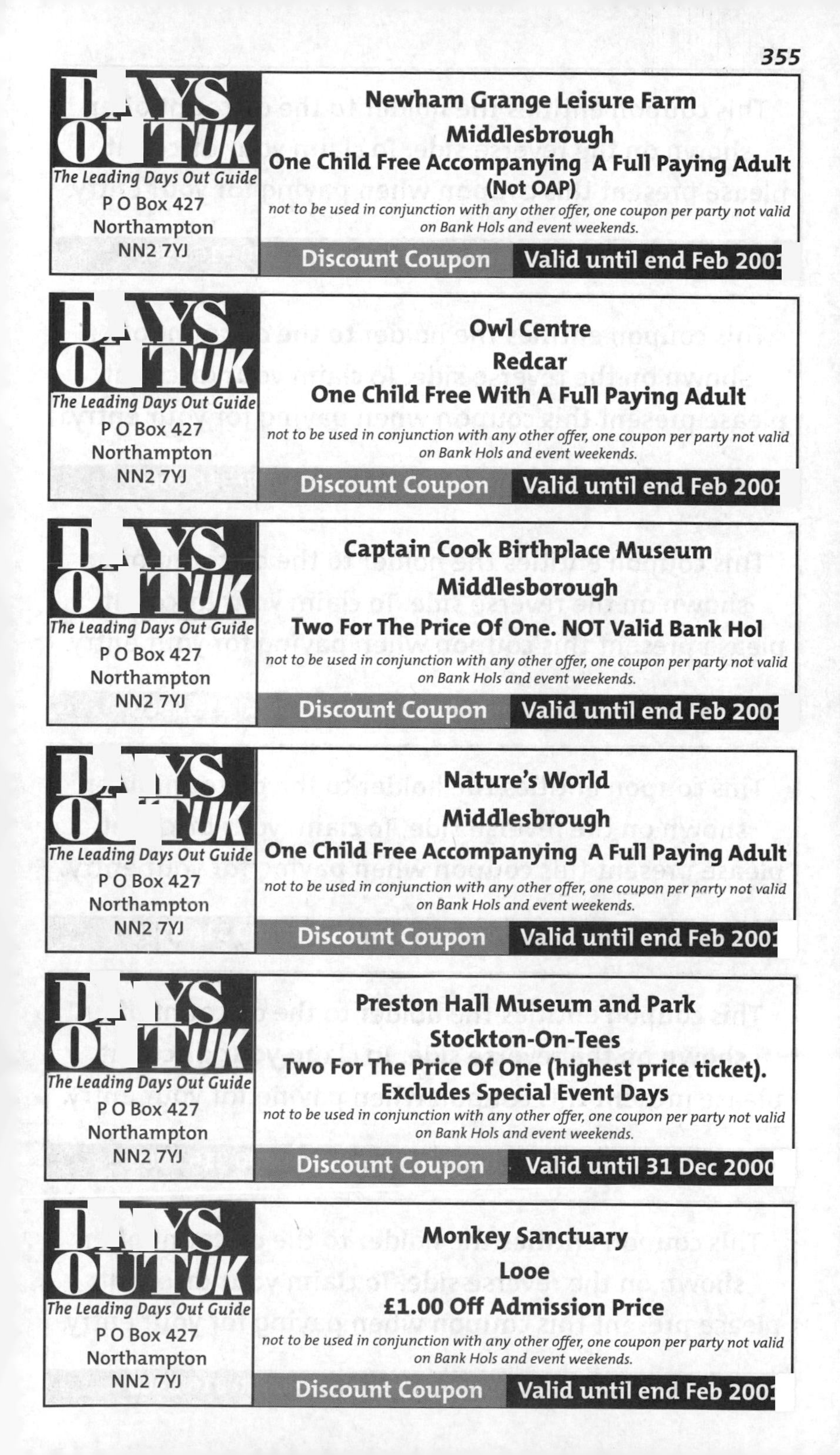
DAYS OUT UK
The Leading Days Out Guide
P O Box 427
Northampton
NN2 7YJ
Newham Grange Leisure Farm
Middlesbrough
One Child Free Accompanying A Full Paying Adult
(Not OAP)
not to be used in conjunction with any other offer, one coupon per party not valid on Bank Hols and event weekends.
Discount Coupon
Valid until end Feb 2001
The Leading Days Out Guide
P O Box 427
Northampton
NN2 7YJ
Owl Centre
Redcar
One Child Free With A Full Paying Adult
not to be used in conjunction with any other offer, one coupon per party not valid on Bank Hols and event weekends.
Discount Coupon
Valid until end Feb 2001
The Leading Days Out Guide
P O Box 427
Northampton
NN2 7YJ
Captain Cook Birthplace Museum
Middlesborough
Two For The Price Of One. NOT Valid Bank Hol
not to be used in conjunction with any other offer, one coupon per party not valid on Bank Hols and event weekends.
Discount Coupon
Valid until end Feb 2001
The Leading Days Out Guide
P O Box 427
Northampton
NN2 7YJ
Nature's World
Middlesbrough
One Child Free Accompanying A Full Paying Adult
not to be used in conjunction with any other offer, one coupon per party not valid on Bank Hols and event weekends.
Discount Coupon
Valid until end Feb 2001
The Leading Days Out Guide
P O Box 427
Northampton
NN2 7YJ
Preston Hall Museum and Park
Stockton-On-Tees
Two For The Price Of One (highest price ticket).
Excludes Special Event Days
not to be used in conjunction with any other offer, one coupon per party not valid on Bank Hols and event weekends.
Discount Coupon
Valid until 31 Dec 2000
The Leading Days Out Guide
P O Box 427
Northampton
NN2 7YJ
Monkey Sanctuary
Looe
£1.00 Off Admission Price
not to be used in conjunction with any other offer, one coupon per party not valid on Bank Hols and event weekends.
Discount Coupon
Valid until end Feb 2001

This coupon entitles the holder to the discount offer shown on the reverse side. To claim your discount please present this coupon when paying for your entry.

Customer care line number *free* phone 0800 316 8900

This coupon entitles the holder to the discount offer shown on the reverse side. To claim your discount please present this coupon when paying for your entry.

Customer care line number *free* phone 0800 316 8900

This coupon entitles the holder to the discount offer shown on the reverse side. To claim your discount please present this coupon when paying for your entry.

Customer care line number *free* phone 0800 316 8900

This coupon entitles the holder to the discount offer shown on the reverse side. To claim your discount please present this coupon when paying for your entry.

Customer care line number *free* phone 0800 316 8900

This coupon entitles the holder to the discount offer shown on the reverse side. To claim your discount please present this coupon when paying for your entry.

Customer care line number *free* phone 0800 316 8900

This coupon entitles the holder to the discount offer shown on the reverse side. To claim your discount please present this coupon when paying for your entry.

Customer care line number *free* phone 0800 316 8900

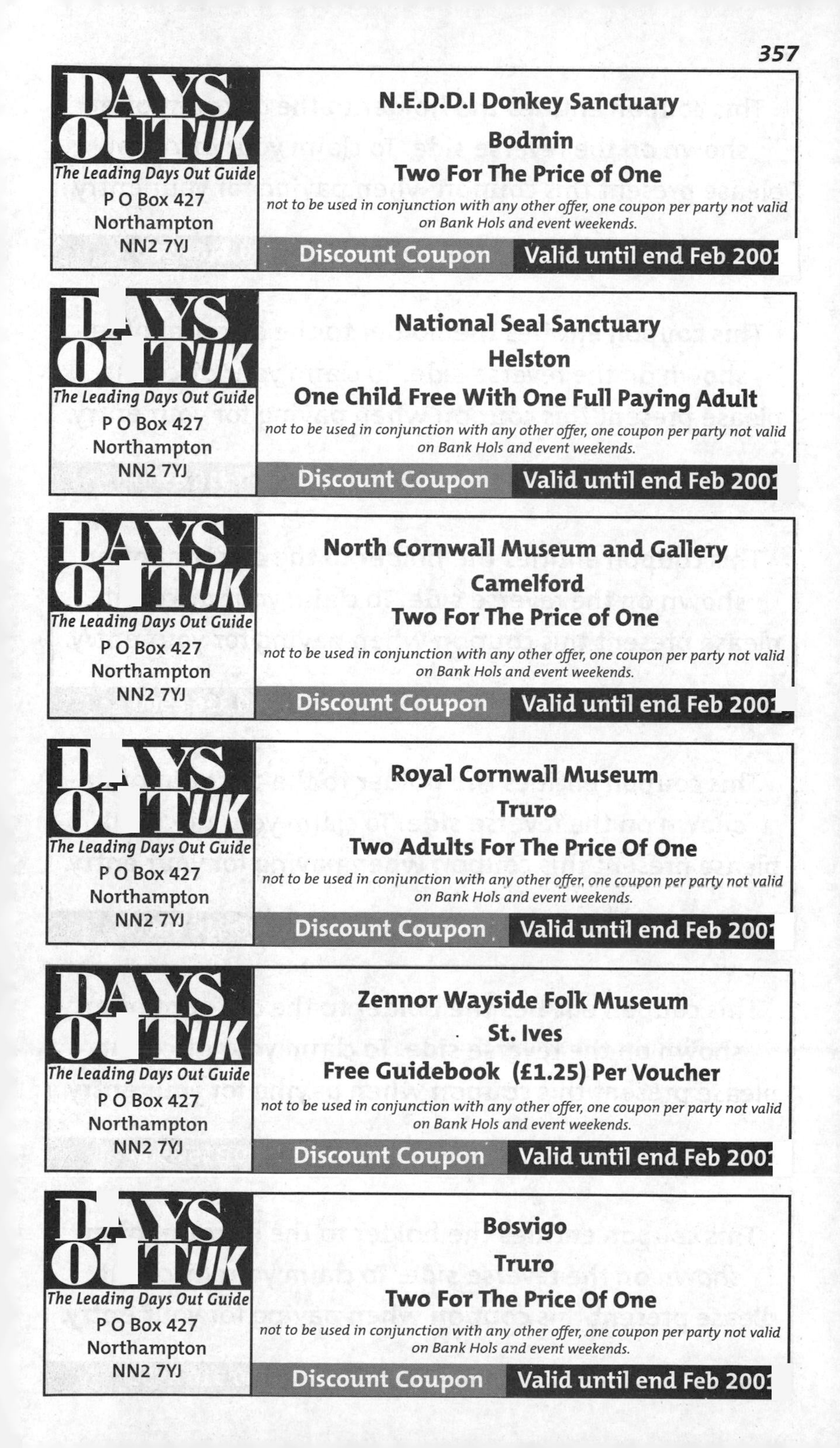
DAYS OUT UK
The Leading Days Out Guide
P O Box 427
Northampton
NN2 7YJ
N.E.D.D.I Donkey Sanctuary
Bodmin
Two For The Price of One
not to be used in conjunction with any other offer, one coupon per party not valid on Bank Hols and event weekends.
Discount Coupon
Valid until end Feb 2001
DAYS OUT UK
The Leading Days Out Guide
P O Box 427
Northampton
NN2 7YJ
National Seal Sanctuary
Helston
One Child Free With One Full Paying Adult
not to be used in conjunction with any other offer, one coupon per party not valid on Bank Hols and event weekends.
Discount Coupon
Valid until end Feb 2001
DAYS OUT UK
The Leading Days Out Guide
P O Box 427
Northampton
NN2 7YJ
North Cornwall Museum and Gallery
Camelford
Two For The Price of One
not to be used in conjunction with any other offer, one coupon per party not valid on Bank Hols and event weekends.
Discount Coupon
Valid until end Feb 2001
DAYS OUT UK
The Leading Days Out Guide
P O Box 427
Northampton
NN2 7YJ
Royal Cornwall Museum
Truro
Two Adults For The Price Of One
not to be used in conjunction with any other offer, one coupon per party not valid on Bank Hols and event weekends.
Discount Coupon
Valid until end Feb 2001
DAYS OUT UK
The Leading Days Out Guide
P O Box 427
Northampton
NN2 7YJ
Zennor Wayside Folk Museum
St. Ives
Free Guidebook (£1.25) Per Voucher
not to be used in conjunction with any other offer, one coupon per party not valid on Bank Hols and event weekends.
Discount Coupon
Valid until end Feb 2001
DAYS OUT UK
The Leading Days Out Guide
P O Box 427
Northampton
NN2 7YJ
Bosvigo
Truro
Two For The Price Of One
not to be used in conjunction with any other offer, one coupon per party not valid on Bank Hols and event weekends.
Discount Coupon
Valid until end Feb 2001

This coupon entitles the holder to the discount offer shown on the reverse side. To claim your discount please present this coupon when paying for your entry.

Customer care line number *free* phone 0800 316 8900

This coupon entitles the holder to the discount offer shown on the reverse side. To claim your discount please present this coupon when paying for your entry.

Customer care line number *free* phone 0800 316 8900

This coupon entitles the holder to the discount offer shown on the reverse side. To claim your discount please present this coupon when paying for your entry.

Customer care line number *free* phone 0800 316 8900

This coupon entitles the holder to the discount offer shown on the reverse side. To claim your discount please present this coupon when paying for your entry.

Customer care line number *free* phone 0800 316 8900

This coupon entitles the holder to the discount offer shown on the reverse side. To claim your discount please present this coupon when paying for your entry.

Customer care line number *free* phone 0800 316 8900

This coupon entitles the holder to the discount offer shown on the reverse side. To claim your discount please present this coupon when paying for your entry.

Customer care line number *free* phone 0800 316 8900

DAYS OUT UK
The Leading Days Out Guide
P O Box 427
Northampton
NN2 7YJ

Trebah Garden
Falmouth
Two For The Price Of One Adult
not to be used in conjunction with any other offer, one coupon per party not valid on Bank Hols and event weekends.

Discount Coupon | Valid until end Feb 2001

DAYS OUT UK
The Leading Days Out Guide
P O Box 427
Northampton
NN2 7YJ

Charlestown Shipwreck and Heritage Centre
St. Austell
10% Off Admission Price
not to be used in conjunction with any other offer, one coupon per party not valid on Bank Hols and event weekends.

Discount Coupon | Valid until end Feb 2001

DAYS OUT UK
The Leading Days Out Guide
P O Box 427
Northampton
NN2 7YJ

Land's End Visitor Centre
Penzance
One Child Free With One Normal Admission
For Top Five Attractions Only
not to be used in conjunction with any other offer, one coupon per party not valid on Bank Hols and event weekends.

Discount Coupon | Valid until end Feb 2001

DAYS OUT UK
The Leading Days Out Guide
P O Box 427
Northampton
NN2 7YJ

Hidden Valley
Launceston
Two For The Price Of One
not to be used in conjunction with any other offer, one coupon per party not valid on Bank Hols and event weekends.

Discount Coupon | Valid until end Feb 2001

DAYS OUT UK
The Leading Days Out Guide
P O Box 427
Northampton
NN2 7YJ

Launceston Steam Railway
Launceston
One Child Free With Two Full Paying Adults
not to be used in conjunction with any other offer, one coupon per party not valid on Bank Hols and event weekends.

Discount Coupon | Valid until end Feb 2001

DAYS OUT UK
The Leading Days Out Guide
P O Box 427
Northampton
NN2 7YJ

World of Model Railways
Mevagissey
One Child Free With Two Full Paying Adults
not to be used in conjunction with any other offer, one coupon per party not valid on Bank Hols and event weekends.

Discount Coupon | Valid until end Feb 2001

This coupon entitles the holder to the discount offer shown on the reverse side. To claim your discount please present this coupon when paying for your entry.

Customer care line number *free* phone 0800 316 8900

This coupon entitles the holder to the discount offer shown on the reverse side. To claim your discount please present this coupon when paying for your entry.

Customer care line number *free* phone 0800 316 8900

This coupon entitles the holder to the discount offer shown on the reverse side. To claim your discount please present this coupon when paying for your entry.

Customer care line number *free* phone 0800 316 8900

This coupon entitles the holder to the discount offer shown on the reverse side. To claim your discount please present this coupon when paying for your entry.

Customer care line number *free* phone 0800 316 8900

This coupon entitles the holder to the discount offer shown on the reverse side. To claim your discount please present this coupon when paying for your entry.

Customer care line number *free* phone 0800 316 8900

This coupon entitles the holder to the discount offer shown on the reverse side. To claim your discount please present this coupon when paying for your entry.

Customer care line number *free* phone 0800 316 8900

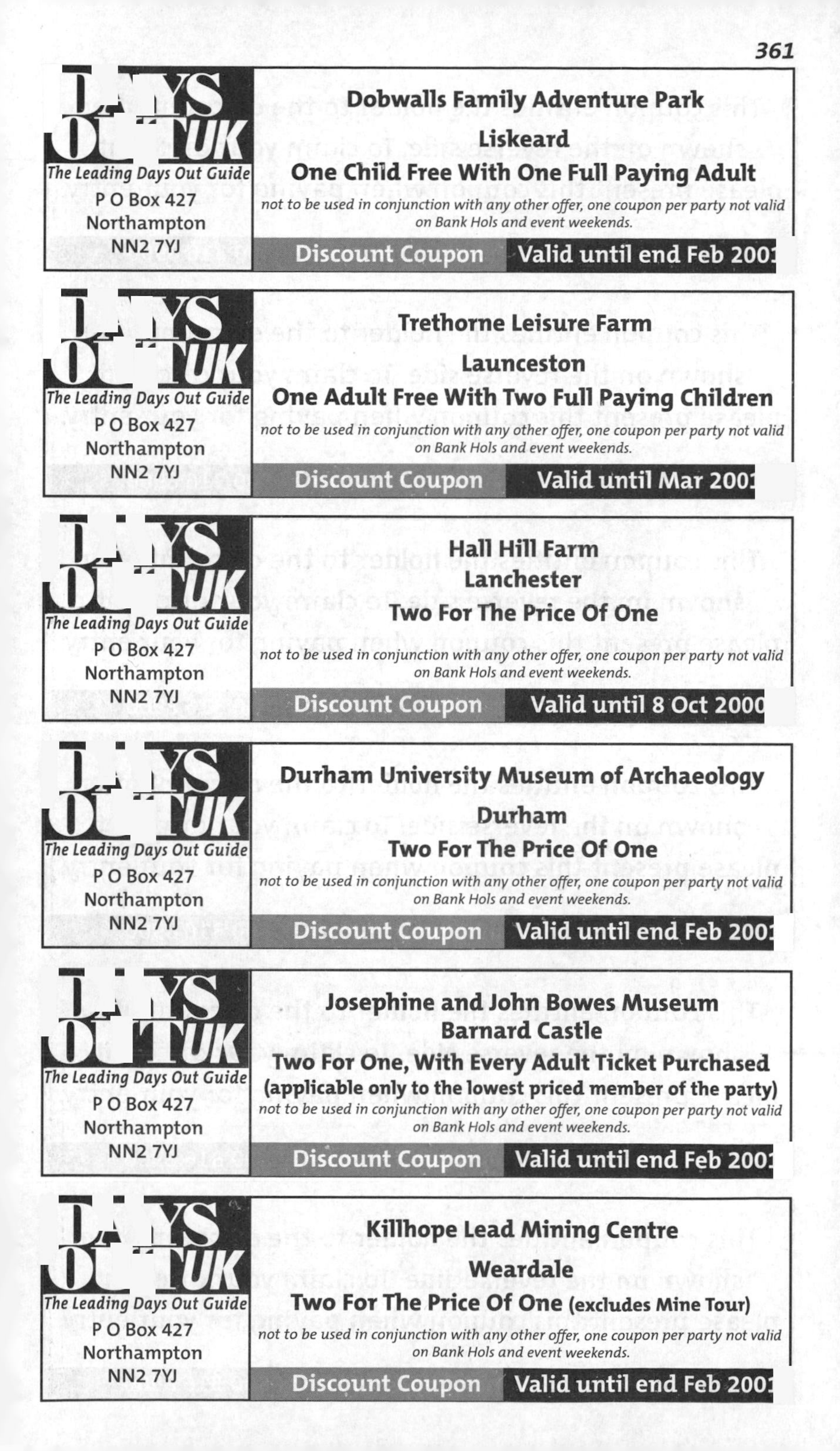

DAYS OUT UK
The Leading Days Out Guide
P O Box 427
Northampton
NN2 7YJ

Dobwalls Family Adventure Park

Liskeard

One Child Free With One Full Paying Adult

not to be used in conjunction with any other offer, one coupon per party not valid on Bank Hols and event weekends.

Discount Coupon **Valid until end Feb 2001**

DAYS OUT UK
The Leading Days Out Guide
P O Box 427
Northampton
NN2 7YJ

Trethorne Leisure Farm

Launceston

One Adult Free With Two Full Paying Children

not to be used in conjunction with any other offer, one coupon per party not valid on Bank Hols and event weekends.

Discount Coupon **Valid until Mar 2001**

DAYS OUT UK
The Leading Days Out Guide
P O Box 427
Northampton
NN2 7YJ

Hall Hill Farm
Lanchester

Two For The Price Of One

not to be used in conjunction with any other offer, one coupon per party not valid on Bank Hols and event weekends.

Discount Coupon **Valid until 8 Oct 2000**

DAYS OUT UK
The Leading Days Out Guide
P O Box 427
Northampton
NN2 7YJ

Durham University Museum of Archaeology

Durham

Two For The Price Of One

not to be used in conjunction with any other offer, one coupon per party not valid on Bank Hols and event weekends.

Discount Coupon **Valid until end Feb 2001**

DAYS OUT UK
The Leading Days Out Guide
P O Box 427
Northampton
NN2 7YJ

Josephine and John Bowes Museum
Barnard Castle

Two For One, With Every Adult Ticket Purchased
(applicable only to the lowest priced member of the party)

not to be used in conjunction with any other offer, one coupon per party not valid on Bank Hols and event weekends.

Discount Coupon **Valid until end Feb 2001**

DAYS OUT UK
The Leading Days Out Guide
P O Box 427
Northampton
NN2 7YJ

Killhope Lead Mining Centre

Weardale

Two For The Price Of One (excludes Mine Tour)

not to be used in conjunction with any other offer, one coupon per party not valid on Bank Hols and event weekends.

Discount Coupon **Valid until end Feb 2001**

This coupon entitles the holder to the discount offer shown on the reverse side. To claim your discount please present this coupon when paying for your entry.

Customer care line number *free* phone 0800 316 8900

This coupon entitles the holder to the discount offer shown on the reverse side. To claim your discount please present this coupon when paying for your entry.

Customer care line number *free* phone 0800 316 8900

This coupon entitles the holder to the discount offer shown on the reverse side. To claim your discount please present this coupon when paying for your entry.

Customer care line number *free* phone 0800 316 8900

This coupon entitles the holder to the discount offer shown on the reverse side. To claim your discount please present this coupon when paying for your entry.

Customer care line number *free* phone 0800 316 8900

This coupon entitles the holder to the discount offer shown on the reverse side. To claim your discount please present this coupon when paying for your entry.

Customer care line number *free* phone 0800 316 8900

This coupon entitles the holder to the discount offer shown on the reverse side. To claim your discount please present this coupon when paying for your entry.

Customer care line number *free* phone 0800 316 8900

DAYS OUT UK
The Leading Days Out Guide
P O Box 427
Northampton
NN2 7YJ
Timothy Hackworth Victorian Railway Museum
Shildon
Two For The Price Of One
not to be used in conjunction with any other offer, one coupon per party not valid on Bank Hols and event weekends.
Discount Coupon
Valid until end Feb 2001
DAYS OUT UK
The Leading Days Out Guide
P O Box 427
Northampton
NN2 7YJ
Trotters and Friends Animal Farm
Keswick
One Child Free With A Full Paying Adult
not to be used in conjunction with any other offer, one coupon per party not valid on Bank Hols and event weekends.
Discount Coupon
Valid until end Feb 2001
DAYS OUT UK
The Leading Days Out Guide
P O Box 427
Northampton
NN2 7YJ
Brantwood
Coniston
Two Children Free With One Full Paying Adult
not to be used in conjunction with any other offer, one coupon per party not valid on Bank Hols and event weekends.
Discount Coupon
Valid until end Feb 2001
DAYS OUT UK
The Leading Days Out Guide
P O Box 427
Northampton
NN2 7YJ
Dalemain Historic House and Gardens
Penrith
Two For The Price Of One (House and Gardens)
Not valid for Special Events
not to be used in conjunction with any other offer, one coupon per party not valid on Bank Hols and event weekends.
Discount Coupon
Valid until 8 Oct 2000
DAYS OUT UK
The Leading Days Out Guide
P O Box 427
Northampton
NN2 7YJ
Hutton in the Forest
Penrith
£0.50 Off Per Adult
not to be used in conjunction with any other offer, one coupon per party not valid on Bank Hols and event weekends.
Discount Coupon
Valid until end Feb 2001
DAYS OUT UK
The Leading Days Out Guide
P O Box 427
Northampton
NN2 7YJ
Mirehouse Historic House and Gardens
Keswick
Two Full Price Adults For One
Valid Sun, Wed (also Fri in Aug) Only
not to be used in conjunction with any other offer, one coupon per party not valid on Bank Hols and event weekends.
Discount Coupon
Valid until end Feb 2001

This coupon entitles the holder to the discount offer shown on the reverse side. To claim your discount please present this coupon when paying for your entry.

Customer care line number *free* phone 0800 316 8900

This coupon entitles the holder to the discount offer shown on the reverse side. To claim your discount please present this coupon when paying for your entry.

Customer care line number *free* phone 0800 316 8900

This coupon entitles the holder to the discount offer shown on the reverse side. To claim your discount please present this coupon when paying for your entry.

Customer care line number *free* phone 0800 316 8900

This coupon entitles the holder to the discount offer shown on the reverse side. To claim your discount please present this coupon when paying for your entry.

Customer care line number *free* phone 0800 316 8900

This coupon entitles the holder to the discount offer shown on the reverse side. To claim your discount please present this coupon when paying for your entry.

Customer care line number *free* phone 0800 316 8900

This coupon entitles the holder to the discount offer shown on the reverse side. To claim your discount please present this coupon when paying for your entry.

Customer care line number *free* phone 0800 316 8900

DAYS OUT UK
The Leading Days Out Guide
P O Box 427
Northampton
NN2 7YJ
Muncaster Castle, Gardens and Owl Centre
Ravenglass
One Child Free With A Full Paying Adult
not to be used in conjunction with any other offer, one coupon per party not valid on Bank Hols and event weekends.
Discount Coupon
Valid until end Feb 2001
DAYS OUT UK
The Leading Days Out Guide
P O Box 427
Northampton
NN2 7YJ
Rydal Mount and Gardens
Ambleside
Two For The Price Of One
not to be used in conjunction with any other offer, one coupon per party not valid on Bank Hols and event weekends.
Discount Coupon
Valid until end Feb 2001
DAYS OUT UK
The Leading Days Out Guide
P O Box 427
Northampton
NN2 7YJ
Windermere Steamboat Museum
Windermere
Two For The Price Of One
not to be used in conjunction with any other offer, one coupon per party not valid on Bank Hols and event weekends.
Discount Coupon
Valid until end Feb 2001
DAYS OUT UK
The Leading Days Out Guide
P O Box 427
Northampton
NN2 7YJ
Lake District Visitor Centre at Brockhole
Windermere
Full Day's Parking For £3.00
Leave Your Coupon In The Windscreen
not to be used in conjunction with any other offer, one coupon per party not valid on Bank Hols and event weekends.
Discount Coupon
Valid until end Feb 2001
DAYS OUT UK
The Leading Days Out Guide
P O Box 427
Northampton
NN2 7YJ
Lowther Leisure and Wildlife Park
Penrith
Three For Two Full Paying Adults/Child
not to be used in conjunction with any other offer, one coupon per party not valid on Bank Hols and event weekends.
Discount Coupon
Valid until end Feb 2001
DAYS OUT UK
The Leading Days Out Guide
P O Box 427
Northampton
NN2 7YJ
The Beacon
Whitehaven
One Child Free With One Full Paying Adult
not to be used in conjunction with any other offer, one coupon per party not valid on Bank Hols and event weekends.
Discount Coupon
Valid until end Feb 2001

This coupon entitles the holder to the discount offer shown on the reverse side. To claim your discount please present this coupon when paying for your entry.

Customer care line number *free* phone 0800 316 8900

This coupon entitles the holder to the discount offer shown on the reverse side. To claim your discount please present this coupon when paying for your entry.

Customer care line number *free* phone 0800 316 8900

This coupon entitles the holder to the discount offer shown on the reverse side. To claim your discount please present this coupon when paying for your entry.

Customer care line number *free* phone 0800 316 8900

This coupon entitles the holder to the discount offer shown on the reverse side. To claim your discount please present this coupon when paying for your entry.

Customer care line number *free* phone 0800 316 8900

This coupon entitles the holder to the discount offer shown on the reverse side. To claim your discount please present this coupon when paying for your entry.

Customer care line number *free* phone 0800 316 8900

This coupon entitles the holder to the discount offer shown on the reverse side. To claim your discount please present this coupon when paying for your entry.

Customer care line number *free* phone 0800 316 8900

DAYS OUT UK
The Leading Days Out Guide
P O Box 427
Northampton
NN2 7YJ
Cumberland Toy and Model Museum
Cockermouth
Two For The Price Of One
not to be used in conjunction with any other offer, one coupon per party not valid on Bank Hols and event weekends.
Discount Coupon
Valid until 30 Nov 2000
DAYS OUT UK
The Leading Days Out Guide
P O Box 427
Northampton
NN2 7YJ
Cars of the Stars Museum
Keswick
One Child Free With Every Two Full Paying Adults
not to be used in conjunction with any other offer, one coupon per party not valid on Bank Hols and event weekends.
Discount Coupon
Valid until end Feb 2001
DAYS OUT UK
The Leading Days Out Guide
P O Box 427
Northampton
NN2 7YJ
South Lakes Wild Animal Park
Dalton-in-Furness
Free Colour Guide With Two Full Paying Adults
not to be used in conjunction with any other offer, one coupon per party not valid on Bank Hols and event weekends.
Discount Coupon
Valid until end Feb 2001
DAYS OUT UK
The Leading Days Out Guide
P O Box 427
Northampton
NN2 7YJ
Rookes Pottery
Buxton
10% On Shop Purchases Over £10.00
not to be used in conjunction with any other offer, one coupon per party not valid on Bank Hols and event weekends.
Discount Coupon
Valid until end Feb 2001
DAYS OUT UK
The Leading Days Out Guide
P O Box 427
Northampton
NN2 7YJ
Heights of Abraham
Matlock
One Child Free For The Cable Car & Caverns With One Full Paying Adult
not to be used in conjunction with any other offer, one coupon per party not valid on Bank Hols and event weekends.
Discount Coupon
Valid until end Feb 2001
DAYS OUT UK
The Leading Days Out Guide
P O Box 427
Northampton
NN2 7YJ
The Old House Museum
Bakewell
Two For The Price Of One
not to be used in conjunction with any other offer, one coupon per party not valid on Bank Hols and event weekends.
Discount Coupon
Valid until 31 Oct 2000

This coupon entitles the holder to the discount offer shown on the reverse side. To claim your discount please present this coupon when paying for your entry.

Customer care line number *free* phone 0800 316 8900

This coupon entitles the holder to the discount offer shown on the reverse side. To claim your discount please present this coupon when paying for your entry.

Customer care line number *free* phone 0800 316 8900

This coupon entitles the holder to the discount offer shown on the reverse side. To claim your discount please present this coupon when paying for your entry.

Customer care line number *free* phone 0800 316 8900

This coupon entitles the holder to the discount offer shown on the reverse side. To claim your discount please present this coupon when paying for your entry.

Customer care line number *free* phone 0800 316 8900

This coupon entitles the holder to the discount offer shown on the reverse side. To claim your discount please present this coupon when paying for your entry.

Customer care line number *free* phone 0800 316 8900

This coupon entitles the holder to the discount offer shown on the reverse side. To claim your discount please present this coupon when paying for your entry.

Customer care line number *free* phone 0800 316 8900

DAYS OUT UK
The Leading Days Out Guide
P O Box 427
Northampton
NN2 7YJ

Heart of the National Forest Visitor Centre
Moira
One Child Free With A Full Paying Adult
not to be used in conjunction with any other offer, one coupon per party not valid on Bank Hols and event weekends.

Discount Coupon | Valid until end Feb 2001

DAYS OUT UK
The Leading Days Out Guide
P O Box 427
Northampton
NN2 7YJ

Eyam Hall
Hope Valley
Two For The Price Of One
not to be used in conjunction with any other offer, one coupon per party not valid on Bank Hols and event weekends.

Discount Coupon | Valid until end Feb 2001

DAYS OUT UK
The Leading Days Out Guide
P O Box 427
Northampton
NN2 7YJ

Melbourne Hall and Gardens
Melbourne
Two For The Price Of One, For House Only
not to be used in conjunction with any other offer, one coupon per party not valid on Bank Hols and event weekends.

Discount Coupon | Valid for Aug 2000 ONLY

DAYS OUT UK
The Leading Days Out Guide
P O Box 427
Northampton
NN2 7YJ

Caudwell's Mill and Craft Centre
Matlock
Two For The Price Of One
not to be used in conjunction with any other offer, one coupon per party not valid on Bank Hols and event weekends.

Discount Coupon | Valid until end Feb 2001

DAYS OUT UK
The Leading Days Out Guide
P O Box 427
Northampton
NN2 7YJ

National Tramway Museum
Matlock
One Child Free With Every Full Paying Adult
not to be used in conjunction with any other offer, one coupon per party not valid on Bank Hols and event weekends.

Discount Coupon | Valid until Sept 2000

DAYS OUT UK
The Leading Days Out Guide
P O Box 427
Northampton
NN2 7YJ

Canonteign Falls and Lakeland
Exeter
One Child Free With A Full Paying Adult
not to be used in conjunction with any other offer, one coupon per party not valid on Bank Hols and event weekends.

Discount Coupon | Valid until end Feb 2001

This coupon entitles the holder to the discount offer shown on the reverse side. To claim your discount please present this coupon when paying for your entry.

Customer care line number *free* phone 0800 316 8900

This coupon entitles the holder to the discount offer shown on the reverse side. To claim your discount please present this coupon when paying for your entry.

Customer care line number *free* phone 0800 316 8900

This coupon entitles the holder to the discount offer shown on the reverse side. To claim your discount please present this coupon when paying for your entry.

Customer care line number *free* phone 0800 316 8900

This coupon entitles the holder to the discount offer shown on the reverse side. To claim your discount please present this coupon when paying for your entry.

Customer care line number *free* phone 0800 316 8900

This coupon entitles the holder to the discount offer shown on the reverse side. To claim your discount please present this coupon when paying for your entry.

Customer care line number *free* phone 0800 316 8900

This coupon entitles the holder to the discount offer shown on the reverse side. To claim your discount please present this coupon when paying for your entry.

Customer care line number *free* phone 0800 316 8900

371
DAYS OUT UK
The Leading Days Out Guide
P O Box 427
Northampton
NN2 7YJ
Escot Country Park and Gardens
Ottery St. Mary
Two For The Price Of One
not to be used in conjunction with any other offer, one coupon per party not valid on Bank Hols and event weekends.
Discount Coupon
Valid until end Feb 2001
DAYS OUT UK
The Leading Days Out Guide
P O Box 427
Northampton
NN2 7YJ
Dartington Crystal
Torrington
One Child Free With Each Full Paying Adult
not to be used in conjunction with any other offer, one coupon per party not valid on Bank Hols and event weekends.
Discount Coupon
Valid until end Feb 2001
DAYS OUT UK
The Leading Days Out Guide
P O Box 427
Northampton
NN2 7YJ
Coldharbour Mill Working Wool Museum
Cullompton
Two For The Price Of One
not to be used in conjunction with any other offer, one coupon per party not valid on Bank Hols and event weekends.
Discount Coupon
Valid until end Feb 2001
DAYS OUT UK
The Leading Days Out Guide
P O Box 427
Northampton
NN2 7YJ
Hemerdon House
Plymouth
Two For The Price Of One
30 days inc May & Aug Bank Hol
not to be used in conjunction with any other offer, one coupon per party not valid on Bank Hols and event weekends.
Discount Coupon
Valid until end Feb 2001
DAYS OUT UK
The Leading Days Out Guide
P O Box 427
Northampton
NN2 7YJ
Powderham Castle
Exeter
Two For The Price Of One
not to be used in conjunction with any other offer, one coupon per party not valid on Bank Hols and event weekends.
Discount Coupon
Valid until end Feb 2001
DAYS OUT UK
The Leading Days Out Guide
P O Box 427
Northampton
NN2 7YJ
Prysten House
Plymouth
Two Adults For The Price Of One
not to be used in conjunction with any other offer, one coupon per party not valid on Bank Hols and event weekends.
Discount Coupon
Valid until end Feb 2001

This coupon entitles the holder to the discount offer shown on the reverse side. To claim your discount please present this coupon when paying for your entry.

Customer care line number *free* phone 0800 316 8900

This coupon entitles the holder to the discount offer shown on the reverse side. To claim your discount please present this coupon when paying for your entry.

Customer care line number *free* phone 0800 316 8900

This coupon entitles the holder to the discount offer shown on the reverse side. To claim your discount please present this coupon when paying for your entry.

Customer care line number *free* phone 0800 316 8900

This coupon entitles the holder to the discount offer shown on the reverse side. To claim your discount please present this coupon when paying for your entry.

Customer care line number *free* phone 0800 316 8900

This coupon entitles the holder to the discount offer shown on the reverse side. To claim your discount please present this coupon when paying for your entry.

Customer care line number *free* phone 0800 316 8900

This coupon entitles the holder to the discount offer shown on the reverse side. To claim your discount please present this coupon when paying for your entry.

Customer care line number *free* phone 0800 316 8900

373
DAYS OUT UK
The Leading Days Out Guide
P O Box 427
Northampton
NN2 7YJ
Tiverton Castle
Tiverton
Two For The Price Of One
not to be used in conjunction with any other offer, one coupon per party not valid on Bank Hols and event weekends.
Discount Coupon
Valid end Sept 2000
DAYS OUT UK
The Leading Days Out Guide
P O Box 427
Northampton
NN2 7YJ
Torre Abbey Historic House and Gallery
Torquay
One Child Free With Every Full Paying Adult
not to be used in conjunction with any other offer, one coupon per party not valid on Bank Hols and event weekends.
Discount Coupon
Valid until end Feb 2001
DAYS OUT UK
The Leading Days Out Guide
P O Box 427
Northampton
NN2 7YJ
Ugbrooke House
Newton Abbot
Two Adults For The Price Of One
not to be used in conjunction with any other offer, one coupon per party not valid on Bank Hols and event weekends.
Discount Coupon
Valid until 7 Sept 2000
DAYS OUT UK
The Leading Days Out Guide
P O Box 427
Northampton
NN2 7YJ
Plymouth Dome
Plymouth
Two For The Price Of One
not to be used in conjunction with any other offer, one coupon per party not valid on Bank Hols and event weekends.
Discount Coupon
Valid until end Feb 2000
DAYS OUT UK
The Leading Days Out Guide
P O Box 427
Northampton
NN2 7YJ
Otterton Mill Centre
Budleigh Salterton
Two For The Price Of One
not to be used in conjunction with any other offer, one coupon per party not valid on Bank Hols and event weekends.
Discount Coupon
Valid until end Feb 2001
DAYS OUT UK
The Leading Days Out Guide
P O Box 427
Northampton
NN2 7YJ
Lydford Gorge
Okehampton
One Child Free With Two Full Paying Adults
not to be used in conjunction with any other offer, one coupon per party not valid on Bank Hols and event weekends.
Discount Coupon
Valid until end Feb 2001

This coupon entitles the holder to the discount offer shown on the reverse side. To claim your discount please present this coupon when paying for your entry.

Customer care line number *free* phone 0800 316 8900

This coupon entitles the holder to the discount offer shown on the reverse side. To claim your discount please present this coupon when paying for your entry.

Customer care line number *free* phone 0800 316 8900

This coupon entitles the holder to the discount offer shown on the reverse side. To claim your discount please present this coupon when paying for your entry.

Customer care line number *free* phone 0800 316 8900

This coupon entitles the holder to the discount offer shown on the reverse side. To claim your discount please present this coupon when paying for your entry.

Customer care line number *free* phone 0800 316 8900

This coupon entitles the holder to the discount offer shown on the reverse side. To claim your discount please present this coupon when paying for your entry.

Customer care line number *free* phone 0800 316 8900

This coupon entitles the holder to the discount offer shown on the reverse side. To claim your discount please present this coupon when paying for your entry.

Customer care line number *free* phone 0800 316 8900

DAYS OUT UK
The Leading Days Out Guide
P O Box 427
Northampton
NN2 7YJ
Exmoor Steam Railway
Barnstaple
10% Off Admission Charges
not to be used in conjunction with any other offer, one coupon per party not valid on Bank Hols and event weekends.
Discount Coupon
Valid until end Feb 2001
DAYS OUT UK
The Leading Days Out Guide
P O Box 427
Northampton
NN2 7YJ
National Marine Aquarium
Plymouth
One Child Free With Two Full Paying Adults
not to be used in conjunction with any other offer, one coupon per party not valid on Bank Hols and event weekends.
Discount Coupon
Valid until end Feb 2001
DAYS OUT UK
The Leading Days Out Guide
P O Box 427
Northampton
NN2 7YJ
Combe Martin Wildlife and Dinosaur Park
Ilfracombe
One Child Free With Every Two Paying Adults
not to be used in conjunction with any other offer, one coupon per party not valid on Bank Hols and event weekends.
Discount Coupon
Valid until 30 Nov 2000
DAYS OUT UK
The Leading Days Out Guide
P O Box 427
Northampton
NN2 7YJ
Abbotsbury Swannery
Weymouth
Up To £3.00 Off. 50p Off Per Adult/OAP
Maximum Of Six Persons
not to be used in conjunction with any other offer, one coupon per party not valid on Bank Hols and event weekends.
Discount Coupon
Valid until 31 Oc 000
DAYS OUT UK
The Leading Days Out Guide
P O Box 427
Northampton
NN2 7YJ
Knoll Gardens and Nursery
Ferndown
One Adult or OAP at Half Price With One Full Paying Adult. Excl Bank Holidays
Maximum Two Persons Per Card
not to be used in conjunction with any other offer, one coupon per party not valid on Bank Hols and event weekends.
Discount Coupon
Valid until 29 Oct 2000
DAYS OUT UK
The Leading Days Out Guide
P O Box 427
Northampton
NN2 7YJ
Mapperton Gardens
Beaminster
Two Adults For The Price Of One
not to be used in conjunction with any other offer, one coupon per party not valid on Bank Hols and event weekends.
Discount Coupon
Valid until 31 Oc 000

This coupon entitles the holder to the discount offer shown on the reverse side. To claim your discount please present this coupon when paying for your entry.

Customer care line number *free* phone 0800 316 8900

This coupon entitles the holder to the discount offer shown on the reverse side. To claim your discount please present this coupon when paying for your entry.

Customer care line number *free* phone 0800 316 8900

This coupon entitles the holder to the discount offer shown on the reverse side. To claim your discount please present this coupon when paying for your entry.

Customer care line number *free* phone 0800 316 8900

This coupon entitles the holder to the discount offer shown on the reverse side. To claim your discount please present this coupon when paying for your entry.

Customer care line number *free* phone 0800 316 8900

This coupon entitles the holder to the discount offer shown on the reverse side. To claim your discount please present this coupon when paying for your entry.

Customer care line number *free* phone 0800 316 8900

This coupon entitles the holder to the discount offer shown on the reverse side. To claim your discount please present this coupon when paying for your entry.

Customer care line number *free* phone 0800 316 8900

DAYS OUT UK
The Leading Days Out Guide
P O Box 427
Northampton
NN2 7YJ

Brewers Quay and the Timewalk Journey

Weymouth

£1.50 Off A Family Ticket To Timewalk Journey

not to be used in conjunction with any other offer, one coupon per party not valid on Bank Hols and event weekends.

Discount Coupon **Valid until end Feb 2001**

DAYS OUT UK
The Leading Days Out Guide
P O Box 427
Northampton
NN2 7YJ

Athelhampton House and Gardens
Dorchester

£1.00 Off Adult/OAP Admision For House & Garden
OR £2.00 Off Family Ticket

not to be used in conjunction with any other offer, one coupon per party not valid on Bank Hols and event weekends.

Discount Coupon **Valid until end Feb 2001**

DAYS OUT UK
The Leading Days Out Guide
P O Box 427
Northampton
NN2 7YJ

Lulworth Castle
Wareham

Two For The Price Of One
(adult or child free with a full paying adult)

not to be used in conjunction with any other offer, one coupon per party not valid on Bank Hols and event weekends.

Discount Coupon **Valid until end Feb 2001**

DAYS OUT UK
The Leading Days Out Guide
P O Box 427
Northampton
NN2 7YJ

Blandford Forum Royal Signals Museum

Blandford Forum

Two For The Price Of One

not to be used in conjunction with any other offer, one coupon per party not valid on Bank Hols and event weekends.

Discount Coupon **Valid until end Feb 2001**

DAYS OUT UK
The Leading Days Out Guide
P O Box 427
Northampton
NN2 7YJ

Dorset County Museum
Dorchester

Second Adult/Child Free
With One Full Admission Paid

not to be used in conjunction with any other offer, one coupon per party not valid on Bank Hols and event weekends.

Discount Coupon **Valid until end Feb 2001**

DAYS OUT UK
The Leading Days Out Guide
P O Box 427
Northampton
NN2 7YJ

James Joyce Museum

Sandycove, Dublin

Two Admissions For The Price Of One

not to be used in conjunction with any other offer, one coupon per party not valid on Bank Hols and event weekends.

Discount Coupon **Valid until end Feb 2001**

This coupon entitles the holder to the discount offer shown on the reverse side. To claim your discount please present this coupon when paying for your entry.

Customer care line number *free* phone 0800 316 8900

This coupon entitles the holder to the discount offer shown on the reverse side. To claim your discount please present this coupon when paying for your entry.

Customer care line number *free* phone 0800 316 8900

This coupon entitles the holder to the discount offer shown on the reverse side. To claim your discount please present this coupon when paying for your entry.

Customer care line number *free* phone 0800 316 8900

This coupon entitles the holder to the discount offer shown on the reverse side. To claim your discount please present this coupon when paying for your entry.

Customer care line number *free* phone 0800 316 8900

This coupon entitles the holder to the discount offer shown on the reverse side. To claim your discount please present this coupon when paying for your entry.

Customer care line number *free* phone 0800 316 8900

This coupon entitles the holder to the discount offer shown on the reverse side. To claim your discount please present this coupon when paying for your entry.

Customer care line number *free* phone 0800 316 8900

DAYS OUT UK
The Leading Days Out Guide
P O Box 427
Northampton
NN2 7YJ

Fry Model Railway
Malahide, Dublin
Two For The Price Of One
not to be used in conjunction with any other offer, one coupon per party not valid on Bank Hols and event weekends.
Discount Coupon | **Valid until 31 Oct 2000**

DAYS OUT UK
The Leading Days Out Guide
P O Box 427
Northampton
NN2 7YJ

Barleylands Farm Museum and Visitors Centre
Billericay
Two For The Price Of One
not to be used in conjunction with any other offer, one coupon per party not valid on Bank Hols and event weekends.
Discount Coupon | **Valid until end Feb 2001**

DAYS OUT UK
The Leading Days Out Guide
P O Box 427
Northampton
NN2 7YJ

Colchester Castle Museum
Colchester
Two For The Price Of One
not to be used in conjunction with any other offer, one coupon per party not valid on Bank Hols and event weekends.
Discount Coupon | **Valid until end Feb 2001**

DAYS OUT UK
The Leading Days Out Guide
P O Box 427
Northampton
NN2 7YJ

Open Garden
Witham
Two For The Price Of One
not to be used in conjunction with any other offer, one coupon per party not valid on Bank Hols and event weekends.
Discount Coupon | **Valid until end Feb 2001**

DAYS OUT UK
The Leading Days Out Guide
P O Box 427
Northampton
NN2 7YJ

RHS Garden Hyde Hall
Chelmsford
Free Child Entry
not to be used in conjunction with any other offer, one coupon per party not valid on Bank Hols and event weekends.
Discount Coupon | **Valid until 29 Oct 2000**

DAYS OUT UK
The Leading Days Out Guide
P O Box 427
Northampton
NN2 7YJ

Hedingham Castle
Halstead
Two For The Price Of One
not to be used in conjunction with any other offer, one coupon per party not valid on Bank Hols and event weekends.
Discount Coupon | **Valid until end Feb 2001**

This coupon entitles the holder to the discount offer shown on the reverse side. To claim your discount please present this coupon when paying for your entry.

Customer care line number *free* phone 0800 316 8900

This coupon entitles the holder to the discount offer shown on the reverse side. To claim your discount please present this coupon when paying for your entry.

Customer care line number *free* phone 0800 316 8900

This coupon entitles the holder to the discount offer shown on the reverse side. To claim your discount please present this coupon when paying for your entry.

Customer care line number *free* phone 0800 316 8900

This coupon entitles the holder to the discount offer shown on the reverse side. To claim your discount please present this coupon when paying for your entry.

Customer care line number *free* phone 0800 316 8900

This coupon entitles the holder to the discount offer shown on the reverse side. To claim your discount please present this coupon when paying for your entry.

Customer care line number *free* phone 0800 316 8900

This coupon entitles the holder to the discount offer shown on the reverse side. To claim your discount please present this coupon when paying for your entry.

Customer care line number *free* phone 0800 316 8900

DAYS OUT UK
The Leading Days Out Guide
P O Box 427
Northampton
NN2 7YJ
Prinknash Abbey
Gloucester
10% Off Pottery Firsts
not to be used in conjunction with any other offer, one coupon per party not valid on Bank Hols and event weekends.
Discount Coupon
Valid until end Feb 2001
DAYS OUT UK
The Leading Days Out Guide
P O Box 427
Northampton
NN2 7YJ
Cotswold Farm Park
Cheltenham
One Child Free With A Full Paying Adult
not to be used in conjunction with any other offer, one coupon per party not valid on Bank Hols and event weekends.
Discount Coupon
Valid until 1 Oct 2000
DAYS OUT UK
The Leading Days Out Guide
P O Box 427
Northampton
NN2 7YJ
Nature in Art
Gloucester
One Child Free With Every Full Paying Adult
not to be used in conjunction with any other offer, one coupon per party not valid on Bank Hols and event weekends.
Discount Coupon
Valid until end Feb 2001
DAYS OUT UK
The Leading Days Out Guide
P O Box 427
Northampton
NN2 7YJ
Birdland
Cheltenham
10% Discount On Admission Prices
not to be used in conjunction with any other offer, one coupon per party not valid on Bank Hols and event weekends.
Discount Coupon
Valid until end Feb 2001
DAYS OUT UK
The Leading Days Out Guide
P O Box 427
Northampton
NN2 7YJ
Clearwell Caves Ancient Iron Mines
Coleford
Two For The Price Of One
not to be used in conjunction with any other offer, one coupon per party not valid on Bank Hols and event weekends.
Discount Coupon
Valid until end Feb 2001
DAYS OUT UK
The Leading Days Out Guide
P O Box 427
Northampton
NN2 7YJ
Robert Opie Collection Museum
Gloucester
30% Off Admission Price
not to be used in conjunction with any other offer, one coupon per party not valid on Bank Hols and event weekends.
Discount Coupon
Valid until end Feb 2001

This coupon entitles the holder to the discount offer shown on the reverse side. To claim your discount please present this coupon when paying for your entry.

Customer care line number *free* phone 0800 316 8900

This coupon entitles the holder to the discount offer shown on the reverse side. To claim your discount please present this coupon when paying for your entry.

Customer care line number *free* phone 0800 316 8900

This coupon entitles the holder to the discount offer shown on the reverse side. To claim your discount please present this coupon when paying for your entry.

Customer care line number *free* phone 0800 316 8900

This coupon entitles the holder to the discount offer shown on the reverse side. To claim your discount please present this coupon when paying for your entry.

Customer care line number *free* phone 0800 316 8900

This coupon entitles the holder to the discount offer shown on the reverse side. To claim your discount please present this coupon when paying for your entry.

Customer care line number *free* phone 0800 316 8900

This coupon entitles the holder to the discount offer shown on the reverse side. To claim your discount please present this coupon when paying for your entry.

Customer care line number *free* phone 0800 316 8900

DAYS OUT UK
The Leading Days Out Guide
P O Box 427
Northampton
NN2 7YJ

Batsford Arboretum

Moreton-In-Marsh

£1.00 Off Two Adults Or Two OAPs Admission

not to be used in conjunction with any other offer, one coupon per party not valid on Bank Hols and event weekends.

Discount Coupon **Valid until end Feb 2001**

DAYS OUT UK
The Leading Days Out Guide
P O Box 427
Northampton
NN2 7YJ

Bourton House Garden

Bourton On The Hill

Two For The Price Of One

not to be used in conjunction with any other offer, one coupon per party not valid on Bank Hols and event weekends.

Discount Coupon **Valid until end Feb 2001**

DAYS OUT UK
The Leading Days Out Guide
P O Box 427
Northampton
NN2 7YJ

Painswick Rococo Garden

Stroud

Two For The Price Of One

not to be used in conjunction with any other offer, one coupon per party not valid on Bank Hols and event weekends.

Discount Coupon **Valid until 30 Nov 2000**

DAYS OUT UK
The Leading Days Out Guide
P O Box 427
Northampton
NN2 7YJ

Cotswold Heritage Centre

Cheltenham

Two For The Price Of One

not to be used in conjunction with any other offer, one coupon per party not valid on Bank Hols and event weekends.

Discount Coupon **Valid until end Feb 2001**

DAYS OUT UK
The Leading Days Out Guide
P O Box 427
Northampton
NN2 7YJ

Dean Heritage Centre

Cinderford

One Child Free With Every Full Paying Adult

not to be used in conjunction with any other offer, one coupon per party not valid on Bank Hols and event weekends.

Discount Coupon **Valid until end Feb 2001**

DAYS OUT UK
The Leading Days Out Guide
P O Box 427
Northampton
NN2 7YJ

Dyrham Park

Chippenham

One Adult Free With One Full Paying Adult

not to be used in conjunction with any other offer, one coupon per party not valid on Bank Hols and event weekends.

Discount Coupon **Valid until end Feb 2001**

This coupon entitles the holder to the discount offer shown on the reverse side. To claim your discount please present this coupon when paying for your entry.

Customer care line number *free* phone 0800 316 8900

This coupon entitles the holder to the discount offer shown on the reverse side. To claim your discount please present this coupon when paying for your entry.

Customer care line number *free* phone 0800 316 8900

This coupon entitles the holder to the discount offer shown on the reverse side. To claim your discount please present this coupon when paying for your entry.

Customer care line number *free* phone 0800 316 8900

This coupon entitles the holder to the discount offer shown on the reverse side. To claim your discount please present this coupon when paying for your entry.

Customer care line number *free* phone 0800 316 8900

This coupon entitles the holder to the discount offer shown on the reverse side. To claim your discount please present this coupon when paying for your entry.

Customer care line number *free* phone 0800 316 8900

This coupon entitles the holder to the discount offer shown on the reverse side. To claim your discount please present this coupon when paying for your entry.

Customer care line number *free* phone 0800 316 8900

DAYS OUT UK
The Leading Days Out Guide
P O Box 427
Northampton
NN2 7YJ
Owlpen Manor
Dursley
Two For The Price Of One
Excludes Sundays and Bank Holiday Mondays
not to be used in conjunction with any other offer, one coupon per party not valid on Bank Hols and event weekends.
Discount Coupon
Valid until end Feb 2001
DAYS OUT UK
The Leading Days Out Guide
P O Box 427
Northampton
NN2 7YJ
Dean Forest Railway
Lydney
Two For The Price Of One
not to be used in conjunction with any other offer, one coupon per party not valid on Bank Hols and event weekends.
Discount Coupon
Valid until end Feb 2001
DAYS OUT UK
The Leading Days Out Guide
P O Box 427
Northampton
NN2 7YJ
Corinium Museum
Cirencester
Two For The Price Of One
not to be used in conjunction with any other offer, one coupon per party not valid on Bank Hols and event weekends.
Discount Coupon
Valid until end Feb 2001
DAYS OUT UK
The Leading Days Out Guide
P O Box 427
Northampton
NN2 7YJ
Cotswold Water Park and Keynes Country Park
Cirencester
Car Parking Discount 50% for Keynes Country Park
not to be used in conjunction with any other offer, one coupon per party not valid on Bank Hols and event weekends.
Discount Coupon
Valid until end Feb 2001
DAYS OUT UK
The Leading Days Out Guide
P O Box 427
Northampton
NN2 7YJ
National Waterways Museum
Gloucester
20% Discount On Single Entry Ticket To Museum
not to be used in conjunction with any other offer, one coupon per party not valid on Bank Hols and event weekends.
Discount Coupon
Valid until 26 Nov 2000
DAYS OUT UK
The Leading Days Out Guide
P O Box 427
Northampton
NN2 7YJ
The Lowry
Salford
25% Discounts On Artwork Tickets
not to be used in conjunction with any other offer, one coupon per party not valid on Bank Hols and event weekends.
Discount Coupon
Valid until end Feb 2001

This coupon entitles the holder to the discount offer shown on the reverse side. To claim your discount please present this coupon when paying for your entry.

Customer care line number *free* phone 0800 316 8900

This coupon entitles the holder to the discount offer shown on the reverse side. To claim your discount please present this coupon when paying for your entry.

Customer care line number *free* phone 0800 316 8900

This coupon entitles the holder to the discount offer shown on the reverse side. To claim your discount please present this coupon when paying for your entry.

Customer care line number *free* phone 0800 316 8900

This coupon entitles the holder to the discount offer shown on the reverse side. To claim your discount please present this coupon when paying for your entry.

Customer care line number *free* phone 0800 316 8900

This coupon entitles the holder to the discount offer shown on the reverse side. To claim your discount please present this coupon when paying for your entry.

Customer care line number *free* phone 0800 316 8900

This coupon entitles the holder to the discount offer shown on the reverse side. To claim your discount please present this coupon when paying for your entry.

Customer care line number *free* phone 0800 316 8900

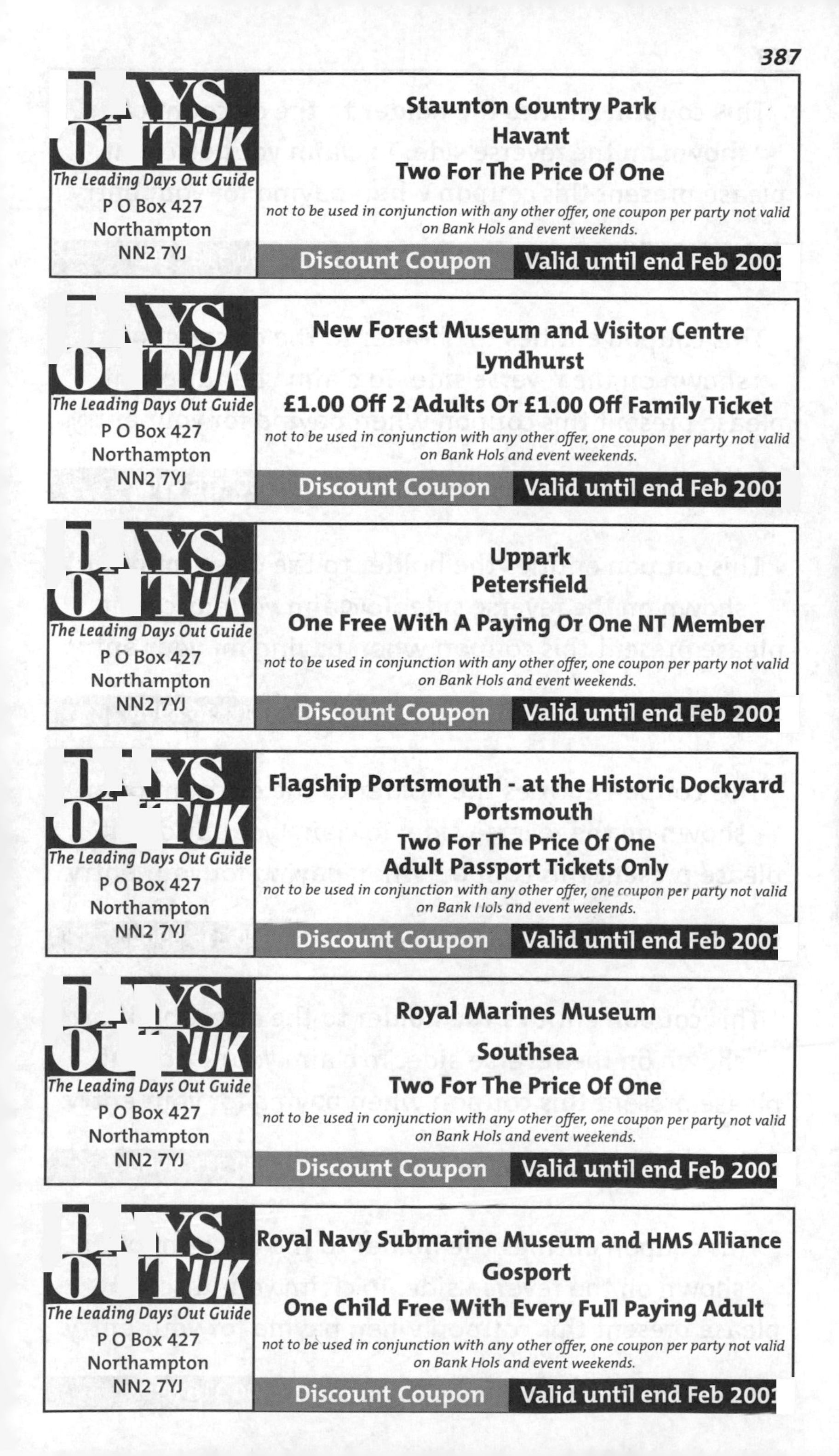

DAYS OUT UK
The Leading Days Out Guide
P O Box 427
Northampton
NN2 7YJ
Staunton Country Park
Havant
Two For The Price Of One
not to be used in conjunction with any other offer, one coupon per party not valid on Bank Hols and event weekends.
Discount Coupon
Valid until end Feb 2001
DAYS OUT UK
The Leading Days Out Guide
P O Box 427
Northampton
NN2 7YJ
New Forest Museum and Visitor Centre
Lyndhurst
£1.00 Off 2 Adults Or £1.00 Off Family Ticket
not to be used in conjunction with any other offer, one coupon per party not valid on Bank Hols and event weekends.
Discount Coupon
Valid until end Feb 2001
DAYS OUT UK
The Leading Days Out Guide
P O Box 427
Northampton
NN2 7YJ
Uppark
Petersfield
One Free With A Paying Or One NT Member
not to be used in conjunction with any other offer, one coupon per party not valid on Bank Hols and event weekends.
Discount Coupon
Valid until end Feb 2001
DAYS OUT UK
The Leading Days Out Guide
P O Box 427
Northampton
NN2 7YJ
Flagship Portsmouth - at the Historic Dockyard
Portsmouth
Two For The Price Of One
Adult Passport Tickets Only
not to be used in conjunction with any other offer, one coupon per party not valid on Bank Hols and event weekends.
Discount Coupon
Valid until end Feb 2001
DAYS OUT UK
The Leading Days Out Guide
P O Box 427
Northampton
NN2 7YJ
Royal Marines Museum
Southsea
Two For The Price Of One
not to be used in conjunction with any other offer, one coupon per party not valid on Bank Hols and event weekends.
Discount Coupon
Valid until end Feb 2001
DAYS OUT UK
The Leading Days Out Guide
P O Box 427
Northampton
NN2 7YJ
Royal Navy Submarine Museum and HMS Alliance
Gosport
One Child Free With Every Full Paying Adult
not to be used in conjunction with any other offer, one coupon per party not valid on Bank Hols and event weekends.
Discount Coupon
Valid until end Feb 2001

This coupon entitles the holder to the discount offer shown on the reverse side. To claim your discount please present this coupon when paying for your entry.

Customer care line number *free* phone 0800 316 8900

This coupon entitles the holder to the discount offer shown on the reverse side. To claim your discount please present this coupon when paying for your entry.

Customer care line number *free* phone 0800 316 8900

This coupon entitles the holder to the discount offer shown on the reverse side. To claim your discount please present this coupon when paying for your entry.

Customer care line number *free* phone 0800 316 8900

This coupon entitles the holder to the discount offer shown on the reverse side. To claim your discount please present this coupon when paying for your entry.

Customer care line number *free* phone 0800 316 8900

This coupon entitles the holder to the discount offer shown on the reverse side. To claim your discount please present this coupon when paying for your entry.

Customer care line number *free* phone 0800 316 8900

This coupon entitles the holder to the discount offer shown on the reverse side. To claim your discount please present this coupon when paying for your entry.

Customer care line number *free* phone 0800 316 8900

The Leading Days Out Guide
P O Box 427
Northampton
NN2 7YJ
Airborne Forces Museum
Aldershot
One Child Free When Accompanied By Full Paying Adults Excludes Bank Holiday Weekends
not to be used in conjunction with any other offer, one coupon per party not valid on Bank Hols and event weekends.
Discount Coupon
Valid until end Feb 2001
The Leading Days Out Guide
P O Box 427
Northampton
NN2 7YJ
Museum of Army Flying
Stockbridge
Two For The Price Of One NOT valid for Special Events & The International Air Show
not to be used in conjunction with any other offer, one coupon per party not valid on Bank Hols and event weekends.
Discount Coupon
Valid until end Feb 2001
The Leading Days Out Guide
P O Box 427
Northampton
NN2 7YJ
Sandham Memorial Chapel
Burghclere
Two For The Price Of One
not to be used in conjunction with any other offer, one coupon per party not valid on Bank Hols and event weekends.
Discount Coupon
Valid until 26 Nov 2000
The Leading Days Out Guide
P O Box 427
Northampton
NN2 7YJ
Rockbourne Roman Villa
Fordingbridge
Two For The Price of One
not to be used in conjunction with any other offer, one coupon per party not valid on Bank Hols and event weekends.
Discount Coupon
Valid until end Feb 2001
The Leading Days Out Guide
P O Box 427
Northampton
NN2 7YJ
Stansted House
Rowlands Castle
Two For The Price Of One on Tue & Wed
(excludes special events)
not to be used in conjunction with any other offer, one coupon per party not valid on Bank Hols and event weekends.
Discount Coupon
Valid until end Feb 2001
The Leading Days Out Guide
P O Box 427
Northampton
NN2 7YJ
Sammy Miller Museum
New Milton
50p Discount On Adult Admission
not to be used in conjunction with any other offer, one coupon per party not valid on Bank Hols and event weekends.
Discount Coupon
Valid until end Feb 2001

This coupon entitles the holder to the discount offer shown on the reverse side. To claim your discount please present this coupon when paying for your entry.

Customer care line number *free* phone 0800 316 8900

This coupon entitles the holder to the discount offer shown on the reverse side. To claim your discount please present this coupon when paying for your entry.

Customer care line number *free* phone 0800 316 8900

This coupon entitles the holder to the discount offer shown on the reverse side. To claim your discount please present this coupon when paying for your entry.

Customer care line number *free* phone 0800 316 8900

This coupon entitles the holder to the discount offer shown on the reverse side. To claim your discount please present this coupon when paying for your entry.

Customer care line number *free* phone 0800 316 8900

This coupon entitles the holder to the discount offer shown on the reverse side. To claim your discount please present this coupon when paying for your entry.

Customer care line number *free* phone 0800 316 8900

This coupon entitles the holder to the discount offer shown on the reverse side. To claim your discount please present this coupon when paying for your entry.

Customer care line number *free* phone 0800 316 8900

DAYS OUT UK
The Leading Days Out Guide
P O Box 427
Northampton
NN2 7YJ
Hergest Croft Gardens
Kington
Two For The Price Of One
(except 1 May - Flower Fair)
not to be used in conjunction with any other offer, one coupon per party not valid on Bank Hols and event weekends.
Discount Coupon
Valid Apr-Oct 2000
DAYS OUT UK
The Leading Days Out Guide
P O Box 427
Northampton
NN2 7YJ
Berrington Hall
Leominster
Two For The Price Of One
not to be used in conjunction with any other offer, one coupon per party not valid on Bank Hols and event weekends.
Discount Coupon
Valid until end Feb 2001
DAYS OUT UK
The Leading Days Out Guide
P O Box 427
Northampton
NN2 7YJ
Kinnersley Castle
Kinnersley
Two For The Price Of One
not to be used in conjunction with any other offer, one coupon per party not valid on Bank Hols and event weekends.
Discount Coupon
Valid until end Feb 2001
DAYS OUT UK
The Leading Days Out Guide
P O Box 427
Northampton
NN2 7YJ
Knebworth House, Gardens and Country Park
Knebworth
Two For The Price Of One
not to be used in conjunction with any other offer, one coupon per party not valid on Bank Hols and event weekends.
Discount Coupon
Valid until end Feb 2001
DAYS OUT UK
The Leading Days Out Guide
P O Box 427
Northampton
NN2 7YJ
Gardens of The Rose (Royal National Rose Society)
St. Albans
Two For The Price Of One
not to be used in conjunction with any other offer, one coupon per party not valid on Bank Hols and event weekends.
Discount Coupon
Valid until end Feb 2001
DAYS OUT UK
The Leading Days Out Guide
P O Box 427
Northampton
NN2 7YJ
Hatfield House, Park and Gardens
Hatfield
Two For The Price Of One
(Excludes Mon & Fri and major special events)
not to be used in conjunction with any other offer, one coupon per party not valid on Bank Hols and event weekends.
Discount Coupon
Valid until end Feb 2001

This coupon entitles the holder to the discount offer shown on the reverse side. To claim your discount please present this coupon when paying for your entry.

Customer care line number *free* phone 0800 316 8900

This coupon entitles the holder to the discount offer shown on the reverse side. To claim your discount please present this coupon when paying for your entry.

Customer care line number *free* phone 0800 316 8900

This coupon entitles the holder to the discount offer shown on the reverse side. To claim your discount please present this coupon when paying for your entry.

Customer care line number *free* phone 0800 316 8900

This coupon entitles the holder to the discount offer shown on the reverse side. To claim your discount please present this coupon when paying for your entry.

Customer care line number *free* phone 0800 316 8900

This coupon entitles the holder to the discount offer shown on the reverse side. To claim your discount please present this coupon when paying for your entry.

Customer care line number *free* phone 0800 316 8900

This coupon entitles the holder to the discount offer shown on the reverse side. To claim your discount please present this coupon when paying for your entry.

Customer care line number *free* phone 0800 316 8900

393
DAYS OUT UK
The Leading Days Out Guide
P O Box 427
Northampton
NN2 7YJ
Forge Museum and Victorian Cottage Garden
Much Hadham
Two For The Price Of One
not to be used in conjunction with any other offer, one coupon per party not valid on Bank Hols and event weekends.
Discount Coupon
Valid until end Feb 2001
DAYS OUT UK
The Leading Days Out Guide
P O Box 427
Northampton
NN2 7YJ
Cromer Windmill
Stevenage
Two Adults For The Price Of One
not to be used in conjunction with any other offer, one coupon per party not valid on Bank Hols and event weekends.
Discount Coupon
Valid until end Feb 2001
DAYS OUT UK
The Leading Days Out Guide
P O Box 427
Northampton
NN2 7YJ
Mill Green Museum and Mill
Hatfield
20p Off A Bag Of Mill Green Flour Any Size
not to be used in conjunction with any other offer, one coupon per party not valid on Bank Hols and event weekends.
Discount Coupon
Valid until end Feb 2001
DAYS OUT UK
The Leading Days Out Guide
P O Box 427
Northampton
NN2 7YJ
Walter Rothschild Zoological Museum
Tring
Two For The Price Of One
not to be used in conjunction with any other offer, one coupon per party not valid on Bank Hols and event weekends.
Discount Coupon
Valid until end Feb 2001
DAYS OUT UK
The Leading Days Out Guide
P O Box 427
Northampton
NN2 7YJ
Verulamium Museum and Park
St. Albans
Two For The Price Of One
not to be used in conjunction with any other offer, one coupon per party not valid on Bank Hols and event weekends.
Discount Coupon
Valid until end Feb 2001
DAYS OUT UK
The Leading Days Out Guide
P O Box 427
Northampton
NN2 7YJ
Welwyn Roman Baths
Welwyn
A Free Colour Postcard
not to be used in conjunction with any other offer, one coupon per party not valid on Bank Hols and event weekends.
Discount Coupon
Valid until 30 Nov 2000

This coupon entitles the holder to the discount offer shown on the reverse side. To claim your discount please present this coupon when paying for your entry.

Customer care line number *free* phone 0800 316 8900

This coupon entitles the holder to the discount offer shown on the reverse side. To claim your discount please present this coupon when paying for your entry.

Customer care line number *free* phone 0800 316 8900

This coupon entitles the holder to the discount offer shown on the reverse side. To claim your discount please present this coupon when paying for your entry.

Customer care line number *free* phone 0800 316 8900

This coupon entitles the holder to the discount offer shown on the reverse side. To claim your discount please present this coupon when paying for your entry.

Customer care line number *free* phone 0800 316 8900

This coupon entitles the holder to the discount offer shown on the reverse side. To claim your discount please present this coupon when paying for your entry.

Customer care line number *free* phone 0800 316 8900

This coupon entitles the holder to the discount offer shown on the reverse side. To claim your discount please present this coupon when paying for your entry.

Customer care line number *free* phone 0800 316 8900

DAYS OUT UK
The Leading Days Out Guide
P O Box 427
Northampton
NN2 7YJ
Willersmill Wildlife Park
Nr Royston
One Child Free With A Full Paying Adult
(One Per Family)
not to be used in conjunction with any other offer, one coupon per party not valid on Bank Hols and event weekends.
Discount Coupon
Valid until end Feb 2001
DAYS OUT UK
The Leading Days Out Guide
P O Box 427
Northampton
NN2 7YJ
Mount Stewart House, Garden & Temple
Newtownards
Two Adults For The Price Of One
not to be used in conjunction with any other offer, one coupon per party not valid on Bank Hols and event weekends.
Discount Coupon
Valid until end Feb 2001
DAYS OUT UK
The Leading Days Out Guide
P O Box 427
Northampton
NN2 7YJ
Newbridge House and Traditional Farm
Donabate
Two For The Price Of One
not to be used in conjunction with any other offer, one coupon per party not valid on Bank Hols and event weekends.
Discount Coupon
Valid until end Feb 2001
DAYS OUT UK
The Leading Days Out Guide
P O Box 427
Northampton
NN2 7YJ
Shaw Birthplace
Dublin
Two For The Price Of One
not to be used in conjunction with any other offer, one coupon per party not valid on Bank Hols and event weekends.
Discount Coupon
Valid until 31 Oct 2000
DAYS OUT UK
The Leading Days Out Guide
P O Box 427
Northampton
NN2 7YJ
Dublin Writers Museum
Dublin
Two For The Price Of One
not to be used in conjunction with any other offer, one coupon per party not valid on Bank Hols and event weekends.
Discount Coupon
Valid until end Feb 2001
DAYS OUT UK
The Leading Days Out Guide
P O Box 427
Northampton
NN2 7YJ
Dublin's Viking Adventure
Temple Bar, Dublin
Two For The Price of One
not to be used in conjunction with any other offer, one coupon per party not valid on Bank Hols and event weekends.
Discount Coupon
Valid until 30 Oct 2000

This coupon entitles the holder to the discount offer shown on the reverse side. To claim your discount please present this coupon when paying for your entry.

Customer care line number *free* phone 0800 316 8900

This coupon entitles the holder to the discount offer shown on the reverse side. To claim your discount please present this coupon when paying for your entry.

Customer care line number *free* phone 0800 316 8900

This coupon entitles the holder to the discount offer shown on the reverse side. To claim your discount please present this coupon when paying for your entry.

Customer care line number *free* phone 0800 316 8900

This coupon entitles the holder to the discount offer shown on the reverse side. To claim your discount please present this coupon when paying for your entry.

Customer care line number *free* phone 0800 316 8900

This coupon entitles the holder to the discount offer shown on the reverse side. To claim your discount please present this coupon when paying for your entry.

Customer care line number *free* phone 0800 316 8900

This coupon entitles the holder to the discount offer shown on the reverse side. To claim your discount please present this coupon when paying for your entry.

Customer care line number *free* phone 0800 316 8900

DAYS OUT UK
The Leading Days Out Guide
P O Box 427
Northampton
NN2 7YJ

Leslie Hill Open Farm
County Antrim
Two For The Price Of One
not to be used in conjunction with any other offer, one coupon per party not valid on Bank Hols and event weekends.
Discount Coupon | Valid Easter-30 Sept 2000

DAYS OUT UK
The Leading Days Out Guide
P O Box 427
Northampton
NN2 7YJ

Ardgillan Castle
Balbriggan
Two Adults For The Price Of One
not to be used in conjunction with any other offer, one coupon per party not valid on Bank Hols and event weekends.
Discount Coupon | Valid until end Feb 2001

DAYS OUT UK
The Leading Days Out Guide
P O Box 427
Northampton
NN2 7YJ

Tower Museum
County Londonderry
Two For The Price Of One
not to be used in conjunction with any other offer, one coupon per party not valid on Bank Hols and event weekends.
Discount Coupon | Valid until end Feb 2001

DAYS OUT UK
The Leading Days Out Guide
P O Box 427
Northampton
NN2 7YJ

Belfast Castle
County Antrim
A Discount Of 10% On The Total Food Bill In Cellar Restaurant (2-10 Persons)
not to be used in conjunction with any other offer, one coupon per party not valid on Bank Hols and event weekends.
Discount Coupon | Valid until end Feb 2001

DAYS OUT UK
The Leading Days Out Guide
P O Box 427
Northampton
NN2 7YJ

Carrickfergus Castle
County Antrim
Two For The Price Of One
not to be used in conjunction with any other offer, one coupon per party not valid on Bank Hols and event weekends.
Discount Coupon | Valid until end Feb 2001

DAYS OUT UK
The Leading Days Out Guide
P O Box 427
Northampton
NN2 7YJ

Castle Coole
County Fermanagh
Two For The Price Of One
not to be used in conjunction with any other offer, one coupon per party not valid on Bank Hols and event weekends.
Discount Coupon | Valid until 26 Sept 2000

This coupon entitles the holder to the discount offer shown on the reverse side. To claim your discount please present this coupon when paying for your entry.

Customer care line number *free* phone 0800 316 8900

This coupon entitles the holder to the discount offer shown on the reverse side. To claim your discount please present this coupon when paying for your entry.

Customer care line number *free* phone 0800 316 8900

This coupon entitles the holder to the discount offer shown on the reverse side. To claim your discount please present this coupon when paying for your entry.

Customer care line number *free* phone 0800 316 8900

This coupon entitles the holder to the discount offer shown on the reverse side. To claim your discount please present this coupon when paying for your entry.

Customer care line number *free* phone 0800 316 8900

This coupon entitles the holder to the discount offer shown on the reverse side. To claim your discount please present this coupon when paying for your entry.

Customer care line number *free* phone 0800 316 8900

This coupon entitles the holder to the discount offer shown on the reverse side. To claim your discount please present this coupon when paying for your entry.

Customer care line number *free* phone 0800 316 8900

DAYS OUT UK
The Leading Days Out Guide
P O Box 427
Northampton
NN2 7YJ
Dunluce Castle
County Antrim
Two For The Price Of One
not to be used in conjunction with any other offer, one coupon per party not valid on Bank Hols and event weekends.
Discount Coupon
Valid until end Feb 2001
DAYS OUT UK
The Leading Days Out Guide
P O Box 427
Northampton
NN2 7YJ
Malahide Castle
Malahide
Two For The Price Of One
not to be used in conjunction with any other offer, one coupon per party not valid on Bank Hols and event weekends.
Discount Coupon
Valid until end Feb 2001
DAYS OUT UK
The Leading Days Out Guide
P O Box 427
Northampton
NN2 7YJ
Curraghs Wildlife Park
Ballaugh
One Third Off Admission Prices
A£2.40 C£1.20
not to be used in conjunction with any other offer, one coupon per party not valid on Bank Hols and event weekends.
Discount Coupon
Valid until end Feb 2001
DAYS OUT UK
The Leading Days Out Guide
P O Box 427
Northampton
NN2 7YJ
Appuldurcombe House
Ventnor
One Child Free With A Full Paying Adult
(for Appuldurcombe House only)
not to be used in conjunction with any other offer, one coupon per party not valid on Bank Hols and event weekends.
Discount Coupon
Valid until 31 Oct 2000
DAYS OUT UK
The Leading Days Out Guide
P O Box 427
Northampton
NN2 7YJ
Haseley Manor
Newport
One Child Free With A Full Paying Adult
not to be used in conjunction with any other offer, one coupon per party not valid on Bank Hols and event weekends.
Discount Coupon
Valid 31 Oct 2000
DAYS OUT UK
The Leading Days Out Guide
P O Box 427
Northampton
NN2 7YJ
Morton Manor
Sandown
Two For The Price Of One
not to be used in conjunction with any other offer, one coupon per party not valid on Bank Hols and event weekends.
Discount Coupon
Valid until end Feb 2001

This coupon entitles the holder to the discount offer shown on the reverse side. To claim your discount please present this coupon when paying for your entry.

Customer care line number *free* phone 0800 316 8900

This coupon entitles the holder to the discount offer shown on the reverse side. To claim your discount please present this coupon when paying for your entry.

Customer care line number *free* phone 0800 316 8900

This coupon entitles the holder to the discount offer shown on the reverse side. To claim your discount please present this coupon when paying for your entry.

Customer care line number *free* phone 0800 316 8900

This coupon entitles the holder to the discount offer shown on the reverse side. To claim your discount please present this coupon when paying for your entry.

Customer care line number *free* phone 0800 316 8900

This coupon entitles the holder to the discount offer shown on the reverse side. To claim your discount please present this coupon when paying for your entry.

Customer care line number *free* phone 0800 316 8900

This coupon entitles the holder to the discount offer shown on the reverse side. To claim your discount please present this coupon when paying for your entry.

Customer care line number *free* phone 0800 316 8900

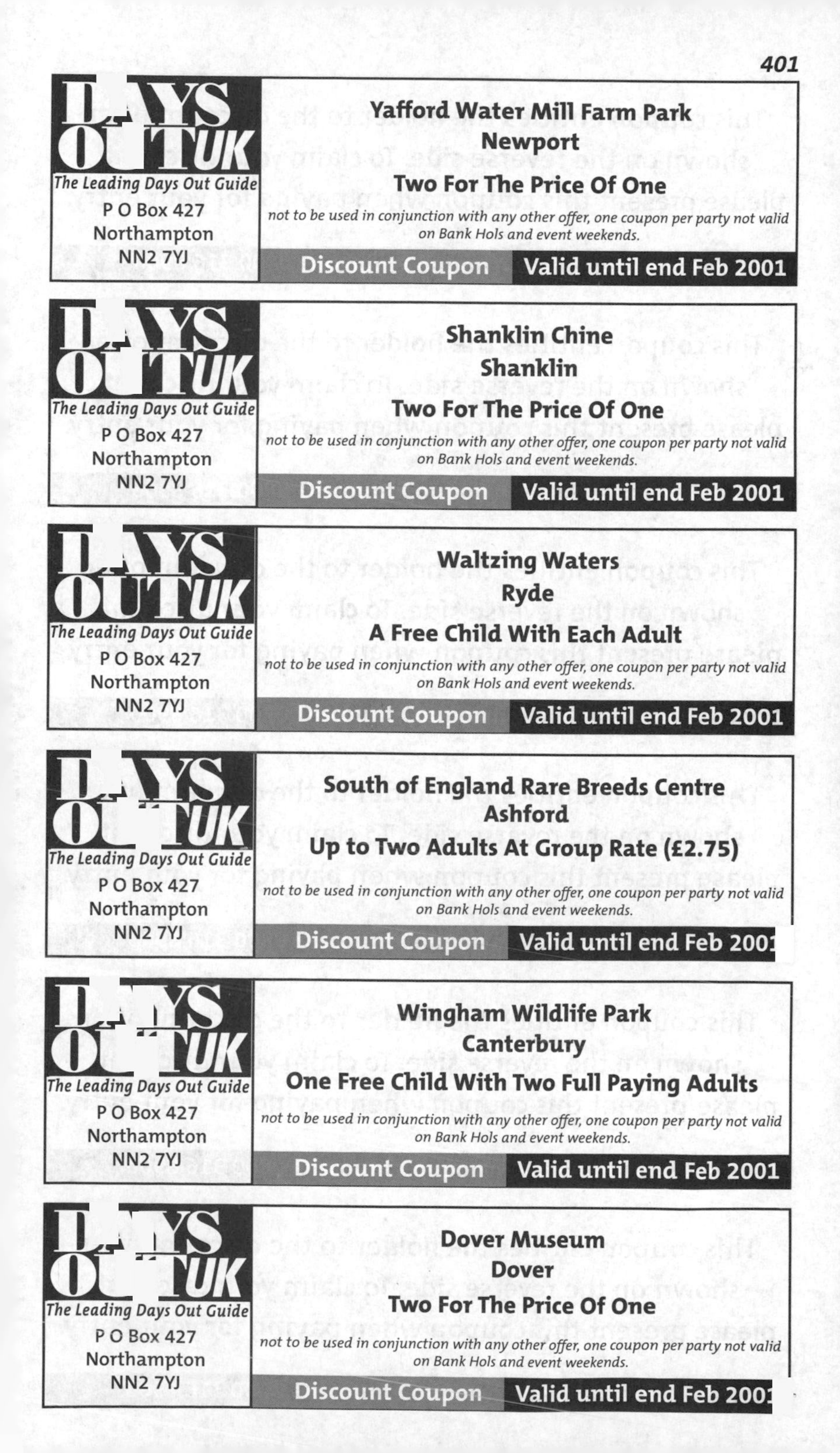
DAYS OUT UK
The Leading Days Out Guide
P O Box 427
Northampton
NN2 7YJ
Yafford Water Mill Farm Park
Newport
Two For The Price Of One
not to be used in conjunction with any other offer, one coupon per party not valid on Bank Hols and event weekends.
Discount Coupon
Valid until end Feb 2001
DAYS OUT UK
The Leading Days Out Guide
P O Box 427
Northampton
NN2 7YJ
Shanklin Chine
Shanklin
Two For The Price Of One
not to be used in conjunction with any other offer, one coupon per party not valid on Bank Hols and event weekends.
Discount Coupon
Valid until end Feb 2001
DAYS OUT UK
The Leading Days Out Guide
P O Box 427
Northampton
NN2 7YJ
Waltzing Waters
Ryde
A Free Child With Each Adult
not to be used in conjunction with any other offer, one coupon per party not valid on Bank Hols and event weekends.
Discount Coupon
Valid until end Feb 2001
DAYS OUT UK
The Leading Days Out Guide
P O Box 427
Northampton
NN2 7YJ
South of England Rare Breeds Centre
Ashford
Up to Two Adults At Group Rate (£2.75)
not to be used in conjunction with any other offer, one coupon per party not valid on Bank Hols and event weekends.
Discount Coupon
Valid until end Feb 2001
DAYS OUT UK
The Leading Days Out Guide
P O Box 427
Northampton
NN2 7YJ
Wingham Wildlife Park
Canterbury
One Free Child With Two Full Paying Adults
not to be used in conjunction with any other offer, one coupon per party not valid on Bank Hols and event weekends.
Discount Coupon
Valid until end Feb 2001
DAYS OUT UK
The Leading Days Out Guide
P O Box 427
Northampton
NN2 7YJ
Dover Museum
Dover
Two For The Price Of One
not to be used in conjunction with any other offer, one coupon per party not valid on Bank Hols and event weekends.
Discount Coupon
Valid until end Feb 2001

This coupon entitles the holder to the discount offer shown on the reverse side. To claim your discount please present this coupon when paying for your entry.

Customer care line number *free* phone 0800 316 8900

This coupon entitles the holder to the discount offer shown on the reverse side. To claim your discount please present this coupon when paying for your entry.

Customer care line number *free* phone 0800 316 8900

This coupon entitles the holder to the discount offer shown on the reverse side. To claim your discount please present this coupon when paying for your entry.

Customer care line number *free* phone 0800 316 8900

This coupon entitles the holder to the discount offer shown on the reverse side. To claim your discount please present this coupon when paying for your entry.

Customer care line number *free* phone 0800 316 8900

This coupon entitles the holder to the discount offer shown on the reverse side. To claim your discount please present this coupon when paying for your entry.

Customer care line number *free* phone 0800 316 8900

This coupon entitles the holder to the discount offer shown on the reverse side. To claim your discount please present this coupon when paying for your entry.

Customer care line number *free* phone 0800 316 8900

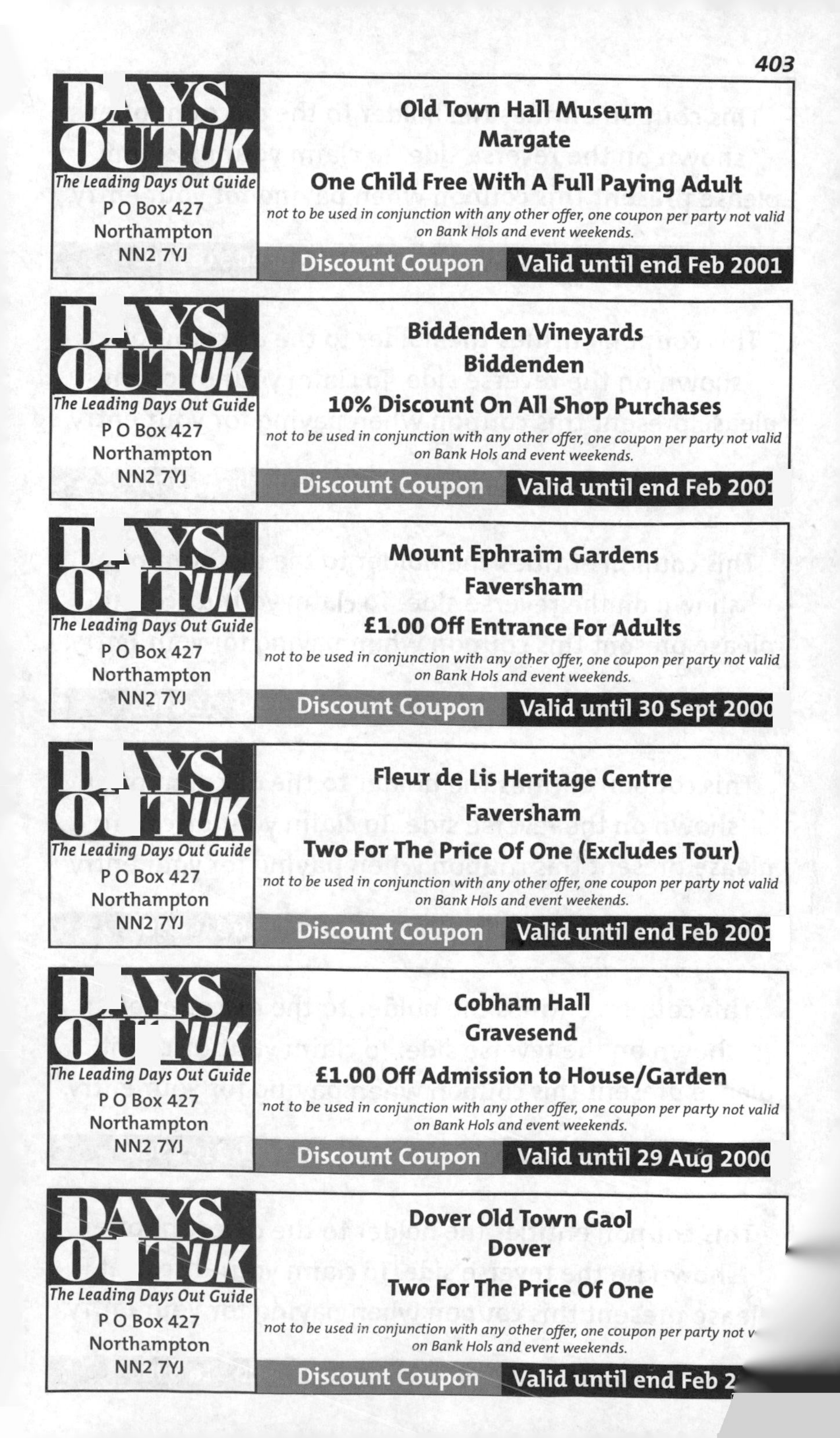
DAYS OUT UK
The Leading Days Out Guide
P O Box 427
Northampton
NN2 7YJ
Old Town Hall Museum
Margate
One Child Free With A Full Paying Adult
not to be used in conjunction with any other offer, one coupon per party not valid on Bank Hols and event weekends.
Discount Coupon
Valid until end Feb 2001
DAYS OUT UK
The Leading Days Out Guide
P O Box 427
Northampton
NN2 7YJ
Biddenden Vineyards
Biddenden
10% Discount On All Shop Purchases
not to be used in conjunction with any other offer, one coupon per party not valid on Bank Hols and event weekends.
Discount Coupon
Valid until end Feb 2001
DAYS OUT UK
The Leading Days Out Guide
P O Box 427
Northampton
NN2 7YJ
Mount Ephraim Gardens
Faversham
£1.00 Off Entrance For Adults
not to be used in conjunction with any other offer, one coupon per party not valid on Bank Hols and event weekends.
Discount Coupon
Valid until 30 Sept 2000
DAYS OUT UK
The Leading Days Out Guide
P O Box 427
Northampton
NN2 7YJ
Fleur de Lis Heritage Centre
Faversham
Two For The Price Of One (Excludes Tour)
not to be used in conjunction with any other offer, one coupon per party not valid on Bank Hols and event weekends.
Discount Coupon
Valid until end Feb 2001
DAYS OUT UK
The Leading Days Out Guide
P O Box 427
Northampton
NN2 7YJ
Cobham Hall
Gravesend
£1.00 Off Admission to House/Garden
not to be used in conjunction with any other offer, one coupon per party not valid on Bank Hols and event weekends.
Discount Coupon
Valid until 29 Aug 2000
DAYS OUT UK
The Leading Days Out Guide
P O Box 427
Northampton
NN2 7YJ
Dover Old Town Gaol
Dover
Two For The Price Of One
not to be used in conjunction with any other offer, one coupon per party not v
on Bank Hols and event weekends.
Discount Coupon
Valid until end Feb 2

This coupon entitles the holder to the discount offer shown on the reverse side. To claim your discount please present this coupon when paying for your entry.

Customer care line number *free* phone 0800 316 8900

This coupon entitles the holder to the discount offer shown on the reverse side. To claim your discount please present this coupon when paying for your entry.

Customer care line number *free* phone 0800 316 8900

This coupon entitles the holder to the discount offer shown on the reverse side. To claim your discount please present this coupon when paying for your entry.

Customer care line number *free* phone 0800 316 8900

This coupon entitles the holder to the discount offer shown on the reverse side. To claim your discount please present this coupon when paying for your entry.

Customer care line number *free* phone 0800 316 8900

This coupon entitles the holder to the discount offer shown on the reverse side. To claim your discount please present this coupon when paying for your entry.

Customer care line number *free* phone 0800 316 8900

This coupon entitles the holder to the discount offer shown on the reverse side. To claim your discount lease present this coupon when paying for your entry.

Customer care line number *free* phone 0800 316 8900

DAYS OUT UK
The Leading Days Out Guide
P O Box 427
Northampton
NN2 7YJ
Squerryes Court
Westerham
Two For The Price Of One
not to be used in conjunction with any other offer, one coupon per party not valid on Bank Hols and event weekends.
Discount Coupon
Valid 1 Apr-30 Sept 2000
DAYS OUT UK
The Leading Days Out Guide
P O Box 427
Northampton
NN2 7YJ
Canterbury Tales
Canterbury
One Child Free With Each Full Paying Adult
not to be used in conjunction with any other offer, one coupon per party not valid on Bank Hols and event weekends.
Discount Coupon
Valid until end Feb 2001
DAYS OUT UK
The Leading Days Out Guide
P O Box 427
Northampton
NN2 7YJ
Maritime Museum
Ramsgate
One Child Free With A Full Paying Adult
not to be used in conjunction with any other offer, one coupon per party not valid on Bank Hols and event weekends.
Discount Coupon
Valid until end Feb 2001
DAYS OUT UK
The Leading Days Out Guide
P O Box 427
Northampton
NN2 7YJ
Royal Engineers Museum
Gillingham
One Child Free With One Full Paying Adult
not to be used in conjunction with any other offer, one coupon per party not valid on Bank Hols and event weekends.
Discount Coupon
Valid until end Feb 2001
DAYS OUT UK
The Leading Days Out Guide
P O Box 427
Northampton
NN2 7YJ
Crabble Corn Mill
Dover
50p Off Adult Ticket or £1.00 Off Family Ticket
not to be used in conjunction with any other offer, one coupon per party not valid on Bank Hols and event weekends.
Discount Coupon
Valid until end Feb 2001
DAYS OUT UK
The Leading Days Out Guide
P O Box 427
Northampton
NN2 7YJ
Romney Hythe & Dymchurch Railway
New Romney
One Person Free With A Full Paying Adult, all Stations Return Ticket. One Coupon Per Day
not to be used in conjunction with any other offer, one coupon per party not va
on Bank Hols and event weekends.
Discount Coupon
Valid until end Feb 20

This coupon entitles the holder to the discount offer shown on the reverse side. To claim your discount please present this coupon when paying for your entry.

Customer care line number *free* phone 0800 316 8900

This coupon entitles the holder to the discount offer shown on the reverse side. To claim your discount please present this coupon when paying for your entry.

Customer care line number *free* phone 0800 316 8900

This coupon entitles the holder to the discount offer shown on the reverse side. To claim your discount please present this coupon when paying for your entry.

Customer care line number *free* phone 0800 316 8900

This coupon entitles the holder to the discount offer shown on the reverse side. To claim your discount please present this coupon when paying for your entry.

Customer care line number *free* phone 0800 316 8900

This coupon entitles the holder to the discount offer shown on the reverse side. To claim your discount please present this coupon when paying for your entry.

Customer care line number *free* phone 0800 316 8900

This coupon entitles the holder to the discount offer shown on the reverse side. To claim your discount please present this coupon when paying for your entry.

Customer care line number *free* phone 0800 316 8900

DAYS OUT UK
The Leading Days Out Guide
P O Box 427
Northampton
NN2 7YJ
Folkestone Racecourse
Folkestone
£2.00 Discount Per Person
not to be used in conjunction with any other offer, one coupon per party not valid on Bank Hols and event weekends.
Discount Coupon
Valid until end Feb 2001
DAYS OUT UK
The Leading Days Out Guide
P O Box 427
Northampton
NN2 7YJ
Dreamland Fun Park
Margate
One Child Wristband Free With Every Full Paying Adult Wristband
not to be used in conjunction with any other offer, one coupon per party not valid on Bank Hols and event weekends.
Discount Coupon
Valid until end Feb 2001
DAYS OUT UK
The Leading Days Out Guide
P O Box 427
Northampton
NN2 7YJ
White Cliffs Experience
Dover
One Child Free With One Full Paying Adult
not to be used in conjunction with any other offer, one coupon per party not valid on Bank Hols and event weekends.
Discount Coupon
Valid until end Feb 2001
DAYS OUT UK
The Leading Days Out Guide
P O Box 427
Northampton
NN2 7YJ
Eurotunnel Education Service
Folkestone
10% Discount On All Group Bookings
not to be used in conjunction with any other offer, one coupon per party not valid on Bank Hols and event weekends.
Discount Coupon
Valid until end Feb 2001
DAYS OUT UK
The Leading Days Out Guide
P O Box 427
Northampton
NN2 7YJ
Druidstone Wildlife Park
Canterbury
Two For The Price Of One
not to be used in conjunction with any other offer, one coupon per party not valid on Bank Hols and event weekends.
Discount Coupon
Valid until 30 Nov 2000
DAYS OUT UK
The Leading Days Out Guide
P O Box 427
Northampton
NN2 7YJ
Howletts Wild Animal Park
Canterbury
£2.00 Off Adult or Child Admission With A Fu
Paying Adult
not to be used in conjunction with any other offer, one coupon per party
on Bank Hols and event weekends.
Discount Coupon
Valid until end Fe

This coupon entitles the holder to the discount offer shown on the reverse side. To claim your discount please present this coupon when paying for your entry.

Customer care line number *free* phone 0800 316 8900

This coupon entitles the holder to the discount offer shown on the reverse side. To claim your discount please present this coupon when paying for your entry.

Customer care line number *free* phone 0800 316 8900

This coupon entitles the holder to the discount offer shown on the reverse side. To claim your discount please present this coupon when paying for your entry.

Customer care line number *free* phone 0800 316 8900

This coupon entitles the holder to the discount offer shown on the reverse side. To claim your discount please present this coupon when paying for your entry.

Customer care line number *free* phone 0800 316 8900

This coupon entitles the holder to the discount offer shown on the reverse side. To claim your discount please present this coupon when paying for your entry.

Customer care line number *free* phone 0800 316 8900

This coupon entitles the holder to the discount offer shown on the reverse side. To claim your discount please present this coupon when paying for your entry.

Customer care line number *free* phone 0800 316 8900

DAYS OUT UK
The Leading Days Out Guide
P O Box 427
Northampton
NN2 7YJ

British Lawnmower Museum
Southport

Two For The Price Of One

not to be used in conjunction with any other offer, one coupon per party not valid on Bank Hols and event weekends.

Discount Coupon **Valid until end Feb 2001**

DAYS OUT UK
The Leading Days Out Guide
P O Box 427
Northampton
NN2 7YJ

Astley Hall
Chorley

Two For The Price One

not to be used in conjunction with any other offer, one coupon per party not valid on Bank Hols and event weekends.

Discount Coupon **Valid until end Feb 2001**

DAYS OUT UK
The Leading Days Out Guide
P O Box 427
Northampton
NN2 7YJ

Leighton Hall
Carnforth

Two For The Price Of One

not to be used in conjunction with any other offer, one coupon per party not valid on Bank Hols and event weekends.

Discount Coupon **Valid until end Feb 2001**

DAYS OUT UK
The Leading Days Out Guide
P O Box 427
Northampton
NN2 7YJ

Turton Tower

Bolton

Half Price Tea, Coffee and Cream Teas

not to be used in conjunction with any other offer, one coupon per party not valid on Bank Hols and event weekends.

Discount Coupon **Valid until end Feb 2001**

DAYS OUT UK
The Leading Days Out Guide
P O Box 427
Northampton
NN2 7YJ

Camelot Theme Park and Rare Breeds Farm
Chorley
One Child Free Accompanied By Two Full Paying Adults At £8.99 Excl Bank Hol Weekends

not to be used in conjunction with any other offer, one coupon per party not valid on Bank Hols and event weekends.

Discount Coupon **Valid 29 Apr-20 Oct 2000**

DAYS OUT UK
The Leading Days Out Guide
P O Box 427
Northampton
NN2 7YJ

Frontierland - Western Theme Park
Morecambe

Two For The Price Of One

not to be used in conjunction with any other offer, one coupon per pa on Bank Hols and event weekends.

Discount Coupon **Valid until end**

This coupon entitles the holder to the discount offer shown on the reverse side. To claim your discount please present this coupon when paying for your entry.

Customer care line number *free* phone 0800 316 8900

This coupon entitles the holder to the discount offer shown on the reverse side. To claim your discount please present this coupon when paying for your entry.

Customer care line number *free* phone 0800 316 8900

This coupon entitles the holder to the discount offer shown on the reverse side. To claim your discount please present this coupon when paying for your entry.

Customer care line number *free* phone 0800 316 8900

This coupon entitles the holder to the discount offer shown on the reverse side. To claim your discount please present this coupon when paying for your entry.

Customer care line number *free* phone 0800 316 8900

This coupon entitles the holder to the discount offer shown on the reverse side. To claim your discount please present this coupon when paying for your entry.

Customer care line number *free* phone 0800 316 8900

This coupon entitles the holder to the discount offer
hown on the reverse side. To claim your discount
e present this coupon when paying for your entry.

stomer care line number *free* phone 0800 316 8900

DAYS OUT UK
The Leading Days Out Guide
P O Box 427
Northampton
NN2 7YJ

Granada Studios
Manchester
Two For The Price Of One. Adult Ticket Must Be Purchased. Please check the info line for year 2000 opening dates & times - ref: MISC/BOGOF.
not to be used in conjunction with any other offer, one coupon per party not valid on Bank Hols and event weekends.
Discount Coupon | Valid until end Feb 2001

DAYS OUT UK
The Leading Days Out Guide
P O Box 427
Northampton
NN2 7YJ

Louis Tussauds Waxworks
Blackpool
One Child Free With Two Full Paying Adults
(excludes the Anatomy Exhibition)
not to be used in conjunction with any other offer, one coupon per party not valid on Bank Hols and event weekends.
Discount Coupon | Valid until end Feb 2001

DAYS OUT UK
The Leading Days Out Guide
P O Box 427
Northampton
NN2 7YJ

Farmworld
Oadby
One Child Free With Two Full Paying Adults
not to be used in conjunction with any other offer, one coupon per party not valid on Bank Hols and event weekends.
Discount Coupon | Valid until end Feb 200

DAYS OUT UK
The Leading Days Out Guide
P O Box 427
Northampton
NN2 7YJ

Halstead House Farm and Nature Trail
Tilton-on-the-Hill
One Child Free With A Full Paying Adult
not to be used in conjunction with any other offer, one coupon per party not valid on Bank Hols and event weekends.
Discount Coupon | Valid until end Feb 2001

DAYS OUT UK
The Leading Days Out Guide
P O Box 427
Northampton
NN2 7YJ

Kayes Garden Nursery
Leicester
Half Price Admission
not to be used in conjunction with any other offer, one coupon per party not valid on Bank Hols and event weekends.
Discount Coupon | Valid until end Feb 200

DAYS OUT UK
The Leading Days Out Guide
P O Box 427
Northampton
NN2 7YJ

Snibston Discovery Park
Coalville
One Child Free With One Full Paying Adult
not to be used in conjunction with any other offer, one coupon per party not va on Bank Hols and event weekends.
Discount Coupon | Valid until end Feb 20

This coupon entitles the holder to the discount offer shown on the reverse side. To claim your discount please present this coupon when paying for your entry.

Customer care line number *free* phone 0800 316 8900

This coupon entitles the holder to the discount offer shown on the reverse side. To claim your discount please present this coupon when paying for your entry.

Customer care line number *free* phone 0800 316 8900

This coupon entitles the holder to the discount offer shown on the reverse side. To claim your discount please present this coupon when paying for your entry.

Customer care line number *free* phone 0800 316 8900

This coupon entitles the holder to the discount offer shown on the reverse side. To claim your discount please present this coupon when paying for your entry.

Customer care line number *free* phone 0800 316 8900

This coupon entitles the holder to the discount offer shown on the reverse side. To claim your discount please present this coupon when paying for your entry.

Customer care line number *free* phone 0800 316 8900

This coupon entitles the holder to the discount offer shown on the reverse side. To claim your discount please present this coupon when paying for your entry.

Customer care line number *free* phone 0800 316 8900

DAYS OUT UK
The Leading Days Out Guide
P O Box 427
Northampton
NN2 7YJ

Rockingham Castle
Market Harborough

Two For The Price Of One To House & Garden

not to be used in conjunction with any other offer, one coupon per party not valid on Bank Hols and event weekends.

Discount Coupon | **Valid until end Feb 2001**

DAYS OUT UK
The Leading Days Out Guide
P O Box 427
Northampton
NN2 7YJ

Skegness Natureland Seal Sanctuary
Skegness

One Child Free With A Full Paying Adult

not to be used in conjunction with any other offer, one coupon per party not valid on Bank Hols and event weekends.

Discount Coupon | **Valid until end Feb 2001**

DAYS OUT UK
The Leading Days Out Guide
P O Box 427
Northampton
NN2 7YJ

Cleethorpes Humber Estuary Discovery Centre
Cleethorpes

One Child Free With A Full Paying Adult/OAP

not to be used in conjunction with any other offer, one coupon per party not valid on Bank Hols and event weekends.

Discount Coupon | **Valid until end Feb 2001**

DAYS OUT UK
The Leading Days Out Guide
P O Box 427
Northampton
NN2 7YJ

Church Farm Museum
Skegness

Two For The Price Of One

not to be used in conjunction with any other offer, one coupon per party not valid on Bank Hols and event weekends.

Discount Coupon | **Valid until end Feb 2001**

DAYS OUT UK
The Leading Days Out Guide
P O Box 427
Northampton
NN2 7YJ

Springfields Gardens
Spalding

Two For The Price Of One

not to be used in conjunction with any other offer, one coupon per party not valid on Bank Hols and event weekends.

Discount Coupon | **Valid until end Feb 2001**

DAYS OUT UK
The Leading Days Out Guide
P O Box 427
Northampton
NN2 7YJ

National Fishing Heritage Centre
Grimsby

One Child Free With Every Full Paying Adul

not to be used in conjunction with any other offer, one coupon per party no on Bank Hols and event weekends.

Discount Coupon | **Valid until end Feb**

This coupon entitles the holder to the discount offer shown on the reverse side. To claim your discount please present this coupon when paying for your entry.

Customer care line number *free* phone 0800 316 8900

This coupon entitles the holder to the discount offer shown on the reverse side. To claim your discount please present this coupon when paying for your entry.

Customer care line number *free* phone 0800 316 8900

This coupon entitles the holder to the discount offer shown on the reverse side. To claim your discount please present this coupon when paying for your entry.

Customer care line number *free* phone 0800 316 8900

This coupon entitles the holder to the discount offer shown on the reverse side. To claim your discount please present this coupon when paying for your entry.

Customer care line number *free* phone 0800 316 8900

This coupon entitles the holder to the discount offer shown on the reverse side. To claim your discount please present this coupon when paying for your entry.

Customer care line number *free* phone 0800 316 8900

This coupon entitles the holder to the discount offer shown on the reverse side. To claim your discount please present this coupon when paying for your entry.

Customer care line number *free* phone 0800 316 8900

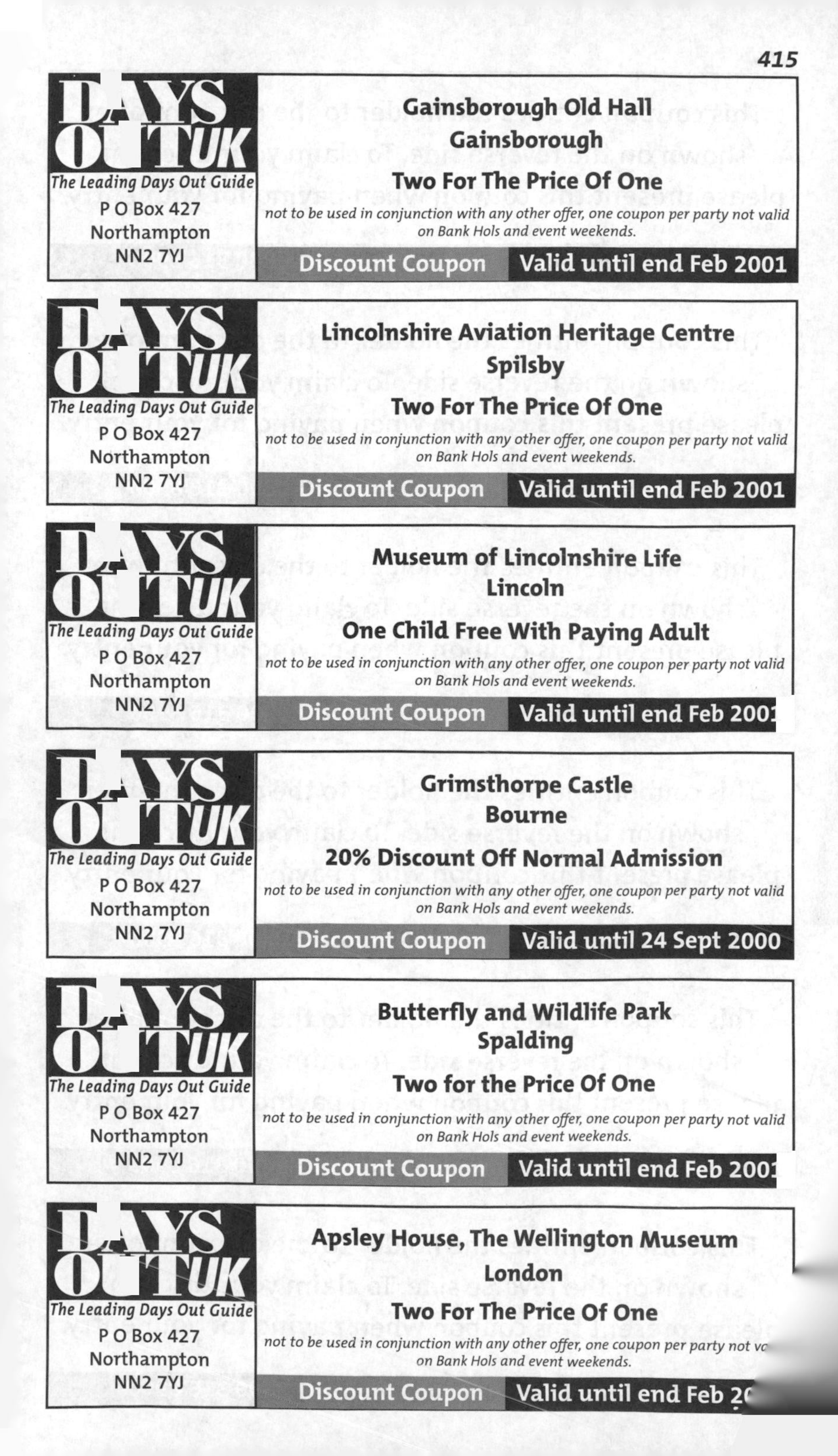
DAYS OUT UK
The Leading Days Out Guide
P O Box 427
Northampton
NN2 7YJ
Gainsborough Old Hall
Gainsborough
Two For The Price Of One
not to be used in conjunction with any other offer, one coupon per party not valid on Bank Hols and event weekends.
Discount Coupon
Valid until end Feb 2001
DAYS OUT UK
The Leading Days Out Guide
P O Box 427
Northampton
NN2 7YJ
Lincolnshire Aviation Heritage Centre
Spilsby
Two For The Price Of One
not to be used in conjunction with any other offer, one coupon per party not valid on Bank Hols and event weekends.
Discount Coupon
Valid until end Feb 2001
DAYS OUT UK
The Leading Days Out Guide
P O Box 427
Northampton
NN2 7YJ
Museum of Lincolnshire Life
Lincoln
One Child Free With Paying Adult
not to be used in conjunction with any other offer, one coupon per party not valid on Bank Hols and event weekends.
Discount Coupon
Valid until end Feb 2001
DAYS OUT UK
The Leading Days Out Guide
P O Box 427
Northampton
NN2 7YJ
Grimsthorpe Castle
Bourne
20% Discount Off Normal Admission
not to be used in conjunction with any other offer, one coupon per party not valid on Bank Hols and event weekends.
Discount Coupon
Valid until 24 Sept 2000
DAYS OUT UK
The Leading Days Out Guide
P O Box 427
Northampton
NN2 7YJ
Butterfly and Wildlife Park
Spalding
Two for the Price Of One
not to be used in conjunction with any other offer, one coupon per party not valid on Bank Hols and event weekends.
Discount Coupon
Valid until end Feb 2001
DAYS OUT UK
The Leading Days Out Guide
P O Box 427
Northampton
NN2 7YJ
Apsley House, The Wellington Museum
London
Two For The Price Of One
not to be used in conjunction with any other offer, one coupon per party not va
on Bank Hols and event weekends.
Discount Coupon
Valid until end Feb 2

This coupon entitles the holder to the discount offer shown on the reverse side. To claim your discount please present this coupon when paying for your entry.

Customer care line number *free* phone 0800 316 8900

This coupon entitles the holder to the discount offer shown on the reverse side. To claim your discount please present this coupon when paying for your entry.

Customer care line number *free* phone 0800 316 8900

This coupon entitles the holder to the discount offer shown on the reverse side. To claim your discount please present this coupon when paying for your entry.

Customer care line number *free* phone 0800 316 8900

This coupon entitles the holder to the discount offer shown on the reverse side. To claim your discount please present this coupon when paying for your entry.

Customer care line number *free* phone 0800 316 8900

This coupon entitles the holder to the discount offer shown on the reverse side. To claim your discount please present this coupon when paying for your entry.

Customer care line number *free* phone 0800 316 8900

This coupon entitles the holder to the discount offer shown on the reverse side. To claim your discount please present this coupon when paying for your entry.

Customer care line number *free* phone 0800 316 8900

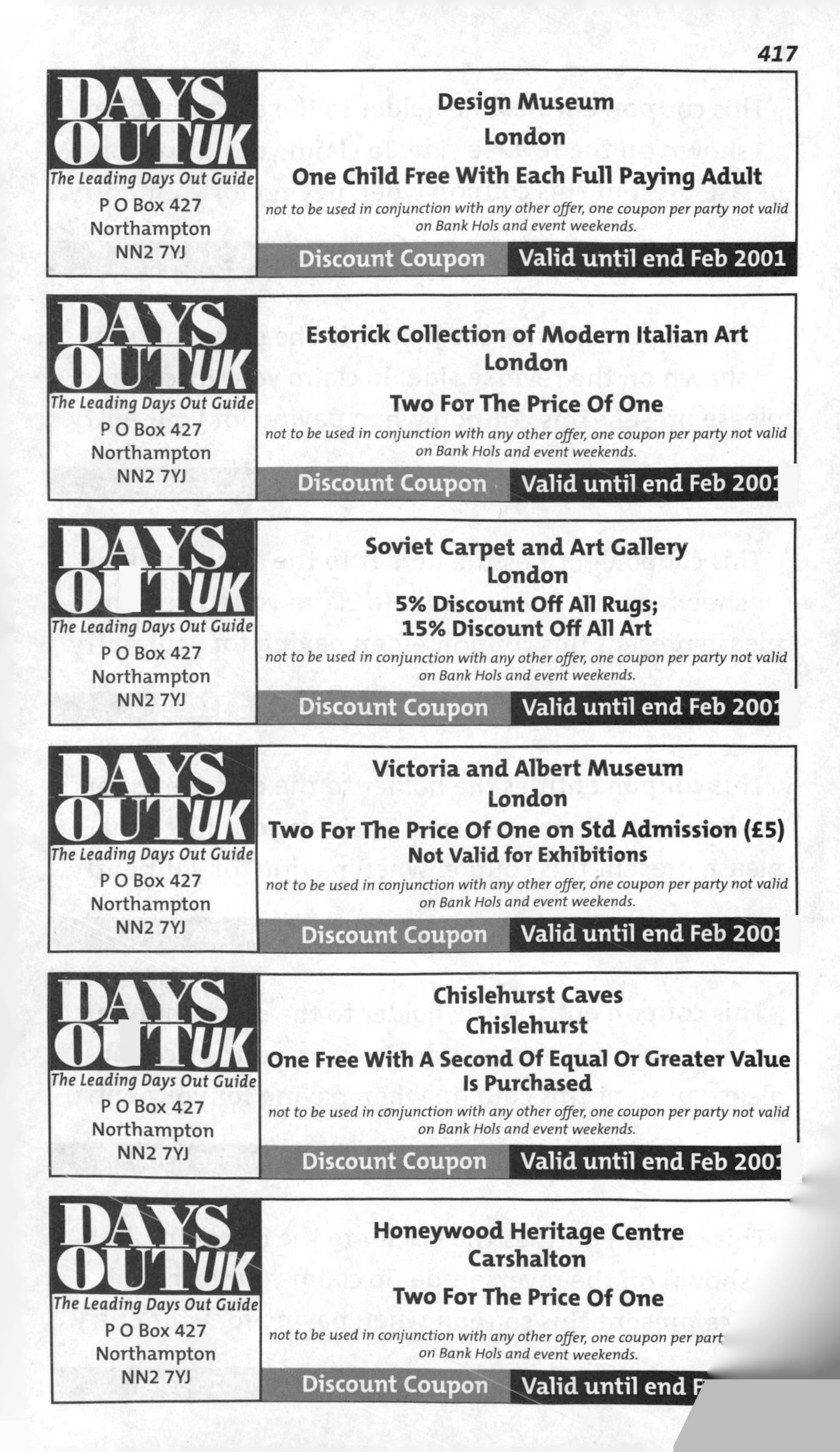
DAYS OUT UK
The Leading Days Out Guide
P O Box 427
Northampton
NN2 7YJ
Design Museum
London
One Child Free With Each Full Paying Adult
not to be used in conjunction with any other offer, one coupon per party not valid on Bank Hols and event weekends.
Discount Coupon
Valid until end Feb 2001
DAYS OUT UK
The Leading Days Out Guide
P O Box 427
Northampton
NN2 7YJ
Estorick Collection of Modern Italian Art
London
Two For The Price Of One
not to be used in conjunction with any other offer, one coupon per party not valid on Bank Hols and event weekends.
Discount Coupon
Valid until end Feb 2001
DAYS OUT UK
The Leading Days Out Guide
P O Box 427
Northampton
NN2 7YJ
Soviet Carpet and Art Gallery
London
5% Discount Off All Rugs;
15% Discount Off All Art
not to be used in conjunction with any other offer, one coupon per party not valid on Bank Hols and event weekends.
Discount Coupon
Valid until end Feb 2001
DAYS OUT UK
The Leading Days Out Guide
P O Box 427
Northampton
NN2 7YJ
Victoria and Albert Museum
London
Two For The Price Of One on Std Admission (£5)
Not Valid for Exhibitions
not to be used in conjunction with any other offer, one coupon per party not valid on Bank Hols and event weekends.
Discount Coupon
Valid until end Feb 2001
DAYS OUT UK
The Leading Days Out Guide
P O Box 427
Northampton
NN2 7YJ
Chislehurst Caves
Chislehurst
One Free With A Second Of Equal Or Greater Value Is Purchased
not to be used in conjunction with any other offer, one coupon per party not valid on Bank Hols and event weekends.
Discount Coupon
Valid until end Feb 2001
DAYS OUT UK
The Leading Days Out Guide
P O Box 427
Northampton
NN2 7YJ
Honeywood Heritage Centre
Carshalton
Two For The Price Of One
not to be used in conjunction with any other offer, one coupon per part
on Bank Hols and event weekends.
Discount Coupon
Valid until end

This coupon entitles the holder to the discount offer shown on the reverse side. To claim your discount please present this coupon when paying for your entry.

Customer care line number *free* phone 0800 316 8900

This coupon entitles the holder to the discount offer shown on the reverse side. To claim your discount please present this coupon when paying for your entry.

Customer care line number *free* phone 0800 316 8900

This coupon entitles the holder to the discount offer shown on the reverse side. To claim your discount please present this coupon when paying for your entry.

Customer care line number *free* phone 0800 316 8900

This coupon entitles the holder to the discount offer shown on the reverse side. To claim your discount please present this coupon when paying for your entry.

Customer care line number *free* phone 0800 316 8900

This coupon entitles the holder to the discount offer shown on the reverse side. To claim your discount please present this coupon when paying for your entry.

Customer care line number *free* phone 0800 316 8900

This coupon entitles the holder to the discount offer shown on the reverse side. To claim your discount se present this coupon when paying for your entry.

ustomer care line number *free* phone 0800 316 8900

DAYS OUT UK
The Leading Days Out Guide
P O Box 427
Northampton
NN2 7YJ
Chelsea Physic Garden
London
Two For The Price Of One
not to be used in conjunction with any other offer, one coupon per party not valid on Bank Hols and event weekends.
Discount Coupon
Valid until 29 Oct 2000
DAYS OUT UK
The Leading Days Out Guide
P O Box 427
Northampton
NN2 7YJ
Royal Mint Sovereign Gallery
London
10% off ANY product displayed
not to be used in conjunction with any other offer, one coupon per party not valid on Bank Hols and event weekends.
Discount Coupon
Valid until end Feb 2001
DAYS OUT UK
The Leading Days Out Guide
P O Box 427
Northampton
NN2 7YJ
Alexandra Palace
London
Two For The Price Of One For Ice Rink
not to be used in conjunction with any other offer, one coupon per party not valid on Bank Hols and event weekends.
Discount Coupon
Valid until end Feb 2001
DAYS OUT UK
The Leading Days Out Guide
P O Box 427
Northampton
NN2 7YJ
Queen Elizabeth's Hunting Lodge
London
Two Adults For The Price Of One
not to be used in conjunction with any other offer, one coupon per party not valid on Bank Hols and event weekends.
Discount Coupon
Valid until end Feb 2001
DAYS OUT UK
The Leading Days Out Guide
P O Box 427
Northampton
NN2 7YJ
Rose Theatre Exhibition
London
Two For The Price Of One
not to be used in conjunction with any other offer, one coupon per party not valid on Bank Hols and event weekends.
Discount Coupon
Valid until end Feb 2001
DAYS OUT UK
The Leading Days Out Guide
P O Box 427
Northampton
NN2 7YJ
Syon House and Gardens
Brentford
Two For The Price Of One Full Paying Adult For Combined Ticket Only
not to be used in conjunction with any other offer, one coupon per party no
on Bank Hols and event weekends.
Discount Coupon
Valid until end Feb

This coupon entitles the holder to the discount offer shown on the reverse side. To claim your discount please present this coupon when paying for your entry.

Customer care line number *free* phone 0800 316 8900

This coupon entitles the holder to the discount offer shown on the reverse side. To claim your discount please present this coupon when paying for your entry.

Customer care line number *free* phone 0800 316 8900

This coupon entitles the holder to the discount offer shown on the reverse side. To claim your discount please present this coupon when paying for your entry.

Customer care line number *free* phone 0800 316 8900

This coupon entitles the holder to the discount offer shown on the reverse side. To claim your discount please present this coupon when paying for your entry.

Customer care line number *free* phone 0800 316 8900

This coupon entitles the holder to the discount offer shown on the reverse side. To claim your discount please present this coupon when paying for your entry.

Customer care line number *free* phone 0800 316 8900

This coupon entitles the holder to the discount offer shown on the reverse side. To claim your discount ease present this coupon when paying for your entry.

Customer care line number *free* phone 0800 316 8900

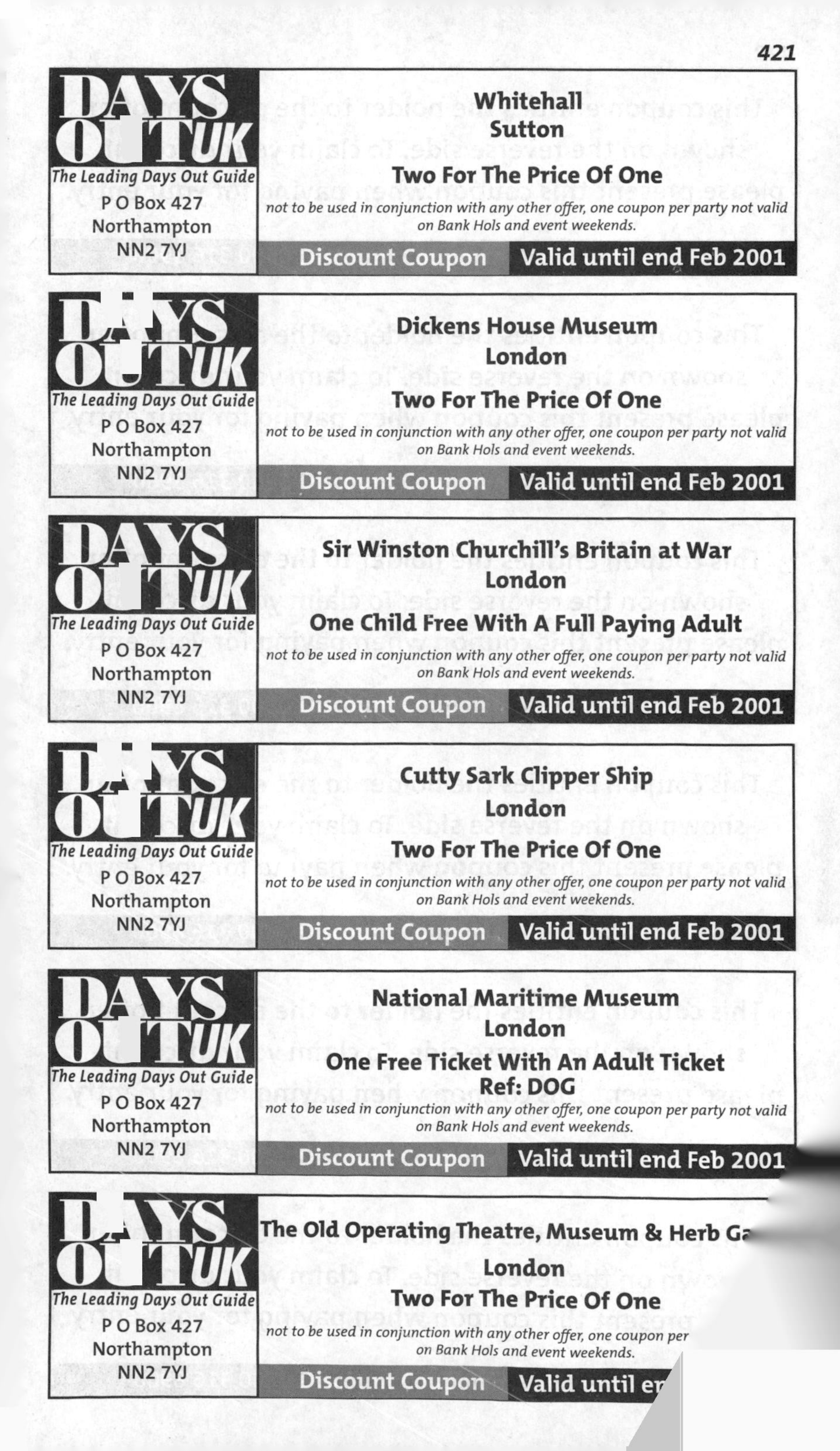
DAYS OUT UK
The Leading Days Out Guide
P O Box 427
Northampton
NN2 7YJ
Whitehall
Sutton
Two For The Price Of One
not to be used in conjunction with any other offer, one coupon per party not valid on Bank Hols and event weekends.
Discount Coupon
Valid until end Feb 2001
DAYS OUT UK
The Leading Days Out Guide
P O Box 427
Northampton
NN2 7YJ
Dickens House Museum
London
Two For The Price Of One
not to be used in conjunction with any other offer, one coupon per party not valid on Bank Hols and event weekends.
Discount Coupon
Valid until end Feb 2001
DAYS OUT UK
The Leading Days Out Guide
P O Box 427
Northampton
NN2 7YJ
Sir Winston Churchill's Britain at War
London
One Child Free With A Full Paying Adult
not to be used in conjunction with any other offer, one coupon per party not valid on Bank Hols and event weekends.
Discount Coupon
Valid until end Feb 2001
DAYS OUT UK
The Leading Days Out Guide
P O Box 427
Northampton
NN2 7YJ
Cutty Sark Clipper Ship
London
Two For The Price Of One
not to be used in conjunction with any other offer, one coupon per party not valid on Bank Hols and event weekends.
Discount Coupon
Valid until end Feb 2001
DAYS OUT UK
The Leading Days Out Guide
P O Box 427
Northampton
NN2 7YJ
National Maritime Museum
London
One Free Ticket With An Adult Ticket
Ref: DOG
not to be used in conjunction with any other offer, one coupon per party not valid on Bank Hols and event weekends.
Discount Coupon
Valid until end Feb 2001
DAYS OUT UK
The Leading Days Out Guide
P O Box 427
Northampton
NN2 7YJ
The Old Operating Theatre, Museum & Herb Ga
London
Two For The Price Of One
not to be used in conjunction with any other offer, one coupon per
on Bank Hols and event weekends.
Discount Coupon
Valid until e

This coupon entitles the holder to the discount offer shown on the reverse side. To claim your discount please present this coupon when paying for your entry.

Customer care line number *free* phone 0800 316 8900

This coupon entitles the holder to the discount offer shown on the reverse side. To claim your discount please present this coupon when paying for your entry.

Customer care line number *free* phone 0800 316 8900

This coupon entitles the holder to the discount offer shown on the reverse side. To claim your discount please present this coupon when paying for your entry.

Customer care line number *free* phone 0800 316 8900

This coupon entitles the holder to the discount offer shown on the reverse side. To claim your discount please present this coupon when paying for your entry.

Customer care line number *free* phone 0800 316 8900

This coupon entitles the holder to the discount offer shown on the reverse side. To claim your discount please present this coupon when paying for your entry.

Customer care line number *free* phone 0800 316 8900

his coupon entitles the holder to the discount offer hown on the reverse side. To claim your discount present this coupon when paying for your entry.

omer care line number *free* phone 0800 316 8900

423
DAYS OUT UK
The Leading Days Out Guide
P O Box 427
Northampton
NN2 7YJ
Royal Air Force Museum
London
Two For The Price Of One
(based on highest priced ticket)
not to be used in conjunction with any other offer, one coupon per party not valid on Bank Hols and event weekends.
Discount Coupon
Valid until end Feb 2001
DAYS OUT UK
The Leading Days Out Guide
P O Box 427
Northampton
NN2 7YJ
Jewish Museum - Finchley
London
Two For The Price Of One Full Paying Adult
not to be used in conjunction with any other offer, one coupon per party not valid on Bank Hols and event weekends.
Discount Coupon
Valid until end Feb 2001
DAYS OUT UK
The Leading Days Out Guide
P O Box 427
Northampton
NN2 7YJ
Cabaret Mechanical Theatre
London
£1.00 Off Family Ticket
not to be used in conjunction with any other offer, one coupon per party not valid on Bank Hols and event weekends.
Discount Coupon
Valid until end Feb 2001
DAYS OUT UK
The Leading Days Out Guide
P O Box 427
Northampton
NN2 7YJ
Musical Museum
Brentford
Two For The Price Of One
not to be used in conjunction with any other offer, one coupon per party not valid on Bank Hols and event weekends.
Discount Coupon
Valid until 31 Oct 2000
DAYS OUT UK
The Leading Days Out Guide
P O Box 427
Northampton
NN2 7YJ
Puppet Theatre Barge
London
One Ticket Free With Every Four Seats Booked
not to be used in conjunction with any other offer, one coupon per party not valid on Bank Hols and event weekends.
Discount Coupon
Valid until end Feb 2001
DAYS OUT UK
The Leading Days Out Guide
P O Box 427
Northampton
NN2 7YJ
Polka Theatre for Children
London
Two For The Price Of One
For Saturday 2nd Main House Performanc
not to be used in conjunction with any other offer, one coupon per
on Bank Hols and event weekends.
Discount Coupon
Valid until en

This coupon entitles the holder to the discount offer shown on the reverse side. To claim your discount please present this coupon when paying for your entry.

Customer care line number *free* phone 0800 316 8900

This coupon entitles the holder to the discount offer shown on the reverse side. To claim your discount please present this coupon when paying for your entry.

Customer care line number *free* phone 0800 316 8900

This coupon entitles the holder to the discount offer shown on the reverse side. To claim your discount please present this coupon when paying for your entry.

Customer care line number *free* phone 0800 316 8900

This coupon entitles the holder to the discount offer shown on the reverse side. To claim your discount please present this coupon when paying for your entry.

Customer care line number *free* phone 0800 316 8900

This coupon entitles the holder to the discount offer shown on the reverse side. To claim your discount please present this coupon when paying for your entry.

Customer care line number *free* phone 0800 316 8900

his coupon entitles the holder to the discount offer hown on the reverse side. To claim your discount present this coupon when paying for your entry.

tomer care line number *free* phone 0800 316 8900

DAYS OUT UK
The Leading Days Out Guide
P O Box 427
Northampton
NN2 7YJ
Royal Observatory Greenwich
London
One Free With Adult Ticket
Ref: DOG
not to be used in conjunction with any other offer, one coupon per party not valid on Bank Hols and event weekends.
Discount Coupon
Valid until end Feb 2001
DAYS OUT UK
The Leading Days Out Guide
P O Box 427
Northampton
NN2 7YJ
London Aquarium
London
£2.00 Off Published Admission Price
not to be used in conjunction with any other offer, one coupon per party not valid on Bank Hols and event weekends.
Discount Coupon
Valid until end Feb 2001
DAYS OUT UK
The Leading Days Out Guide
P O Box 427
Northampton
NN2 7YJ
Gunnersbury Park Museum
London
Any Three Postcards Free
not to be used in conjunction with any other offer, one coupon per party not valid on Bank Hols and event weekends.
Discount Coupon
Valid until end Feb 2001
DAYS OUT UK
The Leading Days Out Guide
P O Box 427
Northampton
NN2 7YJ
Chelsea Football Club
London
4th Child Free When Family Ticket Purchased
not to be used in conjunction with any other offer, one coupon per party not valid on Bank Hols and event weekends.
Discount Coupon
Valid until end Feb 2001
DAYS OUT UK
The Leading Days Out Guide
P O Box 427
Northampton
NN2 7YJ
UK Bungee Club
London
One Person Jumps Free - The Other Pays Full Price
(All Jumpers MUST Pay The £15 Membership and Insurance)
not to be used in conjunction with any other offer, one coupon per party not valid on Bank Hols and event weekends.
Discount Coupon
Valid until end Feb 2001
DAYS OUT UK
The Leading Days Out Guide
P O Box 427
Northampton
NN2 7YJ
M.C.C. Museum and Tour of Lord's
London
Two For The Price Of One
not to be used in conjunction with any other offer, one coupon per part
on Bank Hols and event weekends.
Discount Coupon
Valid until end

This coupon entitles the holder to the discount offer shown on the reverse side. To claim your discount please present this coupon when paying for your entry.

Customer care line number *free* phone 0800 316 8900

This coupon entitles the holder to the discount offer shown on the reverse side. To claim your discount please present this coupon when paying for your entry.

Customer care line number *free* phone 0800 316 8900

This coupon entitles the holder to the discount offer shown on the reverse side. To claim your discount please present this coupon when paying for your entry.

Customer care line number *free* phone 0800 316 8900

This coupon entitles the holder to the discount offer shown on the reverse side. To claim your discount please present this coupon when paying for your entry.

Customer care line number *free* phone 0800 316 8900

This coupon entitles the holder to the discount offer shown on the reverse side. To claim your discount please present this coupon when paying for your entry.

Customer care line number *free* phone 0800 316 8900

This coupon entitles the holder to the discount offer shown on the reverse side. To claim your discount se present this coupon when paying for your entry.

ustomer care line number *free* phone 0800 316 8900

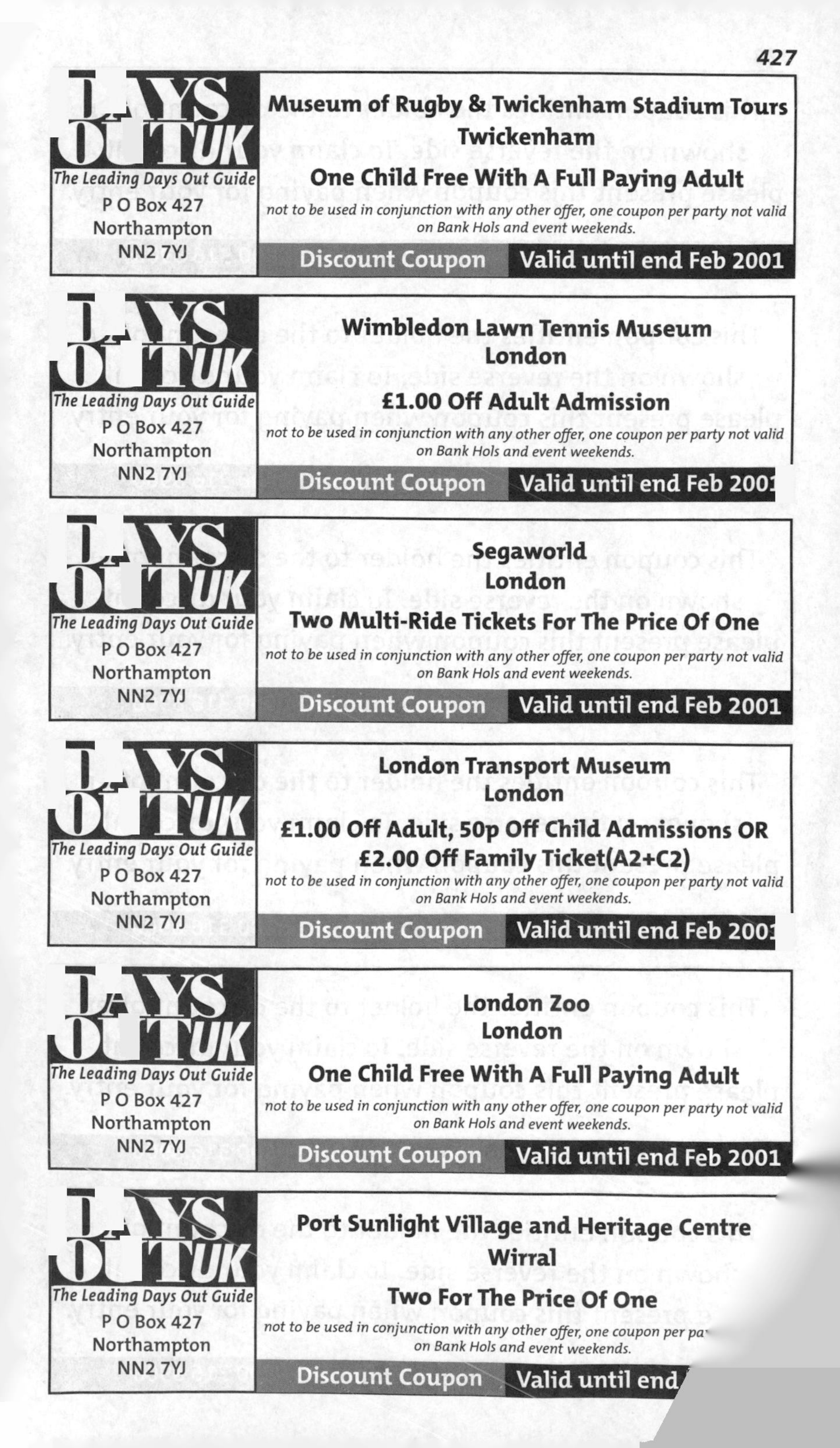
DAYS OUT UK
The Leading Days Out Guide
P O Box 427
Northampton
NN2 7YJ
Museum of Rugby & Twickenham Stadium Tours
Twickenham
One Child Free With A Full Paying Adult
not to be used in conjunction with any other offer, one coupon per party not valid on Bank Hols and event weekends.
Discount Coupon
Valid until end Feb 2001
DAYS OUT UK
The Leading Days Out Guide
P O Box 427
Northampton
NN2 7YJ
Wimbledon Lawn Tennis Museum
London
£1.00 Off Adult Admission
not to be used in conjunction with any other offer, one coupon per party not valid on Bank Hols and event weekends.
Discount Coupon
Valid until end Feb 2001
DAYS OUT UK
The Leading Days Out Guide
P O Box 427
Northampton
NN2 7YJ
Segaworld
London
Two Multi-Ride Tickets For The Price Of One
not to be used in conjunction with any other offer, one coupon per party not valid on Bank Hols and event weekends.
Discount Coupon
Valid until end Feb 2001
DAYS OUT UK
The Leading Days Out Guide
P O Box 427
Northampton
NN2 7YJ
London Transport Museum
London
£1.00 Off Adult, 50p Off Child Admissions OR
£2.00 Off Family Ticket(A2+C2)
not to be used in conjunction with any other offer, one coupon per party not valid on Bank Hols and event weekends.
Discount Coupon
Valid until end Feb 2001
DAYS OUT UK
The Leading Days Out Guide
P O Box 427
Northampton
NN2 7YJ
London Zoo
London
One Child Free With A Full Paying Adult
not to be used in conjunction with any other offer, one coupon per party not valid on Bank Hols and event weekends.
Discount Coupon
Valid until end Feb 2001
DAYS OUT UK
The Leading Days Out Guide
P O Box 427
Northampton
NN2 7YJ
Port Sunlight Village and Heritage Centre
Wirral
Two For The Price Of One
not to be used in conjunction with any other offer, one coupon per pa
on Bank Hols and event weekends.
Discount Coupon
Valid until end

This coupon entitles the holder to the discount offer shown on the reverse side. To claim your discount please present this coupon when paying for your entry.

Customer care line number *free* phone 0800 316 8900

This coupon entitles the holder to the discount offer shown on the reverse side. To claim your discount please present this coupon when paying for your entry.

Customer care line number *free* phone 0800 316 8900

This coupon entitles the holder to the discount offer shown on the reverse side. To claim your discount please present this coupon when paying for your entry.

Customer care line number *free* phone 0800 316 8900

This coupon entitles the holder to the discount offer shown on the reverse side. To claim your discount please present this coupon when paying for your entry.

Customer care line number *free* phone 0800 316 8900

This coupon entitles the holder to the discount offer shown on the reverse side. To claim your discount please present this coupon when paying for your entry.

Customer care line number *free* phone 0800 316 8900

This coupon entitles the holder to the discount offer shown on the reverse side. To claim your discount please present this coupon when paying for your entry.

Customer care line number *free* phone 0800 316 8900

DAYS OUT UK
The Leading Days Out Guide
P O Box 427
Northampton
NN2 7YJ
Speke Hall
Liverpool
Two For The Price Of One - Tue-Fri Only
not to be used in conjunction with any other offer, one coupon per party not valid on Bank Hols and event weekends.
Discount Coupon
Valid until end Feb 2001
DAYS OUT UK
The Leading Days Out Guide
P O Box 427
Northampton
NN2 7YJ
Historic Warships: HMS Plymouth & HMS Onyx
Birkenhead
One Child Free With Full Paying Adult
not to be used in conjunction with any other offer, one coupon per party not valid on Bank Hols and event weekends.
Discount Coupon
Valid until end Feb 2001
DAYS OUT UK
The Leading Days Out Guide
P O Box 427
Northampton
NN2 7YJ
Western Approaches
Liverpool
50p Off Full Adult Admission Price
not to be used in conjunction with any other offer, one coupon per party not valid on Bank Hols and event weekends.
Discount Coupon
Valid until end Feb 2001
DAYS OUT UK
The Leading Days Out Guide
P O Box 427
Northampton
NN2 7YJ
Mersey Ferries Ltd
Wallasey
One Child Free With Every Full Fare Paying Adult On River Cruise
not to be used in conjunction with any other offer, one coupon per party not valid on Bank Hols and event weekends.
Discount Coupon
Valid until end Feb 2001
DAYS OUT UK
The Leading Days Out Guide
P O Box 427
Northampton
NN2 7YJ
Awesome Walls Climbing Centre
Liverpool
One Adult Admission (per card) At £4.00
not to be used in conjunction with any other offer, one coupon per party not valid on Bank Hols and event weekends.
Discount Coupon
Valid until end Feb 2001
DAYS OUT UK
The Leading Days Out Guide
P O Box 427
Northampton
NN2 7YJ
Liverpool Football Club and Stadium Tour
Liverpool
£1.00 Off All Tickets
not to be used in conjunction with any other offer, one coupon per p
on Bank Hols and event weekends.
Discount Coupon
Valid until en

This coupon entitles the holder to the discount offer shown on the reverse side. To claim your discount please present this coupon when paying for your entry.

Customer care line number *free* phone 0800 316 8900

This coupon entitles the holder to the discount offer shown on the reverse side. To claim your discount please present this coupon when paying for your entry.

Customer care line number *free* phone 0800 316 8900

This coupon entitles the holder to the discount offer shown on the reverse side. To claim your discount please present this coupon when paying for your entry.

Customer care line number *free* phone 0800 316 8900

This coupon entitles the holder to the discount offer shown on the reverse side. To claim your discount please present this coupon when paying for your entry.

Customer care line number *free* phone 0800 316 8900

This coupon entitles the holder to the discount offer shown on the reverse side. To claim your discount please present this coupon when paying for your entry.

Customer care line number *free* phone 0800 316 8900

his coupon entitles the holder to the discount offer hown on the reverse side. To claim your discount e present this coupon when paying for your entry.

tomer care line number *free* phone 0800 316 8900

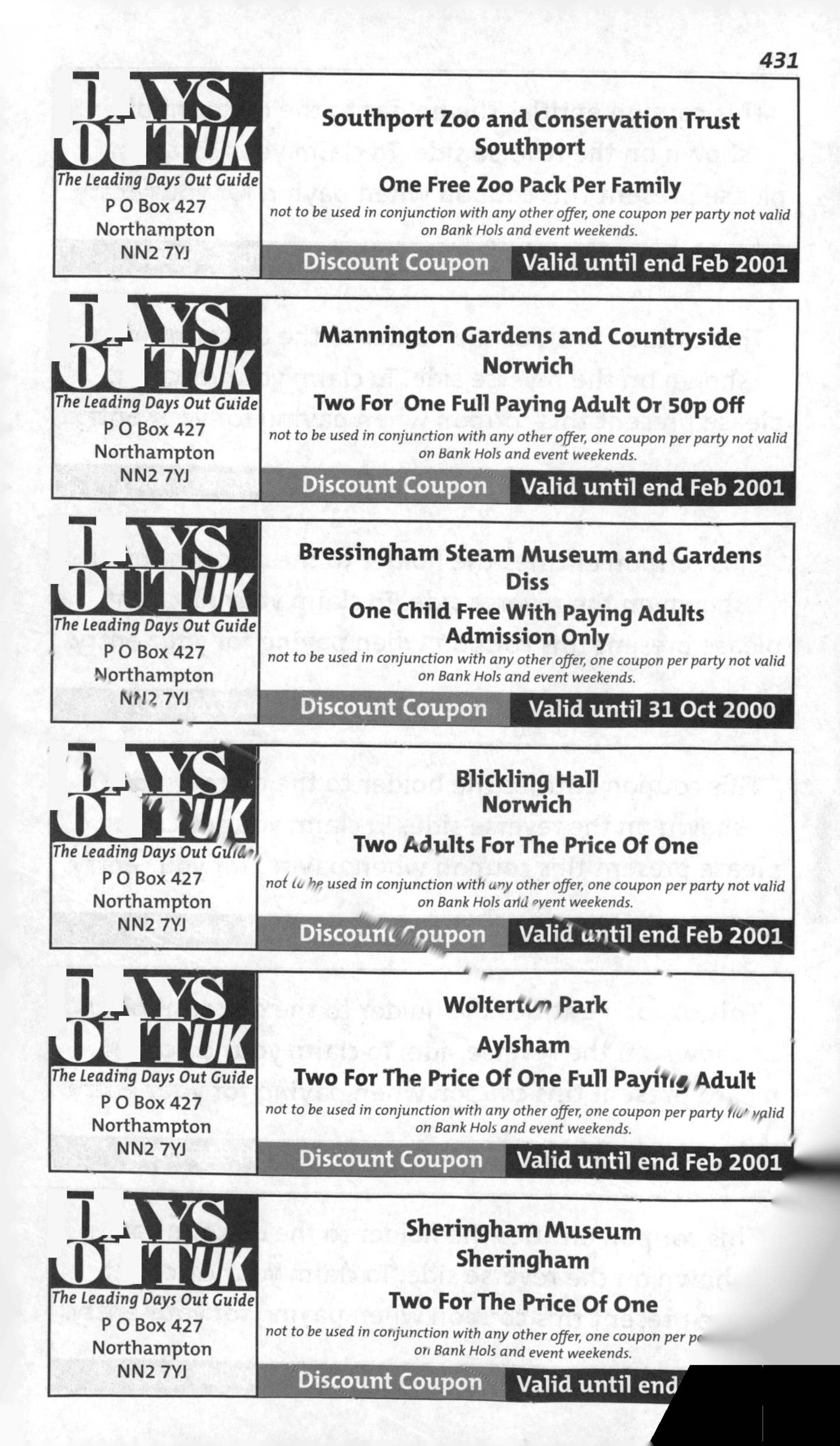

DAYS OUT UK
The Leading Days Out Guide
P O Box 427
Northampton
NN2 7YJ

Southport Zoo and Conservation Trust
Southport

One Free Zoo Pack Per Family

not to be used in conjunction with any other offer, one coupon per party not valid on Bank Hols and event weekends.

Discount Coupon | **Valid until end Feb 2001**

DAYS OUT UK
The Leading Days Out Guide
P O Box 427
Northampton
NN2 7YJ

Mannington Gardens and Countryside
Norwich

Two For One Full Paying Adult Or 50p Off

not to be used in conjunction with any other offer, one coupon per party not valid on Bank Hols and event weekends.

Discount Coupon | **Valid until end Feb 2001**

DAYS OUT UK
The Leading Days Out Guide
P O Box 427
Northampton
NN2 7YJ

Bressingham Steam Museum and Gardens
Diss
One Child Free With Paying Adults Admission Only

not to be used in conjunction with any other offer, one coupon per party not valid on Bank Hols and event weekends.

Discount Coupon | **Valid until 31 Oct 2000**

DAYS OUT UK
The Leading Days Out Guide
P O Box 427
Northampton
NN2 7YJ

Blickling Hall
Norwich

Two Adults For The Price Of One

not to be used in conjunction with any other offer, one coupon per party not valid on Bank Hols and event weekends.

Discount Coupon | **Valid until end Feb 2001**

DAYS OUT UK
The Leading Days Out Guide
P O Box 427
Northampton
NN2 7YJ

Wolterton Park

Aylsham

Two For The Price Of One Full Paying Adult

not to be used in conjunction with any other offer, one coupon per party not valid on Bank Hols and event weekends.

Discount Coupon | **Valid until end Feb 2001**

DAYS OUT UK
The Leading Days Out Guide
P O Box 427
Northampton
NN2 7YJ

Sheringham Museum
Sheringham

Two For The Price Of One

not to be used in conjunction with any other offer, one coupon per pe on Bank Hols and event weekends.

Discount Coupon | **Valid until end**

This coupon entitles the holder to the discount offer shown on the reverse side. To claim your discount please present this coupon when paying for your entry.

Customer care line number *free* phone 0800 316 8900

This coupon entitles the holder to the discount offer shown on the reverse side. To claim your discount please present this coupon when paying for your entry.

Customer care line number *free* phone 0800 316 8900

This coupon entitles the holder to the discount offer shown on the reverse side. To claim your discount please present this coupon when paying for your entry.

Customer care line number *free* phone 0800 316 8900

This coupon entitles the holder to the discount offer shown on the reverse side. To claim your discount please present this coupon when paying for your entry.

Customer care line number *free* phone 0800 316 8900

This coupon entitles the holder to the discount offer shown on the reverse side. To claim your discount please present this coupon when paying for your entry.

Customer care line number *free* phone 0800 316 8900

his coupon entitles the holder to the discount offer hown on the reverse side. To claim your discount e present this coupon when paying for your entry.

tomer care line number *free* phone 0800 316 8900

DAYS OUT UK
The Leading Days Out Guide
P O Box 427
Northampton
NN2 7YJ

Banham Zoo
Norwich
One Child Free With Two Full Paying Adults
not to be used in conjunction with any other offer, one coupon per party not valid on Bank Hols and event weekends.

Discount Coupon | **Valid until end Feb 2001**

DAYS OUT UK
The Leading Days Out Guide
P O Box 427
Northampton
NN2 7YJ

Thrigby Hall Wildlife Gardens
Great Yarmouth
50p Off Standard Rates
not to be used in conjunction with any other offer, one coupon per party not valid on Bank Hols and event weekends.

Discount Coupon | **Valid until 31 Dec 2000**

DAYS OUT UK
The Leading Days Out Guide
P O Box 427
Northampton
NN2 7YJ

Sherwood Forest Farm Park
Mansfield
One Person Free With A Full Paying Adult
not to be used in conjunction with any other offer, one coupon per party not valid on Bank Hols and event weekends.

Discount Coupon | **Valid until end Feb 2001**

DAYS OUT UK
The Leading Days Out Guide
P O Box 427
Northampton
NN2 7YJ

Caves of Nottingham
Nottingham
50p Off Adult & 25p Off Concessionary
not to be used in conjunction with any other offer, one coupon per party not valid on Bank Hols and event weekends.

Discount Coupon | **Valid until end Feb 2001**

DAYS OUT UK
The Leading Days Out Guide
P O Box 427
Northampton
NN2 7YJ

Tales of Robin Hood
Nottingham
Two For The Price Of One
not to be used in conjunction with any other offer, one coupon per party not valid on Bank Hols and event weekends.

Discount Coupon | **Valid until end Feb 2001**

DAYS OUT UK
The Leading Days Out Guide
P O Box 427
Northampton
NN2 7YJ

Nottingham Castle Museum & Art Gallery
Nottingham
One Child Free With Two Full Paying Ad
Weekends & Bank Holidays
not to be used in conjunction with any other offer, one coupon per on Bank Hols and event weekends.

Discount Coupon | **Valid until en**

This coupon entitles the holder to the discount offer shown on the reverse side. To claim your discount please present this coupon when paying for your entry.

Customer care line number *free* phone 0800 316 8900

This coupon entitles the holder to the discount offer shown on the reverse side. To claim your discount please present this coupon when paying for your entry.

Customer care line number *free* phone 0800 316 8900

This coupon entitles the holder to the discount offer shown on the reverse side. To claim your discount please present this coupon when paying for your entry.

Customer care line number *free* phone 0800 316 8900

This coupon entitles the holder to the discount offer shown on the reverse side. To claim your discount please present this coupon when paying for your entry.

Customer care line number *free* phone 0800 316 8900

This coupon entitles the holder to the discount offer shown on the reverse side. To claim your discount please present this coupon when paying for your entry.

Customer care line number *free* phone 0800 316 8900

his coupon entitles the holder to the discount offer hown on the reverse side. To claim your discount e present this coupon when paying for your entry.

omer care line number *free* phone 0800 316 8900

DAYS OUT UK
The Leading Days Out Guide
P O Box 427
Northampton
NN2 7YJ
Galleries of Justice
Nottingham
Two For The Price Of One
not to be used in conjunction with any other offer, one coupon per party not valid on Bank Hols and event weekends.
Discount Coupon
Valid until end Feb 2001
DAYS OUT UK
The Leading Days Out Guide
P O Box 427
Northampton
NN2 7YJ
Newark Air Museum
Newark
50p Off Normal Admission Per Person
not to be used in conjunction with any other offer, one coupon per party not valid on Bank Hols and event weekends.
Discount Coupon
Valid until end Feb 2001
DAYS OUT UK
The Leading Days Out Guide
P O Box 427
Northampton
NN2 7YJ
The Oxford Story Exhibition
Oxford
£1.00 Off Normal Admission Prices
(offer does not apply to groups)
not to be used in conjunction with any other offer, one coupon per party not valid on Bank Hols and event weekends.
Discount Coupon
Valid until end Feb 200
DAYS OUT UK
The Leading Days Out Guide
P O Box 427
Northampton
NN2 7YJ
Broughton Castle
Banbury
Two Adults For The Price Of One
not to be used in conjunction with any other offer, one coupon per party not valid on Bank Hols and event weekends.
Discount Coupon
Valid until end Feb 2001
DAYS OUT UK
The Leading Days Out Guide
P O Box 427
Northampton
NN2 7YJ
Sulgrave Manor
Banbury
Two For The Price Of One
not to be used in conjunction with any other offer, one coupon per party not valid on Bank Hols and event weekends.
Discount Coupon
Valid until end Feb 200
DAYS OUT UK
The Leading Days Out Guide
P O Box 427
Northampton
NN2 7YJ
Didcot Railway Centre
Didcot
One Adult or Child Free With Full Paying Adu
not to be used in conjunction with any other offer, one coupon per party not
on Bank Hols and event weekends.
Discount Coupon
Valid until end Feb

This coupon entitles the holder to the discount offer shown on the reverse side. To claim your discount please present this coupon when paying for your entry.

Customer care line number *free* phone 0800 316 8900

This coupon entitles the holder to the discount offer shown on the reverse side. To claim your discount please present this coupon when paying for your entry.

Customer care line number *free* phone 0800 316 8900

This coupon entitles the holder to the discount offer shown on the reverse side. To claim your discount please present this coupon when paying for your entry.

Customer care line number *free* phone 0800 316 8900

This coupon entitles the holder to the discount offer shown on the reverse side. To claim your discount please present this coupon when paying for your entry.

Customer care line number *free* phone 0800 316 8900

This coupon entitles the holder to the discount offer shown on the reverse side. To claim your discount please present this coupon when paying for your entry.

Customer care line number *free* phone 0800 316 8900

This coupon entitles the holder to the discount offer shown on the reverse side. To claim your discount ease present this coupon when paying for your entry.

Customer care line number *free* phone 0800 316 8900

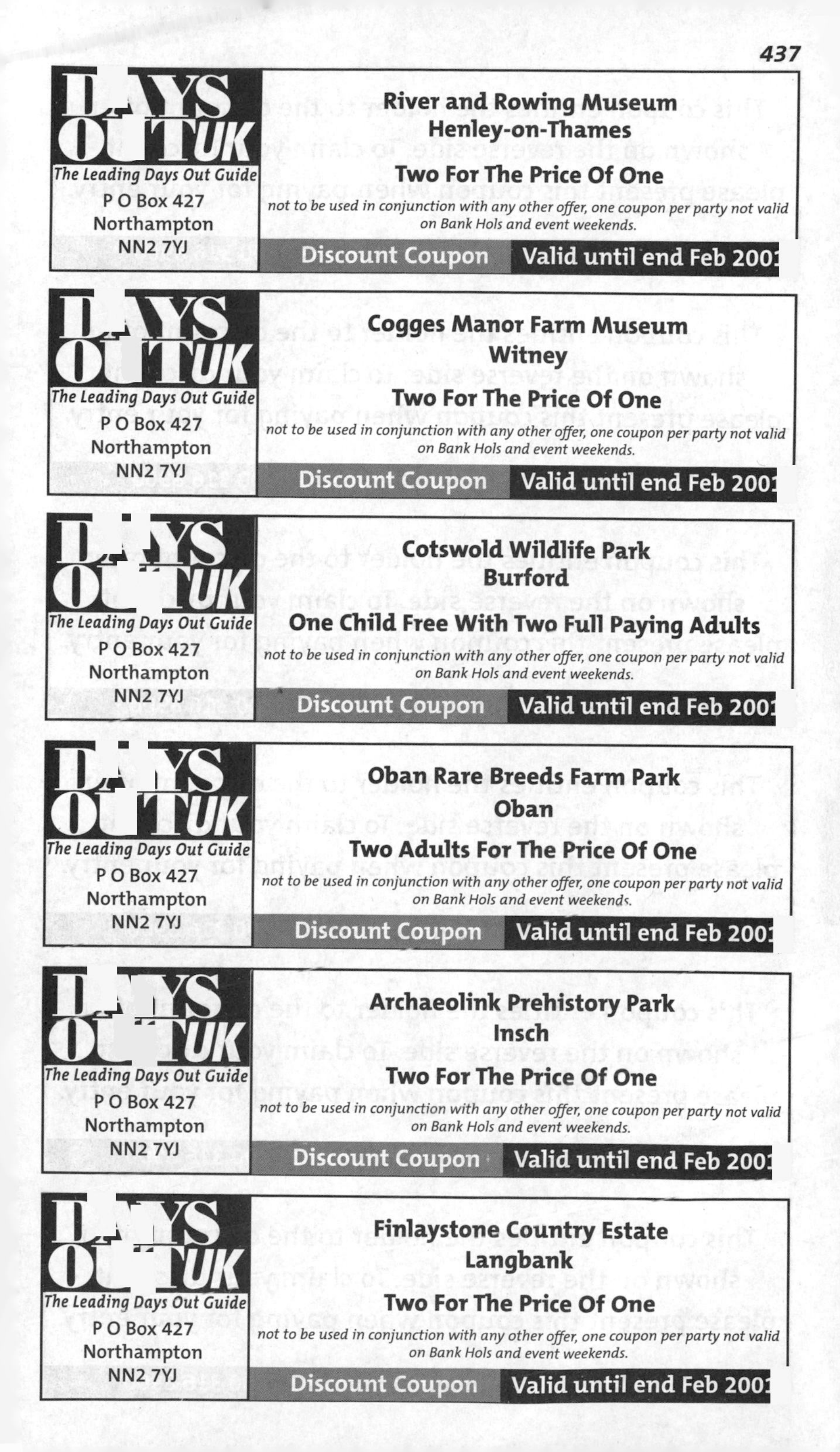
The Leading Days Out Guide
P O Box 427
Northampton
NN2 7YJ
River and Rowing Museum
Henley-on-Thames
Two For The Price Of One
not to be used in conjunction with any other offer, one coupon per party not valid on Bank Hols and event weekends.
Discount Coupon
Valid until end Feb 2001
The Leading Days Out Guide
P O Box 427
Northampton
NN2 7YJ
Cogges Manor Farm Museum
Witney
Two For The Price Of One
not to be used in conjunction with any other offer, one coupon per party not valid on Bank Hols and event weekends.
Discount Coupon
Valid until end Feb 2001
The Leading Days Out Guide
P O Box 427
Northampton
NN2 7YJ
Cotswold Wildlife Park
Burford
One Child Free With Two Full Paying Adults
not to be used in conjunction with any other offer, one coupon per party not valid on Bank Hols and event weekends.
Discount Coupon
Valid until end Feb 2001
The Leading Days Out Guide
P O Box 427
Northampton
NN2 7YJ
Oban Rare Breeds Farm Park
Oban
Two Adults For The Price Of One
not to be used in conjunction with any other offer, one coupon per party not valid on Bank Hols and event weekends.
Discount Coupon
Valid until end Feb 2001
The Leading Days Out Guide
P O Box 427
Northampton
NN2 7YJ
Archaeolink Prehistory Park
Insch
Two For The Price Of One
not to be used in conjunction with any other offer, one coupon per party not valid on Bank Hols and event weekends.
Discount Coupon
Valid until end Feb 2001
The Leading Days Out Guide
P O Box 427
Northampton
NN2 7YJ
Finlaystone Country Estate
Langbank
Two For The Price Of One
not to be used in conjunction with any other offer, one coupon per party not valid on Bank Hols and event weekends.
Discount Coupon
Valid until end Feb 2001

This coupon entitles the holder to the discount offer shown on the reverse side. To claim your discount please present this coupon when paying for your entry.

Customer care line number *free* phone 0800 316 8900

This coupon entitles the holder to the discount offer shown on the reverse side. To claim your discount please present this coupon when paying for your entry.

Customer care line number *free* phone 0800 316 8900

This coupon entitles the holder to the discount offer shown on the reverse side. To claim your discount please present this coupon when paying for your entry.

Customer care line number *free* phone 0800 316 8900

This coupon entitles the holder to the discount offer shown on the reverse side. To claim your discount please present this coupon when paying for your entry.

Customer care line number *free* phone 0800 316 8900

This coupon entitles the holder to the discount offer shown on the reverse side. To claim your discount please present this coupon when paying for your entry.

Customer care line number *free* phone 0800 316 8900

This coupon entitles the holder to the discount offer shown on the reverse side. To claim your discount please present this coupon when paying for your entry.

Customer care line number *free* phone 0800 316 8900

DAYS OUT UK
The Leading Days Out Guide
P O Box 427
Northampton
NN2 7YJ

Edinburgh Crystal Visitor Centre
Penicuik
Two For The Price Of One
not to be used in conjunction with any other offer, one coupon per party not valid on Bank Hols and event weekends.

Discount Coupon | **Valid until end Feb 2001**

DAYS OUT UK
The Leading Days Out Guide
P O Box 427
Northampton
NN2 7YJ

Glenturret Distillery
Crieff
Two Adult/OAPs Guided Tours For The Price Of One; or 10% Discount Off Tasting Tour
not to be used in conjunction with any other offer, one coupon per party not valid on Bank Hols and event weekends.

Discount Coupon | **Valid until end Feb 2001**

DAYS OUT UK
The Leading Days Out Guide
P O Box 427
Northampton
NN2 7YJ

Kailzie Gardens
Peebles
£1.00 Off Per Person. Max 2 Persons
not to be used in conjunction with any other offer, one coupon per party not valid on Bank Hols and event weekends.

Discount Coupon | **Valid until end Feb 2001**

DAYS OUT UK
The Leading Days Out Guide
P O Box 427
Northampton
NN2 7YJ

Torosay Castle and Gardens
Isle Of Mull
Two For The Price Of One
not to be used in conjunction with any other offer, one coupon per party not valid on Bank Hols and event weekends.

Discount Coupon | **Valid until end Feb 2001**

DAYS OUT UK
The Leading Days Out Guide
P O Box 427
Northampton
NN2 7YJ

Almond Valley Heritage Centre
Livingston
One Child Free With Each Full Paying Adult
not to be used in conjunction with any other offer, one coupon per party not valid on Bank Hols and event weekends.

Discount Coupon | **Valid until end Feb 2001**

DAYS OUT UK
The Leading Days Out Guide
P O Box 427
Northampton
NN2 7YJ

Braemar Castle
Ballater
Three For The Price Of Two
not to be used in conjunction with any other offer, one coupon per party not valid on Bank Hols and event weekends.

Discount Coupon | **Valid until 31 Oct 2000**

This coupon entitles the holder to the discount offer shown on the reverse side. To claim your discount please present this coupon when paying for your entry.

Customer care line number *free* phone 0800 316 8900

This coupon entitles the holder to the discount offer shown on the reverse side. To claim your discount please present this coupon when paying for your entry.

Customer care line number *free* phone 0800 316 8900

This coupon entitles the holder to the discount offer shown on the reverse side. To claim your discount please present this coupon when paying for your entry.

Customer care line number *free* phone 0800 316 8900

This coupon entitles the holder to the discount offer shown on the reverse side. To claim your discount please present this coupon when paying for your entry.

Customer care line number *free* phone 0800 316 8900

This coupon entitles the holder to the discount offer shown on the reverse side. To claim your discount please present this coupon when paying for your entry.

Customer care line number *free* phone 0800 316 8900

This coupon entitles the holder to the discount offer shown on the reverse side. To claim your discount please present this coupon when paying for your entry.

Customer care line number *free* phone 0800 316 8900

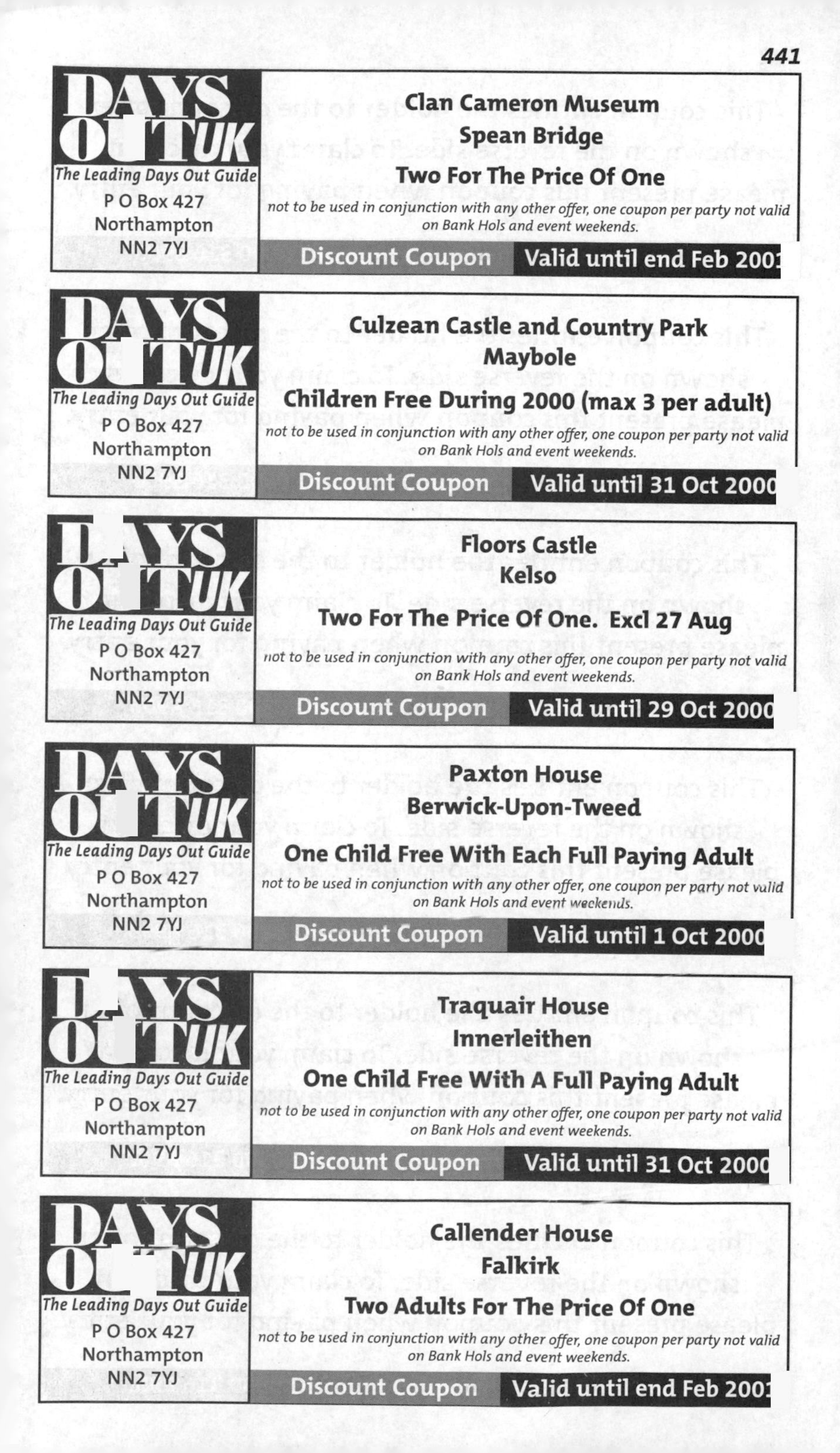
441
DAYS OUT UK
The Leading Days Out Guide
P O Box 427
Northampton
NN2 7YJ
Clan Cameron Museum
Spean Bridge
Two For The Price Of One
not to be used in conjunction with any other offer, one coupon per party not valid on Bank Hols and event weekends.
Discount Coupon
Valid until end Feb 2001
DAYS OUT UK
The Leading Days Out Guide
P O Box 427
Northampton
NN2 7YJ
Culzean Castle and Country Park
Maybole
Children Free During 2000 (max 3 per adult)
not to be used in conjunction with any other offer, one coupon per party not valid on Bank Hols and event weekends.
Discount Coupon
Valid until 31 Oct 2000
DAYS OUT UK
The Leading Days Out Guide
P O Box 427
Northampton
NN2 7YJ
Floors Castle
Kelso
Two For The Price Of One. Excl 27 Aug
not to be used in conjunction with any other offer, one coupon per party not valid on Bank Hols and event weekends.
Discount Coupon
Valid until 29 Oct 2000
DAYS OUT UK
The Leading Days Out Guide
P O Box 427
Northampton
NN2 7YJ
Paxton House
Berwick-Upon-Tweed
One Child Free With Each Full Paying Adult
not to be used in conjunction with any other offer, one coupon per party not valid on Bank Hols and event weekends.
Discount Coupon
Valid until 1 Oct 2000
DAYS OUT UK
The Leading Days Out Guide
P O Box 427
Northampton
NN2 7YJ
Traquair House
Innerleithen
One Child Free With A Full Paying Adult
not to be used in conjunction with any other offer, one coupon per party not valid on Bank Hols and event weekends.
Discount Coupon
Valid until 31 Oct 2000
DAYS OUT UK
The Leading Days Out Guide
P O Box 427
Northampton
NN2 7YJ
Callender House
Falkirk
Two Adults For The Price Of One
not to be used in conjunction with any other offer, one coupon per party not valid on Bank Hols and event weekends.
Discount Coupon
Valid until end Feb 2001

This coupon entitles the holder to the discount offer shown on the reverse side. To claim your discount please present this coupon when paying for your entry.

Customer care line number *free* phone 0800 316 8900

This coupon entitles the holder to the discount offer shown on the reverse side. To claim your discount please present this coupon when paying for your entry.

Customer care line number *free* phone 0800 316 8900

This coupon entitles the holder to the discount offer shown on the reverse side. To claim your discount please present this coupon when paying for your entry.

Customer care line number *free* phone 0800 316 8900

This coupon entitles the holder to the discount offer shown on the reverse side. To claim your discount please present this coupon when paying for your entry.

Customer care line number *free* phone 0800 316 8900

This coupon entitles the holder to the discount offer shown on the reverse side. To claim your discount please present this coupon when paying for your entry.

Customer care line number *free* phone 0800 316 8900

This coupon entitles the holder to the discount offer shown on the reverse side. To claim your discount please present this coupon when paying for your entry.

Customer care line number *free* phone 0800 316 8900

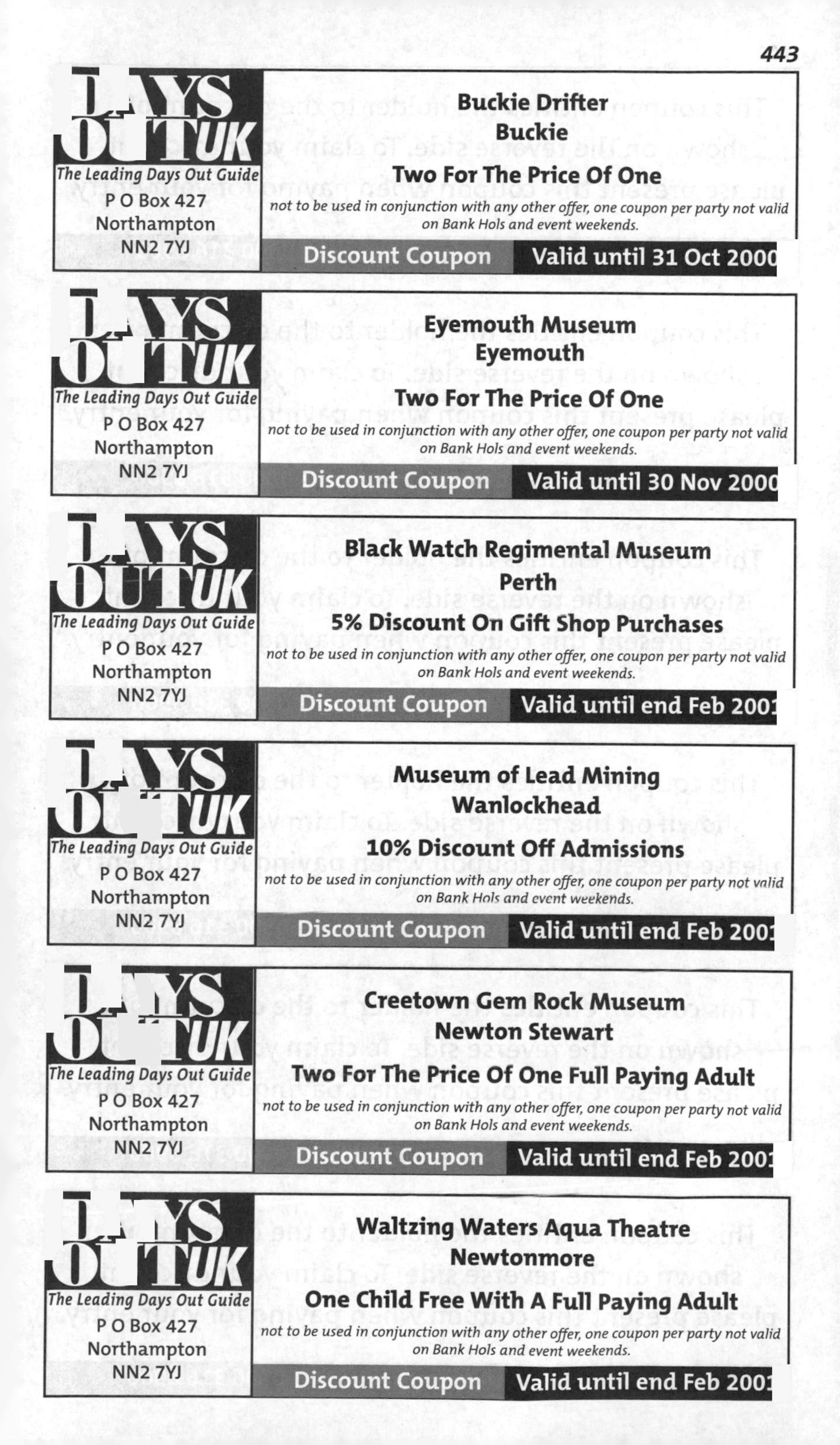
DAYS OUT UK
The Leading Days Out Guide
P O Box 427
Northampton
NN2 7YJ
Buckie Drifter
Buckie
Two For The Price Of One
not to be used in conjunction with any other offer, one coupon per party not valid on Bank Hols and event weekends.
Discount Coupon
Valid until 31 Oct 2000
DAYS OUT UK
The Leading Days Out Guide
P O Box 427
Northampton
NN2 7YJ
Eyemouth Museum
Eyemouth
Two For The Price Of One
not to be used in conjunction with any other offer, one coupon per party not valid on Bank Hols and event weekends.
Discount Coupon
Valid until 30 Nov 2000
DAYS OUT UK
The Leading Days Out Guide
P O Box 427
Northampton
NN2 7YJ
Black Watch Regimental Museum
Perth
5% Discount On Gift Shop Purchases
not to be used in conjunction with any other offer, one coupon per party not valid on Bank Hols and event weekends.
Discount Coupon
Valid until end Feb 2001
DAYS OUT UK
The Leading Days Out Guide
P O Box 427
Northampton
NN2 7YJ
Museum of Lead Mining
Wanlockhead
10% Discount Off Admissions
not to be used in conjunction with any other offer, one coupon per party not valid on Bank Hols and event weekends.
Discount Coupon
Valid until end Feb 2001
DAYS OUT UK
The Leading Days Out Guide
P O Box 427
Northampton
NN2 7YJ
Creetown Gem Rock Museum
Newton Stewart
Two For The Price Of One Full Paying Adult
not to be used in conjunction with any other offer, one coupon per party not valid on Bank Hols and event weekends.
Discount Coupon
Valid until end Feb 2001
DAYS OUT UK
The Leading Days Out Guide
P O Box 427
Northampton
NN2 7YJ
Waltzing Waters Aqua Theatre
Newtonmore
One Child Free With A Full Paying Adult
not to be used in conjunction with any other offer, one coupon per party not valid on Bank Hols and event weekends.
Discount Coupon
Valid until end Feb 2001

This coupon entitles the holder to the discount offer shown on the reverse side. To claim your discount please present this coupon when paying for your entry.

Customer care line number *free* phone 0800 316 8900

This coupon entitles the holder to the discount offer shown on the reverse side. To claim your discount please present this coupon when paying for your entry.

Customer care line number *free* phone 0800 316 8900

This coupon entitles the holder to the discount offer shown on the reverse side. To claim your discount please present this coupon when paying for your entry.

Customer care line number *free* phone 0800 316 8900

This coupon entitles the holder to the discount offer shown on the reverse side. To claim your discount please present this coupon when paying for your entry.

Customer care line number *free* phone 0800 316 8900

This coupon entitles the holder to the discount offer shown on the reverse side. To claim your discount please present this coupon when paying for your entry.

Customer care line number *free* phone 0800 316 8900

This coupon entitles the holder to the discount offer shown on the reverse side. To claim your discount please present this coupon when paying for your entry.

Customer care line number *free* phone 0800 316 8900

DAYS OUT UK
The Leading Days Out Guide
P O Box 427
Northampton
NN2 7YJ

Isle of Mull Railway
Isle Of Mull
15% Discount On Normal Fares- Adults & Children
not to be used in conjunction with any other offer, one coupon per party not valid on Bank Hols and event weekends.
Discount Coupon | Valid until end Feb 2001

DAYS OUT UK
The Leading Days Out Guide
P O Box 427
Northampton
NN2 7YJ

Deep Sea World
Fife
One Child Free With Each Full Paying Adult
not to be used in conjunction with any other offer, one coupon per party not valid on Bank Hols and event weekends.
Discount Coupon | Valid until end Feb 2001

DAYS OUT UK
The Leading Days Out Guide
P O Box 427
Northampton
NN2 7YJ

Scottish Fisheries Museum
Anstruther
Free Guide Book Worth £1.00
not to be used in conjunction with any other offer, one coupon per party not valid on Bank Hols and event weekends.
Discount Coupon | Valid until end Feb 2001

DAYS OUT UK
The Leading Days Out Guide
P O Box 427
Northampton
NN2 7YJ

Highland Mysteryworld
Ballachulish
Two For The Price Of One
not to be used in conjunction with any other offer, one coupon per party not valid on Bank Hols and event weekends.
Discount Coupon | Valid until 31 Oct 2000

DAYS OUT UK
The Leading Days Out Guide
P O Box 427
Northampton
NN2 7YJ

M & D's Scotland's Theme Park
Motherwell
Two Wristbands For The Price Of One
Ref BOGOF
not to be used in conjunction with any other offer, one coupon per party not valid on Bank Hols and event weekends.
Discount Coupon | Valid until end Feb 2001

DAYS OUT UK
The Leading Days Out Guide
P O Box 427
Northampton
NN2 7YJ

Storybook Glen
Maryculter
10% Discount On Admission Prices
not to be used in conjunction with any other offer, one coupon per party not valid on Bank Hols and event weekends.
Discount Coupon | Valid until end Feb 2001

This coupon entitles the holder to the discount offer shown on the reverse side. To claim your discount please present this coupon when paying for your entry.

Customer care line number *free* phone 0800 316 8900

This coupon entitles the holder to the discount offer shown on the reverse side. To claim your discount please present this coupon when paying for your entry.

Customer care line number *free* phone 0800 316 8900

This coupon entitles the holder to the discount offer shown on the reverse side. To claim your discount please present this coupon when paying for your entry.

Customer care line number *free* phone 0800 316 8900

This coupon entitles the holder to the discount offer shown on the reverse side. To claim your discount please present this coupon when paying for your entry.

Customer care line number *free* phone 0800 316 8900

This coupon entitles the holder to the discount offer shown on the reverse side. To claim your discount please present this coupon when paying for your entry.

Customer care line number *free* phone 0800 316 8900

This coupon entitles the holder to the discount offer shown on the reverse side. To claim your discount please present this coupon when paying for your entry.

Customer care line number *free* phone 0800 316 8900

DAYS OUT UK
The Leading Days Out Guide
P O Box 427
Northampton
NN2 7YJ
Finlaystone Doll Collection
Langbank
Two For The Price Of One
not to be used in conjunction with any other offer, one coupon per party not valid on Bank Hols and event weekends.
Discount Coupon
Valid until end Feb 2001
DAYS OUT UK
The Leading Days Out Guide
P O Box 427
Northampton
NN2 7YJ
Grampian Transport Museum
Alford
Two Adults For The Price Of One
not to be used in conjunction with any other offer, one coupon per party not valid on Bank Hols and event weekends.
Discount Coupon
Valid Apr-Oct 2000
DAYS OUT UK
The Leading Days Out Guide
P O Box 427
Northampton
NN2 7YJ
Blair Drummond Safari and Leisure Park
Stirling
One Child Free With Two Full Paying Adults - One Coupon Per Car
not to be used in conjunction with any other offer, one coupon per party not valid on Bank Hols and event weekends.
Discount Coupon
Valid until 2 Oct 2000
DAYS OUT UK
The Leading Days Out Guide
P O Box 427
Northampton
NN2 7YJ
Highland Wildlife Park
Kingussie
£1.00 Off One Single Admission
not to be used in conjunction with any other offer, one coupon per party not valid on Bank Hols and event weekends.
Discount Coupon
Valid Apr-Oct 2000
DAYS OUT UK
The Leading Days Out Guide
P O Box 427
Northampton
NN2 7YJ
Hawkstone Park
Shrewsbury
Half Price Family Ticket (A2+C3)£6.25 (Usually £12.50) Not Valid on Sun Or Bank Hol
not to be used in conjunction with any other offer, one coupon per party not valid on Bank Hols and event weekends.
Discount Coupon
Valid until 31 Oct 2000
DAYS OUT UK
The Leading Days Out Guide
P O Box 427
Northampton
NN2 7YJ
Attingham Park
Shrewsbury
Free Entry To The Park For Children Under 16
not to be used in conjunction with any other offer, one coupon per party not valid on Bank Hols and event weekends.
Discount Coupon
Valid until end Feb 2001

This coupon entitles the holder to the discount offer shown on the reverse side. To claim your discount please present this coupon when paying for your entry.

Customer care line number *free* phone 0800 316 8900

This coupon entitles the holder to the discount offer shown on the reverse side. To claim your discount please present this coupon when paying for your entry.

Customer care line number *free* phone 0800 316 8900

This coupon entitles the holder to the discount offer shown on the reverse side. To claim your discount please present this coupon when paying for your entry.

Customer care line number *free* phone 0800 316 8900

This coupon entitles the holder to the discount offer shown on the reverse side. To claim your discount please present this coupon when paying for your entry.

Customer care line number *free* phone 0800 316 8900

This coupon entitles the holder to the discount offer shown on the reverse side. To claim your discount please present this coupon when paying for your entry.

Customer care line number *free* phone 0800 316 8900

This coupon entitles the holder to the discount offer shown on the reverse side. To claim your discount please present this coupon when paying for your entry.

Customer care line number *free* phone 0800 316 8900

Weston Park
Shifnal

Two For The Price Of One

not to be used in conjunction with any other offer, one coupon per party not valid on Bank Hols and event weekends.

Discount Coupon | **Valid until 19 Sept 2000**

DAYS OUT UK
The Leading Days Out Guide
P O Box 427
Northampton
NN2 7YJ

Royal Air Force Museum, Cosford
Shifnal

£1.00 Off Adult/OAPs & 50p Off Child

not to be used in conjunction with any other offer, one coupon per party not valid on Bank Hols and event weekends.

Discount Coupon | **Valid until end Feb 2001**

DAYS OUT UK
The Leading Days Out Guide
P O Box 427
Northampton
NN2 7YJ

Holbourne Museum of Art
Bath

10% Discount On Admission Prices

not to be used in conjunction with any other offer, one coupon per party not valid on Bank Hols and event weekends.

Discount Coupon | **Valid until end Feb 2001**

DAYS OUT UK
The Leading Days Out Guide
P O Box 427
Northampton
NN2 7YJ

Royal Photographic Society
Bath

Two For The Price Of One

not to be used in conjunction with any other offer, one coupon per party not valid on Bank Hols and event weekends.

Discount Coupon | **Valid until end Feb 2001**

DAYS OUT UK
The Leading Days Out Guide
P O Box 427
Northampton
NN2 7YJ

Cheddar Caves and Gorge
Cheddar

50p Off Per Person For 'Caves & Gorge Explorer Ticket' (max 6 persons)

not to be used in conjunction with any other offer, one coupon per party not valid on Bank Hols and event weekends.

Discount Coupon | **Valid Oct 2000-Mar 2001**

DAYS OUT UK
The Leading Days Out Guide
P O Box 427
Northampton
NN2 7YJ

Wookey Hole Caves and Papermill
Wells

£1.00 Off Full Single Price (max 6 persons)
Not Family Ticket

not to be used in conjunction with any other offer, one coupon per party not valid on Bank Hols and event weekends.

Discount Coupon | **Valid until end Feb 2001**

This coupon entitles the holder to the discount offer shown on the reverse side. To claim your discount please present this coupon when paying for your entry.

Customer care line number *free* phone 0800 316 8900

This coupon entitles the holder to the discount offer shown on the reverse side. To claim your discount please present this coupon when paying for your entry.

Customer care line number *free* phone 0800 316 8900

This coupon entitles the holder to the discount offer shown on the reverse side. To claim your discount please present this coupon when paying for your entry.

Customer care line number *free* phone 0800 316 8900

This coupon entitles the holder to the discount offer shown on the reverse side. To claim your discount please present this coupon when paying for your entry.

Customer care line number *free* phone 0800 316 8900

This coupon entitles the holder to the discount offer shown on the reverse side. To claim your discount please present this coupon when paying for your entry.

Customer care line number *free* phone 0800 316 8900

This coupon entitles the holder to the discount offer shown on the reverse side. To claim your discount please present this coupon when paying for your entry.

Customer care line number *free* phone 0800 316 8900

DAYS OUT UK
The Leading Days Out Guide
P O Box 427
Northampton
NN2 7YJ
Chard and District Museum
Chard
Two For The Price Of One
not to be used in conjunction with any other offer, one coupon per party not valid on Bank Hols and event weekends.
Discount Coupon
Valid until 31 Oct 2000
DAYS OUT UK
The Leading Days Out Guide
P O Box 427
Northampton
NN2 7YJ
The Time Machine Museum
Weston-super-Mare
Two Adults For The Price Of One
not to be used in conjunction with any other offer, one coupon per party not valid on Bank Hols and event weekends.
Discount Coupon
Valid until end Feb 2001
DAYS OUT UK
The Leading Days Out Guide
P O Box 427
Northampton
NN2 7YJ
Gaulden Manor
Taunton
Two Children Free With Two Full Paying Adults
not to be used in conjunction with any other offer, one coupon per party not valid on Bank Hols and event weekends.
Discount Coupon
Valid 8 June-28 Aug 2000
DAYS OUT UK
The Leading Days Out Guide
P O Box 427
Northampton
NN2 7YJ
Secret World-Badger & Wildlife Rescue Centre
Highbridge
Two For The Price Of One
not to be used in conjunction with any other offer, one coupon per party not valid on Bunk Hols and event weekends.
Discount Coupon
Valid until end Feb 2001
DAYS OUT UK
The Leading Days Out Guide
P O Box 427
Northampton
NN2 7YJ
Forde Abbey
Chard
50p Off Full Admission Prices
not to be used in conjunction with any other offer, one coupon per party not valid on Bank Hols and event weekends.
Discount Coupon
Valid until end Feb 2001
DAYS OUT UK
The Leading Days Out Guide
P O Box 427
Northampton
NN2 7YJ
Haynes Motor Museum
Yeovil
One Adult/Child Free With Two Full Paying Adults
not to be used in conjunction with any other offer, one coupon per party not valid on Bank Hols and event weekends.
Discount Coupon
Valid until end Feb 2001

This coupon entitles the holder to the discount offer shown on the reverse side. To claim your discount please present this coupon when paying for your entry.

Customer care line number *free* phone 0800 316 8900

This coupon entitles the holder to the discount offer shown on the reverse side. To claim your discount please present this coupon when paying for your entry.

Customer care line number *free* phone 0800 316 8900

This coupon entitles the holder to the discount offer shown on the reverse side. To claim your discount please present this coupon when paying for your entry.

Customer care line number *free* phone 0800 316 8900

This coupon entitles the holder to the discount offer shown on the reverse side. To claim your discount please present this coupon when paying for your entry.

Customer care line number *free* phone 0800 316 8900

This coupon entitles the holder to the discount offer shown on the reverse side. To claim your discount please present this coupon when paying for your entry.

Customer care line number *free* phone 0800 316 8900

This coupon entitles the holder to the discount offer shown on the reverse side. To claim your discount please present this coupon when paying for your entry.

Customer care line number *free* phone 0800 316 8900

453
DAYS OUT UK
The Leading Days Out Guide
P O Box 427
Northampton
NN2 7YJ
Helicopter Museum
Weston-Super-Mare
One Child Free With A Full Paying Adult
not to be used in conjunction with any other offer, one coupon per party not valid on Bank Hols and event weekends.
Discount Coupon
Valid until end Feb 200
DAYS OUT UK
The Leading Days Out Guide
P O Box 427
Northampton
NN2 7YJ
Tropiquaria
Watchet
One Child Free With A Full Paying Adult
(2 per coupon)
not to be used in conjunction with any other offer, one coupon per party not valid on Bank Hols and event weekends.
Discount Coupon
Valid until end Feb 200
DAYS OUT UK
The Leading Days Out Guide
P O Box 427
Northampton
NN2 7YJ
Ash End House Children's Farm
Tamworth
One Adult Free When A Child Pays Full Price
not to be used in conjunction with any other offer, one coupon per party not valid on Bank Hols and event weekends.
Discount Coupon
Valid until end Feb 200
DAYS OUT UK
The Leading Days Out Guide
P O Box 427
Northampton
NN2 7YJ
Gladstone Working Pottery Museum
Stoke-On-Trent
One Child Free With Every Full Paying Adult
not to be used in conjunction with any other offer, one coupon per party not valid on Bank Hols and event weekends.
Discount Coupon
Valid until end Feb 200
DAYS OUT UK
The Leading Days Out Guide
P O Box 427
Northampton
NN2 7YJ
Royal Doulton Visitor Centre
Stoke-On-Trent
Two Adults For One To Visitor Centre Only
not to be used in conjunction with any other offer, one coupon per party not valid on Bank Hols and event weekends.
Discount Coupon
Valid until end Feb 200
DAYS OUT UK
The Leading Days Out Guide
P O Box 427
Northampton
NN2 7YJ
Bass Museum
Burton-On-Trent
Two For The Price Of One
not to be used in conjunction with any other offer, one coupon per party not valid on Bank Hols and event weekends.
Discount Coupon
Valid until end Feb 200

This coupon entitles the holder to the discount offer shown on the reverse side. To claim your discount please present this coupon when paying for your entry.

Customer care line number *free* phone 0800 316 8900

This coupon entitles the holder to the discount offer shown on the reverse side. To claim your discount please present this coupon when paying for your entry.

Customer care line number *free* phone 0800 316 8900

This coupon entitles the holder to the discount offer shown on the reverse side. To claim your discount please present this coupon when paying for your entry.

Customer care line number *free* phone 0800 316 8900

This coupon entitles the holder to the discount offer shown on the reverse side. To claim your discount please present this coupon when paying for your entry.

Customer care line number *free* phone 0800 316 8900

This coupon entitles the holder to the discount offer shown on the reverse side. To claim your discount please present this coupon when paying for your entry.

Customer care line number *free* phone 0800 316 8900

This coupon entitles the holder to the discount offer shown on the reverse side. To claim your discount please present this coupon when paying for your entry.

Customer care line number *free* phone 0800 316 8900

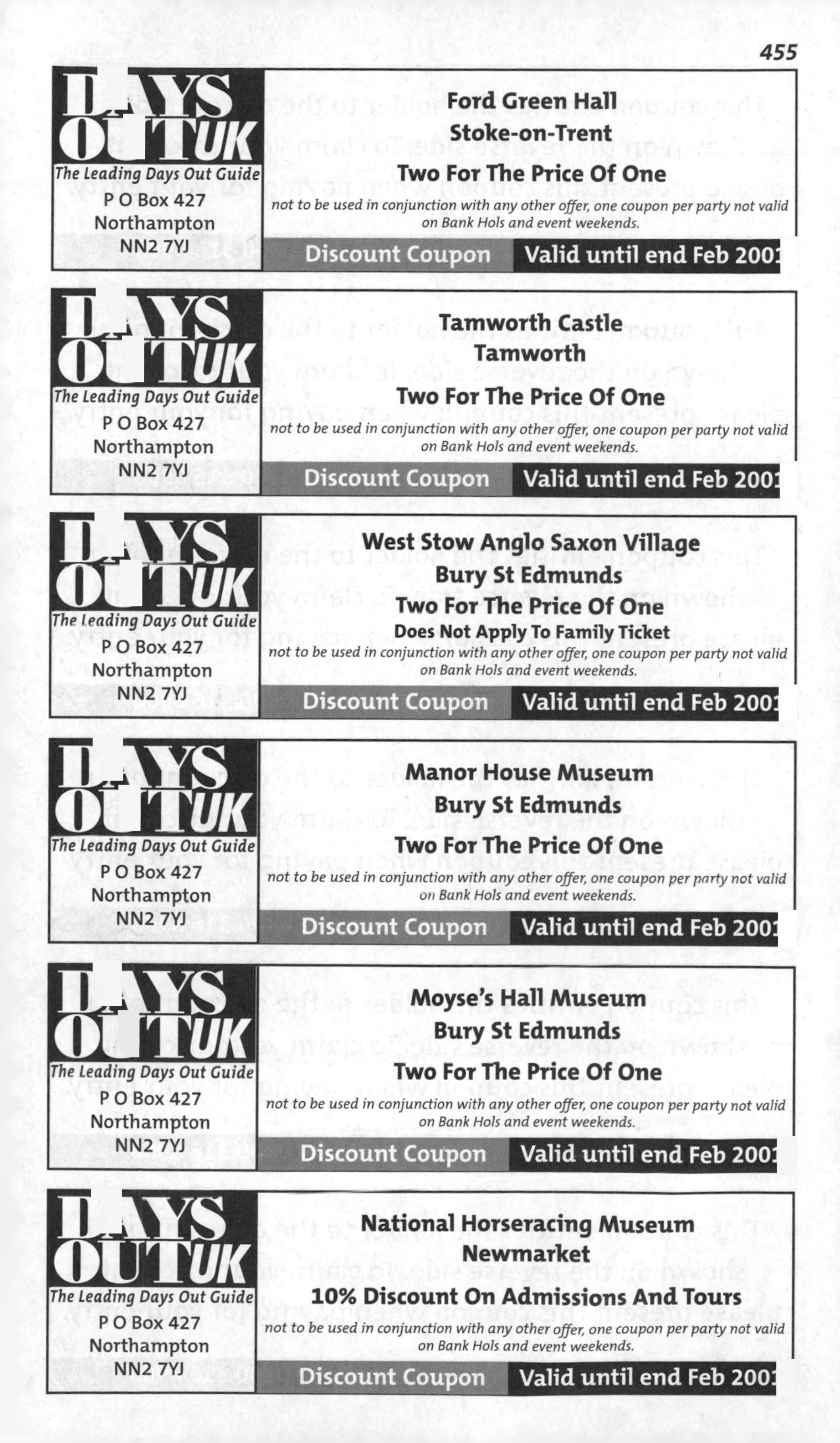
DAYS OUT UK
The Leading Days Out Guide
P O Box 427
Northampton
NN2 7YJ
Ford Green Hall
Stoke-on-Trent
Two For The Price Of One
not to be used in conjunction with any other offer, one coupon per party not valid on Bank Hols and event weekends.
Discount Coupon
Valid until end Feb 2001
DAYS OUT UK
The Leading Days Out Guide
P O Box 427
Northampton
NN2 7YJ
Tamworth Castle
Tamworth
Two For The Price Of One
not to be used in conjunction with any other offer, one coupon per party not valid on Bank Hols and event weekends.
Discount Coupon
Valid until end Feb 2001
DAYS OUT UK
The Leading Days Out Guide
P O Box 427
Northampton
NN2 7YJ
West Stow Anglo Saxon Village
Bury St Edmunds
Two For The Price Of One
Does Not Apply To Family Ticket
not to be used in conjunction with any other offer, one coupon per party not valid on Bank Hols and event weekends.
Discount Coupon
Valid until end Feb 2001
DAYS OUT UK
The Leading Days Out Guide
P O Box 427
Northampton
NN2 7YJ
Manor House Museum
Bury St Edmunds
Two For The Price Of One
not to be used in conjunction with any other offer, one coupon per party not valid on Bank Hols and event weekends.
Discount Coupon
Valid until end Feb 2001
DAYS OUT UK
The Leading Days Out Guide
P O Box 427
Northampton
NN2 7YJ
Moyse's Hall Museum
Bury St Edmunds
Two For The Price Of One
not to be used in conjunction with any other offer, one coupon per party not valid on Bank Hols and event weekends.
Discount Coupon
Valid until end Feb 2001
DAYS OUT UK
The Leading Days Out Guide
P O Box 427
Northampton
NN2 7YJ
National Horseracing Museum
Newmarket
10% Discount On Admissions And Tours
not to be used in conjunction with any other offer, one coupon per party not valid on Bank Hols and event weekends.
Discount Coupon
Valid until end Feb 2001

This coupon entitles the holder to the discount offer shown on the reverse side. To claim your discount please present this coupon when paying for your entry.

Customer care line number *free* phone 0800 316 8900

This coupon entitles the holder to the discount offer shown on the reverse side. To claim your discount please present this coupon when paying for your entry.

Customer care line number *free* phone 0800 316 8900

This coupon entitles the holder to the discount offer shown on the reverse side. To claim your discount please present this coupon when paying for your entry.

Customer care line number *free* phone 0800 316 8900

This coupon entitles the holder to the discount offer shown on the reverse side. To claim your discount please present this coupon when paying for your entry.

Customer care line number *free* phone 0800 316 8900

This coupon entitles the holder to the discount offer shown on the reverse side. To claim your discount please present this coupon when paying for your entry.

Customer care line number *free* phone 0800 316 8900

This coupon entitles the holder to the discount offer shown on the reverse side. To claim your discount please present this coupon when paying for your entry.

Customer care line number *free* phone 0800 316 8900

457
DAYS OUT UK
The Leading Days Out Guide
P O Box 427
Northampton
NN2 7YJ
Newmarket Equine Tours
Newmarket
10% Discount Off Tour Prices
not to be used in conjunction with any other offer, one coupon per party not valid on Bank Hols and event weekends.
Discount Coupon
Valid until end Feb 2001
DAYS OUT UK
The Leading Days Out Guide
P O Box 427
Northampton
NN2 7YJ
Kentwell Hall
Sudbury
One Child Free With Two Full Paying Adults
not to be used in conjunction with any other offer, one coupon per party not valid on Bank Hols and event weekends.
Discount Coupon
Valid until 31 Oct 2000
DAYS OUT UK
The Leading Days Out Guide
P O Box 427
Northampton
NN2 7YJ
Somerleyton Hall and Gardens
Lowestoft
One Child Free With Two Full Paying Adults
not to be used in conjunction with any other offer, one coupon per party not valid on Bank Hols and event weekends.
Discount Coupon
Valid until end Feb 2001
DAYS OUT UK
The Leading Days Out Guide
P O Box 427
Northampton
NN2 7YJ
National Horseracing Museum & Tours
Newmarket
10% Discount On Admissions And Tours
not to be used in conjunction with any other offer, one coupon per party not valid on Bank Hols and event weekends.
Discount Coupon
Valid until end Feb 2001
DAYS OUT UK
The Leading Days Out Guide
P O Box 427
Northampton
NN2 7YJ
Pleasurewood Hills Leisure Park
Lowestoft
£2.00 Discount Off Standard Admission
not to be used in conjunction with any other offer, one coupon per party not valid on Bank Hols and event weekends.
Discount Coupon
Valid until 31 Oct 2000
DAYS OUT UK
The Leading Days Out Guide
P O Box 427
Northampton
NN2 7YJ
Bury St Edmunds Tourist Information Centre
Bury St. Edmunds
Two For The Price Of One
For Blue Badge Guided Tours
not to be used in conjunction with any other offer, one coupon per party not valid on Bank Hols and event weekends.
Discount Coupon
Valid until end Feb 2001

This coupon entitles the holder to the discount offer shown on the reverse side. To claim your discount please present this coupon when paying for your entry.

Customer care line number *free* phone 0800 316 8900

This coupon entitles the holder to the discount offer shown on the reverse side. To claim your discount please present this coupon when paying for your entry.

Customer care line number *free* phone 0800 316 8900

This coupon entitles the holder to the discount offer shown on the reverse side. To claim your discount please present this coupon when paying for your entry.

Customer care line number *free* phone 0800 316 8900

This coupon entitles the holder to the discount offer shown on the reverse side. To claim your discount please present this coupon when paying for your entry.

Customer care line number *free* phone 0800 316 8900

This coupon entitles the holder to the discount offer shown on the reverse side. To claim your discount please present this coupon when paying for your entry.

Customer care line number *free* phone 0800 316 8900

This coupon entitles the holder to the discount offer shown on the reverse side. To claim your discount please present this coupon when paying for your entry.

Customer care line number *free* phone 0800 316 8900

The Leading Days Out Guide
P O Box 427
Northampton
NN2 7YJ
Suffolk Wildlife Park - The African Adventure
Lowestoft
One Child Free With Two Full Paying Adults
not to be used in conjunction with any other offer, one coupon per party not valid on Bank Hols and event weekends.
Discount Coupon
Valid until end Feb 2001
The Leading Days Out Guide
P O Box 427
Northampton
NN2 7YJ
Rural Life Centre
Farnham
Two For The Price Of One
not to be used in conjunction with any other offer, one coupon per party not valid on Bank Hols and event weekends.
Discount Coupon
Valid until end Feb 2001
The Leading Days Out Guide
P O Box 427
Northampton
NN2 7YJ
RHS Garden Wisley
Woking
Two For The Price Of One. Mon-Sat only
not to be used in conjunction with any other offer, one coupon per party not valid on Bank Hols and event weekends.
Discount Coupon
Valid Oct 2000-Mar 2001
The Leading Days Out Guide
P O Box 427
Northampton
NN2 7YJ
Lingfield Park Racecourse
Lingfield
£2.00 Off Per Person
not to be used in conjunction with any other offer, one coupon per party not valid on Bank Hols and event weekends.
Discount Coupon
Valid until end Feb 2001
The Leading Days Out Guide
P O Box 427
Northampton
NN2 7YJ
Brooklands Museum
Weybridge
One Child Free With Each Full Paying Adult
not to be used in conjunction with any other offer, one coupon per party not valid on Bank Hols and event weekends.
Discount Coupon
Valid until end Feb 2001
The Leading Days Out Guide
P O Box 427
Northampton
NN2 7YJ
Seven Sisters Sheep Centre
Eastbourne
Two For The Price Of One
not to be used in conjunction with any other offer, one coupon per party not valid on Bank Hols and event weekends.
Discount Coupon
Valid until end Feb 2001

This coupon entitles the holder to the discount offer shown on the reverse side. To claim your discount please present this coupon when paying for your entry.

Customer care line number *free* phone 0800 316 8900

This coupon entitles the holder to the discount offer shown on the reverse side. To claim your discount please present this coupon when paying for your entry.

Customer care line number *free* phone 0800 316 8900

This coupon entitles the holder to the discount offer shown on the reverse side. To claim your discount please present this coupon when paying for your entry.

Customer care line number *free* phone 0800 316 8900

This coupon entitles the holder to the discount offer shown on the reverse side. To claim your discount please present this coupon when paying for your entry.

Customer care line number *free* phone 0800 316 8900

This coupon entitles the holder to the discount offer shown on the reverse side. To claim your discount please present this coupon when paying for your entry.

Customer care line number *free* phone 0800 316 8900

This coupon entitles the holder to the discount offer shown on the reverse side. To claim your discount please present this coupon when paying for your entry.

Customer care line number *free* phone 0800 316 8900

DAYS OUT UK
The Leading Days Out Guide
P O Box 427
Northampton
NN2 7YJ
Bentley Wildfowl and Motor Museum
Lewes
Two For The Price Of One
not to be used in conjunction with any other offer, one coupon per party not valid on Bank Hols and event weekends.
Discount Coupon
Valid until end Feb 2001
DAYS OUT UK
The Leading Days Out Guide
P O Box 427
Northampton
NN2 7YJ
Battle & District Historical Society Museum Trust
Battle
Two For The Price Of One
not to be used in conjunction with any other offer, one coupon per party not valid on Bank Hols and event weekends.
Discount Coupon
Valid until end Feb 2001
DAYS OUT UK
The Leading Days Out Guide
P O Box 427
Northampton
NN2 7YJ
Weald and Downland Open Air Museum
Chichester
One Child Free With Two Full Paying Adults.
not to be used in conjunction with any other offer, one coupon per party not valid on Bank Hols and event weekends.
Discount Coupon
Valid until 31 Oct 2000
DAYS OUT UK
The Leading Days Out Guide
P O Box 427
Northampton
NN2 7YJ
Denmans Garden
Arundel
Two Full Paying Adults For The Price Of One
Excl Weekends & Bank Holiday
not to be used in conjunction with any other offer, one coupon per party not valid on Bank Hols and event weekends.
Discount Coupon
Valid 1 Mar-31 Oct 2000
DAYS OUT UK
The Leading Days Out Guide
P O Box 427
Northampton
NN2 7YJ
Holly Gate Cactus Garden and Nursery
Ashington
Two For The Price Of One
not to be used in conjunction with any other offer, one coupon per party not valid on Bank Hols and event weekends.
Discount Coupon
Valid until 3 Sept 2000
DAYS OUT UK
The Leading Days Out Guide
P O Box 427
Northampton
NN2 7YJ
Nymans Garden
Haywards Heath
Two For The Price Of One
not to be used in conjunction with any other offer, one coupon per party not valid on Bank Hols and event weekends.
Discount Coupon
Valid until end Feb 2001

This coupon entitles the holder to the discount offer shown on the reverse side. To claim your discount please present this coupon when paying for your entry.

Customer care line number *free* phone 0800 316 8900

This coupon entitles the holder to the discount offer shown on the reverse side. To claim your discount please present this coupon when paying for your entry.

Customer care line number *free* phone 0800 316 8900

This coupon entitles the holder to the discount offer shown on the reverse side. To claim your discount please present this coupon when paying for your entry.

Customer care line number *free* phone 0800 316 8900

This coupon entitles the holder to the discount offer shown on the reverse side. To claim your discount please present this coupon when paying for your entry.

Customer care line number *free* phone 0800 316 8900

This coupon entitles the holder to the discount offer shown on the reverse side. To claim your discount please present this coupon when paying for your entry.

Customer care line number *free* phone 0800 316 8900

This coupon entitles the holder to the discount offer shown on the reverse side. To claim your discount please present this coupon when paying for your entry.

Customer care line number *free* phone 0800 316 8900

DAYS OUT UK
The Leading Days Out Guide
P O Box 427
Northampton
NN2 7YJ
Story of Rye
Rye
Two For The Price Of One For: The Story of Rye OR The Personal Stereo Tour
not to be used in conjunction with any other offer, one coupon per party not valid on Bank Hols and event weekends.
Discount Coupon
Valid until end Feb 2001
DAYS OUT UK
The Leading Days Out Guide
P O Box 427
Northampton
NN2 7YJ
1066 Story in Hastings Castle
Hastings
Two For The Price Of One
not to be used in conjunction with any other offer, one coupon per party not valid on Bank Hols and event weekends.
Discount Coupon
Valid until end Feb 2001
DAYS OUT UK
The Leading Days Out Guide
P O Box 427
Northampton
NN2 7YJ
Goodwood House
Chichester
£1.00 Off Entry Price For Adults And Children
not to be used in conjunction with any other offer, one coupon per party not valid on Bank Hols and event weekends.
Discount Coupon
Valid until end Feb 2001
DAYS OUT UK
The Leading Days Out Guide
P O Box 427
Northampton
NN2 7YJ
Hammerwood Park
East Grinstead
Three For The Price of Two
not to be used in conjunction with any other offer, one coupon per party not valid on Bank Hols and event weekends.
Discount Coupon
Valid until end Feb 2001
DAYS OUT UK
The Leading Days Out Guide
P O Box 427
Northampton
NN2 7YJ
Petworth House and Park
Petworth
50p Group Rate Reduction
not to be used in conjunction with any other offer, one coupon per party not valid on Bank Hols and event weekends.
Discount Coupon
Valid until end Feb 2001
DAYS OUT UK
The Leading Days Out Guide
P O Box 427
Northampton
NN2 7YJ
Tangmere Military Aviation Museum Trust
Chichester
Two For The Price Of One
not to be used in conjunction with any other offer, one coupon per party not valid on Bank Hols and event weekends.
Discount Coupon
Valid until end Feb 2001

This coupon entitles the holder to the discount offer shown on the reverse side. To claim your discount please present this coupon when paying for your entry.

Customer care line number *free* phone 0800 316 8900

This coupon entitles the holder to the discount offer shown on the reverse side. To claim your discount please present this coupon when paying for your entry.

Customer care line number *free* phone 0800 316 8900

This coupon entitles the holder to the discount offer shown on the reverse side. To claim your discount please present this coupon when paying for your entry.

Customer care line number *free* phone 0800 316 8900

This coupon entitles the holder to the discount offer shown on the reverse side. To claim your discount please present this coupon when paying for your entry.

Customer care line number *free* phone 0800 316 8900

This coupon entitles the holder to the discount offer shown on the reverse side. To claim your discount please present this coupon when paying for your entry.

Customer care line number *free* phone 0800 316 8900

This coupon entitles the holder to the discount offer shown on the reverse side. To claim your discount please present this coupon when paying for your entry.

Customer care line number *free* phone 0800 316 8900

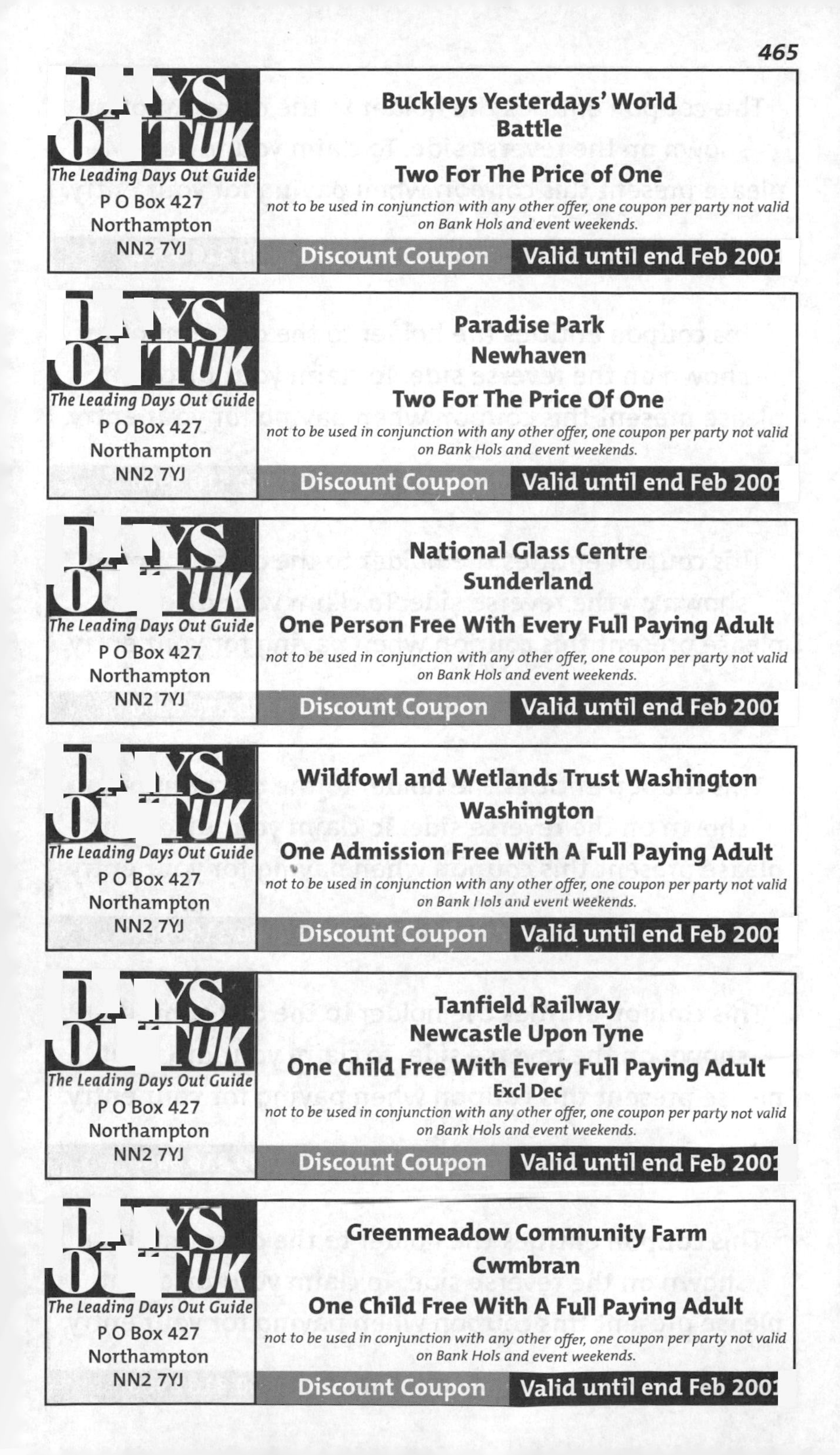
The Leading Days Out Guide
P O Box 427
Northampton
NN2 7YJ
Buckleys Yesterdays' World
Battle
Two For The Price of One
not to be used in conjunction with any other offer, one coupon per party not valid on Bank Hols and event weekends.
Discount Coupon
Valid until end Feb 2001
The Leading Days Out Guide
P O Box 427
Northampton
NN2 7YJ
Paradise Park
Newhaven
Two For The Price Of One
not to be used in conjunction with any other offer, one coupon per party not valid on Bank Hols and event weekends.
Discount Coupon
Valid until end Feb 2001
The Leading Days Out Guide
P O Box 427
Northampton
NN2 7YJ
National Glass Centre
Sunderland
One Person Free With Every Full Paying Adult
not to be used in conjunction with any other offer, one coupon per party not valid on Bank Hols and event weekends.
Discount Coupon
Valid until end Feb 2001
The Leading Days Out Guide
P O Box 427
Northampton
NN2 7YJ
Wildfowl and Wetlands Trust Washington
Washington
One Admission Free With A Full Paying Adult
not to be used in conjunction with any other offer, one coupon per party not valid on Bank Hols and event weekends.
Discount Coupon
Valid until end Feb 2001
The Leading Days Out Guide
P O Box 427
Northampton
NN2 7YJ
Tanfield Railway
Newcastle Upon Tyne
One Child Free With Every Full Paying Adult
Excl Dec
not to be used in conjunction with any other offer, one coupon per party not valid on Bank Hols and event weekends.
Discount Coupon
Valid until end Feb 2001
The Leading Days Out Guide
P O Box 427
Northampton
NN2 7YJ
Greenmeadow Community Farm
Cwmbran
One Child Free With A Full Paying Adult
not to be used in conjunction with any other offer, one coupon per party not valid on Bank Hols and event weekends.
Discount Coupon
Valid until end Feb 2001

This coupon entitles the holder to the discount offer shown on the reverse side. To claim your discount please present this coupon when paying for your entry.

Customer care line number *free* phone 0800 316 8900

This coupon entitles the holder to the discount offer shown on the reverse side. To claim your discount please present this coupon when paying for your entry.

Customer care line number *free* phone 0800 316 8900

This coupon entitles the holder to the discount offer shown on the reverse side. To claim your discount please present this coupon when paying for your entry.

Customer care line number *free* phone 0800 316 8900

This coupon entitles the holder to the discount offer shown on the reverse side. To claim your discount please present this coupon when paying for your entry.

Customer care line number *free* phone 0800 316 8900

This coupon entitles the holder to the discount offer shown on the reverse side. To claim your discount please present this coupon when paying for your entry.

Customer care line number *free* phone 0800 316 8900

This coupon entitles the holder to the discount offer shown on the reverse side. To claim your discount please present this coupon when paying for your entry.

Customer care line number *free* phone 0800 316 8900

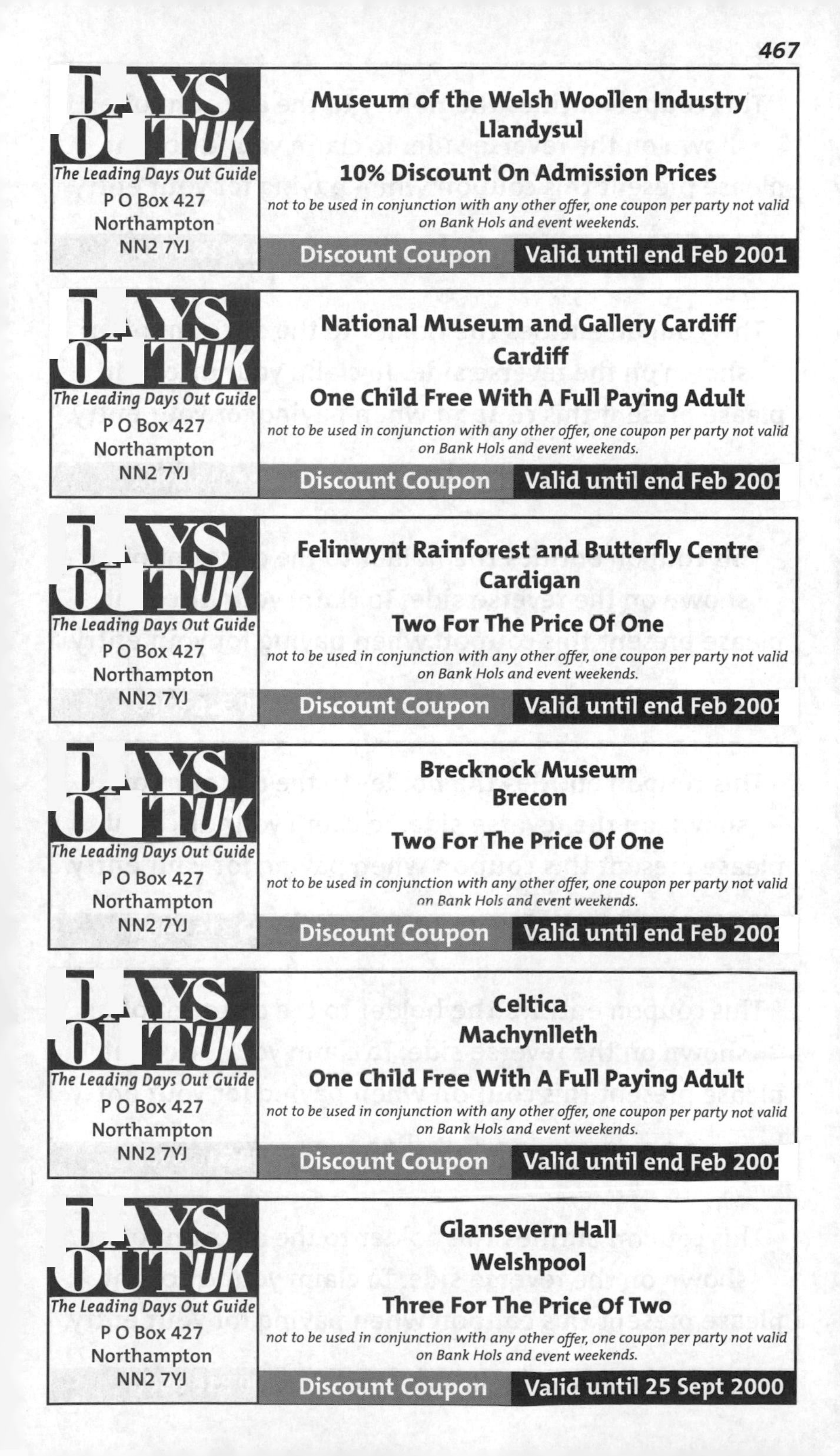
DAYS OUT UK
The Leading Days Out Guide
P O Box 427
Northampton
NN2 7YJ
Museum of the Welsh Woollen Industry
Llandysul
10% Discount On Admission Prices
not to be used in conjunction with any other offer, one coupon per party not valid on Bank Hols and event weekends.
Discount Coupon
Valid until end Feb 2001
DAYS OUT UK
The Leading Days Out Guide
P O Box 427
Northampton
NN2 7YJ
National Museum and Gallery Cardiff
Cardiff
One Child Free With A Full Paying Adult
not to be used in conjunction with any other offer, one coupon per party not valid on Bank Hols and event weekends.
Discount Coupon
Valid until end Feb 2001
DAYS OUT UK
The Leading Days Out Guide
P O Box 427
Northampton
NN2 7YJ
Felinwynt Rainforest and Butterfly Centre
Cardigan
Two For The Price Of One
not to be used in conjunction with any other offer, one coupon per party not valid on Bank Hols and event weekends.
Discount Coupon
Valid until end Feb 2001
DAYS OUT UK
The Leading Days Out Guide
P O Box 427
Northampton
NN2 7YJ
Brecknock Museum
Brecon
Two For The Price Of One
not to be used in conjunction with any other offer, one coupon per party not valid on Bank Hols and event weekends.
Discount Coupon
Valid until end Feb 2001
DAYS OUT UK
The Leading Days Out Guide
P O Box 427
Northampton
NN2 7YJ
Celtica
Machynlleth
One Child Free With A Full Paying Adult
not to be used in conjunction with any other offer, one coupon per party not valid on Bank Hols and event weekends.
Discount Coupon
Valid until end Feb 2001
DAYS OUT UK
The Leading Days Out Guide
P O Box 427
Northampton
NN2 7YJ
Glansevern Hall
Welshpool
Three For The Price Of Two
not to be used in conjunction with any other offer, one coupon per party not valid on Bank Hols and event weekends.
Discount Coupon
Valid until 25 Sept 2000

This coupon entitles the holder to the discount offer shown on the reverse side. To claim your discount please present this coupon when paying for your entry.

Customer care line number *free* phone 0800 316 8900

This coupon entitles the holder to the discount offer shown on the reverse side. To claim your discount please present this coupon when paying for your entry.

Customer care line number *free* phone 0800 316 8900

This coupon entitles the holder to the discount offer shown on the reverse side. To claim your discount please present this coupon when paying for your entry.

Customer care line number *free* phone 0800 316 8900

This coupon entitles the holder to the discount offer shown on the reverse side. To claim your discount please present this coupon when paying for your entry.

Customer care line number *free* phone 0800 316 8900

This coupon entitles the holder to the discount offer shown on the reverse side. To claim your discount please present this coupon when paying for your entry.

Customer care line number *free* phone 0800 316 8900

This coupon entitles the holder to the discount offer shown on the reverse side. To claim your discount please present this coupon when paying for your entry.

Customer care line number *free* phone 0800 316 8900

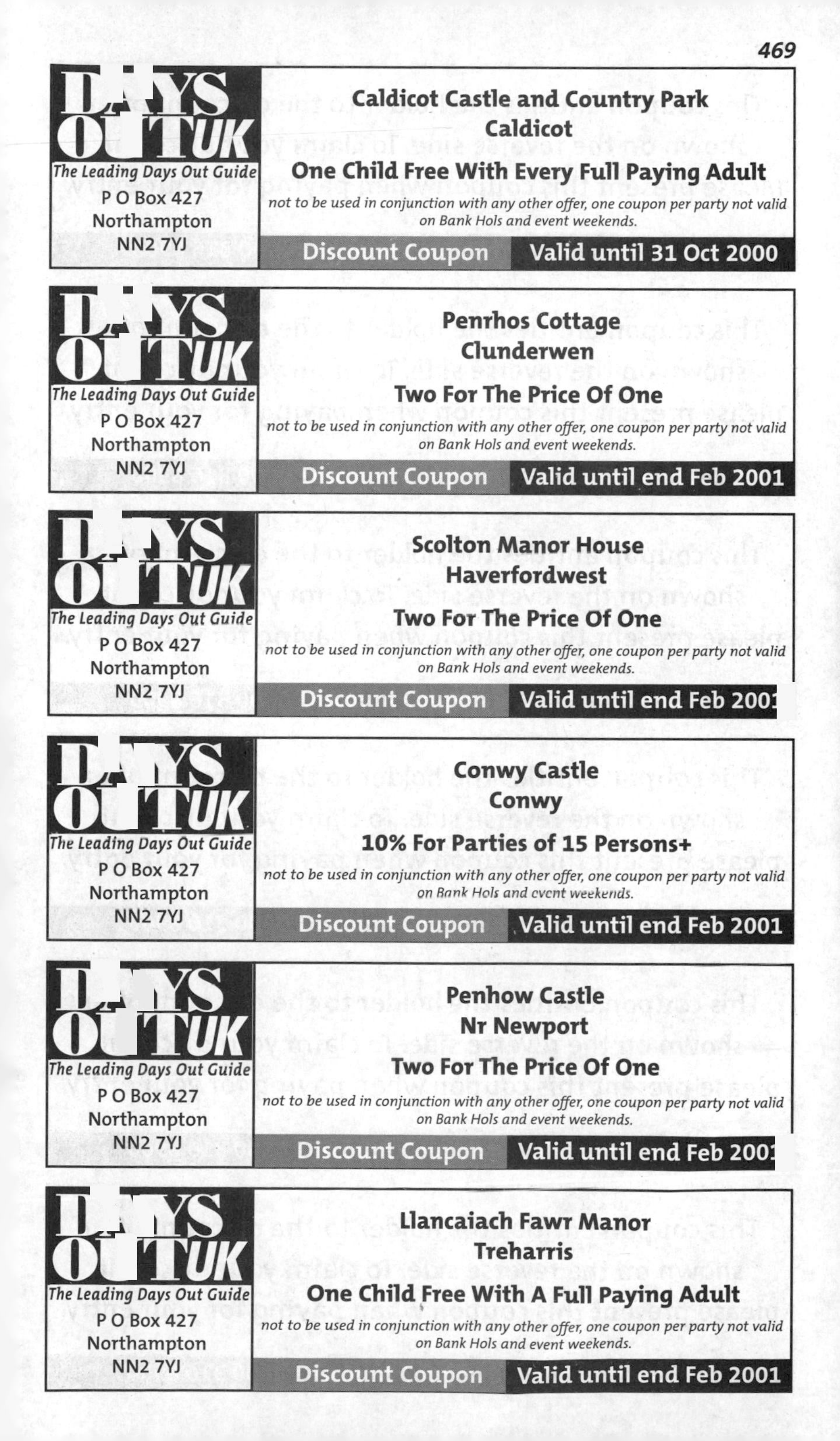
DAYS OUT UK
The Leading Days Out Guide
P O Box 427
Northampton
NN2 7YJ
Caldicot Castle and Country Park
Caldicot
One Child Free With Every Full Paying Adult
not to be used in conjunction with any other offer, one coupon per party not valid on Bank Hols and event weekends.
Discount Coupon
Valid until 31 Oct 2000
DAYS OUT UK
The Leading Days Out Guide
P O Box 427
Northampton
NN2 7YJ
Penrhos Cottage
Clunderwen
Two For The Price Of One
not to be used in conjunction with any other offer, one coupon per party not valid on Bank Hols and event weekends.
Discount Coupon
Valid until end Feb 2001
DAYS OUT UK
The Leading Days Out Guide
P O Box 427
Northampton
NN2 7YJ
Scolton Manor House
Haverfordwest
Two For The Price Of One
not to be used in conjunction with any other offer, one coupon per party not valid on Bank Hols and event weekends.
Discount Coupon
Valid until end Feb 2001
DAYS OUT UK
The Leading Days Out Guide
P O Box 427
Northampton
NN2 7YJ
Conwy Castle
Conwy
10% For Parties of 15 Persons+
not to be used in conjunction with any other offer, one coupon per party not valid on Bank Hols and event weekends.
Discount Coupon
Valid until end Feb 2001
DAYS OUT UK
The Leading Days Out Guide
P O Box 427
Northampton
NN2 7YJ
Penhow Castle
Nr Newport
Two For The Price Of One
not to be used in conjunction with any other offer, one coupon per party not valid on Bank Hols and event weekends.
Discount Coupon
Valid until end Feb 2001
DAYS OUT UK
The Leading Days Out Guide
P O Box 427
Northampton
NN2 7YJ
Llancaiach Fawr Manor
Treharris
One Child Free With A Full Paying Adult
not to be used in conjunction with any other offer, one coupon per party not valid on Bank Hols and event weekends.
Discount Coupon
Valid until end Feb 2001

This coupon entitles the holder to the discount offer shown on the reverse side. To claim your discount please present this coupon when paying for your entry.

Customer care line number *free* phone 0800 316 8900

This coupon entitles the holder to the discount offer shown on the reverse side. To claim your discount please present this coupon when paying for your entry.

Customer care line number *free* phone 0800 316 8900

This coupon entitles the holder to the discount offer shown on the reverse side. To claim your discount please present this coupon when paying for your entry.

Customer care line number *free* phone 0800 316 8900

This coupon entitles the holder to the discount offer shown on the reverse side. To claim your discount please present this coupon when paying for your entry.

Customer care line number *free* phone 0800 316 8900

This coupon entitles the holder to the discount offer shown on the reverse side. To claim your discount please present this coupon when paying for your entry.

Customer care line number *free* phone 0800 316 8900

This coupon entitles the holder to the discount offer shown on the reverse side. To claim your discount please present this coupon when paying for your entry.

Customer care line number *free* phone 0800 316 8900

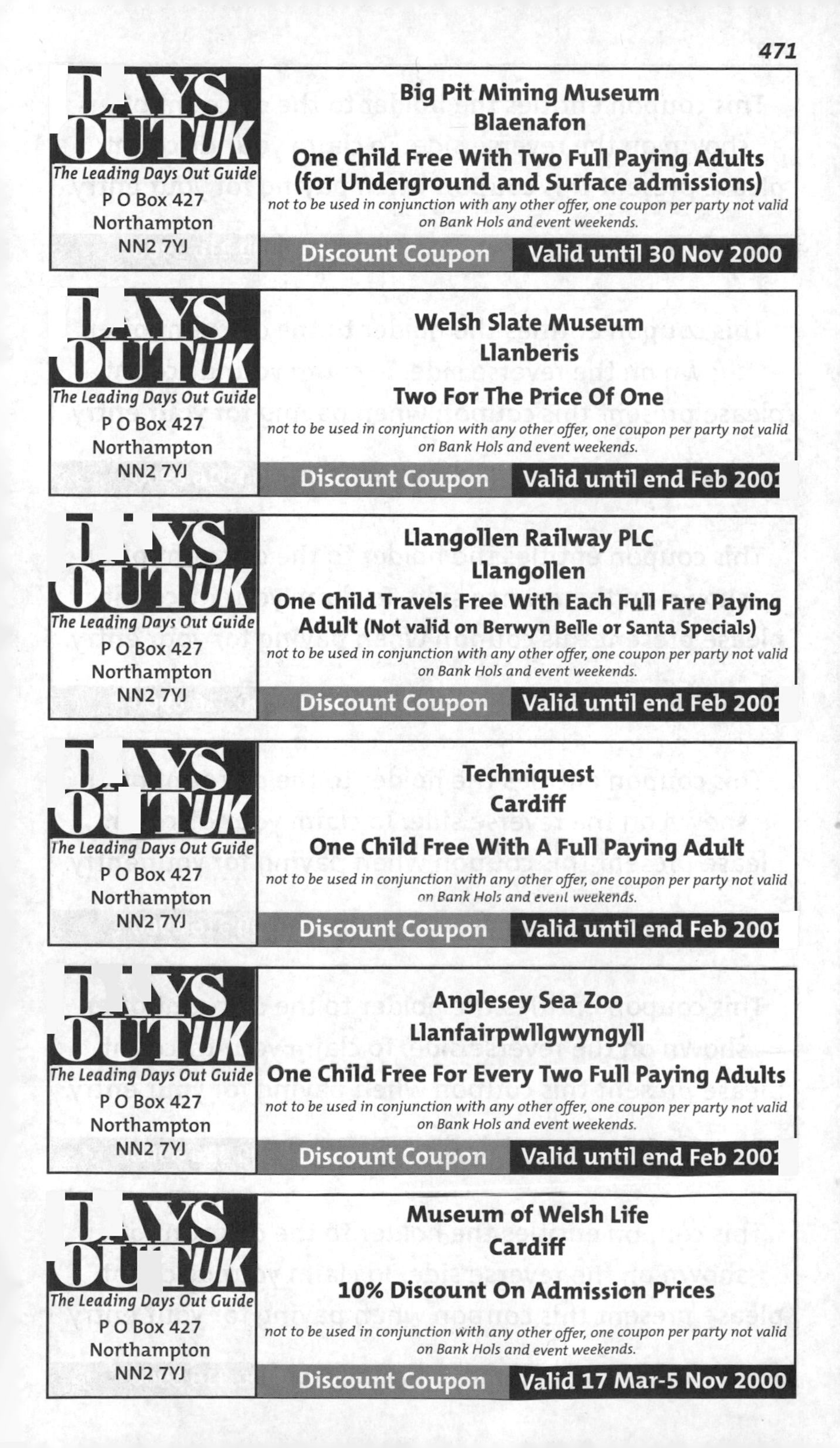
DAYS OUT UK
The Leading Days Out Guide
P O Box 427
Northampton
NN2 7YJ
Big Pit Mining Museum
— Blaenafon
One Child Free With Two Full Paying Adults
(for Underground and Surface admissions)
not to be used in conjunction with any other offer, one coupon per party not valid on Bank Hols and event weekends.
Discount Coupon
Valid until 30 Nov 2000
DAYS OUT UK
The Leading Days Out Guide
P O Box 427
Northampton
NN2 7YJ
Welsh Slate Museum
Llanberis
Two For The Price Of One
not to be used in conjunction with any other offer, one coupon per party not valid on Bank Hols and event weekends.
Discount Coupon
Valid until end Feb 2001
DAYS OUT UK
The Leading Days Out Guide
P O Box 427
Northampton
NN2 7YJ
Llangollen Railway PLC
Llangollen
One Child Travels Free With Each Full Fare Paying Adult (Not valid on Berwyn Belle or Santa Specials)
not to be used in conjunction with any other offer, one coupon per party not valid on Bank Hols and event weekends.
Discount Coupon
Valid until end Feb 2001
DAYS OUT UK
The Leading Days Out Guide
P O Box 427
Northampton
NN2 7YJ
Techniquest
Cardiff
One Child Free With A Full Paying Adult
not to be used in conjunction with any other offer, one coupon per party not valid on Bank Hols and event weekends.
Discount Coupon
Valid until end Feb 2001
DAYS OUT UK
The Leading Days Out Guide
P O Box 427
Northampton
NN2 7YJ
Anglesey Sea Zoo
Llanfairpwllgwyngyll
One Child Free For Every Two Full Paying Adults
not to be used in conjunction with any other offer, one coupon per party not valid on Bank Hols and event weekends.
Discount Coupon
Valid until end Feb 2001
DAYS OUT UK
The Leading Days Out Guide
P O Box 427
Northampton
NN2 7YJ
Museum of Welsh Life
Cardiff
10% Discount On Admission Prices
not to be used in conjunction with any other offer, one coupon per party not valid on Bank Hols and event weekends.
Discount Coupon
Valid 17 Mar-5 Nov 2000

This coupon entitles the holder to the discount offer shown on the reverse side. To claim your discount please present this coupon when paying for your entry.

Customer care line number *free* phone 0800 316 8900

This coupon entitles the holder to the discount offer shown on the reverse side. To claim your discount please present this coupon when paying for your entry.

Customer care line number *free* phone 0800 316 8900

This coupon entitles the holder to the discount offer shown on the reverse side. To claim your discount please present this coupon when paying for your entry.

Customer care line number *free* phone 0800 316 8900

This coupon entitles the holder to the discount offer shown on the reverse side. To claim your discount please present this coupon when paying for your entry.

Customer care line number *free* phone 0800 316 8900

This coupon entitles the holder to the discount offer shown on the reverse side. To claim your discount please present this coupon when paying for your entry.

Customer care line number *free* phone 0800 316 8900

This coupon entitles the holder to the discount offer shown on the reverse side. To claim your discount please present this coupon when paying for your entry.

Customer care line number *free* phone 0800 316 8900

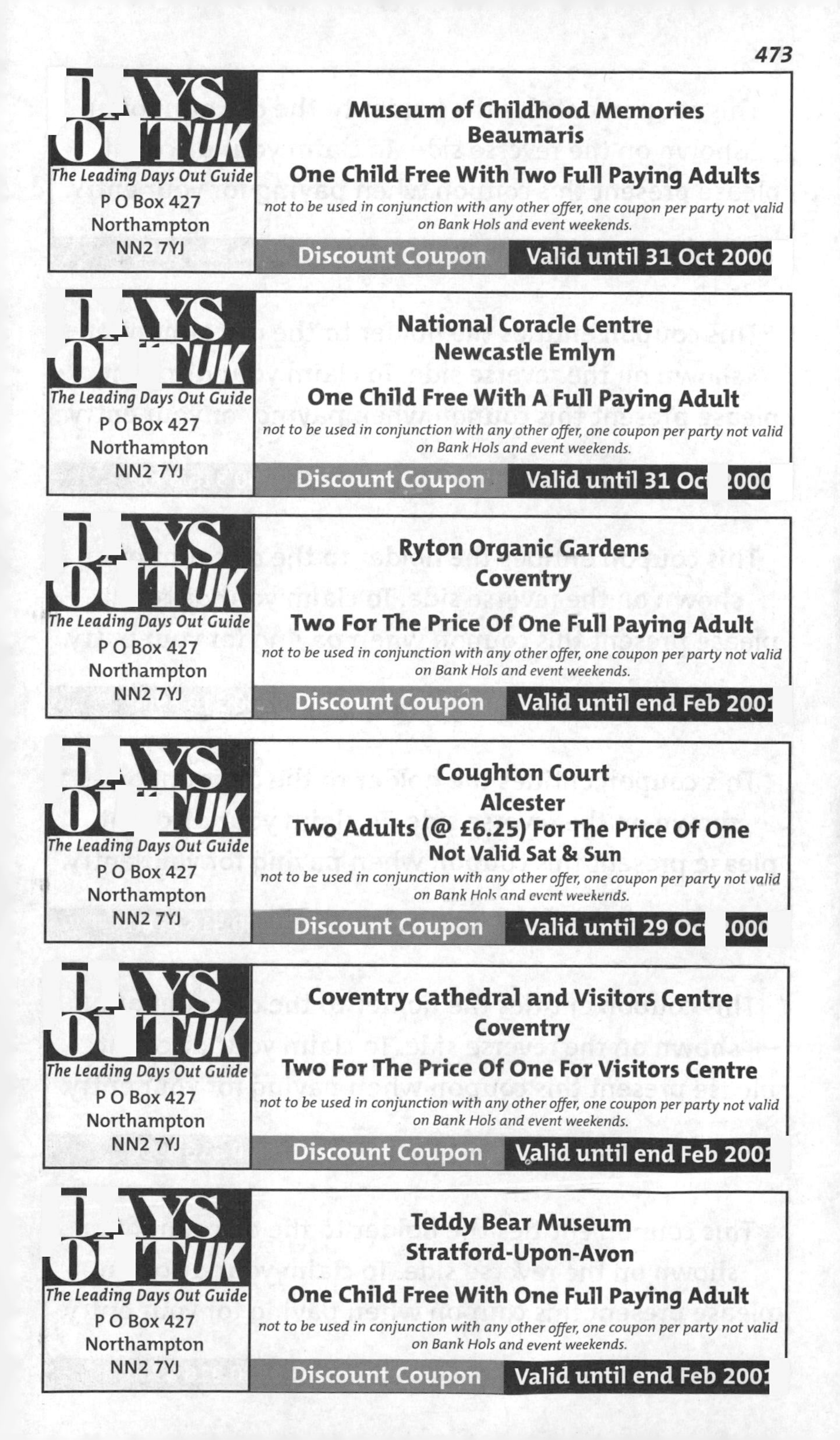
DAYS OUT UK
The Leading Days Out Guide
P O Box 427
Northampton
NN2 7YJ
Museum of Childhood Memories
Beaumaris
One Child Free With Two Full Paying Adults
not to be used in conjunction with any other offer, one coupon per party not valid on Bank Hols and event weekends.
Discount Coupon
Valid until 31 Oct 2000
DAYS OUT UK
The Leading Days Out Guide
P O Box 427
Northampton
NN2 7YJ
National Coracle Centre
Newcastle Emlyn
One Child Free With A Full Paying Adult
not to be used in conjunction with any other offer, one coupon per party not valid on Bank Hols and event weekends.
Discount Coupon
Valid until 31 Oct 2000
DAYS OUT UK
The Leading Days Out Guide
P O Box 427
Northampton
NN2 7YJ
Ryton Organic Gardens
Coventry
Two For The Price Of One Full Paying Adult
not to be used in conjunction with any other offer, one coupon per party not valid on Bank Hols and event weekends.
Discount Coupon
Valid until end Feb 2001
DAYS OUT UK
The Leading Days Out Guide
P O Box 427
Northampton
NN2 7YJ
Coughton Court
Alcester
Two Adults (@ £6.25) For The Price Of One
Not Valid Sat & Sun
not to be used in conjunction with any other offer, one coupon per party not valid on Bank Hols and event weekends.
Discount Coupon
Valid until 29 Oct 2000
DAYS OUT UK
The Leading Days Out Guide
P O Box 427
Northampton
NN2 7YJ
Coventry Cathedral and Visitors Centre
Coventry
Two For The Price Of One For Visitors Centre
not to be used in conjunction with any other offer, one coupon per party not valid on Bank Hols and event weekends.
Discount Coupon
Valid until end Feb 2001
DAYS OUT UK
The Leading Days Out Guide
P O Box 427
Northampton
NN2 7YJ
Teddy Bear Museum
Stratford-Upon-Avon
One Child Free With One Full Paying Adult
not to be used in conjunction with any other offer, one coupon per party not valid on Bank Hols and event weekends.
Discount Coupon
Valid until end Feb 2001

This coupon entitles the holder to the discount offer shown on the reverse side. To claim your discount please present this coupon when paying for your entry.

Customer care line number *free* phone 0800 316 8900

This coupon entitles the holder to the discount offer shown on the reverse side. To claim your discount please present this coupon when paying for your entry.

Customer care line number *free* phone 0800 316 8900

This coupon entitles the holder to the discount offer shown on the reverse side. To claim your discount please present this coupon when paying for your entry.

Customer care line number *free* phone 0800 316 8900

This coupon entitles the holder to the discount offer shown on the reverse side. To claim your discount please present this coupon when paying for your entry.

Customer care line number *free* phone 0800 316 8900

This coupon entitles the holder to the discount offer shown on the reverse side. To claim your discount please present this coupon when paying for your entry.

Customer care line number *free* phone 0800 316 8900

This coupon entitles the holder to the discount offer shown on the reverse side. To claim your discount please present this coupon when paying for your entry.

Customer care line number *free* phone 0800 316 8900

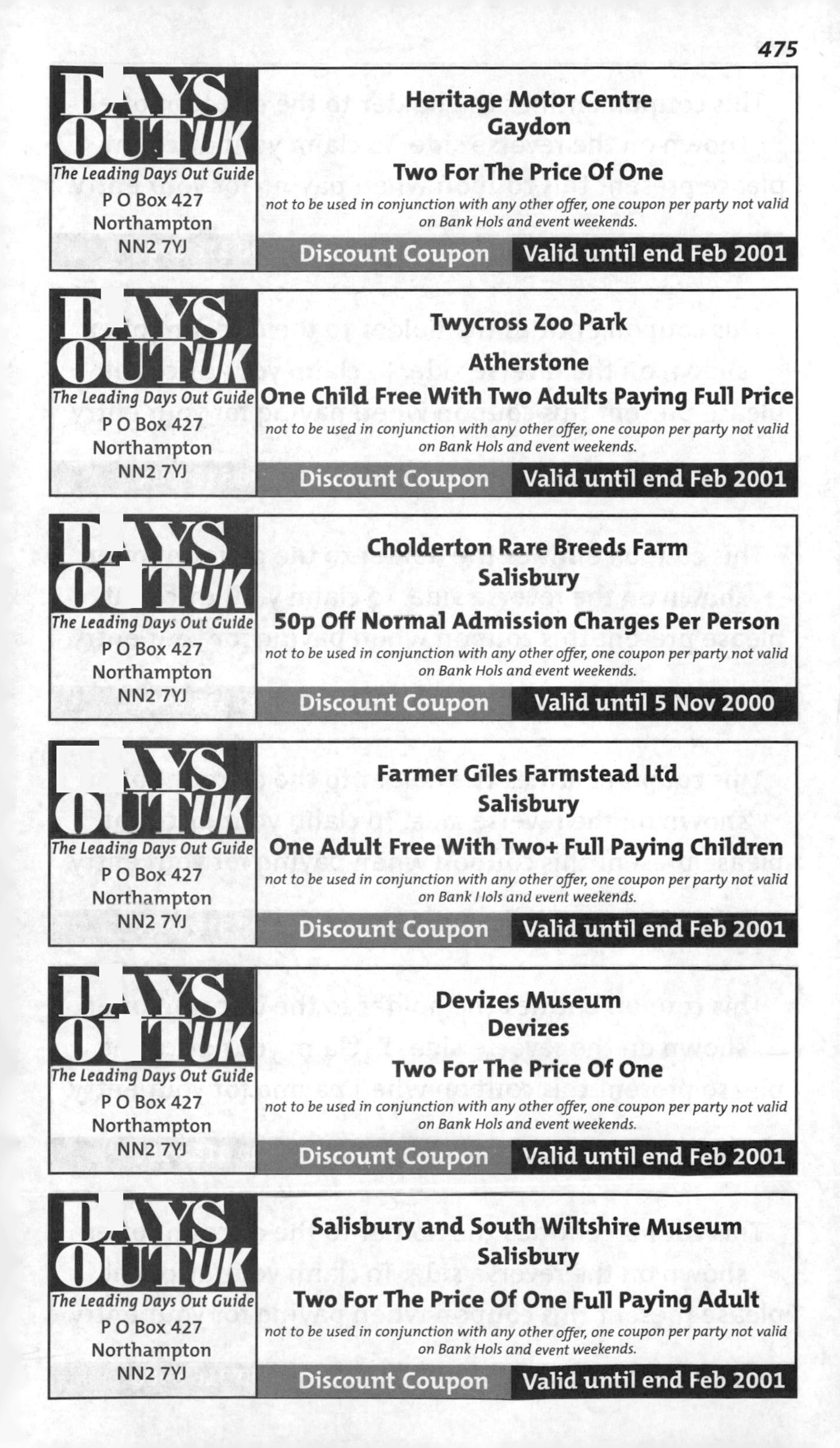
DAYS OUT UK
The Leading Days Out Guide
P O Box 427
Northampton
NN2 7YJ
Heritage Motor Centre
Gaydon
Two For The Price Of One
not to be used in conjunction with any other offer, one coupon per party not valid on Bank Hols and event weekends.
Discount Coupon
Valid until end Feb 2001
DAYS OUT UK
The Leading Days Out Guide
P O Box 427
Northampton
NN2 7YJ
Twycross Zoo Park
Atherstone
One Child Free With Two Adults Paying Full Price
not to be used in conjunction with any other offer, one coupon per party not valid on Bank Hols and event weekends.
Discount Coupon
Valid until end Feb 2001
DAYS OUT UK
The Leading Days Out Guide
P O Box 427
Northampton
NN2 7YJ
Cholderton Rare Breeds Farm
Salisbury
50p Off Normal Admission Charges Per Person
not to be used in conjunction with any other offer, one coupon per party not valid on Bank Hols and event weekends.
Discount Coupon
Valid until 5 Nov 2000
DAYS OUT UK
The Leading Days Out Guide
P O Box 427
Northampton
NN2 7YJ
Farmer Giles Farmstead Ltd
Salisbury
One Adult Free With Two+ Full Paying Children
not to be used in conjunction with any other offer, one coupon per party not valid on Bank Hols and event weekends.
Discount Coupon
Valid until end Feb 2001
DAYS OUT UK
The Leading Days Out Guide
P O Box 427
Northampton
NN2 7YJ
Devizes Museum
Devizes
Two For The Price Of One
not to be used in conjunction with any other offer, one coupon per party not valid on Bank Hols and event weekends.
Discount Coupon
Valid until end Feb 2001
DAYS OUT UK
The Leading Days Out Guide
P O Box 427
Northampton
NN2 7YJ
Salisbury and South Wiltshire Museum
Salisbury
Two For The Price Of One Full Paying Adult
not to be used in conjunction with any other offer, one coupon per party not valid on Bank Hols and event weekends.
Discount Coupon
Valid until end Feb 2001

This coupon entitles the holder to the discount offer shown on the reverse side. To claim your discount please present this coupon when paying for your entry.

Customer care line number *free* phone 0800 316 8900

This coupon entitles the holder to the discount offer shown on the reverse side. To claim your discount please present this coupon when paying for your entry.

Customer care line number *free* phone 0800 316 8900

This coupon entitles the holder to the discount offer shown on the reverse side. To claim your discount please present this coupon when paying for your entry.

Customer care line number *free* phone 0800 316 8900

This coupon entitles the holder to the discount offer shown on the reverse side. To claim your discount please present this coupon when paying for your entry.

Customer care line number *free* phone 0800 316 8900

This coupon entitles the holder to the discount offer shown on the reverse side. To claim your discount please present this coupon when paying for your entry.

Customer care line number *free* phone 0800 316 8900

This coupon entitles the holder to the discount offer shown on the reverse side. To claim your discount please present this coupon when paying for your entry.

Customer care line number *free* phone 0800 316 8900